ns of the City

LEICHHARDT

On the Margins of the City

A social history of Leichhardt and the former municipalities of Annandale, Balmain and Glebe

Max Solling and
Peter Reynolds

ALLEN & UNWIN

Copyright ©1997 Max Solling and Peter Reynolds

All rights reserved. No part of this book may be reproduced or transmitted in any form or by any means, electronic or mechanical, including photocopying, recording or by any information storage and retrieval system, without prior permission in writing from the publisher.

First published in 1997 by
Allen & Unwin
9 Atchison Street
St Leonards NSW 2065
Australia
Phone: (61 2) 9901 4088
Fax: (61 2) 9906 2218
E-mail: frontdesk@allen-unwin.com.au
URL: http://www.allen-unwin.com.au
National Library of Australia
Cataloguing-in-Publication entry:
Solling, Max, 1942-.
Leichhardt : on the margins of the city : a social history of Leichhardt and the former municipalities of Annandale, Balmain and Glebe.

Includes index.
ISBN 1 86448 408 X.

1. Leichhardt (N.S.W. : Municipality) - History. I. Reynolds, Peter L. II. Title.
994.41

Endpapers: Gibbs Shallard & Co's Map of the City of Sydney & Suburbs 1885 (*Maps Collection, Mitchell Library*)
Set in 11/14 pt Bembo
Printed by South Wind Productions, Singapore
10 9 8 7 6 5 4 3 2 1

Contents

Foreword		vi
Preface with acknowledgements		vii
Conversion tables		x
List of abbreviations		xi
1	The land of the Eora	1
2	The physical environment	8
3	Life in the semi-rural retreats, 1830–1841	11
4	Village life, 1841–1871	26
5	Influences shaping suburban development	42
6	The framework of local government	55
7	Building the suburbs	68
8	Institutions of daily life	93
9	Industry and commerce	121
10	Unions, Labor Leagues and working-class mobilisation	134
11	Pollution, pestilence and plagues	149
12	Coming and going	157
13	A call to arms, 1914–1918	168
14	Local politics: fit and proper people	178
15	The slum stigma: life in the inter-war years	190
16	Popular recreation	202
17	Visions of a better post-war world	214
18	A life apart: Italian Leichhardt	222
19	'Chardonnay Socialists' and 'yuppie Trotskyites': Leichhardt 1990	231
20	Traditional and new politics in Leichhardt	239
Appendix A: Census figures		252
Appendix B: Local elected representatives		255
Notes		263
Index		311

Foreword

I am very pleased to introduce the history of Leichhardt: *Leichhardt: On the Margins of the City*. Council decided that a comprehensive history of the area was needed. We were very pleased that Max Solling and Peter Reynolds, well-respected local historians, expressed their interest in the project. In 1994 they were commissioned to research and write a social and political history of the municipality.

The history traces the changes that have taken place from Aboriginal beginnings, through war, depression and immigration to the resident action and community participation of the 1970s and through to the present.

Council has for a long time been committed to the protection of our historic buildings and the publishing of the history is an extension of that commitment to record our past.

With its proximity to the harbour, its city views and its cultural diversity, Leichhardt is an interesting area in which to live and work. It has an active and vital community. The authors have shown how that community was built and have managed to capture its moods and its essence.

I feel sure this work will add greatly to the knowledge of those interested in Australian history. Leichhardt has good reason to be proud of its past and to look forward to its future.

Councillor Kristine Cruden
MAYOR

Preface with acknowledgements

Sydney's physical limits were defined by boundary stones in 1833 but by then villa retreats were appearing just beyond the urban perimeter. The embryonic pattern of European settlement in Leichhardt had begun. Balmain and Glebe were accorded the title of 'suburb' in 1846 though Leichhardt and Annandale did not acquire a definite shape on the map until 30 years later. These dormitory suburbs were inextricably linked to, and dependent upon, the city proper and, as it grew in size and heterogeneity, the functional role of its suburbs changed.

About 29 Aboriginal clans occupied the Cumberland Plain in 1788, each with its own distinct tribal area. The territory that embraced Leichhardt belonged to the Wangal clan, with the Balmain peninsula separating them from the Cadigal. Deprived of their territorial lands and decimated by smallpox, the remnants of these hunters and fishers withdrew further inland.

Leichhardt took its name from a Prussian-born naturalist who went exploring in Northern Queensland in 1848 and was never seen again. The suburb of Leichhardt achieved municipal status in 1871 but its administrative area was much enlarged in 1948 to absorb Balmain and Annandale and twenty years later, Glebe. The whole process of making the suburbs that now comprise Leichhardt Municipality took place against a background of demographic change, improved modes of transportation and the availability of land and capital to sustain residential growth. Measured simply in terms of physical fabric and aggregate population, the period between 1871 and 1891 was one of intensive residential development, as housing increased from 2,547 to 12,191 and Leichhardt's population soared from 11,993 to 57,617.

By 1901, one-third of Sydney's population was concentrated within two miles of the city centre. Schools, churches, pubs, retail stores and other institutions dotted suburban landscapes as they reached sufficient size and wealth and although residents lived together they inhabited different worlds, divided by social class and religion.

From the 1890s, the advance of industry into suburbs adjoining the city proper meant some deterioration in living conditions and the extension of tram and train tracks facilitated an exodus by the better-off to the outer fringes of development. Rooms in the large houses they left behind were let, and boarding houses provided more affordable accommodation. The tendency was, it seems, for these places to provide lodgings for widows, deserted wives and hard-up families.

The response of Leichhardt's residents to the 1914–1918 war was eager and immediate. The deaths of more than 900 of its residents who volunteered for overseas service inflicted great deprivation on their dependents, left without sufficient money to mitigate the hardships of war.

Leichhardt has had its ups and downs. The emergent town-planning movement condemned, in the name of hygiene, much housing in inner Sydney as obsolete and ready for demolition. For more than 60 years Australian preferences were overwhelmingly in favour of low-density suburban living and the streetscapes of Balmain, Glebe, Annandale and Leichhardt were seen as dilapidated and unfashionable.

A visible ruling class of businessmen and professionals had enjoyed a near absolute sway through the whole range of suburban institutional life and they remained firmly ensconced in council chambers to 1920. As Sydney's inner suburbs became more distinctly working-class in their identity, the manner and dress of Labor men elected to council was in marked contrast to that of their predecessors. The social pattern of Leichhardt Municipality was set in a way that would not be drastically revised until the formation of resident action groups in the late 1960s signalled the arrival of the new middle class. The municipality's social and physical fabric has undergone a dramatic transformation and battles within Leichhardt's Labor branches reflected the changing character of local politics. The 1971 Open Council at Leichhardt was a radical departure from the way council previously conducted its affairs and since then participatory democracy has become a feature of local government in Leichhardt.

For help in writing this book we owe much to many people. We are especially indebted to Professor Walter Moore who read and commented on the manuscript at various stages. We have drawn heavily on a mass of archival material housed in the New South Wales Archives; NSW Land Titles Office; NSW Lands Department; Fisher Library; the Mitchell and Dixson Libraries, the State Library of New South Wales; the Noel Butlin Archives Centre, Australian National University; the Royal Australian Historical Society; the Society of Australian Genealogists; the Sydney Water Archive; and the J.G. Park Collection, Macleay Museum.

Records created by the municipality's churches, and preserved by them, were also a fertile source and we acknowledge the assistance of the Good Samaritan Generalate, Glebe Point; Church Records & Historical Society (Uniting Church); the Ferguson (Presbyterian) Memorial Library; and local church archives retained within the municipality.

We particularly wish to acknowledge the assistance and support of the staffs of the Leichhardt Library and of the Mitchell and Dixson Libraries. We thank Dr Shirley Fitzgerald and Rebecca Reynolds for checking the manuscript.

Theses by Jean-Claude Bertoni, Stephen Carrick, Anthony Cusick, George Jetis, Ken Leong, Paul Mazza, and Don Truman at the School of Architecture, University of New South Wales in the 1980s were invaluable in illuminating aspects of suburban development. We acknowledge, with thanks, Dr Lesley Muir, for allowing us to draw on her thesis, 'Shady Acres: Politicians, Developers and the Design of Sydney's Public Transport System 1873–1891', and Dr Benno Engels for providing access to his thesis 'The Gentrification of Glebe: The Residential Restructuring of an Inner Sydney Suburb 1960 to 1986'.

We also benefited from the generosity of the following, who provided illustrations, information and advice: Victor Alberts, Standard Publishing House Pty Ltd, Rozelle; Gary Bennell;

PREFACE WITH ACKNOWLEDGEMENTS

Judy Birmingham; Colin Bowes; Jon Breen; Anthony Browell and the Film Australia National Interest Program; the *Bulletin*; John Darroch; Frank Del Duca; Gwen Dundon; Frank Ehlert; Paul Feain; Patricia Fin; John Flitcroft; Barry Groom; Kath Hamey, Balmain Association; Chris Heine, John Heine & Sons Pty Ltd; David R. Keenan; the late David Kernohan; Bruce Lay; Dr Carol Liston; Betty Mason; Bert Melocco; Robert Mills; Solomon Mitchell; Alan Moir, *Sydney Morning Herald*; Judy Newton, Lever Rexona Division of Unilever Australia; NSW Fire Brigades; A.M. Prescott and R.H. Parsons; Alan Roberts; John Shakespeare, *Sydney Morning Herald*; A. Sharp, Dominion Publishing; Senior Sergeant Peter Smith, Balmain Police Station; Jack Stitt; the late Ada Stokes; June Tomlinson; Tranby Aboriginal College; Tyrrell Collection; Catherine Warne, Kingsclere Books; Peter and Anne Waugh; Barry Williams; Jane Worthy; and Zuliani Studios. We thank them all.

Sources of the illustrations have been acknowledged in the captions which accompany the reproductions and every effort has been made to identify copyright owners for images reproduced in the book. Should anyone have any queries regarding the copyright of any image reproduced in this book, the authors request them to contact the publishers.

Conversion tables

Australia converted to the metric system in 1966. Pre-metric measurements used in historical documents and in an historical context have been retained throughout the text. The following tables will assist in converting them to metric measures.

Length
1 mile	=	1.6 kilometres
1 yard	=	91.4 centimetres
1 foot	=	30.5 centimetres
1 inch	=	2.54 centimetres
12 inches (in)	=	1 foot (ft)
3 feet	=	1 yard (yd)
22 yards	=	1 chain
220 yards	=	1 furlong
5280 feet	=	1760 yards
	=	8 furlongs
	=	1 mile

Area
1 acre	=	0.40 hectares
1 square yard	=	0.84 square metres
9 square feet	=	1 square yard
30 ¼ square yards	=	1 rod, pole or perch
40 perches	=	1 rood
4 roods	=	1 acre
4840 square yards	=	1 acre
640 acres	=	1 square mile

Temperature
100° Fahrenheit	=	37.7° Celsius

Weight
1 ton	=	1.02 tonne
1 pound (lb)	=	0.45 kilograms
1 ounce (oz)	=	28.35 grams
16 ounces	=	1 pound
14 pounds	=	1 stone
112 pounds	=	8 stone
	=	1 hundredweight
20 hundredweights	=	1 ton

Volume
1 gallon	=	4.5 litres
1 bushel	=	36.37 litres
8 pints	=	1 gallon (liquids)
8 gallons	=	1 bushel (solids)

Currency

In 1966 sterling currency was converted to decimal currency at the rate of:

1 penny (d)	=	1 cent
1 shilling (s)	=	10 cents
10 shillings	=	$1
1 pound (£)	=	$2
12 pence (d)	=	1 shilling (1/-)
20 shillings	=	£ (one pound)
£1 1s 0d	=	1 guinea

List of abbreviations

ACM	Annandale Council Records, Minutes
ADB	*Australian Dictionary of Biography*
AJPH	*Australian Journal of Politics & History*
ANUHJ	*ANU Historical Journal*
ANZHES	*Australian and New Zealand History of Education Society Journal*
ATCJ	*Australian Town & Country Journal*
Aust	*The Australian*
BCM	Balmain Council Records, Minutes
Bk	Conveyance Book
BO	*Balmain Observer & Western Suburbs Advertiser*
CPP	*Commonwealth Parliamentary Papers*
DM	*Daily Mirror*
DT	*Daily Telegraph*
GCM	Glebe Council Records, Minutes
GPO	Government Printing Office
GSBE	Graduate School of the Built Environment, University of NSW
ISN	*Illustrated Sydney News*
JNSWLC	*Journal of the New South Wales Legislative Council*
JRAHS	*Journal of the Royal Australian Historical Society*
LCM	Leichhardt Council Records, Minutes
LHJ	*Leichhardt Historical Journal*
LTO	Land Titles Office, New South Wales
ML	Mitchell Library, Sydney
MOA	*The Mirror of Australia*
NSWA	NSW Archives
NSWGG	*NSW Government Gazette*
NSWPD	*NSW Parliamentary Debates*
NSWPP	*NSW Parliamentary Papers*
NSWSR	*NSW Statistical Register*

NT	*National Times*
OST	Old System Title, NSW Land Titles Office
PSCPW	Parliamentary Standing Committee on Public Works
Sands	*Sands's Sydney & Suburban Directory*
SDC	Sydney District Council Assessment Books (1843–46) ML D67
SEM	*Sydney Evening Mail*
SM	*Sydney Mail*
SMH	*Sydney Morning Herald*
TT	Torrens Title, NSW Land Titles Office
V&P NSWLA	*Votes & Proceedings, NSW Legislative Assembly*
V&P NSWLC	*Votes & Proceedings, NSW Legislative Council*
VHJ	*Victorian Historical Journal*
WSWB	*Western Suburbs Weekly Budget*

The land of the Eora

Naval captain Arthur Phillip, with a fleet of eleven ships, set out across the world in May 1787 with 759 convicts—568 men and 191 women—and reached Botany Bay in January 1788. He placed his new settlement on the shore of Port Jackson instead of the intended site, Botany Bay, because, he wrote, it was 'the finest harbour in the world'.[1] The penal colony of New South Wales was the British government's solution to its overcrowded gaols after the American War of Independence ended English transportation of convicted felons to North America.[2]

On 21 January 1788, when the First Fleet entered Port Jackson, the voyagers were about to confront the coastal Aboriginal bands of the harbour. The pale-skinned people from Britain anchored their craft some eleven kilometres from the harbour entrance, where they found a freshwater creek and several areas which appeared suitable for cultivation. They named the place Sydney Cove, after the Secretary of State for the Colonies, Thomas Townshend, 1st Viscount Sydney.[3]

Alf Clint and Clive Williams. Clint, an Anglican Bush Brother, founded Tranby Co-operative College, Mansfield Street, Glebe, in 1958, a centre for training Aborigines to run their own co-operatives. Williams, a major figure in the co-operatives movement at Coraki, was an early director of Tranby. (Tranby Aboriginal College)

The Aborigines saw the newcomers cutting down trees, taking their fish and game and occupying grounds with tribal and spiritual significance.[4] Their bewilderment increased as they witnessed floggings and hangings – and the invaders had the gall to open up burial mounds and bark tombs. Were these barbarians, or were they not living people at all, but white-faced spirits of the dead? The Aborigines were also bemused as to the sex of the clean-shaven and clothed strangers. 'They wanted to know what sex we were,' P.G. King wrote in his journal, 'which they explained by pointing where it was distinguishable. As they took us for women, not having our beards grown, I ordered one of the people to undeceive them in this particular, when they made a great shout of admiration.'[5]

Phillip's instructions directed him to establish friendly relations with the Aborigines, 'enjoining all our subjects to live in amity and kindness with them'. Aborigines speared to death two convicts who had been cutting rushes for thatching at Rushcutters Bay. After this incident Phillip and a party of twelve men went to Botany Bay and Phillip was convinced of the 'necessity of placing a confidence in these people as an only means of avoiding a dispute'.[6]

Relations with the Aborigines deteriorated once they realised the invaders were here to stay; there never was any possibility that the Aboriginal and the imported ways of life could coexist, for a chasm divided the two cultures. It was a clash of nomadic and sedentary societies.

Bound by custom to share their food with all their people, the nomads maintained a balance between their populations and the available resources. Their lives were shaped by their Dreamtime stories, which were both an explanation of how their world came to be, and how people must conduct their behaviour and social relations, things that had changed little from one generation to the next.[7] The rules of their society allowed no person to enslave or dominate another. The British, cultivators of the soil for thousands of years, were individualistic and acquisitive. They assumed power without negotiation and acted from the beginning as the rulers of the country and of all who lived in it. Under the invaders' law Australia was deemed to be 'terra nullius', no person's land, and therefore the rights of the indigenous people were non-existent. By planting the flag the foreigners proclaimed sovereignty over 'territory in which live uncivilised inhabitants in a primitive state of society'.[8]

James Cook, searching for the Great South Land, had sailed into a sheltered bay on 29 April 1770 and a party, including botanists Banks and Solander, went ashore. They gathered so many plants that Cook named it Botany Bay, and during the voyage home he named the coast he had been charting New South Wales. *Terra Australis Incognita* would be the last continent to be occupied by Europeans.

The concepts of Aboriginality and the first Australians came into being only with the arrival of the British.[9] Prehistorians suggest that the first Australians arrived from south-east Asia about 50,000 years ago. The last part of their journey was by simple water craft, perhaps a sea voyage of less than 100 kilometres at a time when sea levels were about 150 metres lower than they are today. Radiocarbon datings of charcoal from fires and food remains left by the early Australians on the beaches of large freshwater lakes are between 35,000 and 40,000 years old. About 30,000 years ago there were perhaps 100,000 people scattered across much of a continent that covered 15 million square kilometres.[10]

When the first Aborigines arrived, eucalypts and acacias dominated the landscape and some large animals—diprotodons and kangaroos and koalas, larger than the fauna of today—still inhabited the land. They seem to have disappeared less than 40,000 years ago. Some animal species evolved into smaller forms (wombat, Tasmanian devil, grey kangaroo) and vegetation patterns altered. Vegetational changes, the extinction of some animals and dwarfing of others may be explained partially in climatic terms, but human impact was also significant. It was only in the use of fire, as a management tool to burn off old vegetation and encourage the regrowth of hunting pasture, that the Aborigines were active in transforming the landscape.[11]

At least 20,000 years ago Aborigines occupied the Sydney region, then a river valley. A rise in sea level in the last glacial period (18,000 years ago) drowned the river valley, creating a ria and destroying evidence of early campsites. People visited large rock shelters in the Blue Mountains while the area was relatively open during the cool conditions of 20,000 to 10,000 years ago. The extent of Aboriginal occupation of coastal areas from 15,000 to 6,000 years ago is difficult to assess since these areas now lie beneath the sea.[12] Estuarine sites, however, do provide some clues; 8,000 years ago at Bobadeen in the Hunter Valley people were eating freshwater shellfish, emu eggs, bandicoots, possums, wallabies and kangaroos.

The diaries, letters and journals of members of the First Fleet contain valuable evidence of traditional Aboriginal life in Sydney at the time of first contact.[13] The basic unit of organisation was the band, which ranged from small family units to groups of up to 100 people centred around married and related individuals. Everyone belonged to a clan, which bound people spiritually to a particular territory and its sacred sites. Twenty-nine bands have been identified as living in the Sydney region in 1788.[14]

Aboriginal artists at work at Tranby College. (Tranby Aboriginal College)

On white settlement it is estimated that 750,000 people were scattered across the country and their societies differed from each other in their organisations, beliefs and practices. They were separated by traditional territories and a plurality of languages; possibly some 600 tribes with 200 to 250 languages and dialects.[15]

In the Sydney region diarist David Collins observed:

> each family has a particular place of residence from which is derived its distinguishing name. This is formed by adding the monosyllable Gal to the name of the place; the southern shore of Botany bay is called Gwea, and the people who inhabit it style themselves Gweagal. Those who live on the north shore of Port Jackson are called Cam-mer-ray-gal, that part of the harbour being distinguished from others by the name of Cam-mer-ray.[16]

Within their tribal boundaries Aborigines moved constantly in search of food. Campsites of coastal Aborigines in the Sydney region were located near the sea and foreshores. Their diet of fish was supplemented by shellfish—mud and rock oysters, mussels, cockles, crabs, octopus and turtles, gathered from the bays of the harbour and rock shelters. A range of local plant foods featured in their diet in spring together with small animals. They developed a sophisticated range of implements and devices for fishing—multi-pronged spears and throwing sticks, shell hooks and scrapers, lines made from the inner bark of trees and various wooden artefacts. Stone tools around the harbour are conspicuous by their absence.[17] Canoes were generally fashioned from the bark of casuarinas. A division of roles existed in fishing—women fished with shellfish hooks and lines, whereas spearing fish was men's work.

Aborigines travelled light for they regarded possessions as encumbrances. West of Parramatta stone implements were more common, together with the digging stick and spears, spear-thrower, club and boomerang. Further inland kangaroos, possums, ducks, fish and countless plants were eaten and, according to prehistorian D.J. Mulvaney, 'Aborigines ate a better-balanced diet than most European town or country dwellers of the time'.[18] Their bark shelters, adequate for their way of life, appeared flimsy to the sedentary Europeans, and the canoes were also regarded as primitive, but they were only used in the search for food, and not to travel long distances.

The spiritual life of the Aborigines was rich: the essence of their belief was the oneness of the land and all that moved upon it. They had a strong sense of place. Tribal lore gave special significance to the creation and resting places of the great ancestors who moved across the tribal territory. As they travelled over their landscape they saw a rich symbolic and religious world and they had named every feature on it. These were not simply rocks, trees and waterholes, but places which the great ancestors had created and where they still lived. Europeans could not comprehend the Aborigines' attachment to the land and the spiritual values they imbued it with.[19]

Tranby Aboriginal College offers skills-based training for carpentry, bricklaying, motor repairs, bookkeeping, agriculture and plumbing, and the principles of co-operatives form the basic syllabus. In 1991, 563 Aborigines—1 per cent of the population—lived in Leichhardt Municipality. (Tranby Aboriginal College)

Aborigines believed in the survival of the human spirit, and spectacular initiation ceremonies served to reinforce ties to sacred sites or to pass on traditional lore to younger generations. As Christianity formed a fixed element in European life, the absence of deity in Aboriginal beliefs puzzled the newcomers. David Collins wrote of two distinct mortuary practices: 'young people they consign to the grave, those who have passed the middle age are burnt'.[20]

Three major Aboriginal languages were spoken in the Sydney region. Dharug was the predominant language on much of the Cumberland Plain. Ku-ring-gai was the language between the Lane Cove River and the coast from the north shore of Port Jackson across Broken Bay. The south side of Botany Bay, extending down to Nowra, was the territory of the Dharawal language.[21] Lieutenant William Dawes was the first to record Aboriginal words in a written form, but Dawes and other early observers—Philip Gidley King, David Collins and Watkin Tench— were not skilled in their own language let alone in other languages. Nevertheless, the imperfect records of these early vocabularists do provide some insight into languages long lost and give us some idea of the things that interested Europeans about Aboriginal life and culture.

There were probably eight Dharug-speaking clans near the coast and they referred to themselves as Eora, derived from the term 'E-e', meaning 'yes', and 'ora', meaning 'country or place'.[22] Within each language group different dialects, which shared a common grammar but had slightly different vocabularies, were spoken.[23] Speakers within a group had little difficulty understanding each other. It is thought that less than one thousand people comprised each language group, making the total number of Aborigines around Sydney about 3,000. Apart from the difference in territories and languages, dances, songs, weapons and implements also varied between groups. Distinctions were drawn between 'coasters' and 'woods tribes'—subgroups of the Dharug in the Sydney region and the 'mountaineers' who inhabited the Blue Mountains.

The Cadigal clan occupied a territory that embraced Sydney Cove and stretched along the southern side of Port Jackson from South Head to about Petersham. The tract of land from Petersham westwards to Rosehill, embracing the present Leichhardt municipality, belonged to the Wangal clan; the boundary that separated them from the Cadigal seems to have been the Balmain peninsula.[24]

Within eighteen months of the arrival of the First Fleet, smallpox, introduced by the Europeans, swept through the Sydney bands, killing over half the local indigenous population. Many were found dead in the rock shelters and bays of the harbour. The disease, named 'gal-gal' by the Aborigines, spread so rapidly that many were dead before they had a chance to see the 'gubbas' (white ghosts) who invaded the land.[25] Captain Hunter, returning from the Cape of Good Hope in May 1789, was surprised to see no Aborigines or their canoes as his ship sailed up the harbour. In his journal Lieutenant Bradley wrote of the terror and panic that smallpox caused as it decimated the Aboriginal population.[26]

Deprived of their lands, their traditional food supply seriously disrupted, and many of the Sydney bands destroyed by smallpox, small remnants of bands combined to form new groups. It brought a drastic change to Aboriginal social relations and occupation patterns, with remnants of the Sydney bands withdrawing from the settlement, suspicious of whites and executing 'vengeance on unfortunate stragglers'.[27] In 1790 the 50-strong Cadigal clan had been reduced to three members and it seems likely that the adjoining Wangal clan, so close to Sydney Cove, was also decimated.

In 1790, Pemulwuy, a warrior of the Botany Bay tribe, killed Governor Phillip's gamekeeper. Phillip directed Captain Watkin Tench and soldiers to shoot any six Aboriginal men of Botany Bay in revenge for the murder. The task was abhorrent to Tench and the expedition was unsuccessful. Pemulwuy continued his attacks on convicts and settlers in the Parramatta, Toongabbie and Georges River areas until he was shot dead in 1802.[28] As white settlement spread Aborigines fought hard to defend their territory and practised guerrilla warfare—plundering crops, burning huts and driving away stock. There was violent conflict on the Hawkesbury–Nepean river flats where Aborigines killed 26 settlers in the 1790s. The European response was punitive expeditions of great ferocity in which bands of Aborigines were indiscriminately killed. By 1820, the numbers of Hawkesbury Aborigines were greatly reduced and their resistance was broken.[29]

The tribal life of the Aboriginal people of the Sydney region had also been effectively destroyed by 1820. Bishop Broughton later told a House of Commons Select Committee that by taking over the land and driving away the kangaroos and other game European settlement had made Aboriginal life in the traditional manner impossible.[30] Survivors of the various clans around Port Jackson combined into a kind of 'Sydney tribe' with their main camp on the north shore of the harbour; remnants of the clans on the southern side gathered on a campsite near the heads at Botany.

The Parramatta 'feast' which attracted seven or eight tribes from as far away as Broken Bay, Jervis Bay, the Monaro and possibly Port Macquarie, could muster only 400 Aborigines in 1824.[31] By 1838, of the 500 Aborigines estimated to be living in the Nineteen Counties most had come from outside the district. Even though dispossessed, Aborigines retained their belief in their rights to the traditional lands. Thaddeus Bellingshausen noted when he visited Sydney in 1820:

> The natives remember their former independence. Some expressed their claims to certain places, asserting that they belonged to their ancestors. It is easy to understand that they are not indifferent to having been expelled from their own favourite localities. Despite all the compensation offered them, a spark of vengeance still smoulders in their hearts.[32]

The British government instructed governors to civilise the Aborigines and convert them to Christianity ('civilisation' and 'Christianity' were synonymous terms). Early painters and engravers depicted Aborigines as noble savages—tall, elegant and handsome.[33] These early images contrast sharply with the caricatures of the 1830s which convey the profound effect that dispossession and the influence of white society was having on the Sydney Aborigines. Lithographs of Charles Rodius and John Carmichael depict Aborigines as symbols of degradation. Within his lifetime, Mahroot, the last male of the once 400-strong Botany Bay tribe, saw his people pass into oblivion. He told a parliamentary committee in 1845:

> Well, Mitter [Mr] . . . all black-fellow gone! All this my country! Pretty place Botany! Little Pickaninny, I run about here. Plenty black-fellow then; corrobborry; great fight; all canoe about. Only me left now, Mitter . . . Poor gin mine tumble down [die]. All gone! Bury her like a lady, Mitter . . . all, put in coffin, English fashion. I feel lump in throat when I talk about her but . . . I buried her all very genteel, Mitter . . .[34]

Those Aborigines who survived in the Sydney region had to develop methods of existing within the totally dominant white culture. They lived as beggars and prostitutes, doing odd jobs and occasionally fishing. They lived in camps at the Government Boat Shed at Circular Quay, at Manly Beach, Lavender Bay, Botany Bay and La Perouse.[35] Inland tribes were encountering whites as settlement spread and everywhere the frontier was the scene of bitter conflict between European settlers and Aboriginal occupants.

Disease, alcohol and malnutrition accounted for perhaps two-thirds of the massive decline in Aboriginal populations. With no inherited immunity from pathogens introduced by Europeans, they died in large numbers from smallpox, measles, influenza, whooping cough and tuberculosis. In some regions, where there were massacres, white violence played a large part and, overall, contributed to about one in five deaths.[36] Everywhere throughout the continent, as white settlement spread, Aborigines were ultimately subdued by disease, alcohol and the gun. Deprived of their land, and reduced to living on the margins of settlements, they continued to resist covertly by retaining some of their traditional knowledge, languages, stories and sacred sites, as well as some of their social mores. An 1888 census collected by police throughout New South Wales recorded 4,718 Aborigines, and by 1900 the 'full-blood' Aboriginal population had decreased by 1,610. A total of 3,108 remained but this ignored an increasing number of 'part' Aboriginal people who identified with the Aboriginal community.[37]

Thousands of engraving sites exist within 100 kilometres of Port Jackson; the most lasting examples of Sydney Aboriginal art are to be found on the soft Hawkesbury sandstone rock which surrounds the Cumberland Plain. In the rock shelters and overhangs there are representations of wallabies, fish and eels; there are also images or stencils of hands, boomerangs, hatchets and spears.[38]

The only known Aboriginal sites within Leichhardt, eight altogether, are located in two areas: at Callan Point within the grounds of Rozelle Hospital, and at Yurulbin Point—parts of the municipality's natural shoreline that have remained largely undisturbed. Evidence of whatever other sites existed has been destroyed by extensive reclamation of the shoreline and development.[39] The five sites identified at Callan Point are shell middens in sheltered areas close to the water's edge where groups camped or stopped for a meal. These middens which, like other sites in Port Jackson, contain rock oysters, cockles, mussels and Terrebralia shells, have been dated at about 4,500 years old. The three other sites have been identified on private land at Yurulbin Point. Two are midden sites located under rock overhangs, and the other is an art site with hand stencils and a charcoal outline of a shark.[40]

2 The physical environment

Before he entered the ministry the Reverend Richard Johnson had worked on farms; and, in the opinion of diarist Captain Watkin Tench, he was 'the finest farmer in the colony'. In November 1788 Johnson wrote to a friend:

> As to the Country in general I confess I have no very great opinion of nor expectation from it. The greatest part of it is poor and barren and rocky and requires a great deal of labour to clear it of trees, roots, etc., and to cultivate it, and after all, the Corn in general that has been sown hitherto looks very poor and unpromising—I think I can say none have given it a fairer trial than myself . . . burning wood, digging, sowing, etc, but did not expect to reap anything nearly adequate to my labour. Others seem to be in the same predicament and almost, at least with but few exceptions, are heartily sick of the expedition, and wish themselves back in old England.[1]

Much of the harbour and its immediate hinterland was explored in the early months of settlement. Other early accounts wrote of the problem of water supply, poor soils, the difficulty of felling large eucalypts, the climate and the unfamiliarity with the new landscape.[2] Beyond Sydney Cove the new settlers found a gently undulating plain extending westwards to a river that flowed at the foot of the steep scarp of the Blue Mountains. At the north-east and south-east edges of, the plain, foothills fringe the sandstone Hornsby (275 m) and Woronora plateaux (450 m), which are every bit as rugged as the Blue Mountains (900 m) on the western periphery. The Cumberland Plain, covering 1,400 square kilometres, stretches about 65 kilometres from north to south and 32 kilometres from east to west. It is surfaced by Wianamatta shales from which its relatively heavy clay and loam soils are derived. These soils are shallow and are underlain by a stiff yellow clay subsoil, which, combined with the low relief of the plain, results in their being poorly drained. In wet weather they are saturated; in dry they become desiccated, cracked and intractable. There are, however, several rich alluvial areas along the rivers.[3]

J.C. Crawford's watercolour of part of Glebe in 1844 reveals a landscape that Reverend Richard Johnson had earlier described as being 'full of large green trees'. The original types of vegetation in the current* Leichhardt Municipality were influenced by shale-derived soils. (J.C. Crawford, *Views of NSW & NZ, 1844–50*, Dixson Library)

* Authors' Note: 'current' refers to the present-day 'Municipality of Leichhardt' (now a combination of the suburbs of Annandale, Balmain, Glebe and Leichhardt) as opposed to the former 'Municipality of Leichhardt' (now the 'suburb of Leichhardt')

The main types of vegetation that existed in pre-European Sydney were influenced by shale-derived soils. Most of the plain was an open eucalypt woodland, with widely spaced trees and grass-covered ground in between. On either side of Sydney Cove, low bluffs of Hawkesbury sandstone jutted out into Port Jackson, just as they did at the mouth of each of the port's inlets. The soils near Sydney Cove were poor and acidic, but better soil was discovered at Parramatta, and here in 1789 the first successful attempt at cultivation was made.[4]

A variety of eucalypts grew in the small valleys that ran back from each of the harbour's many bays. The common eucalypts near Sydney were scribbly gums (*Eucalytus haemastoma*), on the plateau country, and red bloodwoods (*Eucalyptus gummifera*) and Sydney red gums (*Angophora costata*), on broken sandstone country. On deeper soils in the gullies Sydney peppermint (*Eucalyptus piperita*), blackbutt (*Eucalyptus pilularis*), forest red gums (*Eucalyptus tereticornis*) and turpentine (*Syncarpia glomulifera*) could be found. Swampy areas carried swamp mahogany (*Eucalyptus robusta*) and bangalay (*Eucalyptus botryoides*), and mangroves (*Avicennia marina*) flourished in the intertidal zones of protected bays, fringed on their landward side by swamp oak (*Casuarina glauca*).[5] Small trees and large shrubs in the understorey included several acacias, yellow tea-tree (*Leptospermum flavescens*) and blackwattle (*Callicoma serratifolia*). Distributed throughout the valley was the Port Jackson fig (*Ficus rubiginosa*) together with bangalow palms (*Archontophoenix cunninghamiana*) and cabbage trees (*Livistona australis*).[6]

Topography and original vegetation of Leichhardt Municipality

Located just to the west of the centre of Sydney, the Municipality of Leichhardt, covering about twe;ve square kilometres, is a seemingly shapeless tract of suburban Sydney. Its southern limits stretch from Blackwattle Bay along Wattle and Bay streets and then follow Parramatta Road about four kilometres to Long Cove Creek (Hawthorne Canal). From there an imaginary line drawn in a northerly direction marks its westernmost extremity. The northern physical boundaries of the municipality are the harbour waterfrontages of Leichhardt, Balmain, Annandale and Glebe.

Three separate sandstone ridges dominate its landscape. These form peninsulas that were created when Port Jackson became a drowned river valley. Hawkesbury sandstone, the major geological formation and the underlying deposit, runs in a south-westerly to north-easterly direction through Leichhardt to Balmain, with a small ridge in Annandale running in the same direction. The sandstone ridge in Glebe runs from south-east to north-west. The sandstone geology of the Balmain peninsula exceeds 40 metres at its highest parts, and deep below the strata lie the coal seams of the Sydney basin. In Annandale and Glebe the soft Wianamatta shale capping the sandstone has weathered to produce gently rolling slopes and rounded summits, with contours ranging from 20 to 30 metres. Steep cliff faces appear throughout the municipality where the underlying sandstone suddenly outcrops. The ridges were drained by Blackwattle Creek, Orphan School and Johnston creeks, White's Creek and Long Cove Creek (Hawthorne Canal), which carved shallow valleys into the landscape. The natural downslope drainage from the shale deposits over lower sandstone slopes created silt, sand and mud intertidal zones or swamps where creeks met the tidal waters. The shape of the original waterfront in much of the

Reclamation of Leichhardt's shoreline by fill to 1970. From an early date, topography was an important social and sanitary consideration in suburban development. The earliest residences were located on elevated sites. The original shape of the current Municipality of Leichhardt's waterfront has been altered perceptibly by extensive reclamations by fill. (Redrawn from Map of Parish of Petersham, 1970)

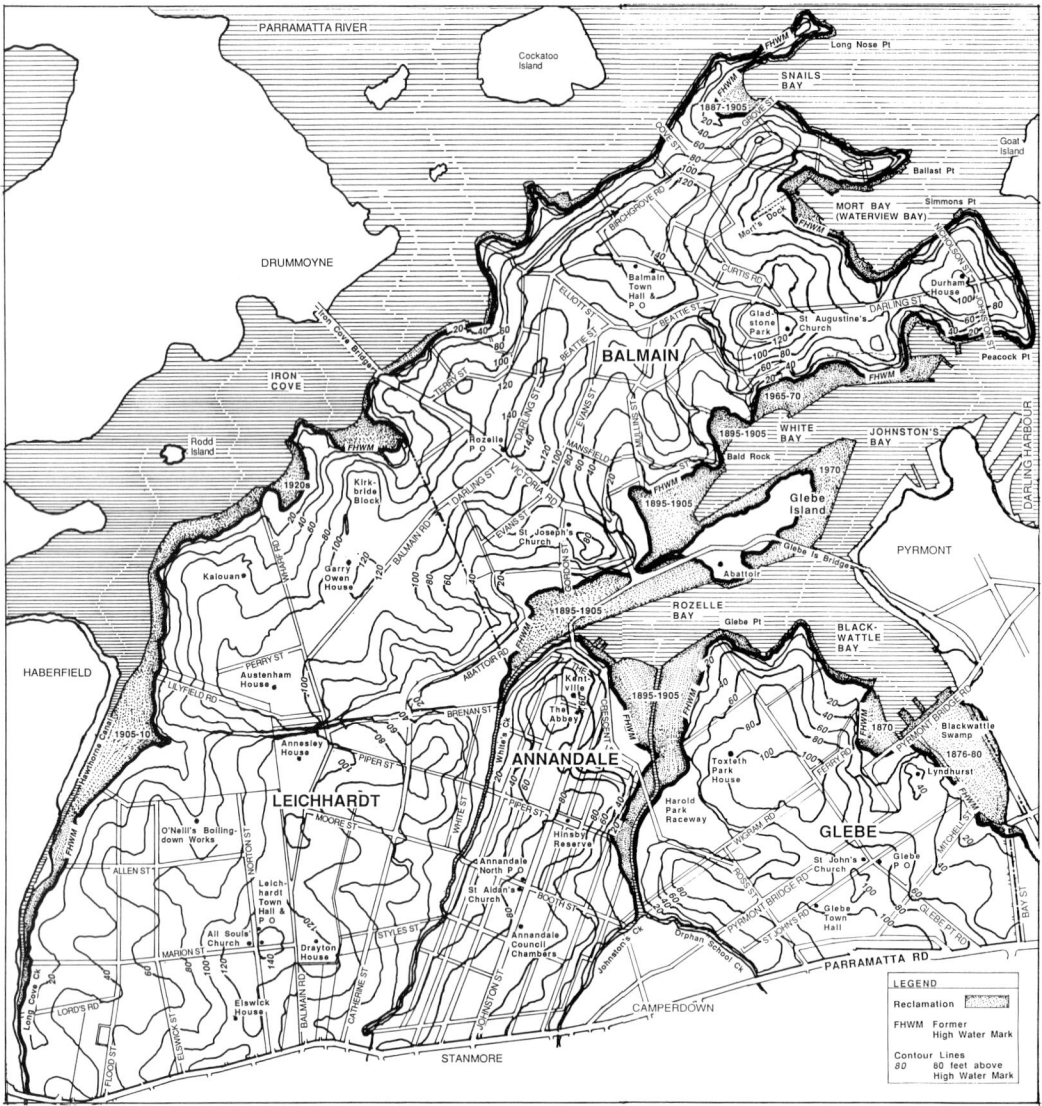

municipality has been radically altered as a result of extensive reclamations by man-made fill, of mangrove and swamp zones at Blackwattle Swamp and on the southern and northern parts of Rozelle Bay, which embrace Glebe Island and the original high water line at Mort's Dock. Parts of Birchgrove and the Hawthorne Canal have also been altered perceptibly.

Open woodlands flourished on the poorer sandstone geology and plateau country. On the ridge areas of shale-derived soils were found grey ironbarks (*Eucalyptus paniculata*), turpentine (*Syncarpia glomulifera*), blackbutt (*Eucalyptus pilularis*), red mahogany (*Eucalyptus resinifera*) and white stringybark (*Eucalyptus globoidea*). On the drier parts of the shale-derived soils forest red gums (*Eucalyptus tereticornis*) grew with an understorey of leptospermum and melaleuca thickets. Red bloodwoods (*Eucalyptus gummifera*) and scribbly gums (*Eucalyptus haemastoma*) were the principal species of the sandstone geology. Swamp oaks (*Casuarina glauca*) grew at the heads of bays with blackwattles (*Callicoma serratifolia*) and grey mangroves (*Avicennia marina*).[7]

Life in the semi-rural retreats, 1830–1841

In 1788 the broad slope behind Farm Cove failed to produce any significant return from the nine acres of corn planted there. The clay soil of Parramatta was better than the sand of Sydney, but, without manuring, it too was expected to return little for the labour expended in farming it.[1] Phillip recognised the value of the alluvial soils on the Hawkesbury, but he hesitated to settle the area because of the lack of suitable people to take charge and of small craft to convey produce to Sydney, and also because he was convinced that, for a time, it would be undesirable to disperse his people too widely.[2]

The British government's policy of free grants, subject to quitrents, sought to encourage permanent settlement of the colony. However it gave substantial power of patronage to governors, developed free of supervision from London. The first convicts who had served their sentences by 1791 were granted farms near Parramatta, and by the time Phillip left the colony in 1792 at least 68 settlers had been placed on small farms, each of 25 to 30 acres. In 1793 the new administration of Major Francis Grose unlocked large tracts of land in five separate clusters—in the original districts of Toongabbie, Liberty Plains, Concord, Bulanaming and Petersham, all in close proximity to Parramatta Road or Parramatta River.[3]

Civil and military officers were the principal beneficiaries of the land patronage system, though merchants, emancipists and a few immigrants with substantial capital also received grants. By 1807, 50 officer settlers had received 22.9 per cent of the 119,676 acres that had been granted. The purpose behind the grants was not achieved, as lack of experience, capital and application led most of the original grantees to sell their land to speculators, who built up large estates. For example, by 1828 only 208 of the original 1,226 emancipist grantees, or 16.9 per cent of them, were still on their land.[4]

Up to 1814, only 14,000 unwanted felons were dumped in this outpost of Britain's empire. When the Napoleonic War ended, the flow of convicts rose dramatically. Between 1815 and 1829, 30,880 men and women were transported to New South Wales, and during the 1830s an average of more than 3,000 convicts a year were sent to New South Wales. More than half had been sentenced for seven years, about a quarter for life, and most of the rest for fourteen years. The majority were transported for stealing and very few of them went back home. Largely drawn from working-class or peasant backgrounds, they formed the basis for the creation of a proletariat in the colony.[5]

There were anxieties about the desirable composition of colonial society. Edward Gibbon Wakefield called it the 'shovelling out of paupers'.[6] Wakefield, who had critically studied emigration during his stay in Newgate gaol, advocated schemes for systematic colonisation, hoping to restore old England in the Antipodes, a place where a young man of breeding but no means could make his way. The prospects of making a fortune at home were slight and here was a treatise on how to acquire wealth and status in the Australian colonies. The proceeds of Wakefield's land sale could be used for the shipment of migrants who would upgrade colonial society, making it 'extensions of the old society'.[7] Those with a vision of Empire had advocated encouragement of free settlement but it was not until 1831 that the government began directly to assist immigration from the British Isles. 'I consider', wrote Governor Bourke, 'that as Great Britain has so long made use of Australia for the convenience of the Empire that the convenience and interests of the colonists should now be considered.'[8] The colony would begin to shed its convict characteristics and emerge as a free enterprise economy between 1837 and 1843 when 50,000 assisted immigrants disembarked at Sydney.

The nature of Sydney society began to alter in the 1820s as a new establishment of civil servants replaced the old military elite. Between 1821 and 1824 the British government appointed a Colonial Secretary, Chief Justice and Attorney-General, and an Archdeacon of the Church of England was created.

A growing import and a small export through Port Jackson made Sydney the focus of trade which, in turn, stimulated the development of commercial enterprise. Expanding trade stimulated the construction of wharves, stores and shipping facilities, and shipping and transport services grew as paddle-steamers were added to the colonial fleet. Associated with this increase in local enterprise was the growth of merchant houses, agencies, shipping offices and retail stores.[9] In the early 1820s the mercantile and retail groups lived within a central core surrounding the main artery of George Street. To the east of George Street the well-to-do resided; west of it the labouring poor, servants, sailors and vagrants.

Sydney was characterised by a static and clearly articulated social structure. Its society was headed by 'Government officials, the Military and Naval Officers and their wives and some few of the leading colonists'. Men engaged in any kind of trade or business, observed Lady Forbes, were not admitted to this inner circle.[10] Below this stratum were the merchants, the administrative elite and professional men with education. 'Government officers don't know merchants,' wrote Louisa Meredith, 'merchants with "stores" don't know other merchants who keep "shops" and then shopkeepers have, I doubt not, a little code of their own prescribing the proper distances to be observed between drapers and haberdashers, butchers and pastrycooks'.[11]

Occupying the next rung of the social ladder were clerks in lodgings and other young men of education but no property, artisans, and those who possessed skilled crafts. Firmly planted at the bottom of the ladder, sharply differentiated from the groups above, were the labourers, servants and vagrants.

Those occupying the top of Sydney's social pyramid were anxious to live separate and apart from ordinary townsfolk, tradesmen and retail merchants. Villa allotments on the Woolloomooloo ridge, ranging from eight acres to ten acres, offered pleasant views westwards

LIFE IN THE SEMI-RURAL RETREATS, 1830–1841

to the town, and to the east overlooked the harbour entrance. From 1828 this became Sydney's exclusive suburban area—with an elite composed of heads of civil service departments and lesser officials. Among the Woolloomooloo gentry were Supreme Court judges Sir James Dowling and John Stephen, the Surveyor General Thomas Livingstone Mitchell, Colonial Architect Ambrose Hallen and High Sheriff Thomas Macquoid.[12]

The 'volume of business,' Dyster has observed, 'allowed men of low talents and little probity to prosper vulgarly.'[13] Certainly a motley collection of people had acquired extensive property holdings in and around Sydney. For example most of the new industrial ventures—distilleries, flour mills, breweries, tanneries and soap and candle works—were promoted by men who had arrived in the colony as convicts: James Underwood, Simeon Lord, William Hutchinson, Samuel Terry, Robert Cooper, Solomon Levey and Daniel Cooper.

Division between free settlers and convicts remained the major cleavage in colonial society. Godfrey Charles Mundy noted that the emancipist remained 'a class apart from the untainted'.

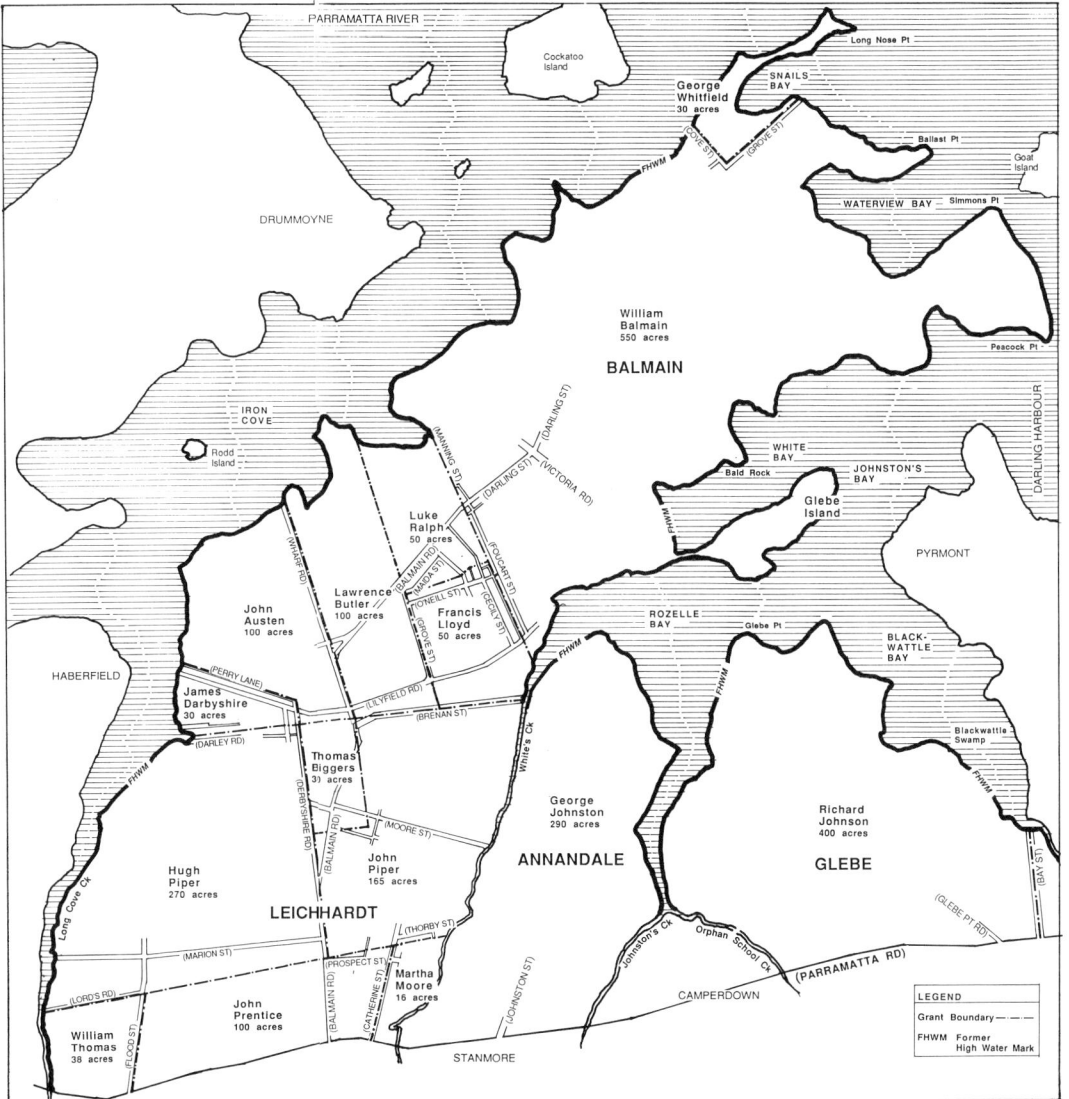

Land grants in Leichhardt Municipality. Leichhardt Municipality is a collection of fifteen separate land grants made between 1789 and 1821. Most of the original grantees did not occupy the land they received. (Redrawn from Map of Parish of Petersham, 1970)

Some ticket-of-leave men did possess handsome residences and other symbols of affluence and met regularly with merchants and men in business on equal terms for the negotiation of affairs. But when the transaction was completed, Colonel Mundy wrote, they 'fell back into their prescribed position'. He saw the society of Sydney as 'cut up into parties and cliques'.[14]

Sydney grew outwards in all directions, its population almost doubling in the years 1828 to 1836. Greatly increased demands for space for non-residential purposes within the physical limits of the Town of Sydney, defined in 1833, inevitably meant some deterioration in living conditions. The earliest villa clusters in Sydney were along the harbour's eastern waterfront. As the traveller left George Street and rode out of town along Parramatta Road, he passed Ultimo House, built about 1800 for Surgeon John Harris, set back on a 34-acre estate, and, about the same time two miles down the road, horsemen passed the gates leading to George Johnston's Annandale estate.

The present Municipality of Leichhardt is a collection of fifteen original grants made between 1789 and 1821, but it was not until the 1830s that a growing number of men moving up in colonial society began to seek retreats along the peninsulas on the western side of town (Table 1). The timing and density of development of the fifteen original landholdings during the nineteenth century varied enormously, but in this chapter it is intended to outline the emergence of semi-rural retreats at the frontier of suburban development.

Balmain, in the northern portion of the Parish of Petersham, and Glebe, in the parish's eastern corner, were the first neighbourhoods to appear on the map. An itinerary of roads incorporated in James Raymond's *New South Wales Calendar and General Post Office Directory* (1833) noted:

> on the right the Glebe road, so named because it leads through lands sold about three years ago by the Church, several good houses have been erected lately and gardens formed. At the junction of the roads is the Archdeaconry; a portion of land where it is contemplated to erect a residence for the Archdeacon of New South Wales.

Raymond did not include Balmain in the directory; as it was off the beaten track, its early residents relied on the water to travel to Sydney.[15]

In 1789 instructions had been given to grant 400 acres 'in or near each town . . . for the maintenance of a minister'.[16] The Sydney Glebe lands were measured out the following year and income derived from the land was to sustain the first clergyman appointed to the colony, Richard Johnson. The church reserve remained heavily timbered and largely unoccupied until 1828 when, to relieve the 'pressing needs of clergy', the Church and School Corporation subdivided Glebe into 28 allotments and all but three parcels were offered for sale.[17]

William Balmain arrived with the First Fleet, an assistant surgeon on the convict transport *Alexander*. He received a 550-acre grant in 1800 of the peninsula that bears his name. Born on 2 February 1762 at Balhepburn, Scotland, Dr Balmain was principal surgeon of the colony when he received his grant. By 1801 he had become a substantial landholder, owning 1,480 acres of which 975 acres had been granted and the rest purchased. Balmain did not reside on or make any use of his 550-acre grant. The preamble in this grant described the land as 'Gilchrist Place', after John Gilchrist, an 'orientalist' of Calcutta. A little more than three months before

Governor Hunter granted 'Gilchrist Place' to the surgeon, Gilchrist had been involved in the export of rum to Sydney on board the *Thynne*, for a syndicate which included Balmain. Dr Balmain transferred the peninsula to Gilchrist for a token five shillings on 7 July 1801.[18] He sailed from Sydney on 26 August 1801 and died in London on 17 November 1803, leaving, in England, a de facto ex-convict wife and two of the three children she bore him.[19]

Table 1   Land grants in the municipality of Leichhardt

Grantee	Occupation	Year	Area (acres)	Estate
Richard Johnson	Chaplain	1789	400	Sydney Glebe lands
John Prentice	Free Settler	1794	100	Hampton Farm
Thomas Biggers	–	1794	30	Biggers' Farm
George Whitfield	Private NSW Corps	1796	30	Whitfield's Farm (later Birchgrove)
George Johnston	Captain NSW Corps	1799	290	(later North Annandale)
William Balmain	Principal Surgeon Colony of NSW	1800	550	Gilchrist Place (later Balmain & Rozelle)
William Thomas	Guard	1810	38	(Later Kegworth)
Martha M. Moore	–	1810	16	–
Hugh Piper	Captain NSW Corps	1811	270	Macquarie Gift
John Piper	Captain NSW Corps	1811	165	Piperston
James Darbyshire	–	1819	30	–
John Austen	Engraver	1819	100	Spring Cove (later Austenham)
Lawrence Butler	Cabinetmaker	1819	100	–
Francis Lloyd	–	1819	50	–
Luke Ralph	–	1821	50	Fairlight

At the auction of the Glebe lands in 1828, 25 allotments ranging from three acres to 42 acres, were offered for sale.[20] Twelve of the smaller lots (9 to 20), near Blackwattle Swamp, attracted the strongest bidding, with prices varying from £95 to £125 per acre being paid by slaughterhouse proprietors Thomas May and Edward Owens, by distiller Robert Cooper and landowner James Mudie. Proximity to a freshwater creek, and to the city, and legislative restrictions that affected the location of industry made Blackwattle Swamp an ideal site for slaughterhouses and boiling-down works.[21]

The larger, more elevated blocks in the northern part of Glebe, with views of harbour and city, would become villa retreats. The purchasers—Alexander Spark, William Dumaresq, Alexander McKenzie, Thomas Harrington, Charles Cowper, George Williams and George Allen—paid between £12 and £16 per acre.

Private George Whitfield of the New South Wales Corps received a 30-acre grant 'at Snails Bay' in 1796. Located on a long spit of sandstone, and almost entirely surrounded by water, Whitfield's Farm was acquired by Lieutenant John Birch, paymaster of the 73rd Regiment, in 1810. Birch built a two-storey timber-shingle-roofed house of sandstone, probably quarried on the site. Birch Grove House, the first residence to appear on the Balmain peninsula, offered seclusion and a view of the Flagstaff. The 'men's huts', located a discreet distance from the residence, housed convicts who laboured on the estate, maintaining its large orchard and vegetable garden and looking after the cattle that grazed there. Apart from this intrusion, the remainder of the peninsula was owned by John Gilchrist. As late as 1818, however, the trustees of William Balmain's estate were acting in a manner that suggested they considered Dr Balmain to be the proprietor of the land, but by 1823 any uncertainty as to Dr Gilchrist's title seems to have disappeared.[22]

John Gilchrist, like Balmain, had trained as a surgeon in Edinburgh and entered the Royal Navy in 1782, but he joined the Indian Medical Service shortly afterwards. While in Calcutta he became fluent in Hindustani and Urdu and published several works to facilitate its study. From 1796, he put aside his medical practice to concentrate on producing grammatical and related works to teach the native language to the East India Company's India-based employees. He was appointed Professor of Hindustani at Fort William College in Calcutta in 1800, but ill-health forced him to return to Edinburgh in 1804. He continued to teach and publish authoritative works on Hindustani and died in Paris in 1841. Gilchrist never visited Australia, but the initial subdivision and sale of his 550-acre parcel took place in 1836. Litigation in English courts over the terms of Gilchrist's will was protracted, and it was not until 1852 that the remainder of his Balmain estate could be released for subdivision and disposal.[23]

The early attraction of Balmain was its steep, sheltered shoreline and deep water close to shore, ideal for docking. An array of people engaged in maritime and waterfront activities was drawn to this 'extraordinary rising Deptford of New South Wales'. Ship captains John Nicholson, James Pearson and George Buddivant moved there and boatbuilders Henry and Edward Gardiner, Joseph Looke, John Bell, William Burnicle, William Howard and Andrew Reynolds established yards on the waterfront. As it emerged as a centre for maritime industry, other related businesses appeared—George Canniss, sailmaker; Daniel Munro, marine surveyor; and Thomas Rowntree, ship repairer.[24]

The healthfulness, scenery and seclusion of Balmain also made it a resort for mercantile men, clerks and bankers who worked in the city.[25] Among those to find a home or lodgings on the peninsula were merchants Michael Metcalfe, John Edye Manning, Adam Wilson and Joshua Young; Anglican clergyman Robert Allwood; accountant John Fraser Gray; Chief Clerk of the Supreme Court Alfred Elyard; William Vallack of the Colonial Secretary's Office; and Robert Blake, speculative builder. Other occupants of Balmain villas were banker John Hunter Baillie, auctioneer Henry Davy, surveyor Leslie Moodie, stonemason John Cavill and cabinetmaker Edward Hunt.[26]

Glebe Point's topography and shallow waterfront ensured that it developed differently from Balmain. It was extolled as a:

> place not inferior to Woolloomooloo for a quiet retirement after business hours and a delightful spot for rural recreation and good society. The soil is good and much improved from having been successfully cropped. There can be no place better suited to the character or tone of respectability than what is constituted in this neighbourhood.[27]

Solicitors, doctors and a collection of businessmen with retail establishments in the city—John Betts, David Jones, John Wood, Ambrose Foss, Thomas Bowden and Edward Pollard, banker

George Miller and accountant George Robinson and brother Robert, a soap manufacturer – were among the occupants of the Glebe villas in the 1830s.

Proceeding west from Glebe along Parramatta Road, a rough track known as Balmain Road branched off to the right at the Bald Face Stag Hotel and weaved in a north-easterly direction across three kilometres of undulating countryside to link up with Darling Street. The territory Balmain Road passed through was occupied, according to an advertisement, by 'numerous gentlemen's seats, and residences of influential persons connected in daily occupations with Sydney'. It was described as a 'neighbourhood not only of choice but of popular enquiry'.[28] Among the prominent officials and professionals residing here were Deputy Surveyor General Samuel Perry, attorney John Ryan Brenan, solicitor James Norton and coal merchant John Piper Mackenzie. Abraham Hearn, publican, and Charles Hughes, butter and cheese monger, were two of the locality's earliest identities.[29]

Private carriage and ferry and, later, the horse-drawn omnibus, would enhance physical continuity between the city and emerging hamlets. Rugged dirt roads connected outlying settlements, and as the city crept closer to these suburban frontiers, open fields were enclosed and the number of market gardeners and keepers of horses, cows and pigs grew.

The first residents of Balmain, Glebe and Leichhardt were solid middle-class citizens whose roots were attached to the commercial hub of the city. Occupants of Glebe and Leichhardt villas journeyed daily by carriage into the city but at Balmain first the watermen and then the ferry remained the quickest way into town. Early settlement at Balmain was confined until the 1850s to the eastern end of Darling Street, and around Waterview Bay. Clusters of villas in Glebe tended to be located on more elevated sites, favoured by natural drainage. Leichhardt remained a retreat of the wealthy and respectable until the 1870s when it gradually began to be denuded of its leafy features.

The 1830s was a period of economic prosperity in the colony. In the neighbourhoods just beyond the urban perimeter the villa allotment remained the predominant landholding.[30] The wealth that some colonists acquired was reflected directly in the new hamlets. Many of the homes were large, befitting the owners' station in society, and they changed hands at premiums that reinforce claims of affluence. 'The private residences of the richer class of gentry,' wrote C.J. Baker, 'are also a little removed from the town, and are very surprising for their number and costliness. They are substantial, handsome buildings, many of them indeed of considerable pretension.' Their occupants set the tone of polite society, and shaped the early character of these neighbourhoods.[31]

Many of the craftsmen who built these early homes remain anonymous. Some were designed by John Verge, John Bibb, Edward Hallen, Henry Ginn, Henry Robertson and probably Mortimer Lewis. A collection of owner-builders and specialist tradesmen, of which carpenters were the most numerous, can however be identified from contemporary directories. In the early 1840s carpenters Thomas Moore, Donald Nicholson, William Phillips, James Reynolds, Thomas Spence and Bill Stewart were busy constructing dwellings in Balmain. Quarrymen, too, found plenty of work on the peninsula and five of them lived locally. Bricklayer Hall, builders Fowler and Milligan, painter Hill and glazier McAnley worked beside carpenters and quarrymen, and Thomas Ellis earned a living sinking wells in Balmain.[32]

The names of the tradesmen who sought to meet the expanding market for houses in Glebe

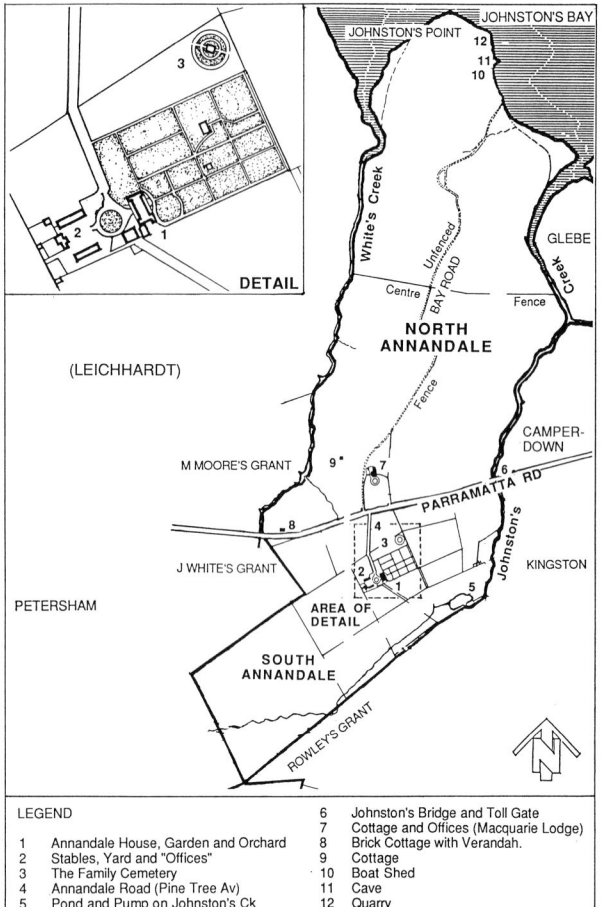

Plan of the Annandale Estate, 1843. The location of Annandale House gave it a commanding view of the surrounding countryside. The estate contained all the pre-requisites for maintaining a lifestyle that demonstrated the occupant's wealth and social standing—convict quarters, orchard and gardens, beehives, quarry and boat shed. (Re-drawn from Map of the Estate Named Annandale . . . the Property of Robert Johnston, RN, 1843, Maps Collection, Mitchell Library)

can also be identified. Builder Thomas Tipple Smith and cabinet-maker William Elphinstone were prominent in the local building industry from an early date, together with bricklayers Ebenezer Dibley and Iddo Oxley and carpenters Jeremiah Baker, John Jackson and John Stanton.[33] Initially building materials were procured from the immediate neighbourhood. Large eucalypts quickly disappeared from the landscape and soon timber was being shipped in to Booth's and Goodlet's mills. Quarries at Balmain and Pyrmont yielded an abundant supply of sandstone blocks for cottages, seawalls and wharves. The Johnstons' brickfield at Annandale was a thriving local enterprise and brickmakers near Blackwattle Swamp obtained clay from William Bryan's brickpits to produce rough bricks in small kilns. An early source of chimney pots, pipes and other building materials was Fowler's Queen Street pottery in Glebe.[34]

The Johnstons of Annandale were the earliest permanent European residents of the present Leichhardt municipality. George Johnston, a veteran of the American War of Independence, arrived in Sydney as a marine officer on the *Lady Penrhyn* in the First Fleet. The governors treated him generously in dispensing land; altogether he received 4,162 acres in grants.[35]

In 1799 Johnston was allotted 290 acres on the northern side of Parramatta Road, an area now known as Annandale. Six years earlier he had received a 100-acre grant on the south side of Parramatta Road, the first of four parcels in this precinct which now forms part of the suburb of Stanmore. These grants Johnston called Annandale, after his home town in Dumfriesshire, Scotland, where he was born in 1764. On board the *Lady Penrhyn* Johnston met milliner Esther Abrahams, transported for seven years for stealing lace. She became his de facto wife and bore him three sons and four daughters.

Annandale House, erected on a ridge on the southern side of the road in about 1800, was approached along an avenue of Norfolk Island pines. A single-storey dwelling, designed in the Georgian style and built of bricks baked from clay on the estate, it was surrounded by a formal garden, an orchard and vineyard, beehives and stables, a summer house and a two-storey convict barracks. In 1820 a burial vault, designed by Francis Greenway, was added for son George junior.[36] George Johnston had given the overseer of the estate, George Platt, a detailed list of instructions relating to tasks to be performed by the convict workers from dawn till dusk.[37] Five acres were set aside as brickfields and a pit and kiln maintained for manufacture and sale to the public.

For his part in the Rum Rebellion in 1808, George Johnston was court-martialled, found guilty and cashiered from the army in 1811, but he retained possession of his extensive landholdings. The Duke of Northumberland, an old commander and patron of Johnston, presented him with fine horses and ewes, greatly assisting him in becoming one of the colony's most successful graziers.[38] On his death in 1823, the second son, Robert, took over the management of their estates. Robert had sailed to England with his father in 1800, joined the Royal Navy in 1807, and was lucky to survive the Napoleonic War. Robert became a patriarchal figure on the Annandale estate, a squire who patrolled his bailiwick on a large white horse. Despite development closing in on all sides, Annandale remained intact until 1876 when, with Robert approaching 84 years, the process of subdividing began.[39]

George Allen acquired the largest tract of Glebe in 1828, a consolidated holding of 95 acres.[40] He established his own legal practice in the city and, in 1830, only eight years after his admission as a solicitor when he had no capital, Allen owned property valued at between £6,000 and £10,000. He had John Verge design a gentleman's residence on his Glebe land which he called Toxteth Park after a village near Liverpool in England. The landed lawyer moved to his new home in 1831 and observed 'my only employment after the business of the day is to retire to my room (for I am the only one of the family left in Sydney) and read my books of which I am sorry to say I have but a slender stock'.[41] The Methodist Society gave him the spiritual nourishment he was seeking and in 1843 a Wesleyan chapel was built on his estate.

Samuel Elyard's watercolour of Annandale House and Estate, 1877. George Johnston and his family occupied the Annandale Estate from about 1800 and, despite development closing in on all sides, their estate remained intact until 1876. (Pictures Catalogue, ZDVG SP COLL/Elyard/ 8, Dixson Library)

There were fifteen convict servants on Toxteth Park. Servants were regarded as chattels and were often treated by their masters with a proprietary air. George Allen told his journal:

> The servants of this colony are the greatest drawback to comfort that I know of. It is our plan to treat them with every kindness but I find we receive only ingratitude in return. By government laws our assigned servants are not entitled to wages but only to certain clothing and rations. I give my servants far beyond the ration allowed and wages and yet I find they are no better than those who are treated with every hardship.[42]

John Crawley, one of Allen's assigned convicts, was taken before the court in 1835 and given 25 lashes for pretending to be deaf. Of this incident, Allen wrote, 'I am averse to getting my men punished but I think that when they are so wicked as to pretend to be sick merely to get rid of their work, they well deserve it'.[43] Draper David Jones, a close friend of Allen's, overstepped the mark when he assaulted two of his women convict servants. Jones pleaded guilty but argued 'outrageous conduct' as a mitigating factor. He was fined 40 shillings.[44]

The relationship between master and servant was not always an unhappy one. Josiah Slater, transported for highway robbery, identified his interests with squire Allen. The baker, and sometime gardener on Toxteth Park, he raised a family in a cottage within his master's domain. Another of Allen's assigned servants, Francis Burgess, worked for many years as a clerk in his law firm. He had been sent to the colony for embezzlement. A small army of working people was required to allow full enjoyment of the comforts and delights that a villa retreat offered. 'I often wish we could do without them,' Allen wrote, 'but it is impossible.'[45]

For much of his long life George Allen kept a diary, and although it throbs with a passion for moral rectitude, it gives us an insight into the life of a rising professional man. He regularly read the Bible, occasionally went on picnics, gave up taking snuff and smoking, disliked

George Allen (1800–1877). Solicitor George Allen was the squire of the 95-acre Toxteth Park Estate, Glebe, from 1831 to 1877. He continued to control the way his estate developed after his death through his will. Title covenants ensured that no public houses appeared on the Wesleyan lawyer's domain. (GPO Videodisc-1 Still No 10516, Mitchell Library)

horse racing and strongly disapproved of dancing: 'I know of the dreadful consequences to which it often leads . . . How many families have been ruined by balls and assemblies.'[46]

Lyndhurst, another Verge Regency villa with Tuscan columns, built between 1833 and 1837, was an imposing sight and overlooked Blackwattle Swamp.[47] It was the residence of the Inspector of Colonial Hospitals, James Bowman, but in 1836, when hospital administration was placed under military control, the surgeon's services were no longer required. No expense had been spared by Bowman on his marine villa with its landscaped grounds and sweeping coach drive, but his income was insufficient to maintain such a lifestyle.[48] By 1842 the ambitious surgeon was almost bankrupt; his brothers-in-law James and William Macarthur bought Lyndhurst and then sold it to the Church of England, which established St James' College there in 1846.

The first villa residence erected in Glebe was Hereford House, and the respectable urban businessmen who made it their home had a magnificent view of Sydney as it acquired a definite shape on the horizon. The house had been built for George Williams, who died shortly after its completion in 1829.[49] The first occupant was probably John Kinchela, who took up his appointment as Attorney-General in New South Wales in 1831 at a salary of £1,200. Kinchela left Hereford House in 1833 and, affected by debt and increasing deafness, retired from the bench in 1837.[50] Chemist Ambrose Foss moved from Hereford House in 1836 to an eight-room colonial style cottage on the brow of the hill just to the west. Foss called this retreat, which was complete with stables and coach house, Forest Lodge. It reflected his aspirations of leafy solitude and privacy, remote from the bustling centre of commerce.[51]

The well-to-do who moved to neighbourhoods on the city's outskirts were not great arbiters of taste but they brought in experts, specialist craftsmen of the day, to design elegant homes, symbols of the stage the owner had reached in his quest for material betterment. The villas, which for social and sanitary reasons were invariably located on elevated sites, featured regular, often square, ground plans with high-ceilinged rooms. The homes were consciously oriented for sunlight (generally facing Flagstaff Hill), for summer breezes and a view. 'Every house has its garden,' wrote a contemporary observer, 'of greater or less extent in which the fruits and flowers of Europe vie with those of Asia.'[52]

The gardens of the new villas were influenced by the picturesque landscaped gardening movement developed as an art form in England by Humphrey Repton. 'Rural scenery and water views seem to be the favourite subject of taste,' wrote Thomas Shepherd in 1836, for these were 'the means of retiring from town to their village or country cottage.' Trained as a landscape gardener in Scotland, Shepherd established the Darling nursery in Chippendale and supplied occupants of semi-rural villas with trees, shrubs and annuals. In Shepherd's view, the way Lyndhurst estate was landscaped was a fine example for a genteel marine residence.[53]

The squires of all the large estates—Annandale (280 acres), Elswick (123 acres), Toxteth (95 acres), Garry Owen (68 acres), Lyndhurst (32 acres) and Birchgrove (30 acres)—had a retinue of assigned convicts to keep them in a manner to which they had become accustomed. 'Men's huts', too, existed on more modest landholdings. However, the supply of convicts ended in 1840 when transportation to New South Wales ceased. The respectable and wealthy owners hired domestic servants to perform the cooking, cleaning and washing in their households, and no family thinking of itself as middle class could be without at least one servant, an ambition that was easily satisfied since help could be had for a pittance.

LIFE IN THE SEMI-RURAL RETREATS, 1830–1841

Ready access by ferry and its 'exposure to pure air' made Balmain a 'singularly desirable and healthy place of residence for those people who are detained during the day by the business of the metropolis'.[54] No home had a finer aspect than Birch Grove House, whose 30 acres of grounds made it the peninsula's largest holding. Early occupants—merchants Rowland Walpole Loane, Captain Samuel Augustus Perry and Superintendent of Convicts John McLean— reflect its desirability as an abode for the wealthy and respectable.

Early residential development in Balmain was clustered around the eastern end of Darling Street and Waterview Bay. The precinct between Nicholson Street and The Avenue, where large allotments predominated, was a favourite marine neighbourhood. Between 1839 and 1844 five substantial sandstone villas—Duke's Cottage, Durham House, Spring Hill, Pine Villa and Alfred Elyard's house—were constructed here. Durham House ranked as one of Balmain's finest. A seventeen-room, two-storey sandstone dwelling, surrounded by large grounds and gardens, it was the home of Harbour Master John Nicholson and his family. Nicholson joined the Royal Navy as a teenager and arrived in Sydney in 1817 as Chief Officer on the convict transport *Lord Melville*. However by 1842, unable to met the demands of creditors, Captain Nicholson's estate was sequestered and Durham House became the Captain Cook Inn. Palatial Durham House, together with the nearby Unity Hall Hotel and St Mary's Church, were conspicuous landmarks on this early townscape.[55] The owner of Spring Hill was Michael Metcalfe. Educated for commerce, he became a customs agent after he arrived in Sydney in 1837 and shortly thereafter he founded the Australian Steam Navigation Co.[56] He was attracted to Balmain by boatbuilder John Bell, his brother-in-law.

Boats, boatbuilding yards and wharves stretched along the waterfront from Simmons Point to Peacock Point. Bass, Burnicle, Buddivant, Howard, Looke, Bell, Pearson, Beattie, Talbot and Chape were prominent names in Balmain's emerging maritime industry. Set back a little from the waterfront between Darling Street Wharf and Simmons Point were the stone cottages of Joseph Looke and William Howard. A little west of Darling Street Wharf, waterside workers could quench their thirst at the Shipwright's Arms and the Waterford Arms.[57]

The St Patrick's Inn (Burnbank Hotel), located in the territory between Ternen and Killeen Streets, acquired a licence in 1836, and nearby J.F. Gray's Elgin Cottage, Canterbury Cottage and Darling Lodge adorned this precinct. But generally landowners here favoured intensive development.[58] The narrow and steep streets that laced this territory combined with countless small timber houses squeezed on to narrow-fronted blocks, made this predominantly a neighbourhood for blue-collar folk. By the mid-1840s the built fabric of Balmain was a mixture of sandstone, brick and timber cottages. Sandstone was the preferred building material of the well-to-do; more modest cottages were constructed of timber.

About 1835 Waterview House was built for Frederick Parbury on the slope of a hill, well back from the water. This one-storey, six-room house, set in ten acres of grounds, contained a stable, coach house and a fenced garden and was the first villa to appear on the Balmain estate. Comptroller of Customs George Cooper acquired the residence but after his bankruptcy in 1841 the Waterview estate was carved into modest building blocks.[59]

Waterview House, built for merchant Frederick Parbury about 1835, the first villa on the Balmain Estate. Demolished after 1905, it stood near the corner of Colgate Avenue and Caroline Street. (Mary Stephen's drawing dated 1875, Wilkinson Family Papers, Dixson Library)

Across the ridge that Darling Street followed, on a parcel of land bounded by Darling, Adolphus and Wallace streets and Johnston's Bay, speculative builder Robert Blake set out to provide gentlemen's residences for those with the means to buy or rent. His first venture, Mount Shamrock, was completed in 1837 and he then commissioned John Bibb to design Moorefield, a Regency cottage of brick, for £1,200. An even grander sandstone house, Wallscourt Lodge (1840), built by Blake, served as the residence of Robert Allwood, rector of St James' Church, Sydney.[60]

Public houses were valuable pieces of real estate and publicans influential local figures. William Ternen, the owner–builder, and licensee, of St Patrick's Inn, had arrived in the colony as a (less than) ten-year-old drummer with the Second Fleet. Boatbuilder John Bell and storekeeper John Beattie were both attracted to the liquor trade, diversifying their businesses to acquire the Dolphin Inn and the Masonic Arms, respectively.[61]

The prospect of enjoying some of the physical comforts associated with middle-class life and, no less important, the feelings of status that came with possessions, were effective stimuli for those moving upwards in colonial society. In their quests for respectability, William Vallack and Alfred Elyard, clerks in the civil service, found cottages in Balmain with essential prerequisites for any self-respecting clerk—coach houses and stables.[62] Members of bourgeois society filled the sandstone villas that dotted the landscape. William Howard, son of a convict, and Joseph Looke, struggling boatbuilder, perhaps did not possess all the ingredients of respectability but they had acquired wealth by building boats and were much admired as self-made men and examples of free enterprise.[63]

Many fortunes vanished during the depression of the early 1840s. Included among local landholders who were declared insolvent were A.B. Spark, J.H. Grose, J.J. Peacock, J. Nicholson, R. Duke, G. Cooper, J.T. Hughes, A. Wilson, J. Edye Manning and A. Foss.[64] Their landholdings were subdivided and intensively developed to satisfy creditors, and this helped to accelerate suburban growth.

The eleven grants that comprised the suburb of Leichhardt ranged from sixteen acres to 270 acres, covering a total area of 952 acres. From about 1832, when the first gentleman's residence appeared, until the late 1860s, the area retained its rustic charm and character as a genteel semi-rural address where a handful of professional and mercantile people had settled.[65] Ownership of several of its large landholdings changed during the buoyant economic conditions of the 1830s. By 1844 some fourteen substantial buildings had been constructed on the Leichhardt estates.[66]

About 1847, merchant Walter Beames acquired a portion of the Piperston estate and a subdivision of this land appeared on plans in 1849 as 'Leichhardt'. Beames was a friend and supporter of the Prussian explorer Ludwig Leichhardt who disappeared in north Queensland in 1848.[67] However, it would be some time before the general area was widely known as Leichhardt. As late as 1870, *Sands's Sydney and Suburban Directory* called the area Petersham.[68]

James Norton, born in 1795 in England where he qualified as an attorney, arrived in Sydney in 1818, ready to seek a fortune in a new land. Norton lived and worked in the city where he established his legal practice. His managing clerk, James Foster, began building a large house in 1832, overextended his finances and sold the Elswick estate to his employer in 1834. The Elswick estate embodied the essence of respectability, wealth and physical comfort. A handsome two-storey stone mansion, complete with coach house and stables, orchard, vineyard and long barracks for the convicts, stood on the 123-acre estate. The house was approached by a carriage drive, curving in from Parramatta Road and passing through ornamental iron gates. The kitchen, laundry and servants' quarters were separate from the house. Its landscaped grounds contained roses, bamboos and gardenias, as well as peacocks and ponds rich in eels.[69] Its valuation suggests it was the municipality's grandest home. The outspoken and rough-mannered Norton had a flourishing legal practice and was registrar of the Archdeaconry of Sydney for 30 years. The squire of the neighbourhood's largest estate died at Elswick on 31 August 1862.[70]

It seems likely that Norton induced his brothers-in-law, John and William Mackenzie, to settle in the area. In 1840 they acquired villa allotments from their uncle, John Piper. William had Bagshot built and Drayton became the abode of coal merchant John who, like Norton, was a fervent Anglican. Both villas fronted Balmain Road.

Welsh-born Samuel Perry, appointed Deputy Surveyor General on a salary of £500, arrived in Sydney in 1829. For 24 years he endured being deputy to an objectionable superior, Major Thomas Livingstone Mitchell.[71] A tenant of Birch Grove House, Perry became the squire of the 100-acre Austenham estate in 1835. By 1844 Perry had moved from Austenham House to Kalouan, a much larger villa with convict barracks and extensive gardens. He remained on the Austenham estate until his retirement in 1853. In 1841 Perry conceived and had pegged out the 'Township of Broughton' between Long Cove and Perry Street, an early attempt at the creation of a marine villa development in the neighbourhood. John Ryan Brenan bought a three-acre lot at this auction and had Broughton House constructed. It was the home of John Adam Walpole in 1844.[72]

Shortly after his arrival in Sydney, Brenan set up in private practice as an attorney and the following year he became City Coroner and later Magistrate. Between 1837 and 1839 he acquired 150 acres near Balmain Road and built a Regency house, possibly designed by Mortimer Lewis. It became known as Garry Owen after Brenan's birthplace in County Limerick, Ireland. Facing north, with views of Iron Cove, it was a two-storey stuccoed house with eight bedrooms on the first floor, reception room, ballroom and cellar, with servants' quarters, kitchen and scullery located across the courtyard. The estate also contained a summer house and bathing house on Iron Cove.[73] The affable and witty Brenan furnished Garry Owen in the most luxurious manner and entertained there in grand style. Later speculative ventures left Brenan heavily in debt and in 1865 Garry Owen was sold by his mortgagee. Brenan died at Petersham on 5 June 1868, aged about 70 years.[74]

Respectability, an ill-defined notion clearly understood by polite society, gave colonial gentry much of their cohesion. Apart from property ownership, the concept had some relation to education and involvement in responsible enterprise, and embraced such attributes as thrift, good manners, cleanliness of person, tidiness of home and honesty in business affairs.[75] The respectable were good people and, it need hardly be said, the pillars of society. They did not get drunk (thus eliminating most of the working class), were independent and law-abiding and maintained a certain propriety of speech and decorum of bearing. All respectable men wanted to be called

Elswick House, Leichhardt, the residence of solicitor James Norton from 1834 to 1862, stood on a 200-acre estate. Elswick Estate embodied the essence of respectability, wealth and comfort and its valuation in 1844 suggests it was the municipality's grandest semi-rural retreat. (Royal Australian Historical Society Glass Slide Collection No 1815)

The Johnstons having tea on the terrace at Annandale House in the late 1880s. (GPO Videodisc-1 Still 10339, Mitchell Library)

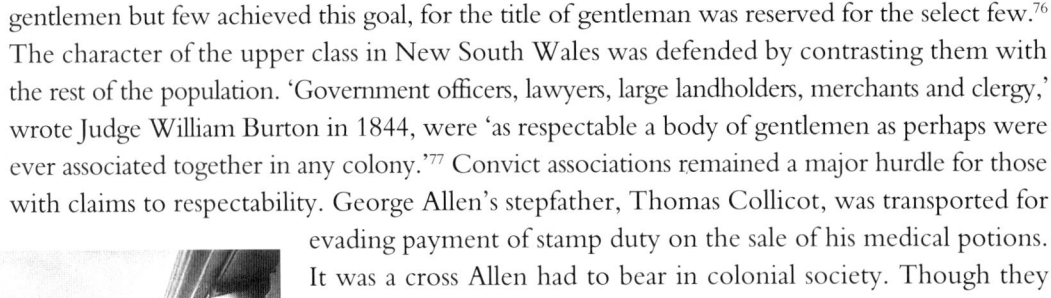

gentlemen but few achieved this goal, for the title of gentleman was reserved for the select few.[76] The character of the upper class in New South Wales was defended by contrasting them with the rest of the population. 'Government officers, lawyers, large landholders, merchants and clergy,' wrote Judge William Burton in 1844, were 'as respectable a body of gentlemen as perhaps were ever associated together in any colony.'[77] Convict associations remained a major hurdle for those with claims to respectability. George Allen's stepfather, Thomas Collicot, was transported for evading payment of stamp duty on the sale of his medical potions. It was a cross Allen had to bear in colonial society. Though they were large landholders, the Johnstons of Annandale had a questionable respectability since Esther Johnston was a transportee.

There is ample evidence to support claims of affluence and social status for occupants of the grandest colonial Georgian and Regency villas that graced the landscapes. However, for more modest retreats, occupied by those climbing the economic and social ladder, the only evidence by which some assessment can be made of their values are the Sydney District Council Assessment Books. In Glebe, Salem House, Forsyth Cottage, Kew Cottage, Guildford Lodge and Rose Cottage, and villas owned by George Miller, John Betts and Randolph Want, are identified as valuable pieces of real estate. High-status areas in Balmain generally corresponded with clusters of handsome sandstone cottages, but almost half of the peninsula's habitations were of timber construction, generally occupied by blue-collar workers. The most visible and picturesque homes in the sparsely populated neighbourhood traversed by Balmain Road were Elswick and Garry Owen, and almost as conspicuous were the locality's three pubs. On the smaller landholdings, Kalouan, Broughton House, Austenham House, Drayton, Kegworth Villa, Bagshot, Maida and cottages owned by Abraham Hearn and Charles Hughes satisfied demands for physical comfort and privacy, and their coach houses, stables and gardens exemplified middle-class aspirations.[78]

The first to move to neighbourhoods just beyond the city limits were those with the economic means to commute daily to their workplaces in the city. A miscellaneous collection of occupational groups had acquired sufficient capital or were in receipt of a salary sufficient to maintain a lifestyle that demonstrated their wealth and social standing.

In colonial Sydney, occupation was the surest criterion of social class and it was reflected directly in the social landscape. Possession of a Balmain or Glebe Point address, or a directory listing as Petersham (which embraced the Balmain Road precinct) was a source of satisfaction to these escapees from urban congestion and pollution. Surrounded by landscaped gardens and orchards, the occupants of elegant villas sought to fulfil dreams of self-importance and respectability.[79] Acquisition of a semi-rural retreat was, however, only the first step in the quest for respectability.

Within the ranks of the new bourgeois, gradations of wealth and status could be discerned. In directories, and on committee lists, John Hunter Baillie, Alfred Elyard, Samuel Perry, John McLean, George Allen, George Miller, John Betts, James Norton, Randolph Want, James

Bowman, John Panton and David Jones had the title 'Esquire' appended to their names, a sure sign they ranked high in colonial society. Among the professional men and prosperous shopkeepers turned merchants who acquired residences in these neighbourhoods of the 'first respectability and stamp', several were associated with responsible enterprise—John Mackenzie, Norton, Metcalfe, Want, Betts, Miller, Allen and Jones all held public directorates.[80]

The Church of England, the religion of about one-half of colonial society, occupied a privileged position as the established church in England.[81] A number of the landed suburban elite—Norton, Mackenzie, Metcalfe, Betts, Bowman and John Wood—played prominent roles in the life of the Anglican Church.

Wesleyan Methodism and the Independents generally drew support from people lower on the social and economic ladder. In Glebe, however, they claimed a coterie of respectable citizens—Ambrose Foss, William Boyce, Ralph Mansfield, Thomas Bowden and, of course, Allen—and they were at the forefront of temperance and teetotal movements.[82] Catholics were conspicuous by their absence among these men of property; an exception was J.R. Brenan of Garry Owen.

In a society that believed in different ranks or order, activities were usually organised so that different classes did not mingle. Protestant churches, for example, segregated their congregations according to status and money, the well-to-do sitting in rented pews, separated from those occupying benches at the rear. Clothing, bearing, manners and accent were differences that distinguished a poor working man from a gentleman employer. The semi-rural retreats of Glebe and Balmain in the 1830s mirrored this type of world, satisfying the social requirements of those who occupied the upper levels of the social pyramid. But the isolation and privacy these exclusive neighbourhoods boasted began to change as they emerged as villages.

4 Village life, 1841–1871

Sydney had spread out in all directions by 1828 when it housed 10,815 inhabitants; at that stage 43 per cent of the population of New South Wales were convicts, 13 per cent were free immigrants, 20 per cent were emancipists and 24 per cent had been born in the colony. Greatly increased demand for space for non-residential purposes within the physical limits of the Town of Sydney, defined by Richard Bourke in 1833, inevitably meant some deterioration in living standards.[1] The first movement towards subdivision of land on the urban perimeter began in the late 1820s and throughout the prosperous times of the 1830s and those with economic means, the professional men and merchants able to sport a horse and carriage and coachman, were first to flee the befouled metropolis and create small segregated communities just beyond the city's outskirts. Here the well-to-do found privacy and solitude in the semi-rural villa retreats.[2]

The 1830s was a period of extraordinarily rapid economic growth in which capital inflow had furnished the material for a vast expansion of the wool industry.[3] By 1835 James Maclehose wrote of buildings spreading like ribbons out from Sydney along the road to Parramatta.[4] The first neighbourhoods within the present Leichhardt municipality to experience an assault on the extensive estate system, the basic unit of landholding, were Balmain and Glebe. It was not until the mid-1870s that intensive subdivision of the large Leichhardt estates began and residential expansion in Annandale did not get under way until about 1880.

The first opportunity for those wishing to acquire a villa allotment on the Balmain peninsula came on 24 October 1836 when 22 waterfront lots were offered for sale. Agent Frederick Parbury was pleased that all the Balmain lots had been disposed of to master mariners, merchants, the Comptroller of Customs, a storekeeper, an innkeeper and a solicitor. Limited in communication with the city proper and separated from other settled areas, Balmain's physical isolation initially made it attractive for villa development.[5] As it was some three and a half to six and a half miles from the city by land transport, Balmain's early and sustained growth was inextricably linked with its steam ferry service to the city.

Three men who acquired villa allotments at Balmain in 1836 subdivided their land in the early 1840s and put it on the market. Just before the onset of the depression late in 1840, auctioneer George Paul carved his land into ten blocks and it proved a very profitable speculative venture for him.⁶ Master mariners, boatbuilders and merchants were especially attracted to the Balmain land sales, some to speculate, others to settle there.

In May 1841 the four-acre Balmain estate of Captain John Jenkins Peacock, who was struggling to meet the demands of his creditors, went under the auctioneer's hammer. The sale notice advertising the 38-lot subdivision claimed 'Balmain is to the town of Sydney, what Deptford is to the City of London, and the daily increase of ferry boats, successfully plying and in constant demand, shows that there is a rising connection and mutual benefit taking place between both places. Ten minutes only are taken in passing to and fro.'⁷ The size of the allotments brought them within the financial reach of 'the tradesman and careful operative', who, it was claimed, had 'now as a good a chance as his neighbour of improving his circumstance and exercising his foresight and prudence'.⁸ Perhaps release of the Peacock land gave working men an opportunity to climb the social ladder, but the proceeds of the sale were not sufficient to forestall the bankruptcy of Peacock in 1843.

From late 1840 an acute depression spread throughout the colonies: 'alarm and panic prevailed; over-speculation, and all credit and confidence are gone. The demand for money is unexampled, but there is none to be had and the bill system will go no further'.⁹ The Balmain holding of another sailing ship skipper, James Pearson, came on the market in June 1841. An abode here, it was claimed, had a special attraction to 'Industrious Tradesmen and Operative mechanics', those with sober and thrifty habits, to join 'the valuable Class of Freeholders of the Colony'.¹⁰

The estate system in areas beyond city limits remained largely intact throughout the 1830s but the economic recession precipitated an assault on these large holdings.¹¹ Some speculators who acquired holdings at the auctions of the Sydney Glebe lands were among those to feel the effects of the contraction of credit.

Merchant and shipping proprietor Joseph Grose, the owner of a thirteen-acre parcel of land fronting Bay, Glebe and Parramatta streets, Glebe, was declared insolvent after the collapse of the Victoria Mills. The Glebe estate of merchant Grose, called Bishopgate after a suburb of London, was subdivided into 154 building blocks and first offered for sale in 1841. A by-product of the economic catastrophe was the appearance of a proliferation of newspaper advertisements offering small plots in Glebe for sale. Prospective purchasers were told that Bishopgate had been laid out:

> to meet the wants of Shopkeepers, Mechanics, and small Capitalists, affording them the opportunity of escaping from the heavy rents of the more crowded parts of town and therefore should not be neglected by so thriving a portion of our citizens . . . The air is salubrious and bracing, water pure and plentiful and the situation most convenient for building operations on account of brick, stone and wood being procurable in the immediate vicinity.¹²

It was to this place that the second wave of escapees from urban congestion, people generally of modest means, moved in search of a home or lodgings.

The trustees of St Phillip's, Glebe (a 32-acre allotment retained by the church from the original grant) were in need of money for diocesan purposes and cut up its land into 32 blocks varying from half an acre to one and three-quarter acres and offered it for lease in 1842. Builders and contractors were told that they could 'put up tenements to hold out 28 years . . . and let weekly at an enormous remunerating price. Weatherboards will be sufficient'.[13]

John Terry Hughes, a wealthy emancipist, was declared bankrupt in 1843, with an individual debt of £55,498. Hughes's four-acre estate, wedged between Bishopgate and St Phillip's, was cut into 46 narrow-frontage allotments. The misfortunes of Grose and Hughes had the effect of accelerating the migration to the suburbs as they off-loaded property to cover debts. Ralph Mansfield, in his analysis of the 1841 census, observed: 'to the west Balmain, Pyrmont and The Glebe and to the south Petersham and New Town already exhibit clusters of elegant dwellings and pleasure grounds and promise in a few years to become populous villages'.[14]

In Sydney the urban proletariat were kept in a subordinate position. Committees of the colonial legislature examined unemployment and general grievances among skilled and unskilled workingmen. The 'distress' and 'monetary confusion' resulted in schedules of bankruptcy being filed by the hundreds during the depth of the recession from 1841 to 1843, and unemployment was the counter to bankruptcy for many artisans and labourers.

The Assessment Sheets of the Sydney District Council compiled for rating purposes in 1844 provide the first detailed record of housing and population in Balmain and Glebe.[15] Some 198 buildings, largely confined to the east end of Darling Street and Waterview Bay were identified on the Balmain peninsula in 1844, and 151 buildings in Glebe; 55 per cent of these constructions in both districts were of brick or stone. Industry in Balmain focused on its waterfront—five boatbuilding establishments, two timber yards and a tannery. At Glebe there was a pottery and a brickmaking venture but the predominant commercial activities were slaughterhouses, boiling-down works and piggeries at Blackwattle Swamp. Since 1830, Thomas May, John Neale, and Thomas Holmes had been operating slaughterhouses at the Swamp, supplying Sydney with one-half of its beef and mutton requirements. The Swamp's sluggish waters extended almost to Parramatta Street, and springs in Surry Hills and Newtown meant Blackwattle Creek was an important source of fresh water and crucial to the continued existence of the slaughterhouses.

Many poor families moved to the swamp because they could live there at about one-quarter of the cost in the city centre, as Thomas May told the 1848 inquiry into Sydney's slaughterhouses. A petition signed by 200 local people claimed that they relied heavily for their sustenance on 'receiving donations of heads, tails, skirts and other parts'. Floodgates at Blackwattle Creek opened periodically to wash away the blood, offal and other refuse from the boiling-down works, piggeries and slaughterhouses. The sluggish tide deposited quantities of offal on the mud flats and, exposed to the sun, these soon became putrid. In hot, windy weather Glebe residents complained of the swamp's vile odours. Slaughterhouse labourers, noted Dr Francis Campbell, living in poorly ventilated timber cottages, were particularly susceptible to attacks of typhoid fever. But not all the inhabitants of this locale were impoverished. 'A great number of brickmakers,' Glebe Road resident Captain Croft observed, 'earn good wages and live pretty comfortably.'[16]

In 1848 there were 78 places within the City of Sydney where animals were being butchered, and as the population density within the city climbed to 10,000 per square mile, measures had to be taken to curb unpleasant smells. The legislative attack on noxious trades in 1849 gave the proprietors of the swamp slaughterhouses ten years' grace to make alternative arrangements.[17]

Colonial Architect Edmund Blacket designed a complex of stone buildings for a public abattoir at Glebe Island between 1850 and 1854 and the siting of the abattoir there attracted meat-preserving firms to the west end of Balmain; its presence was a powerful influence in shaping the character of that part of the suburb.[18]

'So rapidly has population spread and multiplied in the suburbs,' wrote Ralph Mansfield in 1846, 'that its aggregate numbers are now but little short of one-fifth of the population within the city.'[19] To areas where scattered villas had been constructed five years earlier, Mansfield now accorded the title of suburb, a term that defies precise definition. The five largest 'suburbs' ringing the city in 1846 were Balmain (1,337), Newtown (1,215), Glebe (1,055), Redfern (865) and Paddington (826).

Early directories reveal the emergence of a miscellaneous collection of consumer and service trades to cater for the needs of the emerging communities—shoemaker, butcher, grocer, cabinetmaker, blacksmith, dealer, and so forth, and small churches and public houses that appeared in the 1840s were the only communal buildings in the new housing estates.[20]

Members of the middle class, able to command both building skills and capital, could construct elegant homes on elevated sites. Cottages for the mass of the people in the 1840s and 1850s were usually built by men who had saved a little money and risen from the working class of artisans, cabinetmakers, bricklayers, carpenters, plasterers and masons. They used as materials 'brick, stone and wood procurable in the immediate vicinity'.[21] The Sydney Building Acts increased building costs within the city boundaries, making speculative ventures beyond its limits increasingly attractive.[22]

Building construction was not policed, nor were landlords oppressed by building codes, for such hindrances to free enterprise were as yet inconceivable. The end product was much substandard housing. Speculative building on low-lying Bishopgate estate in Glebe was a difficult proposition at any time, though only the briefest descriptions survive of this working-class housing. The absence of drains and a good water supply in this precinct created serious health hazards.[23]

For the great majority of working men—mechanics, labours and artisans, the 'non-elect' as Joseph Furphy called them—economic success was rarely achieved. The wage of the ordinary working man in regular employment was just enough to make him content with the social order, but made little provision for old age or unforeseen distress. Irregularity of earnings among manual workers meant that they lived from week to week. With little capital, they were unable to compete for desirable location or space in the emerging villages on the urban periphery. Home ownership was rare among this class, which was constantly on the move.

Nevertheless, a few of the more successful skilled workers are listed in Sydney's early directories and they left behind some evidence of how they fared. Enoch Fowler and James Pemell, among the wave of immigrants arriving in the mid-1830s, established enterprises in Glebe. Fowler, from County Tyrone, was producing domestic pottery at his Queen Street kiln from 1837, but later made pipes, chimney pots and other building materials as well as varieties of earthenware and stone.[24] Pemell, from London, established his Brisbane Steam Flour Mills on the corner of Glebe Road and Parramatta Street. From 1847 this important landmark served as a polling booth, Sunday school and a general meeting place.[25] Ambrose Thornley moved to Bishopgate not long after his arrival in the colony in 1841. Born in Lancashire in 1819, he earned his living as a greengrocer, but by 1851 had joined the local building industry as a stonemason and soon became one of the most prominent small-time builders.[26]

Among respectable early residents of Balmain whose names appeared in directories were John Cavill, Thomas Rowntree and Robert Blake. Cavill, a Cornish stonemason, arrived in Sydney in 1839 and earned his living supplying Balmain inhabitants with dwellings of stone (often quarried locally); evidence of his work between 1841 and 1871 remains scattered across its rugged landscape.[27]

English-born Captain Thomas Stephenson Rowntree skippered sailing ships in the English, Baltic and Mediterranean trade for ten years from 1842. By 1852 he was navigating the *Lizzie Webber* between Melbourne and Sydney, but he then sold this vessel and joined Thomas Sutcliffe Mort and James Sutherland Mitchell to found the Waterview Bay Dry Dock and for the remainder of his long life remained a prominent figure in Balmain's affairs.[28] In 1831 another immigrant in a new land, Robert Blake, embarked as a quartermaster, but he soon enlisted in the colonial civil service. As a sheriff's officer he criticised the judiciary and was forced to find a new career. Energetic and ambitious, this native of County Galway turned to speculative building activities in Balmain from 1837 and prospered by providing a dozen substantial buildings for the well-to-do on the peninsula.[29]

The pace of unregulated suburban expansion in Balmain and Glebe between 1841 and 1851 was steady as the colonial economy slowly recovered from the recession. By 1851 Balmain housed 1,397 people and Glebe 1,575 (Table 2). The discovery of gold had a dramatic effect on colonial society, doubling the population of New South Wales between 1851 and 1861. Lower middle-class and skilled working-class immigrants poured into Sydney, spilling over into its suburbs, which increased by 73 per cent between 1851 and 1856, compared to only 20 per cent in the city. There was much overcrowding as builders were unable to meet the heavy demand for housing while high costs for both labour and materials produced much substandard building.[30] The absence of any kind of control on spatial development beyond the City of Sydney, an incorporated area from 1842, attracted comment in the press:

> Along these undrained, unlevelled, unshaped ways and passages, misnamed streets, habitations are springing up by hundreds and thousands, many of them quite inaccessible to wheeled vehicles and the whole of them exposed to the nuisances and dangers generated by the want of drainage.[31]

Continued residential expansion in the suburbs was dependent upon more land becoming available for intensive development.[32] Between 1836 and 1851 development in Balmain was

The rustic character of Balmain in 1853 is reflected in J.W. Hardwick's sketch. St Augustine's Catholic Church occupies the most prominent site, overlooking an emerging city. (GPO Videodisc-1 Still 13047, Mitchell Library)

confined largely to the east end of Darling Street and around Waterview Bay. Following the death of John Gilchrist in 1841, disputes over his will in English courts meant his assets were frozen and no additional Balmain land could be released. A decision by the Rolls Court was sufficient to free the land for sale in 1852. Charles Edward Langley's plan of Balmain subdivided the remainder of Gilchrist's Balmain estate—about 400 acres—into 46 sections and this land was disposed of in an intermittent way between 1852 and 1882.[33] Activities by a miscellaneous assortment of carpenters, stonemasons and builders increased in tempo to accommodate the demand for housing in Balmain, and 418 dwellings were constructed between 1851 and 1861 (Table 2).

The Bishopthorpe estate in Glebe was subdivided and offered on long term leases by the Bishop of Sydney from 1856. The number of allotments released on Bishopthorpe helped sustain Glebe residential growth in the 1860s.[34]

The gold rush initially caused dislocation to the economy and builders and speculators could not meet the heavy demand for housing. By 1856, however, the amount of surface gold being won declined, and as the economy slowly readjusted the wool industry and agriculture improved and the number of grain mills, tanneries, saw mills, iron, brass and copper foundries grew. During the 1850s building in the suburbs exhibited marked regional variations, probably because local circumstances affected the tenure of land and the development of estates. Residential building in Balmain was at a low ebb up to 1855 but experienced a marked boom from 1856 to 1861. Glebe experienced a pronounced peak in residential building in the early 1850s and then a slump between 1856 and 1861.[35]

Life in Sydney in 1858 is illuminated by William Jevons' remarks on its social geography. The young assayer at the Sydney Mint recorded personal observations made on exploratory walks, describing the types of houses, sanitary conditions, the social status of the inhabitants and other aspects of urban life. In the suburbs he saw 'thousands of frail and small habitations . . . in many or most cases belonging to and built by those who inhabit them . . . In a great majority of cases the first plan only includes two small rooms, to which others are sometimes added afterwards.'[36]

He divided the inhabitants of the city and suburbs into three social ranks. The first rank included gentlemen and ladies, mercantile men, clerks and other chief employees, professional men and chief shopkeepers. The second included most mechanics or skilled artisans and shopkeepers, and labourers and what he called the 'indefinable lower orders' made up the third rank.

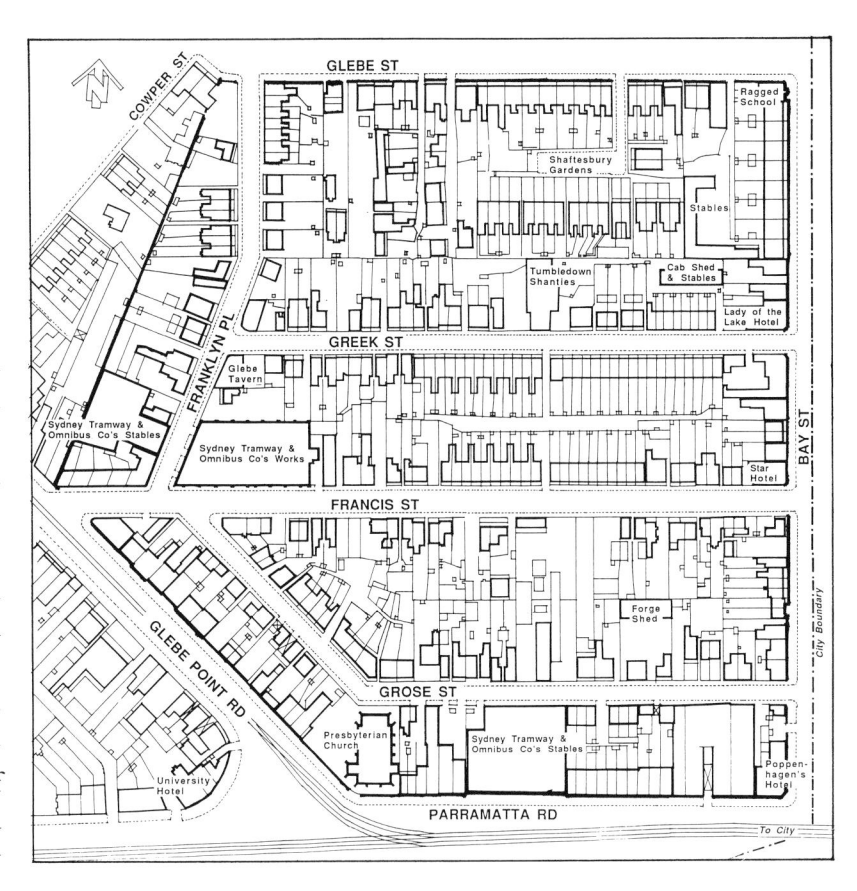

Bishopgate Estate, Glebe, and its environs, c.1890. Cheap cottages were squeezed onto narrow frontage blocks on Bishopgate estate between 1841 and 1861. The end result was the worst type of speculative development. (Re-drawn from Glebe Sheets 1 & 2, Metropolitan Detail Survey, Sydney Water Archive)

Table 2   **Population and housing in Balmain and Glebe 1851–61**[37]

	Population		
	1851	1856	1861
Balmain	1,397	2,224	3,482
Glebe	1,575	3,107	3,712
	Housing		
	1851	1856	1861
Balmain	319	400	737
Glebe	351	651	720

The suburban first-class districts, according to Jevons, followed the trend of the high land, and were generally distinctly separated from the lower-class residences. A large proportion of the first-class residences, he observed, were country villas or mansions situated quite beyond the limits of the town. The second-class residences were to be found in intermediate districts at a short distance from the central part of town. Woolloomooloo, Surry Hills, Strawberry Hill, Redfern, Chippendale, Glebe, Pyrmont, Balmain and the upper part of the Rocks formed the principal second-class districts. There were also thickly populated areas at Newtown, Paddington and Camperdown.

The third-class residences formed 'a part of the town peculiar to themselves' and collected at a few centres, generally in the lowest and least desirable localities. One such locality was around Blackwattle Creek, where Jevons noted:

> the creek's water carried away all the filthy refuse of the slaughter houses, becoming thereby thickened and coloured of a light coffee-brown tint. The foul mud deposited in the channel giving off a fearful stench renders this place as unhealthy and disgusting to one and all the senses as can well be conceived. Yet on one side are a number of small streets or alleys thickly built up with small cottages situated but a few feet above the creek waters; they are almost entirely as might be expected of the third class.[38]

Churchmen, sanitary reformers and police gave evidence about the hidden world of Sydney's rookeries and back lanes to a parliamentary Select Committee, chaired by Henry Parkes, on 'The Condition of the Working Classes of the Metropolis'. This committee concluded that 'even in the more recently erected dwellings the means of drainage and ventilation are almost entirely neglected'.[39]

In 1861 less than half the population of Balmain and Glebe was colonial-born. Immigrants from the British isles built houses, pubs and churches in the manner of their homeland and their social life reflected associations that immigrants brought with them. In Balmain the Irish congregated at St Patrick's Inn for company, drink and song and nearby Scottish immigrants met at the Rob Roy Hotel, built in 1858. The names of many pubs in Glebe and Balmain were direct transpositions of romantic names from the British Isles—Ancient Briton, Honest Irishman, Queen of the Thames, Forth and Clyde, Rose Shamrock and Thistle, Tower of London, Tynemouth Castle and so forth. The names of homes too reflected memories of the lands they had left behind.[40]

Some immigrants had strong feelings of oppression. The Irish had memories of famine and rack-renting of absentee landlords and Highland clearances affected many Scots. In their new land the Irish were well aware they were a minority group. Half of Balmain and Glebe were Anglican and three out of four of their inhabitants were Protestant. Irish Catholics were to remain very much a group apart, largely concentrated among the landless, unskilled working class. About 30 per cent of Balmain and Glebe residents in 1861 were born in England, about 15 per cent were born in Ireland and 5 per cent in Scotland. On the streets that laced these emerging communities the accents of London and Lancashire, Tipperary and Clare, and the Lowlands of Scotland gave them the diversity and vitality of frontier villages.

The territorial distribution of housing and population is contained in the 1861 census. In Balmain, the smallest area, East Ward (1,719 people) was the most populous, while the other areas, both about three times the size of East Ward, were much less densely populated (Table 3). South Ward had 898 inhabitants and North Ward 865. There were 311 houses in East Ward, 181 in South Ward and 161 in North Ward (Table 3). In Glebe, there was a growing concentration of population in Outer Ward (2,043); the intermediate zone, Bishopthorpe, housed 1,180 people; and the largest precinct, Inner Ward, was thinly peopled with only 489 inhabitants (Table 4).[41] Tables 3 and 4 indicate the type of housing construction.

Table 3   Balmain: population and houses per ward, 1861

Population				
East Ward	North Ward	South Ward	Total	
1,719	865	898	3,482	

Houses					
Ward	Brick or stone	Metal	Weatherboard or inferior	Total	Rooms
East	153	7	151	311	1,579
North	64	1	96	161	692
South	75	8	98	181	749
TOTAL	292	16	345	653	3,020

Table 4   Glebe: population

Population			
Outer Ward	Inner Ward	Bishopthorpe Ward	Total
2,043	489	1,180	3,712

Houses					
Ward	Brick or stone	Metal	Weatherboard or inferior	Total	Rooms
Outer	322	7	98	427	1,578
Inner	49	6	15	70	525
Bishopthorpe	135	0	88	223	1,031
TOTAL	506	13	201	720	3,134

There were 255 people in Glebe who gave their occupation as hired servant, 97 of whom resided in thinly-peopled Inner Ward, a sure sign of that neighbourhood's respectability.

Similarly 178 hired servants lived in Balmain's East Ward. Here many Irish domestic servants did the cooking, washing and cleaning for their middle-class sisters.

At Glebe Point and in Balmain's East Ward, where the villa allotment was predominant, a wealthy and respectable elite was housed in comfort. A concentration of professional and commercial occupations and people in government service were to be found to the south and east of the city at Woollahra, Paddington and Randwick in 1861, generally too far from work for those without a horse and carriage.[42] Jevons wrote that there were notable concentrations of working-class folk at Balmain and Glebe.

The construction of the Waterview Bay Dry Dock (Mort's Dock) in 1854 had created about 200 jobs for local workers by 1861, and the character of Balmain's development as a suburb was powerfully influenced by its industrial enterprises. The early location of Mort's Dock, Booth's shipyard and sawmills and the public abattoir at Glebe Island attracted blue-collar workers and stimulated further residential and industrial growth.[43]

Glebe had no distinctive industrial character of the kind emerging in Balmain. There was no manufacturing industry in Glebe in 1861 apart from a corn mill and a few small dressmaking and tailors' workshops. The majority of its employed residents walked to work along the main pedestrian routes into the city.

Excavation work began on Mort's Dock in 1854. It was a venture that powerfully influenced the industrial and residential character of Balmain. (*Mort's Dock 50 Years Ago and Today*, 1905, Mitchell Library)

Sydney's first council was incorporated under its own Act in 1842, but it soon ran into difficulties and was dissolved in 1854. Earlier experiments in local government, the Parish Road Trusts and District Councils were failures. Balmain and Glebe came within the jurisdiction of the Sydney District Council which was empowered to provide roads and schools and required to pay half the cost of police administration. By 1850 the Police Act was extended to suburbs, and though it made provision for local services, little was achieved.[44]

New South Wales was granted self-government in 1856 and there was agitation for some form of local government for areas just beyond the city limits, and in country towns, so that they could be required to contribute towards the upkeep of the town infrastructure. The *Municipalities Act,* 1858, provided for a permissive system of incorporation. If at least 50 householders signed a petition, a municipality would be proclaimed by the Governor, provided that within three months no counter-petition containing a greater number of signatures had been presented.

The borough councils had to provide the entire physical setting for urban growth and they often assumed control of districts that had no water supply. The absence of sewerage and drainage facilities meant that the stench in some neighbourhoods was of a vileness that the euphemistic language of contemporary accounts, 'noxious effluvia', did nothing to sweeten. The so-called roads were dirt tracks that became quagmires in wet weather. Imposing some physical order on their new bailiwicks was no mean task for the councils.

In April 1859 the pro-municipal faction in Glebe clashed with the anti-incorporationists at a meeting at Margaret Onan's hotel. Those opposing adoption of a municipal system argued that owners of large blocks of unoccupied and unimproved land would benefit from municipal expenditure without making any contribution toward it.[45] Glebe was proclaimed a municipality on 1 August 1859 and nine councillors were elected from seventeen candidates at the first Glebe elections held on 29 August 1859.[46] The chairman was elected annually from and by the councillors, one-third of whom retired annually.

The faction seeking to have Balmain proclaimed a municipality met with staunch opposition. Four petitions seeking incorporation, signed by 593 householders, were matched by no less than 837 Balmain signatories to four counter-petitions.[47] Balmain was incorporated as a municipality on 21 February 1860 and some 24 candidates contested the first election on 3 April 1860.[48]

The creation of a borough council helped promote the notion of corporate identity but the low percentage of eligible voters who cast a vote at by-elections suggests that local government generated little interest among the populace. The municipal franchise was essentially a ratepayer franchise; those who paid the rates had the right to vote.[49]

As councils sought to leave their imprint on the landscape by creating physical order through the provision of roads and other works, the promulgation of by-laws for 'the suppression of nuisances and houses of ill-fame'[50] was aimed at creating economic, social and moral order. The growing regulation of colonial society was designed to inculcate habits of orderliness and regularity.[51]

The colonial legislature showed little interest in building regulations and public health, and the first standard 'town planning regulations' were issued in New South Wales in 1829. The basic ground plan, a standard gridiron pattern, was laid down regardless of ridges, swamps and other considerations.[52] The alignment and direction of the street network that laced Balmain and Glebe were dictated by the earlier patterns of land ownership, which tended to act as morphological frames to condition the genesis and growth of streets. (Darling Street, following the Balmain ridge, and Palmer Street, winding around difficult terrain, were surveyor Charles Langley's responses to local topography.)

The basic urban infrastructure was taking shape in the 1860s. Suburban streets were aligned and gazetted, and pounds created. A little earlier, postal services, through general stores, had been established. After disputes over charges, the City Council agreed to extend its water main to Glebe in 1862, when local consumption so increased that it was necessary to shut off the water supply nightly.[53] The Glebe water supply was neither regular nor sufficient and demands were made for a share of the revenue to compensate for tearing up the streets.[54] For a long time water carts, tanks and wells were the main sources of water for Sydney's hamlets. All residences in Glebe were connected to town water pipes in the later 1870s, about the same time mains were extended to Balmain.

Glebe's streets were first lit by gas from 1860 and from 1867 gas, used almost exclusively for street illumination and simple domestic lighting, was available to most Glebe residents. Gas mains were extended to Balmain in 1873.[55]

The outward spread of Sydney's suburbs was clearly defined by the available means of transport. Glebe was very much a walking suburb; regular horse bus travel into the city was beyond the means of most of the population.[56] The speed, regularity and cost of the Balmain

Margaret Onan (1810–1862), bounty immigrant from Letterkenny, County Donegal, became licensee of the Victoria Inn, Glebe, in 1850. A widow with five children, running a pub was one of the natural extensions of housekeeping—the provision of food and drink and accommodation. (Max Solling Collection)

The pattern of development and industry in suburbs now comprising the Leichhardt Municipality, c.1875. The street networks in Balmain and Glebe, dictated by earlier patterns of land ownership, were firmly established by 1875. Leichhardt suburb, however, remained a suburban frontier and the Annandale Estate is untouched by residential development. (Re-drawn from Map of Parish of Petersham, 1970)

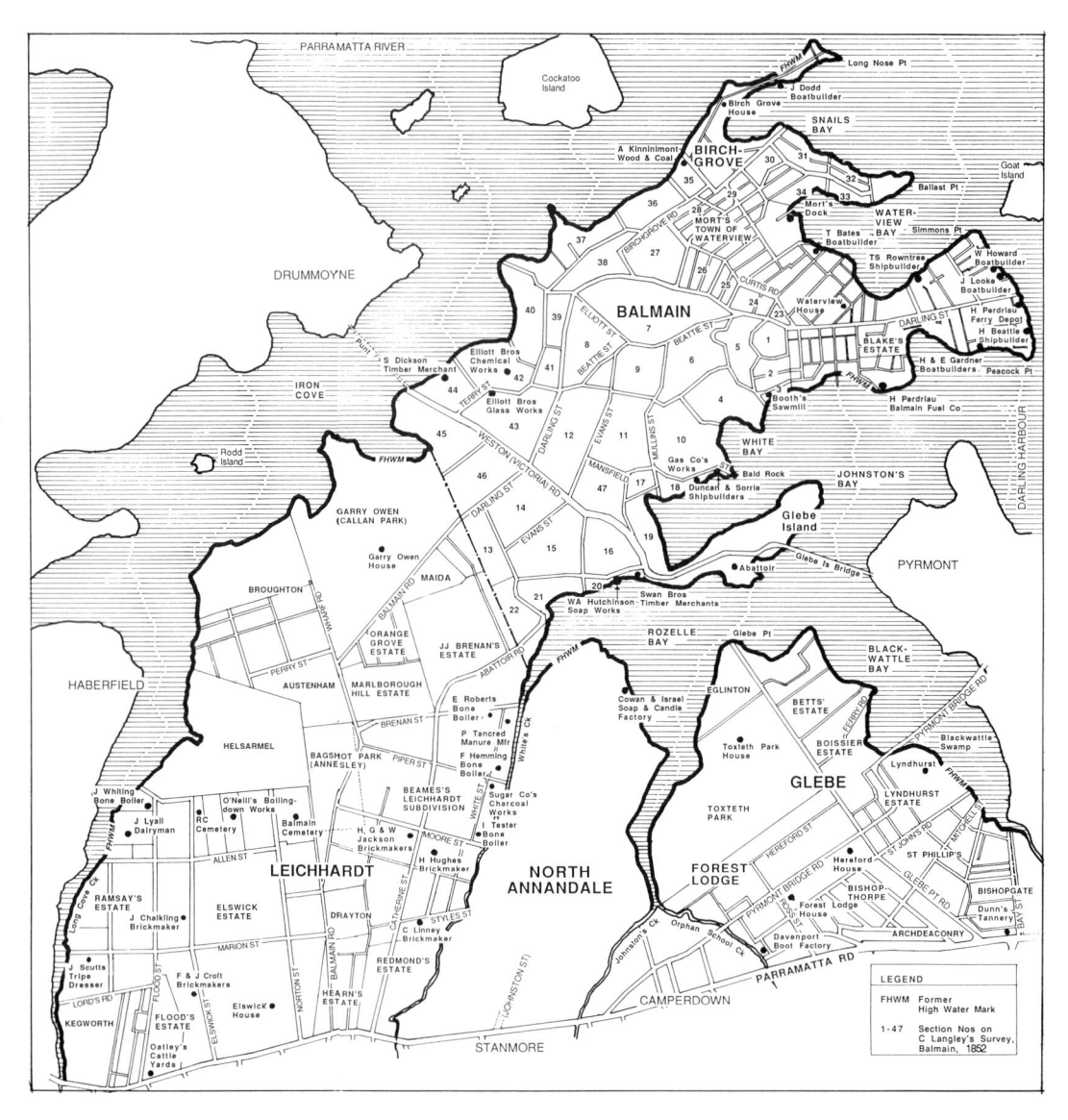

steam ferry service, the main form of conveyance for commuters into the city, compared favourably with land transport by the 1860s.[57]

The migration to the suburbs that ringed Sydney increased in tempo during the 1850s. Those in full employment were expected to fill six days with work and to rest on the Sabbath. Casual labour gave the worker more spare time but for him poverty was a constant companion. 'The single men do not want wives and the responsibilities and encumbrances of family life,' Godfrey Mundy wrote in 1852. 'They prefer working hard—working like slaves—four or five days, and "larking the rest of the week".'[58] Married manual workers had little time for recreation. Apart from the demands of home and family, in a society relatively starved of recreation the pub and the chapel, vigorously competing for the attention of the masses, symbolised alternative lifestyles. There was nowhere else to go. The pub was seldom closed, the chapel was not quite so accessible.

Public houses

Public houses of the 1840s, open from 4 a.m. to 10 p.m. in 1849, were single-storey buildings, usually located on street corners. The law prohibited societies that required oaths of observance of solemn rites to meet at these drinking outlets; the government was concerned they might become centres for subversive activities.[59] The long room, a feature of larger pubs, was used for public meetings, church services, court sessions, dances and concerts. It was also the main gathering place for sports clubs, volunteer corps, friendly societies and penny banks. From about 1860 it became the most important forum for municipal aspirants seeking success at a ward by-election to harangue ratepayers from that particular precinct.[60]

Publicans in Glebe organised rat-baiting and cock-fighting on Saturday afternoons. As pubs existed basically for commercial gain, so the more people attracted through the doors, the more drink was sold. In the 1850s publicans provided a variety of facilities for patrons: quoits, bagatelle, billiards, skittles and darts. The pub, always close by and, from 1862, open from 6 a.m. to 11 p.m., was the only place outside the home where the drinker could find comfort, relaxation and company. Working men turned to alcohol to celebrate life's pleasures and dull its pains. In the benign world of the pub, patrons were known by name and often had their own seats. The offer of a drink was something that could not easily be refused, as 'shouting' was a common form of hospitality.[61]

It was not only drink that drew customers to the corner pub; there was also the attraction of good talk combined with smoking and the observation of street life. During the convict era, drinking and smoking were common among men and women, but from the 1850s the cult of domesticity made it unacceptable for women to drink in public. Temperance imposed new restrictions on the public behaviour of women, increasingly tying them to the home, making the pub an institution for working-class males.[62]

The relatively open and flexible nature of the 'local' was its strength and its attraction, for overcrowded and impermanent housing made any stable family life difficult for labouring folk. There were sufficient Balmain working men to support a pub from 1842, and by 1851 there were five corner pubs there serving alcoholic drinks.[63] Glebe men too found the attractions of the neighbourhood bar irresistible and its first pub, the Glebe Tavern, began trading in 1844. The number of Glebe pubs grew steadily from three in 1851 to thirteen in 1858 and to sixteen in 1870.[64] In 1847 some Balmain and Glebe pubs were supplied by Tooths, but up to the 1870s most beer, wines and spirits sold in these outlets were imported. Imported beer—Bass or Whitbread's or Worthington's—sold in bottles, was safe to drink, but colonial beer, sold in bulk, was not. Colonial beer was 'much drugged after it got in the hands of publicans', claimed policeman John McLerie.[65]

Lady of the Lake Hotel, corner of Greek and Bay streets, Glebe, in 1884. Built in about 1847 it was an especially popular drinking place in the 1860s when Bobby Hancock was licensee. The Option Vote forced its closure in 1908. (Max Solling Collection)

A committee inquiring 'into the cause of the alarming increase in Intemperance', found that in 1854 there were some 370 public houses clustered at street corners in the heart of the metropolis and in the emerging neighbourhoods on the city fringe. After the inquiry, police made a concerted effort to curb the proliferation of drinking places. Around Blackwattle Swamp pubs lost their licences for a variety of reasons—for being conducted in a disorderly manner, for having insufficient stables, or because there were too many pubs in the immediate vicinity.[66]

Drinking was not without its subtle social gradations. A parliamentary committee in 1870 distinguished 'better class' public houses from mere 'drinking shops, dancing saloons and singing saloons'.[67] Respectable tradesmen did not frequent dancing saloons, observed George Reid; they were patronised by 'the lowest order of men and by young girls on the verge of prostitution'. Joseph Barnier, the second rector of St Barnabas's, drew a sharp distinction between the respectable artisan and the class of people who lounged about the doors of local pubs. Barnier claimed that on his route to and from church on the Sabbath he was confronted by 'reeling men and blaspheming youth' on the street corners outside pubs. 'Parramatta Street,' he said, 'is unpleasant to walk through on Sunday.'[68]

Churches

No other institution in colonial society claimed as many members as the churches. The building of a church or chapel was a physical symbol of a denomination's distinctive identity and of its commitment to shape the moral landscape. The size, elegance and location of a place of worship were testimony to the wealth and aspirations of its members. Edmund Blacket drew up plans for two Anglican churches in Balmain in 1843. The first was a temporary chapel for rector Frederick Wilkinson, and the other, expanding on this chapel, was a permanent stone church, begun in 1845. It was consecrated as St Mary's by Bishop Broughton in 1848.[69]

Religion tended to follow an ethnic pattern. Anglicans, Methodists and Baptists were mainly English; Presbyterians, Scottish; Roman Catholics, Irish; and Lutherans, Germans.[70] The Church of England, the religion of about half of Australians in the nineteenth century, leaned towards social conservatism and was closely linked with Sydney's ruling elite. Catholics, on the other hand, were acutely aware of the political oppression and religious persecution they had suffered in Ireland. Though they comprised about one-quarter of the population, their national origins and religion made them very much a group apart. Catholics, most numerous among the ranks of unskilled labour and domestic service, gathered together on 5 May 1851 when Archbishop Polding consecrated St Augustine's Church, Balmain. They quickly formed strong local networks in a parish where they worshipped, educated their children and sought fellowship and recreation.

The Anglican, Presbyterian and Congregationalists were middle class in nature and composition and the Anglican Bishop of Sydney, Frederic Barker, doubted 'whether any denomination of Protestants have hold of the working men of the colonies'.[71] Congregationalists, though numerically small, opened a large stone church in Balmain in 1855, capable of seating 500 worshippers in its pews. A little earlier local Presbyterians had united with them but a schism took place in 1857 and the Presbyterians moved into their own modest timber chapel in 1858.

Wesleyan Methodism, largely lower middle class in adherence, was strong among shopkeepers and small tradespeople. It was the first to take its religion to the masses in Glebe and by 1864 three of its churches were built. Wesleyans had gathered together in a timber chapel in Balmain in 1845 and its growing congregation moved to a new church designed by George Allen Mansfield, in 1860. Primitive Methodism, born on the pottery fields of Staffordshire, was solidly working class in composition.[72] It established a chapel in Bay Street, Glebe, in 1860. It flourished in Forest Lodge from 1874 and later congregations developed at Balmain, Annandale and Leichhardt.

Labouring families had congregated around Blackwattle Swamp from the early 1840s and for those working-class migrants from southern Ireland, St Benedict's (Chippendale) became an important focal point.[73] Anglicans set out to evangelise poor Protestants living in this precinct. Thomas Smith attracted large congregations to 'Parson Smith's barn' and firmly established St Barnabas's as a centre of evangelism. Glebe's Anglicans could attend a church–school from 1857; the congregation at St John's Bishopthorpe (1870) was of a very different character from St Barnabas's. Its worshippers were solidly middle class and two-thirds of its seats were subject to payment of pew rent.[74] The local Sunday school was part of a middle-class civilising mission.[75]

There is little detailed evidence of church life in Balmain and Glebe in the 1850s, but the 1861 figures indicate nominal adherence. Anglicans comprised half the population of Balmain and Glebe in 1861 but there was a greater concentration of Catholicism in Glebe (28 per cent) compared to 18 per cent on the Balmain peninsula. There was a higher proportion of Scottish Presbyterians in Balmain—nearly 15 per cent compared to 7.7 per cent in Glebe. Some 9.64 per cent of Glebe residents counted themselves as Wesleyan or Primitive Methodists; Methodists comprised 6.4 per cent of the Balmain population.[76]

Some 269 pupils were enrolled at Balmain National School and 333 at Glebe in 1862.[77] The education the offspring of locals received at the Catholic or Protestant denominational schools was also of an elementary nature, little different from the state system, except that parents paid more, and five hours a week was devoted to religious instruction.

The Anglican Church, Glebe, built in 1857. Photographed here in 1870, it served as a place of worship until St John's Bishopthorpe was completed (1870), as well as being a denominational school up to 1882, when 359 pupils were enrolled there. (GPO Videodisc-1 Still No 05812)

Attempts at moral improvement

Between 1844 and 1859 anxieties among Sydney's well-to-do and respectable led to the appointment of committees to inquire into 'The Insecurity of Life and Property' (1844), 'Intemperance' (1854) and the 'Condition of the Working Classes' (1859). The propertied classes were troubled about the behaviour and attitudes of the working class. There was, in the early 1860s, an uneasiness among middle-class residents of Balmain and Glebe about perceived threats to life and property. Mounted police patrols in the suburbs were considered inadequate and in Glebe locals called on the Inspector General of Police for three resident policemen to protect this 'exposed and unguarded locale'.[78] Their complaints fell on deaf ears. A public meeting in Balmain in 1863 echoed similar concerns about the unprotected state of its residents and 'riotous behaviour'.[79]

The first Anglican minister appointed to the Glebe parish, William Cowper, wrote of 'a population greatly demoralised' living near Blackwattle Swamp. 'Drunkenness and all the attendant evils were rife and dominant. The holy day of Rest was often desecrated by scenes of riot and disorder.'[80] Cowper, who believed poverty and distress to be the result of intemperance, told a select committee in 1860 that 'those who are sober, steady and industrious are generally able to get enough employment to maintain themselves respectably'. Edward Wise, on the other hand, who had studied housing and sanitary conditions in Britain, maintained that it was the poor social conditions and unhealthy locations that produced intemperance: 'Filth and foul air had the effect of causing nervous depression,' argued Wise, 'and a morbid appetite was thus created by those evils for stimulating drinks.' Those previously temperate, he said, would become drunkards if required to live in filthy dwellings and unhealthy surroundings.[81]

Religious and philanthropic bodies, in their quest to eliminate poverty and drunkenness, sought to reform the manners of the working class and their attempts to nourish habits of thrift, temperance and industry centred on active missionary work. Evangelical Protestants united to form the Sydney City Mission. Their concern for the offspring of the poor led to the establishment of Ragged Schools in areas of chronic want. Thomas Smith saw the Glebe Ragged school as an important medium of social reform; dirty and ragged as the children were, he said, they could be heard singing hymns on Sunday evening. Smith had been allotted the task of saving the souls of the residents of Blackwattle Swamp. Largely self-educated, Smith knew nothing, and cared less, for the nicer points of theology and his sermons consisted of a Biblical or topical story, dramatically told, followed by some moral principle extracted from it.

The local penny bank was designed to encourage thriftiness; the Temperance Society, Band of Hope and Mutual Improvement Society provided organised entertainments, readings, lantern lectures and musical evenings, a deliberate and systematic attempt to counteract the influence of the pub. Rector Smith told the seventh anniversary meeting at St Barnabas's that in his 'outlawed neighbourhood notorious for its disregard for God and disrespect for order . . . there had been a remarkable improvement in the social and moral condition of the people'.[82]

Solicitor Nicol Drysdale Stenhouse moved to Balmain in 1856, the year its School of Arts was formed. He became a prominent literary patron and his home, Waterview House, became a centre for colonial writers and intellectuals.[83] The working man, bent on self-improvement, could enjoy an array of literary and dramatic activities in Balmain during the 1860s—an active Mechanics Institute, Musical Union, Amateur Dramatic Association and St Mary's Literary Institute. The Total Abstinence Society (1860) vigorously sought converts and their Workingmen's Institute (1863) was especially active;[84] in June 1868 Henry Parkes told 250 men at an Institute tea meeting that 'in Balmain where so many of the better portions of the working class reside the Institute should have 500 members'.[85]

In October 1860 a literary coterie set out to enrich the lives of Glebe's working men. A certain Dr Walker exhorted working men at a meeting at the University Hotel to employ their time meaningfully to improve their chances of mounting the ladder of success. There were 'very many men of intellect and means resident at the Glebe who would, he was sure, readily come forward and help the working man in the establishment of the School of Arts in the locality'.[86] He had repeatedly seen the advantage they had conferred upon the labourer and mechanic elsewhere. However the proud skilled workmen and artisans of Glebe stayed away in droves, repelled by the patronage of the middle-class worthies seeking to impose their standards.

In the early 1860s members of friendly societies met at local pubs. These societies were known for their organisation of medical services, for organising the supply of medicines, for their sick pay and for the help they gave to those who fell on hard times. They also offered their members a variety of social activities.[87]

In Sydney the volunteer movement was nurtured as a means of colonial self-defence and upwardly mobile young men enrolled to defend Queen and Country. In England Charles Kingsley described the volunteer corps as 'centres of cordiality between class and class' and it was no different in the colonies.[88] On the drill ground a man might make useful connections as well as defend his country. An incentive to join the Balmain or Glebe volunteers was a grant of 50 acres after five years' service. On weekends volunteers practised their shooting or went on excursions and they joined in impressive parades on the Queen's Birthday. In 1869 Sydney battalions claimed 527 members—South Sydney 100, Paddington and Surry Hills 82, Balmain 66 and Glebe 63.[89]

Another symbol of progress and prosperity in Balmain was the appearance of the *Balmain Reporter* in February 1867. In an era of hand presses, hand setting, small staffs and the clipping of news from other papers, the capital requirements of a local newspaper were modest.

Balmain Volunteer Rifles, c.1860. After enrolling to defend Queen and Country, riflemen received land grants and often established connections on the parade ground that were useful in business. Soldier turned Balmain freeholder Patrick Killeen is standing second from left. (Wain Family Collection, Dixson Library, Pictures Accession No 6468, Mitchell Library File No 2211/78)

5 Influences shaping suburban development

Sydney in 1861 exhibited the characteristics of a mercantile city with a rudimentary manufacturing sector. Its roads and transport systems were primitive, and clustered along the streets in the city proper was an intermixture of retail shops, manufacturing ventures and residences. At the 1851 census 82 per cent of the metropolitan population lived within the boundaries of the Sydney City Corporation, a settlement largely confined to the tongue of land stretching from the base at Darling Harbour east to Woolloomooloo and Rushcutters Bay. Ten years later it housed 43 per cent of those engaged in trade and commerce, and half those in the 'Learned and Educated Professions'.[1]

The mid-nineteenth-century walking city would soon experience the full transforming effect of the interacting influences of new technology, new demands and changing taste. In the second half of the nineteenth century there would be a dramatic shift in population distribution from within the municipal boundaries of the City of Sydney to the suburbs, and an increasing conversion of city land from residential to business use.[2] New and improved modes of public transport radically changed the old verities of time and distance within Sydney while the growth of industry, and the concentration of labour, created new demands and opportunities which altered permanently the city's economic structure.

Neighbourhoods within a radius of five kilometres of the city centre – Balmain, Paddington, Glebe, Redfern, Newtown, North Sydney, Leichhardt and Marrickville—were the arena for changes which dramatically altered the shape and character of their landscapes as these areas were transformed into bricks and mortar to accommodate the demand for housing.

The pace of suburban development was determined by five important influences. The first was demographic, for the overcrowding and congestion in Sydney caused its population to overflow into suburbs that ringed the city proper.[3] Secondly, the size of Sydney and its residential districts was clearly defined by the available means of transport. Suburbs close to the city experienced steady rates of growth between 1841 and 1871 when transport was limited to the public omnibus, private carriage and ferry. From the 1880s the tram and train, new and more efficient modes of urban transportation, and a significant lowering in the cost of daily suburban travel, made the outer fringes of development more accessible and enabled the suburbs to spread much further outwards.⁴ The city was where people worked, and the suburbs where the bulk of the population had their homes. The cost of transport to and from the city was important in shaping the social structure of suburban communities, for the nature of commuter travel had the effect of separating the working and lower middle classes from the more affluent sections of the community. With the horizontal growth of Sydney, suburbs became much more socially differentiated, and this was reflected in the wide range of housing prices. Thirdly, the rate of suburban expansion was powerfully influenced by advanced technology and methods in the building industry, and the availability of capital with which to finance the process. Lagging behind in the suburban development process was a fourth element in this expansion: the providers of essential services – roads, gas, water and sanitation. Finally, the tempo of events was governed by the local circumstances that affected the tenure of land and the development of estates.

The demographic pattern of Sydney

The five largest suburbs that ringed the City of Sydney in 1861 were Newtown with 10.9 per cent of the suburban population, Redfern with 10.2 per cent, Glebe with 9.5 per cent, Balmain with 8.9 per cent and Paddington with 6.9 per cent. Measured simply in terms of population statistics these suburbs remained among the largest residential districts of Sydney from 1861 to 1891, although their order was to alter significantly throughout the three inter-census periods.⁵

All these inner-suburban districts experienced high population growth rates and profound changes in their physical superstructure and social content during this period of rapid development. By 1881 the aggregate population of Sydney's suburbs (124,787) overtook the city for the first time, but such was the intensity of the building boom that by 1901 the suburban municipalities (with 369,721 residents) housed more than three times the number of people living in the city proper.⁶

By 1901, within the present Municipality of Leichhardt, Glebe had the highest population density, with 36.9 persons per acre, followed by Balmain 32.3, Annandale 23.2 and Leichhardt 14.9. Census data on the number of persons per room reflected the extent of overcrowding.⁷

Transport

Sydney's transport system before the goldrush was rudimentary. 'There were no cabs, porters or coaches in Sydney,' wrote John Hood in 1843. 'A dray may be had to transport heavy goods landed at this place if you walk a quarter of a mile into the town but the lesser conveniences are not to be found.'⁸ Sydney remained essentially a walking city in 1858, supporting no less than 277 boot and shoemakers.⁹ Land transport was slow and expensive, road maintenance was minimal, and, in wet weather, access to outlying areas was not always possible. Nevertheless, enterprises associated with the horse and carriage trade grew, and locally built wagons outnumbered imported vehicles.

The first railway line, from Sydney to Parramatta, was opened in 1855 but the railway had little impact on suburban development prior to 1880.[10] 'Balmain,' wrote W.H. Wells in 1848, 'lies on the opposite side of Sydney and by land it is distant about 7 miles.'[11] Steam ferries began operating on the Parramatta River in 1831 and the ferries on this run called at Balmain en route, only two kilometres from the city by water. Former British naval officer, Henry Perdriau, began financing watermen's boats when he moved to Balmain in 1841, and two years later expanded his service by establishing the Balmain Steam Ferry. James Palmer told a committee in 1853 that communication between Sydney and Balmain was 'very inefficient' and the Balmain Steam Ferry Co. proposed to improve the type of ferry and increase the fleet to three.[12] The interests of another ferry operator, Samuel Crook, were acquired in 1858 by Perdriau, who effectively gained a monopoly of the Balmain run until 1882.[13]

The service remained expensive—one shilling to the city, and half-fare return in 1870—and this restricted its regular use to the middle class. Its small ferries, navigated by 'steady Scotchmen', left as early as 5 a.m. but the service was not fettered by regulations. Balmain Mayor Josiah Mullens observed that the ferries 'go when they like, come when they like and charge what they like'. After the ferry ceased running the only way to town was by the small boats of watermen.[14]

Balmain's early and sustained growth was closely linked with its steam ferry service to the city. Paddle steamers the *Balmain* and the *Bald Rock* operating on the Balmain service in about 1905.
(J. Darroch Collection)

The pace of development in Balmain increased after 1862 when a bridge was constructed from Pyrmont to the newly opened Glebe Island Abattoirs. However, although Balmain residents could now travel to and from the city by horse-drawn omnibus, a government-imposed toll on bridge use limited the amount of traffic.

The quickest way into the city from Glebe was by road transport. The first horse omnibus service in Glebe, established by Jonathan Howard in 1846, conveyed passengers from the lower end of George Street to Bay Street. Howard's horse bus, 'The Fitzroy', was described as being 'a packing case on wheels, roughly constructed and most uncomfortable to ride in'.[15] Few in Glebe's working population could afford to use the omnibus or hackney cab, and those who could not find work locally walked daily along the principal roads to their place of employment in the city.

The unshaped streets of Bishopgate, described as inaccessible to wheeled vehicles, had been aligned and gazetted in 1862.[16] In the early 1860s the principal task of the new councils was to let tenders to kerb and gutter the miles of streets that laced their areas. Maintenance of suburban streets remained a constant drain on municipal funds. In 1867, according to S.T. Leigh, Balmain's streets were in a 'perfect state of repair', and Glebe Point Road was ballasted and macadamised.[17]

Sydney's first successful attempt at an urban transport system was the Pitt Street horse-car tramway, opened in 1861. In ran along Pitt Street from Circular Quay to the old Redfern railway station but continuous complaints led to its closure in 1866. Sydney's major form of urban transport until the early 1890s was the privately owned horse-drawn omnibus.[18]

The Sydney populace was dependent on the horse for personal mobility and it became an integral part of the work ethic. The horse provided the main motive power for transport of goods and in Balmain and Glebe many earned their living as dray, delivery cart and cart proprietors. Apart from the omnibus, the middle class travelled the streets in their hansom cabs, broughams and buggies.[19]

The opening of an alternative route from the city made Glebe more accessible. In 1857 a private company, the Pyrmont Bridge Company, bridged Darling Harbour and then constructed a causeway and bridge across Blackwattle Swamp, linking Glebe to the city. Pyrmont Bridge Road pushed on through Glebe to the hamlet of Camperdown and the company imposed a toll on users of their road; a pedestrian was charged twopence at the toll gate, a horse and rider threepence, and the driver of a two-horse chaise paid a fee of ninepence. The toll restricted the use of the road, especially by manual workers walking to work.[20]

The demand for more regular horse-bus services in the suburbs meant that a growing number of omnibuses plied the streets. The number of omnibus proprietors in Glebe jumped from five in 1859 to 45 some eight years later. The horse-bus fare of sixpence was beyond the means of the average working man and in the early 1860s the omnibus service did not begin running until 8 a.m., well after the time working people began work.[21]

Public transport was geared to the needs of middle-class office workers, and the timetabling generally made commuter services inaccessible to the working classes. However, by 1872 the intensity of competition between horse-bus proprietors in Glebe was reflected in a drastic reduction in the fare from sixpence to threepence. In 1876 an omnibus journey from Glebe to the city took 30 minutes; an omnibus ride to Forest Lodge took 41 minutes, and a trip to Balmain took 50 minutes.

Throughout the 1870s, public transport continued to be geared to the needs of the office workers and remained inaccessible to the blue-collar folk, who worked from 6 a.m. to 6 p.m.[22] There were frequent complaints that many vehicles were unfit for service, that more than the certified number of passengers were packed into the vehicles and that lives were endangered by the use of the omnibus as a way of breaking in young horses.

The operations of horse omnibuses serving the city and suburbs were unregulated. Omnibus transport, privately owned, serviced areas that returned a profit and ignored other precincts. In 1870, for example, Thomas Hale, with nine licensed omnibuses, had a monopoly of the run

The building of the Glebe Island Bridge in 1862 connected Pyrmont to the new government abattoir and provided Balmain residents with a quicker route into the city by horse-drawn omnibus. (GPO Videodisc-1 Still 05720)

Hansom cab stop, corner of Glebe Point and St John's roads, c.1903. Horse-drawn public transport began to decline in the 1890s. The increasing cost of fodder and cheaper electric tram fares made it harder for the horse bus to survive against the new technology. (Max Solling Collection)

from Glebe Point to Wynyard Square. The report of the Select Committee on Public Vehicles and Boats led to the establishment of the Metropolitan Transit Commissioners in 1873.[23]

Between 1875 and 1888 private interests vigorously lobbied for construction of a bridge from Glebe Point to Balmain West, and though the scheme received municipal support, it was never implemented.[24]

Businessman Henry Hoyt floated the Reform Bus Company, which began operating in Francis Street, Glebe, in 1872. It bought out Henry Vickers' Invincible Coach Works and by 1877 most inner-city horse buses were controlled by this company, now called the Sydney Tramway and Omnibus Company. The Transit Commissioners controlled buses within an eight-mile radius of the city and, together with a consolidation of the industry, helped improve services. The Sydney Tramway and Omnibus Company had a real presence in Glebe. At its four-storey building near the corner of Glebe and Parramatta roads, 32 wheelwrights, body-makers, painters and trimmers turned out a two-horse bus every fortnight. The Glebe depot was also the company's largest, with 316 horses stabled there in 1888. Each two-horse bus operated for 13 hours a day, with four changes of horses daily. Company drivers drove the horses along the main roads for ten hours a day. They received a weekly wage of £2 to £2 10s 0d.[25]

The respectable middle class generally did not favour travel by omnibus. They regarded horse buses as 'small, narrow and dirty with no stuffing to the seats', and the conductors were seen as a scruffy lot, clothed in 'an absolutely indecent manner and apparently didn't wash themselves'.[26] It could also be a risky affair: in 1881, for instance, passengers in a horse bus which went out of control en route to Glebe found themselves having to swim for safety after being catapulted into the waters of Blackwattle Bay.[27]

In 1878 the government examined the usefulness of trams as a mode of urban transport and their suitability for Sydney's narrow streets.[28] Two years later the New South Wales government became the sole proprietor of Sydney's tramways. Between 1879 and 1884 about 30 miles of tram tracks were laid; lines were extended to the wealthy eastern suburbs. In August 1882 one track branched off Parramatta Road along Glebe Road to the Glebe Point terminus at Cook Street. The tram line to Forest Lodge passed along Derwent, Catherine and Mt Vernon streets, turning into St John's Road and Ross Street, with the Forest Lodge terminus being just north of Bridge Road. This dramatic new mode of personal mobility, the steam tram, was described as a 'demon of steam and iron with a great flaring eyeball at night time ... a machine calculated to frighten the horses by day and children by night', but within a two-mile radius of the city the steam tram could not compete with the frequency and overall speed of the horse bus.[29]

Work began on a double tram track from Forest Road along Parramatta Road to Johnston

Steam tram in Broadway travelling into the city in the 1880s. Steam tram services to Glebe began in 1882, to Annandale in 1883, and Leichhardt in 1884. It was not until 1892 that steam tram tracks were extended to Balmain West. (Max Solling Collection)

Street, Annandale, and the line was opened for traffic in 1883. The tentacles of the double tram track proceeded up Parramatta Road to Norton Street, Leichhardt, and northerly to Marion Street in May 1884 but the high plateau and steep foreshores of the Balmain peninsula made a tramway connection difficult. Balmain Council sought a private enterprise initiative to build a cable or electric tramway through the suburb.[30] Agitation for a tram line to provide both internal transport and to link it with the tramway network continued in Balmain throughout the 1880s. Finally, in April 1892, the Forest Lodge tram line was constructed around Rozelle Bay to Balmain West Public School and then to Gladstone Park.[31] Balmain Mayor James Brodie told a parliamentary committee that this was an indirect route to the city and only a single track. Balmain, he said, needed a swift access by tram into the city across Glebe Island and Pyrmont bridges.[32]

Though generally uncomfortable, the four major bus services operating in Glebe and Forest Lodge provided passengers with a wider area of coverage than the tram as well as stopping more frequently. The Millers Point to Lyndhurst omnibus route serviced an area untouched by the steam tram. The Sydney Tramway and Omnibus Company had a monopoly of the Forest Lodge route and was closely integrated with the other services that ran to Glebe. Each horse bus had its own destination sign; the Glebe bus, for example, carried a green destination sign and carried two green lamps, one on each side of the vehicle at night.[33] The horse bus provided 'an excellent service' in Glebe in 1887, 'starting at six minute intervals' and operating at comparable rates to the tram; two years later it was attracting traffic away from the twopenny journey by tram into the city.[34]

The horse bus in Balmain in 1891 provided a service every twenty minutes into the city, between 8 a.m, and 11 p.m., the journey taking about 55 minutes. It was estimated that 720 passengers used this service every day but, although Balmain residents could also catch horse buses on the Ryde route, the number of passengers carried by horse bus was insignificant compared to the number that travelled by ferry.[35]

The steam tram started to come into its own in districts like Leichhardt, four miles from the city. In 1891 it took 35 minutes from Norton Street to Bridge Street and cost only twopence on a special workmen's fare. Here horse bus proprietors were struggling to compete.[36]

Residents of Sydney's waterside suburbs had been commuting to work in the city from an early date. The Balmain Steam Ferry Company, a limited liability company which refined the double-ended wooden ferry, colluded with the Balmain Steam Ferry service in 1882 to fix a single fare at threepence, but ferry commuters benefited from intense competition between these two companies between 1885 and 1887 when a ferry trip fare was reduced to a penny. The monopoly, re-established in 1887, was again challenged that year by the formation of the Balmain

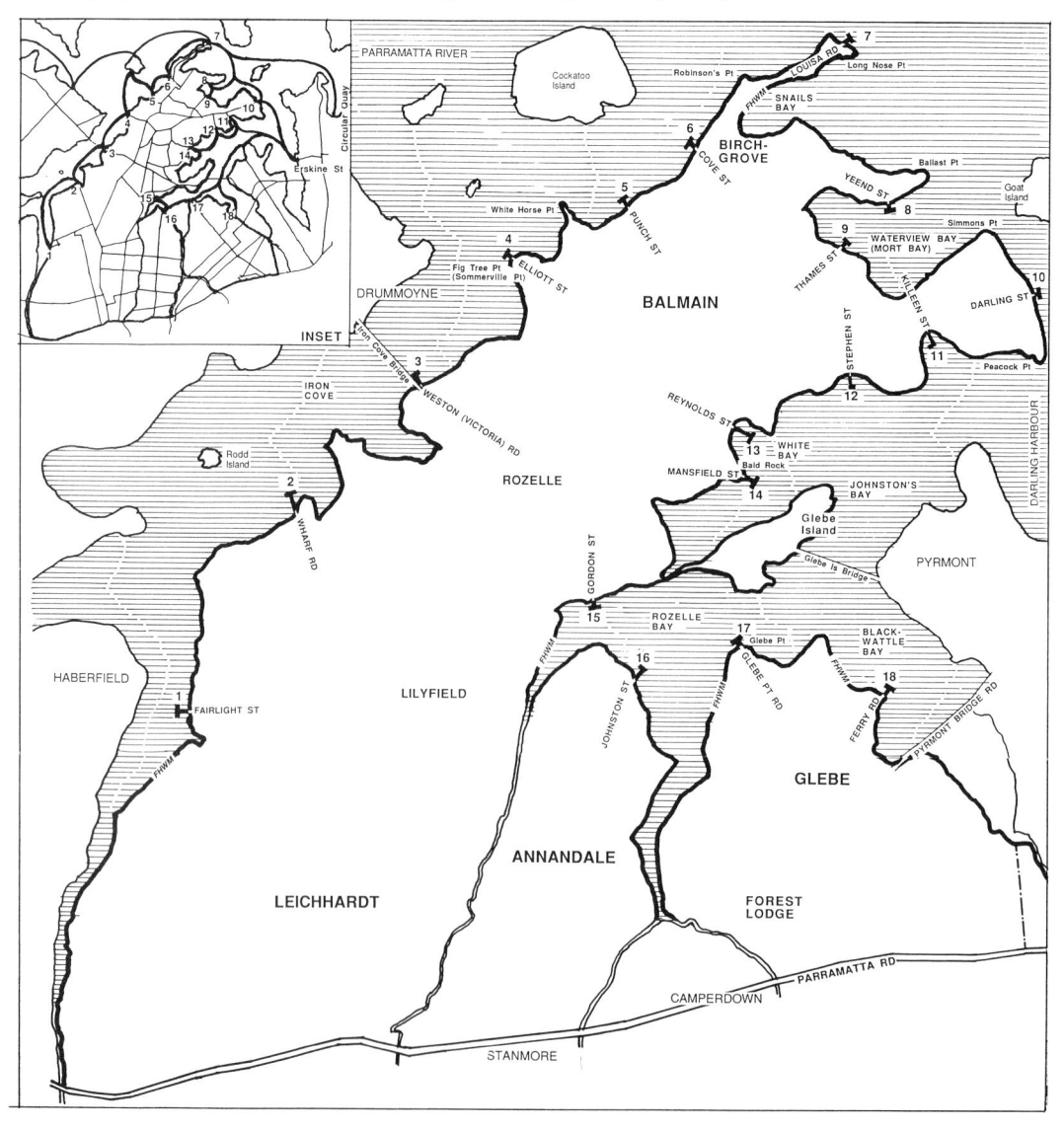

In about 1900 there were no less than eighteen places where passengers could board or alight from ferries serving Annandale, Balmain, Glebe and Leichhardt. (Redrawn with permission from A. M. Prescott, *Sydney Ferry Fleets* (published by R.H. Parsons, Magill, SA, 1984)

and Western Suburbs Steam Ferry Cooperative which offered a penny service. But the people's cooperative lacked the resources to compete against established interests and was wound up in 1888. For much of the 1880s a fare to Erskine Street wharf cost threepence but regular users received some concessions. A worker's weekly cost one shilling and sixpence in 1887, an ordinary weekly two shillings and a monthly ticket seven shillings.[37] The New Balmain Ferry Co. undercut its competitor in 1892 by offering a penny fare and eight years later it had taken over the Balmain Steam Ferry Co. Ltd. It was estimated that in 1891 between 20,000 and 24,000 people travelled daily on the sixteen ferries that conveyed passengers between Balmain and the city.[38]

Matthew Byrnes, anxious to get a slice of the lucrative transport industry, began operating the Annandale & Glebe Point Steam Ferry Co. in 1880. Double-ended paddle steamers ran from the city to Blackwattle and Rozelle Bays, stopping at wharves in Ferry Road, Glebe Point, Annandale and Gordon Street, and though the service was not as frequent as that of the omnibus or the tram, the speed and fares of the steamboat services compared favourably.[39] In 1897, ownership of the service operated by Byrnes passed to the Annandale Cooperative Ferry Co. Ltd, which introduced a penny fare into the city.[40] However, the ferry service to Glebe was finding it increasingly difficult to compete with the tram, and in August 1903, the *Glebe Gazette* reported that the Annandale & Glebe Point Steam Ferry Co. had gone into liquidation.[41] The ferry, too, was conveying passengers from Leichhardt into the city in the 1890s.

Horses remained the principal means of transport in Sydney in the second half of the nineteenth century and the tempo of life was geared to their pace. Each morning they hauled wagons loaded with fresh food and fodder, and at night they hauled drays loaded with nightsoil from the city's back lanes. They pulled delivery vans and milk carts, fire engines and hearses; they carried cargoes from the port to warehouses and from warehouses to retail shops; and they hauled materials to building sites.

Suburban directories in the 1880s were filled with the names of independent carters. In 1887 there were 864 horses stabled in Glebe and 960 in Balmain.[42] In an increasingly competitive business, a growing number of previously self-employed carters had, by 1901, become wage labourers driving carts or lorries. Large general carrying firms emerged to dominate the industry. By 1890 there were six large firms operating in the city, the biggest with between 80 and

Electric tram, Parramatta Road and Johnston Street, Annandale. From about 1900 the electric tram quickly established itself as the main form of transport in the inner suburbs of Sydney. (R.J. Mills Collection)

The tramway network in the current municipality in 1927 showing single and double tracks. The metropolitan electric tramway network gave ordinary people greater mobility than ever before. (Map by David R. Keenan, *The Western Lines of the Sydney Tramway System*, 1993)

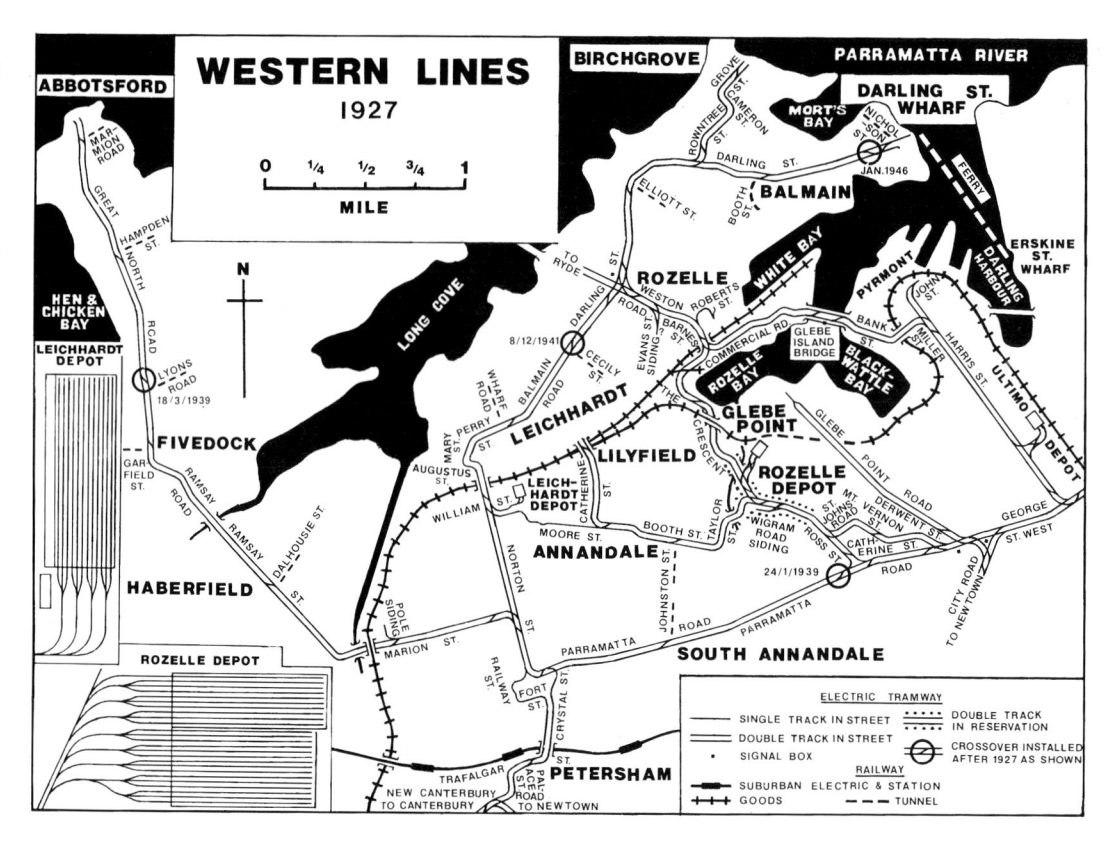

100 horses, and a further eight large firms spread around the inner suburbs, including William McKeown and John Meloy, each with 25 to 45 horses.[43] Horse-drawn public transport began to decline in the 1890s though private horse-drawn transport continued to grow. The increasing distance between fodder-producing areas and the inner city pushed up the cost of feed, making it harder for the horse-bus proprietor to survive. The number of licensed horse cabs operating in Sydney dropped from 1,299 in 1892 to 1,100 in 1895; there were 1,365 licensed cabbies in 1895, 136 fewer than three years earlier, and from then on their ranks became progressively thinner.[44]

Each working horse consumed about five tons of fodder a year, and large quantities of manure were deposited on suburban streets, creating a major pollution problem.[45] Apart from the increasing direct and social costs of the horse, the improving technology of steam hastened a revolution in urban transport. Steam power remained the dominant mode of propulsion for Sydney's tramways until the early 1900s when it was overhauled by electric traction. The heavily subsidised penny electric tram was quickly established as the main form of urban transport. There was a dramatic expansion of the metropolitan tramway network between 1901 and 1914 when Sydney's population grew rapidly from 482,000 to over 750,000. By 1914 a tramway network of over 200 miles conducted nearly 300 million passenger journeys annually.[46]

The cost and shackles of the public transport system meant residents of the inner suburbs remained closely tied to their neighbourhood, but the spreading tentacles of the tramways, by giving ordinary people greater mobility than ever before, helped to break down a parochialism that characterised suburban life.

In Glebe, Annandale and Leichhardt ferry proprietors were unable to compete against the cheaper fares of the electric tram, or the frequency of its service. However, the tram did not pose the same threat in Balmain, and the introduction of the penny ferry fare there in the 1890s ensured the survival of the ferry service.

Builders and contractors

Most of the dwellings in mid-nineteenth-century Sydney were the creations of owner–builders and specialist tradesmen. They faced few barriers to entry into the building trade but the failure rate was high. Tradesmen competed with each other for contracts which were often negotiated in the nearest pub. Carpenters were the largest group of urban tradesmen, and they worked around sawyers, brickmakers and quarrymen who fashioned timber, bricks and stone, hauled to the site by horse and cart. Bricklayers, masons and labourers worked beside them, and shinglers, plumbers, glaziers and painters completed construction work.[47]

The increased demand for housing in the 1870s and 1880s brought significant changes in building materials and techniques. The more basic the cottage, the more prefabricated materials were used as suburban house builders increasingly resorted to machine-produced timber and bricks.[48] With the introduction of powered machinery in the 1890s, employers desired to coordinate more closely the work of separate trades so as to maximise machine use.

The organisation of building businesses and contracts began to change. Owner–builders and specialist tradesmen working on their own account, who were so predominant before 1870, gradually gave way to general contractors who tendered for the whole of the construction work. Initially contractors were small-scale builders, but a number became large-scale speculators.[49]

In the last quarter of the nineteenth century residential construction was the most important source of capital investment. In 1891, the building industry, which was predominantly urban, absorbed about one-third of all investment—more than that of any other single activity—and directly employed 14 per cent of the workforce.

After a recession in 1870, residential investment rose sharply to a peak in 1875. In 1877, building activity experienced a downturn but in 1879 rents rose and remained on a high plateau until 1883. By 1884, building activity was declining but the so-called 'long boom' continued unabated to 1889. The year 1890 marked the beginning of a severe depression.[50] A contemporary wrote of the frenetic pace of the building boom:

> Everywhere the sound of the workmen's tools is heard, all through the busy day. Brickyards are worked to their utmost capacity; iron foundries are taxed to their greatest powers, sawmills and joinery establishments are in full activity . . . Areas have to be circumscribed—societies, speculators, jobbers, have bought up all the estates, and vacant blocks around Sydney.[51]

Some 600 builders and 100 architects were active in the metropolitan area of Sydney in 1888. Some 61,630 permanent dwellings were constructed in Sydney between 1861 and 1891, 80 per cent of which were either of brick or stone.

By 1891 there were 21,117 habitations in the City of Sydney and 58,338 in its suburbs. Residential finance remained cheap throughout the 1880s and funds from banks, building societies, individuals and mortgage companies helped sustain house building. Investment in building societies was attractive because they paid higher rates of interest on deposits than banks. Their main depositors were the well-to-do and most of their clients were commercial borrowers.[52] In Glebe, Leichhardt and elsewhere an extraordinarily close relationship existed between building societies and successful builders. As directors on the boards of the building societies, builders had a guaranteed source of capital.

Provision of essential services

The provision of piped water, roads, sewered streets and gas lagged well behind the private developer in the suburban development process. Arrangements for adequate drainage and sewers were casually contrived as there was no obligation on the builder or developer to provide these services, but the building boom of the 1880s accentuated the need for comprehensive sanitation and water supply systems to be established and vested in a central authority. Before 1850 water carts and pumps were the main source of supply outside the city limits. Springs, rain tanks and windlass-drawn wells supplied Balmain residents with water and, according to City Engineer Edward Bell, a well in Kensington Street near Tooth's brewery was the principal source of water for the mass of Glebe's population.[53] Only 1,000 of the 8,000 houses within the City Corporation area in 1851 were supplied with water. 'Half the time of the poor is taken up in obtaining water from pumps,' noted the *Herald*, and some working-class consumers who obtained their water from water carriers paid up to one-third of their wages for their weekly supplies.[54]

The Botany Swamps scheme, carried out by the City Council, improved the city water supply when it became operational in 1859; water was pumped to a brick reservoir at Crown Street and the City Council negotiated with neighbouring municipalities on terms to extend its water mains to them. Pumped supplies of town water reached Glebe in 1862, but Balmain was unable to agree to City Council conditions and remained reliant on wells and tanks until 1880 when it received a supply from Botany Swamps. The water supply to Balmain remained intermittent to 1886, and higher parts of the suburb experienced problems up to 1891.[55]

Distribution to the more elevated parts of Glebe was neither constant nor efficient in 1869.[56] Professor Liversidge's 1875 reports of faecal matter, undigested food and human hair in the Crown Street reservoir, the source of Glebe's water supply, cast doubts on its quality.[57] By the late 1870s all Glebe residences were connected to town water pipes and between 1878 and 1882 mains were extended to Leichhardt and Marrickville.[58] The Botany scheme in the 1880s had difficulty coping with increased demands, especially in the summer months, but the supply improved in 1888 when water from the Upper Nepean scheme first reached Sydney.

The absence of underground drainage meant that suburban gutters flowed with household wastes which grew in volume from street to street, banking up at intersections, overflowing the carriageways and eventually finding an outlet into the harbour. One of the City Council's principal sewers emptied stormwater and sewage into Glebe's sink, Blackwattle Bay.[59] And in 1876 the Sewage and Health Board found that filth and sewage running down narrow lanes at the southern end of Glebe were 'positively sickening' and infrequent visits by the corporation cart, which swept away all the rubbish, added up to 'studied neglect'.[60] The main means of sanitation was a separate backyard outhouse with a removable pan; water closets which discharged into a brick cesspit were less numerous. Nightsoil disposal was a flourishing business; it was usually undertaken by contractors who collected the soil in carts, having gained access to the pan along narrow back lanes. The nightsoil was deposited at Moore Park, Botany and Homebush.[61]

The process of substituting underground drains for open ditches began in the early 1880s and, as the typhoid toll mounted, local councillors became vociferous about the danger their unsewered streets posed, calling for replacement of the inefficient and expensive system of pan collecting by a system of underground sewerage.[62] By 1885 Glebe Council could wait no longer and in 'a spirit of self reliance and with the warm approbation of the ratepayers' undertook its own sewerage works.[63] Contractors began laying pipes in 1886, and in 1889, when most of the work was completed, only 200 houses were connected to the sewer.

Edward Harman Buchanan, the Mayor of Balmain, told a Parliamentary Standing Committee in 1889 there were 4,300 pans in his municipality (which each cost £1 a year to empty) and 300 to 400 cesspits. Leichhardt had 2,700 pans and 750 cesspits and it was clear that the cartage of nightsoil and its disposal were becoming more difficult and unhygienic.[64] Progressively increasing discharge of raw sewage into the harbour forced the government to draw up a comprehensive sewerage system which would convey sewage by gravitation to an outfall in the ocean off Bondi. The extension of the Bondi Sewer to Glebe, Annandale, Balmain and Leichhardt was built in the mid-1890s with more tunnel work and the construction of two reinforced concrete aqueducts over Johnston's Creek and White's Creek, Annandale.[65] The high death rates in the inner suburbs from typhoid and other epidemic diseases declined after connections were made to the Nepean water supply and the Bondi sewer outfall.[66]

The function of the Board of Water Supply and Sewerage, formed in 1888, was to maintain the major works completed by the Public Works Department, and to extend and amplify the reticulation system. This dual control, from planning to operation, continued until 1924 when the Metropolitan Water, Sewerage and Drainage Board became the central authority for all water and sewerage works in Sydney.[67]

The formation, kerbing and guttering of streets was the responsibility of the municipal council. It was a constant and continuing drain on council funds and accounted for a significant proportion of the total revenue.[68] Corner posts with street names printed on galvanised iron were erected and efforts made to keep

The White's Creek sewer aqueduct, completed in 1898, looking towards Annandale. The sewerage system to Annandale, Balmain and Leichhardt was made possible by Monier reinforced concrete aqueducts over White's Creek and Johnston's Creek. (Sydney Water Archive)

goats, pigs and other animals off the streets. The Australian Gas Light Co. signed a contract with Glebe Council in 1860 to light its streets and by 1867 gas was used almost exclusively for street illumination although some simple domestic lighting was available.[69] The gas company began building gas works in Balmain in 1874 and two years later its streets were gaslit.[70]

Dust on earth and gravel streets was controlled to some extent by seawater sprayed from horse-drawn carts. More offensive was the manure that dried and powdered on suburban streets, to be converted by rain into muck which wheels threw up on to the footpath. Main arteries like Darling Street and Glebe Point Road were ballasted and macadamised, but bitumen- or asphalt-sealed streets remained the main form of road construction until the 1920s. The tram took a heavy toll on the median, adding to maintenance costs.[71]

Road construction and maintenance and other public works in the boom years forced councils to borrow heavily. By 1890, 70 miles of streets traversed Leichhardt, there were 52 miles in Balmain and about 21 miles in Glebe.[72] Private companies competed for the right to supply electric current to Sydney hotels, libraries and warehouses. Country centres led the way in lighting streets with electricity. Tamworth was the first in 1888.[73] Gas remained the street illuminant in Balmain until 1908 when the Balmain Electric Light and Power Supply Corporation became one of the private concerns that supplied the suburbs.

The framework of local government

6

Balmain Municipal Offices, 1887, in the former cottage on the site now occupied by the Balmain Post Office and Court House. Balmain Mayor, William Burns JP (*at left*) and Alderman James McDonald (*fourth from left*) pose with Council Clerk H.B. Macintosh (*second from left*), Assistant Council Clerk J.M. Hetherington (*third from left*), Junior Clerk A.W. Sommerville (*fifth from left*) and the Borough Engineer and Surveyor, J. Goodsir. Council's salaried officers and assistants were paid £1,009 in 1887. (By courtesy of Frank Ehlert)

Local government came to Glebe and Balmain in 1859 and 1860 respectively, making them among the earliest districts to have this framework imposed on them. However, this occurred only after opposing factions had engaged in robust debate, and a series of local petitions and counter-petitions, had been circulated.[1] Burdened with the administrative and financial responsibilities of new settlements, the colonial government wanted to force local communities to contribute towards the cost of establishing and maintaining their basic physical infrastructure.[2]

Introduction of a municipal system in semi-rural Leichhardt drew support from sectional interests but even among these groups there were concerns about the benefits of incorporation. A petition signed by 113 local householders in October 1870 seeking incorporation was matched six months later by a counter-petition with a greater number of signatories, many from Petersham.[3] The Petersham precinct was then excluded from the proposed municipal district, reducing the area to 1,300 acres, and on 14 December 1871, after a further petition was received, Leichhardt was proclaimed a municipality. The six newly-elected aldermen held their first meeting at the local Working Men's Institute on 16 February 1872.[4]

Early by-laws, which empowered councils to regulate activities, dealt with the suppression of nuisances and houses of ill fame, required householders to keep their premises free from offensive or unwholesome matters, allowed councils to curb noisome and offensive trades, and sought to prevent the spread of contagious and infectious diseases. By-laws for Glebe were first proclaimed in 1864, followed by Balmain (1868) and Leichhardt (1872). The basic structure of councils, and their functions, can be discerned from their committees—Finance, Works, By-Laws and General Purposes.[5]

The Council Clerk, responsible for the efficient administration of the municipality, had to possess a knowledge of legislation under which Council operated and maintain proper books for rating purposes. Throughout the 1860s and 1870s the affairs of councils were conducted from modest chambers geographically located at the centre of their communities.[6] Their lack of financial resources, and staff who were often unqualified for their tasks, meant their achievements were limited, and the populace was represented by people anxious to accommodate the municipality's men of wealth and influence. The Inspector of Nuisances, paid a pittance to safeguard the people's health, faced a daunting task.[7]

Both Balmain and Glebe housed more than 3,000 people in 1861 and their councils had to provide a basic infrastructure of roads, drains, bridges and so forth. Rates were the main source of municipal finance, and though government endowments were significant contributions in the early years after incorporation, they were far from adequate (Table 5).[8] In 1876, for example, Leichhardt Council sought an increased endowment; otherwise, it claimed, Council would be 'utterly unable to properly and permanently make necessary public works'.[9]

Road construction and maintenance, including lighting and other borough works, absorbed most of Council's revenue and, as a consequence, fortnightly meetings were preoccupied with these matters. Without any other significant source of revenue, councils had an inbuilt constraint on what they could do.[10]

Table 5   Receipts, expenditures and registered voters 1861–70

Year	Rates (£s)	Endowments (£s)	Total (£s)	Expenditure (£s)	Registered voters
Balmain					
1861	1,777	1,865	3,642	4,801	690
1862	1,598	1,401	2,999	6,474	690
1865	1,582	1,315	2,897	2,826	700
1867	1,554	803	2,357	2,114	1,116
1870	1,541	972	2,513	1,537	969
Glebe					
1861	1,858	1,522	3,380	3,244	–
1862	1,497	1,439	2,936	3,313	771
1865	1,669	1,237	2,906	2,598	698
1867	1,846	757	2,603	2,637	809
1870	1,823	759	2,582	2,689	1,335

About half of Balmain's fifteen miles of streets were kerbed and guttered in 1873, its busiest streets laid with blue metal. Hard white metal obtained from local quarries provided a surface for its other roads.[11] Government gave Balmain no assistance for its street network; those who benefit, the government said, must bear the cost. Balmain, without piped water, was entirely dependent on 'private individual catches and stores by means of tanks and wells'. Glebe, closer to the city, had water pipes extended to it from 1862 and was connected to town gas; its streets had been aligned and gazetted and a pound established by 1865.[12] The type of activities that engaged the time of councils—letting tenders for kerbing and guttering; erecting street signs; seeking to keep pigs, goats and other animals off the streets; petitioning about an inadequate water supply; grubbing out tree stumps; and negotiating with the Gas Company about lighting the streets—can be culled from the minutes.[13]

The early running of Glebe Council was not without its problems. Its first Clerk and Surveyor, Henry Sanderson, slipped away in the dark of the night with some Council property; he was apprehended and brought before the Police Court.[14] Council salaries absorbed a small proportion of its expenditure. The Council Clerk of Glebe received £13 per month in 1868, a foreman was paid at a daily rate of seven shillings and casual labourers six shillings. Leichhardt's first Council Clerk, W.J. Howe, received £45 per annum.[15]

Rate revenues climbed steadily during the 1870s. By 1878 Balmain collected £4,078 in ordinary rates, Glebe £2,765 and Leichhardt only £594.[16] House building increased in the 1880s, boosting council revenues, as rating was based on improved value, and councils were forced to borrow from loan markets with a ready supply of funds. Borrowing by councils 'became a mania' and interest on these loans moved steadily upwards.[17]

Table 6   Rates and endowments 1874[18]

Municipality	Rates	Endowment
Balmain	£1,810	£465
Glebe	£2,346	£459
Leichhardt	£391	£391

The extent of both borrowings and public works in Balmain peaked between 1884 and 1888 (Tables 7 and 8). Though municipal financial returns were insufficiently detailed to permit close analysis, street construction, it seems, absorbed much of its expenditure. Glebe first went into debt in 1883 to undertake local improvements, and the extent of its municipal works and borrowing rose sharply in 1887–88.[19] Leichhardt Council went heavily into debt from 1885 as its local improvements sought to keep pace with the municipality's rapid residential growth. Maintenance of 52 miles of made streets in 1888, and some fourteen miles of dirt tracks, imposed a heavy burden on Leichhardt.[20]

Every year between 1884 and 1888 Balmain borrowed twice the amount it collected in rate revenue. In Glebe in 1887 and 1888 rate revenue represented 70 per cent of the amounts borrowed; loans Leichhardt negotiated between 1885 and 1888 were about two and a half times the rate revenue.[21]

In 1887 the Casual Labour Board was established to provide work for a growing number of unemployed men. About 1,000 men were employed by suburban municipalities on half wages, performing local relief works. In 1887 Balmain Council engaged 30 day labourers and 59 men from the Casual Labour Board to form, maintain and repair roads and footpaths and to do kerbing and guttering.[22] Glebe contributed one half the wages of 75 labourers from the Labour Board in the same year.[23] Substantial concreting work at Johnston's Creek, Helsarmel and Elswick at Leichhardt was carried out under the Casual Labour Board. Initially most municipal work was done by day labour but later it was contracted out.[24]

Table 7   Municipal expenditures 1881–88

Year	Office & salaries (£s)	Public works (£s)	Lighting (£s)	Total (£s)
Balmain				
1881	494	6,987	1,444	11,457
1883	1,115	8,600	1,745	19,575
1884	1,303	16,838	1,599	26,921
1885	1,137	18,553	1,907	29,603
1887	1,009	17,864	2,042	34,840
1888	1,300	24,337	2,206	37,962
Glebe				
1881	421	4,662	1,276	10,219
1883	574	12,137	1,382	15,937
1884	511	6,277	1,744	10,646
1885	555	6,585	1,038	13,077
1887	631	10,500	2,201	16,521
1888	930	26,544	1,303	32,135
Leichhardt				
1881	813	4,136	–	5,115
1883	756	6,641	702	8,602
1884	1,018	7,117	793	10,063
1885	1,020	9,908	1,112	16,299
1887	868	22,382	1,185	27,235
1888	760	14,990	1,334	20,764

Glebe Town Hall, St John's Road. Designed by Ambrose Thornley Junior in the Victorian Second Empire style, the building was opened on 24 June 1880 by Mayor T.J. Dunn and photographed in 1887. It remains as a symbol of local wealth, pride and independence though Glebe lost its municipal identity in 1948. (GPO Videodisc-1 Still 05335)

The years of heavy municipal expenditure came to an abrupt end with the onset of the depression. Councils were now confronted with declining land values upon which rates were levied. Outstanding loans by councils were about four times the general rate in 1891.[25] These councils' indebtedness amounted to £1,083,775 and they held assets valued at £4,644,120.[26] There was a constant demand on municipal purses to maintain streets and undertake other public works, but as land values continued to fall into 1897, and debt repayment and interest charges increased, councils were forced to borrow simply to maintain basic services.[27]

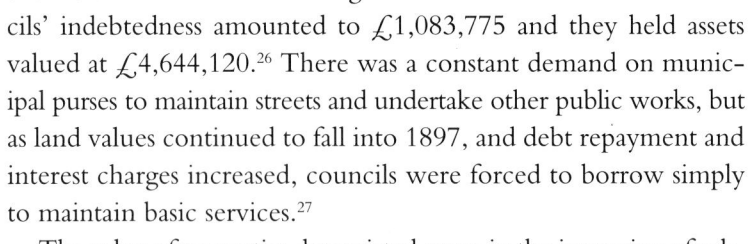

The value of properties depreciated more in the inner ring of suburbs than in settlements on the periphery of development and rate arrears became chronic. In 1893, for example, Balmain was owed £10,036, more than a year's rate revenue; Leichhardt was owed £2,916 and Glebe £1,176. Balmain was the largest debtor of all the metropolitan councils, owing £68,915 in 1897. Leichhardt had a debt of £41,418, Glebe £39,060, and Annandale £12,154.[28]

The town halls built in the prosperous 1880s remain as lasting monuments to local pride, wealth and independence, embodying every flamboyance that appealed to the taste of that period. Glebe people celebrated the opening of their town hall on 24 June 1880 with a grand concert.[29] At Balmain, Mayor Edward Buchanan opened the new hall he had designed on 25 August 1888, and the official opening of Leichhardt Town Hall by Governor Carrington on 26 September 1888 attracted 5,000 people.[30] Construction of these edifices was at a significant cost to the ratepayers of Glebe, Balmain and Leichhardt; the buildings alone cost £5,000, £4,500 and £5,600 respectively and the sites about half these amounts. More modest council chambers for Annandale, designed by architect John Richards, were opened on 20 September 1899.[31]

The town hall was not only the centre of local administration but also a venue for meetings of Oddfellows and Masons, concerts and bazaars, and for an array of other activities. It was, as well, a place where people congregated to debate matters of local concern. Aldermen vigorously pursued concerns of their ward when Council met, and the municipal council reflected the views of local residents in dealings with the government.[32]

Table 8 Municipal receipts 1881–88

Year	Rates (£s)	Lighting (£s)	Loan (£s)	Government (£s)	Total receipts (£s)
Balmain					
1881	4,884	1,617	4,200	2,608	15,094
1883	6,679	2,226	3,000	3,841	18,255
1884	6,607	2,199	12,000	3,339	27,830
1885	6,462	2,152	15,000	3,303	31,116
1887	9,709	3,230	21,000	2,512	17,864
1888	5,308	1,743	14,903	1,421	10,426
Glebe					
1881	4,252	1,417	–	2,530	9,468
1883	5,251	1,750	3,000	3,751	13,753
1884	5,697	1,899	–	2,625	12,420
1885	6,592	2,197	–	2,848	14,012
1887	7,104	2,368	10,000	1,797	1,356
1888	7,181	2,394	10,000	1,776	13,843
Leichhardt					
1881	1,921	334	–	1,614	4,589
1883	2,449	851	–	2,153	6,313
1884	3,479	1,160	–	3,107	10,518
1885	4,253	1,306	16,000	2,548	26,274
1887	5,736	1,905	14,000	1,729	9,996
1888	4,954	1,419	10,000	1,358	8,412

Annandale was the last of the four incorporated areas to acquire its own permanent centre of administration. Annandale Council Chambers in Johnston Street served as a major venue for Annandale residents to debate matters of local concern as well as the municipal centre from its opening in 1899 to 1948. (Photograph by David Liddle)

A strong sense of belonging to a local community developed and any club that took the name of the suburb received strong support. Councillors exuded municipal pride when appearing before parliamentary inquiries and fiercely defended their suburb against any criticism. The spirit of voluntary effort was nurtured by councils through rate concessions and donations to sporting clubs, brass bands, local distress societies, mechanics' institutes and churches. The civic self-consciousness that became apparent in the 1880s led to a competitive spirit between municipalities.[33]

In the early years of their administration, councils were parsimonious in the salaries they offered a handful of senior officers and their assistants. However by the 1880s these salaries were more attractive (Table 7) and in 1888 they comprised 5–8 per cent of municipal expenditure.[34] The remaining council workers were classified as outdoor or labouring staff; their numbers were reduced in the hard times of the 1890s, though councils ensured local labourers were given preference for available work.[35]

Leichhardt Council workmen (1921) were the most visible face of Council, repairing roads, cleaning the streets, collecting garbage and maintaining the parks and reserves. The names of these workmen were not recorded for posterity. (J.G. Park Collection, Macleay Museum)

Salaried council officials played a crucial role in developing their municipality and setting standards of administration. The growth of the occupation of town clerk, borough engineer, health inspector and auditor, as organised professions, imposed their standards on the running of councils. In Annandale, John Golden Hinsby shaped the council's structure from 1903 to 1926 when he was Town Clerk, and Thomas Glasscock left an indelible imprint on Glebe Municipality during his exceptionally long period as Town Clerk from 1884 to 1933.[36] Alexander Sommerville filled the position of Town Clerk on Balmain Council from 1918 to 1940. Phillip Newland, Walter Beames and Thomas Devenish Meares were powerful figures in the administration of Leichhardt Council.[37]

Public health

Councils were local law makers in matters of public health and amenity, but the municipalities were powerless to make any significant impression on the public health hazards their residents faced. They lacked resources, both financial and in terms of personnel, and there was an urgent need for a central health authority.

The Inspector of Nuisances roamed the municipality reporting on health hazards. Poorly paid, he was often required to perform additional tasks such as rate collection. Policemen such as Constable Davies at Leichhardt combined nuisance inspection with their normal duties.[38] John Reilly was an inspector, pound keeper and councillor at Glebe.[39]

People in Sydney lived in mortal fear of the childhood infections—scarlet fever, measles, whooping cough and diphtheria—and from the 1870s these scourges were joined by tuberculosis, influenza, typhoid and, most frightening of all, bubonic plague.

Mains water was extended to Glebe in the 1860s but Balmain and Leichhardt remained largely reliant on tanks and ground wells until about 1882. Piped water was far from pure. Professor Liversidge tested samples of water drawn from the city mains in 1875 in six different areas and found faecal matter in three of them. He was puzzled why there had not been widespread disease caused by drinking city water.[40]

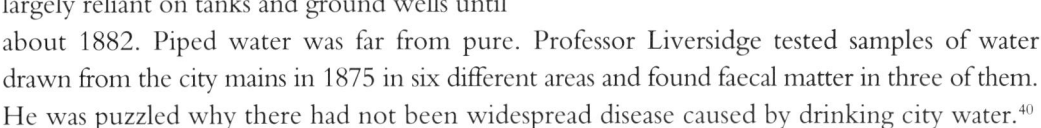

Until the 1880s, Glebe, Balmain and Leichhardt were not connected to any sewerage system. The main form of sanitation in these suburbs was the pan system and, to a lesser extent, the cesspit.[41] As it was common practice to dig wells and cesspits next to each other, there was a higher incidence of water-borne infectious diseases in neighbourhoods not supplied with mains water.

In 1875 the Sydney City and Suburban Sewage and Health Board set out to make a comprehensive inquiry into the general condition of the urban population and sources of danger to its health. Over two years the Board produced a series of revealing reports. It found there was inadequate care taken over the collection and disposal of human excreta, euphemistically referred to as nightsoil.[42]

This work was undertaken by contractors on behalf of councils which either levied a special rate or included the cost in the general rate. Competition for council contracts was intense, and a deodorant, it was claimed, had been developed to overcome the stench emanating from metal night carts as they passed along suburban streets.[43] Residents of cottages without any rear lane access watched the nightman shouldering the pan down their hall.

As population spread, it became increasingly difficult to find places to bury the nightsoil. Balmain contractors dumped their nightsoil in the grounds of Callan Park for a time until Dr Manning complained it was not being disposed of in the agreed manner.[44] Glebe nightmen disposed of their putrid loads far from the municipality but resentment grew in other neighbourhoods over 'foreign' night carts using their streets.[45] Sewage collection and disposal posed such a threat to health in Glebe, 'with typhoid and other diseases rife', that the local council undertook their own sewerage works, completed at a cost of £11,779.[46] The cartage of

Top left: T.D. Glasscock (1862–1944). The name of Thomas Glasscock was synonymous with the administration of Glebe Council. He was Glebe Council's Town Clerk from 1884 to 1933. (Max Solling Collection). *Top right*: J. Golden Hinsby (1858–1926). A prominent Anglican and Freemason, Hinsby was a dominant figure at Annandale Council from 1903 to his death in 1926 when he was Town Clerk. Born in England and once a schoolteacher, he is remembered by Hinsby Park in Annandale. (Annandale Council Chambers). *Bottom left*: Alexander Sommerville (1869–1943). All Sommerville's working life was with Balmain Council beginning as a junior clerk in about 1887 and serving as its Town Clerk from 1918 to 1940. (Balmain Council Chambers). *Bottom right*: Phillip Newland, a prominent local builder in the 1880s was the Overseer of Works from 1890 to 1913 at Leichhardt Council and also its Inspector of Nuisances from 1899 to 1905. (Leichhardt Town Hall).

nightsoil became more onerous, and its disposal more difficult, until the mid-1890s, when the present municipality of Leichhardt was linked to a comprehensive, modern sewerage system.

The emergence of industry and noxious trades exposed many suburban residents to a variety of occupational risks and hazards. From the 1840s slaughterhouses, boiling-down works, tanneries and other noxious trades were major polluters which contributed to the spread of infectious disease. Blackwattle Swamp, into which one of the city sewers discharged, was described as a 'fever bed'.[47] William Pinhey, chemist and Glebe councillor, told a meeting that the 'effluvia which arose' from the swamp 'was at times intolerable giving rise to miasmatic and other fevers and placing Glebe in an unenviable position in mortality tables of the Statistical Register'.[48] After reclamation of the swamp was completed in 1880, legislation decreed the land be reserved and residential development prohibited because of inadequate drainage.[49]

The government abattoir at Glebe Island, a place neither government nor city authorities were anxious to manage, was a major source of pollution. Residents from adjoining suburbs in 1873 petitioned that 'the stench arising from gut cleaners, tripe boilers, and from the Island, is often so abominably suffocating that the residents within a mile are compelled to close their doors and windows'.[50] Without a permanent water supply, the abattoir had to rely on storage tanks, and when they ran dry, carcasses were washed in the polluted harbour water. The dumping of offal in Leichhardt by butchers from Glebe Island was another source of trouble. The Sewage and Health Board recommended the collection of blood in proper receptacles for burying; this would remove 'at a trifling cost one of the grossest sources of pollution in the harbour'.[51] The abattoir would remain a constant source of agitation until its closure.

The Select Committee on the 'Conditions of the Working Classes of the Metropolis' reported in 1860 that 'the house accommodation of the working classes of Sydney is admitted on all hands to be deplorably bad'.[52] Sixteen years later little had changed; the Health Board then found many 'wretched hovels' in its house-to-house survey of poorly-drained, low-lying localities. In Glebe it reported on 'the most glaring cases of overcrowding and its concomitant evils'.[53] The heat and stench from cow yards, common stinking cesspits and streams of filth and sewage running from backyards into Francis Street and Franklyn Place made this neighbourhood 'positively sickening' while nearby the gutters of Queen Street were filled with dead dogs and cats, dead fowls, bones and decayed vegetable matter of all sorts. Dead walls at the back of small rooms prevented any ventilation, while many dwellings had insufficient air and floor space and made little or no provision for drainage.[54]

Five epidemics of infectious disease swept through Sydney between 1867 and 1900. A childhood measles epidemic occurred in 1867, and in 1875–76 an outbreak of a much dreaded disease, scarlet fever, provoked considerable public reaction.[55] The influenza epidemic of 1891 was the first time Sydney was caught up in a major pandemic of infectious disease. But it was the smallpox epidemic in 1881–82 and the bubonic plague in 1900 that produced scenes of hysteria and panic.[56] Middle-class anxieties about these epidemics led to the formation of the Health Society in 1876, and the *Infectious Diseases Act*, 1882, was the legislative response to the smallpox outbreak. Soon a Central Board of Health came into being, and a Medical Adviser to the government was appointed to oversee public health matters. By the late 1880s sewerage and drainage systems had improved and legislation was enacted regulating the removal of nightsoil, the supervision of milk products, the prevention of nuisances and the location of noxious industries.[57] The *Public Health Act*, 1898, empowered municipalities to undertake surveys of housing conditions as well as to cleanse and disinfect premises considered dangerous to health.

Municipalities were divided into wards based on population. Districts with between 1,000 and 4,000 people were divided into three wards. There were three separate administrative areas in Glebe—Outer, Bishopthorpe and Inner wards—and in 1871 a fourth ward, Forest Lodge, was added.[58] Balmain also contained three wards—North, South and East—and as its population grew its municipal administrative boundaries were reorganised in 1874 into four wards—South East, North East, South West and North.[59]

In December 1878 Leichhardt municipality was divided into East, Middle and West wards and a fourth ward, North, came into being in 1886. There was widespread dissatisfaction among the residents of East Ward (Annandale) about the way they were administered by Leichhardt Council. In December 1892, 677 residents and ratepayers petitioned the Colonial Secretary requesting that their ward be separated from the district.[60] On 2 January 1894 the area between White's and Johnston's Creeks was proclaimed the Borough of Annandale. Leichhardt retained the remaining three-ward structure (West, North and Middle) and the boundaries of Annandale municipality were substantially the same as the old East Ward. In 1894 Leichhardt municipality was again divided into four wards: the Kendall, Cook, Norton and Wentworth wards.[61]

Apart from providing basic services, councils exercised an important influence over the physical and social environment of their suburbs. Control over the physical process of suburban development came through housing by-laws, and under the 1897 Act some degree of control over building construction then came within the ordinance framework.[62]

Municipal councils responded to the wider concept of social needs by providing free libraries, parks, open spaces and swimming pools for the health, recreation and pleasure of their citizens. Wealthy and influential people lent their patronage to activities that were healthy and harmless, and satisfying to local patriotism.

The first free library was opened in Newtown in 1869.[63] These libraries received a government subsidy which was spent on the purchase of books, but to fill their library shelves they had to rely heavily on donations from benefactors. The size of the Glebe Free Library, established in the local town hall in 1881, was enlarged by donations from G.W. Allen, George Sutherland and from William Munro's estate.[64] Balmain Council opened its own library in 1888 and Annandale in 1899.[65] These municipal libraries fared poorly in competing for the attention of the masses. The Glebe library was so little used in 1901 that Council dispensed with the services of its librarian and the following year Mayor Nosworthy sought local views on what should be done to make the library more useful and attractive. The Mayor's call generated little interest and in 1907 the local Workingmen's Institute asked Council to hand over the books from the municipal library to the institute.[66]

Before 1914 the Workingmen's Institutes emerged as thriving institutions with large numbers of members, healthy bank balances and substantial libraries. Most of the revenue the institutes generated came from their main attraction, billiards.

In 1912 the Balmain and Annandale municipal libraries, with 800 and 628 books respectively, still had their doors open but they were rapidly losing ground to the rival institutes. The Balmain Workingmen's Institute claimed 696 members and 6,540 books in 1912; the Glebe Institute 320 members and 2,543 books; and Leichhardt 215 members and 2,300 books. The Rozelle

Mechanics' Institute, which earned a huge £1,908 from billiards in 1912 (and only £151 from subscriptions) had 309 members and 2,451 books.[67]

The municipal library in Annandale seems to have closed by 1915 while Balmain Council maintained its library until 1926. The largest suburban municipal library, at Paddington, was no longer operating in 1940.

Councils were empowered to provide baths for recreational purposes. Balmain opened shark-proof baths, about 33 yards long, at White Horse Point in 1883.[68] Leichhardt Council constructed a larger tidal pool at Iron Cove, about 66 yards long and 55 yards wide, in 1905.[69] Glebe residents lobbied unsuccessfully for a pool in Blackwattle Bay in 1879 and despite further efforts in 1900 and 1912, Glebe never acquired its own pool; residents used the baths at the foot of Point Street, Pyrmont.[70]

As the tempo of development quickened in the 1870s areas were not set aside for parks and recreation grounds (Table 9). However, the *Land for Public Purposes Acquisition Act*, 1880, recognised the need for open space and Henry Parkes sought to ensure that wastelands were dedicated for public recreation purposes.[71] The inhospitable Blackwattle Swamp was reclaimed and named Wentworth Park, a public reservation for the residents of Pyrmont and Glebe.[72] Boggy land at Snails Bay was infilled to create Birchgrove Park[73]; a mangrove swamp at Rozelle Bay was reclaimed between 1895 and 1904 and these new public lands were called Federal Park and Jubilee Park. Leichhardt Park, more than 24 acres of elevated land overlooking Iron Cove, was an exception—a prime piece of real estate that became a public park in 1882. It was enlarged five years later when seven and a half acres of reclaimed land were added to it. The main suburban parks all featured rotundas where the local brass band performed on weekends.[74]

The landscaped grounds of Wentworth Park with its trees, shrubs and flowerbeds looking south-west to Glebe with Sydney University beyond. (*ATCJ*, 13 Oct. 1900, between pages 29 and 35)

Balmain Council created three public reserves from low-lying wastelands (Easton Park, Punch Park and White Bay Reserve) and further improved the local amenity by the addition of Gladstone Park and Elkington Park.[75] The privately owned Balmain Cemetery came under the control of Leichhardt Council in 1886 and the old eleven-acre cemetery became Pioneers Memorial Park in 1941.[76]

Investment in water or sewerage works had not attracted private enterprise but it did involve itself in the provision of other utilities. The Australian Gas Light Company (AGL), formed in 1837, controlled the supply of gas in Sydney but many claimed it abused its monopoly position to extract large profits.[77] AGL built gas works at White Bay, and in 1875 Balmain Council arranged with the company to light its streets with gas. Glebe had entered into a similar agreement some fifteen years earlier.[78] In 1887 the streets of Balmain, Glebe and Leichhardt were lit by 323, 308 and 312 gas lamps respectively. Balmain argued for years that the price of gas was excessive and considered taking over the White Bay plant.

Table 9   Parks and recreation grounds

Location	Land area (a)	Date
Glebe		
Wentworth Park	32. 2.15	10 November 1885
Jubilee Park	13. 1. 0	23 September 1908
Annandale		
Reserve Piper Street	0. 3.28	Private dedication
Federal Park	–	–
Reserve No 30122	16. 1.20	Private dedication Notified 11 November 1889 (4 January 1929)
Balmain		
Easton Park	4. 3.17	Resumed 13 December 1889 Proclaimed 9 May 1890
Gladstone Park	5. 0. 04	Resumed 22 September 1882 Proclaimed 28 July 1885
Birchgrove Park	13. 2.18	Proclaimed 13 October 1893
White Bay Recreation Reserve	8. 0.17	Dedicated 9 September 1899
Punch Park	2. 0.20	Purchased by Balmain Council 14 December 1887
Elkington Park	6. 3.06	Purchased by Balmain Council 4 May 1880, 9 June 1880
Leichhardt		
Leichhardt Park	31. 3.00	Proclaimed 20 September 1887
Reserve No 30970 Long Cove	4. 1.39	Notified 19 May 1900
Pioneers Memorial Park	11.0.00	1941 Formerly Balmain Cemetery

Balmain decided to generate its own electricity and from 1909 a private enterprise, the Balmain Electric Light and Power Supply Corporation, supplied the municipality with electricity.[79] AGL, with many friends in parliament, argued vigorously that it would be outrageous to allow councils to generate electricity for domestic consumption in direct competition with private capital.[80] Glebe Council, anxious to replace its gas lamps with electric lights, held a referendum on the issue in 1905. The majority voted for electric lights, and these were installed by the end of 1911.[81]

The disposal of mounting quantities of garbage and rubbish, collected in horse-drawn municipal drays, posed increasing problems for councils. Initially garbage was dumped in unoccupied areas on the periphery of development, but as with nightsoil disposal, dumping grounds in close proximity became harder to find. Four council carts provided Leichhardt residents with a garbage service twice a week.[82] The outbreak of bubonic plague in 1900 brought heightened public awareness of haphazard methods of garbage disposal. The Balmain Garbage Destructor, which became operational in 1908, was claimed to have the capacity to 'deal with the refuse from three other municipalities the size of Balmain'. Leichhardt too had its own incinerator built.[83] Disposal of manure left by the large horse population in the metropolis contributed further to urban pollution.[84] In the increasingly congested suburbs near the city, sea dumping, tipping and open-air burning of garbage all added more pollutants to the atmosphere and ocean and by the 1920s public agitation forced councils to consider alternative methods of garbage disposal. An assortment of Glebe's garbage, dumped at sea by its contractor, ended up on the city's beaches in 1929.[85] The outcry was such that the Glebe Council opted for an incinerator to solve its problem. The Reverberatory Incinerator and Engineering Company won contracts to build electrified incinerators at Glebe (1932) and Leichhardt (1936). These were two of twelve incinerators designed by Walter Burley Griffin between 1929 and 1937.[86]

By 1900 the rise of the statutory authorities deprived councils of control over some functions that had been regarded as properly municipal. The licensing of public vehicles for hire was given to the Transit Commission in 1873, and the Metropolitan Water Sewerage and Drainage Board was constituted to take over water supply and sewerage. Port control and fire prevention had never been placed under local control. The Metropolitan Fire Brigades Board did provide some municipal representation, but the Sydney Harbour Trust, established in 1900, was a wholly appointed body with no local government members.[87]

Glebe Council yard and Walter Burley Griffin designed incinerator, 1937, Forsyth Street, Glebe. (*Municipality of Glebe, The Mayor's Report, 1935–1937*)

In the late nineteenth century an alderman agonised over councils' lack of control over local services:

> There is no municipal control of traffic, gas companies and Government Departments tear up streets at their pleasure, parks are controlled by irresponsible trustees, boards control water and fire extinction services, the Government runs the tramways and abattoirs.[88]

The proposal for a larger city, loosely named 'Greater Sydney', was first raised by suburban councils at a conference in 1898, perhaps stimulated by the visit to Sydney at this time by Sidney and Beatrice Webb, who advocated the establishment of a large city council to supersede the functions of the 40 municipalities.[89] Incorporated areas, such as Darlington, which covered only 40 acres, were too small, it was argued, for any but the most minor local functions. City council representatives favoured a unified form of metropolitan government; suburban aldermen favoured a federated model. The City Council wanted an enlarged city which would extend its own power, and would not accept any proposal whereby it would be only one municipality among many equals.

The Royal Commission for Greater Sydney, set up in 1912, heard evidence from representatives of 36 municipalities and shires, including Mayors Thomas Colebrook of Annandale, George Clubb of Balmain, Frederick Artlett of Glebe and James Treadgold of Leichhardt.[90] In all, 83 witnesses were examined. Suburban councils remained strongly opposed to unification. There was little possibility of compromise and a Greater Sydney bill, prepared by a Labor government in 1915, was lost in the political turmoil of the war. In 1926 Glebe attempted, without success, to unite with the City of Sydney, but amalgamation of several working-class municipalities with the City finally came in 1948.[91] Annandale and Balmain lost their municipal identity in 1948 when they were incorporated into Leichhardt Municipality and Glebe, too, was subsumed by council amalgamations, coming within the jurisdiction of Sydney City Council. In 1968, when the city of Sydney's boundaries were restructured, Glebe became part of Leichhardt Municipality.

7 Building the suburbs

The process of carving up open farmland in the municipality of Leichhardt and transforming it with bricks and mortar extended over a period from 1830 to 1918. It took place against the background of a population explosion in the metropolis, improved modes of transportation and the availability of land and capital to sustain residential growth. The 7,200 residents in 1861 were largely concentrated in Balmain and Glebe, but the peopling of the many new streets that served the municipality filled the pages of *Sands's Sydney and Suburban Directory* in the second half of the nineteenth century.[1]

Measured simply in terms of physical fabric and aggregate population, the most intensive residential development occurred between 1871 and 1891. Although the supply of new houses varied from year to year, the magnitude of residential expansion in Leichhardt Municipality is evidenced by an overall growth in the number of buildings—from 1,457 in 1861 to 12,192 in 1891—and a population that had increased to 57,617 by 1891.[2]

A host of local circumstances affected the tenure of land and, as a consequence, residential development varied, in both its timing and density, from place to place. The proximity of Balmain and Glebe to the city meant that they were the first neighbourhoods to experience intensive development. The rest of the municipality remained suburban frontiers but by 1881 the semi-rural precincts were on the threshold of spectacular expansion.[3]

Building activity in the 1860s, a period of economic stagnation, merely kept pace with population growth, and an acute housing shortage persisted throughout this decade. Tradesmen, many of whom had not even served an informal apprenticeship, were attracted by an expanding market for houses.[4] A motley collection of workers entered the building industry, which required no specialised skills and little or no capital. The careers of some so-called carpenters, joiners, masons and plasterers were histories of jerry-built cottages and bad debts. But the solid and solemn cottages of Balmain builders George Chidgey, Peter McBeath and William Thornton and the dwellings of the Elphinstone brothers, Thomas Tipple Smith and Ambrose Thornley in Glebe, earned them reputations as competent builders.[5]

Two tracts of Glebe land that the Church of England retained, St Phillip's and Bishopthorpe, were developed by building leases. For small-scale operators it was a convenient device: the initial outlay was small, and high rentals obtained for residential accommodation promised a handsome return. However the builder generally paid higher interest rates for capital borrowed on leasehold property.[6] The landlord retained control, and received a rental return with little capital outlay. The short-term (28-year) leases granted by the trustees of St Phillip's from 1842 imposed no minimum building standards. The end result was the worst type of speculative venture: cheap timber cottages that ceased being fit for habitation long before the leases expired.[7]

Bishopthorpe estate, on the other side of Glebe Road, developed in a different way. Bishopthorpe was cut up into 238 allotments and offered on 99-year leases by the Anglican Bishop of Sydney from 1856.[8] The long-lease term, larger allotments, covenants excluding timber dwellings, and a more elevated terrain produced a much better standard of housing than in St Phillip's.[9]

Among the speculative builders of Bishopthorpe was an array of occupations – dairyman, engraver, whip maker, commission agent, greengrocer and newsagent, together with a collection of specialist tradesmen.[10] Its more substantial domestic buildings—Ramelton House, Chesterfield House, Stonehouse, Aysleigh and others—were the work of architects Blacket and Mansfield and builders Elphinstone, Thornley and Walker. By 1874 the process of building up Bishopthorpe was largely complete, with Derwent, Catherine, Westmoreland, and Mount Vernon streets filled with unadorned brick Victorian Georgian one- and two-storey terraces and houses.[11] The landlord's failure to specify the type of land-use saw five pubs appear on Bishopthorpe, much to the chagrin of Synod.[12]

Shortly after Thomas Sutcliffe Mort acquired an interest in the Waterview Dry Dock, Thomas Holt and Thomas Rowntree bought most of the land surrounding the dock and then conveyed this land to Thomas Mort. 'Allotments at Mort's Dock Balmain,' an advertisement in 1857 read, 'for disposal on 99 years lease with option of purchase at any time during 7 years, a portion of the allotments which as sites for business premises for private residence is not to be surpassed. Will be disposed of on highly favourable terms.' Lease rentals were £5 to £8 per annum.[13] In his dual role as industrial entrepreneur and large-scale developer, Thomas Mort had a considerable impact on Balmain, though he was never a resident.[14] The locality, he thought, was in debt to him. 'I am doubling, trebling, quadrupling the value of their property,' he told a parliamentary committee in 1855. 'Land which at the time I commenced my Dock was only worth 5 shillings a foot they are now asking £6 for.'[15]

Mort's Town of Waterview was a very large development, embracing some 700 allotments. Surveyor Ferdinand Hamilton Reuss had the subdivision pegged out and roads formed. The allotments were mostly 33-foot frontage, with depths ranging from 84 to 109 feet but subsequent resubdivision produced many smaller parcels. Perhaps Mort initially sought to provide rental accommodation near the dock to attract skilled labour and he indicated that a building society might be formed to assist purchasers.[16] The building up of Mort's estate stretched out over a 40-year period. Though the developer spoke of 'the great increase in the number of buildings' on Mort's Estate in 1867, a little over half the subdivision had been sold in 1878. By 1896 the streets that laced Waterview—Mort, Church, Phillip, Short, College, Rowntree, Curtis, Spring, and Cameron streets—were filled with an assortment of houses, 796 in all: 396 brick, 348 weatherboard, 51 stone and one iron.

The Scottish Australian Investment Company was the only investment company to subdivide and sell land in Glebe. It acquired a sixteen-acre portion of the Lyndhurst estate in 1851.[17] Robert Morehead, a director of the Aberdeen-based company, knew the value of this

Ewenton, 1 Blake Street, Balmain, 1895. The Victorian Regency wing built in 1860 for businessman Ewen Wallace Cameron is at left. Cameron purchased the other twelve houses on the Blake Estate during 1856–61. He added the Victorian Free Classical wing (at right) in 1872 and died there in 1876. (By courtesy of Peter and Anne Waugh, Guyra)

Alfred Hancock (1835–1919) and family in the garden of Mertonville, Beattie and Elliott streets, Balmain. Estate agent Hancock bought up large tracts of Balmain West and the 'Homes for the People' scheme he introduced enabled many people of limited means to become freeholders. As a Balmain councillor in 1873–82 and 1884–86 he was ideally placed to guide his developments through Council. (Balmain Association Collection)

property would be substantially enhanced when the Pyrmont Bridge Company's road sliced through their Glebe freehold.[18] He was privy to this information from an early date since he was also on the board of the Pyrmont Bridge Company. The company initially granted 99-year leases with an option to purchase within seven years, provided certain capital improvements were carried out, and the lessee was required to pay the company £145, the equivalent of twenty years' rental. Between about 1869 and 1880 the 21- to 26-foot frontages in Brougham, Gottenham and Talfourd streets and a portion of Bridge Road were filled with rows of terraces.[19] Forest Lodge emerged with a local life and character of its own between 1865 and 1871 when a syndicate of four politicians—the ubiquitous George Wigram Allen, his great friend Thomas Holt, Thomas Smart and Randolph Want, solicitor and Legislative Councillor—subdivided and disposed of this 45-acre estate.[20] A mixture of socioeconomic groups inhabited Forest Lodge: small workingmen's cottages clustered around Davenport's boot factory while Pyrmont Bridge Road was lined with picturesque villas and cottages occupied by people in commercial occupations, the professions, and clerks in government service.[21]

Early development on the Balmain peninsula gravitated to the eastern end. Proximity to the city and water views initially made it an elite marine resort, though by 1855 it began to acquire an industrial character when the dry dock was opened. The western end of the suburb, a physically distinct neighbourhood, remained a suburban frontier in 1870.[22] The decision to locate the government abattoir at Glebe Island was critical in determining the way Balmain West developed.[23] The other end of Balmain offered more space, and better houses, but the abattoir, tripe-dressing sheds and other animal-based noxious trades combined with rotting refuse on the low-lying, swampy foreshores of White Bay and Rozelle Bay to fill the neighbourhood's 'fresh breezes' with a pungent aroma.

The auctions of subdivisions in this locality were never going to attract large bids. Allotments in Balmain West were narrow-fronted, generally fifteen feet to 25 feet, and the depths of blocks rarely exceeded 75 feet. 'The rents are higher and the class of residents better at the eastern than the western end,' observed William Alston Hutchinson, 'where land is cut up into smaller blocks and sold on very easy terms to working men.'[24]

Alfred Hancock, born in London in 1835, migrated to Sydney in the late 1850s. He became a land and estate agent at Balmain West, where building land was plentiful and cheap.[25] Between 1867 and 1880 Hancock bought up large parcels of land in the area for subdivision and sale.[26] A number of speculators joined him in his ventures—partner William Cross, piano importer William Henry Paling, surveyor Ferdinand Reuss, medical practitioner Louis Foucart and publican Robert Symons. Hancock's marketing strategy was a simple one—a large turnover of building plots at a modest price. He initiated the 'Homes for the People' scheme, offering 'some hundred' building blocks for £4 cash and 21 quarterly instalments of £2. Timber was supplied to purchasers for ten shillings weekly.[27] It has been estimated that Hancock sold at least 1600 sites in Balmain West, and the system he introduced enabled many people of limited means to become freeholders.[28] Developer Hancock was an alderman on Balmain Council from 1873 to 1882 and 1884 to 1886, and costs associated with his subdivisions (formation of roads and provision of drainage) appear to have been minimal during his period on Council. Single-storey stone or brick cottages, ten to fifteen feet wide, in sets of four to six, filled the streets of Balmain West, with terrace housing and small wooden dwellings interspersed among them.[29]

These cottages squeezed on to the narrow-fronted blocks were of minimal standards of amenity but in most cases were probably adequate for the needs of the people, at a price that the great majority of the working classes could afford. Hancock continued to sell land under the 'Homes for the People' slogan till at least 1907, leaving his imprint throughout Balmain West—on the Park View and River View estates, in Foucart Street, the Merton, Bridgewater, Bridge and Bayville estates, and on the corner of Darling Street and Victoria Road.[30]

Hancock's advertisements named 'the Great Coal Mine, Lever Bros Great Works, the Reclamations, Levelling of Glebe Island, the New Bridges, Extensions of Trams, etc' as good reasons to invest in Rozelle.[31] Callan Park Hospital for the Insane and Iron Cove Bridge were also being erected at this time. This brought into the area mechanics and tradesmen who needed houses close to their work. In his 'Homes for the People' advertisement, Hancock was offering blocks of land for £2 deposit and £1 monthly in Percy, Evans, Callan, Foucart, Alfred and Albert streets and Weston (Victoria) Road.

A rising market for houses, and the availability of capital to finance house-building gradually transformed the nature, methods and business organisation of the industry in the suburbs. Before, most suburban houses were the products of a small army of tradesmen operating on their own account, but as the migration to the suburbs increased a number of large contractors, with local addresses, emerged tendering for the whole of the construction work. Even these operators, however, were still relatively small employers; in 1891, for example, each building contractor employed, on average, only 5.6 wage earners.[32]

The building industry was hierarchical in structure, with the architect at the apex. 'Architects were Lords absolute,' recalled builder George Parker Jones, and 'George Mansfield', he said, 'was the mightiest autocrat I have ever met.'[33] Under the architect, the master builder occupied the second rung of the building ladder; he entered into contracts with the client to carry out the project according to the architect's specifications. The journeyman came next, training himself under a master and learning his trade under the direction of an experienced journeyman. David Elphinstone and Ambrose Thornley Junior, under the tutelage of their fathers, started by constructing modest cottages, rose from the ranks of carpenters and builders to master builders and eventually called themselves architects.[34] They had plenty of experience in the trade, though they lacked the formal qualifications of a traditional architect.

The supply of capital for suburban house-building ebbed and flowed, as its profitability depended on the potential alternative earnings of the funds used to supply it. Fluctuations in house-building synchronised closely with the general trend in the colonial economy; peaks in building activity were reached in 1875 and from 1879 to 1884, and house-building was at its lowest ebb in the intervening years, though the so-called 'long-boom' continued unabated to 1889. As a consequence, the supply of new houses varied considerably from one phase of the building cycle to another.[35]

On exploratory walks of the suburbs in the 1850s William Jevons observed brick, stone or timber verandahless cottages, the majority with two small rooms, to which others were added later.[36] Most were built with the front wall flush to the street alignment and with the doorstop abutting the street. Early verandahed cottages featured broad, flat timber verandah posts, small-paned sash windows, valance board and picket fence. Much of the small-scale town and suburban domestic architecture of the third quarter of the nineteenth century survives in Glebe's Bishopthorpe and St Phillip's estates. The basic Victorian Georgian terraced cottage here is symmetrical double-fronted, unadorned, with shared chimney stacks placed in the party walls. In Balmain and Glebe three early terrace types began to appear from about 1870—the terrace with verandahs, terrace with verandah and balconies, and the terrace with cantilevered balconies.[37] The straight lines of Georgian and Regency began to give way to the Italianate terrace style in the 1880s which preferred round-arch or segmental arch window and door heads. Three distinctive Italianate types could be discerned – parapet type, party-wall type and the elaborate one.[38]

Not only was the terrace the most suitable building form for regular and continuous development, but significant economies could be derived from terrace building. The suburban landlord, aiming to maximise the return on his capital, could reduce physical construction costs in a number of ways by building two or more adjoining houses. Unit cost was cut by the use of the party wall and multi-flued, common chimneys which served two adjoining houses in a terrace. With land prices rising, savings were also made on land costs. Jackson estimates that, in the early 1880s, a fifteen-foot inner-suburban allotment sold for about £10 per foot. Therefore, Jackson deduces, for a detached house on a single allotment, land costs may have amounted to £150, while three houses in a terrace on two adjoining lots would have reduced this figure to £100 per house; sometimes even five houses were accommodated on three lots.[39]

The supply of suburban homes could either be retarded for lack of capital or it could be expanded far beyond current needs. Until the mid-1870s, it seems, building societies were small, co-operative self-help organisations where most borrowing was done by wage earners. They were popular institutions; between 1865 and 1880, 80 building societies were formed in New South Wales.

The form of building societies changed to meet financial needs and business opportunities created by the prosperity of the 1880s. Many societies converted to company status and it was rare for new societies to be formed after 1877. Building companies supplanted building societies in the late 1870s as the main source of funds for residential development in the Sydney metropolitan area. By 1888, 44 building companies and societies provided finance primarily for Sydney business. Of these, only fourteen had the nominal title of 'society', and the remainder were 'companies'.[40]

The records of very few of the building companies and societies have survived, but their mortgages, registered at the Land Titles Office, reveal the scale of their operations. The extent of involvement by building companies and, to a lesser extent, by building societies, in the subdivision of estates and financing of house-building ventures reveals how important they were in shaping development in Balmain, Glebe, Leichhardt and Annandale.[41] Banks, insurance companies, friendly societies and benevolent institutions played minor roles in the finance of house-building, but in the particular localities the role of wealthy private individuals cannot be ignored.

Some lending institutions were closely identified by name or association, with the development of different parts of Sydney. The board of the Balmain Building Society and Savings Bank Ltd, formed in 1885, was filled with local worthies—Darling Street estate agent William Moffatt Burns, Captain Thomas Heselton and Henry Perdriau of the Balmain Steam Ferry Company, and master mariners John Greenway Punch and John Lyons. Burns, Perdriau and Punch were, or had been, Balmain aldermen. Offering handsome returns to investors, the society declared that one of its aims was to allow 'the industrial and thrifty classes to participate in the distribution of real estate'.[42]

The functions of the Industrial Provident Permanent Building Society, formed in 1871, were akin to those of a bank; it took in savings and made loans. Between 1871 and 1880 the society advanced £591,000, principally to people 'among the working class or to those', its manager said, 'who have raised themselves a little above their fellows and who require houses of their own'. The average housing loan ranged from £200 to £500.[43] William Jarrett, a Kentish carpenter and joiner who worked on St Phillip's, Glebe, in the 1860s, was the society's first manager, and his Glebe neighbour, Ambrose Thornley Junior, its architect.[44] Its directors, William Cary, John Roseby, George Renwick and William Day, sat on the boards of several other lending institutions. The society approved countless housing loans in Balmain and Glebe and was perhaps the largest housing loan society of its kind in Sydney (it lent £143,000 in 1882) but it did not seek to broaden its functions.

The broad expanse of what became the suburbs of Annandale and Leichhardt, covering about 1,300 acres, remained largely undeveloped, and the prospect of reaping rich rewards by developing these farmlands excited local land speculators and financiers. Profits could be maximised by the formation of building and land companies, institutions that not only bought, subdivided and sold land but also undertook the complete program of development.

The North Annandale estate attracted the attention of John Young. Born in Kent in 1827, he acquired architectural and engineering experience in England and became superintendent for the Crystal Palace. He migrated to Victoria in 1855, where he prospered as a building contractor, constructing many metropolitan churches. He arrived in Sydney in 1866 and he obtained many large contracts, which included St Mary's Cathedral, the General Post Office and the Department of Lands building.[45] The contract for the 1879 Exhibition Building alone

Building contractor and entrepreneur John Young (1827–1907), a dynamic personality, left his imprint on Annandale's development. A Leichhardt councillor from 1879 to 1886, he was prominent in the incorporation of Annandale Municipality and he became its first Mayor in 1894. (Annandale Council Chambers)

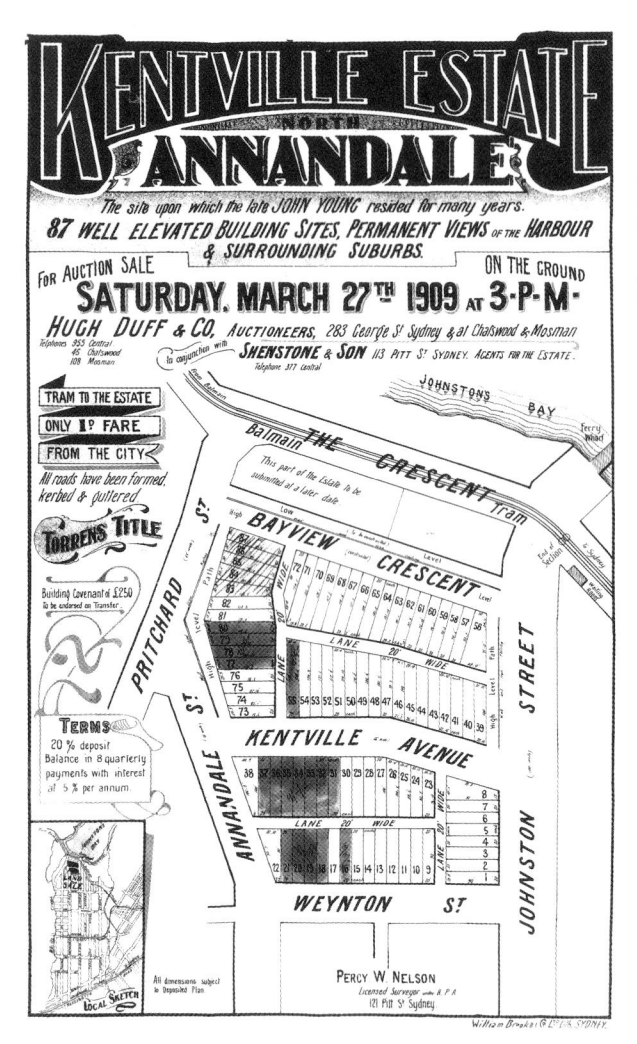

Subdivision and sale of the Kentville Estate, Annandale, 1909. (Maps Collection, Mitchell Library)

earned Young an estimated fee of £2,500, more than the Colonial Secretary's salary.[46] John Young acquired the remainder of the North Annandale estate from the Johnston family in 1877 for just under £121,000. He then formed the Sydney Freehold Land and Building Investment Co. Ltd to subdivide and sell the 280 acres.[47] To assist prospective purchasers of the estate the North Annandale Building and Investment Society was formed in 1878. There is, however, no evidence that this society ever operated as a lending institution.

The Sydney Freehold Land and Building Investment Co. was a tribute to Young's business acumen, the first example of a building company that owned the freehold, laid it out for building and undertook to finance residential development. Other directors of the company were politicians Samuel Gray and Robert Wisdom, developers John North and A.W. Gillies, Balmain soap and candle manufacturer William Hutchinson, and Henry Hudson of Hudson Brothers.[48] However, it was Young, large-framed and with a goatee beard, who remained the dominating figure as company chairman and its second-largest shareholder. He moved to Kentville at Annandale in about 1877 and quickly became active in local affairs. He was first elected to Leichhardt Council in 1879 and became Mayor in the same year. From 1884 to 1886 he was again Mayor and was the prime mover in the secession movement that led to the incorporation of the Annandale Borough Council in 1894.[49]

In 1878 Young's company offered a prize of £150 for the best design for Annandale.[50] The competition was won by architect and surveyor Ferdinand Reuss Junior, who was retained by the company to design many of the houses. Annandale was laid out for 'villas and the better class of houses as much as possible by themselves; for clerks, smaller ones also by themselves; and blocks for the erection of artisans' houses'.[51]

Streets in the subdivision, in a grid pattern, were wider that the 30- to 40-feet streets in adjoining suburbs. All the new suburb's streets were 66 feet wide, except Annandale Street, which was 80 feet wide, and the main artery, Johnston Street, was 100 feet wide. The majority of the building allotments were generous—mostly 66-foot frontages with depths of about 190 feet, ideal for bungalows and freestanding houses.[52] The broad design catered for middle-class incomes and tastes and it was only the low-lying, less attractive building plots that came within the financial reach of ordinary working people. The plan also featured three large reserves and six smaller ones.

Building plots in Annandale sold slowly in the depressed real estate market of the late 1870s, forcing the company to revise its original policy and resubdivide many of the subdivisions. The proliferation of smaller lots created by these resubdivisions attracted an increasing number of working-class residents.[53] Only Johnston Street remained typical of the kind of suburb the company originally envisaged.

By the mid-1870s most of the dwellings on St Phillip's, Glebe, had been reduced to rubble. The Metropolitan Mutual Permanent Building and Investment Association acquired new leases from trustees of the Church of England and set out to redevelop the area. It provided the capital for the new development that made David Elphinstone the largest contractor to operate in Glebe.[54] Between 1877 and 1885 Elphinstone called tenders for 211 houses and new shops, which stretched from Norton Street to St John's Road on the eastern side of Glebe Road.[55] Operating as an architect from 1879 at 246 Pitt Street, he formed a remunerative association with Metropolitan Mutual which numbered among its directors his brother James, W.A. Hutchinson of the Sydney Freehold Society, John Hardie of Hardie & Gorman, Alexander Thomson and Humphrey Richardson. Hutchinson seems to have played an important role in determining the way Metropolitan Mutual approached this redevelopment.

The solid and respectable one- and two-storey terraces that lined Cowper, Campbell, Broughton, Mitchell, Phillip, and Glebe streets and St John's Road were produced with the mechanical fidelity of the production line, the only concession to decoration being the ironwork and incised plaster work on party walls. Little room was left for garden plots. The blocky chimney stacks, with their chamfered edges and hooded mouldings, are an Elphinstone trademark and although his Italianate terraces do not contain a parapet (unlike his commercial buildings), most of them have a pitched roof.[56]

In polite colonial society the Leichhardt neighbourhood was remembered as a place where a respectable elite resided, including the Norton, Perry and Brenan families. Their elegant villas, sited to take advantage of the views and surrounded by extensive grounds, remained largely intact and the landscape retained its leafy features. The locale had achieved municipal status in 1871, though it housed a mere 614 residents, but the neighbourhood had acquired sufficient shape on the map for the Sydney directory to recognise its existence.[57]

There was a dispersal of industry to the fringes of development. Cowan & Israel's soap and candle factory on the North Annandale shores of Rozelle Bay followed the new abattoir.[58] Noxious trades such as tanning, tripe making, and boiling-down works were ideally sited on the edge of Long Cove, well away from close settlement. Their pungent odours, a source of increasing complaints within the subdivision of Helsarmel in Leichhardt, led to their expulsion in the mid-1880s. Brickmaking became a thriving local enterprise, small dairy herds dotted the rural landscape, and from 1868 some eleven acres were set aside on Elswick estate for a general cemetery.[59] By 1881 a miscellaneous collection of consumer and service trades clustered around Parramatta Road and Norton Street, but invasion of the farmlands around Leichhardt village had just begun, as the municipality at this stage had only 1,866 residents.[60]

The Elswick estate, subdivided into five large sections, had been offered for sale in 1867, with five new streets staked out on a grid pattern. Norton Street, the suburb's main artery, ran in a northerly direction from Parramatta Road to the boundary of Helsarmel estate. A little to the west, Elswick Street also ran in a north–south direction. Marion Street, following the east–west

David Elphinstone (1847–1916). Elphinstone joined the building industry as a carpenter under the tutelage of his father in 1868. Operating as an architect from 1879, the scale of redevelopment of St Phillip's, Glebe, made him the suburb's largest contractor. (Max Solling Collection)

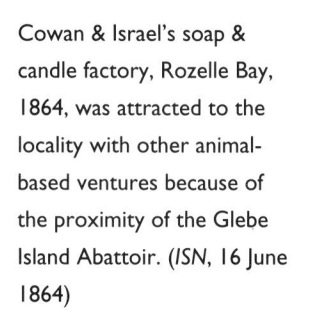

Cowan & Israel's soap & candle factory, Rozelle Bay, 1864, was attracted to the locality with other animal-based ventures because of the proximity of the Glebe Island Abattoir. (ISN, 16 June 1864)

ridge, was a major cross street. Two other one-chain (66-foot) streets were included in the plan—Allen and Short streets. The auction was held in a time of economic stagnation and only one allotment was sold. A radically amended subdivision plan of Elswick was prepared between 1868 and 1874. It featured two large allotments: the 53-acre parcel became the Excelsior estate, and the 42-acre allotment, Whaleyborough. There were sixteen smaller allotments, ranging from one acre to almost twelve acres.[61]

The municipality of Leichhardt, shorn of the Annandale precinct, covered 1,120 acres; the process of subdividing the farmlands of Leichhardt, and building up its streets, stretched out over a period of 40 years to 1914 and beyond. At least 29 separate subdivisions can be identified in Leichhardt between 1875 and 1906, and the nomenclature of the countless streets that lace Leichhardt recalls early landowners, their houses and estates, developers and local political figures.[62]

The years between 1881 and 1891 were a particularly intensive phase in Leichhardt's development. Building activity slowed in the 1890s, though there were three subdivisions, and levels of house-building activity fluctuated from Federation up to the outbreak of war.[63]

An insight into suburban estate development can be gleaned by tracing the operations and fortunes of an important building company in Leichhardt, the Excelsior Land Investment & Building Company. Registered in August 1880, the company had earlier purchased the Elswick House estate, which comprised James Norton's mansion and surrounding land—in all about 53 acres. This first venture occupied former orchards and cultivated land bounded by Parramatta Road to the south, Elswick Street to the west, Marion Street to the north, and Norton Street to the east. Building plots, ranging from 40-foot to 16-foot frontages were pegged out and streets formed. Allotments fronting Parramatta Road were 20 feet wide.[64]

Estate agents Mills, Pile & Gilchrist promoted the subdivision as possessing all the amenities for a modest suburban home with the advantages of proximity to the city and relatively cheap rent. It was only a brisk walk to Petersham Railway Station or to horse-omnibus stops. During the developmental stage of the Excelsior subdivision the selling agents advertised 'TO THOSE IN SEARCH OF A HOME' a once-in-a-lifetime opportunity. 'Why pay rent?' became the company's catchcry. On payment of 10 per cent of the value of the property, the member would be let into possession, and the balance of the purchase price could be spread over a period of twelve years by way of rent.[65] Ambrose Thornley Junior and John Smedley were retained by the company as architects, and members could avail themselves of standard and individual house designs prepared in their office and purchasers could enter into building agreements with a contractor to erect a house of a stipulated value. Continuing involvement by the company in the whole development process meant the ultimate gain to its shareholders was likely to exceed, by a good margin, profits obtained by simply selling the land outright.

The Excelsior Building Company was in the advance party in seeking to provide working men with the opportunity of acquiring a home. This ideal was strongly shared by a number of the company's directors, including its manager, William Jarrett, who had arrived in the colony as working-class tradesmen, full of energy and ambition but with little or no capital. Modesty, however, did not preclude directors William Day, George Renwick, William Jarrett, Alfred Rofe, John Roseby and Ambrose Thornley Senior and Junior from naming the streets of the 596-lot subdivision after themselves.[66] The company's name and that of Ferdinand Reuss Senior and Junior were also imprinted on the subdivision.

Four-roomed semi-detached houses in Day Street sold for £420 while terrace houses in Rofe and Junior streets with two main rooms cost £230.[67] Narrow-fronted dwellings attracted much attention from an array of blue-collar families as the price and the company's flexible terms brought these cottages within their financial reach. Thirteen feet wide, they comprised two rooms, kitchen and washhouse. The pan was in a separate brick outhouse which stood like a sentinel in the backyard.

Between 1881 and 1890, 426 blocks on the Excelsior subdivision were sold and it was not uncommon for three terrace houses to be squeezed on to a 40-foot allotment. Many of the occupants of a variety of predominantly brick building types (600 in all in 1890) that filled the estate's ten streets were solid working class, though there was a fair representation of lower middle-class folk. Along Norton and Renwick streets especially, architects Thornley & Smedley left behind fine examples of one- and two-storey houses, some Victorian Filigree in style, others Victorian Italianate.

A significant proportion—56 per cent—of Excelsior dwellers were owner–occupiers, and about one-quarter of the home owners were women.[68] The favourable terms of purchase offered to members by the Excelsior Building Company seem in part to explain the extent of home ownership in this working-class precinct in 1890. In the inner-suburban areas of Sydney between 1871 and 1891, R.V. Jackson found that only about one-quarter of the population owned their homes.[69]

A variety of shops appeared in the 1880s along Parramatta Road between Elswick and Norton streets: the Bongiorno brothers' fruitery, a hatter, a boot-importer, a newsagent, watchmaker Maurice Fienberg, two confectionery stores, a draper, butchers Wilson & Franklin, baker John Marker, tobacconist Francis Alexander and chemist Harrie Brothwood.[70] The Elswick Hotel, on the corner of Parramatta Road and Rofe Street, began trading in 1882; the publican, John Whiting, was also the proprietor of a boiling-down works and a local alderman.

Provision was made within the subdivision for corner shops—an integral part of domestic retailing—and by 1890 its six corner stores were evenly distributed. The proprietors, each of whom had a cluster of loyal customers, reflect an interesting ethnic mix: Italian Andrea Fontana, German Frederick Weit, Moses Selig, Isiah Whitehouse, John Ward and George Watson.[71]

Estate agent George Pile was able to use his considerable political influence to persuade Secretary for Public Works John Lackey to extend tram tracks the full length of Norton Street; by 1884, with trams servicing the estate, land sales rose perceptibly.[72] In 1891 many land and building companies suspended operations with the onset of the depression. The Excelsior Company, unable to meet demands on deposits, called a meeting where shareholders were told by William Cary that with the shareholders' forbearance the company could pay twenty shillings in the pound. The company had a surplus of assets over liabilities of £107,289. It became

Profusely decorated in the Victorian Filigree style, 14 Thornley Street, Leichhardt, was built in 1883 on the Excelsior Company's subdivision. (Photograph by Solomon Mitchell)

involved in completing some 26 houses on which they had to foreclose. The last sale of the Excelsior subdivision was made to contractor John Barker in 1924.[73]

Immediately to the north of Excelsior, a 42-acre tract of land bounded by Norton, Allen, Elswick and Marion streets was bought by solicitor and speculator William Whaley Billyard. He called the estate Whaleyborough. An affection for the land of his birth moved the landed lawyer to name the streets after famous English figures—Cromwell, Marlborough, Carlisle and Macauley.[74] Its wide streets, northerly aspect and generous 50-foot frontage building plots, with depths of about 142 feet, made Whaleyborough a much more desirable precinct than the Excelsior Company development. Though it was ideal for freestanding cottages, a mixture of housing types appeared on the subdivision's 213 blocks. In Marlborough Street two or three terrace houses were squeezed on to single allotments and the terrace became the predominant form in Norton Street. Separate single-storey brick cottages could be found throughout the estate.

The most eligible sites on Billyard's subdivision were excellent locations for local institutions. A modest Primitive Methodist chapel (1883) appeared in Cromwell Street and the much grander All Souls' Church, designed by Blacket & Son, on the corner of Norton and Marion streets opened in 1884. A police station in Marlborough Street dates from about 1885.[75]

Just to the west of Whaleyborough, building lots fronting Edith and Regent streets in Isaac Doust's subdivision were of similarly generous proportions.[76] The developer left behind his harsh imprint on a 50-acre parcel near the western extremity of Rozelle Bay. Justin Joseph Brenan was determined to squeeze as much money as possible from this land his father bequeathed to him. Brenan's estate was carved into eighteen- to twenty-foot frontage lots, 875 in all, and tiny freestanding weatherboard cottages (comprising 64 per cent of all dwellings in 1890) filled the new streets of this subdivision—O'Neill, Grove, Halloran, Justin, Lamb, and Ryan streets, and Brockley, Joseph and Cecily streets were extended into the subdivision.[77]

Building and land companies took an interest in several pieces of farmland in Leichhardt. Helsarmel estate, some 92 acres of indifferent country on the western edge of Leichhardt, was developed by the Anglo-Australian Investment & Finance Company in two stages. Influential members of Sydney's business houses filled the company's board room—Andrew McCulloch, a solicitor to the company, and its friend in parliament; Henry Gorman, estate agent of Hardie & Gorman; Francis Wright of Wright, Heaton & Co., carriers; Benjamin James Junior, John H. Newman; and Charles Skarratt. Some 564 allotments were pegged out in the first portion of 61 acres in 1884, and the streets formed bore the Christian and surnames of the company's directors—Charles, Hubert, Francis, James, Henry, William, and Augustus streets, and Park Road. The remaining 31 acres embraced Falls, Flat, Fairlight, Recreation, Wharf and Cove streets, and the 318 lots were offered for sale from 1888.[78] Land on the whole estate sold slowly and only 116 houses—59 timber, 56 brick and 1 stone had been built by 1889. Much of the poorly-drained land near Iron Cove remained unattractive to buyers until reclamation work began in 1904 and the Hawthorne Canal was built.

Nine other building companies, as well as the Anglo-Australian Investment & Finance Company, featured prominently in estate development in Leichhardt. Between 1882 and 1915 the Haymarket Permanent Land Building & Investment Company developed the Bellevue, Town Hall, Whiting and Verdun estates, about 224 building allotments in all, and the Intercolonial Investment Land & Building Co. Ltd, operating at a similar time and on a comparable scale, was involved in the building up of four parcels of land, including the Tram Terminus subdivision and part of Flood's estate.[79]

The Kegworth estate, covering about 24 acres, was subdivided and sold off by the New South Wales Property Investment Co. Ltd in two stages. Beeson, Hathern, Tebbutt and Kegworth streets, all 66 feet wide, were formed in 1883. Only half the lots were disposed of, and in 1889 the residue of the estate was resubdivided into 25-foot frontage lots. Prospective purchasers could pay a £3 deposit and the balance of purchase monies by monthly instalments.[80]

In 1890 Edward Flood's estate, close to Kegworth in Leichhardt's south-western corner, was carved up into 191 lots, each with a 20-foot frontage, by the National Building Land & Investment Co. Ltd. However, the process of building up Albert, National and Flood streets, and part of Myrtle Street, proceeded slowly and few houses covered the ground when the Intercolonial Investment Land & Building Co. Ltd acquired the unsold portions of this estate in 1901. Keen to attract families of blue-collar workers, the company offered sale terms very similar to those on Kegworth estate. Proximity to the electric tram stop and Lewisham Railway Station featured prominently in estate agents' advertising.[81]

Smaller building company ventures were undertaken by the Mutual Provident Land Investment and Building Society Ltd on the Annan View estate (1884), by the Town and Country Land Building & Investment Co. on the Marion estate (1887) and by the New South Wales Realty Co. on the Waratah Street precinct (1911).[82]

Alfred Hancock and Louis Foucart set about subdividing the Orange Grove estate into 170 lots and forming Point, Helena, May and Carrington streets and The Boulevarde in 1883. By 1889, at the second auction sale of Orange Grove, the Upwood Land Building & Investment Co. Ltd was promoting the development, and in 1891 the indefatigable Alfred Hancock reappeared on the scene as manager of the people's friend, the Hand-in-Hand Mutual Permanent Investment & Building Society.[83]

People from a range of occupational groups, most of whom lived locally, participated in land speculation and the names of some of them are remembered in the suburb's streets—John Wetherill (draper), Charles Burfitt (auctioneer), John Whiting (bone boiler), John Lyall (dairyman), Frederick Thorby (contractor), William Pritchard (auctioneer), Walter Beames (grocer), William McAleer (police constable), Herbert Rayner Steward (builder and estate agent), Frederick Henry Emmerick (builder) and John Frazer (engineer).

People of capital from Balmain West extended their speculative ventures into land on the eastern perimeter of Leichhardt where land was ripe for development. Hancock and Foucart promoted the Orange Grove estate and William Henry Paling joined Hancock in the building up of Percival, Starling, Gladstone and White streets on the Leichhardt Hill estate (1880).[84] Anne Case Paling, a relative of the piano importer, was involved in building up Ilka, Edna and Paling streets from 1887, and in the same year W.H. Paling had the Annan Hill subdivision pegged out.[85]

Alfred Hancock's last foray into Leichhardt was with timber merchant George Holdship on the City View estate (1903). They offered 83 narrow-fronted lots for sale and created Pretoria, Russell and Lonsdale streets.[86]

The business of estate development was pragmatic in character. Promoters endowed new streets and neighbourhoods with their own unique character, and in Leichhardt the building companies and men and women of means—W.H., R.J. and A.C. Paling, W. Billyard, J. Wetherill, A. Hancock, L. Foucart, J.P. Starling and J.J. Brenan in particular—left their own indelible mark.

The upwardly mobile had a clear preference for freestanding villas in garden settings or, failing that, for detached cottages. Such properties often looked grander than they actually were. The terraced house catered for a range of incomes and tastes.[87] The larger terraced house featured bay windows, often in the Classical or Italianate idiom. The lower the income the plainer the terraced house and many were devoid of all ornamentation—the only concession to decoration being in the ironwork and the incised plaster work in firewalls. The most humble of these buildings were usually constructed of timber.

Charles Langley's plan of Balmain in 1852 determined the basic street pattern of the suburb, incorporating existing routes and shaped by topographic features. The surveyor numbered the new subdivision sections from 1 to 46, and a further section 47 was added after the realignment of Weston Road and Mansfield Street. Piecemeal disposal of estates and the nature of the terrain tended to increase the complexity of the street pattern. The westernmost limit of Balmain zigzagged from Sommerville Point to White Bay near Crescent Street, and from 1862 all land south-west of this line was called Balmain West.

From 1841, when the owner of the Balmain peninsula, Dr John Borthwick Gilchrist, died, until 1852 none of his Balmain estate was subdivided and sold. From 1852, when sales resumed, until 1882 the Gilchrist Trust disposed of land to some 230 initial purchasers.[88]

The rate at which farmland on the urban perimeter was coming under the shadow of settled areas stirred capitalistic instincts. Not only were men of property anxious to acquire suburban land that was ripe for development, but others with enterprise but no money were also keen to participate in speculative ventures. The first people on the scene at the Balmain land sales between 1852 and 1882 were not dissimilar to the developers of Leichhardt.[89] Some were wealthy and respectable predators who cast avaricious eyes over land throughout the metropolitan area—two were knights of the realm: lawyers William Montagu Manning and George Wigram Allen. Others were the Paling brothers, William and Richard; their offsider in the piano importing business, John Penny Starling; Thomas Holt; and, of course, the insatiable Alfred Hancock. Also among the speculative builders were surgeons (O.S. Evans, Arthur a'Beckett), lawyers (J.B. Darvall, Charles Davis), stonemasons (James and William Burt, John Cavill), shipwrights (John Booth, William Bruce), dealers (Robert Brent, Edward Pyne), gentlemen (Thomas Buchanan, Robert Ennis), grocers (Alexander Chape, William Cavill), as well as the builder William White and the wholesale druggists George and Frederick Elliott.[90]

About forty people acquired holdings exceeding six acres at the Balmain sales, and smaller operators could also enter the suburban house-building business because of ready finance. The nature of the processes involved have already been identified in the building up of Balmain East, and especially in Mort's Town of Waterview estate. As the trend to an ever-increasing number of owners in Balmain increased, there were smaller and smaller divisions of holdings. The plethora of land transactions is reflected in dramatic changes in Balmain's landscape. To attempt here to trace these changes in detail would be a herculean and unnecessary labour.

Balmain Road linked the western part of Balmain to Leichhardt but the Drummoyne peninsula remained inaccessible until a punt service began operating across Iron Cove in 1864.

Resumptions created a route for a main artery from Glebe Island to the eastern part of Iron Cove. The Government Road, as it was called, climbed the hill to the Darling Street ridge and then descended to the ferry punt.[91] Horse-drawn omnibuses rumbled down this road (renamed Weston Road in the 1870s) on their way to the city, and in the other direction a bridge over Iron Cove (1882) quickened the pace of development in the emerging hamlet of Drummoyne.[92]

A miscellaneous collection of service and consumer trades appeared along Evans Street as speculators led an assault on this suburban frontier, and as the neighbourhood's population grew its commercial centre shifted to Darling Street.

The emerging settlement of Balmain West was now providing sufficient basic services to form community focus. Edmund Blacket's St Thomas's Church of England (1874) was an early English rural brick design, and opposite this edifice, on the other side of Darling Street, St Paul's Presbyterian Church appeared two years later.[93] Primitive Methodism, whose membership was predominantly working class, also established a chapel there in 1880. Some 266 enrolled in Balmain West Public School in 1878, and further evidence of the precinct's growing social and economic sophistication was provided by the opening of a branch of the Bank of New South Wales (1885), a Masonic Hall (1888) and a new post office (1894) on the corner of Darling Street and Weston Road. The name Balmain West remained in use until about 1907; it is now generally known as Rozelle.

Weston Road carved through Balmain West, creating two distinctive residential precincts on opposite sides of the road. This main thoroughfare was renamed Victoria Road in 1939.

The eastern portion of the Merton Estate and its environs, Rozelle, c.1905. The 14-acre portion was developed between 1874 and 1890 by developers William Paling and John Starling and selling agent Alfred Hancock. This precinct adjoins what was the Rozelle civic centre with two schools, two churches and a post office. (Re-drawn from Balmain Sheets 55–57 & 60–61, Metropolitan Detail Survey, Sydney Water Archive)

On the eastern side of Victoria Road, a broad belt of land bounded by Elliott, Reynolds and Crescent streets, and then extending right along Victoria Road to Iron Cove, comprises ten portions in Langley's subdivision plan.[94] Though many of these sections were acquired between 1855 and 1862, little intensive development occurred until the early 1870s. The largest subdivision, the Merton estate, covering almost nineteen acres, was carved into 197 building plots, generally 30 feet wide with a depth of 100 feet. It was auctioned off from 1874 by Alfred Hancock, whose land promotions have already been examined. By 1890 much of Terry, Wellington, Merton and Nelson streets were filled with one- and two-storey brick terraces, as well as two pubs, the Bridge and the Welcome and some shops.[95] The earliest residences here were the products of Robert Gordon, William Whitehorn, James Gibson, Alexander Kerr, George Light, George Folster, Arthur Pinchen and James Walker, local builders who operated on a small scale.[96]

The owners of the Merton estate—piano importers William Paling and John Starling—bought up large parcels of land bounded by Crescent, Reynolds and Evans streets and Victoria Road, and this precinct was covered with houses by 1891. Other developers operating on a smaller scale in Rozelle East were David Ramsay Junior, druggists George and Frederick Elliott, dealer Robert Brent, shipwright William Bruce and stonemason John Cavill.[97]

Land on the western side of Victoria Road, covering nine sections on Langley's plan, were further subdivided into some 21 residential precincts, mostly during the period between 1875 and 1882. Section 20, an area of about five acres along Abattoir (Lilyfield) Road, was established from 1861 as an industrial locality. Tracts of cheap land in the territory wedged in between Foucart and Manning streets to the west, and Victoria Road to the east, attracted W.H. Paling's brother-in-law, Andrew Maney, publican Robert Symons, shipwrights Joseph Gosling and William Bruce, dealer Robert Bruce, and engineer John Barnes. George Wigram Allen joined with these people in estate developments along Gordon, Hornsey, Maney and Graham streets and Lilyfield Road.[98] But the largest developers on the other side of Victoria Road were also predominant in Rozelle West—William and Richard Paling, John Starling and Alfred Hancock, who was in partnership with Louis Foucart, a Scottish-born medical practitioner and the Port of Sydney Health and Quarantine Officer from 1883 to 1889.[99] Foucart acquired seven acres on Section 13 in 1877 and land agent Hancock promoted the development.

Four estates—the Bridge, Springside, Cambridge and Longview estates—and part of the Merton estate, which extended across Victoria Road, were embraced within a neighbourhood that stretched from Iron Cove to Darling Street. As land was subdivided and Byrnes, Clubb, Toelle, Callan, Springside, Manning, Park, Oxford, Moodie, Cambridge and Waterloo streets formed, local builders William Daniels, William Mesher, James Walker, William Thornton and Henry Toelle struggled to keep pace with the demand for housing.[100]

The central part of Rozelle West was occupied by Sections 14 and 15. The twelve-acre tract bounded by Darling Street, Victoria Road, Evans Street and Denison Street (Section 14) contained four separate estate developments, and the building up and peopling of Percy, Albion, Red Lion, Belmore, Hancock, Withecombe and Ellen streets stretched over a 30-year period from 1874.[101]

The Bona Vista, Bayview, Dalley and Park View estates were on Section 15, a much larger portion of some 26 acres encircled by Gordon, Burt, Denison and Evans streets and Victoria

Road. The Paling brothers and Hancock, together with publican Robert Symons, were central figures in the subdivision and sale of these four estates, but by 1896 the streets in the area—Charlotte, Alfred, Elizabeth and Prince streets as well as those on the perimeter—were only half covered by a mixture of brick terraces and detached houses, timber cottages and shops.[102] Albert, Mary and Easton streets were formed between 1875 and 1880 when the Brockley and Hutcheson subdivisions near Rozelle Bay were pegged out, and just to the east small pieces of land owned by James Flood and Edward and Jane Pyne went under the auctioneer's hammer. Almost five acres were dedicated for public recreation purposes in 1890 and called Easton Park.[103]

The first subdivision of the Birchgrove estate in 1860 carved the area into ten sections with many 'villa lots'. Louisa Road followed the ridge, creating the maximum number of lots in a single row with deep water access. Street frontages varied from 50 feet to 70 feet with a depth of about 150 feet. The rugged terrain in this precinct made it ideal for substantial free-standing dwellings on blocks of generous dimensions but by 1882 only 53 residences stood on the estate.[104] Devoid of any encroachment by industry, few vacant allotments remained by 1894.

One large estate, the 103-acre Garry Owen estate, was acquired by the Parkes government in 1873, on advice from Colonial Architect James Barnet, for a hospital for the insane. Local residents objected that such an asylum would be 'a great worry, injury and annoyance'; their peace of mind and lives would be endangered and they 'would be subject to constant annoyance and horror'. It was known as Callan Park, and by 1879 nearly 120 patients were undergoing treatment there. The extensive new buildings erected on Callan Park between 1880 and 1884 were in a picturesque setting and were similar in conception to a grand English country house.[105]

The last of the Glebe estates was about to be transformed. The twenty-acre grounds of Lyndhurst, the Benedictine Academy, were carved into 16-foot to 30-foot frontage lots at auctions in 1878 and 1882. By 1889 the process of building up Darghan, Darling Bellevue, Cardigan and Lyndhurst streets and peopling these streets was largely complete.[106]

George Allen retired from his legal practice in 1855. He enjoyed strolling around Toxteth Park before breakfast and found solace in his library. Although developers were closing in on all sides, he resisted any onslaught on his domain and, even after he was laid to rest in the family vault at Rookwood, he continued to control development of his estate from the grave through directions in his will.[107] The first major subdivision of the 95-acre Toxteth Park estate took place in April 1884, six years after Allen's death. Italianate and Queen Anne style houses, with their spacious drawing rooms and servants' quarters, filled the streets on Toxteth Park. Reflecting a leisurely style of living, they were promoted as ideal gentlemen's residences. Title covenants stipulated the types of building materials and prohibited erection of public houses. The estate, built up by 1914, remained an entirely residential area.[108]

Callan Park Hospital for the Insane, covering 103 acres, was designed by Colonial Architect James Barnet in a picturesque setting not unlike a grand English country house. Built in 1880–84, the patients were enclosed by sloping banks or ha-has with walls out of sight at the bottom. Later part of the Rozelle Hospital and now occupied by the Sydney College of the Arts, the ward blocks and related buildings were conceived as interconnected pavilions. (From the original photograph in the Archives Office of New South Wales, COD 121, No 940)

Very few of those engaged in house-building in Balmain and Glebe between 1851 and 1865 were still operating when the building cycle began its upturn in the later 1870s. Easy money, and a demand for living accommodation, boosted by a rising birth-rate and immigration, precipitated the sale and subdivision of cheap and plentiful land on the urban fringe.[109]

A feature of the building industry was the predominance of small-scale operators who, lacking capital and other resources, perhaps built no more than two or three houses. After completing one house in a terrace, the builder would occupy the dwelling and then proceed to build a second or third house. If this enterprise returned a reasonable profit, the builder might raise the scale of his operations. Andrew McGovisk bought two acres in Forest Lodge, on the corner of Bridge Road and Junction Street, erecting one house in a terrace and then arranging a further mortgage with the Government Savings Bank so he could continue the process. Between 1877 and 1883 he completed Avoca, Auburn and Magnolia terraces—a total of 22 houses and a hotel.[110]

The names of hundreds of builders filled the trade section of *Sands's Sydney and Suburban Directory* in the mid-1880s and the careers of a good number were to end in bankruptcy. Nevertheless perhaps three-quarters of the total houses built in the Leichhardt municipality between 1881 and 1901 were the products of men operating on a shoestring budget.[111] A broad distinction was drawn between two types of builder. Competition was fierce for contract (jobbing) builders who tendered for jobs advertised in the Sydney press. Eager to get the work, they cut profit margins to a minimum. They in turn often sub-contracted to others who operated on even tighter margins, and any miscalculation in costing, inclement weather or injury could lead to bankruptcy. Though stonemasons were the first to win the eight-hour day in 1856, most builders laboured from 6 a.m. to 6 p.m. six days a week for £2 to £3 weekly.[112]

The builder who had purchased a vacant lot was in a slightly better position. Invariably he had a mortgage to service but he could pitch a tent there for his family and then move to a hastily erected stable at the rear of the block before getting to work on his cottage.

A rising market in the 1880s led to overbuilding from time to time when suburbs where glutted with new but tenantless houses. 'People have been building very largely in the suburbs of Sydney lately and it may be overdone,' observed William Jarrett in 1880. 'There are many more houses now empty than there were.'[113] In this climate, it seems, speculative ventures were much more common than building under contract.

Many loosely described as 'speculative builders' did not appear in trade directories. In fact they were not builders at all but people recruited from the most unlikely sources—butchers and bone boilers, grocers and tobacconists, bank clerks and publicans, police constables and drapers, and others with no connection with the industry, all influenced the shape of suburban development.[114] Their entry into the house-building business was made easier by the availability of capital to finance their enterprises. They sub-contracted all the work out to carpenters, bricklayers, plumbers and others, and whether they rented or sold the completed house depended on the extent of their indebtedness.[115] More diligent 'speculators' read architectural pattern books like J.C. Loudon's *Encyclopaedia of Cottage Farm & Villa Architecture* (1833) and other technical literature to acquire some knowledge of an industry of which they possessed no practical experience.

Evidence culled from the Purchaser's Index and tender notices indicates that most builders had local addresses and those who did not rarely came from further away than Ultimo, Petersham, Redfern or Newtown.

The number of Balmain builders listed in *Sands's Sydney and Suburban Directory* climbed from 31 in 1879 to 53 in 1885. Skilled stonemasons were attracted to Balmain by the availability of local sandstone and by 1901 some 595 stone cottages represented about 10 per cent of all its housing.[116] Solomon Wakfer, John Cavill and James and William Burt especially left behind fine examples of their work.

Architect James McDonald, a Scot who arrived in Sydney in 1851, was a prominent figure in the local industry. He began by tendering for domestic buildings from 1857, designed the Darling Street Presbyterian Church (1858), Campbell Street Presbyterian Church (1868) and Balmain Council Chambers (1878) and retained the right of private practice during his eight years as Council Clerk.[117]

Edward Harman Buchanan began his architectural practice in Balmain in 1880 and designed an array of local buildings—Ellerslie Terrace (35–37 Ballast Point Road), terraces at 2–8 Rose Street and St John's Church, Balmain North (1881–82). Elected an alderman in 1883 and Mayor (1888–89), Buchanan is remembered for his design of Balmain Town Hall (1888), a Victorian Free Classical style building which included the centenary hall capable of seating 1,000 people.[118]

The most intensive house building phase in Balmain was between 1871 and 1881 when 2,039 new houses were constructed. The so-called building boom of the 1880s saw another 1,122 dwellings added to the landscape but residential expansion in Balmain West meant that house building activity between 1891 and 1901 was in fact a little more intensive than in the preceding ten-year period. Altogether during the major phase of local domestic building between 1871 and 1901 some 4,400 new houses were erected.[119] Land title data indicates that among those especially prominent in building up the suburb's physical superstructure were William Halfknights, William Mesher, John Oag, Thomas Batty, Thomas Henley, Alexander Bowen, James Sherratt, William Schultz, Henry Toelle, George Milham, Charles Clymer, George Stewart, George Clubb, George Chidgey, William Thornton and James Reynolds.

Unlike adjoining suburbs Balmain had a predominance of timber housing to 1881, but by 1891 this had declined to 46 per cent of all its housing.[120] A concentration of timber yards and sawmills in Balmain from the 1850s is a partial explanation, but the use of timber as the main building material also strongly suggests the influence of owner–builders, especially in Balmain West. For these 'one-off' builders, most of them battlers, timber provided the cheapest housing.

The number of builders living in Glebe grew steadily from sixteen in 1870 to 26 nine years later, and had reached 42 by 1885. The most intensive building phase in Glebe's development was between 1871 and 1891 when 2,069 new houses were completed, but building activity slowed perceptibly during the 1890s when only 386 houses were constructed.[121]

The scale of redevelopment of St Phillip's, Glebe, made David Elphinstone the largest contractor in the suburb and from 1868 to 1884 he was building throughout Glebe.[122] Ambrose Thornley

The Hermitage, 154 Bridge Road, Glebe, was designed in the Victorian Italianate style by civil engineer, architect and surveyor Ferdinand Hamilton Reuss Senior, who lived there from 1866 until his death in 1896. (Max Solling Collection)

A striking pairing of two asymmetrical houses to make a symmetrical composition in which the towers are placed toward the central party wall. The houses, 13–15 Collins Street, Annandale, were built in the Victorian Italianate style, c.1890. (By courtesy of Betty Mason, Annandale)

Junior also was a significant figure shaping streetscapes. Operating as a master builder from 1864 until 1872, when he was elected architect for the Industrial Provident Building Society, Thornley called tenders for 87 houses, eleven corner shops and dwellings combined, and two bakeries in Glebe between 1871 and 1893. The pinnacle of his architectural career was the Second Empire style Glebe Town Hall.[123]

Thomas Sinclair, a Balmain boat builder, entered into a partnership with Glebe builder Joseph Walker. These Scottish-born Presbyterian lay preachers became the most active builders in Glebe Point throughout the 1880s, building in the Italianate idiom and using a chimney design which is unmistakable evidence of their work.[124] Ferdinand Hamilton Reuss Senior was involved in surveys for T.S. Mort and, as an architect, designed The Hermitage in Bridge Road, where he lived, Reussdale and other elegant buildings. Like his father, Ferdinand Hamilton Reuss Junior was also a surveyor and architect. He built up a flourishing practice between 1875 and 1908 and was responsible for a significant number of buildings in Glebe.[125]

Some 897 houses dotted the Annandale landscape in 1891, and a further 764 houses were constructed in the ten-year period to 1901, a boom comparable to the 1880s there. The house-building industry in Annandale remained busy between 1901 and 1911 when the number of residences increased from 1,661 to 2,363. The Intercolonial Land & Building Co. Ltd was the only building company operating in Annandale, acquiring some 70 allotments throughout the suburb. The imprint John Young left on Annandale's development has been briefly examined. A group of buildings centred on The Abbey in Johnston Street, near Young's home, Kentville, are particularly interesting. Oybin, next to the Abbey, was built for the architect C.H.E. Blackmann, and two of the 'Witches Houses' – Hockingdon and Highroyd, built as a pair, with side spires—were erected by John Young to provide income for his daughters. The other pair, Kenilworth and Claremont, had centre spires and were built for leasing.[126]

It appears that John Young built The Abbey between 1881 and 1883 for his own residence but never lived there. Young was a high-ranking mason, and The Abbey, rich in masonic symbols and having a layout similar to that of a typical lodge, may have been a place where Young could express his views with like-minded men.[127]

Among other significant builders of Annandale were the partners Herbert Bartrop, John Henry Wise and John Rawson, who are especially remembered for the five pairs of bay-fronted Italianate houses at 41–59 View Street. Also significant were Robert Shannon of Albion Street, William Nicholls, William Baker, Albert Packer, Owen Ridge, George McDonald, George Bates, Hans Christensen, Cornelius Gorton, William Wells and Phillip Newland.[128]

Prosperity in the housing industry came to an end in the early 1890s when new housing in

Leichhardt contracted sharply with the severe economic downturn. However, residential expansion in the old Leichhardt Municipality continued unabated for twenty years after Federation; the extent of house-building at this time is reflected in the fact that by 1921 the number of residences had climbed from 3,393 to 6,047.[129]

Thomas Madge, builder and member of Leichhardt Council, was prominent on the Excelsior subdivision, erecting residences and shops until 1884 when, unable to pay mortgage instalments, he ceased operating. Simon Davies was also busy in this precinct and his large semi-detached Victorian Filigree pair at 2–4 Thornley Street with their hipped gable roof are handsome buildings and unique to Excelsior.[130] Among the array of builders operating on a small scale were Thomas and William McCredie, Thomas Winkle, Henry Walters, William Harries, James Wilson, John Findlay and a Norton Street builder who rejoiced in the name of Richard Augustus Bastard. Between 1891 and 1900 Hepburn Pollock of Carlisle Street was especially active in Leichhardt, and in the late 1890s Herbert Steward and Frederick Emmerick were involved in many land dealings.[131] Steward, a local alderman, was shot dead in 1904, apparently over a property dispute.

Hard manual labour remained a feature of much building work—digging foundations and drains, laying bricks, lining interiors and so forth—and materials were hauled to the building sites by horse and cart. New building materials and technology were important elements in quickening the tempo and scale of house-building. The use of prefabricated plasterwork, door frames, window sashes and fascias, and of Wunderlich pressed-metal ceilings meant suburban houses could be completed in a shorter time than previously.[132] The number of suburban brickmakers, sawmills and timber merchants increased to meet the demands of the building industry.

The Johnstons' Annandale kilns were an early source of local bricks. Enoch Fowler established a pottery near rich clay beds at Blackwattle Swamp in 1837 and rough hand-made bricks were being produced nearby.[133] By 1858 George Blackhall was still making bricks at Glebe but the pits were struggling to meet local demand and firewood had to be brought from further afield. Blackhall moved to more easily exploited Wianamatta shale deposits at Leichhardt (and a better supply of firewood) and, by 1871, no less than ten brickmakers were busy at their kilns there.[134] Builders were increasingly turning towards brick construction rather than timber or stone. The Leichhardt brickyards of Henry Hughes, Charles Linney, John Chalkling and others were busy places throughout the 1870s and at Taylor Street, Annandale, in 1882 the Sydney Land and Building Co.'s brickworks was operating.[135]

The brick industry at Leichhardt reached its peak in 1882 with fourteen operators. Clay dug from the pit was pugged in a horse-drawn pugmill, then taken to the moulding table. A brickmaker pressed the pugged clay into the mould by hand to produce 'green' bricks which were cured for several hours and fired in wood-fuelled kilns.[136] Clamp kilns and Scotch kilns,

This plan of Hinsby Reserve and its environs, c.1910, a portion of the North Annandale Estate with Johnston, View, Trafalgar and Piper streets reflects the kind of suburb the building company originally envisaged—large blocks and wide streets and a reserve catering for middle-class incomes and taste. (Redrawn from Leichhardt Sheets 5–7 & 12–14, Metropolitan Detail Survey, Sydney Water Archive) producing bricks of variable shape and qualities, began to give way to more efficient down-draught kilns but all were intermittent kilns. The small-scale brickmakers could make 1,000 to 2,000 daily but the introduction of steam-powered brickmaking machines effectively eliminated the local cottage industry by 1890. The new Hoffman steam kilns operated continuously and had the capacity to burn over 200,000 a week.[137]

Enoch Fowler moved from Glebe in 1855 to establish a large pottery and brickworks at Camperdown, and this and other brickworks at Newtown, Alexandria, Marrickville, Waterloo and St Peters became the main sources. Conlon & Cotter's Glebe pottery and Carter's Leichhardt pottery continued operating into the new century.[138]

Other activities associated with building and construction—sawmilling, joinery and furniture—sprang up on suburban frontiers. By 1870 John Booth's sawmills at Balmain, which had been operating for sixteen years and included a joinery and a turner's shop, employed about 60 men and turned out about 60,000 feet of timber a week. The mills were destroyed by fire in 1874. Rebuilt on a much larger scale, John Booth & Co. Ltd's nine-acre establishment had doubled its number of employees and increased production to 200,000 feet of timber a week by 1885. Booth's steam sawmills and joinery and timber works had branch offices at Wharf Street, Sydney, and on the Manning River.[139] The company imported building materials, glass and iron and advertised that it sold 'sawn pine, kauri, cedar, hardwood, doors, sashes and all kinds of joinery'.[140] From 1882 new sawmills began competing with Booth for business—James Fludder's Forest Lodge mills, Chidgey Brothers' Gainsbro steam sawmills on Balmain West's Iron Cove shore, the Kauri Timber Co. at Glebe and the Nicholson Street sawmills of Alexander Burns.[141] The number of timber merchants climbed to 22 in 1886—eleven in Balmain, four in Leichhardt, four in Glebe and three in Annandale—and by 1896 builders had three Balmain and two Glebe steam joinery works to choose from. From 1901 local paint manufacturers were operating.[142]

By 1901 brick was clearly the predominant building material in Glebe (87 per cent), Annandale (85 per cent) and Leichhardt (70 per cent). Balmain was the exception, with timber dwellings comprising 54 per cent of all housing in 1861, a figure which climbed to 58 per cent in 1881; it would be another twenty years before the number of brick dwellings (50 per cent) in Balmain eclipsed the number of timber homes (42 per cent) for the first time.[143]

The developers of Leichhardt Municipality built up an intricate network of contacts with colonial governments and lending institutions. As Lesley Muir has demonstrated, their subdivisions closely followed, and sometimes anticipated, where tram tracks and railway lines were laid.[144] For example, George Pile, selling agent for the Excelsior subdivision and Toxteth Park estate, brought influence to bear to ensure that tram tracks were extended to these areas, greatly enhancing property values.[145] The councils of Annandale, Balmain, Glebe and Leichhardt were filled with elected representatives with a vested interest in unbridled development—builders and contractors, land agents, solicitors, large landowners, financiers of enterprises and so forth. The same people ensconced in local town halls reassembled elsewhere as directors on boards of road-building companies, tram corporations, building companies and societies, and were prominent on such bodies as the Metropolitan Railway Extension Committee.

In the absence of strong party organisations in the nineteenth century, local government became a means for candidates to gain the acceptance necessary to launch a career into colonial politics. Municipal voting was confined to ratepayers, and they wanted representatives capable of trading political support for local advantages.[146] A combination of self-interest and public service attracted energetic and ambitious men to municipal institutions, and these bodies became a focus for social and political cohesion. In Balmain local elected representatives John Booth, George Elliott, Thomas Rowntree, Alfred Hancock, Solomon Hyam, William Hutchinson, George Clubb, Edward Buchanan, Charles Clymer and William Schultz all participated in local developments. George Wigram Allen was the most outstanding example in Glebe while Ambrose Thornley Senior and Junior, Joseph Walker, David Elphinstone, William Jarrett and Joseph Stimson were prominent figures in the building up of Glebe.[147] Most of the twelve aldermen on Annandale's first council in 1894 were closely associated with the local building industry. John Wetherill, William Pritchard, John Young and Sydney Smith, all Mayors of Leichhardt, were active participants in the whole process of development, as were Thomas Madge, James Lonsdale and Herbert Steward.[148]

The ability of local government representatives to extract concessions from government was an important credential for them to achieve parliamentary honours. Many moved from the municipal arena to state parliament. Freemasons exercised a pervasive influence at all levels of government and counted among members of this fraternity in the suburban house-building industry were John Young, John and Percy Lucas, John Sutherland, William Cary, David Elphinstone and Ambrose Thornley Junior.[149]

In 1886 the number of Sydney builders listed in *Sands's Sydney and Suburban Directory* reached a peak of 816 but by 1890 the number had shrunk to 471.[150] As house-building reached its lowest ebb, small speculative builders, with little experience or capital, were the first to bear the brunt of the recession and turned to other pursuits. Many newly-completed houses remained empty, and builders who had overextended themselves with mortgages lined up to file for bankruptcy. In Annandale and Balmain, where demand for housing remained relatively strong, builders with local addresses continued to find work. In Glebe building activity slowed perceptibly and by 1890 the number of builders listed in Leichhardt had fallen to fifteen.[151] Certainly, plenty of the boom builders vanished when the economy contracted sharply but by 1894 building activity in the metropolitan area seems to have revived with 705 builders listed in trade directories.[152]

Who reaped the largest monetary rewards from the making of Annandale, Balmain, Glebe and Leichhardt? An examination of the estates of builders, sworn for probate purposes, reveals that none of them left fortunes. For example Andrew McGovisk left £17,080, David Elphinstone £15,565 and William Jarrett £22,652. Ambrose Thornley Junior, unable to sell houses, was declared bankrupt in 1895 and he became the licensee of the Grand Hotel at Rockdale while Joseph Walker, the largest builder at Glebe Point, left only £527 in 1904. Architects fared little better. The great Edmund Blacket left only £3,100 and James Barnet, the Colonial Architect for 28 years, died with £10,672. Ferdinand Reuss Senior left £6,286, John Kirkpatrick £5,944, A.L. Elphinstone was made bankrupt in 1893 and Thomas Rowe lost heavily in the 1890s and died penniless. On his death in 1898, timber merchant John Booth left £71,000.[153]

Those who reaped the largest profits were astute buyers who acquired large pieces of land on suburban frontiers, when land was cheap and plentiful, and unloaded on a rising housing market, and financiers of enterprises.

George Wigram Allen (1824–1885). The Allen family owned one-quarter of Glebe and as Mayor from 1859 to 1877 George Allen occupied pride of place at meetings of Glebe Council. Member of Parliament, money lender, land speculator and slum landlord, James Froude described Allen as 'one of the millionaires of Sydney'. (John Clarke Album of Portraits, Pictures Catalogue, PXA 549 Photo 11c, Dixson Library)

William Henry Paling (1825–1895). Dutch-born piano importer Paling reaped large rewards from land speculation in Balmain, Balmain West and Leichhardt. He left a net estate of £208,563 in 1895. (*Australian Men of Mark*)

Four politicians were prominent among the early land speculators in Balmain and Glebe. Thomas Holt's land transactions added to interests acquired as a merchant before 1870 and on his death in Kent in 1888 he left an estate of £330,000.[154] A friend and associate of Thomas Sutcliffe Mort, Thomas Smart was a self-made businessman and MLA for Glebe in 1860–69. Part of a syndicate that subdivided and sold the Forest Lodge estate, he left personal property valued at £243,000.[155] William Montagu Manning, who also sat on the Supreme Court bench, was busy in his spare time buying Balmain land between 1854 and 1861. The family of George Wigram Allen owned about one-quarter of Glebe. Allen became a substantial money-lender and speculator, in Glebe and on the south coast especially. Admitted as a solicitor in 1851, he was a director of many public companies and was described by James Froude as 'one of the millionaires of Sydney'. He left an estate of £300,000 in 1885.[156]

But none of these men's speculation in Leichhardt Municipality was on the scale of William Henry Paling's. Dutch-born, Paling arrived in Sydney in 1853 and quickly attracted attention as a music teacher and entrepreneur. At his Sydney store he sold European pianos and sheet music and his business flourished. William and his brother Richard, who operated a similar store in Melbourne, used profits from the music business to buy up large tracts of land ringing the city. Between 1868 and 1882 William Paling bought extensively in both Balmain and West Balmain and was also prominent in developing Leichhardt.[157] The Paling brothers were joined in their land ventures by John Penny Starling, a director of W.H. Paling & Co. Ltd. A resident of Stanmore, William Paling was an alderman on Petersham Council from 1876 to 1889 and its Mayor from 1881 to 1882. He left a net estate of £208,563 in 1893.[158]

Thomas Sutcliffe Mort developed the 700-lot Town of Waterview subdivision at Balmain and Mort's Dock made him by far the largest employer in Balmain. Mort's wealth multiplied through inflation and successful speculation and on his death in 1878 income and capital realisations distributed to his beneficiaries totalled some £600,000.[159]

John Booth was involved in an array of activities in Balmain; he was a local alderman in 1862–63 and from 1865 to 1869, Mayor in 1867 and MLA in the 1870s. As well as being a large employer of local labour at his sawmills and joinery works, Booth also owned extensive landholdings in Balmain and was a significant local landlord.[160]

Dairyman turned builder William Cox and Registrar General and solicitor Theodore James Jaques were active buying and selling land, but not on the same scale as Alfred Hancock and Louis Foucart, whose activities in Balmain West and Leichhardt brought them large rewards.[161] Soap and candle manufacturer William Alston Hutchinson, who was involved in the Sydney Freehold Company's development of Annandale and in land dealings in Balmain, left an estate of £36,000. William Cary, director of the Excelsior Building Company and a Glebe alderman for eighteen years, owned a George Street firm which supplied builders with roofing slates, cements, plaster, sheet and pipe lead, corrugated and plain iron, marble and slate mantelpieces, slate slabs and other building materials. The ornamental plasterer and inventor died in 1906 leaving an estate of £162,444.[162] The extent of building contractor and entrepreneur John Young's involvement in Annandale and Leichhardt has already been mentioned; he left an indelible impression on the development of the area and was Mayor of both municipalities. Draper John Wetherill and solicitor William Billyard were also successful developers in Leichhardt.[163]

Generally terrace rows did not exceed six or seven houses and it appears that it was not until the end of the boom that large developers built terraces exceeding eight houses. The number of rooms in a house generally reflects something of the means and lifestyle of its occupant. Three- to four-room houses were the most common dwellings in Leichhardt (57 per cent), Annandale (55 per cent) and Balmain (49 per cent) in 1901. Houses of these dimensions comprised 41 per cent of Glebe dwellings; 43 per cent of Glebe's houses in 1901 had five or six rooms.[164]

A diversity of houses and styles catered for a range of incomes and tastes. In the late nineteenth century, an unadorned two-room brick terrace house could be acquired for £230 and a four-room semi-detached brick house cost from £420. Housing prices in Sydney's suburbs indicate their increasing social differentiation. Prices ranged from £4,000 at Darling Point to more than £1,000 at Randwick and Mosman. The average price in the current Leichhardt Municipality appears to have been between £400 and £700.[165]

For unskilled or casual workers with little capital home ownership was rare. Often they could pay no more than five or six shillings per week for rent. Invariably the poorest houses—small cottages with tiny yards—were occupied by the poorest families.[166] The unskilled male worker received about seven shillings for working an eight-hour day, and the basic-needs wage of a labourer, the Harvester Judgment of 1907 decreed, was two guineas a week. He paid from 10s 6d to 12s 6d a week rent (a quarter of his wage) to house his family in a basic two-bedroom terrace house.[167] A little further up the economic ladder, skilled craftsmen earning between £150 and £180 per year could afford to rent a more spacious house while members of the professions and people who owned and staffed their own businesses had the capacity to buy or rent houses with drawing rooms and servants' quarters.[168]

The ideal of owning a home with a garden plot in the suburbs was extolled by many but the dream could only become a reality for those with the capacity to pay. The majority of people did not achieve home ownership. R.V. Jackson, relying largely on rate books, examined patterns of home ownership in the inner suburbs of Sydney between 1871 and 1891. In 1891 84 per cent of Glebe houses and 73 per cent of residences at Glebe Point were tenanted. Elsewhere, too, he found a high proportion of tenanted houses—Paddington 77 per cent, Newtown 71 per cent and Darlington 78 per cent.[169] Lynch, who had no rate books to cull in Balmain, established that between 1853 and 1882 more than half the suburb's landowners were non-residents, but lack of sound source material makes assessment of home ownership in Balmain a matter of conjecture.[170] Levels of home ownership in Annandale and Leichhardt await detailed rate book research. Large absentee landlords were not common. The great majority of houses were owned by small landlords, most of whom lived in or near the suburb, since landlordism and speculative ownership seem to have been the natural focus of petit bourgeois investment.

Many influences shaped the character of suburban development. After land was released, covenants often influenced the type of dwelling built. In high-status areas like Glebe Point, restrictive covenants that ran with the land were imposed by the developer. Brick and stone covenants were placed on the title of land at North and South avenues, Leichhardt, and elsewhere undesirable activities were expressly prohibited.[171]

The preference by the well-off for better drained sites with commanding views on higher ground meant that topography was an important determinant of social geography, and land at Johnston Street, Annandale, at Birchgrove, Glebe Point, and on the (A.C.) Paling and

Scarvell Estate and its environs, Leichhardt, c.1910. Brick or stone covenants were inserted on titles of land at North and South Avenues, subdivided in 1902, to ensure a certain standard of building. (Redrawn from Leichhardt Council Planning Scheme, 1974)

Whaleyborough estates in Leichhardt changed hands at premiums that reflected their social desirability.[172] Conversely, lower sites that were subject to flooding and poor drainage—such as the Bishopgate estate in Glebe, the Iron Cove shore of Helsarmel and Happy Valley in Balmain—were the least sought after.[173] Invasion of residential areas by unattractive industrial land uses, such as the building of Mort's Dock and Glebe Island Abattoirs, also exerted a powerful influence on the character of a neighbourhood.

The casual observer may gain the impression that the houses which fill the streets of Leichhardt Municipality are products of large contractors working by methods of mass production. But closer examination of the creation of these artefacts reveals that the physical fabric of Annandale, Balmain, Glebe and Leichhardt was largely the work of literally hundreds of builders who operated on a small scale. The making of each suburb was not a conscious creation, nor was it the work of a homogeneous band. Among those who influenced the shape and character of suburban developments were landowners, financiers of enterprises, house and land agents, surveyors, landlords, clerks, solicitors and shopkeepers—as well as all other members of these suburban communities.

Institutions of daily life

Pubs

The pub represented an alternative lifestyle in colonial society, competing vigorously with its great rival, the chapel, for the attention of the masses. Swinging gas or oil lamp above the main door, wooden horse trough and hitching rail outside and painted sign boards made it an institution that could be readily identified. Inside, little of the surface was left plain.[1] Throughout the nineteenth century and beyond, the pub was a dominant institution in suburban life, a centre for neighbourhood socialising that many found necessary to their lives; its attraction was not only the beer that brought a slow fuddled joy, but the warmth, bright lights and comradeship of the neighbourhood bar.

'The working man,' wrote Friedrich Engels,

> comes home from his work tired, exhausted, finds his home comfortless, damp, dirty, repulsive; he has urgent need for recreation, he must have something to make his work worth his trouble to make the prospect of the next day endurable. His enfeebled frame, weakened by bad air and bad food, violently demands some external stimulus; his social need can be gratified only by the public house, he has absolutely no other place where he can meet his friends. How can he be expected to resist temptation?[2]

The home and family symbolised the middle-class emphasis on the ownership of private property and the bourgeois division of sex roles. Anxieties about the stability of home and family life stirred the 'Mothers and Daughters of The Glebe', 1,376 in all, to claim in 1870 that 'the sacredness of domestic life is profaned, the peace of the fireside invaded, the nurture and education of the children neglected' and, in their petition, to implore the government to curtail the granting of licences for the sale of the demon drink.[3] The number of pubs in Balmain climbed from fourteen in 1870 to 33 in 1880; in Glebe only five new pubs appeared in the same period, reaching 21 in 1880.[4]

The location of pubs in these areas, concentrated as they were in working-class neighbourhoods, reflected the social life of communities, for respectable residents neither needed pubs nor encouraged them. The ideal of domesticity, fostered by evangelical Protestants, meant that by about 1870 the pub had become very much a male preserve. Women worked as publicans and barmaids as the pub was one of the natural extensions of housekeeping. The barmaid was an essential part of pub culture 'both as staff . . . and as a further item of allurement among its mirrors and mahogany, its brassware and coloured tile'.[5] Certainly publicans sought sexually attractive women to serve behind the bar. F.B. Boyce regarded barmaids as nothing more than a lure—'a pretty girl is frequently engaged to attract soft young men, and keep them hanging about the bar'—and berated the occupation of barmaid as 'so dishonourable and lowering a calling'.[6] The lavish trappings of the pub, Peter Bailey argues, gave it the 'dramatic properties of the stage' which provided the barmaid with a 'framing effect', making her both 'conspicuous and seductive'.[7]

As the number of pubs in New South Wales swelled from 2,182 in 1870 to 3,829 in 1880 temperance forces were marshalled to fight the good fight.[8] The temperance movement helped to introduce guilt in the minds of pleasure-seekers, and Nonconformist ministers, with a professed goal of rescuing working men from the pub, led the way in seeking legislative restriction or prohibition of the liquor trade.[9] Temperance drew heavily on evangelical religion for its rhetoric and fervour. Protestant denominations believed that drink was the main cause of poverty and misery and joined in a series of campaigns denouncing alcoholic drinks. Catholics regarded drinking as a serious problem, but urged moderation rather than prohibition.

The *Liquor Act*, 1882, embraced some of their demands. By making Sunday trading illegal, it forced drinkers to buy more bottled beer to see them through the weekend and also had the effect of changing the physical shape of the pub to accommodate this more leisurely style of beer drinking. The Act also introduced the concept of local option by which electors in local government elections could vote on whether they wanted to reduce or maintain hotel licences.[10]

Up to the 1870s most beer, wines and spirits sold in pubs were imported products as local brewers experienced technical and economic problems producing commercial quantities of beer of acceptable quality.[11] Colonial beer was widely drunk from the 1880s and small suburban breweries competed with large city operators for a slice of the expanding beer trade. Bogie's Annandale brewery was established in 1884, and three appeared in Leichhardt between 1886 and 1890—the Edinburgh, Yorkshire and King & Company's Centennial Brewery, which doubled its output between 1896 and 1899.[12] W.H. Bogie's brewery produced a light dry ale, 'as pure a quality as English but not so heavy', as well as a variety of non-alcoholic drinks such as horehound champagne.[13] By 1900 few of Sydney's 21 small breweries had survived and the metropolitan market was dominated by Tooth's Kent Brewery (1835) and Toohey's Standard Brewery (1876). Robert and Frederick Tooth were English-born Anglicans; their great rivals, John and James Toohey, were Irish Catholics.

Temperance reformers argued there were too many pubs in Sydney (820 in 1887) selling too much liquor. Churchmen, convinced that drink was ruining the country, induced the government to set up the Intoxicating Drink Inquiry in 1886 but its findings cast doubt on any increase in insobriety.[14] The amount spent per capita on liquor fell from five guineas in 1882 to three guineas in 1899 and arrests for drunkenness declined from 39 per to 23 per thousand.[15]

The number of Balmain pubs had reached 42 in 1891, which represented one public house for every 559 people. The ratio in Glebe, with 28 pubs, was one pub for every 610 people. Pubs were much less numerous in Leichhardt and Annandale, suburbs that developed at a time of vigorous temperance activity and the impact of the option vote. Within the Protestant churches temperance had become a passport to social respectability.[16] In 1901 Leichhardt supported eight pubs and Annandale three, ratios of 1:2,182 and 1:2,783 respectively. Liquor consumption fell in the 1890s depression and forced the closure of four Glebe pubs and one in Balmain. Publicans, backed by the breweries, fought back, making the neighbourhood bar more attractive, with cheerful lighting and food to eat, quite often free, on the counter.[17]

Drinking was not without its subtle social gradations. The 'better class' public houses were distinguished from 'mere drinking shops' and dancing and singing saloons.[18] Respectable tradesmen did not frequent dancing saloons, observed George Reid; they were patronised by 'the lowest order of men and by young girls on the verge of prostitution'.[19] In the 1870s most locals were small single-storey drinking outlets, and often found lounging around their doors were 'reeling men and blaspheming youth'.[20] The large and highly ornamental two- and three-storey pubs constructed in the 1880s were much more comfortable establishments which featured extensive cellars, many bedrooms, stables, billiard and club rooms, public bars and parlours.[21]

The police estimated in 1900 that 80 per cent of Sydney's pubs traded illegally on Sundays though the small number of convictions each year gave little support to this claim.[22] The amount of liquor consumed increased in the early years after Federation as the economy improved. In Glebe, however, publicans faced a threat to their trade when, in 1901, James Hogg, a fair-haired former member of the Scottish constabulary, moved to the district. Policeman Hogg set out to catch publicans trading on Sunday or after hours. In a predatory mood, Hogg dispensed with his heavy boots for sandshoes, and invariably conducted his raid on a wet evening when, with an umbrella pulled down over his head, he was not readily detected by cockies.[23]

'Hogg by name, Hogg by nature,' drinkers muttered as the dedicated sergeant's successes mounted. This intolerable interference with local drinking habits could not continue; in 1902 allegations were made that the terror of imbibers had used a skeleton key to gain entry to Mary Gee's Excelsior Hotel at 101 Bridge Road, Glebe. A Royal Commission found the allegations against Hogg were without foundation and were simply an attempt to have him removed from the district.[24]

In 1901 Peter Brennan told an inquiry that 'when a man gets out of his bed at 6 o'clock to see his house opened and is kept up until 12 o'clock in the night or 1 o'clock in the morning, it is not a bed of roses for him'.[25] Brennan went on to tell the inquiry that 'as the brewer gets no profit running the hotel himself, the middleman gets no profit and he gives these large counter lunches, lollies and other things of that nature, out of what otherwise would be the publican's profit while he is controlling the beer trade in that locality'.[26]

Publicans laboured long hours to earn a living. From 1843 to 1881 pubs were open from 6 a.m. to 12 p.m. seven days a week. In 1882, when Sunday trading was prohibited, drinking hours were 6 a.m. to 11 p.m. and this situation continued till 1916. A publican's lot under the tied-house system, where many were bound to buy all their supplies from a particular brewery, was not an easy one. Stephen Davoren, for example, licensee of the Hand and Heart, Glebe, was compelled to buy all his beer, wines, spirits and cordials from supplying brewer Tooth &

Co., and they drove a hard bargain. Davoren, who sold eight to ten 36-gallon barrels a week and paid Tooth's 8 per cent interest on a loan of £1,750, told an inquiry that he made nothing out of the hotel business: 'I gave 16 years of my life to Tooth & Co.', he said.[27] Tooth's dominated the drink trade in Glebe and Newtown while Balmain was a stronghold of Toohey's.[28]

In 1905 the Liquor Amendment bill denied compensation to publicans who lost their licences under the local option vote. The liquor trade found a friend in W.A. Holman who perceived temperance in class terms; it was, he said, a middle-class attempt to suppress the centre of working-class social life, the pub. In the debate on the bill, Holman denounced the middle-class view that 'the working man must be protected; the man who goes into a bar to get a drink must be fenced around with safeguards to protect his morals and his manners, but the member of the club or the man who can keep his own sideboard need not be interfered with'.[29]

The Temperance Alliance's efforts to impose its middle-class morals and manners on the working man triumphed at the local option polls in 1907[30]; by 1912, nine pubs in Balmain and six in Glebe were forced to close their doors. However, Tooth's Town Barrel Beer books indicate that a reduction in the number of drinking outlets was more than offset by a spectacular increase in draught beer sales between 1900 and 1914.[31] The sphere of influence of publicans remained strong in the immediate vicinity of their pub, and the term 'local' signified patronage by an established clientele who shaped its drinking patterns.

Between 1898 and 1940 Tooth's and Toohey's breweries acquired the freeholds of hundreds of pubs, largely taking control of the drink trade in Sydney. During this time, Tooth's became the owners of sixteen pubs in Balmain, nine in Glebe and two each in Annandale and Leichhardt.[32]

In three successive temperance referenda in 1907, 1910 and 1913, the 'no licence' vote peaked at 39 per cent while the vote for continuance of current licensing regulations grew into a solid majority.[33] Publicans came under renewed pressure to shorten hours of business when a campaign for early closing gathered momentum during the war. A referendum, held in June 1916, introduced six o'clock closing.[34] It destroyed the pub as a centre of working-class social life in a society where people worked a 48-hour week. Now, at sunset, their temple stood darkened and lifeless, shuttered and barred at the most accessible time for most workers.

The character of the 'local' changed radically as it became a high-pressure drinking house, with little pretence of service, amiability and personal contact between publican, barman and drinker. Now every part of the pub that could be used for either public, private or saloon bar space was annexed to accommodate the avalanche of drinkers in the hour before closing time; it was estimated that 90 per cent of alcohol consumed in pubs was drunk between 5 p.m. and 6 p.m.[35]

Just before the outbreak of war publicans were grumbling that an exciting new attraction, the picture show, was ruining their trade; after 1916 with their opening time reduced from seventeen to twelve hours a day the primacy of the pub was threatened by the increasing popularity of the cinema and a trend towards home-centred leisure.[36] The interior of the pub altered. Bars, previously occupying only a small part of the establishment, now took up most of the ground floor, and more beer, either bottled or fetched from the pub in jugs, was consumed at home. The artistic 'play the game' advertisements which appeared on pub exteriors promoted the amber fluid as being good for you.[37]

In the interwar years counter lunches returned to many pubs. The fare was plain but for threepence patrons could eat their fill of bread, cheese, boiled mutton or German sausage, and for a short time after work the pub was a place of noisy and hurried conviviality as crowds of men, most wearing hats, struggled to attract the barmaids' attention. Only in a few pubs with decent lounges could women join the men.[38]

A multiplicity of temperance associations remained active throughout the 1920s. Prohibitionists argued drunkenness was rife in Sydney, that liquor interests were able to corrupt and influence parliamentarians and, in calling for prohibition of alcohol, argued that drink was destroying the nation.[39] Their exhortations were rejected at the Prohibition referendum in 1928.[40] In the depression it was reported that close to half of Sydney publicans were on the verge of bankruptcy. In the 1920s the number of pubs in the current Leichhardt Municipality remained stable; there were 59 pubs altogether: 32 in Balmain, seventeen in Glebe, seven in Leichhardt and three in Annandale.

From the mid-1930s the United Licensed Victuallers Association foresaw that the bar would give way to the lounge, where men and women could mingle, drinking quietly in comfort—a return to earlier times when the pub was a leisurely community centre. The new mobility afforded by the car worked to the advantage of some pubs but not others.

It was difficult to buy beer during the 1939–45 war, when the production of liquor was under government control and, as a consequence, a vigorous black market flourished. There was widespread dissatisfaction with the conditions of public drinking but anti-liquor forces opposed any extension of drinking hours or increase in the number of outlets. Arrests for drunkenness increased dramatically between 1945 and 1948 despite frequent shortages of beer.[41]

Before 1939 the small number of registered clubs, with a solid middle-class clientele, enjoyed much more liberal drinking conditions than working men experienced in pubs. In 1954 New South Wales abandoned the 'six o'clock swill' after a referendum favoured the extension of pub trading hours to 10 p.m., but it retained for several years a one-hour closure to allow drinkers the opportunity of going home for a meal.[42] In 1956 clubs were able to install poker machines on their premises, and with the takings could expand the facilities and entertainment clubs could provide. Clubs added new dimensions to the living standards of ordinary people and by 1972 one in three adults in New South Wales was a member of a licensed or registered club.

The growth in registered clubs threatened the pub's existence. But the pub showed itself to be a resilient institution, and the number of pubs in New South Wales has remained fairly stable since the war. There were 2,028 pubs in 1954, 1,979 in 1975, and 1,907 in 1984.

The pub in nineteenth-century Sydney had three major roles as a meeting place, a centre for recreation, and as a stopping place for travellers on their journey. Until the 1880s aspirants for municipal office announced their intention to stand for council in their local pubs, advertising when they would be available for voters to hear their views on how the suburb should be run.[43] A number of

The Bald Rock Hotel, 17 Mansfield Street, Balmain, with its corner pediment and iron lace verandahs, was built in 1876 and became a Tooth's pub in 1902. In 1910, when this photograph was taken, the genial licensee was Balmain councillor George Peters. (Balmain Association Collection)

Leichhardt Hotel, 1888. The freehold of this hotel, a Victorian Filigree style building on the corner of Balmain Road and Short Street, was acquired by Tooths in 1901. The hotel was rebuilt in 1923. (J.G. Park Collection, Macleay Museum)

publicans—Fred Vale, James Brodie and Peter McBeath in Balmain; John Walton, James Simpson, William Jarrett, Alfred Tye, and William Burton in Glebe; and John Whiting in Leichhardt—were all sufficiently well known to be elected to council.

Initially the church complemented the pub, using its facilities for meetings and other functions, but from the late 1870s, drinking, more than any other recreation, attracted criticism from the organised forces of respectability. Offspring of church and chapel, Band of Hope, Good Templars, Temperance Alliance and so forth, developed their own social activities to offset the influence of the pub.[44] Beer, the average working man's beverage, cost threepence a pint and many men could always find time to socialise with friends at the bar and to escape. Before the town halls were built the larger pubs served very much as community centres for a whole suburb. Large meetings in Balmain were often held in Dick's Hotel and the Exchange, both located at the suburb's geographical heart.[45] The University Hotel, on the corner of Glebe Road and Broadway, provided the largest venue for public meetings in Glebe.[46] Pubs were great places for Labor activists to meet from the early 1890s and none more so than the North Annandale Hotel. The Bald Faced Stag, associated with the Hearn family, was an integral part of the emergence of Leichhardt as a suburb, while the central position the Royal occupied from 1888 made it a popular place for tradesmen to drink.

Smaller pubs were focal points for particular neighbourhoods and occupations. Men tended to congregate at the pubs nearest their place of work. Wharfies spilled over onto the footpath at the Forth and Clyde and the Dry Dock Hotel. Dock workers, abattoir workers and butchers met at the White Bay Hotel and Irish Catholics congregated at the Rose, Shamrock and Thistle. After the 1914–18 war, Annandale's 'lovely Vic' was a popular SP pub, and the Burton Family in Glebe remained true to its name, a place where a generation of fathers and sons have drunk, with Mum sending the children to the Burton to tell Dad dinner was ready.

The Harold Park, once a sleazy bloodhouse, blossomed into a cultural Mecca, a performing arts complex funded by beer instead of taxpayers. It is now a place to eat, drink, talk and mix with writers, poets and comics and enjoy their performances.[47] Pubs have adapted to social changes by becoming taverns, introducing trattorias or ristorantes in what used to be the backyard beer garden, by going gay, hiring rock bands, showing Sky Channel TV and widespread videos, all a far cry from the Friday night chook raffle.

As working families increasingly fled from the inner city, the traditional

Pubs were far less numerous in Annandale and Leichhardt than in Balmain and Glebe. In 1884 the Victoria Hotel ('the lovely Vic') on the corner of Young and Collins streets, shown here in 1930, became the first pub to begin trading in Annandale. (Noel Butlin Archives Centre, Australian National University, Tooth & Co. Ltd, N60 (Yellow Cards)) working man's pubs of tiled walls and cigarette-proof carpets, Toohey's on tap and Sky Channel in the corner, came under siege. Some hoteliers embarked on extensive refurbishment and upgrading of the establishments; the traditional pub acquired a new image to match a changing clientele. The new upmarket boutique pub offers a wide range of imported beers, better food and an intimate style—but some pubs in Balmain, Glebe and Leichhardt have remained resolutely blue-collar places.[48]

Table 10 Number of pubs 1870–1995

Suburb	1870	1880	1891	1901	1914	1947	1995
Balmain	14	33	42	41	32	31	23
Glebe	16	21	28	26	17	17	11
Leichhardt	1	1	7	8	8	7	7
Annandale	–	–	3	3	3	4	4

Publican Jack Flitcroft, wife Ettie and son Jack Junior (in pram) with others outside the Burton Family Hotel, corner St John's Road and Gottenham Street, Glebe, 1903. The Flitcroft family has had a continuous association with this hotel since 1897. The hotel is remembered as a popular meeting place for the Glebe District Rugby League Club and for unionists. (By courtesy of John Flitcroft)

Educating the young

The type of schooling the young received in nineteenth-century Sydney was fundamentally a matter of social class. There was during this time a long and acrimonious debate on the scope and meaning of education and on the role of the state in the education system.[49] For the great mass of suburban children what school they attended was largely governed by the parents' capacity and willingness to pay. The offspring of ordinary folk attended elementary schools while secondary schools were the prerogative of the middle class. University was for the rich.

Government schools in New South Wales dated from 1848, when a Board of National Education was created to establish and run elementary schools and, at the same time, a Denominational School Board came into being to distribute government funds to church schools.[50] Glebe children first had the opportunity of receiving a public education in 1858. Balmain followed in 1860 and Leichhardt in 1862. By 1862 there were five government-supported church schools: Anglican schools in Balmain, Glebe and Parramatta Street (Broadway) and Catholic schools in Balmain and Parramatta Street.[51]

The facades of the national schools were impressive Gothic designs with sheltering verandahs and high windows. The interiors were much less generous—long, cold rooms with rows of backless desks, bad ventilation, poor lighting and rows of hooks for hats and coats at the rear, symbolising an obsession with order, economy and efficiency.[52]

The curriculum of public schools revealed a reluctance to teach students anything more than was assumed to be proper to their station in life. George Allen told a parliamentary committee that he saw no reason why the offspring of the lower orders should not be made as learned as the higher classes of society.[53] There was a fear, however, that poorer children would be given ideas above their station in the social pyramid. The type of education the vast majority received was more concerned with stability than social mobility. The curriculum offered by the state schools covered reading, writing, arithmetic, grammar and geography; sometimes singing and military drill were added and girls were taught needlework.[54]

Attendance by children of working people in the mid-nineteenth century was characterised by short periods of enrolment and very irregular patterns of attendance; fees also discouraged poor or apathetic parents. The children of the middle classes were sent to a variety of independent schools, often run by a principal single-handed or with the help of a few assistants. In Glebe well-to-do Protestants could send their sons to the Glebe Point Grammar School, under Anglican patronage. It advertised that it prepared students for 'University and the learned professions, but attention is also especially paid the requirements of those who are destined to enter on mercantile pursuits'.[55] Lyndhurst, a Benedictine academy, provided a classical and literary education for wealthier Catholics and on its closure in 1877 it had prepared for matriculation 35 of the 45 Catholics who had graduated at the University by that time. The majority of Irish Catholics could not understand the value of education of the Lyndhurst kind, maintaining that it bred snobbery and pretension.[56] The Christian Brothers movement in Ireland was founded by a layman, explicitly to bring a sound education to the poorer classes.

Most church schools were adjuncts to the local church and subsidised by public money, something that aroused passions in colonial politics. It also had to be resolved whether the education offered in government schools should be compulsory, free and secular. By 1869, 258 pupils were enrolled at the Balmain Catholic School and 159 and 139 pupils respectively at the Balmain and Glebe Church of England schools.[57]

By 1866 the churches had built and were running 317 schools in New South Wales, about one half Anglican and a third Catholic, but by 1872 the number of denominational schools under the Council of Education had shrunk to 106.[58] The dual system of education was not only wasteful but socially divisive and inspectors' reports paint an unflattering picture of denominational schools as being inferior in teaching, curriculum and apparatus to state schools.[59]

Under the *Public Instruction Act*, 1880, attendance became compulsory for children between six and fourteen years but the minimum attendance requirement of only 70 days each half year meant that for many children schooling remained a part-time activity.[60] More children came to school in autumn and winter, when the annual examination was held, but even then barely half the children attended for 50 days and a large minority failed to attend for the minimum 35 days in each quarter. Children often stayed away through illness—epidemics of measles, scarlet fever and whooping cough could empty a school. Some parents had difficulty providing adequate clothes or footwear or in paying the weekly fee.[61]

The new Act established the Department of Public Instruction and reforms included a degree of compulsion upon parents to send their children to school, provision for remedial evening education and for secondary education. After state aid was withdrawn from the end of 1882 only 70 denominational schools, mostly Catholic, continued to operate.[62] The Catholic bishops set out to create a separate independent school system, a network of schools staffed by religious orders. Catholic parents were urged to remove their children from state schools. A dramatic school population increase—a result of compulsory clauses in the 1880 Act, compounded by the withdrawal of state aid to church schools—created heavy demands on public education. The period from 1880 to 1885 was one of extraordinary school building, when the number of government schools in New South Wales climbed from 1,115 to 2,046. By 1900 there were 2,745 government schools.[63]

Eighty per cent of all elementary school pupils were educated in government schools in 1885 and most of the remainder were in the Catholic system. Fees, though reduced in 1880, continued until 1906 when they were abolished in primary schools.

Most state school teachers were poorly trained and educated. After completing an elementary schooling at fourteen or fifteen, they served a four-year apprenticeship as a pupil–teacher, teaching by day and studying by night. These women and men toiled for a meagre salary. Departmental inspectors exercised rigid control over teachers, curriculum and students.[64] Pupils were offered a narrow and unappealing fare dominated by the three Rs, taught rigidly and by rote in an atmosphere of stern and sometimes brutal discipline. Levels of attendance suggest that an elementary schooling was an ordeal many pupils sought to avoid.

In the final quarter of the nineteenth century government schools struggled to keep pace with the extraordinary increase in enrolments. The number of children in government schools exceeded 1,000 in 1880 in Balmain, in 1885 in Leichhardt, in 1886 in Glebe, in 1895 in Forest Lodge and in 1900 in Annandale. From the mid-1890s a tremendous surge in enrolments meant that roll books at both Leichhardt and Glebe contained the names of more than 2,000 children. Fortunately for the size of all classes anything from a quarter to one-half of all pupils stayed away.[65]

The average school site covered only two acres and the buildings, designed by the Department's architect from 1880 to 1894, William Kemp, were dim and stuffy, with high windows of blue tinted glass and little ventilation. The stark utility of Rozelle school was softened by architect J. Horbury Hunt's coloured glass windows, which featured beautiful birds and animals and through which the sunlight glowed.[66] Kemp adopted a classic style that made his schools externally very different from George Mansfield's Gothic buildings.[67]

Large schoolrooms were designed to accommodate about 120 pupils each. They were furnished with desks and forms about ten feet long, arranged in three blocks of five on a stepped gallery, and provided seating for 90–105 pupils. In these rooms two or three teachers would work simultaneously with the various classes, although some relief from classroom noise could be obtained by moving pupils into an adjoining room.[68] Mounting enrolments forced the Department to keep extending school buildings but schools remained crowded places. Not only were 400 infants squeezed into two classrooms, two hat rooms and a shed at Birchgrove school, after 1902 they also had to contend with noise and dust from the adjoining coalmine.[69] In a delightful piece of understatement, Inspector John McCredie solemnly pronounced in his 1886 report that Glebe and Forest Lodge schools were 'uncomfortably full'.[70]

Inspectors, who travelled around in pairs, like comedians, were feared by teaching staff, but they were conscious of the appalling conditions under which teachers worked. In 1894 at Birchgrove, Inspector Thompson noted:

> the marked improvement in the general proficiency of the pupils, and in details shown at this year's inspection, points conclusively to constant, persistent effort, together with considerable tact and discretion, on the part of Mrs De Lambert, who under such discouraging and disadvantageous circumstances has, in barely 12 months, achieved so much.[71]

Thomas Herlihy took over Kegworth school in 1894 from the Principal who 'belched forth his drunken guilt . . . The school was in a wretched condition. Many parents withdrew their children, others refused to send them'.[72]

Barren playgrounds were slowly transformed from 1890 when Arbor Day was introduced. Gardens and experimental plots were created as part of the beautification of school sites. The highlight of Arbor Day was extensive planting by children of trees and shrubs supplied by the Department.

Most of Kegworth's staff between 1887 and 1907 were pupil–teachers, boys and girls who began their apprenticeship at only thirteen and learned on the job. They taught classes all day and received lessons before and after school from the headmaster and one of the mistresses. Children were required to pay school fees of threepence a week, up to a maximum of one shilling for a family.[73] The public school system emphasised order, obedience and respect for authority; rolls were marked daily and at the end of the day rows of backless desks had to be straightened. Few wore school uniforms in public schools and footwear was optional. Children wrote in ink with steel nibs and each desk had an earthenware inkwell filled with a bottle kept in the corner of the room.[74]

Parents of Catholic children were told from the pulpit, and on parish visitations, that it was their unchallenged duty to send their children to Catholic schools. The Good Samaritan order, founded by Archbishop Polding, grew out of the work of the Pitt Street Refuge in Sydney, and from the 1870s the sisters played an important role in the development of Catholic education, especially among the poor.[75] A Catholic school had been established at St Augustine's, Balmain, from 1852 and by 1877 a boys', girls' and infants' school, as well as a high school, were being run there by ten Good Samaritan sisters. Total enrolments at these schools remained at around 400 pupils for the next fifty years.[76]

Archbishop Vaughan, speaking in 1879, at St Joseph's, Balmain West, was delighted that so many of the local working people made sure their children received a Catholic schooling and congratulated them for providing the school buildings and convents. Most of the money had come from the weekly subscriptions, but for fifteen months local people had worked late into the night, in addition to their usual employment, to construct these buildings with their own hands.[77] St Joseph's, on the corner of Victoria Road and Gordon Street and opened in 1876, was another school staffed by the Good Samaritan order. Some 300 pupils filled their two schools in 1883, a year after St Joseph's was made a separate parish from St Augustine's.[78] On the closure of St Joseph's in 1994, some children went to St Augustine's (renamed the Father John Therry Primary School) and others were sent to Leichhardt. 'If our Catholic people,' declared Archbishop Vaughan, 'bring up their children thorough Catholics, that is, educate them in thorough Catholic schools, the victory is ours; if, on the contrary, the State takes possession of them and they are thrown into Public Schools, the victory will eventually be with our opponents.'[79]

Catholic schools were intent on protecting their flock from a world that was hostile or indifferent to the true faith. Catholics felt that they were an embattled minority and Patrick O'Farrell has described their attitude as 'a religiosity which emphasised duty, obedience, loyalty, hard rules, the black of sin, the white of purity with no areas of grey'.[80]

On laying the foundation stone at Forest Lodge school Vaughan returned to his old theme, the resourcefulness of the Church and its ability to provide education for its children at its own cost.[81] Good Samaritan sisters walked daily from their Pitt Street convent to the new Forest Lodge school in 1880, teaching the girls in the school's upper level; the boys, under a lay principal, were educated downstairs. St James' Boys School was taken over by Irish Patrician Brothers in 1892 and they continued to run the school until 1967. A high school for girls transferred its pupils to St Scholastica's Convent at Glebe Point, which opened in March 1902 as a day and boarding school in Toxteth House, acquired the previous year by the Good Samaritan order.[82] Mother M. Berchmans McLaughlin reported that 55 pupils (44 girls and eleven boys) attended the school in 1915. Enrolments at St Scholastica's school grew from 100 in 1930 to 400 in 1966. In 1996 about 700 girls, including 80 boarders, attended the school.

The primary school at St James claimed some 404 pupils in 1915. A small brick school in Bellevue Street, Glebe, named after St Ita, the patron saint of Munster, and founded by the Good Samaritans, opened in 1900. It provided an elementary education for poorer Catholics who were unable to pay the fees of the Glebe Point college. In 1915, 250 children were squeezed into St Ita's; the school eventually closed in 1955.[83]

The parish of St Fiacre in Leichhardt, formed in 1887, had established three Catholic schools within ten years—St Fiacre's (1894), St Columba's (1896) and St Martha's Industrial Home for orphan girls.[84] A total of 557 children attended these primary schools in 1897.[85] The Sisters of St Joseph, an order founded by Mary McKillop, laid down that 'schools of the Sisters would be in no way inferior to those conducted by the state'.[86] In 1881, the sisters also formed St Brendan's School in Johnston Street, Annandale.

The Christian Brothers established a school at Thames Street, Balmain, in 1887, with 150 boys on the roll. 'The nuns keep a class of little fellows,' wrote Brother O'Hagan. 'I got a few from the state school and I must say they are well taught.'[87] The boys who received a primary and secondary schooling at Balmain Christian Brothers were drawn from an array of occupational groups—blacksmiths, publicans, dairymen, shoemakers, bakers, rent collectors, plumbers, labourers and so forth—and up to its closure in 1990 enrolments varied from 250 to 460.[88]

The separate education Catholics received set them apart from public school children and generally precluded any genuine friendship between the groups. Catholic and Protestant children met on the street and taunted each other with rhymes: 'Catholic Catholic ring the bell, Protestant Protestant go to hell' was met with the rejoinder 'Catholic dogs they jump like frogs and don't eat meat on Friday'.

Apart from the religious component, the curriculum in the government schools was little different from that in Catholic parish schools. Nevertheless, there was a different perspective reflected in public and Catholic school textbooks between 1880 and 1914. In the government schools children learned they were heirs to a tradition of invincible English superiority. 'Catholics,' S.G. Firth has observed, 'learned that their forefathers had suffered under the English yoke; whereas the heroes of public school children were the builders of the British Empire, those of the Catholic children were saints and martyrs building the Faith.'[89] Both kinds of schools taught the virtue of being hard-working, thrifty and prudent. The public system could claim to make good citizens while Catholics had to be content with making good Catholics.

The public school system was a great purveyor of imperial sentiment. Proud that their race had sprung from the great British Empire, colonists demonstrated a growing affection for their British heritage, bound together by what Henry Parkes called the 'crimson thread of kinship', the tie of blood and race.[90] School children celebrated Queen Victoria's 60 years on the throne in 1897, affirming the strength of identification between the Empire's subjects and their monarch, and in May 1910 public school children were called together and told with great solemnity that the ruler of the Empire, King Edward VII, had passed away.

From 1905, Empire Day was celebrated on 24 May and within three years it had become a major attraction in the schools.[91] The young heard great stories of race and Empire, were given maps of the world and asked to colour the Empire red. After hearing a patriotic homily from the Mayor, they sang patriotic songs and were presented with a rock cake, apple and sandwich and received free rides on the merry-go-round, razzle-dazzle and swinging-boats. Empire Day, however, was not universally celebrated. Catholics resented it as an Anglophile initiative, a day when toadies waxed lyrical about the glories of a foreign country. The *Bulletin*, a vigorous producer of anti-imperial rhetoric, called it Vampire Day: 'To mark this official feast of St Jingo, the children in the public schools will gather together to sing hymns of blood and battle, in glory of a country which is not their own.'[92]

In 1891 Annandale, Balmain, Birchgrove, Forest Lodge, Glebe, Kegworth and Leichhardt had between 10 and 72 boys drilling regularly in their cadet corps. The standard remedy for idleness, indiscipline and bad associations was military training.[93] The Education Department encouraged a martial spirit, conducting camps for boys, and the Defence Acts introduced compulsory service. Cadet corps and the boy scouts aimed at instilling order, regularity and patriotic duty in local youth. From 1911 unruly suburban youth, forced to wear a uniform and to train and drill, did so only from legal compulsion, and not for patriotic self-sacrifice. However, in 1914, when the nation was called on to defend England, hundreds of former pupils of the public schools especially rushed to enlist for service.[94]

The system of manly and compulsory games was an important part of the curricula in private and public schools; one special virtue which sport was supposed to have was 'manliness', a term which defies precise definition.[95] In their formal education children were bombarded with manliness and its offshoots, service to friend, king and country. At Forest Lodge school, for example, headmaster William Bardsley sought to instil in all his pupils the sporting spirit; he encouraged the children to swim and play football and tried, with limited success, to interest them in lacrosse and baseball. But it was cricket that captured Bardsley's imagination; any boy with no interest in cricket was an infidel with no hope of salvation.[96]

The very poor and unruly, refused admittance to state schools, could attend one of Sydney's four Ragged Schools, found in the poorest localities. The Glebe Ragged School opened on the corner of Bay and Glebe Streets in 1862, providing a mixture of elementary education and industrial training for the offspring of unskilled and underpaid adults. The Ragged School movement tried to reform and improve the poorest elements in society, visiting the homes of their pupils, inspecting their mothers and dispensing advice. The Glebe Ragged

School, which moved to premises in Water Street, Glebe, in 1896, had closed its doors by 1927.[97]

Between 1882 and 1906 evening public schools, largely designed for neglected or uncontrolled adolescents who had received little schooling, were established at Annandale, Balmain, Birchgrove, Glebe, Leichhardt and Rozelle. Usually conducted by the headmaster three nights a week, the schools offered a narrow curriculum and enrolments rarely exceeded 30 pupils.[98]

In 1911 these schools were replaced by evening continuation schools which offered courses in technical, commercial and domestic science subjects from 7 p.m. to 9.30 p.m. three evenings a week. The new schools operated at Annandale (1912–41), Glebe (1912–45), Balmain (1911–38), Rozelle (1911–41) and Leichhardt (1912–45) and provided working-class boys with an opportunity to improve their skills and prospects in life.[99]

Maintaining order in a crowded schoolroom was no mean feat. Classes of 45 to 50, which progressed at the pace of the bottom slow learners, could swell to 100 pupils if a teacher was absent; this was done by opening the dividing doors between classrooms. Corporal punishment was a method of maintaining order and respect. The cane was used not only for disobedience or inattention but also for failing to spell a word or work a sum correctly. At Glebe school the somewhat menacing figure of Mr Donahue saw to it that children were caned regularly while he was on playground duty; his favourite ploy was to cane anyone who looked on while others got it. A colleague, red-headed Mr Bradley, a thin-cane man, also quick to administer punishment, was known as 'Gingerlep', from his 'lep right, lep right' when marching children into school.[100]

Balmain (1881), Glebe (1884), Leichhardt (1885) and the other government schools achieved Superior School status under the 1880 Act, providing a secondary schooling for a handful of boys and girls who progressed beyond primary level.[101] The elementary schooling most received was no more than a basic education in literacy and numeracy. Children were taught by rote how to read and write, add and subtract. From 1913 the school system was again reorganised and it was agreed that pupils should be given a post-primary education best suited for their future vocation. After leaving school at twelve or thirteen it was assumed pupils would enter a skilled trade, commerce, the professions or the home. The high schools continued to offer a narrow academic course in preparation for university. Commercial schools were established for boys intent on entering the business world. They were taught book-keeping, shorthand, business principles and practice so they could meet the demands of the office. Junior technical schools gave special emphasis to technical drawing, woodwork and metalwork. The two-year course for girls in domestic science covered practical aspects of cookery, home

Balmain Trades School, Darling Street (now Balmain Police and Community Youth Club), established in 1914. Here boys could acquire special skills three nights a week as part of their apprenticeship. (GPO Videodisc-1 Still 33072)

management, dressmaking and millinery.[102] There were also special trades schools established from 1914, at Balmain and elsewhere, where boys could acquire special skills, three nights a week, as part of their apprenticeship.[103]

Between one-quarter and one-half of children stayed away from school regularly in the late nineteenth century, but by 1914 more children were getting used to regular and prolonged attendance, and to increased dependence on their parents.[104] Though enrolments tended to stabilise up to 1910, some Sydney metropolitan schools were bursting at the seams. Between 1914 and 1918, 755 teachers out of a total New South Wales teaching force of 7,800 enlisted for service and some 200 were killed in action or died of wounds.[105] Children in the public school system had drummed into them the virtues of patriotism and duty to Empire and during the war they demonstrated their loyalty to king and country, involving themselves in humanitarian causes—collection for relief works, concerts and knitting socks for soldiers. At Glebe school, for example, children financed their own memorial by donating a penny a week.[106]

The pandemic of influenza that swept into the country in January 1919 claimed 12,000 victims, and led to the closure of most public schools for about twelve weeks as authorities sought to isolate the disease.

Increased enrolments and the unwillingness of the Department to undertake extensions or even maintain existing buildings led to much temporary or makeshift accommodation. The infants department at Kegworth took over the Baptist church hall and in 1928 the headmaster of the boys department, Thomas McAuley, complained of overcrowded classes, makeshift classrooms, the lack of staffrooms and the fact that his office was a converted hat room.[107] Birchgrove school rented two classrooms from St John's church to house their students in 1922. The neighbouring coalmine was a source of constant complaints, driving 'out to the other suburbs all who can get away, practically [closing] the local church, [menacing] the health of the children and seriously [affecting] the attendance'. Birchgrove headmaster, William Easton, agonised that his classrooms were 'streaked with coaldust—nothing could be more depressing, more debasing, than to have to work in these rooms'.[108]

Between 1900 and 1937 Leichhardt, Rozelle and Glebe schools retained extraordinarily high levels of enrolments. At Leichhardt enrolments altered little from 2,137 in 1900 to 1,971 in 1937. Enrolments at Rozelle were also fairly constant: 1,731 in 1900 and 1,630 in 1937. Glebe Public School's enrolments fell from 2,088 in 1900 to 1,311 in 1937. The average class size at each school was about 42.[109]

Enrolments at Kegworth and Orange Grove remained stable between 1910 and 1937; Kegworth had 667 children on its rolls in 1910 and 647 in 1937 and Orange Grove enrolments fell from 939 in 1910 and 881 in 1937 but there were significant fluctuations in enrolments at Annandale's two public schools in the 37 years after 1900.[110] Generally enrolments at most of these schools peaked in the early 1920s. Annandale had 1,591 enrolled in 1900 but with the opening of North Annandale School (1906), Annandale numbers fell dramatically. By 1937 North Annandale had 787 pupils and Annandale 619, with average class sizes about 46. At Balmain and Forest Lodge public school enrolments were halved between 1900 and 1937. Balmain dropped from 1,326 to 750 and Forest Lodge from 1,485 to 692 in 1937.[111] Numbers at Birchgrove school also declined from 1,162 in 1900 to 730 in 1937.[112] Smith Street, Balmain, with some 1,335 pupils in 1900 declined steadily to only 357 enrolments in 1937. Smith

Leichhardt public school in 1921 had 2,231 pupils on its roles and a teaching staff of 52. Enrolment figures indicate that the local public schools were crowded places. (A. Vialoux and C.M. Reeves, *The Jubilee History of Leichhardt*, 1921)

Street closed in 1945 and became the Balmain Teachers College.[113] Nicholson Street, Balmain, always had the smallest number of enrolments of all the twelve local public schools. It reached a peak of 499 in 1900 but by 1937 only 190 pupils were enrolled there, with average class sizes of 47.[114] Falling enrolments led to the closure of the girls department at Annandale (1935) and Birchgrove (1943) and both schools were then conducted as two departments—primary and infants. Declining enrolments meant Kegworth was reclassified as a Central School and remained so until 1960.[115]

Each public school began as one department but as the number of pupils increased, a combined boys' and girls' primary department was created, with a separate department for infants and then, as enrolments and accommodation allowed, the schools were divided into three separate departments. Segregation in the state's primary schools continued until 1960, when co-educational classes were encouraged.

Many young married women teachers or permanent staff in New South Wales (about 600 between 1930 and 1935), whose husbands were in employment, were dismissed under a special Act, and the salaries of teachers were reduced in 1930 and 1931.[116]

Economic conditions in the inter-war period required only a small minority of the population to have advanced training or formal qualifications. The vast majority joined the workforce in their teens as apprentices, juniors or assistants and acquired their occupational skills on the job. Generally government schools prepared most of their charges for their stations in life, and served as a means of social mobility for a fortunate few.[117] Before the 1939–45 war less than half of all children in Australia received any secondary education at all. By the end of the 1960s, however, four in every five remained in secondary school for at least four years.[118]

About four out of five children attended the local public school in the early post-war years.

Some 90,766 people lived within the present Municipality of Leichhardt in 1947, with many large families being raised on a single income in a rented terrace.[119] But from the later 1960s the social complexion of the inner suburbs underwent change. By 1976 Leichhardt Municipality's population had declined to 62,540 and this decline had significant impact on enrolments in primary schools, with average class sizes falling to around 30 and below.[120] Especially dramatic were declining enrolments at the three largest schools. In 1980, Leichhardt Public School had 682 pupils on its rolls, compared with 1,971 43 years earlier. At Rozelle, enrolments fell from 1,630 in 1937 to 353 in 1980 and the numbers enrolled at Glebe fell from 1,311 in 1937 to 300 in 1980.

Catholic leaders argued for the superiority of their education over that of the government by extolling Christianity and condemning secularism. Catholic schools faced a critical shortage of resources caused by the increased demand for secondary education and a decline in recruitment to religious orders, with the proportion of lay teachers rising from 25 per cent in 1965 to 70 per cent in 1975.[121] Expansion of Catholic schools lagged behind that of the government schools to the extent that by 1970 only three-fifths of Catholic children attended Catholic schools.[122]

In the post-war years machinery replaced many workers in farming and construction, and in some factory jobs. Expansion of industry into processing and manufacturing industries called for a growing number of technicians, and there was a rapid growth in the professional and salaried groups of the new middle class. In these expanding occupations there was an increasing emphasis on specialised training and formal qualifications for which a high level of secondary education was an essential preliminary.[123]

In New South Wales those receiving a Catholic schooling increased from 94,000 in 1945 to 195,000 in 1975. Enrolments in government education in New South Wales rose from 350,000 in 1945 to 800,000 in 1975; the transformation was the most dramatic in secondary education.[124] The Wyndham scheme led to an expansion of secondary enrolments (which affected Catholic as well as government schools), larger high schools and from the 1970s average class sizes fell below 30.[125] At Leichhardt, Ibrox Park Boys High began enrolling pupils from 1960, and two years later Leichhardt Girls High opened. These two schools merged in 1976 to form Leichhardt High School. The need for more secondary schools in the municipality persisted. Two magnificent waterfront sites formerly occupied by timber companies were acquired by the Department. School architecture underwent radical changes and this was reflected at Balmain High at Terry Street, which opened in 1974 and Glebe High, on Blackwattle Bay, which had its first intake of pupils in 1979.[126]

Local high schools no longer recruit students of every range and ability from their particular neighbourhood. The practice of competitive entry by examination to selective high schools began in the 1930s, providing the advantages of a private school education without the attendant cost.[127] Fort Street, where offspring of the professional and business classes predominate, measures its success in competition with the private schools in terms of the number of university places gained.[128] Governments have presided over a systematic assault on educational equality. They have fostered middle-class alienation from state education by very generous increases in funding to non-government schools compared with the amounts received by state schools.[129]

Table 11 School enrolments and average attendances 1900–1937

School	1900 Enrol	Av Att.	1910 Enrol	Av Att.	1921 Enrol	Staff	Av Att.	1931 Enrol	Staff	Av Att.	1937 Enrol	Staff	Av Att.
Annandale	1,591	839	742	510	1,038	19	833	762	19	622	619	13	494
Annandale North	–	–	538	382	882	16	677	919	18	736	787	17	638
Balmain	1,326	736	862	633	1,068	26	864	977	28	822	750	20	582
Birchgrove	1,162	669	860	618	991	18	818	764	19	659	730	15	522
Forest Lodge	1,485	750	914	643	979	21	775	697	21	692	555	22	547
Glebe	2,088	1,069	1,268	949	1,380	32	1,152	1,359	37	1,124	1,311	31	1,044
Kegworth	1,066	641	667	487	739	19	575	736	20	590	647	15	547
Leichhardt	2,137	1,281	1,745	1,250	2,231	52	1,813	2,175	62	1,758	1,971	47	614
Nicholson St Balmain	499	264	284	215	268	5	217	214	6	175	190	4	139
Orange Grove	1,083	631	939	680	1,104	20	901	1,106	26	918	881	18	725
Rozelle	1,731	1,012	1,337	1,004	1,712	41	1,420	1,852	52	1,544	1,630	39	1,303
Smith St Balmain (Closed 1945)	1,335	700	842	555	810	17	652	483	14	398	357	9	283

The bond of religion

The period between 1860 and 1890 was a time of religious growth and renewal in Balmain, Glebe, Leichhardt and Annandale. Church building was sustained by mortgages, large donations and much congregational effort, and initially congregations appeared to keep pace with local population growth. Often the physical location of places of worship not only mirrored the denominations' position in society, but also stood as testimony to the wealth and aspirations of their members.[130]

No less than five denominations—Anglican, Roman Catholic, Wesleyan Methodist, Presbyterian and Congregationalist—had a physical presence in Balmain as early as 1861. Church or chapel was a symbol of each group's distinctive identity, and its commitment to shape the moral landscape. Profession of faith had obligations – church attendance, a financial commitment to maintain church buildings, to support Sunday schools and help pay stipends. Wesleyans and Primitive Methodists were the first to take religion to the masses in Glebe, with the evangelical Anglicans just behind. The two Anglican chapels were for very different congregations— St Barnabas's was strictly working class, the other was for the respectable and well-to-do.[131]

There were significant ethnic concentrations. In Balmain, Scottish Presbyterians were active and influential, comprising 18.3 per cent of the population in 1871, twice the colonial average.[132] Irish Catholicism too had a strong presence in Balmain. Father George Dillon, a parish priest at St Augustine's church from 1864 to 1869 and 1878 to 1881, was a vigorous promoter of the Irish Catholic cause in an electorate dominated by Protestant employers.[133]

By 1901 there were in the municipality 37 churches, chapels, missions and other institutions holding religious services on Sunday. Though a large number of people rarely or never set foot in a church, they continued to profess allegiance to a Christian denomination; their failure to take up the churchgoing habit was a result more of indifference than of hostility to organised religion.[134]

The churches played a stabilising role in providing people with spiritual guidance, the companionship of the congregation in times of need and trouble, as well as the setting for important rituals in the lives of ordinary people—baptisms, marriages and funerals.[135] Most offered regular recreational activities and a social life based around the church. Apart from choir practice, prayer meetings, Bible readings and recitations, the churches provided ample diversions in the form of sports clubs, debating societies, amateur dramatics, youth organisations, temperance and mutual improvement societies, and all sorts of musical recitals and lantern lectures. People also found employment through connections established within the churches, for they were very much an integrated part of the local economy.[136]

Throughout the nineteenth century Sydney Anglican diocese was strongly Protestant and evangelical in outlook, with each church developing its own style and traditions.[137] Anglican views on what their parish church should look like was largely determined by Edmund Blacket. Between 1843 and 1874 Blacket designed St Mary's, Balmain; St Barnabas's, a school-church and St John's Bishopthorpe at Glebe; St Thomas's, Rozelle; and All Souls', Leichhardt.[138]

Synod continued to elect an urbane Englishman with an Oxbridge degree as Bishop of Sydney; he shared with the colonial governor the same upper-class accent. Anglicanism retained much of the ethos of the established Church of England and had close links with the urban elite, which told against them in their attempts to evangelise the masses.[139] Anglicans generally sanctioned the prevailing social order, teaching that since everything was according to God's divine plan, all people should be content with the lot assigned to them in this world. Sandstone Anglican churches adopted pew rents to supplement the offertory, and on Sundays rented pews were invariably occupied by solid middle-class folk. Working people turned their backs on this resort of the well-to-do. Sydney's Anglican Bishop, Frederic Barker, doubted 'whether any denomination of Protestants have hold of the working men of the colonies'.[140] St Barnabas's, styled the working man's church, located in a very poor neighbourhood, was a different type of Anglican ministry. All its seats were free, and the colourful and topical preaching style of the rector appealed to working-class people who flocked there.[141]

Three clergymen at St Mary's, Balmain—Henry Langley, Thomas Tress and Mervyn Archdall—brought with them an Irish tradition of militant Protestantism. Ulsterman and Cambridge MA, Canon Archdall was a prominent evangelical and leader of the Australian Protestant Defence Association, which believed that Catholicism was conspiring to usurp Protestantism's rightful place in society. His erudite sermons were beyond most of his parishioners, one worshipper recalling that he was kept awake only because the address was like listening to a song in some foreign language.[142] Archdall was tireless in his parish. The 1890 report, for example, listed the year's work as 345 services, 200 sermons, 175 Bible lectures, 8,400 visits, 1,300 at Holy Communion and 230 school classes.[143] Congregations at St Mary's were about 175 in 1890 and at St John's, Balmain North, in 1889 about 256 people listened to W.A. Charlton's sermons.[144] Balmain Anglicans were more diligent churchgoers than their Glebe brethren. Reverend E.M. Saliniere served about 40 communicants at St John's Bishopthorpe in 1886, with perhaps a congregation of 70 to 80. All Souls', Leichhardt, claimed a congregation of 350 in 1884 attracted by the 'zeal and enthusiasm' of its first rector, Thomas Holme.[145]

The pews of Presbyterian churches were filled largely by migrants from around Edinburgh, the Lothians and Fife, and some from Caithness and Dumfries. They retained a strong attachment to their kirk, congregating there on Sunday with fellow Scots. Many prospered in their new land. They were conspicuous as builders, architects and merchants in Glebe and Balmain, and they were strong among the ranks of employers, the self-employed, bankers and teachers, especially in government schools.[146] Presbyterians were diligent churchgoers. In 1900, for example, average attendance on Sunday was 450 at Balmain, 180 at Rozelle, 400 at Glebe, 245 at Annandale and 120 at Leichhardt.[147]

The Presbyterian church strove hard to obtain learned ministers and was a little proud that a much larger proportion of its ministers (35 per cent in 1898) were university graduates than was the case in any other denomination.[148] James Cosh (Balmain), George Grimm (Rozelle) and Thomas Clouston (Glebe) were noted for their broad scholarship. Cosh and Clouston became professors in Theology.[149]

A Gothic sandstone edifice at Annandale with a 182-foot spire became a spectacular physical symbol of Presbyterianism. Completed in 1889 as a memorial to banker John Hunter Baillie, who had died 35 years earlier, it dominated the landscape. There was no debt on the church, which was funded by Hunter Baillie's widow, Helen.[150]

The *Bulletin* in 1890 noted that a Presbyterian minister's minimum stipend of £300 per annum was considerably above the wage of an artisan and accused the clergy of wealth and avarice, calling for apostolic poverty. Others went further and called the clergy physical weaklings: 'The clergymen were all very mild young men, some milder than others but a typical "curatical" mildness pervaded them all. Their eyes were mostly weak, their

Hunter Baillie Presbyterian Church, Johnston Street, Annandale. Designed by Cyril and Arthur Blacket, it was completed in 1889, 35 years after the death of John Hunter Baillie, to whom it is a memorial. The 182-foot spire of this Victorian Academic Gothic sandstone church makes it a dominant feature on the Leichhardt landscape. (Photograph by Solomon Mitchell)

walk more or less a shuffle and their clothes built with a clerical amplitude and disregard for wrinkles'.[151]

The occupations of Sunday school superintendents, lay preachers, stewards, trustees and other prominent members reveal that Wesleyan Methodism drew its strength from the lower middle class, especially small businessmen and skilled workers. Many Methodists, through industry, frugality and sobriety, moved away from their working-class origins and rose to positions of wealth and eminence.[152] In the process some Methodists acquired the blessing (and curse) of respectability.

In Balmain, Glebe, Leichhardt and Annandale circuits lay preachers played an important role in expanding church agencies and spreading the word. Prominent members of the Methodist laity included Thomas Colebrook, Charles Field, Henry Carruthers, and Jacob Garrard, who was for 30 years a Methodist Sunday school superintendent and teacher in Balmain.[153] The three-year itinerary rule, which Wesleyans rigidly applied, made it difficult for ministers to familiarise themselves with the problems of the circuit.

The *Bulletin* took great delight in making fun of unrelenting Methodist campaigns against the demon drink.[154] A prominent Wesleyan minister, Richard Sellors, was very proud that 'seldom had he seen on any table of the houses he had visited intoxicating liquors of any kind'.[155] Many Methodists did abstain. Wesleyans also had strong things to say about the evils of gambling, public dances, cheap literature and prostitution, seeking not only to impose their standards on their members but also on the unchurched masses. As a result of its opposition to important sources of pleasure among working-class people, the limited appeal of Methodism to this group gradually declined.

Many Nonconformists were bitterly opposed to Catholics, and the cleavage among these two groups was the widest religious division in society, and the source of the sectarianism which figured prominently in the politics of the colony.

In 1882 W.G. Taylor brought to Glebe the fervent Methodism of Yorkshire. An evangelist with a vigorous and picturesque preaching style, his mission was to win converts and he did so in a spectacular way. Winter was the best time for revivals, when the circuit minister sought to warm his congregation to sufficient fervour and expectancy. In the winter of 1883 Taylor threw himself into a revival, in which he claimed over 100 Glebe people confessing conversion in a fortnight.[156] Later Taylor adopted unorthodox methods—street preaching, brass bands, posters and handbills to advertise services.[157]

Protestant denominations saw one another as part of a 'common Christianity', and increasingly they were becoming more like one another, though Anglicans enjoyed a social prestige denied the Nonconformists. But interdenominational co-operation did not extend to Catholics. Protestants and Catholics continued to view each other with suspicion. Loyal Orange Lodges established branches at Balmain, Glebe and Leichhardt, and these agents of militant Protestantism stoked sectarian fires.[158] The hard core of their members were Presbyterian Ulster migrants and Wesleyan Methodists, and their mission was to resist Catholic encroachments on civil and religious liberties. No group sang the national anthem with more fervour than these defenders of Protestantism. Lodges of Freemasons too opposed everything that the Roman Catholic church stood for. Like the Orangemen, they wore aprons, gloves and regalia, and preached service to society and the cultivation of brotherhood while practising exclusivity. This powerful and secretive Protestant business fraternity recognised each other by codes and handshakes, displayed a fondness for the observation of status, ceremony and ritual, and erected social barriers against Catholics.[159]

The building of churches, primary schools, convents and orphanages was testimony of the social and spiritual unity of Catholics, but the creation of these suburban structures placed a heavy burden on the purse of the ordinary churchgoer.[160] The Catholic church that emerged in New South Wales inherited the character of the Irish faith. Acutely aware of their national origins and of the political and religious persecution they or their forebears had suffered in Ireland, Catholics were very much a group apart.[161] Concentrations of Irish immigrants in Balmain, Forest Lodge, Leichhardt and elsewhere created their own social and economic structures, such as the Hibernian Australasian Catholic Benefit Society, St Joseph's Building Society, the Sydney Shamrock Club and the Catholic Young Men's Society. Catholics were numerous among the ranks of unskilled labour and domestic service, and although some Catholics aspired to middle-class goals, it required capital to enter commerce and industry, or to obtain the education which was the key to the professions. The civil service was opened to competitive entry only in the 1890s.[162] The strong local networks Catholics built up in the parishes where they worshipped, educated their children and sought fellowship, were their greatest protection in times of stress, illness or unemployment. By 1900 an alignment of Catholic Christianity with Irish and working-class sections of society sharpened trade union militancy and contributed to the emergence of organised labour as a party political force. In the inevitable conflict between labour and capital, Protestant Christianity was perceived as being on the side of the capitalists, and a bulwark of bourgeois respectability.[163]

Catholic priests identified themselves with the political aspirations of their flock and their power was rarely challenged. Priests rarely made public pronouncements on the condition of their church and the strength of Catholic allegiance is difficult to assess. At St James', Forest Lodge, in 1891 Father Hugh Callachor reported that 1,400 regularly attended Mass.[164] Reports of Mass attendance at St Fiacre's, Leichhardt, varied from 650 in 1896 to 2,600 in 1917.[165] Between 1915 and 1918 Father Michael Rohan, parish priest at St Augustine's, Balmain, recorded the number attending Mass as ranging from 1,600 to 2,000.[166] Perhaps six out of ten Catholics regularly attended Mass, and their religious observance was well in front of other denominations.

The number of Catholics in Sydney's inner suburbs was 10 per cent above their state average in 1901, while in the outer suburbs Protestant numbers were 10 to 15 per cent above the state-wide concentration.[167] Religion added another social dimension to occupational stratification, and although Catholics were over-represented among labourers and the unemployed, by 1914 they were filling more diversified roles in inner-city life. They were well represented in the liquor trade, and as the Labor Party grew in strength Catholics became prominent in municipal, state and federal politics.[168]

The Salvation Army, founded in England by William Booth, offered a faith hostile to social pretension, and succeeded in mobilising the religiosity of labouring folk.[169] Tailor Tom Mudiman declared war on the sins of Sydney in 1882. New corps were quickly formed at Balmain (1883), Forest Lodge (1885) and Leichhardt (1885). Though regarded as a disruptive element in the religious climate, they nevertheless made a strong impression.[170] Crowds followed the bands with their martial music or watched with curiosity or contempt the tambourine-beating throng. They hired halls until barracks were opened but the respectable Anglicans and Presbyterians resented their shock tactics and noisy activities on the streets. The Salvation Army was born in working-class neighbourhoods and General Booth made it clear that the streets were not to be surrendered to the enemy. The Army's concern was to evangelise the working classes but by 1890 there was more emphasis on social work among the submerged tenth, those below the working classes who needed a bath, a bed and a bowl of soup.[171]

Within a stone's throw of the Army's barracks at Balmain, Forest Lodge and Leichhardt, Primitive Methodist chapels were established. The Primitives, who had their origins in out-door preaching, also drew their strength from labouring folk. More democratic in their principles and practice than the Wesleyans, they used the camp meeting as a feature of their religion, together with their brass bands.[172] The ethos of social reform among Primitives fitted in well with the aims of the new Labor Party. Their ministers strongly espoused Christian Socialism. 'The greatest problem of the day,' declared James Blanksby, 'was the inequitable distribution of the wealth that was produced.'[173] Forest Lodge, Leichhardt, Balmain and Annandale remained strongholds of the Primitive Methodists until they merged with the Wesleyans in 1902.

The Congregationalists, an influential minority largely confined to the metropolitan area, established churches in Balmain (1855), Glebe (1880) and Leichhardt (1912). In the early years of Federation, Congregationalism flourished in middle-class suburbs, just beyond the populous areas.[174]

Baptists recruited most strongly among the lower middle class. Baptists were prominent in Newtown, Petersham and Stanmore, they established churches at Balmain (1881) and Leichhardt (1888) and had strong links with the City Mission in Glebe, though they never founded a church there.[175]

The inner-suburban districts were rapidly being built up in the 1880s, and improved modes of transportation allowed the more affluent to flee to the outer fringes of development. In London, Charles Booth observed a similar phenomenon with 'the tendency for the better-to-do classes to fly furthest off centrifugally, with the result that residential London tends to be arranged by class in rings with the most uniform poverty at the centre'.[176] The Sydney middle classes, with their rising fortunes, abandoned Balmain, Glebe, and other inner-residential areas, and built substantial homes and elegant Protestant churches in the new suburbs just beyond the main centres of population.[177]

From the 1890s clergymen lamented from the pulpit a steady exodus of members to newer residential areas and implored their congregations to be loyal, sympathetic and regular in their church attendance.[178] More working people arrived in inner Sydney to take the place of the migrating middle class, and the Pleasant Sunday Afternoon and other campaigns were evidence of efforts to attract them to church. In 1896 Reverend S.S. Tovey, rector of St John's,

In the early years of Federation, Methodists embarked on open-air evangelism and missionary activity in the inner city. The opening of the Methodist Helping Hand Mission Hall at Evans and Ewell streets, Rozelle, in 1903, was a direct result of tent evangelism the previous year. (J. Colwell, The Illustrated History of Methodism in NSW, 1904)

Glebe, adopted novel methods to attract working men to his church, 'advertising talks by moonlight under the shadows of the church and amidst the perfume of flowers on Christianity and Socialism'.[179]

By 1900 the empty pews left behind were not being filled, stimulating Anglicans and Methodists to search for ways to arrest the decline. A report on suburban Methodism by Reverend J.E. Carruthers contrasted the depressed state of inner-city Methodism with the vigorous and vital church life in the outer suburbs.[180] The Anglican rector of St Paul's, Redfern, F.B. Boyce, chaired a committee in 1901 investigating the condition of Anglicanism; it recommended that prime consideration be given to the poor and crowded inner-city parishes 'consisting almost wholly of the working classes of people'.[181]

The Protestant churches embarked upon vigorous missionary activity in the inner suburbs in the early years of Federation but, for the most part, it took the form of a moral crusade to root out evil and impose righteousness. Scottish-born Wesleyan minister Patrick Stephen, an emotional fundamentalist preacher, founded the Montague Street, Balmain, mission in 1890. With the support of lay preacher W. Druce, Stephen, using outdoor services and brass bands, transformed an ailing cause into a strikingly successful one, as evening congregations climbed to 850.[182] A staunch advocate of trade unionism, temperance and Protestant defence movements, Stephen successfully undertook evangelistic work between 1903 and 1907 at Leichhardt, where he established a mission. In 1902–03 William Woolls Rutledge brought new life and vigour to the Glebe circuit through open-air evangelism and missionary activity, and at Rozelle the Methodist Helping Hand Mission developed in 1902 as a direct result of tent evangelism.[183]

The Sunday school was conceived as a part of a middle-class civilising mission, bringing religion and moral standards to the working class; it became an important instrument for the religious instruction of children within each congregation and made a significant contribution to families who had very little association with any other aspect of church life.[184] By any standard, efforts by the various denominations to induce children to join the Sunday school were an overwhelming success. Many non-churchgoing adults were in the habit of sending their children to Sunday school, sometimes both morning and afternoon. Backsliders salved their conscience by strict insistence that children attend Sunday school. For mothers it was a device to get their children out of the house on the weekend; for the young it was often a pleasant break in the week's routine, a place for picnics, magic lantern shows, concerts and suppers.[185]

Teachers strove to provide the rising generation with a moral education but there is evidence of playful resistance to the type of instruction received in the Sunday School. Some children viewed the religious worship and instruction provided there with humorous detachment, gaining comic relief by inverting oaths and pledges.[186] One parody of 'Fight the Good Fight' went:

Reverend S.S. Tovey (*middle row, fifth from left*), boys and teachers from St John's Bishopthorpe Glebe Sunday school on a picnic, *c.*1896. Many non-churchgoing adults salved their conscience by strict insistence on their children attending Sunday school. (Max Solling Collection)

> Fight the good fight with all thy might,
> Sit on a box of dynamite.
> Light the fuse and you will see
> The quickest way to the cemetery.[187]

Available evidence suggests that the period between 1880 and 1920 was the heyday of the Sunday school. The best records of Sunday school attendance and enrolments were kept by the Methodists and Presbyterians.[188] The number of children at Balmain Methodist Sunday schools grew from 934 in 1890 to 1,369 by 1900 and to 1,124 scholars in 1910. Methodist Sunday schools at Glebe ranged from 749 enrolments in 1890 to 600 thirty years later. Leichhardt had 626 young Methodists on their rolls in 1920 and Annandale 390. The proportion of children in Methodist Sunday schools was far higher than the percentage of Methodists in the community.[189]

Presbyterian Sunday schools peaked about 1900—Balmain 532, Rozelle 344, Glebe 376, Hunter Baillie 271 and Leichhardt 288.[190] Anglicans kept Sunday school journals, but few have survived. What records exist indicate that their Sunday schools were also bursting at the seams. Average attendance at St John's Bishopthorpe's Sunday school in 1898 was 490 in the morning and 563 in the afternoon, and St Aidan's, Annandale, claimed 700 in 1899.[191] About 300 scholars attended St Mary's, Balmain, in 1897, and All Souls', Leichhardt, claimed 542 scholars in 1909.[192]

The Sunday school retained its hold on the young into the early 1930s but ministers continued to agonise over the failure to convert hundreds of Sunday school scholars into church members once they reached wage-earning status. By the time of the 1939–45 war enrolments had fallen away and the Sunday school was no longer the vibrant institution of earlier years.

The majority of Australians identified with a Protestant god, a British king and an Anglo-Australian country. The Protestant churches were unequivocal in their support of the British Empire's civilising mission; they perceived the 1914–18 war as a life or death struggle and took a patriotic stance. The high level of enlistments in the war had a dramatic impact on church life and the honour rolls and memorials within the churches are visible evidence of this time of trial and tragedy.[193] Clergymen and parish priests delivered casualty telegrams to families of soldiers. Reverend H.G. Howe, rector of All Souls', Leichhardt, who delivered 200 notifications of deaths to relatives well knew the horror of war.[194] Every time a parishioner of the Hunter Baillie church was reported as killed in action, a piper in full dress stood in the church's foyer and piped a lament.[195] To Reverend Rook at St Aidan's, Annandale, the war had a spiritual significance. He considered society to be decadent, as it had turned to pleasure instead of God, while Reverend McDowell at Hunter Baillie said that any eligible young man who failed to enlist should be passed 'by when you meet them in the street as unworthy to be recognised as citizens of our glorious Constitution'.[196]

Throughout the nineteenth century, and until the 1920s, four out of ten people in New South Wales claimed nominal adherence to the Church of England, and it remained the largest group to 1981. The percentage distributions of religion in Annandale, Balmain, Glebe and Leichhardt in 1891 and 1933 and changes in nominal adherence over the 42-year period are indicated in Table 12. Catholics comprised about 25 per cent of the state's population, Presbyterians 9 per cent, Methodists, 8 per cent, Congregationalists, 3 per cent and Baptists 2 per cent.[197]

Census figures, however, tell us nothing about what proportion of the suburban population were active church members. It is clear that most adult Protestants did not take up the churchgoing habit. Among the Protestants, Presbyterians showed the strongest loyalty, with Sunday morning attendance being about 25 per cent of nominal adherents. The Methodists, like the Presbyterians, were diligent record keepers and they had an average attendance of about 20 per cent of nominal adherents. Some measure of weekly attendance at Anglican churches can be gleaned from their parish service books which, when compared with census figures, suggest attendance levels ranging from 5 to 15 per cent of total nominal adherence.[198]

Patterns of religious practice among Catholics are more difficult to determine since priests ignored requests of colonial and state authorities for censuses of churchgoers. However, limited Catholic records that survive in the parishes, and in their church archives, provide some clue to levels of attendance at Masses. The picture that emerges is that a much higher proportion of Catholics than of any Protestant denomination attended church. Another sign of Catholic fidelity was the way they supported their schools.[199]

Average attendances at Presbyterian churches in 1880 reveal they were the most diligent Protestant churchgoers—350 at Balmain, 450 at Glebe and 170 at Rozelle, with evening services more popular than morning ones.[200] Presbyterian attendance remained high in the early years of Federation despite the continuing middle-class exodus. The Hunter Baillie had an average attendance of 300 in 1910, Balmain 240, Glebe 240, Rozelle 110 and Leichhardt 105.[201] Some twenty years later Annandale, Balmain and Rozelle congregations, with average attendances of 350, 350 and 260 respectively, were healthier than in 1910. Leichhardt's congregation in 1930 remained fairly stable at 120 but the number of Glebe Presbyterians had been more than halved to 100.[202] Presbyterian congregations at Annandale, Balmain and Glebe were significantly larger than the Anglican ones, even though Presbyterians comprised only about 9 per cent of the population.

Anglican clergymen S.S. Toovey and E.G. Cranswick in Glebe, Mervyn Archdall, W.A. Charlton and W.J. Cakebread in Balmain, Thomas Holme and H.G. Howe in Leichhardt and F.W. Reeve and 'Daddy' Rook in Annandale often took the lead in local affairs. They also received slight precedence at local functions, something that rankled with the other denominations. The average number of communicants at All Souls', Leichhardt, on a Sunday varied from 96 in 1922 to 59 in 1930 to 67 in 1940.[203] Parishioners at St John's, Balmain North, were not so numerous, with the average number of communicants ranging from 23 to 29 between 1905 and 1920, increasing to 67 in 1930 but falling to 57 by 1940.[204] At St John's Bishopthorpe, Glebe, between 1915 and 1940 the average number taking communion ranged from 40 to 50.[205]

Membership of Methodist churches in Glebe peaked in 1883, during the ministry of W.G. Taylor, with 175 members; it fell to 87 in 1900 but recovered markedly to reach 160 by 1910. Glebe's two Methodist churches claimed 107 members in 1930, with the proportion of Methodists in the local population shrinking dramatically from 8.3 per cent in 1891 to 3.4 per cent in 1933.[206] Both Balmain and Leichhardt also supported two Methodist churches and their membership remained relatively stable over a long period. Balmain claimed 329 members in 1900, and this rose to 392 in 1910; by 1940 the Balmain mission had 259 senior and 98 junior members on its rolls.[207] Leichhardt's membership rose slightly from 267 in 1910 to 294 senior members in 1940. From about 1940 attendances at all Protestant churches were on a downward slide.[208]

During the inter-war period especially, the Sydney City Mission had a very real presence in the municipality. Founded by Protestant businessmen in 1862 as a non-denominational mission, it was essentially an evangelistic agency which responded to the physical needs of the poor.[209] Initially its missioners spent most of their time making house-to-house visitations, handing out tracts, reading the Bible and praying for people, especially the sick and the poor. They conducted street services but soon established mission halls in areas of greatest need. During the depression years, the Glebe and Balmain mission halls devoted all their resources to aiding the poor, operating soup kitchens and distributing meals, food, clothing and blankets.[210]

The churches were the mainspring of much charitable activity, providing short-term relief in hard times. St Vincent de Paul, run by Catholic laymen, distributed food orders and money for rent, and Our Lady's Nurses of the Poor, known as the 'brown Sisters', were familiar figures in the inner city, caring for the frail, aged, ill and poor in their daily struggle.[211] Methodist missions were visible in their efforts to meet the needs of the poor and unemployed. In 1929 the Glebe Methodist minister, F. McGowan, wrote that 'where want exists a practical Gospel of help alone is effective . . . Pathetic causes come to our notice of homes without light or fuel, insufficient food, scanty clothing and practically everything in pawn, even to blankets'.[212]

R.B.S. Hammond, rector of St Barnabas's, Broadway, mixed evangelism with a social concern for working people, and became involved in a range of welfare activities: 'I spent a lot of time cultivating the non-churchgoer. I liked him. I soon found that interesting sinners were much better company than some "stale" saints. I found among the non-churchgoers willingness to serve—often a fine generosity, a kindly consideration and a delightful frankness.'[213] Concerned at widespread evictions, Hammond suggested the problem could be solved by moving inner-city families into the country. He established an outer settlement, which became known as Hammondville and which offered families the opportunity to purchase homes at low rates.

The Protestant churches' numerical decline accelerated in the post 1939–45 war period. In 1947 Methodists, Presbyterians and members of the Church of England comprised just over 60 per cent of the population of New South Wales; in 1966 they comprised 54 per cent and in 1986 only 35 per cent. After the war Protestant churches in the inner city were unable to arrest the already marked decline in membership. 'Ministers are facing a heartbreaking task,' the *Methodist* observed in 1941, 'in maintaining the work under existing conditions and the remnant of loyal people sometimes feel that the task of continuing the work appears to be hopeless.'[214] The Methodist Conference, determined to grapple with what

The Glebe Volunteer Fire Brigade at the Mitchell Street station, c.1897. Up to 1910, local fire brigades were largely run by volunteers. Thereafter stations were manned by permanent staff. (By courtesy of the NSW Fire Brigades)

was referred to euphemistically as the 'inner city circuit problem', appointed Reverend Ralph Sutton to Glebe in 1942. With little financial resources, Sutton introduced the community church concept and soon had 270 boys and girls involved in an array of club activities; he also stimulated debate on contemporary social issues. But this vibrant community life was not sustained after Sutton's departure.[215]

In 1967 the Methodist Home Mission department amalgamated Glebe with Balmain–Rozelle under the name of West Sydney Mission. The St John's Road Methodist church was sold in 1969, and Glebe Presbyterians, with only a handful of worshippers, abandoned their church in the same year and moved to 244 Glebe Road, Glebe.[216] A similar pattern of church closures and struggling parishes was also a feature of other inner suburbs. Protestantism was very much in retreat.

In 1969 Sydney Synod appointed a commission to examine the life and work of Anglican churches in the inner city. The existing system was found to be inadequate and the commission claimed that 'a radical change must take place if the Church is to have any real impact in the proclamation of the Gospel'. The commission noted the small size of the congregations in most parishes; average attendance was less than 100 in thirteen parishes and less than 60 in seven parishes. In fourteen parishes there were less than 35 weekly communicants.[217]

By 1986 Catholics, comprising 29 per cent of the population in the metropolitan area, had overtaken the Anglicans (26 per cent). The Catholic Church too was no longer the monolith of old. A decline in the recruitment to the religious orders meant their school system was increasingly run by lay teachers, and parishes were being amalgamated because of a shortage of resources.[218]

Table 12   Percentage distribution of religions 1891 and 1933

Suburb	Anglican	Roman Catholic	Presbyterian	Methodist	Congregational	Salvation Army
Annandale						
1891	–	–	–	–	–	–
1933	44.69	25.03	7.18	3.76	0.15	0.08
Balmain						
1891	44.58	21.27	14.88	8.37	3.59	0.78
1933	42.95	20.24	10.69	3.83	0.38	0.17
Glebe						
1891	48.68	23.41	9.36	8.29	3.33	0.69
1933	42.28	28.54	5.96	3.40	0.29	0.28
Leichhardt						
1891	44.25	17.92	10.97	11.34	5.53	0.78
1933	47.52	21.76	8.32	5.90	0.79	0.61

Hans Mol estimated in 1985 that no more than 26 per cent of Australians could be described as even moderately regular churchgoers, and at the 1991 census some 23 per cent of the population in Annandale–Leichhardt said they had no religion.[219] A survey of attendance at Annandale's four churches—Anglican, Presbyterian, Catholic and Uniting Church—on Easter Sunday in 1995 was revealing. Of the 342 adults who worshipped, two-thirds (210) attended St Brendan's Catholic church, 45 attended the Uniting Church (which has a part-time minister), there were 44 at the Presbyterian church and 43 at the Anglican church. Clearly there were too many churches and too few faithful.[220]

Table 13   Centres of religious worship in Annandale, Balmain, Glebe and Leichhardt

Suburb	Anglican	Roman Catholic	Presbyterian	Methodist	Congregational	Salvation Army	Baptist	Primitive Methodist
Annandale	St Aidans's 1892	St Brendan's 1912	Hunter Baillie 1889	1883 1891	—	—	—	1883?
Balmain	St Mary's 1845, 1856–59; St Thomas's 1874, 1880–81; St John's 1882	St Augustine's 1848–51, 1906–07; St Joseph's 1876, 1906	Darling St 1841–55; Darling St 1858; Campbell St 1868; St Paul's 1876, 1894	1863 1914 1909	1855–57*	1883	1881	1880
Glebe	St John's 1868–70; St Barnabas's 1858, 1872	St James's 1878; St Ita's 1901	Broadway 1879–1927, Bridge Rd 1928–69	Toxteth Park 1843; Glebe Rd 1864–1923; St John's Rd 1923–69	St John's Rd 1880–1901	1885	—	Bay St 1861; Forest Lodge 1875, 1892; Mitchell St 1888
Leichhardt	All Souls' 1881–83	St Fiacre's 1984; St Columba's 1896	Marion St 1885	1888 1905	Elswick St 1911	Jarrett St 1885; Carlisle St 1916	Foster St 1888	Cromwell St 1883

* The Balmain Congregational Church, Darling Street and Curtis Road, was a place of joint worship for Congregationalists and Presbyterians from 1855 to 1857.

Industry and commerce   9

To the west of the city, Balmain's deep and sheltered waterfront suited boatbuilders and repairers who moved there in the early 1840s, and an associated enterprise, timber milling, came in the wake of the boatbuilders.[1] The number of industries operating in the Balmain and Glebe districts in the 30 years after 1840 was relatively small—boatbuilders and repairers, an abattoir, tannery and other animal-based concerns, a chemical works, bootmaking factory and small brick kilns on the periphery of these emerging villages. The government resumed land for a public abattoir at Glebe Island in 1850, and within a decade tanners, tripemakers and soap and candle manufacturers were operating in close proximity to the abattoir. Glebe Island abattoirs, two long sandstone buildings, one to slaughter sheep, and the other for cattle, stood out on the landscape. Agitation for removal of the abattoir became more strident with residential expansion, culminating in lengthy parliamentary inquiries in 1878 and 1903. Construction of a new abattoir at Homebush Bay was authorised in 1906 to replace Glebe Island: 'a noxious nuisance . . . a source of serious loss to the government . . . and hopelessly out of repair'.[2] It had gone by 1916.

Captain T.S. Rowntree came ashore in 1853 and acquired land at Waterview Bay for a slipway. Rowntree had transacted business with T.S. Mort, who, impressed with the sheltered bay, joined the captain in a new venture.[3] They initiated construction of a dry dock at Waterview Bay in 1854 and this was hailed as an 'example of individual enterprise conducted with unflinching vigour'.[4] By 1861 the dock was being leased to various shipping companies, ship repairers and engineers. Mort became directly involved in the dock's operation from 1866 and poured in new capital to build iron and brass foundries, a patent slip and new facilities for boilermaking, blacksmithing and

The office and sawmill at Mort's Dock, Balmain, c.1905. The dock was the largest single private employer in nineteenth-century Sydney, with about 1,350 workers. (*Mort's Dock 50 Years Ago and Today*, 1905)

121

engineering. J.P. Franki became dock manager in 1867, and his experience in railway and mining engineering drew orders for the manufacture of equipment for sugar crushing and refining, and retorts for mining and refrigeration. A feature of the dock throughout the 1870s was the more general nature of engineering work it undertook.[5]

Mort saw piece-work as a means of increasing profit and 'breaking down' wages, though in 1870 he did offer foremen and leading hands a half-share in the dock to improve labour relations. Some agreed to buy shares, and for two years the dock was managed by a committee of Mort, Franki, Benjamin Buchanan and foremen and leading hands. These men were shareholders in 1872 when Mort's Dock & Engineering Co. was created, and three years later the company was incorporated with limited liability.[6]

Plutocrat Mort withdrew from active participation in dock affairs in 1873 and died five years later. The dock undertook much more marine work in the buoyant conditions of the 1880s but an economic downturn meant its workforce fluctuated from 1,100 in 1885 to 450 in 1887. The sheer size of Mort's Dock, and its workforce, had a pervasive influence on Balmain, a place where generations of local families earned their living. The average number of hands at Balmain factories in 1889 was 26, while the dock employed 1,350.[7]

Maritime unions, the largest in Sydney, played an important role in the urban labour movement. Mort's Dock was the largest private employer in the colony. Casual and unskilled workers from the dock formed the backbone of the Balmain Labourers Union and its first representatives took the initiative in forming the first Labour Electoral League. The Balmain Labourers met at the Working Men's Institute in 1900 when the union changed its name to the Ship Painters and Dockers. The workforce embraced by this union now met regularly at Dick's Hotel in Beattie Street, Balmain.[8] Ship painters and dockers were employed on a casual basis, generally performing 'one-off' tasks and then returning to the pool of unemployed labour. Their principal pick-up place was a paddock adjacent to Mort's Dock.[9] The dock, which covered some eighteen acres, had by 1923 provided 1,300 men with apprenticeships. Under the management of the extraordinary J.P. Franki, the dock engaged in diverse activities, its marine and engineering section making locomotives, ships and machinery, ironwork for bridges and buildings and components for mining and resource development. Welded steel pipe for the Water Board was also made there. During the 1939–45 war the dock manufactured fourteen corvettes, four frigates, tugboats and a 1,000-ton capacity floating dock. On 12 November 1958 the dock closed its operations and the following year it went into liquidation. In 1968 the area was levelled, the dry dock filled in and the site became a shipping container facility.[10]

Most wooden-hulled ships were built by specialist yards, and there was often a close tie between shipbuilders and timber mills. John Booth, who established his Balmain works in 1854, operated steam-powered sawmills and built ships. Booth temporarily retired in 1870 but his sawmills, joinery and timber works continued to flourish, employing 60 people at the

John Booth began operating a sawmill at Balmain in 1854. The business flourished and, by 1889 when this illustration was made, Booth's sawmill, joinery works and timber yard dominated White Bay and employed 300 men on the company's eight-acre site. (*ISN*, 11 July 1889)

company's eight-acre site at White Bay. The main driving wheel of the 500 hp engine at Booth's mill was cast at Mort's Dock; it drove the sawing, planing and moulding machines which produced up to 200,000 feet of timber each week. After Booth's death in 1898 the company leased parts of the site to various enterprises and the mill was sold to the Sydney Harbour Trust in 1912.[11]

The London-born Elliott brothers, George, Frederick and James, unable to import adequate supplies of sulphuric acid for their wholesale druggist business, decided to purchase an isolated eighteen-acre site at Iron Cove and manufacture their own acid. In 1866 their factory commenced operation and by 1872 the Balmain Chemical Works was producing sulphuric, nitric and hydrochloric acid, powdered sulphate of iron, superphosphate of lime and soft soap. Registered as a public company in 1883, its capital had increased to £700,000 by 1911 and Elliott Brothers became a part of Drug Houses of Australia in 1929.[12]

Sydney's factories were concentrated in and to the south and west of the city proper. On the harbour the dockyards, stretching from Circular Quay to Balmain, maintained vessels moored in Port Jackson. Close by were the shunting and repair yards that made and serviced the trains that carried goods to and from the port of Sydney. Steam power revolutionised land and sea transport as well as manufacturing, and in the period between 1881 and 1901 the industrial structure of Sydney experienced rapid but uneven growth.[13] Population growth and increasing urbanisation stimulated industrialisation. Small-scale craft-based industry remained important but a growing number of large-scale industries brought larger numbers of workers together under one roof. Four factories employed more than 500—the Eveleigh railway workshops, Mort's Dock, the Colonial Sugar Refinery at Pyrmont, and Hudson Brothers at Clyde.

In 1889 some 15,425 of the 25,000 metropolitan factory jobs were concentrated within the city limits. Redfern provided 2,822 jobs for factory workers, followed by Balmain (1,537), Newtown (1,458), Paddington (698) and Glebe (351).[14]

Comparatively cheap land and low suburban rents for industrial premises were powerful reasons for small workshops to move beyond the city limits. A growing market led to an expanding demand for local labour in local factories, workshops and mills and also to a rising employment in the local retail trades. Dispersal of industry to the suburbs had begun in the 1880s. The number of factories in the Balmain electorate (which embraced Leichhardt) fluctuated: 61 in 1881, 45 in 1883, 93 in 1887 and 73 in 1888, which employed 1,619 workers.[15] Mort's Dock was synonymous with shipbuilding and repair, but there were eleven other concerns engaged in this industry including Rowntree's Floating Dock and the Balmain Ferry Co.'s works at Waterview Bay and Foster & Minty and Gardiner Brothers at Peacock Point. Other significant employers of local labour were eight foundries and seven engineering workshops in Balmain in 1888 as well as six sawmills, five steam joineries, five dry docks and four soap and candle works.

Booths' steam sawmill and joinery was an impressive building, dominating White Bay. Freezing, desiccating and meat-preserving firms clustered around the abattoir. Box and glass companies faced Rozelle Bay. On either side of Weston Street was a collection of iron foundries, soap manufacturers and beverage firms, and on Balmain's north-western boundary, along Iron Cove, were industrial sites occupied by Elliott Brothers, the boot-making works of J.H. Mills and Chidgey Brothers' timber company.[16]

Langdon, Hopkins & Langdon's timber and joinery works at Rozelle Bay, Annandale, expanded rapidly to employ 120 men, and from 1891 the Kauri Timber Co.'s Blackwattle Bay mill was flourishing. A parliamentary committee recommended the Darling Harbour goods line be linked by a railway goods line to the head of Rozelle Bay in a scheme to redevelop the port functions of Blackwattle and Rozelle bays which, by 1914, had become a centre for the coal and timber coastal trade. The new sawmills received consignments of sawn timber, logs, piles and girders from coastal ports as well as increasing quantities of imported softwoods.[17]

The Sydney Harbour Trust commissioners in 1914 noted the 'pressing needs of increasing trade and the larger modern vessels', and proposed building extensive broadside wharfage in Johnston's, Rozelle and Blackwattle bays, but lack of capital and manpower meant that this work did not take place until 1926.[18] During World War I a railway line proceeded by viaduct across Wentworth Park and by tunnel under Glebe Point to Rozelle Bay. Rozelle railway yards became a feeder for the Darling Harbour line and by 1916 a railway line, along the western boundary of Leichhardt to Wardell Road, Dulwich Hill, was completed. Construction of wharfage around Glebe Island began in 1912, and six years later foundations for grain elevators were laid there. Large grain silos together with wharves to handle bagged wheat dominated Glebe Island by 1922.[19]

Industrial penetration in Glebe was less marked than in Balmain and was strikingly heterogeneous, with the number of factories rising from 30 in 1880 to 41 in 1888.[20] The four-storey factory of the Sydney Tramway & Omnibus Co. in Francis Street drew other coach and wagon builders to the suburb and it remained an important local industry throughout the 1890s.[21] Sawmills, iron and brass foundries and joineries also provided employment for local labour. Industry in Glebe tended to be located on the perimeter of the suburb. There were Hackshall's Centennial Steam Biscuit factory, Lackersteen's Jam and the Upton Soap Works in Parramatta Road near Ross Street; the NSW Magic Soap Works, Sydney Lead Co., and Abrams broom factory in Wentworth Park Road; and, just around the corner in Bridge Road, Brady's revolving shutter factory and Kauri timber mills and coachbuilders. Not far from Franklyn Place was Dunn's tannery and Conlon's Broughton Street pottery, and Thomas Wearne's Cowper Street foundry, which employed about 130 workers in 1889, producing railway carriages, safes, ovens and bridge components.[22]

Brickmaking was a major industry in Leichhardt throughout the 1870s, reaching its peak in 1882 with fourteen brickyards.[23] But new technology in the form of the Hoffman steam kiln revolutionised the industry. By 1891 the Leichhardt brick pits had closed but William Carter's Catherine Street pottery remained. Samuel Harper & Co.'s Marion Street boot factory was listed as one of Leichhardt's main industries in 1890, along with the Queen soap works and Lock Brothers soap factory.[24] Local people also found employment in the suburb's meat-preserving companies and furniture factories, and there were, as well, chair-makers and wood-turners, confectioners, timber and broom factories, iron and brass foundries and three breweries.

Annandale remained largely untouched by industry in 1890 though timber merchants, wharves and a box company were visible around Rozelle Bay, and the smell of fermenting hops pervaded Collins Street where a small brewery was operating.[25]

A report in 1876 on factory conditions noted that while overcrowding and poor working conditions existed in clothing, boot and tobacco factories, conditions were gradually improving because of the practice of 'giving out work'.[26] The system of sub-contracting was open to abuses.²⁷ The clothing industry used many workers employed on piece-work; dressmakers worked alone or employed one or two assistants in small rooms, often in small terraces or cottages where the light and ventilation were bad.

Child labour was a feature of the factory system, especially in woollen mills, boot factories and on Sydney's brickfields. Children laboured long hours carrying clay in suburban brickyards for ten to fourteen shillings a week.²⁸ Dr Arthur Renwick believed the employment of boys and girls close together for long hours made them 'sharp and precocious in things of which they should be ignorant, and physically deteriorates them in many ways . . . the boys become men too soon and the girls women too soon'.²⁹

Industries which contributed directly to the building of the city and suburbs—sawmills, steam joineries and iron and brass foundries – all experienced rapid growth. Shipbuilding and repair had a significant impact on metal-working industries. The size of overseas vessels entering the port stimulated new technical innovations by local foundries because of the complexity of maintenance work. The need to service the increased tonnage of shipping was not the only factor that encouraged growth in engineering and associated trades; these trades also found work providing machinery for the rural sector.³⁰ Foundry proprietors worked to their capacity seeking to meet the demand for ship boilers, engines, shafts and other fittings.

In 1900, 67 per cent of the 2,047 factories in the Sydney metropolitan area employed between four and 30 persons, and only 61 factories had more than 100 workers.³¹ Between 1899 and 1912 the numbers employed in manufacturing in New South Wales grew from 68,000 to 120,000 and much of this expansion took place in Sydney; after 1904 there was an increasing concentration to the south and west of the city proper, though the nature of the manufacturing industry changed little.³² Some of this growth involved making mining and agricultural machinery for primary industries, but many metal-working and engineering plants were really in the repair business. The remainder of manufacturing was largely concerned with making construction materials or non-durable products such as foodstuffs, clothing and drinks.

Overseas supplies of many manufactures were cut off during the 1914–18 war, stimulating expansion of local industry and the rise of new industries—motor cars, electrical appliances and rubber goods—which were supported by protective tariffs.³³

Factory employment statistics in Sydney were not published between 1890 and 1944, but entries in *Sands's Sydney and Suburban Directory* and other sources reflect increasing industrialisation in the inter-war years, when manufacturing took every opportunity to diversify operations but not their locations. The harbour remained a barrier to factory development on the north shore.³⁴ In the period of rapid expansion after 1904 an array of commercial and

Established at White Bay in 1897, Lever Brothers became a vast factory complex covering about 25 acres and employing up to 1,100 workers in the 1960s. The success of this British-owned company, shown here in 1955, was built on the manufacture of Sunlight Soap. (By courtesy of Lever Rexona Division of Unilever Australia)

Going down the mine at Balmain, c.1900. As many as 309 coalminers worked on shifts at Balmain, but the coal was of a poor quality and expensive to extract. The mine closed in 1931. (*NSW LA* 1901, Annual Report Dept of Mines NSW, 1900)

Bird & Lucas Iron Foundry, Phillip Street, Glebe, photographed in 1904. Shipbuilding and repairs provided much work for the metal-working industries. This foundry made a wide range of castings for baker's oven doors, truck and barrow wheels, fireplace surrounds, stoves and iron desk stands for public schools. A. Roberts *Social History of Glebe and Annandale No 2, Men's Work,* Glebe Public School (1982), p21

industrial users invaded parts of the residential areas of Annandale, Balmain, Glebe and Leichhardt municipalities, when there were increasing demands on power generation and the railway system.

In the 1890s new industrial activities were attracted to Balmain. Lever Brothers, established at White Bay in 1897, became a vast factory complex covering 25 acres. It was the municipality's largest industrial site, employing up to 1,100 workers in the 1960s. The company began crushing copra at the Balmain plant, shipping the coconut oil back to its base in England, but soon was manufacturing Sunlight Soap, the foundation of the Lever empire. There were early problems in soap manufacture, as oil exuded from the soap, damaging its packaging and making it unattractive for sale. Once this problem was overcome, the company made a fortune. Balmain master soapmaker, William Wainwright, was Mayor of Balmain in 1922, and one of a coterie of Freemasons at Lever Brothers. At the Balmain complex there was also a glycerine refinery, toilet soap plant, and an oil refining and hardening works.[35]

The search for coal in Balmain began in 1897 when the first shafts were sunk at Birchgrove. After the first coal was won five years later, the Sydney Harbour Collieries Ltd obtained a lease to mine under the harbour. As many as 309 men worked on shifts at the mine but the coal was of a poor quality and expensive to mine. About 850,000 tons of coal were extracted from the mine before it closed in 1931.[36]

The new coal-fired power stations contributed a disproportionately high degree of industrial pollution to the area. Electricity for street lighting and household consumption in Balmain and adjoining municipalities was supplied by a private company, the Electric Light & Power Supply Corporation, which began operating in 1909. The Balmain Power Station at Iron Cove, the largest privately owned power station in Sydney, was taken over by the Electricity Commission in 1957.[37] An expanding railway and tramway network required more power generation and the Department of Railways began the first phase of White Bay Power Station in 1912; it became fully operational in

1917. The longest serving power station in New South Wales, White Bay was transferred to the Electricity Commission in 1953.[38]

The number of Balmain factory entries in *Sands's Sydney and Suburban Directory* increased from 44 in 1918 to 111 in 1932, with growing concentrations around White Bay, Rozelle, Iron Cove, Mort Bay and Johnston's Bay. The Colgate-Palmolive factory (1922), Glebe Island Grain Silos (1922), Commonwealth Oxygen, Adelaide Steamship Co, the Hume Pipe Co., and J.B. Sharp's furniture factory were important parts of this expansion.[39]

The timber industry (George Hudson, Vanderfield & Reid, Hardy Bros and others) emerged as a large employer of local labour in Glebe, and in the early years of Federation, with the expansion of the wool industry, some of Glebe's working-class housing was demolished to make way for multi-storey wool stores and warehouses, hide and skin merchants, flour millers and coal merchants. In the inter-war years a growing number of small mechanical and general engineering workshops—some fourteen in 1936—and printing firms were operating in Glebe. There were also Bird & Lucas's iron foundry, Stone's Waratah stove works, jam and cigar factories, a straw hat workshop and an ostrich-feather works.[40]

Meat packing, preserving and exporting, so prominent in Leichhardt in 1918, had been replaced by jam and fruit preservers like Cottees in 1947 and sauce-maker Lea & Perrins. Among Leichhardt's prominent employers in 1918 were the City Furniture Manufacturing Co., Pilcher's Balmain Road Baking Co., machine-tool maker John Heine & Son and toymakers Cyclops.[41]

Carbolic and sand soap makers, Pearson Brothers, began operating a factory in Henry Street from 1896. Their sandsoap, especially used by domestics for scrubbing table tops and floors, was advertised in the *Worker*, the official organ of the trade union and labour organisations, and their Solvol soap was famous throughout the country, being widely used by tradesmen and factory workers for removing the grime from their hands.[42] Industry was increasingly attracted by Leichhardt's locational advantages between 1918 and 1932 and the number of trade entries more than doubled from 41 to 90 in this period. Furniture making, wood and ivory turning, chair-making and coopers remained prominent, together with hat-maker John Bardsley, box- and case-makers, brush and broom manufacturers, small engineering workshops and foundries, macaroni-maker Italia Australian Delicacies and stove manufacturer Ernest Presdee.[43]

Some 40 factories could be identified in Annandale in 1918. They included T.H. Chapman, saw manufacturer, James Robertson, tinsmith, Marvel Toy Works, a yeast-maker and a marble manufacturer.[44]

Octavius Beale began the manufacture of sewing machines and pianos at Trafalgar Street, Annandale, in 1893. His sewing machines bore the motto 'Advance Australia', but high duty

In 1917, John Heine & Son Pty Ltd established a sheetmetal-working and machine-tool manufacturing firm on the corner of Allen and Francis streets, Leichhardt. Many boys served apprenticeships here, acquiring skills in machine-tool technology. It was the pre-eminent machine-tool manufacturer in the southern hemisphere. (By courtesy of John Heine & Son Pty Ltd, Bankstown)

Above: Beale's Piano Factory, Trafalgar Street, Annandale, in 1902. Octavius Beale began operating from the Annandale complex in 1893. (*SM*, 18 January 1902) *Below*: Craftsmen assembling pianos at the factory in 1911. Annandale's largest industry employed 560 people in 1920. (*ATCJ*, 24 May 1911)

on machine parts forced Beale to abandon their production in favour of pianos. The suburb's largest industry, by the 1920s Beale & Co.'s piano factory employed 560 people, many of whom were superb craftsmen. Octavius Beale and his son, Harold, pioneered the use of Australian timbers and the pianos, furniture and panelling made at Annandale were of the highest standard.[45]

By 1932 Annandale had 69 industrial entities and industry was beginning to encroach upon the suburb's residential precincts. The most numerous firms were furniture-makers, joinery, box and packing-case workshops, piano tuners, small engineering works and dye works. There were also a patent medicine importer and manufacturer; a china, glass and earthenware importer; a grinder; a furrier; a blind-maker; and the Imperial Billiard Table Co.[46]

The process of the industrialisation of the inner suburbs intensified between 1932 and 1944 with a significant growth in the number of factories. This process was supported by the existing system of rail or water-borne transport and other locational advantages.[47] Within the present Municipality of Leichhardt, Balmain had by far the most factory jobs, with some 179 factories employing 10,238 people. In 1944–45 there were 175 factories in Annandale and 4,235 workers, 158 industrial establishments in Leichhardt and 4,121 workers, and 156 factories in Glebe with 4,496 workers.[48] The City of Sydney remained the hub of industry and commerce in 1945, with one-third of all factory jobs and about one-half of all non-factory jobs in the state and in the period between 1945 and 1953 Sydney retained its manufacturing workforce.

The composition of the metropolitan workforce underwent fundamental change between 1921 and 1971. From the 1960s there was a massive decline in the number of manufacturing jobs in both the City of Sydney and in the Leichhardt Municipality. These jobs were shifting westwards where land and buildings more suited to manufacturing's technical requirements were available and where the most rapid population expansion was occurring. By 1971 commerce (including wholesale and retail trading, finance and real estate) had overtaken manufacturing as the most important industry in Sydney. The number of blue-collar jobs was declining though the proportion of the workforce employed in building and construction altered little.[49]

Women, comprising one-quarter of Sydney's paid workforce in 1921, had increased to over one-third in 1971. Between 1971 and 1984 manufacturing employment in some inner-city local government areas declined by more than 50 per cent.[50] Table 14 reveals a dramatic decline in the number of factories and manufacturing employment between 1971 and 1984 in Leichhardt Municipality.[51]

The growth of trucking and containerisation for freight transport promoted this dispersal. Warehouse jobs, too, left the inner city for sites more appropriate for new goods-handling techniques. The closure of Mort's Dock in 1958, the municipality's largest single employer of labour, epitomised the beginning of the decline in the industrial structure of the inner city. In the early 1960s, Beale's factory eventually closed and Balmain and White Bay power stations were being decommissioned. In the 1970s, the timber companies were being expelled from Rozelle and Blackwattle bays; the huge Glebe Island silos were no longer being filled with wheat; and between 1971 and 1990 the Sunlight Soap (Unilever) complex in Balmain was closed down.

Table 14 Leichhardt municipality manufacturing industries (excluding 108 small single-establishment enterprises, ie those with fewer than 4 persons employed)

Year	Number of establishments	Male employees	Female employees	Total employees
1971–72	462	10,662	4,570	15,232
1982–83	222	6,642	2,085	8,727
1983–84	210	6,578	1,913	8,491
Loss 1 Year, 1983–84	12 5.4%	64 1.0%	172 8.3%	236 2.7%
Loss 13 Years, 1971–84	252 54.6%	4,084 38.3%	2,657 58.1%	6,741 44.3%

Retail shops

The earliest suburban retailers, listed in Sydney directories published by Low, Ford, Waugh & Cox, and John Sands between 1844 and the 1870s, probably operated from the front rooms of houses, selling basic necessities. The fancy bazaars and the market-stall holders were disappearing from the directories, replaced, it seems, by shops occupied by small-scale traders who catered only to the needs of surrounding householders.[52] The rise of a new generation of shopkeepers in the municipality can be traced through *Sands's Sydney and Suburban Directory* from about 1880. Businesses concerned with the sale of food were most numerous—grocers, butchers, bakers and fruiterers. There were also those selling clothing and household goods—tailors, dressmakers, milliners and bootmakers—and there was a miscellaneous group that included hairdressers, chemists, tobacconists, mercers, newsagents and fuel and produce merchants.[53] Many small-scale retailers did not survive the depression after 1893 but the number of suburban retailers had recovered by 1904.[54]

Most shops were located in groups on the main roads or on interconnecting side streets and others were in new residential subdivisions away from the main routes. The local grocer, boot- and shoemaker, butcher, baker and greengrocer could count on the continuous patronage of a relatively small but fairly concentrated clientele. Others, such as the musical instrument repairer, costumier and photographer, depended on the occasional custom of a large number of people and were found only along the main thoroughfares—Darling Street, Glebe Road, Parramatta Road, Norton Street and Booth Street.[55]

The appearance of new public buildings—courthouse, police station and post office—often fashioned in the Classical idiom, was a sure sign of a more general sophistication in the economic and social apparatus of each suburb. Irregular mail deliveries were established in Balmain and Glebe from the early 1850s, but the building of a post office by the Public Works Department was official recognition that a locality had attained sufficient size to merit substantial public expenditure. Banks, anxious to capture a share of expanding local economies, opened branches as early as 1875 in Balmain and two years later in Glebe.[56] Leichhardt people had two banks to choose from in 1888, and a branch of the Bank of New South Wales opened in Annandale in 1908. Perhaps the most visible symbol of local progress and prosperity was publication of their own newspaper. The *Balmain Observer* (1880), the *Glebe, Ultimo & Forest Lodge Advocate & Darlington Observer* (1883) and the *Leichhardt & Petersham Guardian* (1886) all possessed an ideology of independence and fierce local patriotism.[57]

A cluster of retailers could be discerned near the junction of Darling, Nicholson and Johnston streets in the 1850s—two pubs, butcher James Beattie, Watkinson's bakery, a draper and a ship grocery and chandlery store.[58] Around Bay Street, Glebe, about this time, small consumer service trades—butcher, grocer and baker—appeared and in the precinct where Glebe Road joined Parramatta Road, a chemist, tailor, ironmonger and bootmaker could be found.[59] An array of retailers, generally in small clusters, was trading on both sides of Darling Street, extending from Stephen Street to Birchgrove Road. A number of these sold basic necessities, and there were also a newsagent, hairdressers, confectioners, tobacconists, a watchmaker, a glass and china warehouse, a chemist, ham and beef shops, as well as pubs, two banks, a building society, the office of the *Balmain Observer*, and upholsterer and undertaker Arthur Wood.[60] A group of shops met the needs of customers living close to the crossing of Rowntree and Cameron streets and estate agents were thick on the ground near the corner of Rowntree and Darling streets. A wide range of Balmain retailers—fruiterers, grocers, butchers, bakers, stationers and newsagents, a fish and oyster saloon and bootmakers—stretched westwards along Darling Street in 1890 with the heaviest concentration around the crossing of Victoria Road and Darling Street.[61]

A similar mix of retailers stretched along Glebe Road in 1890 from Broadway to St John's Road, with the occasional oddity—tea merchant, picture-frame maker and piano tuner. The heavier concentration was on the eastern side of Glebe Road and ended in a small group of shops—jeweller, milliner and dressmaker—near Marlborough Street.[62] A cluster of shops near Ferry Road catered for Point customers, and from about 1928 shop fronts were added to residences near Forsyth Street.[63]

By the end of the 1880s an array of retailers was established in Leichhardt. Parramatta Road, a busy thoroughfare, attracted boot and shoe dealers, booksellers, fuel and produce merchants, a hatter, drapers, tailors and milliners, and a branch of the Bank of Australasia.[64] Fruiterers, grocers, a newsagent, a tobacconist, and a produce dealer traded along Norton Street between Parramatta Road and Carlisle Street. Down Marion Street where it met Flood Street, a grocer and fuel merchant, Thomas West, blacksmith David Shulter and a butcher could be found, and two grocers, a butcher and a draper had small shops in Lamb Street between O'Neill and Joseph streets. The locational advantages of the junction of Parramatta Road and Johnston Street attracted retailers but between 1900 and 1910, in Annandale a mix of retailers gradually appeared along Booth Street from Nelson Street to Annandale Street, with the Johnston and Booth Street crossing being a major focus.[65]

INDUSTRY AND COMMERCE

Retailing accompanied the subdivision of housing estates, and retail establishments grew steadily in numbers from the 1880s. From 1910 the corner store could be found distributed fairly evenly throughout each district, except where covenants on land titles in prestigious neighbourhoods prohibited them from trading.[66] Most corner stores were family businesses, and with the storekeeper and his family living on the premises they were open for long hours. Storekeeping was the one avenue where a worker could achieve a degree of independence, a little status, and hopefully a reasonable living.[67]

The corner store stocked the basic necessities of life—milk, cheese, butter, tea, sugar, Devon sausage, ham and other groceries; all commodities came in bulk and were measured into paper bags on the shop scales. Travellers from Hoffnung's, Walter Reid, Nestlé's and others did the weekly rounds of the corner stores, most suppliers giving the storekeeper 30 days credit, except the Colonial Sugar Refining Co., which sold its sugar cash-on-delivery.[68]

The sheer number of corner stores is ample testimony that they were very much an integral part of domestic retailing. Between 1880 and 1915, in Balmain, for example, no less than 120 corner shops have been identified, though there was not that number at any particular date.[69] Customers of each store generally lived nearby, perhaps within a radius of 500 feet or less. Fifty-eight corner stores dotted Glebe's landscape in 1895 and by the outbreak of the 1930s depression, 55 corner stores (one store for every 371 people) were still operating.[70] Some 66 corner stores can be identified on the map of Leichhardt in 1915, with 33 Annandale corner stores.[71]

The corner store was very much an institution in itself. Its economics demanded a wily system of trading. It had few cash customers. Takings were added up at the end of each day and what was in the till in the morning was subtracted. A wife (never a husband) would apply humbly for tick on behalf of her family and the shopkeeper inquired through local networks on the reliability of a potential customer. Other storekeepers provided candid assessments. 'Don't let them get over ten shillings', 'she has a bit of strife', 'the husband drinks; she will always pay'. If after this scrutiny of her honesty and financial position, the wife passed the test, a credit limit of not more than five shillings worth of foodstuffs in any one week was fixed, with fancy provisions such as biscuits and boiled ham proscribed. On Thursday evening accounts were added up and presented to the customer the next day.[72] A tick book, honoured each week, became an emblem of integrity and a bulwark against hard times. Those shopkeepers who were not astute judges of character, or were simply too kind-hearted, often ended up in the Small Debts Court.

From the early years of Federation to the outbreak of war, the number of small-scale suburban traders grew steadily, and there was a consolidation of this pattern between 1918 and 1932 as the number of retailers in Balmain, Glebe and Annandale continued to increase.[73] The most striking aspect of suburban retailing was the sheer number and diversity of small businesses. In 1932 *Sands's Sydney and Suburban*

Timber verandahs with cast iron lace were a feature of the retail streetscape of Darling Street, Rozelle, in 1924. The verandahs shaded both goods and customers. (Balmain Association Collection)

Directory reveals an incredible number of shops—perhaps as many as 350 in Balmain, about 300 in Leichhardt, about 230 in Glebe and 170 in Annandale.[74]

These suburbs were integrated into Sydney's distributive system and increasingly they felt the pervasive competition of Sydney's central business district. The city proper offered an unrivalled number and variety of specialist retailers which tempted customers away from local shops. Well-to-do ladies could visit the Civil Service Stores and they could post their orders and receive deliveries at home. They could also be clothed at Farmer's numerous departments or buy from the comprehensive range of goods in Anthony Hordern's catalogue.[75]

The odd fish and oyster saloon and ham and beef shop appeared around Federation but by the 1920s these retailers blossomed. Leichhardt, for example, had eighteen ham and beef shops and eleven fish and oyster saloons in 1932.[76] Pawnbrokers too were a vital component of the local economy and a visible sign of the vulnerability of the worker to instability of employment.[77] Among the various retailers in 1932 were grocers, butchers, fruiterers, boot- and shoemakers and confectioners; their numerical strength is revealed in Table 15.[78]

Table 15 Retail trading in 1932

Trader	Annandale	Balmain	Glebe	Leichhardt
Grocer	47	74	51	95
Butcher	11	27	17	27
Fruiterer	18	38	25	45
Boot- & shoemaker	11	21	15	31
Confectioner	24	39	10	30

The delivery of groceries to the back door, and the issuing of accounts, added to the cost of food from the corner store. The introduction of cash-and-carry, in the mind of local storekeepers, was the beginning of the end for them. First adopted by Grace Brothers in 1923, it meant that the customer could buy more cheaply if they paid cash and took the groceries home, eliminating both the credit account and the delivery service. From the depressed 1930s, more people were looking to cheaper ways of buying groceries.[79]

The corner store was an integral part of the rhythms of daily suburban life. But with improved communications after World War II the pattern of neighbourhood life began to alter and this traditional suburban institution began to disappear, replaced by the supermarket. The supplanting of the grocer in his long white apron by a person on the checkout was a direct consequence of the long-term tendencies of capital accumulation and concentration.[80]

Grace Brothers, established in 1885 in Broadway, had taken over three adjoining shops and added glassware and imported boots to the items it sold by 1892. Its removal, storage and shipping division emerged out of the firm's retail furniture business to become the largest of its type in Australia. Grace Brothers, with some 200 employees by 1914, was providing stiff competition to Glebe's seven drapers and sixteen bootmakers and ironmongers.[81]

An outstanding example of working-class co-operation in food retailing was the Balmain Co-operative Grocery Society Ltd, which expanded from its Balmain base to establish stores at Rozelle, Leichhardt, Campsie, Drummoyne, North Sydney and Kensington. A customer bought shares in the Co-op and was allotted a number.[82] When buying over the counter, Co-op customers would state their number and pay for the groceries, or arrange delivery for large orders. Bread was delivered daily. As well as bread and pastries, the Co-op sold kitchenware and cakes (wedding cakes were a specialty); it had a boot and shoe department and departments for clothing and fabrics. Derrin Brothers, too, were successful suburban grocers, with stores at Balmain, Glebe, Leichhardt, Marrickville and Newtown.[83] Bakeries, invariably family concerns with a strong German influence, declined in number after 1914 as a result of increasing mechanisation. Pilchers in Leichhardt and Raith & Purves in Glebe were large and long-established bakeries.

The Balmain Co-operative Society Ltd, Montague Street, Balmain, c.1910. At this time, it was the state's largest Co-operative. An outstanding example of working-class co-operation in food retailing, the Co-op expanded, opening up branches in six other suburbs, but closed in 1936. (G.M. Dundon Collection)

10 Unions, Labor Leagues and working-class mobilisation

Early working men's organisations—the Society of Emigrant Mechanics (1833) and the Mutual Protection Association (1843) were formed to protect the interests of those employed in various trades.[1] Colonial trade unionism was profoundly influenced by the British model, from which its inspiration was drawn. Membership was confined to limited categories of workers but they did co-operate with each other in strikes and petitions. However, none of these bodies survived more than four or five years. From the 1850s craft unions acquired a permanent form and took their place in the political order being formed in the pastoral period. An artisanal form of working-class consciousness could be discerned among some unionists, their radical rhetoric vaguely hinting at the need for democracy and for a redistribution of wealth.[2]

In the colonies there were co-ordinated campaigns for the eight-hour day—labouring eight hours for six days a week was an attractive idea for those working 70 hours or more. In Sydney, stonemasons won the eight-hour day in 1855, an important victory for the emergent union movement.[3] The British immigrants who formed a branch of the Amalgamated Society of Engineers (ASE) on a ship sailing to the colony were committed to self-improvement but were also bearers of a strongly developed and exclusive tradition of craft-conscious unionism.[4] Agitation by craft unions for the eight-hour day continued, but it received a setback in 1861 when iron trades workers, under the wing of the Iron Trades Protection Association and the ASE, failed to achieve eight hours in a long and bitter confrontation at P.N. Russell's iron foundry.[5] Thereafter unions won very few strikes, largely because employers had begun to combine, but they continued their pursuit of improved conditions and there were about fifteen permanent unions in Sydney in 1871.

Organisations with distinct working class interests and ideals emerged in the 1870s when trade unionism was largely confined to three areas: urban crafts, the northern coalminers and maritime labour.[6] The Trades and Labor Council (TLC) was founded in Sydney in 1871 to co-ordinate union activity, with its industrial objective 'to harmonise the various conflicting interests of the whole body of workmen'. Rigid divisions existed between the skilled aristocrats of labour and unskilled workers, and early affiliates to the TLC were not part of a unified labour movement.[7] The total number of unions had grown to between 30 and 40 by 1874 but some of these had collapsed by 1880 as a result of employer resistance and the recession. However during the 1880s union organisation in New South Wales spread rapidly. There were 125 unions in 1891 with about 65,000 members, amounting to 21 per cent of the workforce.

Many joined a trade union hoping to avoid the insecurity imposed on the unemployed and migratory workers. In the early 1880s the Sydney Coal Lumpers Union and the Balmain Labourers Union, which enrolled men in ship maintenance and repair, were especially active. The strength of organised labour was displayed at the 1888 celebrations in Sydney when 13,000 trade unionists marched down George Street. Each society bore emblems of its trade and the day's highlight was Lord Carrington laying the foundation stone of the Trades Hall. Membership of miners, railwaymen, shearers and the older skilled unions expanded. Gas stokers, clothing trade workers, brewery employees and road transport workers were among the urban unskilled who formed unions.[8]

The constitution adopted in New South Wales in 1856 established an institutional framework of government—the British model of two houses of parliament, an upper and a lower house. The upper house emerged as a fortress of conservatism, a check on hasty or ill-considered legislation emanating from the more democratic lower house.[9]

Property qualifications for both members of parliament and electors, and the way in which electorates were drawn up, ensured an upper house which represented property above all. The New South Wales Legislative Council was filled with wealthy squatters.[10] Those qualified to vote were male residents aged 21 and over who could prove they had lived in New South Wales for a certain time.[11]

Payment of members was essential to the entry of ordinary workingmen into parliament. Without it, time and income lost attending to parliamentary duties was simply something they could not afford, and it was not until 1889 that payment of MPs was adopted in New South Wales.

Municipal politics in Balmain and Glebe became a starting point for many with parliamentary aspirations. In the municipal arena one could gain local recognition and, after an interval, a measure of influence and respectability, and from this power base between 1860 and 1883 John Booth, Walter Church and Jacob Garrard from Balmain, and George Wigram Allen, William Redman, George Dibbs and Michael Chapman from Glebe were elected to the New South Wales Legislative Assembly. A successful parliamentary campaign however could be expensive: in 1887 it was estimated to cost about £300.[12]

From 1856 to 1891 there were no less than 27 ministries formed in New South Wales, making the average life of each of them little more than sixteen months.[13] 'Independent' members gathered into factions and the man able to command the greater number of votes through his own faction, and the support of others, became the head of government. Factions were formed around old friendships, loyalties, obligations and shared interests and values, and the strength of the faction depended on its size and on the degree of its cohesion. Factions were not only close-knit, they tended to be heterogeneous in their occupational composition as were, for example, the four factions which operated in the 1860s.[14] The urban, mercantile, trading and professional men comprised 50–60 per cent of the membership of the New South Wales Legislative Assembly between 1856 and 1900. Members drawn from banking, commerce, the professions, journalism, law and medicine always outnumbered the squatters and farmers.[15]

The Free Trade and Protectionist parties formed in the late 1880s were better organised with a more coherent body of principles than the factions of earlier years.

Most of the members of the Legislative Assembly represented respectable bourgeois society which their class, by virtue of its wealth and status, dominated. Merchant and churchman John Campbell, son of Robert Campbell of Wharf House, narrowly won the newly created Glebe electorate seat in 1859 from Balmain businessman E.W. Cameron, who polled well in his own subdivision.[16] Campbell was replaced by Thomas Ware Smart, who represented Glebe from 1860 to 1869 and served as Colonial Treasurer and Secretary for Public Works. The son of a convict, Smart made a fortune as a land agent and banker, and lived in fine style at Mona, Darling Point, which he built on a fifteen-acre site. In parliament he was a liberal, favouring free trade and extension of the franchise.[17]

Glebe patriarch George Wigram Allen became the electorate's parliamentary representative in 1869. The eldest son of Glebe's largest landowner, he saw himself as a natural leader of society and assumed the role of patron and president of many local associations, occupying pride of place at their meetings. At elections in 1869 and 1872, Allen was denounced as an enemy of the working class for his anti-union attitude on wages and his opposition to the eight-hour day and unemployment relief.[18] Balmain timber merchant John Booth contested the Glebe election in 1874 but T.S. Mort's support ensured that Allen easily retained his seat.[19] Speaker of the House from 1875 to 1882, he was knighted in 1877.

Campbell, Smart and Allen regarded politics as a duty or a mark of esteem; they shared the experience of government and administration and at parliamentary elections their pronouncements indicate they perceived themselves as fit and proper representatives for working people as well as for the better off. Allen had a private annual income of £15,000 and Smart was in a comparable income bracket. Lack of payment for parliamentary duties was not a concern.[20]

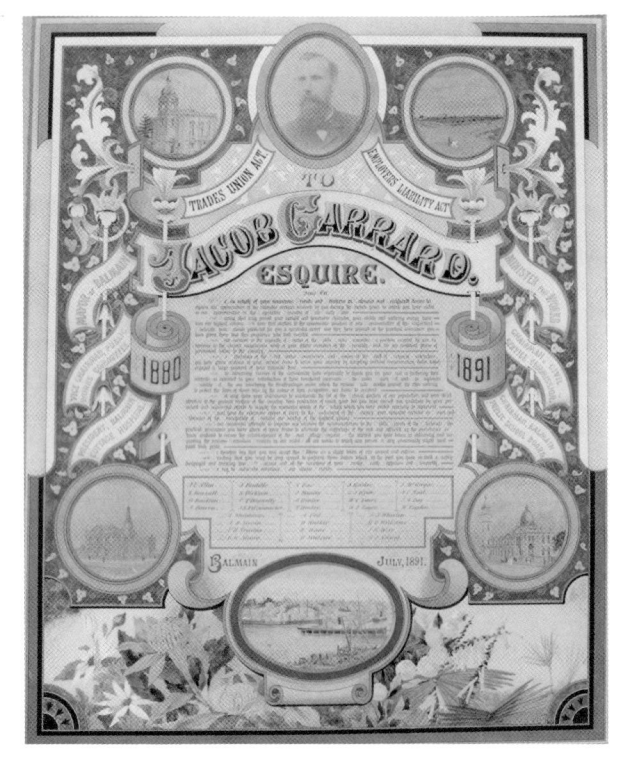

Jacob Garrard, born in England in 1846, migrated to New Zealand about 1859 and worked on coastal ships. Apprenticed in 1861 to an engineer, he moved to Balmain in 1867 where he worked at Mort's Dock.[21] He joined the Amalgamated Society of Engineers, became a delegate to the TLC and led the 1873–74 strikes that won the eight-hour day for iron trades workers. Dock workers were told that unionism was the only bulwark against capitalist oppression and class consciousness emerged through the eight-hour struggles. Garrard's prominence as a trade unionist was enhanced by organising iron trades support for the Seaman's

Illuminated Address to Jacob Garrard, 1891. Balmain councillor from 1879 to 1886 and MLA for Balmain from 1880 to 1890, Garrard moved away from his working-class roots and refused to join the Labor Party in 1891. (Balmain Association Collection)

Union strike in 1878 against the ASN Company. He contested West Sydney in the 1877 election, claiming he was 'no railler against capitalism . . . [but] it was class legislation to have a House composed of capitalists and squatters'.[22] Failure only sharpened his ambition. A prominent Methodist, Garrard was committed to the temperance cause, haranguing Band of Hope and Local Option meetings and his profile was further increased by his election as a Balmain councillor from 1879 to 1886 and as Mayor in 1880. He was also a fervent member of the Loyal Orange Lodge, and Orangemen were numerous enough to make up a potent political force. He was strongly supported by the ASE when he was promoted as the people's candidate for Balmain in 1880, when he narrowly defeated building contractor John Taylor by 789 votes to 777.[23]

Garrard went into parliament exuding pride as a genuine worker's representative. He played a leading role in promoting legislation of interest to trade unions, and won five elections in the 1880s as the representative of labour. In 1883 he left his work as an engineer to become a local estate agent and the respectable but militant labour aristocrat lost touch with rank-and-file workers as he became increasingly acceptable to middle-class voters. He moved away from his working class roots, took on company directorships and his political perspective altered.[24] To many labouring men in Balmain he was a traitor who refused to join the Labor Party. His subsequent career as an estate agent, building society chairman and AMP director clearly demonstrated a political volte-face.

Blacksmith's shop at Mort's Dock, c.1905. The marine and engineering section of the dock undertook diverse work, making locomotives, ironwork for bridges and buildings, ships and machinery, and components for mining and resource development. (*Mort's Dock 50 Years Ago and Today*, 1905)

The residents of Annandale, Balmain, Glebe and Leichhardt were represented in parliament throughout the 1880s by an assortment of conservative local businessmen and professionals. Six of the nine MPs (M. Chapman, G. Clubb, J. Garrard, W.A. Hutchinson, S.H. Hyam and J. Meeks) were also ensconced as local aldermen, and none could be described as a friend of the 'labouring classes'.[25] The TLC sought to defeat retail trader Michael Chapman at the City Council elections in 1873 because of his opposition to the eight-hour day. Socialists attacked Arthur Bruce Smith, barrister and son of ship owner Howard Smith, as an enemy of the working class.[26]

The other parliamentarians included solicitor Frank Smith, medical practitioner W.C. Wilkinson and four who operated businesses in Balmain—soap and candle manufacturer W.A. Hutchinson, auctioneer and estate agent George Clubb, wholesale produce merchant Solomon Hyam and draper turned house and land agent, J.S. Hawthorne. These 'independent' men of property and capital, who monopolised parliamentary representation before 1891, relied on a hard core of loyal supporters within their electorate, and on business associates who often ran their businesses in their absence.[27]

The radical character of politics in Balmain was largely determined by the class structure endowed by its dominant industry, Mort's Dock, the colony's largest private firm. This large employer of labour engaged in ship-building and repair as well as in engineering. Late in 1873 unionists served a log of claims for an eight-hour day and a 16–17 per cent pay rise on the Mort's Dock management. Delegates to the Eight Hour Conference were dismissed by the management and the workers went on strike for several months. The conservative press berated the 1,000 workers but Thomas Mort, perceiving the resolve of the men, capitulated.[28] The conduct of the strike was important in consolidating trade unionism in New South Wales. The continuity of working and social lives in Balmain made for easy industrial action. Unionists walked from work to local pubs to thrash out industrial disputes.

The colonial economy prospered between 1870 and 1890, particularly in manufacturing and mining for both metals and coal. Industries in Sydney changed in response to the city's greater size, complexity and wealth. Breweries, sugar refineries, gas works and woollen mills, for example, brought large numbers of workers together under one roof. The great majority of the 60,000 engaged in manufacturing worked within a mile or so of the city centre in 1891, and clustered along the harbour waterfront was an abattoir, sugar refinery and the dockyards that maintained vessels berthed in Port Jackson.[29] Wharf labourers, dockers, sailors and draymen, most of whom walked daily to their place of employment, lived together near the wharves that stretched from Millers Point to Balmain. At Redfern and Eveleigh, where over 4,000 men were employed in government railway workshops, there was a similar concentration of train crews and railway workshop employees.[30]

Factory jobs in 1891 were concentrated in three municipalities—Sydney (15,425), Redfern (2,822) and Balmain (1,537) where there were 45 large factories. Thirteen factories in Glebe employed 362 hands.[31] Building houses and offices in Sydney (which provided employment for a high proportion of skilled tradesmen), and the construction of public works, accounted for most of the colony's workforce of about 40,000. Small scale, craft-based industries also remained important.

Building workers, road menders, wharf labourers and many others in the city earned their keep by hard and unremitting physical toil. The muscle power of strong men and women was constantly in demand. On the wharves, for example, a minority of very strong men (the 'bulls' as they were called) were capable of lifting 300 pounds. The daily routine of the suburban housewife, cooking on a wood stove, washing clothes in a copper, beating rugs and carpets and so forth, also called for a good deal of muscle power.[32]

In 1883 the Agent-General wrote that there was no country 'where those who live by the sweat of their brow can realise so nearly as in New South Wales the paradise of their class, namely the union of high wages with short hours, good living, and a fine healthful climate'.[33] Wages of labouring men, in real terms, were higher than in England, work was easier to get, the wage

Wharf labourers loading four-gallon tins of kerosene on to motor trucks and horse-drawn carts at Balmain, c.1920. (Small Pictures File, Mitchell Library)

differential between craftsmen and labourers was less and skilled men and labourers alike worked eight hours each day compared to the ten in the society they had left behind.[34]

In Sydney's maritime economy much work was seasonal, and many people survived on casual work. Wool comprised more than half Sydney's exports and shipping movements strongly influenced the daily rhythms of city life. Dock labour was recruited as the demand arose and jobs often became available at short notice.[35] At the height of the wool season stevedores and wharf labourers worked around the clock, and once the season was over this feverish activity suddenly ended. In the busy months of midsummer labourers could earn £3 10s 10d a week, but in the slack winter months, with perhaps only work for two days, they earned no more than fifteen shillings a week.[36]

In parliament, Garrard and other representatives had promoted trade union interests and claimed a special sympathy for the 'labouring classes'.[37] However unionism would be secure only if there was direct labour representation in parliament. Throughout the 1880s the trade union movement had been moving towards a definite commitment to political involvement. The TLC was best equipped to take the steps necessary to achieve this end. The TLC, with unionist Peter Brennan playing a special role, pursued a program for industrial, financial and electoral improvement and the creation of a political party with a clear-cut and detailed reforming policy.[38] The Inter-colonial Congress at Hobart in 1889 unanimously called for the direct representation of the working classes in parliament.[39] The maritime strike, which began in July 1890, was a powerful final stimulus to action. The strike, the greatest industrial conflict the Australian colonies had seen, made clear to the unions their inability to make gains solely by industrial action. It generated a new sense of class conflict among trade unionists and provoked a violently hostile response from conservative critics.[40]

A TLC committee drafted the platform, rules and organisational plan of the Labor Leagues. All but four of the sixteen planks in the platform were limited to trade union demands—three broader demands for electoral reform and the fourth for free and compulsory education. There was nothing here to terrify the bourgeoisie.[41]

Local urban unions took the initiative in the formation of the Labor Electoral Leagues (LEL). Charles Hart, a quarryman resident in West Balmain, joined the Balmain Labourers Union in 1889, a union whose activities were coloured by a radical anti-capitalist ideology. In March 1891 the Balmain Labourers received TLC permission to form a league in Balmain. On 4 April 1891 the first LEL was formed at Balmain, the inaugural meeting being convened and chaired by Hart.[42]

Branches of the LEL were formed at Glebe on 14 April 1891 and Hart chaired a meeting on 18 April 1891 to form a Leichhardt League 'to work in harmony' with the Balmain LEL.[43] Within two months there were 300 members in the Balmain and Leichhardt leagues.[44] Branches were set up in haste and, especially beyond the metropolitan area, their organisation was rudimentary.

In 1891 the Electoral Act provided for multi-member constituencies with larger electorates returning more than one candidate, thereby reducing the number of votes a candidate had to gain to be elected. Labor did very well in inner Sydney, where their organisation was strongest. Labor nominated four candidates at Balmain and won all four seats and in West Sydney also all four candidates were successful. Labor won two of the four seats in both Redfern and

Newtown and one of the two seats at Glebe. Eleven of the sixteen metropolitan Labor seats (including that of E. Clark at St Leonards) were in the inner urban areas.[45] Labor returned 35 members to the Legislative Assembly, which housed 141 members altogether, a remarkable achievement for a party conducting its first campaign within three months of its foundation.[46] The new Labor members were drawn from an assortment of occupations; 'several miners, three or four printers, a boilermaker, three sailors, a plasterer, a journalist, a draper, a suburban mayor, two engineers, a carrier, a few shearers, a tailor, and—with bated breath—a mine owner, a squatter and an MD'.[47] Table 16 sets out the successful LEL candidates for Balmain, West Sydney, Redfern, Newtown and Glebe.

Table 16   LEL candidates elected to NSW parliament 1891

Name	Occupation	Electorate	Religion
G.D. Clark	Temperance Journalist	Balmain	Methodist
F. Cotton	Journalist	Newtown	Methodist
E. Darnley	Plasterer	Balmain	Church of England
T.M. Davis	Seaman	West Sydney	Church of England
J.D. Fitzgerald	Printer	West Sydney	Roman Catholic
T.J. Houghton	Printer	Glebe	Church of England
J. Johnston	Boilermaker	Balmain	Presbyterian
A.J. Kelly	Wharf Labourer	West Sydney	Roman Catholic
J.S.T. McGowen	Boilermaker	Redfern	Church of England
W.A. Murphy	Ship's Officer	Balmain	Church of England
W.H. Sharp	Printer	Redfern	Congregational

Labor aristocrats remained aloof from the rest of the working class. The aristocrats of labour in New South Wales were the tradesmen's unions which were characterised by a lack of militancy, a desire to maintain their privileged position and close ties with employers and a reluctance to organise the unskilled. Included among the labour aristocrats were boilermakers, compositors, shipwrights, shearers and coalminers, but not all trades were regarded as aristocrats.[48] A craftsman could expect to earn about 50 per cent more than a labourer.[49] Worker discontent against employers grew in the 1880s with the decline of apprenticeships, the reorganisation of work and the introduction of new technology which eroded the position of labour aristocrats in a number of trades.[50] Declining opportunities for upward social mobility brought a corresponding increase in industrial militancy.[51]

Sydney became a centre for the reception and circulation of new ideas from abroad as immigrants poured into the city. In 1879 Henry George's *Progress and Poverty* won him repute as a leading American reformer. He questioned why progress meant a minority who grew rich at the expense of the majority who remained poor. George's theories spread in the colonies chiefly through the *Bulletin*.[52] A land tax was proposed to ensure that property was used to its fullest capacity and in 1887 the Land Nationalisation League was founded in Sydney to propagate George's views. Two years later it was reformed as the Single Tax League (STL).[53] Others discovered the social thoughts of Edward Bellamy in his utopian romance, *Looking Backward* (1887), a vision of socialist America where unemployment, the monotony of work and poverty had disappeared. Also to be found in the luggage of immigrants disembarking at Sydney were Smith's *Wealth of Nations*, Marx's *Das Kapital* and Laurence Gronlund's *Co-operative Commonwealth*—works that inspired the formation of societies to debate their ideas.[54] The Australian Socialist League (ASL), founded in 1887, disseminated ideas that challenged the existing capitalist order and sought solutions to fundamental social problems.[55]

Beyond the city limits union men congregated on the corner of Beattie and Darling streets, Balmain, every Sunday night to engage in vigorous political debate; it became an important forum of radical exposition in a politically conscious suburb. A lonely Welsh immigrant, William Morris Hughes, opened a small mixed shop in Beattie Street, Balmain, took on odd jobs and mended umbrellas. He revelled in the suburb's radical sub-culture and found a ready market for political pamphlets and the back room of his shop became a meeting place for young reformers like W.A. Holman and George Beeby. The visit to Sydney in 1890 by Henry George stirred the imagination of Hughes, who made his political debut as a street corner speaker for the Balmain STL.[56]

The *Radical* (renamed the *Australian Radical* in March 1888), mouthpiece of the ASL, was distributed by sympathetic shopkeepers in the city and also in Glebe and Leichhardt. ASL branches were formed in Balmain, Marrickville, Newtown, Leichhardt and Lilyfield during 1892–93.[57] At the Balmain branch, W.A. Holman, a slight, studious figure with an unruly shock of black hair, captivated locals at weekly meetings. Holman lived in Balmain and his father, an actor, coached him in the art of elocution. By day he was a cabinetmaker and by night a speaker at debating societies, at street corners or wherever an audience could be found.[58]

Left: Tom Batho, an active member of the Australian Socialist League, began printing the *Socialist* in 1894 from his home at 41 North Street, Leichhardt. (*Revolutionary Socialist*, State Library)
Right: Artisan/Radical John Grant (1857–1928). A stonemason for fourteen years, Scottish-born Grant became secretary of the Stonemasons Society and Glebe LEL. He was an ALP senator from 1914 to 1920 and 1922 to 1928 (*Co-operator*, 7 December 1912)

The *Australian Radical*, which ceased publication in 1890, was replaced four years later by the *Socialist*, produced by Harry Holland and Tom Batho from a print shop in Leichhardt. The *Socialist*, though without official ASL patronage, was supported by the majority of ASL members who approved its critical approach to the Labor Party.[59]

ASL members were prominent in the formation of LELs and, as trade unionists, in urging their fellow unionists to join the new party. ASL involvement in the election campaign was evident at a meeting on 20 February 1891. When government ministers Bruce Smith, conservative Free Trader and MLA for Glebe, and William McMillan, popularly known as 'Good Iron Mac', entered Glebe Town Hall they were greeted with hoots, groans and hisses. After their exit a motion was passed condemning them as 'enemies of the workers' and calling on them to resign. At least eight of the new Labor MPs in 1891 were members of the ASL.[60]

Radicals in the labour movement who embraced the single tax creed were a respectable lot, generally drawn from the lower middle class, but the brief tour of Henry George in 1890 did capture the imagination of some labouring classes. Frank Cotton, Methodist lay preacher, shearer and editor of several single tax journals, was vocal and tireless in spreading George's views which, he wrote, would determine if the nineteenth century was to end in 'millennium or pandemonium'.[61] J. Grant, G.S. Beeby and A. Ridell, all STL members, were secretaries of LELs at Glebe, Newtown and Annandale, young men who grappled with various combinations of free trade, protectionism and socialism, but were won over to the single tax by Sydney's boom and bust economy which demonstrated the social cost of land speculation. The STL added zest to the period 1887–94, by trying to infiltrate the Free Traders, the TLC and the parliamentary Labor Party, injecting a stream of ideas into the effervescing debates. On the other hand, socialists, moved by the hardships of the working class, were more directly opposed to capitalism than were the followers of Henry George.[62] Socialism had an important inspirational effect on members of the Labor movement; the ASL had fifteen branches and more than 9,000 members in New South Wales in 1893. But neither the STL nor the ASL had any hope of founding a political party.[63]

Few trade unionists shared the single taxers' enthusiasm for free trade since protective tariffs safeguarded many industries and livelihoods. George was antagonistic to socialism and decried trade unionism as a 'class combination' which embittered the relations between master and servant. These beliefs alienated much working-class and radical support.[64] Socialists ridiculed the naive belief that land monopoly was the cause of all social ills. Within branches of the LEL socialists and trade unionists challenged the single taxers on ideological as well as fiscal grounds. Debate was vigorous and at times vitriolic as trade unionists and socialists gained the upper hand.[65] Membership of STL branches began to decline and among those to defect to the socialists were W.A. Holman, G.S. Beeby and W.M. Hughes.

The Stonemason's Society was the first urban union to welcome Henry George to Sydney. John Grant, the Society's and Glebe LEL secretary, a stonemason for fourteen years, gave evidence to the Royal Commission on Strikes where he revealed himself as an extraordinarily well-read artisan radical. His solution to the labour problem lay in ending the private monopolisation of land. Excessive rents, he explained, forced capital and labour into a struggle for survival. The only class to profit were the landlords: 'an army of . . . boozers, loafers and legalised robbers . . . empowered to collect tribute from the toilers'. He ended with an appeal to natural right and divine law: 'What right after all has one man more than another to any part of this planet?'[66]

Charles Hart's staunch protectionism could not accommodate free trade or single tax philosophies. He questioned the single taxers' working class credentials and accused Frank Cotton of 'living off the job', exploiting his position on the TLC for journalistic advantages and wagered £10 that Cotton 'couldn't take the wool off a sheep'.[67] An ASL member and avowed unionist, Hart was unhappy about non-bona fide workers holding office within the unions of the new LELs. Hart failed to gain preselection as one of the four candidates for Balmain; an alliance of single taxers and free traders destroyed his political aspirations.[68] In December 1891 a disgusted Hart declared 'the Leagues were too out of touch with the workers to merit their continued involvement'.[69]

Divisions quickly surfaced in the combined Glebe and Annandale branch as single taxers battled with socialists and unionists for control of the branch. Members quarrelled constantly, eggs were hurled at speakers, and 'foul language' marred debate. The strongly protectionist Glebe branch accused its president, J. Skelton, in May 1892 of lecturing for the STL and referring to fellow members as a 'miserable herd'. Skelton responded by offering 'to settle the matter outside'.[70] Denied this opportunity, Skelton, some of the executive and most of the Annandale members immediately resigned. The League then resolved to hold future meetings in Glebe Town Hall, far from the 'public houses of the neighbouring suburb'.[71]

From 1891 Labor had to build a new party in an economic recession that lasted for a decade. Labor shared the loyalties and time of disparate groups—single taxers, protectionists, Free Traders, socialists and unionists—but during the 1890s they were unable to mould these groups together or create a state-wide movement. Banks failed in 1893, and declining profits forced manufacturers to reduce costs through change and reorganisation. Average real incomes did not reach the peak level of the 1880s until 1909.[72]

Labor's progress through the 1890s was precarious. It endorsed only four of the sitting parliamentarians in the 1894 elections and those not endorsed ran as independent Labor candidates. Multi-member constituencies were abolished, and though Labor received 26 per cent of the vote in 1894 it won only seven seats in Sydney, a little under half the number it won in 1891.[73] It made no progress in the suburbs in 1895 but Labor's electoral nadir was in 1898 when it only received 9 per cent of the vote in Sydney; the Protectionists and Free Traders held sway and the struggling Labor Party could well have gone out of existence.[74]

Labor could run only seven candidates in the 29 Sydney suburban electorates in 1898, winning only five seats (Balmain South, Botany, Redfern, Lang and Pyrmont).[75] Its failure to stand candidates, and win votes, was largely a result of the collapse of the party's organisational base in the trade unions. The TLC was crippled by the depression, and as affiliates withdrew from it, the AWU took over the party. Its organisation was hampered by a series of droughts between 1895 and 1903 which retarded recovery.[76]

Labor needed the Catholic electorate for its political advancement. Cardinal Moran led one-quarter of the population, and perhaps one-third of the workers. Catholics were heavily under-represented in the new party, especially when the working-class nature of the Catholic community was considered.[77] Socialist ideas and movements played an important role as an ideology in working-class mobilisation and the socialist rhetoric of Labor Party leaders gave the party a sense of class identity. Socialism, however, alienated Catholic voters. Nationalisation was promoted by the ASL in 1897 but this objective was discarded in favour of phraseology considered less alarming to electors.[78] Increasingly socialists were excluded from, and moved outside the party. Labor did not challenge the capitalist structure but worked through the capitalist state organisations. It was not a socialist party.[79]

By 1901 the Catholic press was urging Catholics to join Labor Leagues to see that they got 'a fair share of the nominations so that Catholic rights may be guarded in the Legislature'. Labor also benefited from a transfer of the former Protectionist vote. An alliance between the Liberal Free Trade Party, temperance organisations and militant Protestants ensured that most Catholics did not vote for them. At the 1901 elections, seven out of twenty-four Labor men returned were Catholic, compared to only one in 1898.[80]

Underlying Labor's recovery and expansion in the early years of Federation was trade unionism. Only eight unions with a combined membership of 407 were affiliated to the Sydney District Council by the end of the 1890s, but as real wages steadily improved, some unions which had virtually ceased to exist re-formed successfully. The trade union revival was greatly aided by the requirements of a system of compulsory arbitration; the court could hear claims only from registered unions, and this was a powerful stimulus to union organisation.[81] Shop

Draper Sydney Law (1856–1939) in front of his store at Weston Road, Balmain West. Small trader and Orangeman, Law was Labor MLA for Balmain South from 1894 to 1904. He left the party and was elected MLA for Rozelle from 1904 to 1907 as a Liberal candidate. (*ISN*, 11 July 1889)

assistants, public servants and other white-collar employees and female workers, previously unorganised, came within the ambit of unionism. Maritime and associated transport industries experienced significant expansion through the growth of rail and tramway services. The number of unions affiliated with the Sydney Labor Council grew from 71 in 1904 to 93 in 1910.[82]

Cheaper public transport made it easier to organise the support of working people in suburban electorates where Labor branches were growing. The recovery of city unionism helped support a parliamentary Labor strategy which treated voters not only as workers but as tenants, home builders, rate payers, parents and residents with rights to enjoy the amenities of the area they lived in and to exercise control over it.[83]

Labouring men did stand for municipal elections in Glebe, Balmain and Leichhardt before 1891 and occasionally they were successful. They were independents in every sense. 'Honest' John Reilly, Ono Earnshaw and James Gillard became local elected representatives in Glebe; William Davidson entered municipal politics in Balmain and Charles Linney became a Leichhardt councillor. All these men earned their living by the sweat of their brow.[84]

The control of municipal councils aroused interest in the Leagues because it provided an opportunity to secure relief works in times of unemployment and to enforce minimum rates of pay and maximum hours. But the union leadership made sure that municipal socialism was removed from the party's local government program.[85] As the state parliamentary Labor Party grew in strength in the early years of Federation, the endorsement of Labor candidates in municipal elections was debated in suburban Leagues. At Leichhardt Council in 1908 there was concern that the council might be handed over to 'socialists' and when the Labor Party first stood candidates at the Glebe municipal elections in 1911 they finished at the bottom of the poll.[86]

Balmain returned four Labor men to the New South Wales Legislative Assembly in 1891. Balmain North and Balmain South were created in 1894 with the abolition of multi-member constituencies, and for the remainder of the century these two seats were shared by a Free Trader and Labor. Wood and coal merchant, Free Trader and Orangeman William Wilks became the MLA for Balmain North in 1894 and held off Labor challenges in his working-class constituency till 1901 when he was elected MHR for Dalley.[87] Draper Sydney Law, a small businessman who joined the Balmain Labourers Union, won the seat of Balmain South for Labor in 1894. This petit-bourgeois trader retained the seat until 1904 when he won the new seat of Rozelle as a Liberal Reform candidate, maintaining a base among sectarian Protestants and working men until his defeat in 1907.[88] James Mercer came from a background not dissimilar to many Liberal parliamentarians. The Labor MLA for Rozelle from 1907 to 1917, he was a religious man, a long-time Anglican lay reader who embraced the temperance creed.[89] The Grand Chief Templar of New South Wales in 1901–2, Mercer left the party over conscription. He was replaced in 1917 by John Quirk, a foundation member of the Rozelle LEL, and its president. Born and bred in Rozelle, Quirk attended St Joseph's school there, helped establish the Letter Carriers Union (he was a local postman), and was an active member of the Balmain United Friendly Society.[90]

W.A. Holman, Labor's most talented orator, stood for the seat of Leichhardt in 1894. He was opposed by John Hawthorne, MLA for Balmain from 1885 to 1891. Hawthorne, who won, had an unhappy career in business. He filed for bankruptcy as a draper in 1884 and six years later the affairs of his Leichhardt estate agency were also placed in the hands of the trustee in bankruptcy. An Anglican temperance advocate, like J.B. Mercer, Hawthorne remained the Free Trade/Liberal MLA for Leichhardt till 1904.[91] Robert Booth, headmaster of Orange Grove Public School in 1883–94, won endorsement for the Liberal Party in 1904 and retained the seat for the Liberals.

Ambrose Campbell Carmichael, son of Scottish migrants, was trained as an accountant but worked on the land until he moved to Leichhardt and worked as a bookkeeper for Annandale piano maker O.C. Beale. In 1907 Carmichael won Leichhardt, the first time Labor had been successful in this seat. Carmichael quickly became a leading parliamentarian, a forceful and, at times, brilliant speaker with an effective flow of sarcasm. He was appointed to various ministerial portfolios but in March 1915, disturbed by war preparations, he resigned from the ministry. At 49 years of age, Carmichael enlisted in the AIF and announced that he had the support of military and recruiting authorities to carry out his own program 'to raise a thousand rifle reserve recruits' who would join the AIF with him. Promoted to Lieutenant in the 3rd Battalion, he was wounded at Houplines, France, in 1917 in an action for which he was awarded the Military Cross. Invalided home, Carmichael, still a parliamentarian, had become something of a national figure—an over-age and mercurial war hero with panache and courage.[92]

Overseas at the time of the Labor split in 1916, Carmichael favoured conscription and would gradually drift from the party. He raised another 'Carmichael's thousand' and rode at their head when they left Sydney in 1918.[93] On returning home he disclosed his antipathy to 'machine politics' to his constituents, and announced the formation of the People's Party of Soldiers and Citizens. He ran for Balmain as an independent in 1920, but polled only 8 per cent of the vote.

Annandale was a stronghold of militant Protestantism and the Liberal Party. Free Trader/Liberal William Mahony was MLA for Annandale from 1894 to 1910, during which time he repulsed challenges from Protectionists P. Larkin and J.J. Maxwell, Labor men A. Duncan and J. Skelton and independent I.R. Cohen.[94] Former Salvation Army officer Albert Bruntnell, a member of the ultra-Protestant organisation, the Australian Protestant Defence Association (APDA), and a staunch temperance man, succeeded Mahony in 1910 but Labor persuaded the formidable Arthur Hill Griffith to run for Annandale at the 1913 elections. An outstanding sportsman and experienced Labor politician, Griffith won the seat. He saw the war as a crusade against Germany for the preservation of civilisation, refused to accept his party's direction to oppose

Thomas Houghton (1862–1933), first full-time general secretary of the TLC, Labor MLA for Glebe from 1891 to 1894 and proprietor of the *Australian Workman* from 1894 to 1897. (Large Portraits Collection, L Port G/L, Dixson Library)

conscription for overseas service and was expelled in November 1916. He contested seats in 1917 and 1920 as independent Labor, but lost.[95]

Thomas Houghton was an important progenitor of the Labor Party. The TLC's first full-time general secretary, he was on the sub-committee that drafted a scheme of government that became the LEL and was appointed to the Royal Commission on Strikes. At the 1891 elections there were two seats for Glebe and Houghton shared the electorate with Free Trader Arthur Bruce Smith. He lost as a Protectionist Labor candidate for Glebe in 1894 and he then became the proprietor of the *Australian Workman*.[96] Glebe was held from 1894 to 1910 by the dapper Free Trade/Liberal J.A. Hogue, former editor of the *Evening News*. Known to parliamentary colleagues as 'Dismal Jimmy' because he was 'always cheerful', Hogue served as Colonial Secretary, Minister for Public Instruction and for Labor and Industry. A man with broad interests, Hogue was a vice-president of the New South Wales Rowing Association and a state bowls champion.[97]

Protestants and conservatives had been moving together before Labor and Catholics formed an alliance. The APDA was largely a layman's response to the alleged Catholic menace. It believed Catholicism was conspiring to usurp Protestantism's rightful place in society.[98] The APDA's claim of Catholic political influence was a myth, as only 18 per cent of parliamentarians were Catholics.[99]

Militant Protestantism was on the march in 1901 and the strongest branches of the APDA were found in suburbs where sectarianism was most virile—in Annandale, Leichhardt, Balmain and Newtown where many working- and lower middle-class folk aspired to respectability. At the first meeting of the Glebe branch 240 members enrolled and by the end of 1903 there were 135 APDA branches with 22,000 members. At the same time membership of the Loyal Orange Lodges climbed to around 20,000.[100]

Sectarian friction was overt in some electorates where belligerent Orangemen and the APDA men stood. Former Labor man S.J. Law, now Liberal member for Rozelle, told an Orange celebration in Lithgow 'that if Cardinal Moran withdrew his support from Mr McGowen and the members of the party, they would be politically dead'.[101] At Leichhardt the APDA branch put forward Robert Booth, Orangeman and temperance advocate, and sitting Liberal J.S. Hawthorne lost endorsement after supporting state aid for a Catholic orphanage.[102] Protestants got behind the Liberal Party to a man, thus ensuring that book-finisher Walter Anderson, APDA member and Orangeman, unseated Labor man John Storey at Balmain.[103] Re-endorsement of Liberal MLA for Annandale, Methodist solicitor William Mahony, was guaranteed by his APDA membership, and his Presbyterian Liberal colleague at Glebe, J.A. Hogue, had the right credentials.

The election of J.H. Carruthers' Liberal and Reform Party in 1904 made Protestants feel safe from Catholic threats; as a result APDA membership shrank and sectarianism declined. The United Licensed Victuallers' Association mobilised their forces at the next election in 1907, targeting electorates of temperance advocates, 'our determined enemies and we concentrated the whole of our energies to put them out of parliament'.[104] They claimed more than half the Liberal casualties, including Booth at Leichhardt and Anderson at Balmain where Labor won the seats. Rozelle also returned to Labor, with the defeat of S.J. Law.

It took Labor almost twenty years to win office. Not until about 1904 did the party

Womanhood Suffrage League. Leading workers of the Womanhood Suffrage League and branches. *Back row, standing*: Mrs Jackson (President of the Redfern Branch), Mrs Wynn (President of the Annandale Branch), Miss Caldwell (Camperdown), Mrs T. Parkes (President of the Toxteth League), Mrs Hansen (President of the Newtown Branch). *Seated*: Mrs C. Martel (Recording Secretary of the Central League), Mrs McDonald (President of the Glebe Branch), Miss Belle Golding (Secretary of the Newtown Branch), Miss Annie Golding (Organising Secretary of the United Branches), Mrs Dickie (ex-President of the Newtown League), Mrs Chapman (Secretary of the Redfern Branch), Mrs Dwyer (Secretary of the Camperdown Branch). The Golding sisters from Newtown, Belle and Annie, were especially prominent figures in the early political lobbying that led to NSW women celebrating the granting of their right to vote in 1902. (*ATCJ*, 6 September 1902)

achieve the vote it received in 1891, but new support surged after 1907 and at the general elections of June 1910 Labor became the government. It won 50 seats in parliament and Balmain, Glebe, Leichhardt and Rozelle returned Labor men. Annandale finally became a Labor seat in 1913.[105]

State voting patterns reflected the class differences in Sydney. In 1913 Labor's metropolitan strength lay in a south-west sector within two to three miles of the GPO, while the Liberals held all seats north of the harbour.[106]

Labor took practical measures to deal with the rising cost of living. These included regulation of the meat industry, the setting up of a state fishery, measures against monopolies, fair rents court, and new 'Daceyvilles' in other parts of Sydney. In 1913 Labor again mustered 50 votes in an Assembly of 90, and it seems that many voters had by then developed a strong identification with the party.[107]

Tom Keegan, son of an Irish-born miner, was working at the Lighthouse mine, Wyalong, when he was sacked for supporting W.A. Holman's stand against the South African War. He moved to Glebe, where he joined the local LEL and became active in the United Labourers Union. In 1910 he thanked the working people of Glebe from the balcony of Record Reign Hall for voting for him. In parliament he sought to protect labour and fight hardship, seeking relief for the less fortunate. He pursued ministers on the issues of public transport and the working conditions of state and municipal employees. He secured the appointment of a select committee on rents and a bill to establish a fair rents tribunal. Keegan held the seat of Glebe from 1910 to 1920 and from 1927 to 1935, and the seat of Balmain from 1921 to 1927.[108]

John Storey was educated at Darling Road Public School (Rozelle) and night school. At the age of fourteen he was apprenticed to boilermaking with Perdriau & West and then worked as a journeyman at Mort's Dock from 1883 to 1901. An active member of the Boilermakers Union, Storey's political instinct was aroused by the dangerous working conditions at Mort's

John Storey (1869–1921). A boilermaker at Mort's Dock from 1883 to 1901, Storey was Labor MLA for Balmain North from 1901 to 1904 and for Balmain from 1907 to 1921. He became Premier of NSW in 1920. (GPO Videodisc-1 Still 12971)

Dock, and he joined the Balmain LEL in 1891. The gregarious teetotaller won the seat of Balmain North in 1901, lost the new seat of Balmain in a sectarian campaign, but won it back in 1907. Storey never lost the common touch and in parliament he mastered his public shyness and became an entertaining speaker, popular with all members. Storey's leadership of the Labor Party after the split was critical in the party's survival and rehabilitation. He was Premier of New South Wales from April 1920 to his death of nephritis on 5 October 1921.[109]

W.M. Hughes announced that the government would introduce conscription for military service overseas, subject to its approval at a referendum. The unions opposed conscription believing that it had been used overseas to break down working conditions; in fact no substantial section of organised labour supported Hughes' conscription scheme. In September 1916 the New South Wales executive rejected Hughes' proposal by 21 to 5, expelled him and E.S. Carr from the party and withdrew the endorsements of Holman, Griffith, Hall and Bagnall who had announced support for Hughes.[110] At the parliamentary level the casualties were especially heavy. The 1913 state election had returned 49 Labor MLAs; after the 1917 election, only seventeen of these would be state members; 23 would have been expelled.[111] On 28 October 1916 the referendum was held and conscription was defeated. The party hailed the vote as a 'victory of democracy over militarism'.[112]

The split had removed from the Labor Party many of its most experienced and able parliamentary leaders and Holman and his supporters formed a Nationalist coalition with the opposition in November 1916. The Nationalists comfortably won the 1917 election but Labor still won 33 seats with 46 per cent of the vote. In inner Sydney Labor's representation was unchanged.[113]

Pollution, pestilence and plagues

11

From the 1830s those able to flee from Sydney erected elegant villas on their estates just beyond the city limits, an idyllic world of commanding city views, landscaped grounds and retinues of servants to keep the landed proprietors in the manner to which they had become accustomed.[1] But the city soon spread outwards, closing in on the solitude and seclusion of these semi-rural estates. People were pouring into low-lying localities just beyond the city boundary stones and this unregulated suburban expansion in the 1850s produced a number of dead ends on the street plan.[2] Cheap and insanitary cottages lined the narrow lanes and alleys on Glebe's Bishopgate estate; life here was without the advantages of suburban living as enjoyed by the middle class. It was neither rustic nor romantic.[3] In 1851 a *Sydney Morning Herald* reporter was horrified at what he found in a back lane branching off Parramatta Street:

> outside the tenements, ducks, fowls or pigs are diving into the depths of dung heaps, fetid gutters, etc., and the place is altogether stinking—the smells are overpowering—the people cook in dirt and they sleep in it; they are born, bred and they die in dirt; from the cradle to the grave, they pass through life in filth—the society tolerates it and they look upon it as their inheritance—it was so in the old country.[4]

A Select Committee in 1848 found slaughterhouses near Sussex Street and Blackwattle Swamp extremely offensive to people residing near them and injurious to their health.[5] Dr Francis Campbell told the committee that people living nearby were generally poor, and he mistakenly attributed attacks of typhoid fever to the impurity of the air, to the want of ventilation and the filthiness and smallness of the houses. Neglected cow houses and piggeries, Dr Campbell said, were even more pernicious to health than the slaughterhouses.[6] Frances Campbell's evidence reflected the prevailing miasmic theory that disease was communicated by the noxious vapours or gases which collected in damp sheltered localities or where faecal wastes were deposited. The young Listerians were advancing their ideas of bacterial contagion in the 1890s, though the general populace continued to cling to old beliefs for a time.[7]

Topography became a critical element in suburban development. Elevated home sites favoured with natural drainage (and a view), were coveted by the well-to-do from an early date. These sites were exposed to breezes and fresh air and remote from blighting winds and noxious vapours that emanated from nearby swamps and estuaries.

Ill-health among the poor and more crowded parts of the city and adjoining suburbs was documented in 1867 when a measles epidemic raged with great virulence. Thirteen thousand young children caught the disease, and 70 per cent of the 667 who died lived within the city limits.[8]

Smallpox, cholera, typhoid, diphtheria, scarlatina and measles—the miasmic diseases—were largely the product of an unwholesome environment. Most urban epidemics occurred where people lived crowded together in conditions of material deprivation and poverty, often in close proximity to wharves and factories. The poor ran the highest risk of illness or death.[9] 'In 1875,' wrote T.A. Coghlan, 'Sydney was troubled by an extraordinary visitation of sickness; children died, stricken by diarrhoea and atrophy, pneumonia and bronchitis, diphtheria and scarlatina and measles. Its children were literally decimated.'[10] Sydney, wrote the local press, was an unwholesome place. Seasonal mortality levels in the city were now higher than in London. Infant mortality was 75 per 1,000 in 1875, with the March quarter being the worst for infant deaths. Some 47 per cent of all deaths in the city were of children aged under five, and percentages in the suburbs were even higher.[11] Despite widespread agitation about public health in 1875, the colonial legislature failed to enact any health legislation.[12]

Hospitals and benevolent asylums provided an important service for the sick, injured and dying and the Hospital for Sick Children, opened at Glebe in 1879, was set up to isolate sick children from their overcrowded and insanitary environments.[13] The high incidence of industrial accidents at Balmain led to the establishing of a cottage hospital there in 1885 because 'of the great distance of rowing injured work men to Sydney Hospital'.[14]

Anxieties over public health, however, did produce reports on the poor in crowded parts of Sydney by the Sydney City and Suburban Sewage and Health Board. These covered housing, water and sewerage and more general health issues. In a house-to-house survey of working-class accommodation the Board noted 'scenes of filth and wretchedness of which it is impossible to convey an adequate idea by mere verbal description, however forcible'.[15] Dilapidated houses examined had insufficient air and floor space and few had bathrooms. There were coppers in backyard washrooms but less often tubs, taps and drains. Some houses were sub-let, room by room, to whole families. Overcrowding in these tenements meant if one member of a family contracted an infection, they all caught it. The wretched poverty the committee found hidden away in back lanes mocked the economic optimism of the men of property. Michael Chapman, a committee member, observed in a reflective mood:

> It has been well said that half the world does not know how the other half lives. Neither Dr Reid or myself, though we have both of us lived a great many years in Sydney, could have credited without ocular inspection the terrible state of overcrowding which we witnessed.[16]

Chapman's view was reinforced by F.B. Boyce, appointed rector of St Paul's, Redfern, in 1884. 'I have laboured in industrial and congested areas,' Boyce later wrote, 'and my experience has convinced me that bad living conditions foster drunkenness of all descriptions . . . It is in the squalor of a crowded street that strong drink recruits its material. I have known of many cases in which changed living conditions have meant changed lives.'[17] The squalor of working-class life, in Boyce's view, drove the poorly paid to the pub; he embraced the temperance creed for humanitarian reasons and vigorously advocated slum clearance.

The provision of essential services lagged behind residential expansion in the inner suburbs in the 1880s. These still relied on the pan and cesspit for their sanitation and the results were predictably unhealthy and unaesthetic.[18] Raw sewage was discharged into the harbour and open sewers ran along the lanes fronting tenement housing. Supplies of piped water were irregular and drinkingwater wells were often contaminated by seepage from cesspits. The mayors of the municipalities of Glebe, Balmain and Leichhardt were examined in 1889 by a parliamentary committee about the state of their sewerage and drainage systems. P.C. Lucas explained that Glebe undertook its own sewerage scheme in 1886 because of 'the excessive death-rate that then existed in the borough. Landlords and property-owners had difficulty in getting their houses filled because of the unsavouriness of the place'.[19]

The nature of Balmain's terrain created considerable drainage problems. Mayor E.H. Buchanan told the committee that ordinary house and kitchen slops lay on mud flats at Happy Valley and in Beattie Street, the smells being most offensive in summer. Balmain's nightsoil was emptied from carts into punts and dumped six miles out at sea. 'If there is a heavy wind blowing' at this reception area, 'you certainly get the effluvium,' said the Mayor. Leichhardt was relatively free of typhoid, Benjamin Moore told the committee in 1889. There were, he said, 'less deaths from fever than any borough around', but when his municipality's bilious overflow emptied into White Bay, Rozelle Bay and Iron Cove 'at low water, and when the sun is strong, the smell is very bad'.[20]

The city and inner suburbs were connected to the Nepean water supply in 1888, and an underground sewerage system was connected to the Bondi outfall between 1889 and 1897. The benefits of sanitation and a better water supply contributed significantly to a remarkable decline in the infant mortality rate from the 1890s, with deaths from diarrhoea and associated maladies being greatly reduced. Death rates from typhoid and other epidemic diseases remained high in Sydney's unsewered suburbs.[21] Suburban expansion was in part the consequence of growing population and conversion of land near the city from residential to business use.

Industries producing unpleasant smells were believed to be important causes of ill-health. Boiling-down works, tanneries and other industries associated with processing animal hides and carcasses, and sometimes tobacco and chemical factories, were classified as noxious trades. In 1883 a Royal Commission into Noxious and Offensive Trades heard evidence from 312 witnesses and tabled details concerning 108 suburban premises.[22] Glebe Island abattoir, a

Elliott Bros Chemical Works (on left) and the Balmain Garbage Destructor and Power Station dominate the Rozelle waterfront on Iron Cove in the 1930s. (By courtesy of Standard Publishing House Pty Ltd, Rozelle)

massive polluter of the air and harbour, loomed large before the commission, which agreed that offensive industry should be segregated from the centres of population. Blood was converted to fertiliser in a desiccating plant at Glebe Island and other waste materials were boiled down in a tallow factory there. Blood and offal were dumped into the harbour and cattle, sheep and pigs, driven along suburban streets, represented a serious threat to pedestrians.[23] Basic cleaning procedures were ignored at the abattoir and there was clear evidence of mismanagement. Despite agitation for removal of the abattoir in 1879, a parliamentary committee recommended improvements rather than removal.[24] The stench of Glebe Island permeated Balmain and Glebe and the *Balmain Observer* remained an implacable opponent. However in the 1890s Labor members James Johnson and S.J. Law defended the abattoir, with Johnson accusing council inspectors of persecuting butchers and other meat tradesmen.[25] In 1903 secret overflows from the abattoir were still finding their way into Blackwattle Bay, which was described at times as being 'blood red'.[26]

Above: Glebe Island Abattoir began operating in the early 1850s and became a massive polluter of both the air and the harbour. It was a place neither government nor city authorities were anxious to manage. The abattoir remained a constant source of agitation until it finally closed in about 1916. (*SM*, 22 February 1896)

Right: Slaughterman, Glebe Island Abattoir. His working life was one of dirty, unremitting physical labour and low pay. (*SM*, 22 February 1896)

Piggeries attracted to Glebe Island by the offal available there were prosecuted by Balmain Council and forced out of the area. The same council, however, was reluctant to pursue the nuisances created by large enterprises like Elliott's chemical works and Hutchinson's soap manufactory, perhaps because the proprietors of both concerns had occupied the mayoral chair.[27] Other councils too rarely sought to enforce the common nuisance by-laws. Thomas Dunn's Glebe tannery and John Whiting's boiling-down works at Leichhardt seemed immune to prosecution; both proprietors were local elected representatives.

The most putrid smell, that of rotting human corpses, pervaded the general cemetery at Leichhardt—known as Balmain Cemetery—Mayor James Williams told an inquiry, in 1881.[28]

As populations swelled within a two-mile radius of the city centre, residents were massed closer together. In 1890 a witness told the parliamentary inquiry that was considering the extension of railways into the inner city that 'every person who can afford the time and money will live out of town if he can'.[29] Another inquiry heard a government medical officer explain the exodus to areas further afield in terms of 'freedom from the city's noise and a purer atmosphere than they find there'.[30] Certainly the smells and noises of suburban life were among its most evocative elements.

The energy for cooking and heating was supplied by wood, coal and coke, bought from the horse and cart of fuel merchants or collected by children in their billycarts. It fuelled stoves on which family meals were cooked, clothes were washed in a wood-stoked boiler or copper, bathwater heated in a chip bath-heater, and the house warmed in winter.[31] Grit and carbon from burnt fuel poured from a growing number of factory smokestacks and from thousands of domestic chimneys creating a heavy haze that enveloped the suburbs. New power stations added to the great clouds of smoke. In winter countless horse-drawn carts, cabs, and coaches turned the streets into quagmires. The rattle of harnesses, the shouting of drivers controlling their charges and the piercing noise of iron-shod hooves and wagon wheels on asphalt roads were part of daily life, as were the shrill summonses of factory whistles. Machinery in suburban factories hummed away throughout the day and about every ten minutes the clatter of a tram was heard along the main roads.[32]

Smells were as prevalent as sounds. Local geography and local industry gave each district its own particular odour. The noisome smells from Glebe Island assailed the nostrils of the Balmain and Glebe residents for a long time. Residents in different parts of Balmain lived with the smell of the coalmine, the Sunlight Soap complex and the more pungent aromas from Elliott's chemical works. Different precincts in Glebe were familiar with pleasant odours from Hacksall's Biscuit Co, Dunn's Grose Street tannery and the Magic Soap Works. Jam, pickle and sauce manufacturers left their distinctive odours in Leichhardt as did the meat-packing and preserving firms and Pearson's soap factory. In the evening the tantalising odour of yeast hung around bakeries in every suburb and the air was sweetened by confectioners boiling syrup.[33]

In 1885 the landscape of semi-rural Leichhardt was dotted with 33 dairies; in more closely settled Balmain there were 26; and thirteen in Glebe.[34] Suburban dairies were marginal enterprises with seven cows being the size of the average herd. Some kept a cow in the backyard with fowls, scavenging on vegetable scraps supplemented by cheap hay. A serious outbreak of typhoid in Leichhardt in 1886, in which 38 people caught the fever, was traced to a well polluted by sewage from surrounding houses.[35] The epidemiological inquiry into the outbreak, the first of its kind in Australia, was carried out by Dr John Ashburton Thompson, deputy medical adviser to

Elliott Bros Chemical Works, c.1922. The pungent aromas that poured from the works smoke stacks pervaded this industrial precinct for decades. (*The Laboratories & Chemical Works of Elliott Brothers Limited, Rozelle,* 1922)

White Bay Power Station, 1925. Coal-fired power stations provided the power-generating capacity required for an expanding railway and tramway network. However, they contributed a disproportionately high degree of industrial pollution to the current municipality. (GPO Videodisc-1 16137)

The Balmain Colliery headframe adjoined Birchgrove Public School and operated from about 1900 to 1931. Headmaster William Easton observed that the noise and coaldust from the colliery drove 'out to the other suburbs all who can get away'. The headframe stood on the skyline for many years after 1931. (Balmain Association Collection)

the government.[36] The particular well on a Helsarmel dairy was also fed by drainage from two neighbouring cemeteries and Dr Thompson warned people not to drink water from domestic wells. Most dairies operated under insanitary conditions and were considered 'neglected', but by 1889 only five dairies fell into this category. The water supplies of eighteen local dairies were sampled by the Board of Health in 1890. Two had wells fit only for liquid manure, three were doubtful, but the rest were satisfactory.[37]

Milk was found to be an efficient vehicle for the communication of various infectious diseases and, as a direct consequence of the Leichhardt outbreak, the *Dairies Supervision Act* was enacted in 1886. Most of the 537 dairies in the metropolitan combined districts in 1901 used pan closets and only 20 per cent had a ready supply of hot water for cleaning purposes. At corner stores, milk was ladled out to customers from open buckets, exposed to flies and dust, but by 1914 the conditions under which milk was produced and retailed had improved.[38] Eleven dairies were still operating in Leichhardt in 1918 but the number had shrunk to two by 1932.[39]

Francis Adams saw the inner ring of Sydney suburbs as a harsh and sterile environment in 1893: 'a congerie of bare brick habitations . . . an arid desolate waste . . . utterly unrelieved by tree or grass where the shoddy contractor despotises in his vilest and most hateful shape'.[40] Though a well-defined mosaic of middle-class, lower middle-class and working-class neighbourhoods remained within two miles of the city, a gradual change in the social composition of these suburbs was under way.

The bubonic plague outbreak in Sydney in 1900 was concentrated in a precinct between Darling Harbour, George Street and Central Railway where wharf labourers, seamen, unskilled workers and self-employed tradesmen and their families lived cheek-by-jowl in dilapidated small cottages, overcrowded tenements and boarding houses.[41] Intermixed with these dwellings were produce stores, warehouses, insanitary basements and yards and pervading the whole area was the sickly smell of rotten refuse and faeces. It was a quarter described some years earlier as a centre of 'dirt, disease and death'.[42] Plague and poverty were closely associated. Most of the 303 people who contracted the plague were working-class males living in conditions that harboured infected rats and fleas. Of those, 103 died. The plague caused widespread social and economic dislocation.[43] The government placed areas in the city and in Chippendale, Glebe and Redfern under quarantine and undertook a massive clean-up program. Many of the habitations were found to be structurally defective, without adequate ventilation and lacking basic sanitary and washing facilities. Within four months 54,000 tonnes of garbage had been destroyed, nearly 4,000 premises were inspected and cleansed, and about 45,000 rats killed.[44]

The period between 1901 and 1911 in Sydney was one of extraordinary expansion as the metropolitan population swelled by 32.2 per cent and a tramway network covering 200 miles was laid down. The housing shortage was, however, exacerbated by the extension of the city infrastructure and by the demolitions that followed the plague in 1900. Resumption of inner-city housing at Athlone Place and elsewhere dispossessed 9,000 people who lived in 1,760 dwellings.[45] A sense of uneasiness among some parliamentarians led to the appointment in 1908 of a Royal Commission for the Improvement of the City of Sydney and Its Suburbs, and to another commission dealing with local government (1913). John Sulman, J.D. Fitzgerald, F.B. Boyce and other members of the town-planning movement largely set the agenda for the inquiries and these members reflected the hierarchy of concerns expressed. The commission on the city and suburbs sat for twelve months and gave special attention to transport problems. The solution it sought involved a railway system and street widening, as well as improvements designed to beautify the city. The 'provision of decent home conditions for the working classes' was well down the list. Attention was focused especially on Wexford Street and Athlone Place where the commission recommended resumption and wholesale demolition for industrial use.[46] The evangelical zeal and patronising attitude of some of the witnesses ('I do not see why workmen's dwellings should not contain bathrooms') failed to address the shortage of low-income housing. It was only J.D. Fitzgerald's participation in the inquiry that ensured the inclusion of social welfare goals of workers' housing and slum clearance.[47] The commission favoured the suburban ideal on 'social and hygienic grounds'. Those workers whose occupations did not require them to live close to the job, they said, should be moved out of the inner city; their findings represented a condemnation of the pattern of working-class life that had developed in the inner suburbs.[48]

Average weekly rentals of working-class housing surged between 1905 and 1914, and the McGowen Labor government, elected in 1910, concerned that real wages were being eroded by rising rent, established a Housing Board in 1912 and enacted a *Fair Rents Act* in 1915 which stabilised rentals.[49] R.F. Irvine, a radical economics professor, was appointed by W.A. Holman in 1912 to investigate the provision of workingmen's housing in Europe and America. Irvine returned to report on the 'Housing Conditions of New South Wales', where he identified the major problems as lack of planning, overcrowding, sub-standard accommodation and the inability of many to afford suitable housing.[50]

Working-class women were part of the labour force (all able-bodied members of the working class needed to work), and did what they could to help their husbands squeeze out a living. It was difficult for them to sell their labour outside the home, since work places did not cater for children and babies. Mothers took in washing and ironing, did mending, sewed clothes, cleaned lodgings, minded children, did piece-work for the clothing industry or took in boarders.[51]

The average issue of married women in New South Wales was seven in the 1870s, but couples anxious to avoid the strain and economic responsibility of raising children increasingly resorted to contraceptive techniques to curb family size. The 1903 Royal Commission which inquired into the falling birth-rate condemned women for using birth control to avoid their 'natural responsibilities'. The moralising commissioners accused women of putting their selfish desires before the nation's need.[52] The experience of childbirth was fraught with danger, and the wives of blue-collar workers relied on family and neighbourhood networks for support during pregnancy and childbirth. Kin and friends kept the home warm by lighting fires in every room, they did the washing and ironing and cooked meals. Two things could not come quickly enough for many of these women: the change of life, and an old-age pension, which from 1901 they could claim when they reached 60 years of age.[53]

Free kindergartens, begun in 1896 in order to improve the lot of inner-city children, became a tool of urban social reform. Parents of these children were described as being drawn from the 'lowest strata of society', and it was hoped that through the children and the missionary zeal of the teachers families could be taught middle-class norms.[54] Kindergartens were established in Glebe in 1905 and Balmain in 1910.[55]

Dr W.G. Armstrong pioneered infant welfare work in inner Sydney in the early years of Federation. In 1914 Armstrong persuaded the Labor Minister for Public Health, Fred Flowers, to set up a network of government baby health clinics and by 1918 there were 28 baby clinics in existence.[56] The official view was that poorer mothers especially were incapable of rearing their children without guidance. Government measures were taken to encourage women to have more children, with the introduction of a £5 baby bonus in 1912.

Motherhood, according to the official view, was a woman's natural role, but she had to be educated to fulfil it and in 1905 domestic science was made compulsory for girls in public schools. There was a growing awareness of the need for children to have high levels of nutrition, and baby clinics provided inexperienced mothers with education in baby care, and especially feeding techniques. They did not recommend the use of fresh cow's milk, opting for powdered milk supplemented by fresh fruit juice. The quality of the public milk supply was so poor that mothers were advised, as late as 1923, to feed their children with dried milk preparations.[57]

Baby weighing day at Balmain Baby Clinic, 1916. Baby clinics were designed to provide inexperienced mothers with an education in baby care. (GPO Videodisc-1 Still 31710)

Coming and going

12

In the late 1880s the social geography of Sydney's inner suburbs entered another phase, a pattern not unlike a series of rings on the townscape. The extension of tram and train tracks to outlying areas created new suburban alternatives, and Protestant clergymen lamented a steady exodus of members from once genteel suburbs.[1] The middle class found a new way of life well beyond the central business district (according to Balmain's Town Clerk). Most of the 'better class' had left Balmain but dispersal of industry and commerce was largely confined to suburbs immediately adjoining the city proper. The advance of industry into old residential precincts meant some deterioration in living conditions, though noxious trades had come under better control, and sanitary provision and health had improved.

The process of building up Balmain, Glebe and adjoining areas was nearing completion. It was accompanied by a gradual change in the social complexion of these suburbs. All still retained well-to-do streets occupied by people who owned their own enterprises—doctors, lawyers and members of the newer professions. The number of boarding houses was increasing and more rooms in large dwellings were being let. Relatively low rentals provided accommodation for a growing number of widows, deserted wives and other hard-up families.[2]

Contemporary handbooks and directories give some clues to a suburb's social standing. Suburban respectability was largely a matter of the right address, and a residence close to the city was no longer a source of smug satisfaction. Balmain in 1900 was described as the 'Home of the aquatic world and working classes. Some of the most extensive workshops of the colony are located here.'[3] The perceived character of the other three municipalities was much less clearly defined until about 1914. By then the social pattern was set in a way that would not be drastically revised until the 1970s. Glebe, by 1914, was 'mostly a large industrial and manufacturing centre', though it still had a fashionable part, Glebe Point. Annandale had a similar standing – an elite in Johnston and Annandale streets but the rest of the place was 'mostly an industrial centre'; and Leichhardt, by 1921, was proud of its mixed industrial and commercial character.[4]

Casual workers tried to remain close to the city where they could readily pick up a few days' work, walking to and from varying places of employment. Their choice of localities was largely limited by their incomes. This intimacy of work and social life bred a sense of place and made for easy industrial and political organisation. The Labor Leagues in Balmain, Glebe, Leichhardt and Annandale brought with them the rituals of working-class life—a world centred around the pub and union office, and a household dominated by a male bread-winner.[5] Maritime unionists in Balmain thrashed out industrial disputes in local pubs. Politics at the local branch level was volatile in 1891–92, but many Labor men had the distinct perspective of an underclass looking up at a vast and hierarchical network of class relations and institutions. Socialist Francis Adams observed in 1893 that there was an 'ever-widening and ever deepening gulf between rich and poor' and with 'astonishing speed and intensity the process of aggregation of wealth operated to bring labour and capital into bitter conflict'.[6]

Sydney, with a large floating population of dock workers, seamen and seasonal labourers, was a reception centre for thousands of immigrants. They found lodgings in clusters of cheap rooming houses and boarding houses in a narrow transitional zone around the waterfront, railway station and central business district.

Chicago sociologist Ernest Burgess provided a rich sociological image of a typical city divided into physical zones, each of them representing a step in the assimilation process of immigrants, and he presented the concentric zone theory as a universal phenomenon, applicable to all groups in the city. 'In a zone of deterioration and encircling the central business section,' Burgess wrote, 'are always to be found the so-called "slums", a deteriorating area of rooming-house districts, the purgatory of lost souls … The slums are … crowded to overflowing with immigrant colonies.'[7]

Many of the immigrants disembarking at Sydney had come with the idea of bettering themselves, and the belief in upward social mobility was a potent influence. 'The artisan who can earn ten shillings a day,' wrote American journalist Henry Franklyn,

> by eight hours' work in a climate where the interruptions to outdoor work are few and far between, and who can obtain board and lodging for fifteen shillings a week, has only to practise sobriety and thrift, in order to elevate himself into a position of a director of other men's labour in the course of a very few years … No working man who is prudent, temperate and industrious need occupy a house that is not his own.[8]

W.F. Morrison and Everard Digby took up Franklyn's theme in 1888, chronicling stories of immigrants from the British Isles who made good in a new land.[9] As Charles Fahey and Bill Rubenstein have shown, only a few made a fortune and even the 'men of mark' had their share of setbacks.[10]

The development of commerce and finance in the 1880s increased Sydney's clerical workforce by over 130 per cent. Clerical workers were employed by both business and government and, together with an expanding number of schoolteachers, railway and post office officials, they formed a growing lower adjunct to the middle class. In 1891 P.C. Lucas noted the increasing number of people employed 'as assistants in warehouses, clerks, Government officials and suchlike persons whose business brings them into town every morning'.[11] Rapid urbanisation also swelled the demand for labour in transport and communications (telegraphists, tram drivers), services (lift drivers, office boys) and construction (building labourers, railway navvies) and a range of new and mobile occupations.

Respectability underpinned much of the ideology of social class. The clerk sat uneasily

Glebe Championship Eight, 1900. This Glebe crew was composed of white-collar workers and small businessmen. The definition of an amateur oarsman precluded manual workers from competing in Association regattas before 1903. *Rear* (left to right): Bob May, Ainslie Hopkinson, Bill Gillies, Tom Kermode (trainer). *Front* (left to right): Harry Williams, Eugene Renard, Jack McGregor (stroke), Ted Strom, Charlie Paull. *Seated on floor*: Arthur Sewell (cox). (Max Solling Collection)

between the middle and working classes; he possessed a good hat, as well as a fancy waistcoat on which to display his watch. The pay of clerical workers compared unfavourably with that of many trades (bank clerks were paid ten shillings per week in 1888 when labourers were getting six shillings a day), while promotion came slowly within a system that demanded conformity to certain standards of dress and lifestyle. A product of a rigid status system, characterised by deference and authority, a clerk moved cautiously through various levels of authority in the quest for status, respectability and a higher income.[12]

Keeping up appearances was important. Most men possessed a Sunday suit (invariably a blue indigo one made in Germany), and to appear on Sunday in work clothes was to admit impending destitution. Women wore their most elegant outfits on weekends, promenading with their menfolk up and down main suburban thoroughfares.[13] Opportunities for material advancement for most were limited, and the labourer, earning about one shilling and threepence or less per hour, languished at the bottom of the occupational ladder and was likely to remain there. A labourer's wife with dressmaking skills could earn three shillings a day with fares in 1907, but there was little part-time work close to home or available for unskilled married women.

In the 1880s groups of working-class youths, who adopted distinctive patterns of dress, speech and behaviour, gathered on street corners or lounged about the doors of shops. They were called 'larrikins' and they found recruits among those who were unable to find jobs or who rejected the life of monotonous and low-paid labour that confronted them. The men wore short coats with a velvet collars, open vests and narrow ties, bell-bottomed trousers and soft felt hats with broad brims. The women favoured a costume that featured feathers and high-heeled shoes. They often mocked and abused the respectable or made rowdy displays, and their illegal and anti-social acts represented a delinquent way of life that raised middle-class anxieties. Francis Adams regarded the larrikin as more dangerous and brazen than any English hooligan.

The image of delinquents who would avenge themselves on society drew strong responses from the respectable and wealthy:

> The Glebe push . . . are the terrors of the streets after dark. The larrikin has nothing manly about him. He is a sharp, active, horsy-looking, vicious cad; he very rarely does any work but mostly lives upon the lowest means possible—by the vice of others. The 'larrikinesses' are melancholy creatures. One wonders what their mothers could have been. The larrikiness sometimes works; often she lives by bullying her parents and compelling them to support her and her low companions.[14]

But the popular view of the larrikin was at odds with a more sober appraisal by police. Superintendent Larkins claimed in 1900 that most of the young men in the pushes were 'earning an honest livelihood during the day and assemble at street corners in the evenings'.[15]

In the 1890s closely-knit pushes replaced the casual street corner crowds, with each gang drawn from particular streets or pubs. Each push tended to derive its members from, and concentrate its activities in, its own territory. They fought one another for control of communal territory.

As a boy, H.M. Moran had observed the pushes and wrote:

> They were made up of hard swearing violent urchins who waged a sort of guerilla warfare with rival bands and committed isolated acts of terrorism . . . The weapons of the pushes were only sticks and stones; there was an ammunition dump of blue metal on many roads. The two pushes we knew best were the 'Stars' and the 'Darlos', rival denizens of two suburbs which adjoined the University Park, their great battleground . . . they had hard visages and foul tongues. A whistle would be sounded as a signal when the quarry came in sight, and then like Arabs the band would appear from nowhere.[16]

Tom Durkin's cartoon of a larrikin dancing the Schottische, 1894. The larrikin adopted a distinctive pattern of dress, speech and behaviour. Men wore short coats with velvet collars, open vests and narrow ties, bell-bottomed trousers and soft felt hats with broad brims. The women favoured a costume that featured feathers and high-heeled shoes. (Reproduced from the *Bulletin* centenary issue, 29 January 1980)

A sense of place was strong in working-class neighbourhoods, with their banter and 'characters', especially in precincts near Mort's Dock, in Leichhardt South around Excelsior Street, and on St Phillip's and Bishopthorpe estates in Glebe. Although it gradually became less common to live and work in the same locality, urban change tended to accentuate residential solidarities. The working class was not an undifferentiated sociable mass, and housing estates had their own complicated hierarchies of rank and respectability. Streets had their rough and respectable ends, with subtle gradations in between which were properly understood only by the residents. Within their own particular neighbourhood, a resident might often know a large number of people by name, and even more by face.[17]

Only fragmentary evidence survives about ordinary folk who belonged to neighbourhoods close to the city. They rented small dwellings, frequently changed residence and are absent from probate records. These denizens of the inner city were constantly on the move because they needed jobs or hoped to find better paying ones.[18] Moving was not a problem as they had few possessions to take with them, and they leapfrogged from house to house and from neighbourhood to neighbourhood looking for additional space or cheaper rent.

Moving induced a sense of insecurity. Families tried hard to create a social fabric that would afford some measure of security and to fit themselves into some form of network. On moving to a new neighbourhood, the housewife set about learning its ways and standards, be it Short Street, Balmain, Rofe Street, Leichhardt, or Mitchell Street, Glebe. She weighed up acquaintances she made on her daily rounds. A 'good neighbour' would assist in an emergency, but neighbourly solidarity was very much a reciprocal arrangement. Neighbourhood meant more than houses and streets; it meant the mutually beneficial relationship one formed with others. As much work was casual, many working-class families had an uncertain and fluctuating income. The threat of unemployment (and consequent poverty) produced a need to become known and trusted. In times of stress, illness or unemployment, the close-knit pattern of collective life was the working-class family's greatest protection.[19]

The basic-needs wage for labourers in 1907 was two guineas a week, just enough to make them content with the social order, but with little provision for old age or unforeseen distress. In 1913 Justice Heydon heard evidence from eighteen inner-Sydney housewives in an inquiry to establish the living or basic wage. He collected much material on the cost of food and clothing, and on aspects of housing. One housewife, Anne Fairs of 17 Broughton Street, Glebe, told the inquiry, 'we live on bread and butter'. Bread, potatoes and meat were the staple diet for many. A two-pound loaf cost three and one-half pence; the statistician estimated that a family of four people would consume 22 pounds of bread a week; it was eaten at all meals. For Mrs Fairs it was a battle to keep the bellies of her four hungry boys full.[20] She had only one pint of milk a day ladled out to her boys and bought a shilling's worth of fruit on Saturdays, which was gone the next day. Potato was the commonest vegetable but Mrs Fairs bought a cabbage daily because she believed that greens were especially nutritious. In 1914 Justice Heydon declared 48 shillings a week as the living or basic wage.

It was the role of the wife to maintain the stability of the home and she had to exercise both frugality and ingenuity in balancing the family budget. Rent comprised a major part, taking about one-quarter of the family's income. Usually on Thursday evening the husband handed the pay packet to his wife, who gave him an agreed sum for pocket money; she then had to pay the rent and feed and clothe the family with what was left. It was always a struggle to make ends meet, and when the money ran out the housewife would resort to the neighbourhood store for credit or to the pawn shop for a loan.[21] If she had established a reputation for reliability with her storekeeper, her family would not go hungry. The corner store was more than just a source of credit. People found information at

Caroline Janet Miller Kernohan and her father William Miller (joiner) stand behind Annie Miller, who is holding six-months-old David Kernohan, 1912. Extended families, who often lived in the same house or the same street, were a feature of inner-city life. Here, four generations of the Miller family lived within a stone's throw of each other. (Max Solling Collection)

the corner store that was important in helping them face the daily problems of family life. It was also a kind of confessional where the conventional wisdom of the shopkeeper was a source of reassurance, a place where a worried mother could have a chat over all sorts of problems.[22]

The trade union revival from about 1904, stimulated by compulsory arbitration, strengthened inner-city Labor Leagues, but the lives of many workers continued to be plagued by low wages, urban blight, family breakdown and crime. Trade unionism aimed to protect workers' livelihoods, though by 1900 fewer than one worker in ten belonged to a trade union. Poor conditions of work for the 'lower classes' were accepted in colonial society as 'natural' in a laissez-faire state. The Sydney Harbour Trust made no provision for water taps, toilets, or shelter sheds for workers on the city waterfront.[23]

Most wharf labourers were former seamen who accepted lower earnings for the benefits of a more regular home life. Wharf labouring was casual and intermittent, often with heavy demand one day and unemployment the next. It was important for these men to get as much extra money as they could during the season to tide them and their families over the lean spells of the other months. For this dirty, dangerous and heavy work, with a high accident rate, wharf labourers were paid 1s 3d an hour and overtime (at 1s 9d per hour) was paid after eight hours' continuous work. The longer the hours—whether the work involved loading wool, wheat, frozen meat and other foodstuffs, coal, timber, cement and other valuable cargoes—the better the pay. Families of the strongest men ('Bulls'), who earned much more than the basic wage of two guineas a week, had no financial worries.[24]

Wheat-carrying was seasonal summer work and shipping agents were always anxious that ships' holds be emptied as quickly as possible. The wharf labourer caught the wheat bag at the bottom of the chute and deftly swung it across the shoulders. Though the regulation bag was designed to hold 240 pounds, they generally weighed in excess of 300 pounds. The speed at which a bag could be taken and stowed increased the reward a labourer received, and some men could shift a bag a minute—that meant 14,400 pounds an hour, or 50 tons in an eight-hour day.[25] It was work only for strong men, who often worked 24-hour shifts, but it took a heavy toll on their bodies. They were frequently hospitalised. At the beginning of the season, heavy weights, excessive speed and long hours took all the flesh off the shoulders of John Gildea. The heavy bags so damaged his stomach that he was unable to digest his food properly and he rubbed fat into his stiff skin, During the season Gildea's weight fell dramatically from 12.5 stone to 10 stone and he told an inquiry in 1906 that 'I am not as good a man as I was a couple of years ago'. Doctors found the ribs of some wharf labourers overlapped, and 40-year old John McMahon's shoulder had a hole in it big enough to 'put an egg in'. Wharf labouring conditions altered little, the only significant improvement being the limiting of the weight of grain bags to 200 pounds.[26]

Domestic service, the major paid work for women, was a class relationship between a middle-class mistress and the working-class servant. The mistress expected deference and obedience.[27] Girls from poor families were prepared for domestic service at home. They received training in house work, laundry and other chores. They learnt to be resourceful in the care of smaller children. They learnt to expect very little for themselves and to comply with parental decisions, which economically were reinforced by the fact of the family's poverty. These features of a girl's life help to explain why long hours and small financial returns could so often be tolerated.[28]

Domestics were treated as inferiors, often called names that went with the job, made to wear uniforms and paid a pittance for long hours of labour. General servants worked a 68-hour week and were paid between ten and sixteen shillings a week in 1910. The percentage of the population employed in domestic service had declined by 1911 as the prejudice against the occupation of a servant hardened.[29]

The absence of trade unions in the clothing industry and for domestics was a recipe for low wages. Few were more exploited than women outworkers. Mary Edwards, a dressmaker with twenty years' experience, fetched materials from Grace Bros to make blouses and ladies' coats at home at piece rates. For more than 50 hours of labour at her sewing machine she received £1 14s 0d per week, and often less than that.[30]

Left to right, sisters Florence Eliza Stokes and Lydia Starr in 1899. As domestic servants they were treated as inferiors, often called names that went with the job and paid a pittance for long hours of labour. (Max Solling Collection)

Moral and thrifty behaviour was the ethos of a developing, upwardly mobile, middle-class society. Middle-class values stressed the virtues of marriage and family, civility, property and civic pride. This was clearly distinguished from the culture of the working class which, reinforced by a strong Irish influence, displayed an intolerance of respectability and manners, a hostility to authority and an idealisation of male comradeship.[31] The working class enjoyed diversions, such as drinking and gambling, that made life tolerable. Working people had largely turned their backs on the churches and were conspicuous by their absence from an array of mutual improvement associations that peddled recipes for success.[32]

The wife of a working man remained tied to the home, doing all she could to help her husband squeeze out a living. Crowded living conditions and the struggle to make ends meet were her lot in life, and she displayed an extraordinary ability to manage with very little.

The ideal of self-help gave rise to institutions of mutual aid, and friendly societies saved many from the humiliation of receiving charity in times of need, playing a critical role in the network of social welfare in a society with no workers' compensation, unemployment relief or old-age pensions. In 1873 about 83 per cent of lodge members were engaged in manual occupations; few members had a higher social status that those of small tradesmen or clerks.[33] Artisans were well represented in the lodges but the middle class was generally missing. In return for a weekly contribution of one shilling and sixpence friendly societies provided lodge doctors, allowances for time off work and sometimes funeral benefits. Lodge contributions were beyond the financial reach of workers without regular employment. These people had to seek treatment at hospitals staffed by honorary doctors, and if the poor male breadwinner was afflicted by serious injury or illness his family faced certain destitution.[34]

Lively and democratic friendly societies had a social life of their own, meeting weekly or fortnightly, and the dinners, rituals, processions, excursions and festivals helped promote a kind of class consciousness for the respectable tradesman or clerk.

Friendly societies reached their peak in 1913, when their beneficiaries numbered 778,000 in New South Wales, or 42 per cent of the state's population.[35] Glebe had seven local lodges in 1897.[36] There were eight local friendly societies in Leichhardt in 1921, with all the major societies—Grand United, Independent Order, Foresters, the Order of Druids and Catholic Guild—represented. The Leichhardt societies had at least 4,500 members on their rolls, but the lodges cast a much wider net than that since membership figures could be multiplied by four, at least, to determine the total number of people receiving health protection.[37] A number of societies established their own dispensaries because of the high cost of medicines. Within twelve months of the Balmain United Friendly Society Dispensary opening in 1885, there were no less than twelve affiliated lodges with 1,500 members. Freed from the pressure to make profits, and under the direct control of the members, the dispensary, it was estimated, had achieved a 20 per cent saving to members.[38] The two-storey Leichhardt and Petersham United Friendly Societies Dispensary in Parramatta Road was an impressive sandstone building with public halls and lodge rooms. During the 1919 influenza epidemic the 650-member strong Leichhardt lodge paid out £200 of claims in one fortnight.[39] Medical officers in the Balmain dispensary and the Glebe dispensary prescribed drugs to members, wives and families six days a week, and their rooms were frequently filled with people.

Consumer co-operative societies did not develop in New South Wales except in mining areas and in other solid working-class areas like Balmain. Workers' co-operative enterprises sought to replace capitalist relations of production at the workplace level. A large number of co-operative ventures grew out of strikes in the 1890s—laundries, bakeries and cooperages.[40] The objectives of the Balmain Co-operative Society, formed in 1877, were to:

> import or purchase wholesale articles of general consumption and utility and to retail them at the lowest possible prices consistent with proper regard to the protection of the interests of the Association; and to make arrangements with manufacturers, importers and others to supply at wholesale or reduced prices, articles not kept by the Association.[41]

The 1877 co-operative had failed by 1894 but the strength of working-class traits of co-operation and solidarity in Balmain ensured the viability of its successor. Founded in 1902, the new Balmain Co-operative Society established branches in six other suburbs and was the state's third largest co-operative in 1910; it ceased to exist in 1936.[42]

The opening of moving picture shows in the suburbs about 1910 had a dramatic impact on local folk. In the evening more and more husbands were escorting their wives to the 'pictures'. A seat in the stalls cost threepence, and one in the dress circle sixpence.[43] Young men met their girlfriends and romance blossomed in the darkened privacy of the local picture show. But the cinema was not without its detractors. Publicans grumbled that it was ruining their business, while local clergy, and some councillors, saw it as a pernicious influence that would lead residents down the path of moral decay.⁴⁴

Publicans offered a range of games—darts, quoits, billiards and bagatelle—to attract custom and were active in the formation of football and cycling clubs. Some enterprising publicans arranged boxing matches. The working-class tradition of street fighting was embraced by the pastime clubs in the inner suburbs from about 1905 when they underwent a resurgence. Working men rolled up in force to see their local heroes do battle in the hempen square, the main event being a 20-round contest. Singing, exhibitions of skipping and the local brass band enlivened the evening. Admission charges were sixpence and one shilling. The patrons of the pastime clubs were a 'goodly class' who, near the end of 1907, were said to be 'at home practising on their dumb bells and other implements of physical culture in order to get up their muscles for the slaughter of the Christmas rooster'.⁴⁵

Brass bands were a separate part of the musical world, associated with working-class performers and audiences, and largely ignored by orthodox musicians. Primitive Methodist and volunteer rifle corps bands enlivened suburban communities in the 1860s and were soon joined by processions of friendly societies led by their own bands. In 1865, for example, a multitude of Sunday school children from St Barnabas's was accompanied by the German and Fife Band to Market Street Wharf as they headed off on their annual picnic.⁴⁶ The Salvation Army adapted the brass band to its own particular purpose but other bands broke from the socio-religious mould. Town bands, like Balmain Alliance and the Glebe Brass Band were busy playing at regattas and football matches.⁴⁷

Bandsmen enjoyed the camaraderie of this exclusively male institution as well as the pleasures and challenges of making music.⁴⁸ The bands had chequered histories, as these independent entities, created by a strong group of local people, survived only as long as their members had the will and means to carry on. The growth of brass bands was nurtured by instrument makers and music publishers.

The pub, always open and nearby, was the social institution of the male working class, as we have seen in Chapter 8, and occupied a pivotal position in the world of sport. Pubs were places where men both played games and talked about them and where organised team sports were integrated into the pattern of collective life. Games playing was a staple part of local culture.

Rugby League clubs were established at Glebe (1908), Balmain (1908) and Annandale (1910). It was the working man's game, and its structure

Leichhardt Brass Band, winners of the Bathurst contest, 1918. Municipal bands were symbols of local identity and pride and their achievements at the highest competitive level reflected a well-founded brass-band culture. (By courtesy of Carol Liston)

The Unity Hall Hotel, on the corner of Darling and Beattie streets, Balmain, was a conspicuous landmark on the suburb's early townscape. Built in 1875, this photograph was taken in 1907. (Peter Reynolds Collection)

was based on local rivalries. Local supporters were unashamedly partisan; they came to see their men win:

> Wentworth Park crowds are always demonstrative. They never hesitate to show on which side of the fence their sympathies lie. So when the play was at its fiercest on Saturday, the crowd yelled 'Red, red, red', to encourage the local champions. Eastern Suburbs had a good following but it was Glebe's native heath and it was Glebe's day out.[49]

Unskilled and semi-skilled workers were predominant among the men who played for Balmain, Glebe and Annandale. They gained self-esteem by excelling on the playing field.[50] They often received their only chance in the sporting arena. League produced a sub-culture that helped to further a kind of local consciousness; it made men feel they belonged to the community through the activities of the local team. Saturday afternoon League was their food and their drink. 'Chook' Fraser, 'Chunky' Burge, 'Junker' Robinson and 'Bingeye' Benson were fellow sub-urbanites whom supporters often knew personally.

The 'professional' nature of Rugby League was more akin to our meaning of 'semi-professional'. First-graders received a proportion of the gate between 1911 and 1920 and they were happy to get £3 or £4 for a match.[51] League emerged as a major spectator sport by 1911 and the fierce desire of local partisans to see their men win often led to clashes with rival groups of supporters.[52] The value the game placed on masculinity, with its stress on toughness, stamina and independence, was part of League's appeal to working-class communities. It provided for some the only excitement in a week spent in monotonous and exhausting labour, and may also

Balmain Rugby League footballers and supporters. 'Wee Georgie' Robinson (*far left*), Harold Matthews (*hand on hip*), Bill Maizey (*with hat tilted back*), George Bishop (*arms folded*), Harry Witton (*third from right*) and others congregate outside a city court house where some of them had to appear after an 'incident' at Birchgrove Oval. (Balmain Association Collection)

have acted as a safety valve, a socially acceptable means by which labourers could work off their aggressive instincts.

Amateur rowing clubs were established at Glebe (1879), Balmain (1882) and Leichhardt (1887). The sport attracted elite patronage and popular support. The New South Wales Rowing Association adopted a restrictive definition of amateur oarsmen that excluded manual workers.[53] Working men who wanted to row established their own club, the Balmain Working Men's Club (1886), but they were unable to compete in any of the Association's regattas.[54] Their exclusion was justified on the ground that they had an unfair physical advantage over more delicately nurtured competitors. The Leichhardt club was something of a hybrid, run on the 'lines of a true democracy, as the manual labourer and the brain toiler' could both join.[55]

From the beginning the restrictive amateur definition did not lie easily with the Balmain and Glebe clubs, and their delegates were at the forefront of moves to open up the sport to a broader range of occupations. Captains of Balmain and Glebe, John Symington and Cec Farran, were instrumental in 1903 in amending the definition so as to admit workers. The larger city clubs, far from pleased, announced that manual workers would not be admitted 'at any price' to their clubs.[56]

Throughout the nineteenth century neighbourhoods near the city were predominantly pedestrian, street-corner societies, but after Federation improved and cheaper tram and train travel helped break down the parochialism of suburban life. People identified with their community, with its own social network and complement of community facilities, and the pattern of collective life in Annandale, Balmain, Glebe and Leichhardt focused on the church and public house, the corner store and pawnbroker, friendly society and working man's institute.

A distinctive class culture could be discerned in the inner-suburban communities of Sydney on the eve of the outbreak of war in 1914. Any sporting club taking the name of a suburb attracted a tribal loyalty, something clearly displayed at Rugby League games.

13 A call to arms, 1914–1918

Australia was in the middle of an election campaign when war broke out in Europe in the summer of 1914. Residents of working-class communities within the shadow of the City of Sydney had seldom ventured far beyond the confines of street-corner societies, but the European conflict would help break down the cultural isolation of their lives. It also brought suffering, dislocation and change. The response of Australia to the war was immediate and eager. Andrew Fisher, leader of the Labor opposition, pledged his country to 'stand beside our own and help defend her to the last man and last shilling',[1] and the Governor-General informed London of the 'indescribable enthusiasm and entire unanimity throughout Australia' for the Imperial cause.[2] He ignored a few radical socialists who perceived the war as another dimension of capitalist exploitation as workers suffered merely for the economic gain of the ruling class. They denounced it as a conflict between rival capitalist and imperial regimes in Europe. 'We hope no wave of jingo madness will sweep over the land,' the *Australian Worker*, in a cautious mood, wrote, 'unbalancing the judgement of its leaders, and inciting its population to wild measures, spurred on by the vile press'. It went on to warn that 'thousands of unemployed will be created; unscrupulous greed will seize the opportunity to raise the necessaries of life to famine prices'.[3]

Early pro-war rhetoric in the local press, after the country found itself at war on the morning of 5 August 1914, praised the resistance of 'gallant little Belgium' and the nobility of Britain and France in accepting their treaty obligations and opposing the beastliness of the Hun. A contingent of 20,000 soldiers was offered for a conflict that, it was thought, would be over in 1915. It became evident, however, that the allies could expect no quick victory. Municipal representatives in Annandale, Balmain, Glebe and Leichhardt pledged their loyalty to the Empire when the nation was called on to defend England. When Balmain's Mayor Henry Swan proposed the pledge, councillors rose to their feet and 'sang the National Anthem besides giving three cheers for the King', and the Minister for Defence was offered 'all parks, pavilions, buildings and grounds under council's control in Glebe'.[4]

Men began queuing at recruiting tables; the desire to volunteer was strong. Rigorous medical examination rejected many of the Empire's youth who had unfilled teeth, flat feet, corns, puny chests or who were under 5 feet 6 inches tall.[5] Others were too young or too old. Rejected men formed an association and wore a large badge to cover their civilian shame. Working-class men living in the shadow of the city proper were the most likely to enlist, for the frontiers of opportunity had narrowed for many who at or after the age of fourteen years went to work. Boys went out in search of a trade, and once they served their apprenticeship they were sacked. The unemployment rate had reached 11 per cent by Christmas 1914, and the army pay of six shillings a day added to the lure of travel and adventure.[6] Death or incapacitation of breadwinners, whose families often lived from week to week, inflicted great deprivation on their dependants.

Butcher James McGlynn, who enlisted in Balmain, was killed at Lone Pine on 8 August 1915, leaving a wife and five-year-old son. Without the breadwinner, Lillian McGlynn was dependent on the charity of her mother's family with whom they lived. The widow's pension she received, about ten shillings a week, was only one-quarter of the average weekly wage, a level of benefit less than that paid in Britain and France.[7]

Working-class people in the present Municipality of Leichhardt, without money to mitigate the hardships of war, would bear a very heavy burden. The ranks of the first AIF were filled by many unemployed working-class men. Enthusiasm to volunteer can be explained partly in terms of love of Empire and hatred of Germany. The Empire was in crisis and everyone was expected to do their duty. Some were keen 'to get to grips with those inhuman brutes to do something to help wipe out such an infamous nation'.[8] For others it was an overseas trip of a lifetime, a thing of boyhood dreams. Ordinary folk who had grown up with an uncertain future enlisted for many reasons—loneliness, family trouble, public opinion and so forth.

The entry of Turkey into the war persuaded the British command to divert the 'colonial' contingent to Egypt where they were grouped into an army corps, the ANZAC. They trained hard in the sands of Egypt but camp life was dreary. The Wadir, Cairo's brothel quarter, was an exciting place for some of the 'six-bob-a-day tourists', as the AIF men were called, and venereal disease was their reward.[9] Most survived and became part of a larger operation of 75,000 men that attempted to establish an allied beachhead on the Turkish coast. British and French troops, the main force, would occupy Cape Hellas, and, thirteen miles further up, the Anzacs were to come ashore to open country and secure the hills on their flank. Soon after dawn on Sunday, 25 April 1915, the Anzacs stormed ashore on the eastern side of the Gallipoli peninsula to an unrecognisable terrain, for they had landed too far north. The Turks watched the flotilla form at Lemnos and the Anzacs suffered heavy casualties from rifle and artillery fire as they pushed themselves up barren, precipitous ridges. As darkness fell on the first day of the campaign, the Anzacs clung precariously to the foothills of Sadi Bair, about half a mile inland.[10] Very exposed, and unable to withdraw, they set about digging a complex of trenches, overlooked by the Turks, who were often barely

Many men were rejected because of unfilled teeth, flat feet, corns or puny chests, as well as those under 5 feet 6 inches. Others were too young or too old. The men in the photograph, and other rejected recruits, formed an association and wore a large badge to cover their civilian shame. (*Lone Hand*, 1 September 1916)

Butcher James McGlynn and wife Lillian, c.1909. James enlisted in Balmain and was killed at Lone Pine on 8 August 1915. Lillian and her five-year-old son John were dependent largely on the charity of her mother's family, with whom they lived. She received a pension of ten shillings per week. (Max Solling Collection) a hundred feet away. The Anzacs observed the enemy through periscopes, and both sides engaged in a series of hand-bombing attacks but the lines changed little during the next three months. The Anzacs began to mass in the trenches on 6 August 1915 for an assault on Lone Pine. Harold Jackson, a 22-year-old builder's clerk from Glebe, recalled:

> We charged three hills that night. On the first hill I bayoneted a Turk who was feigning death, with a few extra thrusts. He was an oldish man and on the first thrust which did not go right home he tried to get his revolver out at me, but failed . . . coming up the third hill, a gigantic Turk . . . grabbed me round the chest . . . he was a veritable Samson . . . [and] slowly began to crush the life out of me, I was almost gone when a mate of mine called Tippen came up and bayoneted him . . . We made sure of him & then continued up the hill. Poor Tippen got shot just in front of their trench in the stomach with two bullets, he died groaning horribly. I killed his assailant however by giving him five rounds in the head.[11]

Seven Victoria Crosses were won at Lone Pine.

The first account that Australians read of what apparently happened at the landing came from English journalist Ellis Ashmead-Bartlett: 'this race of athletes proceeded to scale the cliffs without responding to the enemy's fire . . . I have never seen anything like these wounded Australians in war before . . . They were happy that they had been tried for the first time and had not been found wanting.'[12] Hearts back home were filled with pride. The Turks and the Anzacs consolidated their defences, strengthening their strategic positions, and the battles that raged on the Gallipoli ridges amounted to successive waves of soldiers climbing out of their trenches and attempting to win more ground. The amount of territory gained by either side was small but casualties were heavy. The most successful part of the ill-fated campaign was the withdrawal in December 1915 which left behind 7,594 dead Australians. Some 19,500 Australians were wounded.[13]

The feats of the first AIF at Gallipoli, an army composed entirely of volunteers, assumed larger-than-life proportions of heroic grandeur. The Anzacs had, said General Hamilton, 'created for their country an imperishable record of military virtue'.[14] Gallipoli was hailed as the finest achievement in the country's history, and from then on the legend became firmly embedded in the popular consciousness. The British had lost three times as many men at Gallipoli as the Anzacs, and the French a comparable number to the Diggers. C.E.W. Bean was the foremost of the writers to sanctify Gallipoli as the site of the creation of Australian nationhood. *The Story of Anzac* became the most extensive manifestation of the Anzac tradition in print, though the accuracy of Bean's analysis has since been challenged.[15]

The first casualty lists published in Sydney newspapers were accompanied by photographs and short biographies of 'the heroes of the Dardanelles'. Local people grieved the death of William Robertson, secretary and senior piper of the Rozelle and Leichhardt Band;[16] Frank Francis, a former cadet at Annandale Public School, whom Reverend Rook remembered as a 'most straightforward and daring young fellow';[17] and Mervyn Lown, who left his father's Balmain grocery to 'don the khaki'.[18] Gallipoli's rugged terrain was strewn with the bodies of literally dozens of local men, including 21-year-old packer Harry Hay and John Rollason, a letter carrier, both Leichhardt boys; Alexander Mackie, a wireman with the City Council; and carpenter Charles Kelly from Glebe.[19]

Empire Day 1915 was an occasion for local MP A.H. Griffith to bombard the children at Annandale Public School with the virtues of patriotism,[20] and A.C. Carmichael was full of patriotic homilies for pupils of Leichhardt school.[21] At Forest Lodge school, Attorney-General D.R. Hall called for a show of hands of those who had relations fighting at the front and when 'quite a forest of hands were raised', he remarked that it was the best show of its kind he had yet seen, adding that 'those who have not yet some of their household at the war ought to take their hats off to those who have'. Hall went on to observe that 'one of the old boys of this school has already given his life in the service of the Empire. That is a noble and glorious action.'[22]

At home people experienced a dramatic fall in living standards. Unemployment doubled in those unions which reported the numbers of their members out of work, and by 1915 prices and rents had risen sharply.[23] The government set out to persuade young men to enlist and many were swept along by the patriotic tide as the number of volunteers peaked at 36,000 in July 1915; it did not again reach such heights.[24] Leichhardt Council formed its own recruitment committee, co-opting Sub-inspector Brooks and Sergeant Corcoran.[25] Patriotic condemnation of spectator sports singled out working-class pleasures (Rugby League and boxing) for continuing their activities while horse racing and cricket did not attract any criticism.[26] By the end of 1915 war-shocked survivors returned to local communities that had little idea of what they had endured, and there was alarm at the delinquency of soldiers on leave. On 14 February 1916 hundreds of soldiers rioted in Sydney. Grace Brothers, Broadway, was barricaded off after some of its windows were smashed. Tom Herlihy, headmaster of nearby Glebe Public School, told pupils: 'I want you to go straight home. There's going to be a big storm.'[27]

Sporting activities had been curtailed by 1916, and the temperance movement intensified its activities, urging their panacea, hotel closures or reduced trading hours. The pub, an important social centre in working-class communities, was under threat; working people did not want to see the trading times of their temple at night reduced. 'Liquor,' wrote R.B.S. Hammond, 'has proved more effective and more cruel than German bullets . . . The bar is the night school where men learn to drink. Close them at 6.00 p.m. and tens of thousands will seek healthier and saner recreation.'[28] Balmain cleric Luke Parr depicted the referendum on hotel closing hours as 'a patriotic struggle'. It was, he said, aimed at 'greater efficiency for our forces who were combating the "frightfulness" of Germany'.[29] New South Wales voted for 6 p.m. closing in pubs in June 1916, though an analysis of polling booth returns in the current Leichhardt municipality indicates that people in working-class neighbourhoods wanted pubs to remain open until 9 p.m.[30]

Mounting casualty lists in 1916 turned simple patriotism at home into something much more grim and ugly. Local patriots investigated the patriotism of local Germans, and councils did not escape the anti-German hysteria, circularising letters among themselves calling for German businesses to be boycotted and German workers to be sacked.[31] The *Mirror of Australia* embarked on a campaign of vilification of anyone who might have a 'Hun' connection, however remote. It wrote scurrilous things about 'Herr Bollard, a Mort's Dock draftsman', chemist Carl Bogenrieder and medical practitioner Franz Breitner, all from Balmain. Dr Breitner's wife, they complained, 'can even give garden parties at a leading Sydney hotel'.[32] Three sons of Henry

Schneider, general manager of the Balmain Co-operative Society, enlisted in the AIF. 'There has been considerable comment in the district at the retention of Mr Schneider's services by the company,' observed the *Mirror*.[33] But not for long; Schneider was sacked. Once this poisonous process gathered momentum no one was safe from denunciation. Rudolph Bohrsmann, the son of a German immigrant who arrived in Sydney in 1854, was a medical graduate from Sydney University. After Dr Bohrsmann put up his brass plate at 36 Glebe Road, Glebe, in 1898 he became active in community affairs. The dux of Glebe Superior Public School from 1900 received the Dr Bohrsmann gold medal. An avid supporter of Empire Day celebrations. Bohrsmann gained 43 per cent of the vote when in 1913 he stood as the Liberal Party candidate for Glebe. But he was caught up in strong communal feelings against the 'square heads', was shunned by local folk and left Glebe in 1918.[34]

No evidence was found of any German disloyalty or treachery undermining Australian society,[35] but that did not stop the Glebe Anti-German League denouncing anyone with a German name; its chairman, Captain Strachan, ranted about 'enemies freely moving about' in their midst, placing 'every British man, woman and child in the community in danger'.[36]

The War Precautions Regulations were extended to include 'all aliens whether enemy or otherwise'. Once the military decided an 'enemy alien' was disloyal, they were placed in a camp behind barbed wire from where there was no recourse to the law and no access to the ordinary processes of judicial appeal. The majority of internees and deportees were of German origin but Irish nationalists, radical socialists and members of the International Workers of the World were also deported.[37]

The jingoism that characterised the beginnings of the war dissipated, and the losses at Gallipoli weakened the commitment at home. Suburban quotas were not being filled and army medical examinations exposed the poor standard of health of many working-class men. The minimum height for recruits was lowered to 5 feet 2 inches and new Prime Minister Hughes called for 50,000 volunteers to form new units of the AIF.[38] Gallipoli was a mere sideshow to the real war being fought on the Western Front. The morass of trench warfare in France was on a scale far beyond anything encountered at Gallipoli, and was an even more horrifying experience where human life would be squandered in an unprecedented manner.

The Town Clerk of Balmain recorded an array of reasons why a growing number refused to volunteer—the refusal of parental consent, physical disabilities. Others said they would only join if compelled to do so and others would not enlist because not all single men had gone to the front.[39] A Balmain hairdresser proudly displayed in his shop window an honour roll containing the names of about 100 'of my customers'.[40] W.M. Hughes, anxious to keep up the flow of recruits to the front, sought to introduce compulsory overseas military service and issued call-up notices so eligible men could begin training even before the referendum was held. Long lists at Balmain and Glebe court houses, filled with the names of young men seeking exemption from the proclamation calling up single men, was evidence that there were many unmoved by any martial or imperial enthusiasm. A garbage carter employed by Leichhardt Council was denied an exemption because the court refused to believe he was employed in an indispensable industry and, in any case, he could be replaced. At the same court a conscientious objector stated 'he was of mild and nervous disposition and liable to collapse at the sight of blood'.[41] Neil McKibbon told Glebe Court he was the sole support of his mother, and added that he sometimes gave her 'ten bob' and sometimes 'a quid' a week. He was granted an exemption. A Toxteth Road postal assistant, who gave his crippled mother £8 a month, was not so lucky.[42]

Much of the impetus in the campaign against conscription came from the socialists, and with the more radical elements of the trade union movement, pacifists, women and Quakers, they formed a united front. The conscription campaigns in October 1916 were marked by violence.[43] Anti-conscriptionists were jostled, harassed, forcibly removed from platforms and pelted with stones by loyalists and soldiers. Both sides arranged thousands of meetings, distributing leaflets and pamphlets and holding open-air meetings on suburban street corners. Local town halls became the main venue for the largest pro-conscription rallies, actively supported by most councillors and chaired by the mayors, H.P. Scott (Balmain), E. Hogan (Annandale), R.W. Stone (Glebe) and T. Hastings (Leichhardt).[44] At Balmain Town Hall J.C. Watson urged locals to support conscription because, he said, Germany was still unbeaten, and on the same platform J. Garland KC, appealed to 'Australia's well-won military honour'.[45] A compulsory-reinforcements meeting at Glebe Town Hall heard that 'if the Empire went down in the struggle, civilisation would fall with it . . . it is our bounden duty to fight for our system. Conscription was an organised and equitable system'. But within a stone's throw of this meeting, William Martin urged people to 'record an emphatic "no" and show the world that while always willing to do their share in the defence of the Empire, they were not going to be forced to the points of German bayonets'.[46] A.H. Griffith told a gathering at Coronation Hall, Annandale, that only 'two men a day needed to be found from an electorate like Annandale until the divisions were brought up to their full strength'.[47] At Balmain, Premier W.A. Holman met with ridicule and abuse, and was asked why he had not joined the colours.[48] The majority of the nation rejected conscription at the referendum held on 28 October 1916.

Loyalty to God, king and country, and the virtue of self-sacrifice were emphasised in local public schools and, as the war continued, school assemblies and speech days attested to these virtues. These schools drew on the imperialist hegemony of the Boer War and the effusiveness of Empire Day celebrations to construct a war ideology. Apart from symbolic observance, schools resorted to practical patriotism with their war relief schemes, fundraising, making comforts for the Red Cross and the continuation of school cadets. The Education Department encouraged a martial spirit, conducting camps for boys, and cadet corps aimed at instilling order, regularity and patriotic duty in the Empire's children. The public schools were vast reservoirs of volunteers and hundreds of former pupils of public schools in Annandale, Balmain, Glebe and Leichhardt responded to the call of king and country and crossed the seas. Their names were recorded in columns on honour rolls and memorials. Catholic schools shared similar wartime ideologies with their public school counterparts, but after Easter 1916 their direction changed. Now Catholic assemblies and

Patriotic girls from Glebe Public School dressed as servicemen and Britannia, Christmas 1915. Left to right, Ivy Phillips, Beryl Ferrier (sailor), Dulcie Cameron (Britannia), Bess Harvie (soldier, standing) and Margaret Gray. (Max Solling Collection)

speech days opened with 'Back to Erin' rather than 'Land of Hope and Glory', and their schools, taking Dr Mannix's lead, embraced both Irish–Australian nationalism and anti-conscriptionist sentiment.[49]

The war helped sharpen conflicts over working conditions and wages. Deteriorating living standards—because wages had fallen behind rising prices—food shortages and growing unemployment all contributed to putting workers in a disadvantaged position. On 2 August 1917 a general strike by railwaymen against the introduction of a card system that workmen regarded as an insidious method of forcing them to greater toil without reward began in New South Wales.[50] The strike soon spread throughout the labour movement and involved about 76,000 workers. Acting Premier G.W. Fuller called the men 'tools of Disloyalists and Revolutionaries', and the government set out to defeat the strikers.[51] 'Free' labour was recruited, and the government established its ability to govern without the unions. The government stood firm for unconditional surrender and the unions had no option but to concede. The bitterness generated by the general strike was due largely to the harsh settlement. 'Loyalist' volunteers were given preference in employment over defeated unionists. Hundreds of railwaymen, miners and waterside workers were refused re-employment. Others, like J.B. Chifley, an engine driver dismissed for his participation in the strike, was grudgingly re-admitted to the railway service with lower pay and status as a fireman.

Australian casualties amounted to 38,000 in the European autumn of 1917, as against 10,000 enlistments. Hughes announced that there would be a referendum proposing to make up the deficiency in recruiting by a ballot among eligible single men. The second campaign in December 1917 was marked by more heated and acrimonious debate than the first, as supporters and opponents of the war became even more sharply divided.[52] At Annandale J.C. Fitzpatrick told a rowdy meeting that 'it is the slackers who won't go that we are after and who we are going to compel to go'.[53] Soldiers disrupted public meetings, and violence and disorder escalated at open-air gatherings as loyalists resorted to force and confrontation to curtail the strong and effective campaign conducted by anti-conscriptionists. Some soldiers interpreted the movement against conscription and war as undermining not only their political purpose, in defending the king and Empire, but also their manliness. They saw socialist women implicitly undermining manly ideals by promoting pacifism and advocating anti-conscription, both of which were considered cowardly and feminine.[54]

W.M. Hughes set out to discredit anti-conscriptionists, particularly the Irish. Sectarianism intensified when Catholics were derided as disloyal by Protestants for not doing their share, but enlistment figures reveal young Catholic men were not under-represented among the volunteers. Archbishop Mannix was not one to resile from a challenge. He poured scorn on Hughes' overtures to support conscription and rallied Catholics to the anti-conscriptionist cause.

Letters from the front possessed an honesty, immediacy and vividness, bringing memories of life in Balmain and Leichhardt from the trenches as well as providing vignettes of foreign parts. Harold Murray told his sister he had 'bumped into a lot of old Forest Lodge boys' in France and informed her how some of his mates were faring.[55] Major J. Doherty from Balmain expressed disappointment at not going back to his battalion: 'I don't think,' he wrote, 'it possible to strike such a fine lot of fellows in civil life.'[56] Some soldiers in France schemed for repatriation. 'Some of the malingerers . . . have a method of making their knees swell by binding them tightly with a towel,' recalled Annandale electrician T.J. Cleary.⁵⁷ A disillusioned Earl Neaves found little to enthuse about in 1917. He told brother Harry, also at the front:

> All my pals . . . I came over with are gone, but seven out of 150 remain, it's simply scientific murder, not war at all. As for seeing Germans it's all lies you never get close enough to do that unless in a charge. I keep smiling but I tell you it takes some doing . . . the premonition I had when leaving Sydney that I will never see home again still hangs about me . . . one would be unnatural to go through uninjured. If I get out with a leg and an arm off I'd be perfectly satisfied'.⁵⁸

Neither Earl nor Harry made it back to Avona Avenue, Glebe.

The funeral of returned soldier John Lynch in 1918. Lynch enlisted with Carmichael's First Thousand and was repatriated after being gassed in France. He left a widow and five children who lived at 13 Junction Street, Forest Lodge. (*SM*, 19 June 1918)

The war took charge of countless thousands of people's lives and reshaped them and the names of Gallipoli, Messines, Menin Road, Passchendaele, Bullecourt and Pozières became etched in local memories as places of death. Everyone knew a neighbour who had been killed and mothers prayed every night that their boys would come home. Some prayers were answered but others were not so lucky. Mrs Wellings, a distraught mother, composed this memoriam:

> Oh the anguish of the mother
> Oh the bitter tears she shed
> When she heard her boy was missing
> And she wondered 'Is he dead?'
> Oh the weeks and months of torture

> Oh the agony and pain
> And she wept and prayed and wondered
> Would he come to her again
> 'Killed in Action' came still later
> Oh the awful truth is bare.[59]

By 1918 the military mission for civilisation was overwhelming the communities of Annandale, Balmain, Glebe and Leichhardt. The defeat of conscription meant the continuance of voluntary recruiting, and ordinary folk, feeling a deepening weariness of war, became critical of things about the war, and especially of those who they believed were making huge profits at the country's expense. Confident pronouncements from local pulpits in 1915 had softened to a greater sense of compassion for those who grieved.[60] The public tried to put the conscription crisis behind it and returned to honouring and supporting the men at the front.

Near the end of the war Leichhardt residents enthused over the news that one of their own boys had won the Victoria Cross. Leichhardt wireworker William Currey, after two unsuccessful attempts to enlist, including giving a false age, finally sailed for France in 1916. At Péronne on 1 September 1918 Currey's 53rd Battalion was suffering from a 77 mm field gun firing at very close range. Currey rushed forward under machine-gun fire, killed the whole crew and captured the weapon, and later in the afternoon he worked around the flank of a German post and opened fire with a Lewis gun, inflicting many casualties. Despite being gassed, Currey saw out the war and returned home in 1919.[61] The field gun he captured became a war trophy which was displayed in the grounds of Leichhardt Town Hall.[62]

On 11 November 1918 church bells rang out throughout the suburbs that this period of trial and tragedy was over, and 'every man, woman and child came into the city to celebrate'.[63] The nation mourned the loss of nearly 60,000 from a population of four million. Of the 417,000 men and women who voluntarily enlisted, 330,000 had served overseas and two-thirds had become casualties. Approximately 40 per cent of all Australian men aged between eighteen and 45 had enlisted in the AIF.[64]

The bodies of Anzacs were buried where they died—at Gallipoli, in the Middle East and in France. Eventually their bodies were exhumed and buried near foreign battlefields in graves made by the Imperial War Graves Commission. As these graves were too far away for most wives, brothers, sisters, mothers and fathers to visit, public mourning was to be expressed in memorials throughout the country. In New South Wales alone, 516 memorials were erected.[65] Mass deaths called for commemoration in conspicuous sites—in public parks, main streets, at intersections and in school yards. Balmain's Unity Square, a busy intersection, was renamed Loyalty Square and on 24 April 1916 a memorial drinking fountain was unveiled there. Featuring the words 'Peace, Honour, Empire and Liberty', it recorded the names of 38 men killed at Gallipoli.[66] It was one of the very few memorials actually erected during the war.

Sydney's inner-suburban communities paid an extraordinary price in their defence of the Empire. There is sufficient evidence to estimate, with some accuracy, the magnitude of each municipality's contribution. A draft roll of honour of enlistments from Balmain contains 791 names, but it seems to be incomplete.[67] In the foyer of Glebe Town Hall there are columns containing 792 names, etched in bronze of those who 'answered the call of King and Country'.

A large crowd gathered at Annandale Town Hall on 25 June 1917 to see Joseph Cook unveil its rosewood honour board which Mayor Hogan said contained the names of 1,000 volunteers.[68]

It seems that perhaps as many as 1,500 people from Leichhardt joined the AIF. The Anglicans, the largest denomination in Leichhardt, recorded 1,200 enlistments.[69] At the 1911 census the present Municipality of Leichhardt housed some 89,475 men, women and children and altogether about 4,000 of its residents enlisted.

Gilbert Doble's magnificent figure of Peace, located in the middle of Norton and Marion streets, Leichhardt, was unveiled on 9 April 1922.[70] Some 379 local men died overseas. Balmain left no memorial of those who died between 1914 and 1918 but honour boards and memorials in Balmain's churches and schools suggest at least 200 of its sons were killed in action or died of wounds, while the trachyte memorial in Hinsby Reserve, fronting Johnston Street, Annandale, contains 90 inscribed names.[71] In Glebe a granite and marble monument in the form of a mausoleum records the names of 174 local men who died. All these public statements of grief and pride were products of local and voluntary initiative.

Gilbert Doble's magnificent figure of Peace was located in the middle of Norton and Marion streets, Leichhardt, when unveiled on 9 April 1922. The names of 379 Leichhardt men who died in the Great War are inscribed on the memorial. It is now located in Pioneers Memorial Park, Leichhardt.
(Photograph by David Liddle)

14 Local politics: fit and proper people

Municipalities created under the 1858 Act faced the daunting task of providing the basic infrastructure for small communities that were appearing on the landscape. Money to finance municipal work came from rates, levied upon annual values, and government endowments. On incorporation, municipal administration and meetings were conducted from modest places, and as the amount of revenue collected until the late 1870s remained small, there were inbuilt constraints on what councils could achieve.[1] The men elected to councils in Glebe (1859) and Balmain (1860) were among the most respectable and wealthy citizens these communities had to offer. Between 1860 and 1870 Methodist missionary and newspaper editor Ralph Mansfield, druggist George Elliott, wholesale grocer Walter Church, master mariner and shipbuilder Captain Thomas Rowntree, lawyer and literary patron Nicol Drysdale Stenhouse, medical practitioner Owen Spencer Evans, timber merchant John Booth, Egyptologist and chairman of the Stock Exchange Josiah Mullens, ferry proprietor Henry Perdriau and ironmonger Frederick Robinson served as chairmen, or from 1867, mayors, of Balmain.[2]

G.W. Allen occupied pride of place at meetings of Glebe Council from incorporation to 1877, a period of eighteen years; on his death, Council recorded that he was 'one whose many good qualities and arduous labours as a Christian Gentlemen and a good citizen rendered him a conspicuous Colonist'.[3] A coterie of councillors who sat at meetings with Allen were every bit as respectable as their Balmain counterparts—shipbuilder John Korff; architects Edmund Blacket, George Allen Mansfield and William Munro; oil-and-colour man Michael Chapman; and surveyor Thomas Harwood. Allen, whose law firm was based in the city, was the eldest son of a pioneer who owned one-quarter of Glebe. Voters, it seemed, preferred to be represented by a businessman with vested local interests, surmising that he would exert his influence in a way that would also bring benefits to the wider community.[4] Perhaps the populace expected to be governed by a leadership of educated gentlemen. The conduct of council affairs, minutes indicate, was akin to that of a gentleman's club, and the keynote of social relationships between the respectable councillors and their ratepayers was deference – deference to the elite. Not all councillors were wealthy or influential, but it was an elite group of merchants and professional men, industrialists and retail traders who had the loudest say in local affairs. Complaints that the early hours of meeting (4.30 p.m.) made them inaccessible to most people fell on deaf ears, and there was a significant number in the community who felt they would be better off if their territory remained unincorporated, free of the financial burdens local government imposed.[5]

The early bourgeoisie of Leichhardt had mostly gone by 1871, when it housed only 614 residents. Its first councillors—salesman Frank Beames, grocer Albert Barrell, house agent Aaron Wheeler, brickmaker Charles Linney and warehouseman Frederick Parsons—were far from well-heeled, though draper John Wetherill was a significant landowner.[6] The other early representatives of sparsely populated Leichhardt in the 1870s were townsfolk with small businesses—an ironmonger, publican, hay and corn dealer, mason, dairyman and boiling-down works proprietor.

The growth of local industry and the emergence of clusters of small retail shops accompanied the residential boom of the 1880s, and the occupational composition of councils mirrored these developments. The first generation of gentlemen councillors in Balmain and Glebe began to withdraw from municipal life from the late 1870s; they were replaced largely by a new breed of businessmen closely associated with the whole process of suburban development.

Annandale, one of the three wards within Leichhardt Municipality, felt it had fared poorly in the distribution of local funds, and petitioned successfully for the creation of a separate municipality, which came into being in 1894.[7] John Young, a dominant figure in shaping Annandale, became its first Mayor. The courtesies and gentlemanly behaviour that characterised early councils gave way to a more robust style of campaigning as ambitious entrepreneurs jostled each other for a seat on Council.[8] These respected creatures of local industry and commerce, the 'self-made men', soon gained influence in municipal life, respectability and, after an interval, a good measure of social recognition. At ward elections they were not backward in informing the public about shortcomings of opponents. On Council they quarrelled about rates and roads. The property-based voting system ensured that a vast majority of the total adult population was denied the municipal franchise and plurality voting, some argued, placed control of municipalities in the hands of the well-to-do, to the detriment of the masses. Ward elections, it seemed, generated little interest, for only a minority of eligible voters bothered to cast a vote.[9]

Business and property owners, with time to spare, held near absolute sway over municipal affairs, though this dominance was interrupted occasionally by a few tradesmen and small retailers, working-class in origin but with social aspirations. Local government represented a narrow range of interests, and the absence of payment for municipal office generally made participation in local affairs inaccessible to wage and salary earners. The typical local councillor was male, Protestant, middle-class, self-employed and conservative in outlook, a guardian of the status quo rather than an agent of social change.[10]

Each year one-third of councillors were required to retire, nominations were called for vacant seats and, if more than one person nominated, a ward election held. This system persisted to 1908, when all councillors had to face triennial elections. Most served out their three-year term; new councillors, in the opinion of P.C. Lucas 'were not worth a twopenny ticket until they had been on council two years'.[11] Those councillors who were regularly returned by ratepayers emerged as prominent local identities. The office of councillor conferred status and local power upon the holder. In the municipal chambers the manner and dress of councillors—their claw-hammer coats, bow ties and fob watches—were visible outward expressions of respectability, something that

Balmain Town Hall, 1888. Balmain councillors wanted an administrative centre appropriate for the size, wealth and concentration of their suburb. They chose their Mayor, architect E.H. Buchanan, to design a Town Hall in the Victorian Free Classical style. (*Souvenir to Commemorate the 50th Anniversary of the Incorporation of the Municipality of Balmain 1860-1910*)

Mr. A. G. Crump Mayor.

Mrs. Crump Mayoress.

was reinforced by the abbreviation 'JP' after their names. They met the credentials of 'fit and proper people'. But not all councillors were held in high esteem; for example, legal proceedings were taken against Patrick Toohey who claimed 'the Mayor and the lot of them [the Council] could be bought for five shillings'.[12]

The town halls were a manifestation of the strong desire for physical improvement. In emerging communities they became the focus for much local activity and the main forums for political campaigns, meetings and rallies as well as centres for local administration. Mayor Field of Glebe, a Wesleyan lay preacher, was concerned about his town hall being used for quadrille dancing in 1881, and J.P. Treadgold thought the use of Leichhardt Town Hall for party political purposes free of charge in 1893 was 'inimical to peaceable municipal government'.[13]

Council meetings in the 1890s were preoccupied with burgeoning debt and unemployment relief schemes. Unemployment caused 'widespread distress' in Balmain in 1893,[14] and about the same time Mayor R.B. Cropley of Leichhardt gave 'sufficient employment to as many as I could find room for so that they could pay rates, believing that this was a better and more humane course than issuing summons against them'.[15]

People were attracted to municipal office by a combination of self-interest and public service. Local councillors filled the boards of local building societies and land companies, friendly societies, free trade and protectionist associations, and temperance societies, and provided social leadership on local voluntary associations. Formation of Labor Leagues was a symptom of fundamental change in local class relations as the working class mobilised and, for the first time, became more visible, but it was not until the 1920s that Labor had any impact on municipal politics.[16]

The local business elites, hailed as self-made men who had proved themselves in the battle of life, remained firmly ensconced in local town halls. Municipal councils, middle class in nature and composition, were held together by social and political ties but each council had its own peculiar social geography.

The industrial character of Balmain pervaded every aspect of its life, and its largest employer, Mort's Dock, had ample representation on council—T.S. Rowntree, E.W. Cameron, W. Davidson, J. Broomfield, S. Briggs and, of course, J.P. Franki. Three other councillors—H. Perdriau, A. Elkington and J. McDonald—had longstanding connections with the dock.[17] Other owners of large enterprises—John Booth, George Elliott, Alfred Hancock and William Hutchinson—were both visible and voluble councillors. In the years up to 1917 Balmain had a good representation of local and professional men on Council (four solicitors, four architects, six engineers, two doctors and two accountants), together with a sprinkling of boatbuilders, butchers, estate agents, publicans, timber merchants and builders.

Business interests in Balmain were well served by Henry Brisbane Swan, a partner of a local timber company. A councillor altogether for 32 years and Mayor in 1893–94 and 1914–15, Swan was chairman of the New Ferry Co. and a long-time member of the Balmain District Hospital committee.[18] A broad cross-section of the local business fraternity stood beside Swan on council for decades, including estate agent George Clubb, architect James McDonald, publican Matthew Cohen, accountant Robert Campbell, ironmonger Thomas Jesson, boot importer Henry Mills, brassfounder Alex Milne, storekeeper Henry Scott and carpenter Henry Cox. A formidable figure at Balmain from 1911 to 1944 was Reginald Thornton, admitted as a solicitor in 1899. Thornton was something of a local historian and, with Alexander William Sommerville, wrote a municipal history of Balmain in 1935. At Balmain Town Hall he was representative of various conservative groupings and was not comfortable with Labor men on Council, a feeling that was reciprocal.[19]

Glebe, without Balmain's industrial base, had a slightly different occupational composition. In the era up to 1917 two groups were strongly represented on Council—the building industry with thirteen representatives, and the real estate industry (house and land agents or commission agents) with ten councillors. Four energetic publicans were vigorous spokesmen for the drink trade (joining in fiery debate with temperance councillors), and three of the five solicitors on Council occupied the mayoral chair. Owners of industries that were locating on Glebe's perimeter from the 1880s—Wearne's foundry, a major employer of labour; Dunn's tannery; the Magic Soap Works; and Conlon's pottery—also took their place on Council along with butchers, carriers and chemists.[20]

P.C. Lucas was very much the archetypal late-Victorian councillor—business proprietor (wine and spirits), protectionist, Protestant, promoter of the school of arts and a founding member of the Glebe Masonic Lodge. He was also a great stayer, being a councillor continuously from 1880 to 1925, ten times Mayor, and representing his suburb at parliamentary inquiries on sewerage, transport and Greater Sydney.[21] Others who shared similar middle-class values included tanner Thomas Dunn, ornamental plasterer William Cary, carriers S.L. Cole and William Robey, oil-and-colour man Michael Chapman and hide merchant Thomas Law. All of them spent many years on Council.

The formation of a local vigilante committee at Leichhardt in 1886, to closely monitor the actions of Council and see that money was properly spent, was a symptom that all were not happy with the way local affairs were being run.[22] A conservative Protestant and Masonic

Henry Brisbane Swan (1858–1926). Swan, a timber merchant, was a Balmain councillor for 32 years (1889–1908, 1911–22, and 1926) and Mayor in 1893–94 and 1914–15. He was chairman of the New Ferry Co. and committeeman on the Balmain District Hospital Board. (Balmain Council Chambers)

Percy Charles Lucas (1845–1930). Very much the archetypal late-Victorian councillor—business proprietor, Protestant and Freemason, Lucas was a member of Glebe Council continuously from 1880 to 1925. He also served ten terms as Mayor. (Max Solling Collection)

Some 5,000 people attended the official opening of Leichhardt Town Hall by Governor Carrington on 26 September 1888. Located at the civic centre of the suburb, the intersection of Norton and Marion streets, the town hall was designed in the Victorian Free Classical style by architects Drake & Walcott. The tower clock was installed in 1897 to mark Queen Victoria's Diamond Jubilee. (GPO Videodisc-1 Still 35597)

fraternity held sway at Leichhardt from 1871 to 1920. These were people drawn from the local business community, with builders (eleven of them, the largest single group), a handful of professionals (three engineers, two accountants and a solicitor), together with three publicans (Charles and Alfred Hearn, and Benjamin Moore), five clerks and a collection of manual workers (three labourers, a stonemason, a wire-worker and an asphalter). The latter were absent from other councils. Bacon curers, brickmakers, confectioners and dairymen were also attracted to Leichhardt's municipal life.[23] Alfred Blackmore entered the municipal arena in Leichhardt in 1911 and the Methodist solicitor remained an imposing figure in the council chamber until 1937.[24] He shared his years on Council with local dairyman William Lambert, clerk William Atkins, accountant James Treadgold and draper James Lonsdale.

The council chambers at the smallest municipality, Annandale, were filled with a miscellaneous collection of small businessmen between 1894 and 1920. Apart from building contractor John Young, three timber merchants—Allen Taylor, Albert Guthrey and John Maxwell—operated large local businesses. Among those who owned and staffed small enterprises were seven builders and contractors, two grocers, two printers, two butchers and a carrier. There were also four clerks and two professionals (accountant, solicitor).[25]

Profiles of T.E. Colebrook and E. Hogan provide some insight into the kind of men who dominated municipal life in Annandale. Thomas Colebrook expressed concern to the Commission on Greater Sydney in 1913 that the scheme threatened the right of small suburban freeholders. A lay preacher for the Methodist Church, worshipful master of the Loyal Orange Lodge and president of the Australian Aborigines Mission, Colebrook was a printer and publisher at Annandale; from 1891 to 1901 he was a Leichhardt councillor, and from 1903 to 1919 and 1923 to 1925 a local councillor at Annandale.[26] From 1906 to 1944 carrier Edward Hogan was a member of Annandale Council, its longest serving representative. He stood as a Nationalist Party candidate for the state seat of Annandale in 1927, and on Council he was the leading figure in the Progressive Party, being Mayor eight times.[27] Hogan had close political ties with his council colleagues—tinsmith Jimmy Robertson, builders Owen Ridge and Arthur Packer, contractor William Wells, sawmaker Thomas Chapman, piano tuner Charles Winkworth, butcher Charles Schofield and electrician James Cummings—all self-employed small businessmen and social leaders of their community.

By the time of Federation the residential character of the inner suburbs, still suffering from the 1890s depression, was increasingly coming under attack from expanding industry. Though many of the better-off had departed for more salubrious suburbs, a visible ruling class of local businessmen and professionals remained. At the peak of the social pyramid within suburban society was an elite of leading families in which doctors, solicitors, estate agents and publicans featured prominently. The kind of businessmen ensconced in the town halls had changed a little and become more petit bourgeois in tone. Now the voices of estate agents, carriers, grocers, storekeepers and other local retailers, closely identified with the immediate community, resounded in the corridors of the town halls.[28] As Balmain and adjoining suburbs became more distinctly working-class in their identity and public life, working people found little solace in the municipal arena; they were simply an audience to a middle-class performance. The vast majority of these communities consisted of tenants who, lacking physical property as a resource, found that their only access to the political system lay within the numbers game of a party which saw the forces of the boss and private property aimed at the suppression of the worker.[29] Councillors were perceived as being on the side of the boss and property.

As the economy grew, a new vigour and life could be discerned within Labor branches from about 1904 and Labor began formulating policies to improve the lot of working-class communities. Hope was kindled among ordinary people that they might be able to exercise some control over what happened in their neighbourhood and its amenities. Adult franchise at municipal elections had yet to come.[30]

By 1908 at Leichhardt the business community was worried that people with 'socialist views' might be elected to Council. Municipal socialism might become a reality. Three 'liberal' councillors, Treadgold, Pearson and Lonsdale, were induced to stand again to keep out the dreaded socialists.[31] Fears were allayed when all twelve conservative councillors were returned, but three years later Labor succeeded in having two men, Hylton Retallack and Monteith Meller, elected. It was, however, something of an aberration as men under the banner of Sound Municipal Government, and the Progressive Party, retained an iron grip on local affairs in Leichhardt at the five elections between 1914 and 1925. At Annandale in 1911, Labor stood eleven candidates at the council election but was unable to capture a solitary seat.[32] It was a disappointing outcome and Labor made little effort for a long time to gain a foothold on Annandale Council, which remained undeviatingly conservative. Glebe Labor mounted a challenge in 1911, fielding a team of eight candidates. They finished at the bottom of the polls and it was not until after 1922 that Labor won a single seat at Glebe.[33]

The Greater Sydney Council proposals threatened the existence of suburban councils. Glebe would not have a bar of it, and in 1902 circularised councils advising them that under such a scheme they 'would have to hand over the whole of their assets, and in return be more heavily taxed'.[34] Mayors of Annandale, Balmain, Glebe and Leichhardt gave evidence to a Royal Commission on Greater Sydney in 1913, strongly opposing the scheme. George Clubb, Mayor of Balmain, told the commission his suburb was 'an island entirely cut off from other municipalities'. 'We are purely a manufacturing suburb,' he said, 'and no works of a general character' needed to be carried out.[35] Annandale ratepayers would pay higher rates, said Mayor T.E. Colebrook: 'Surely this would not be truly democratic in a community where so many of the people are small freeholders.' J.P. Treadgold of Leichhardt told the commission his suburb 'being further away from the centre . . . would not get the same attention', but rates

Thomas Colebrook (1857–1928). Printer and publisher Colebrook was a member of Leichhardt Council from 1891 to 1901 and Annandale Council from 1903 to 1919 and 1923 to 1925. He was a prominent Methodist lay-preacher and Worshipful Master of the Loyal Orange Lodge. (Leichhardt Town Hall)

Edward Hogan (1867–1945). From 1906 to 1944 carrier Hogan was a member of Annandale Council, its longest-serving representative. He was also Mayor for six terms. (Annandale Council Chambers)

would increase. F.L. Artlett was especially concerned about the threats to 'the purity of municipal life' posed by Greater Sydney. The Glebe Mayor considered suburban aldermen possessed 'a higher moral character' than their city counterparts and Greater Sydney 'would tend towards Tammany', he said.[36]

In 1915, when A.H. Griffith introduced the Local Government (Franchise) Bill, some 246 municipalities forwarded petitions of protest.[37] Glebe and Annandale councils petitioned both houses of parliament 'not to extend the Local Government Franchise beyond those who are either owners of land within an area, or are householders, or lessees from the owner', arguing that 'municipal expenditure is purely local. With an adult franchise, a body of persons may be in the area in such numbers as to smother the votes of those who have permanent interests'.[38] The *Herald* regarded the franchise as a 'blot' that would confer civic privileges where there was no civic responsibilities.[39] But 31 resident petitions lauded the Bill, arguing that the existing restrictive franchise had allowed an exclusive class to control municipal affairs, something that had produced administrative 'cliquism, inefficiency and paralysis'.[40] The expulsion of Griffith for his stand on conscription was a major setback and all the electoral provisions were subsequently deleted by the Legislative Council. Women could be elected councillors from 1918 but they were denied the ordinary local franchise unless they held independent qualifications.

The first municipal elections after the 1914–18 war saw Labor gain a majority of seats on Paddington and Redfern councils.[41] Labor had their first representative elected to Balmain Council in 1911 but councillors who presented themselves under the banner of the Progressive Party continued to hold sway in Balmain until 1922, when the working class captured power with election of eight Labor candidates.[42] Labourer Bertie Wheeler became Balmain's first Labor Mayor but his party lost control of council in 1925 when eight Reform Party candidates were returned.[43] Stanley Cole, Glebe councillor for 21 years and a member of the Sane Democracy League, bitterly condemned the intrusion of party politics into local government. Business people, in Cole's opinion, were uniquely capable of transcending particular or sectional interests, of representing the interests of the community as a whole and of providing good government for all.[44] However, many councillors before 1920 had personal interests which they sought to protect, and their notion of 'independence' is difficult to reconcile with the reality of their own political lives. S.L. Cole epitomised the business and mercantile ascendancy in local affairs that the *Herald* categorised as 'non-political'. The founding partner of a carrying firm, Cole was active in both the Liberal and Nationalist parties, was a member of the Protestant Alliance and president of the Local Government Association from 1922 to 1924.[45] Others who claimed to be untainted by political allegiances were P.C. Lucas (Glebe), G.C. Murdoch and W.C. Ward, all of whom stood as Liberals in state elections.

The Labor Party, with an electoral base of working-class voters and blue-collar membership, developed an Irish Catholic image after the 1916 split. There was a strong Irish–Australian presence in inner-city Catholic parishes by 1933, when Catholics comprised about 30 per cent of the population, and they became influential in local municipal and Labor Party politics; after 1920 Catholics held about 50 per cent of Labor seats in New South Wales.[46] Links with communism were explicitly proscribed as early as 1924, the Communist Party being a competitor with Labor for working-class loyalties.

In 1926 John Fitzpatrick attacked the proposed adult franchise. It would, he said, transfer the destinies of local government to the 'tender mercies' of every 'Tom, Dick and Harry and penniless derelict in the community'.[47] A Bill introducing the adult franchise was passed in 1927, although it was initially rejected in the Legislative Council, and there were over 200 councils opposed to the move. The first elections under the new franchise, held in December 1928, did not establish the Labor hegemony in municipal affairs that some had prophesied. The *Labor Daily* noted Labor gains at the expense of 'hidebound conservatism' but accused the government of deliberately discouraging the newly enfranchised occupiers from enrolling by insisting that applications be witnessed by a justice of the peace.[48]

At municipal elections it was clear the conservative press took the view that Labor had no place in local government, headlining any success Labor met with in the municipal arena with such headlines as 'Red Victory'.[49] The *Herald* in particular derived great satisfaction in detailing Labor council affairs with dramatic headlines, 'Wild scenes at Council meeting', 'Glebe: Labor Domination: Graft Charges', 'Ald Gill resigns as protest against alleged maladministration'.[50] Councils at Annandale and Leichhardt, controlled by non-Labor groups, were ignored by the conservative press. Glebe, controlled by Labor from 1925, acquired a reputation for job patronage, irregular letting of contracts and manipulation of tenders. Political patronage, financial kickbacks and finding jobs on council were very much part of working-class culture.[51] By 1931 Leichhardt and Glebe councils in particular struggled with indebtedness.[52] The impecunious state of inner-city municipalities meant that what corruption did exist was petty in nature—'things that fell off the back of trucks'. Allegations of bribery that were proved all involved small amounts of money. There was no large-scale corruption.

Local government had a wide range of responsibilities—providing and maintaining local roads and bridges, providing kerbing, guttering and footpaths, lighting and garbage collection. It also had to protect the health of residents (and now had to pay the health inspector's salary) and cater for recreational needs. It was a burden generally beyond the scope of its financial and human resources.[53]

The classic style of machine politics that emerged in the 1920s was not unlike the ethnic politics in the United States of America. The displaced Irish organised themselves in the face of a hostile and excluding establishment. It was a style of politics that fulfilled functions for the deprived and the worker adopted a Tammany Hall mode of organisation in order to survive; in the inner city Labor stalwarts looked to the Catholic church, and the party, for an almost tribal sense of belonging. Catholic parliamentarians relied heavily on local organisations which were often based on parish networks, and Catholics exercised a strong influence in the trade unions.[54]

Local Labor factions were based primarily on personal loyalties and the development of patron–client relationships between leaders and followers. Ordinary working people without financial resources relied on local networks for support in times of unemployment or illness. Loyalty was a prized virtue in the urban working class, whether it be to kin and friends, church or party. Loyalty was also manifested in the local sports club, bonding people together and making them feel they belonged to the community.

Personal power was the business of local politics, power based on family feuds, faction fights and backroom deals. An individual recruited to a local branch was especially interested in the direct personal benefits that would flow from loyalty to a faction leader. The loyal activist received benefits of a tangible and material kind—clothing, blankets, meals for those in need. Others were found a job on the council and contacts eased the way for people who sought building and other permits. The successful faction leader had to remain constantly active, remaking links with each member of his team. Should the leader's energy flag, and benefits dry up, the prudent member looked for a new leader.[55]

The position of councillor could provide a springboard for higher office; if one supported one's mates, it could lead to several terms as Mayor and access to an allowance for a car. It also meant a chance for public prominence and resources for demonstrating in a variety of ways that one had become a figure of substance. For the less ambitious, years of faithful service to the party could be rewarded by preselection at the municipal election and a certain seat on Council. Machines developed intricate networks and the dominant group of councillors was able to deploy groups of compliant council workers within the party branches.[56]

The manner and dress of the new occupants of Glebe council chambers were in marked contrast to those of the old guard. Many wore blue flannel shirts to work—several were City Council employees. There was a railway worker, printer and union official, together with a schoolteacher, clerk, hairdresser and French polisher.[57] Bookmaker William Walsh served as Mayor from 1925 to 1929. The new Labor men—Bert Ward, Clarence Emblem, Jimmy Diver, Matthew Fitzpatrick, James Lahiff, Bobby Gorman, Frank Dick and Steve Cormack—were an eminently respectable lot. The old guard's fear of radicals running local affairs was without foundation.

At the 1934 elections, medical practitioner H.J. Foley became a member of Glebe Council.[58] Dr Foley's community involvement at a time of hardship, which included, among other things, giving free medical treatment to the poor, earned him local support and a territorial base for a career in local politics. Bill Carlton, a councillor since 1928, and his faction fought bitterly with the Foley faction for control of the local machine. Carlton was elected MLA for Glebe in 1935 and Foley was able to make Glebe his fief.[59] Dr Foley was charged with breaches of the *Local Government Act* in 1938 while he was Mayor, and after investigations into allegations about the administration of Glebe Council it was dismissed in 1939 and an administrator appointed.[60]

Three Labor men, Bertie Wheeler, George Mullins and Thomas Harrington, shared the robes and ritual of mayoral office between 1922 and 1924, but in December 1925 Labor was ousted when eight candidates of the Reform Party were elected to Council.[61] The control of Balmain Council remained in the hands of the Reform Party from 1926 to 1934, with Reg Thornton, Lyle Swan and Gilbert Storey serving as mayors in this period. Labor regained power in 1934 and remained the dominant group to 1948.[62] Compulsory voting was introduced in 1947 by a Labor government.

From the 1940s factional infighting on the Balmain peninsula centred around the three branches, all with large memberships. Rozelle East was the fiefdom of Michael Cashman, George Harris controlled the Balmain branch and Eddie Erwin was the faction leader at Rozelle. Though branch meetings were poorly attended, at elections and other times the Labor Party was able to call upon the faithful to work for the party.

Throughout the 1920s and 1930s Labor representatives were conspicuous by their absence on Leichhardt and Annandale councils. The non-Labor Progressive Party was the dominant group on Leichhardt Council from 1914 to 1941, and all mayors in this period—T. Hastings,

A. Blackmore, W. Lambert, H. Breen, W. Atkins, A. Campbell, W. Stuart, W. Bowmaker and W. Dyer—belonged to this influential business alliance. During that period three Labor men (E. Collins, F. Evans and J. Fisher) were elected in 1928, and another one, Alex O'Hare, in 1937.[63] For the first time in 1941 Labor had the majority of councillors at Leichhardt, and remained in power to 1948.[64]

Annandale was the most conservative of all councils, successfully beating off all attempts by Labor to get a foot in the door of its town hall. However, in the 1940s middle-class and employer interest in municipal politics in Annandale had waned sufficiently to allow for the election of the first Labor Mayor, health inspector James Prendergast JP, in 1945.[65]

Women seemed to threaten the masculine Anglo-Celtic atmosphere of local machines, and they were conspicuous by their absence from key positions. The right to election to councillor or Mayor was not conferred upon women until the *Women's Legal Status Act*, 1918, and in 1920 Fanny Furner (Manly) and Lilian Fowler (Newtown) were the first females to stand at municipal elections in Sydney. Neither was successful.[66] Though women did much of the hard work in the Leagues they were not rewarded by representation on Council.

Labor men brought with them the ritual of working-class life. Social solidarity was expressed in habitual modes of address ('mate' and 'comrade'), deployed in the conviviality of the pub, as well as such devices as caucusing, pledges of solidarity and the election by the whole caucus of leaders and ministers.[67] Labor's sense of mission focused on the male wage worker but from the conscription campaigns an articulate and animated group of women socialists and feminists challenged the continuing subordination of women in the Labor Party. Lilian Fowler, a strong character and outstanding organiser, was elected to Newtown Council in 1928, the first woman to enter the municipal arena. She remained on Council until 1948, operating from her base, the Newtown–Erskineville League, which she had made her fief from 1917.[68] An activist in the anti-conscription campaigns, Mary Ann Dunn was elected to Glebe Council in 1932 and remained on Council until 1937. A representative for Glebe on the West Sydney Electoral Council, Mrs Dunn was also campaign director for H.V. Evatt when he won the state seat of Balmain in 1925.[69] May Pitt also gained preselection at Glebe municipal elections in 1941 and remained there until 1945. No women were elected to either Annandale or Leichhardt councils before 1948, but Balmain had two female representatives—Elizabeth Gallimore from April 1943 to 1948, and Grace Laver from 1944 to 1948.[70]

In these working-class communities women engaged in diverse communal activities. Women's auxiliaries and distress societies formalised and gave official recognition to informal networks that had existed for decades. Mary Quirk gained preselection for the state seat of Balmain on the death of the sitting member, her husband, in 1938, and she remained the local MLA until 1950. At Balmain Dot Lincoln effectively ran the local branch, and elsewhere women were dominant figures at branch level. Sarah Peninton and May Pitt controlled the Glebe branch, and the Toxteth branch was the personal fief of Annie Doyle and Margaret Colbourne.

Mary Ann Dunn (1874–1944). A Glebe councillor from 1932 to 1937, Dunn was the first woman elected to any council in the current Leichhardt Municipality. She was also an active anti-conscriptionist and Glebe ALP representative on the West Sydney Electoral Council. (Municipality of Glebe, The Mayor's Report, 1935–1937)

Elizabeth Gallimore (1889–1958). The first woman elected to Balmain Council from 1943 to 1948 and a Leichhardt councillor in 1956–58. (Leichhardt Town Hall)

Table 17 Long-serving local elected representatives

	Councillor	Years	Occupation
Annandale 1894–1920			
1	T.E. Colebrook	1891–1901 (Leich), 1903–19, 1925–28	Printer
2	J. Robertson	1901–25	Tinsmith
3	C. Schofield	1906–25	Butcher
4	O. Ridge	1894–1912	Builder
5	A.E. Packer	1908–24	Builder
6	W. Wells	1894–99, 1901–16	Contractor
7	T.H. Chapman	1908–22	Sawmaker
8	J.E. Cummings	1908–22	Electrician
9	C.R. Winkworth	1919–33	Piano tuner
10	E. Hogan	1906–44	Carrier
Balmain 1860–1918			
1	H.B. Swan (R)	1889–1908, 1911–22, 1926	Timber merchant
2	R. Thornton (R)	1911–41	Solicitor
3	G. Clubb	1881–96, 1911–22	Estate agent
4	J. McDonald	1872–95	Architect
5	M.H. Cohen	1897–1919	Publican
6	R. Campbell	1895–1916	Accountant
7	T.E. Jesson	1903–22	Ironmonger
8	H. Mills	1895–1913	Boot importer
9	A. Milne	1893–1911	Brassfounder
10	H.P. Scott	1911–31	Storekeeper
11	H. Cox	1896–1910, 1917–19	Carpenter
Glebe 1859–1918			
1	P.C. Lucas	1880–1925	Wine & spirits merchant
2	T.J. Dunn	1876–1907	Tanner
3	T. Law	1889–1915	Hide merchant
4	S.L. Cole	1902–25	Carrier
5	M. Chapman	1866–74, 1878–92	Oil- & colour-man
6	W. Robey	1897–1916	Carrier
7	W. Cary	1878–82, 1892–1905	Ornamental plasterer
8	G.W. Allen	1859–77	Solicitor
9	W.T. Tate	1899–1904, 1908–13, 1920–25	Estate agent
10	A. Thornley senior	1859–64, 1868–83	Builder
Leichhardt 1871–1918			
1	A.B. Blackmore	1911–37	Solicitor
2	W.A. Lambert	1911–35	Dairyman
3	J.P. Treadgold	1892–1913	Accountant
4	J. Lonsdale	1892–96, 1902–13	Draper
5	N.C. Neale	1885–98, 1902–06	Banker
6	B.R. Moore	1885–99	Publican
7	W.B. Wragge	1888–1902	Storekeeper
8	J. Young	1879–87, 1894–99	Building contractor
9	W. Westbrook	1899–1912	Asphalter
10	W.D. Atkins	1914–16, 1920–37	Clerk
Annandale 1920–48			
1	E. Hogan (P)	1906–44	Carrier
2	G.W. Marshall (P)	1926–48	Milk carter
3	T. Douglas (P)	1934–48	Attendant
4	S.C. Francis (P)	1929–44	Engineer
5	C.R. Winkworth (P)	1919–33	Piano tuner
6	G. Law	1937–48	Tram driver
7	M.G. Smith (P)	1929–41	Collar maker
8	W.C. Boyd (P)	1932–41	Cabinetmaker
9	W. Roberts (P)	1919–31	Carriage builder
10	J. Prendergast	1941–48	Health inspector

Balmain 1920–48

1	R.M. Brownlee (L)	1923–25, 1929–48	Greengrocer
2	J.W. Waite (L)	1923–25, 1929–31, 1934–48	Butcher
3	S.H. Burns (R)	1924–39	Insurance
4	R.W. Robinson (R)	1924–38	Bricklayer
5	M.D. Cashman (L)	1932–44	Driver
6	H.G. Tatham (L)	1934–44	Plumber
7	B.L. Wheeler (L)	1920–31	Labourer
8	J.P. Gallen (L)	1919–28	Boilermaker
9	C. Stapleton (L)	1932–37, 1941–43	Foreman
10	L.B. Swan (R)	1926–34	Timber merchant
11	F.B. McIntosh (R)	1926–34	Shipping clerk

Glebe 1920–48

1	A. Ward (L)	1925–39	Schoolteacher
2	C. Emblem (L)	1925–39	Service marker
3	J. Diver (L)	1925–28, 1930–39	Clerk
4	J. Lahiff (L)	1927–39	French polisher
5	M. Fitzpatrick (L)	1929–39	Manager
6	R. Gorman (L)	1925–34	Salesman
7	F. Dick (L)	1925–35	Printer
8	S. McCormack (L)	1932–39	Carrier
9	W. Carlton (L)	1929–35	Railway worker
10	E. Pedersen (L)	1941–48	Storeman

Leichhardt 1920–48

1	W. Bowmaker (P)	1917–41	Builder
2	A.N. Campbell (P)	1919–41	Engineer
3	J.L. Campbell (P)	1920–37	Engineer
4	D.T. Swadling (P)	1923–41	Engineer
5	W.C. Dyer (P)	1925–41	Provision merchant
6	C.G. Harris (P)	1929–41	Labourer
7	W. Sutart (P)	1932–41, 1944–48	Cooper
8	R.S. Hudson (P)	1932–41	Landscape gardener
9	D.J. Beck (P)	1937–41, 1944–48	Coach painter
10	C.F. Gow (P)	1935–41, 1944–48	Chair manufacturer

Party affiliations:

(L) = Labor Party

(P) = Progressive Party

(R) = Reform Party

15 The slum stigma: life in the inter-war years

Peace brought its own challenges. Spanish flu claimed 15 million lives in Europe and there were fears returning troops would infect Australians. Strict quarantine measures were unable to restrict the spread of the virus that closed schools and theatres and overwhelmed hospitals with patients from February 1919.[1] The flu claimed the lives of 12,000 Australians.

In the war Australians suffered the highest casualty rates of any allied nation—60,000 dead and 150,000 wounded—and thousands of AIF men brought back physical and mental scars for the families who had to look after them. Blind and limbless men were familiar sights. Others suffered paralysis, disfigured faces, lung complaints caused by mustard gas and recurring neuroses that resulted in stammering, speechlessness, phobias, suicidal depression or uncontrollable violence.[2] Apart from its legacy of personal problems and social tensions, the war also raised people's expectations. Amidst a wave of strikes, and even housewives' boycotts of overpriced products, the promise made by the Prime Minister, W.M. Hughes, in the 1919 election campaign of a Royal Commission into the basic wage was widely accepted. Unionists saw it as a real chance to improve wages and conditions, and it was tolerated by employers out of fear of more radical and 'Bolshevik' demands.[3]

A.B. Piddington, a champion of the right to a decent living wage, chaired the Royal Commission that inquired into and reported on the living standards of the working population. The commission altogether examined 796 witnesses in all capital cities, and considered 580 exhibits. The Majority Report recommended that to meet the needs of a family with three children, the basic wage should be £5 16s 6d. Piddington accepted that it was unrealistic to assume that all workers could be paid a 'family' wage, and suggested a minimum wage of £4 0s 0d, and a benefit of twelve shillings endowment for every dependent child.[4] Industry howled that it could not afford the wage proposed and the first main test case before Justice Powers saw an outright rejection of the wage—and, as unemployment grew, employers set about driving down wages.[5]

In 1911 one-third of Sydney's population was concentrated within the City of Sydney and adjoining municipalities within two miles of the city centre.[6] The number of residents in these areas just after the war had declined to 32 per cent of the total metropolitan population, and

Red Cross staff distributing food to influenza victims at Balmain in 1919. The epidemic forced the closure of schools, theatres and other public places. (GPO Videodisc-1 Still 13507)

the inner-suburban share had shrunk to only 16 per cent in 1933. Aggregate populations in the municipalities of Annandale, Balmain and Glebe fell between 1921 and 1933, though Leichhardt was still growing.[7] In the inter-war years there were more demolitions than new buildings in Glebe.[8]

Vast tracts of land on the periphery of the metropolis were being carved up and sold off, and during the 1920s such was the magnitude of land subdivision that the shape of Sydney changed radically. To the north and south of the harbour, and especially in the western and southwestern regions, the tempo of property development and house-building quickened. Semi-detached houses and bungalows with gardens took centre stage and many fled to these new environments.[9] Growth in zones between three and thirteen miles from the city centre was facilitated by an expanding tramway network, electrification of railways and growth of motor transport. The heart of the city remained the hub of industry and commerce, with manufacturing industries, protected by tariffs, as major employers.[10]

The steady upward climb of inner-city rents was halted in 1916 with the introduction of the *Fair Rents Act*, and some landlords began to sell their terraces and look for more lucrative avenues of investment. However those landlords who remained in the market still fared well, since between 1919 and 1929 average rent levels rose by 50 per cent.[11] Rent remained a heavy burden for workers, eating into their inadequate wage. Sub-letting in poor localities tended to

Christie Street, Glebe, 1938. With its narrow frontage terraces, Christie Street was a harsh and sterile place, a street synonymous with chronic want. These buildings were demolished in about 1952 and replaced by multi-unit Housing Commission constructions. (GPO Videodisc-1 Still 27788)

increase overcrowding. A shrinking population left vacant some of the oldest housing stock and 'Not Fit for Habitation' notices were being affixed to their doors by health inspectors.[12] Invading industry added to pollution and noise and heavy traffic accelerated the decay of poor residential communities.

Recovery from the effects of war shortages and inflation was uneven and fragile. The urban economy, tied to the fortunes of primary industries, remained subject to seasonal fluctuation. The level of unemployment ranged between 6 and 11 per cent, and there was a permanent residue of unskilled and casual labour.[13]

Underlying much of the criticism of working-class life was an ideological objection to terrace housing. Critics of terraces described them as 'ugly and monotonous beyond expression', and focused on their room size, the size of blocks, their physical condition, alleged overcrowded state and absence of basic amenities.[14] In a sense the terrace became a physical expression of the gulf between the classes.

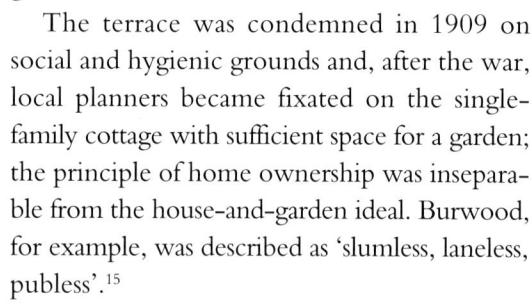

The terrace was condemned in 1909 on social and hygienic grounds and, after the war, local planners became fixated on the single-family cottage with sufficient space for a garden; the principle of home ownership was inseparable from the house-and-garden ideal. Burwood, for example, was described as 'slumless, laneless, publess'.[15]

Wilfred Allen, expressing a distaste for flats and boarding houses in 1924, claimed that the Church of England, a large landowner in Glebe, had 'stopped progress' there by not 'demolishing the slums and erecting modern buildings in their place'.[16] After the death of J.D. Fitzgerald in 1922, the slum eradication and rehousing debate did not revive until about 1932. Nevertheless throughout the 1920s near-city working-class accommodation was increasingly subjected to negative stereotyping. Self-respecting working men and their families, unable to flee to quarter-acre blocks on the suburban landscape, drew upon themselves the stigma of slum-dwellers, denizens of rough and nasty streets and houses, their lives, like their environment, smoky, dirty, and crime-ridden in the eyes of Sydney's better paid, more respectable citizens.[17]

The *Labor Daily*, a critical part of working-class literary culture, shaped the opinions of many in the inner city and in 1935 it entered the anti-slum campaign. N.H. Dick joined in calling for the 'total elimination' of the slums, which in his view stretched from Woolloomooloo Bay through Surry Hills, Paddington, Redfern, Newtown, Glebe, Pyrmont, Balmain, Alexandria, Waterloo and Botany.[18] Even the cartoonists in the *Australian Worker* were depicting the one-storey terrace as being 'not fit for dogs to live in'.[19] Locals vigorously defended any assaults on the respectability of their suburb and resented this public condemnation by a workingman's paper. The tenants' condition was something Labor men knew about and argued against the non-Labor government's pro-landlord stance. William McKell's widowed mother and family were evicted from their Redfern home in 1917, and though untiring in his opposition to landlordism in his political career, McKell became a vocal and persistent slum-eradication advocate.[20] Another product of the inner city, Eddie Ward, born at Surry Hills, had a different perspective to McKell. Dismissed from the tramways for his part in the 1917 strike, Ward was mostly unemployed for seven years until he found security of a kind as a tramway labourer, and was later arrested for picketing at the timber-workers' strike. Elected the federal member for East Sydney in 1931, Ward was an inner-city dweller, and proud of it, and did not want to see the area where he lived demolished or his constituents moved to the outer suburbs.[21]

The inner suburbs were continually portrayed in government reports, novels and newspaper accounts in an unflattering light. To middle-class Sydney these areas had nothing to commend them. Ruth Park depicted working-class accommodation in Surry Hills as having 'hideous backyards, full of garbage cans, tom-cats and lavatories with swinging broken doors and rusty buckled tin roofs' and the womenfolk who lived there complained that 'the rest of Sydney persisted in looking down on them'.[22] After a visit to Glebe in 1932 Marjorie McEvoy found it inhabited by 'vociferous women, dirty, quarrelling children, shabby men vacantly supporting posts or gathered in groups on empty allotments'. She complained of the dirt and noise and claimed that she was almost knocked off her feet by 'lean, dirty, unmannerly dogs (admiringly described by their owners as "ricing dorgs")'.[23] If you lived in the inner suburbs, they thought, you could probably fight or play football, but do blessed little else. The Housing Conditions Investigation Committee stigmatised the inner city as 'blighted zones' that needed to be rehabilitated or demolished. G.R. Gerlach of the Housing Improvement Board wrote in 1937: 'Right through the inner ring of the metropolitan municipalities are thickly populated areas, where property has deteriorated beyond recovery, centres of economic waste and breeding places for crime, disease and social demoralisation.'[24]

Sectarian antagonisms, mobilised during the conscription campaigns, continued to burn fiercely after the war with the election of the militantly Protestant and anti-Catholic Fuller government in New South Wales. There was little open hostility, except among schoolboys in the separate systems who shouted rude rhymes at each other and threw stones. In employment, especially in the public service, the rivalry of Catholics and Masons was a fact of life. Passions were inflamed in 1925 when the government sought to legislate to declare illegal Catholic canon law on mixed marriages.[25] Non-Labor cliques on councils often had militant Protestant members, and Orange and Masonic lodges were part of the machinery of the economic preferment for Protestants in business, the public service and politics. Denominational tribalism extended to some sporting clubs which adopted the black ball test in balloting to ensure Catholics could not get a foot in the door.[26] However from the 1920s a growing number of Catholics exercised power and influence through the Labor machine and as municipal councillors.[27]

Though beer consumption declined dramatically in the depression it still remained one of the few pleasures left for the working class, Some were anxious, however, to deprive them of this pleasure; drink was blamed for unemployment by the temperance advocates in the public debate leading up to the Prohibition poll in September 1928.[28] The anti-prohibitionists counter-attacked claiming prohibition would foster organised crime. The forces of respectability were unable to convince workers that not having a drink was good for them.

The 41 members of Balmain Police Station in 1922 including motor cyclists (extreme left and right). Introduction of motor cycles and vehicles after the 1914–18 war improved the speed and efficiency of the force but slowly eroded the relationship constables on the beat had developed with their local community. (Balmain Police Station)

The main role of the suburban constabulary was to maintain local order by patrolling the streets and apprehending trouble-makers; opening of stations at Balmain (1854), Glebe (1882), Leichhardt (1887) and Annandale (1905) allayed middle-class anxieties about threats to life and property.[29] Though police knew their backstreets and suspicious 'characters' well, working-class neighbourhoods exhibited strong cultures of resistance; attacks by street pushes or gangs on patrolling constables were not infrequent. It was in the enforcement of public order that police most often ran foul of working men. In 1899, 81 per cent of all arrests involved offences against good order.[30]

Many activities policed, including drinking, swearing, fighting, urinating in the streets and vagrancy, came within the province of public propriety and appropriate behaviour, and police were officially equipped with a repertoire of responses—caution, arrest, summons. Constables were required to perform an extraordinary range of social and administrative duties— policing breaches of licensing laws, infractions of public health regulations and truancy, the administration of maintenance payments and the enforcement of municipal Acts.[31]

The close contact police established in reinforcing their presence on the streets was an effective method of maintaining social order in suburban communities. By 1916 early closing legislation and the expansion of summary offences had created further police responsibilities. The introduction of motor cycles and vehicles improved the speed and efficiency of the force but slowly eroded the relationship constables on the beat had developed within their local community.[32]

The introduction of six o'clock closing and the limited range of old off-course tote shops indirectly created a sufficient economic base for the formation of a coherent vice economy. Crime was one industry that boomed in peace.[33] Sly grog, SP bookmaking, narcotics and prostitution emerged in the 1920s as lucrative industries that were able to sustain, for the first time, entrepreneurs who lived by controlling criminals instead of committing crimes. The combined cocaine–prostitution trade, concentrated in East Sydney and Kings Cross, created exceptional profits and led to conflict between syndicates headed by Norman Bruhn, Phil Jeffs, Kate Leigh and Tilly Devine. Between 1927 and 1930 razor gangs fought violent and intensive battles for the control of the cocaine trade. After the tabloid press published graphic accounts of the violence the gangs were quickly eliminated by police.[34]

The present Leichhardt Municipality was largely untouched by the gangs that dominated

Darlinghurst, but sly grog and SP bookmaking were widely dispersed, with shops and outlets in all suburbs. The inner industrial suburbs were a challenging frontier for a young constable sworn to keep the peace. His working life was divided into shifts, and from 10 p.m. to 6 a.m. on the night shift, this uniformed figure, armed with a whistle and a Webley Scott .32 revolver, trudged alone along dimly lit streets. It was mainly the non-respectable part of the working class that came into contact with the law. Ray Blissett, a policeman stationed at Glebe from 1928, recalled that there were plenty of 'quality criminals' in Balmain, including 'Bogan' Dempsey and 'Minties' Skinner (who mused when receiving a ten-year sentence for armed robbery, 'it's moments like these you need Minties'). Glebe, too, had its fair share of 'knock-about criminals', including Harry 'Boo' Stanton, Reg and Stan Flannagan, Brian Kelly, 'Tinker' Wilson, 'Googer' Morton, Raymond Riley and Norman and Robert Connolly.[35] Though he resided in Chippendale, gunman 'Chow' Hayes appeared in Glebe Court charged with offences committed in the neighbourhood.[36]

By 1920, four years after six o'clock closing began, the sly grog trade, it was estimated, had increased tenfold.[37] Bottled beer was bought from hotels on discount and the operator usually doubled his money, paying 1s 2d a bottle and then selling it by the glass at unlicensed premises. Not all supplies were obtained from pubs. Percy Neville and 'Ripper' Robinson, operating in a lane behind the Toxteth Hotel, Glebe, stole their bottled beer from trains travelling by tunnel under Glebe. Eva Casey was always charged when the flourishing Lyndhurst Street sly grog outlet was raided. She took the rap for the real operator, her husband Tom, the City Librarian, who would otherwise have lost his job.[38]

SP bookmaking emerged in response to revolutionary changes in communications. The off-course gambler could now follow the race live through radio broadcasts and the SP bookmaker could contact everyone with access to a telephone.[39] Hotels, barber shops and corner mixed businesses served as SP shops, but the most popular place was the 'Run-In' (you ran in with a few 'bob' and then ran out), a backyard or an empty garage with the door cut in half like the loose box of a stable. 'Cockatoos' kept watch for raiding police, and agents were employed on pushbikes to collect bets. After the industry attracted standover men, police formed an effective Consorting Squad and they were supplied with information of strong-arm tactics. Allegations were made that SP bookmakers were making regular payments to police, and in 1936 a Royal Commission was appointed to investigate these charges. Four local policemen including Sergeant Thomas Dunn of Glebe and Sergeant John Hogan of Balmain, gave evidence to the Commission 'into allegations against the Police in connection with the Suppression of Illegal Betting'. Incorporated in the report was an illuminating lecture on sly grog by Superintendent Mackay.[40] Labor parliamentarians defended sly grog and SP betting, both popular working-class leisure activities, as acceptable social diversions. John Storey, MP for Balmain, in opposing an amendment seeking to ban one-shilling race 'sweeps', said 'Because a man happens to be a worker, and is unable by reason of unfortunate position, to pay three shillings and sixpence to enter the Leger at Randwick, and makes a bet elsewhere, he is designated a criminal'.[41]

In the debate about what was 'fair and reasonable' for 'the humblest class of worker', the balance would be tipped very much in favour of capital in its inevitable conflict with labour.[42] In February 1929 timber workers refused to work under an award handed down by Justice Lukin which provided for 'longer hours, less pay, piecework and substitution of youth for adults'.[43] The award was perceived as a forerunner of a broader attack on the 44-hour week and workers' wages and conditions generally. It was estimated that between 25,000 and 75,000 strikers and supporters gathered at Sydney Trades Hall, and the procession then moved towards Hyde Park to the tune of 'The Red Flag' and 'Solidarity Forever', and in the park a large effigy of the judge was burnt.[44]

The timber strike was remarkable for its tenacity and duration in the mills clustered around Blackwattle, Rozelle and White bays. Locked-out timber workers were able to sustain their industrial militancy because of the strong support traditional networks in their local working-class communities provided.[45] Relief depots, established in areas where workers lived and worked, provided families with about £1 a week for food. Money was raised locally at euchre parties, smoke concerts and evening entertainments, and wives of workers collected at football grounds and boxing stadiums, hotels and theatres. Boycotts and pickets were used against landlords who evicted timber workers and storekeepers who refused to assist the strikers' cause.[46] Without the assistance of shops in Forest Lodge, the Glebe relief depot would have been hard-pressed to supply the families with bread, meat, vegetables, groceries and fish; the public listing of boycotted establishments in the *Labor Daily* was a strong inducement for local businesses to actively support strikers.[47]

Timber workers massed at the Trades Hall, Goulburn Street, Sydney, during their General Strike in 1929. (Max Solling Collection)

Moored logs ready for milling at George Hudson's timber yards, Blackwattle Bay, Glebe, 1913. Timber mills clustered round Blackwattle, Rozelle and White Bays were significant employers of local labour. (Max Solling Collection)

As the strike progressed morale was increasingly undermined by the employers' engagement of strike-breakers who were shuttled by tram into Glebe under heavy police protection. George Hudson's mill at Blackwattle Bay became the scene for violent clashes in July 1929 between police and women and men picketing the site. After the whistle blew at Hudson's mill in the afternoon, strikebreakers had to run the gauntlet of angry strike supporters surrounding the yard and stretching back along Bridge Road. Locals pelted them with stones and charged at them with fence palings, yelling 'you scabbing bastards', and women tossed dirty dish water over 'loyalist' workers.[48] Throughout the strike carloads of police, known as the 'basher gang', would arrive early in the morning as pickets formed and, armed with their waddies, move in and, as one policeman observed, 'God help any strikers who got in the road'.[49] Picketers were charged with assault and seven strike leaders were prosecuted, unsuccessfully, for conspiracy, intimidation and molestation. Glebe Council lodged a complaint that 'the procession of voluntary workers . . . was preventing local residents from using our own streets'.[50] 'The police have been enrolled,' roared alderman Bill Carlton,

> to protect these scabs who are taking the bread and butter out of the mouths of the timber workers and their dependants. I have seen the scabs, well-protected by police, make insulting gestures to people standing around. This protest should have been entered weeks ago to let the world know we have no sympathy with such a scabby outfit as Hudson's.[51]

This trial of strength left timber workers financially and psychologically broken. The last strikers, sustained to the end by local women who established formal and informal networks to retain their living standards, remained out until 17 October 1929, some eight-and-a-half months, but the union had to back down and accept the Lukin award. Very few were re-employed in their mills, and many faced long periods of unemployment.[52]

Again at the end of 1929 the New South Wales Nationalist government, determined to use non-union labour to break the lockout at the Rothbury mine, sent armed police to the coalfields to enforce its decision. In a clash between pickets and 'loyalists', police opened fire, killing a miner. It was an incident that assumed great emotional importance; an outraged Glebe Council protested to Premier Bavin for 'using armed forces of the State for the purposes of shooting down unarmed members of the working class'.[53]

Social welfare provided by government in New South Wales was limited to a pension for widows with dependent children and workers' compensation. In 1927, one of the last acts of the Lang government was to introduce child endowment. There was no government provision for unemployment benefits, but the extent of distress required government efforts to assist the unemployed despite wider economic imperatives to reduce expenditure.

Local government was expected to bear responsibilities for health and social welfare. Councils, already burdened with overdrafts and seeking to balance their budgets, began standing down outdoor employees.[54] Federal and state governments were forced to intervene with grants for relief schemes. An Unemployment Relief Tax, imposed in 1930, was expended in two ways: on food and on relief works. J.T. Lang dominated depression politics. Remembering the humiliation of his own destitute childhood, he made food relief a distinguishing characteristic of his administration. Labor, concerned to avoid any suggestion of stigma, saw the poor or unemployed as ordinary human beings. 'You will have to realise in your home, in your own person,' Lang told his colleagues, 'what the poor devils outside have been suffering months too long.'[55] Non-Labor was less sympathetic; it upheld the traditional virtue of self-help and suspected the moral worth of able-bodied men who sought food relief.

Metropolitan food relief was administered through the Department of Labour and Industry. To qualify, a person had to sign a declaration that their income was below a certain amount. The dole varied according to the size of a family. The permissible income test was severe. A couple earning forty shillings a fortnight got full relief,

Dole queue at Harold Park in 1931. Unemployed men became exposed to public gaze as they lined up to receive the dole. (A. Sharp, *Nostalgia Australia*, Dominion Publishing, 1975)

a couple earning forty-one shillings got nothing. As the value of food relief was counted in, some qualified for relief only in alternate weeks.[56] Men became exposed to public gaze as they lined up in queues to receive the dole. Orders for food were in the form of coupons drawn against local shops, government stores and charity depots.

The level of poverty of those on relief and part-time work was illustrated by the Minority Report of the 1929 Royal Commission into Child Endowment. This stated that the basic wage could barely support a man and wife and one child, let alone the three children the Harvester Judgement laid down as the minimum standard of living.[57] The dole of £1 2s 9d a week in 1934 was clearly well below minimum subsistence requirements; in 1932 the number on the sustenance dole peaked at 600,000.[58] Those reluctant to submit themselves to the indignity of applying for the dole could undertake relief work. Initially this was provided two weeks at a time, but in 1933 the government introduced a scheme in co-operation with local councils. Annandale, Balmain, Glebe and Leichhardt councils all established relief work systems between 1930 and 1934. They involved work on construction or improvement projects that had previously generated employment on public works. Some people simply worked to pay off rate arrears but some schemes were on a large scale; in Leichhardt in 1934, for example, 1,000 men participated in relief work which stretched over fourteen weeks.[59]

Local voluntary social agencies could not cope with the demands relief required. St Vincent de Paul, an organisation of Catholic laymen, and the Salvation Army distributed food parcels, and the Sydney City Mission had a real presence, actively responding to the physical needs of the poor. All the churches, too, assisted the poor and homeless. Strong community spirit in the suburbs meant the poor often received more help from friends and neighbours than from charities; food was shared with neighbours who had fallen on hard times, and savings were pooled to spare a neighbour the indignity of a pauper's funeral. Need also found an outlet in the pawnshops, which were invariably located in poor localities. Balmain supported four private moneylenders in 1915; two each could be found in Rozelle, Glebe and Leichhardt and one in Annandale. Those who relied on the broker to live a week in advance of wages pledged their jewellery, clothes, cutlery and other items and returned home with cash to pay the rent or buy food.[60]

Pleas of demoralised workers were not being heard, for they lacked the effective organisation and clout of trade unions. Nobody wanted to know them, and the Labor Party seemed unable to do much to improve their condition. The appearance of the Unemployed Workers Movement (UWM) in 1930 set it apart from other unemployed organisations, providing an alternative life and hope for the unemployed. Communist-led, the UWM believed unemployment would be permanent under capitalism, and its aims were clearly stated in its organ *Call to Action*: 'our tactics are to organise the workers for mass fights in place of individual and committee fights, for example, mass demonstrations, mass picketing and strikes for evictions, protest meetings, petitions . . .'.[61]

The UWM quickly moulded itself into a tough, skilful and militant political organisation that acquired a reputation for action and fearlessness. It maintained an uneasy relationship with the labour movement, but the more radical hailed its membership as the true socialists in the Labor Party, bent on an equitable redistribution of wealth.[62] The UWM arranged entertainment, including concerts, dances and boxing contests, it established shelters for the homeless and provided comradeship for those who had fallen on hard times. In Annandale its headquarters in a disused Nelson Street hotel provided accommodation for activists, usually single men without family ties.[63] A spectacular form of protest and resistance by the unemployed was their opposition to evictions. The UWM picketed properties where tenants were threatened with eviction for arrears of rent, in order to prevent the agent emptying their belongings into the street.[64]

At Balmain, the home of the cartoonist, writer and orator Jack Sylvester was the centre of debate on communism, wobblyism, socialism, anarchy and Trotskyism, political ideologies that challenged the capitalist order. The Balmain UWM persuaded the local council and Tooheys to allow the delicensed Volunteer Hotel to be used as a hostel and night shelter for 28 men but, along with their Leichhardt colleagues, they were unable to get the Defence Department's agreement for its drill halls to be occupied by the homeless.[65] The ruling non-Labor clique on Balmain Council, however, would have nothing to do with the Friends of the Soviet Union's request to use King George Park to celebrate the fourteenth anniversary of the Russian Revolution.[66]

The Balmain UWM vigorously argued for the dole to be doubled and paid in cash or open order, and its platform contained a rent and clothing allowance. At Leichhardt the UWM enjoyed a good rapport with councillors; they agreed to erect a board in front of the Town Hall where newspapers could be displayed and they handed over some 40 chairs, which were beyond repair, for the unemployed to use as firewood.[67]

Annandale Council allowed the UWM to hold a concert for the unemployed in Hinsby Park and reluctantly agreed to being addressed by communist Ena Stack; but it was much more comfortable dealing with the anti-communist Annandale Workers' Association, whose objects were twofold—taking the unemployed off the streets, and offering them the opportunity to help themselves. The Children's Relief Committee asked Council to openly support the UWM's efforts to supply soup to children. They refused.[68]

The Glebe UWM, led by Stan Moran, was a very active and militant branch; it operated a relief depot which distributed up to one hundred gallons of soup daily.[69] The Glebe Labor Council, dominated by Catholics, was antagonistic to the UWM. In 1930 a UWM member bitterly complained to Council about its insults and insinuations and then walked out.[70] Surprisingly, Council allowed communist Mrs Sharkey's Glebe Workers' Study Circle to hold its lectures in the Town Hall.[71] The unemployed had earlier requested Council to hand over the sheep and goat which grazed in Jubilee Park for them to eat, and suggested that Council employ some of those out of work to mow the grass these animals ate. Mayor Dick was unsympathetic: 'a goat was mentioned in the letter but they forgot to mention the goat that put forward the proposal'.[72]

A celebrated anti-eviction battle occurred at Union Street, Newtown, in June 1930 when 40 police, attempting to execute an eviction order, stormed a house. Picketers replied with stones and other weapons and casualties on both sides were heavy. Police crashed through pickets at Starling Street, Leichhardt, and batoned and severely beat the occupants holed up in the house.[73]

Evictions for arrears in rent were disastrous for people such as this family who, with their belongings, had been emptied on to a Redfern street in 1934. The Unemployed Workers Movement picketed property where tenants fell behind with payment of rent and sought to stop agents evicting them. (Hood Videodisc Still 00870, Mitchell Library)

There was a strong UWM presence at a picketed house in Bridge Road, Glebe, in 1931, but two bus loads of police returned at dawn the next day to catch the squatters napping. One of those arrested is alleged to have said he did it 'to wake up Lang and Gosling'.[74]

Stan Moran, leader of the Glebe UWM, led a deputation in November 1931 to see Glebe's Mayor about Premier Lang's permissible income questionnaire.[75] The questionnaire sought answers to, among other things, whether dole recipients had any livestock. Fleas, some said. Mayor Bert Ward told him it was none of the council's business. Moran then proceeded to address the crowd and police moved in to arrest the activist. They were repelled by angry workers.[76] That evening an estimated crowd of 5,000 surrounded Glebe Town Hall and in an act of defiance began burning about 1,000 dole forms. Inspector Tom O'Brien lined up Glebe police at their station and told them to teach the 'commos' a lesson. R.G. Blissett recalled:

> We were then conveyed on motor lorries to the Town Hall and ordered to clear the streets. It became mayhem with uniformed police, batons drawn, belting the daylight out of any one stupid enough to stand and resist. I recall Inspector O'Brien, whip in hand, chasing and belting across the backside a female, a woman named Eatock, a leading communist of those times.[77]

The demonstration left two police sergeants in hospital with serious injuries and those arrested were charged with summary offences.[78]

Average weekly rentals in Annandale, Balmain, Glebe and Leichhardt in 1933 ranged from 15s 5d to 18s 11d.[79] Those unable to pay rent were constantly on the move, often under cover of darkness. The 'moonlight flit' was born in the depression; those in debt who stayed too long could lose what few possessions they had to the agent.

Basic facilities were lacking in some housing. 'I moved to an upstairs room in a terrace house at Glebe,' Judith Wright remembered. 'There was neither bath nor shower, the landlady indicating that the backyard washtub provided all a Christian should need (she was stronger on Godliness than cleanliness).'[80] The health inspector at Glebe reported that a combination of poverty and a 'lack of proper food and clothing' in overcrowded housing was conducive to lowering resistance and spread of disease.[81] The Balmain Infectious Diseases Register revealed the most common notifiable diseases in 1930 to be scarlet fever, with 43 cases, and diphtheria, 37. Reported cases of diphtheria in Balmain had climbed to 164 in 1937.[82]

For working-class communities in Annandale, Balmain, Glebe and Leichhardt the depression began in the early 1920s and finished in the late 1930s, leaving an indelible imprint on the physical and social fabric of these areas. The human toll is difficult to quantify. Most working-class people alternated between intermittent employment and the dole and these common experiences limited tension and hostility by producing a conviction that all were 'in the same boat'.

The raw statistics taken on census day in 1933 underestimated the full extent of unemployment or underemployment. Broadly, two-thirds of all male employees and three-quarters of all female employees were either unemployed or earning less than the basic wage, which suggests that they were working only part-time or accepting lower wages in preference to unemployment. In 1933 38.1 per cent of Balmain's male workforce was listed as being out of work; in Glebe the figure was 39.5 per cent, in Annandale 32.7 per cent and in Leichhardt 31.0 per cent. Slightly fewer females were listed as unemployed: 23.8 per cent in Balmain, 22.3 per cent in Leichhardt, 21.4 per cent in Glebe and 20.7 per cent in Annandale. Most males had incomes in the £52 to £155 bracket in Annandale, Balmain, Glebe and Leichhardt, and only 3 per cent to 6 per cent had annual incomes exceeding the annual male basic wage of £250.[83]

16 Popular recreation

Evidence of the early patterns of leisure activities is inevitably random, but games of cricket were being played just beyond the city limits in the 1850s, and football games resembling Rugby were nurtured by gentlemen's clubs and private schools from about 1865.[1] Publicans attracted custom by offering patrons skittles, billiards and quoits, and the pub became a venue for blood sports involving animals: cock-fighting, dog-fighting and bull-baiting. These contests were outlawed by legislators who viewed them as barbaric, but the status of rats gave them no legal protection. Ratting pits remained in or near some pubs with prize money offered for dogs who killed the most prey.[2] Organising prize fights was also good for the drink trade, and appealed to the street-fighting tradition of the poor working class. The middle class set the tone of society in Balmain and Glebe, and with games acquiring a new popularity and social purpose, their villa estates featured croquet lawns, bowling greens and bathing houses.[3]

Expansion of recreational 'Sport' was initially inhibited by the lack of playing fields, for unfettered suburban growth made little provision for places where people could play games. Perhaps they were expected to fill six days with work and to rest on the Sabbath. The developers of suburbs did not have to contribute towards public reserves. The parks and playing fields dedicated for public recreation were unsuitable for residential development. Wentworth Park (1885), Easton Park (1890), Birchgrove Park (1893), Federal Park (1899) and Jubilee Park (1908) were tracts of low-lying, swampy 'fever beds' reclaimed by fill from government dredges.[4] The only piece of prime real estate set aside for the people was Leichhardt Park.

Football and cricket provided an outlet for aggression and the competitive instincts of young men. A growing sense of identification with place could be discerned in the inner suburbs from the 1880s and any club, by taking the name of a suburb, attracted strong local support. At the football and cricket, local elders, too old to play, but with emotion to expend, watched, shouted and gained satisfaction from talking over the day's play. Women were largely excluded from this new world of sport. It was a male domain, with its own language, rituals and models of masculinity. Henry Lawson, a little bemused with the passion for sports and games, wrote:

> In a land where sport is sacred,
> Where the Laborer is God,

You must pander to the people,
Make a hero of a clod.[5]

The first sign of increasing organisation and regulation of games in New South Wales was an association controlling cricket (1856). The main winter game, Rugby, had its own governing body in 1874, and soon bodies controlling amateur rowing (1878), bowls (1880), soccer (1882), athletics (1887), and swimming (1892) were established. By the time of Federation a host of formal and strictly organised clubs and associations had succeeded in reshaping and modernising almost every game then in existence.[6]

A Sydney electoral cricket competition, based on residential qualifications, began in 1893. Glebe was represented from the first season, Leichhardt from 1894–95, and Balmain made its entrance into the second-grade competition in 1897. Crowds of 10,000 were reported at Wentworth Park in 1896, but at suburban ovals on Saturday afternoons just before World War I, cricket was unable to attract anything like the numbers who followed their district Rugby League teams.[7] There was little demand for professional cricketers in the domestic competition, where the game remained almost entirely amateur. However some talented cricketers did accrue material benefits without actually signing a contract or being given a pay packet. Testimonials were organised for them and they were given sinecures by their clubs, or employed in ways related to the game.[8] A feature of the pre-war Sydney competition was the graceful batting style of Paddington's Victor Trumper and Glebe, with Australian representatives A. Coningham, T. McKibbin, A. Cotter, W. Bardsley, C. Kelleway and W.A. Oldfield, were three-time premiers up to 1914. In 1902–03 a combined Balmain–Leichhardt XI were runners up, and in 1915–16 Balmain, with A. Mailey, B. Folkard, A. Ratcliffe, H. Love and L. Wall in its line up, won its first premiership.[9]

There were only 23 Rugby clubs in New South Wales in 1877, but Rugby shrugged off the challenge of Victorian Rules and by 1879–80 it was established as the dominant football code in Sydney.[10] The Rugby competition acquired a recognisably modern shape in 1883 with senior and junior premiership matches, but encroachments by partisans on to the unenclosed grounds frequently disrupted club games. A Sydney district Rugby competition began in 1900 with clubs represented and the game continued to be controlled by middle-class gentlemen thoroughly imbued with the amateur ethos. But as more working men took up the game, it was inevitable that the traditional Rugby ideology would face a challenge.[11]

J.W. Fletcher and other British public school old boys promoted soccer in Sydney in the 1880s but they were soon replaced by blue-collar workers from England and Scotland who filled inner-city teams. Pyrmont Rangers dominated the Gardiner Cup, appearing in seventeen finals between 1889 and 1914. 'Pyrmont was rich in the number of her barrackers,' noted the *Australian Star* in 1889, 'who appeared upon the scene with large tickets in the front of their hats, upon which were inscribed words of encouragement to the Rangers.'[12] Balmain, strengthened by workers from Britain, also fielded strong sides in the Gardiner Cup, emerging as premiers in 1895, 1896 and 1897; they were four times cup holders between 1905 and 1915, and, as Balmain–Fernleigh, were premiers in 1919 and 1920. Glebe won the Gardiner Cup in 1906, three years after the club was formed and Leichhardt–Annandale became a force in Sydney soccer from the 1940s, won the State League Cup in 1943, 1948, 1949 and 1956 and won the State League series four times between 1946 and 1955.[13]

Football was not without its critics. In 1896, for example, fighting on and off the field and other disturbances attracted a series of articles in the Sydney press on the alleged brutalising influence of the game.[14] Concerted efforts were made to establish the Victorian code in Sydney and throughout the 1880s and 1890s the West Sydney Australian Football Club played its home games at Wentworth Park. Australian Rules experienced a revival in Sydney in 1903 when Balmain and ten other clubs engaged in a district competition and in 1906 a crowd of 3,000 watched Balmain play YMCA at Wentworth Park.[15] The New South Wales Football League won over many schools to the Victorian game; 58 state schools and thirteen Catholic schools played the game in Sydney in 1908. However, it seems, few went on to play senior football and Australian football was left with a small band of devotees, many of whom were expatriate Victorians and South Australians. The Balmain club battled on to the end of the 1925 season, and has continued to function since it was reformed in 1948.

Clubs for riders of the cumbersome penny-farthing bicycle were formed in the 1880s. This cycle was both expensive and difficult to ride, and enthusiasm waned and clubs disbanded. In the inner city, clubs for the new 'safety bike' flourished. They provided the athlete with a new and exciting form of leisure, and the working man with a new mobility. Local road races became a feature of the cycling calendar, with cyclists wearing tweed suits, caps and stockings peddling furiously along suburban arteries.[16]

Young professionals and men in trade and commerce, together with public servants and bank and insurance clerks were well represented in rowing clubs in Balmain, Glebe and Leichhardt in their formative years. After manual workers became eligible to compete in association regattas from 1903 the social composition of these clubs gradually changed as men in occupations previously conspicuous by their absence—labourers, policemen, stonemasons and publicans—were taking up the sport.[17] The local oarsman in 1912 was 'a man of slender means', according to Gordon Inglis. 'His path is not easy,' he wrote, 'for even in summer the evenings are short and much of his training must be done in the dark.'[18] Balmain, Glebe and Leichhardt all enjoyed considerable success on the water. The Balmain Working Men's Club, renamed Balmain Enterprise in 1892, came to a sudden end in September 1917 after its White Horse Point boatshed was demolished in a storm and its fleet destroyed.

People on the Balmain peninsula revelled in the delights of the sea that surrounded them. From 1849 to 1914 the Balmain regatta was celebrated every year on 9 November. A rowing correspondent in 1876 observed: 'The rocky foreshores of Balmain were literally thronged from morning to dusk. The scene was a particularly lively one. There were flags flying from all the poles and masts to be seen around and the water was alive with a perfect fleet of small

Sailing, Mort Bay, Balmain, c.1900. The people on the Balmain peninsula revelled in the delights of the sea. The Balmain regatta was first held in 1849 and the Balmain Sailing Club had a real presence on the harbour from 1885. (Tyrrell Collection, vol. 1, section 1, No 62, ref 1966, PXA433, Dixson Library)

craft of every description flitting hither and thither.'[19] On the harbour the Balmain Sailing Club (1885) had a real presence. It had all manner of open boats, from 24-footers to 10-footers, on its register and was a club that accommodated both amateurs and professionals. The boats of the Johnston's Bay Sailing Club added to the colour of Balmain's waters at weekends from 1895.[20]

Municipal councils began constructing pools and baths in the 1880s and initially imposed by-laws requiring bathers to cover their bodies from neck to knee. From its foundation in 1884 the Balmain Swimming Club was very active, conducting regular meetings at the White Horse Point pool, and by 1902 three other local clubs, Gladstone, Mort's Dock and Balmain East, were engaging in friendly competition. Inspired by their Balmain neighbours, Leichhardt people were holding swimming carnivals at their Iron Cove pool from 1905.[21]

W.F. Morrison observed in 1888 that although the 'youth of twenty summers and a man of seventy' were found on the bowling green, 'it was a game well adapted for men of years'.[22] John Young was a major influence in the early development of the game. He established the Kentville club at his Annandale residence in 1878, and as president of the New South Wales Bowling Association initiated regular intercolonial matches with Victoria. Bowling clubs were formed at Balmain (1880), Glebe (1882) and Gladstone Park (1896).[23] The new club at Victoria Park absorbed some of Glebe's members when its club closed in 1899. The game flourished in Leichhardt when working men established the Leichhardt Bowling and Recreation Club in Piper Street in 1923.

The church and the pub continued to be dominant suburban institutions up to the 1914–18 war. In the early years of Federation, churches were at their zenith as flourishing centres of leisure. The Sunday school, offering an array of social and recreational activities, had an extraordinary hold on the young, and most religious institutions provided their members with a regular and comprehensive range of activities. They formed cricket, rugby and swimming clubs, and indoor games and pastimes were played in parish halls. Some had an institute and reading room, as well as mutual improvement associations, debating societies and agencies with a strong temperance message. After the war, with the emergence of alternative secular attractions, the number of those who availed themselves of the regular and mostly free recreation which centred on the church began to slide.

Militant Protestantism embraced the temperance creed, and its activities, combined with the option vote, threatened the very existence of the pub; many suburban drinking outlets closed their doors permanently, and six o'clock closing changed the social character of the pub.[24] Both the pub and its main rival, the church, were going through a transition. However, despite a significant reduction in the number of drinking outlets, Tooth's Town Barrel Beer Books suggest that beer continued to be the focus of much leisure.[25]

Each suburb had its own Rugby Union and Rugby League clubs and they developed a fierce loyalty among their players, officials and supporters. Balmain was very proud of its Tiger representatives in their black and gold guernseys. Rugby Union reached unprecedented popularity in Sydney in 1907 when a total of 153,000 spectators attended four international matches against the All Blacks. Its governing body acquired Epping Racecourse (Harold Park) to develop as its own ground. Despite widespread enthusiasm for the game there was disquiet among Sydney footballers over loss of earnings caused by injuries suffered while playing. The Metropolitan Union rejected a claim for compensation made by Glebe forward Alec Burdon.

Not long after, the newly formed New Zealand Rugby League team stopped at Sydney en route to Britain and played three matches against the Sydney Pioneers under union rules; each player received ten shillings a match for travelling expenses. Immediately the Metropolitan Union initiated an inquiry into 'sundry acts of professionalism' and expelled those who played for the Sydney Pioneers. A schism occurred in the Rugby game and a hostile conservative press attacked the new Rugby League, formed in August 1907.[26] Battle lines were drawn by Rugby Union men in Sydney, who legitimised Rugby as 'purely amateur' sport and castigated the so-called professionalism of the League as 'beyond the pale'. They expressed concern about destruction of the amateur ideal, and the contamination of sport by money that professional football would bring.[27]

At the founding of the Glebe District Rugby League Club on 9 January 1908, president Harry Hoyle announced that 'men should play the game without loss to themselves . . . if any of the men lost time, the gates they would draw as footballers would have to make up their wages'.[28] He also told the meeting that 'if they were hurt whilst playing they would receive £2 a week for 16 weeks with free doctor and medicine until they had recovered'.[29] By 1911 the New South Wales Rugby Union was in financial trouble and was forced to sell Epping Racecourse. The League code was popular and growing attendance figures reflected its appeal. League, thriving on inter-suburban rivalry, quickly became a staple part of the working-class communities of inner Sydney.[30] These partisans came to see their men win and rolled up in large numbers when their team was doing battle at the top of the premiership table, but when defeat became a frequent occurrence they also stayed away in droves.

Glebe, known as the 'Dirty Reds', with a reputation for 'serving out stoush', were a leading contender for the premiership in 1911 and 1912, but the goal-kicking prowess of Dally Messenger of Eastern Suburbs deprived them of that honour.[31] Balmain, with a well-balanced side that included Chook Fraser, Pony Halloway, Junker Robinson and Jim Craig in the backs, and Bob Craig and Bill Schultz in the forwards, emerged as premiers in 1915, 1916 and 1917, losing only four games in this period.[32] Rugby League dominated bar-room discussions in winter and supporters displayed amazing knowledge about their favourite players. No one on the Balmain peninsula would hear of a finer player than local boy Charles 'Chook' Fraser. Sturdily built, but only 5 feet 4 inches tall, he was equally comfortable at fullback, in the centres, and at five-eighth. An elusive runner with the ball, Fraser possessed a good sidestep and sure hands; he represented Australia from 1911 to 1922.[33] The Tigers' great rival, Glebe, also possessed a player of great versatility. Frank Burge joined his brothers in the Glebe pack in 1911 and established himself as one of League's outstanding try-scoring forwards. A fast, powerful and long-striding player, 'Chunky' Burge redefined lock-forward play by breaking quickly from the scrum to run with the backs. An Australian representative up to 1922, he scored 141 tries for Glebe between 1911 and 1922.[34]

First-grade League players received one-third of gate takings; few could support themselves on football playing alone and men in second- and third-grade teams received a pittance for their efforts. Games at the Sydney Cricket Ground drew larger crowds through the turnstiles than matches on suburban grounds. In 1909 South Sydney retained the premiership when Balmain refused to play as a protest against the loss of gate receipts caused by the rescheduling of the final as a mere curtain-raiser.[35] It was the last straw for Glebe first-graders in July 1917 when the League transferred their fixture with Balmain from the Sydney Cricket Ground to Birchgrove Oval. A little earlier Glebe felt some players had been harshly treated by suspensions. Glebe decided to go on strike, refusing to take the field in their Balmain match as a protest against what 'the club regards as a set against it by the League committee'. The League responded by suspending the team for the 1918 season.[36]

Glebe remained one of the strongest teams in the competition to 1922, and though unable to win a premiership, they were runners up in 1911, 1912, 1915 and 1922; Glebe was eliminated from the competition in 1929.[37] Annandale entered the competition in 1910, but languished at the bottom of the League table and finally left in 1920. Balmain continued to be one of the League's front runners, winning further premierships in 1919, 1920, 1924, 1939, 1944, 1946, 1947 and 1969; it had a run of successes from 1941 to 1950, during which time they never missed a place in the semi-finals.[38]

Competitive women's cricket was played at the end of the 1920s. Informal matches played in Trafalgar Street, Annandale, often broke windows in the Hudson family home. Mrs Hudson formed the Annandale Waratahs in 1930 so that the girls would be able to play on a field and not in the street.[39] Annandale Council at first deferred laying a cricket pitch in Hogan's Park but in 1930 finally agreed.[40] The Waratahs' demon bowler Amy Hudson helped the team win the state premiership many times. She played in the Australian team which toured Britain. Despite the Waratahs' success, Annandale Council failed to provide facilities and the club acquired an old tram for its dressing room.

After World War I working-class people were increasingly leaving a world where they created their own entertainment in the home. Extension of the tram and railway network

Annandale Waratah Cricket Club, 1930. Amy Hudson and her mother formed the club and it thrived until 1953. Hudson was the outstanding all-rounder, representing NSW at 16 years of age and Australia two years later. She toured England in 1937 and 1951. (R. Cashman et al., Wicket Women, Cricket & Women in Australia, UNSW Press, 1991)

increased the geographical mobility of ordinary people, and new and exciting technological inventions—the cinema, radio, recorded music and motorised transport—became very much a part of everyday life.[41] There was a definite shift towards commercially based mass entertainment, spearheaded by the spectacular development of the cinema, and at the same time there was a reduction in the importance of localised and diverse church-based leisure; working-class male social life focused around the neighbourhood bars.

The picture show had a dramatic impact on the social lives of ordinary people.[42] Pastime clubs, with their boxing contests, dancing, singing and skipping exhibitions, introduced silent movies to Sydney's inner suburbs in about 1908, and at the same time open-air theatres, whose screenings were often disrupted by rain storms, were operating in Annandale, at Epping Racecourse and at Wentworth Park.[43]

Between 1910 and 1912 picture shows appeared along the main arteries in Annandale, Balmain, Glebe, Rozelle and Leichhardt. Initially it was very much entertainment for the working class who were captivated by the cheap thrills and jerky melodrama, and involved in the fantasy of the silent films. It cost threepence for a hard seat in the stalls, and sixpence in the dress circle. After the war as films improved in standard so too did the interest of the middle class.[44] Enterprising local businessmen sought to take a slice of what was fast becoming the most popular form of entertainment. The Broadway theatre sought to capture some of Glebe's Ideal Picture Theatre's patrons by offering free lemonade and biscuits at intermission and the price of admission to the afternoon session was only a penny, or any type of empty bottle.[45]

'The movies,' wrote the *Sydney Morning Herald* in 1920, 'fascinated the masses with a rapidity and completeness unprecedented in the history of amusement,' and there was ample

Children queuing for tickets for a matinee in the 1930s at the Empire Theatre, Quay Street, near Railway Square. Renamed Her Majesty's, the theatre burnt down and was replaced by the present Her Majesty's. (Hood Videodisc Still 03352)

evidence to support this claim.[46] At that time nationally there were more than 68 million admissions to cinemas annually, while combined racing and theatre attendances were about 16 million in 1921.[47] The years between 1919 and 1939 were the heyday of the picture palace.

In the inter-war period the cinema was the best attended, most criticised, liveliest and most influential component of our popular culture. Endless movie publicity provided the public with constant distraction from everyday humdrum. Introduction of the 'talkies' in 1929 meant that theatre design had to change to make them more acoustically sympathetic. Rival entertainment, football, dancing, skating and concerts attracted nothing like the numbers drawn to the motion picture.[48] Suburban cinemas, cheaper than their city counterparts, and more accessible, mushroomed to 115 by 1934, providing the only night out most people knew. They were suburban landmarks easy to identify, being brilliantly lit to sell the image of a good night after the rest of the district had closed down. Shops closed at 5.30 p.m. and the pubs 30 minutes later. Patrons would gather in the foyers to meet their friends before the show and during the interval.[49]

The new Kings Civic Theatre, on the corner of Darling Street and Birchgrove Road, opened on 3 July 1935 and was described as 'strikingly modern and at night, when the flaring neon signs outline it in a blaze of colour, it is a landmark, as well as a milestone in the suburb's progress'. Residents in Annandale felt the same in 1928 when the Royal opened in Johnston Street, and Glebe people, without cinema for several years, rejoiced in 1936 when the Astor in Glebe was built. Balmain's Civic Theatre, with a seating capacity of 974, mirrored the fate of many suburban temples of mass entertainment; attendance declined from the mid-1950s as television began to replace movie-going as a pastime. Balmain's Civic closed in 1959 and was demolished two years later. The palatial Royal was reduced to rubble in 1958.[50]

Throughout the 1920s and 1930s dancing was a great outlet, even a passion, for young men and women and also the middle-aged. Dancing or singing saloons could be found in the roughest localities, but no respectable tradesman or clerk would be seen in these places. The number of music and dancing teachers grew steadily after 1918 as more and more parents wanted their offspring to become competent pianists or dancers. In 1930, for example, fifteen music teachers in Leichhardt, nine in both Balmain and Glebe and two in Annandale made modest livings teaching people to sing and to play the piano and violin.[51] Dancing schools did much to propagate the pastime by holding their own 'evenings' where they showed off their pupils, with tap-dancing dominating the program, in the hope that the proficiency of their protégés would attract custom. Gloves and pumps were obligatory at the Annandale Hall in Young Street where F.A. Reeve taught all 'the latest London and American dances'; ladies and gentlemen paid one shilling each for three hours of ballroom dancing.[52]

Dancing had many venues. People danced in the street and outside the pub, or they went to respectable town hall dances and balls, church dances (though Methodists banned them) and prominent local dance halls. The great temple of dance in Sydney, the Trocadero, with its big bands and crooners, was filled with dancers looking for a night of glitter and glamour.[53] The municipal ball with its debutantes was a more formal occasion, while at the other end of the social scale the Wattle Dancing Assembly reserved the right 'to assert refinement, and an enjoyable Dance Evening to all, [and] the right is reserved to refuse admission to undesirable persons'.[54] Working-class youth could gain admission at assembly halls for sixpence and they could

Young dancer, c.1920. Dancing schools did much to propagate the pastime by holding their own 'evenings' where they showed off their protégés. Their programs were dominated by tap dancing. (J.G. Park Collection, Macleay Museum)

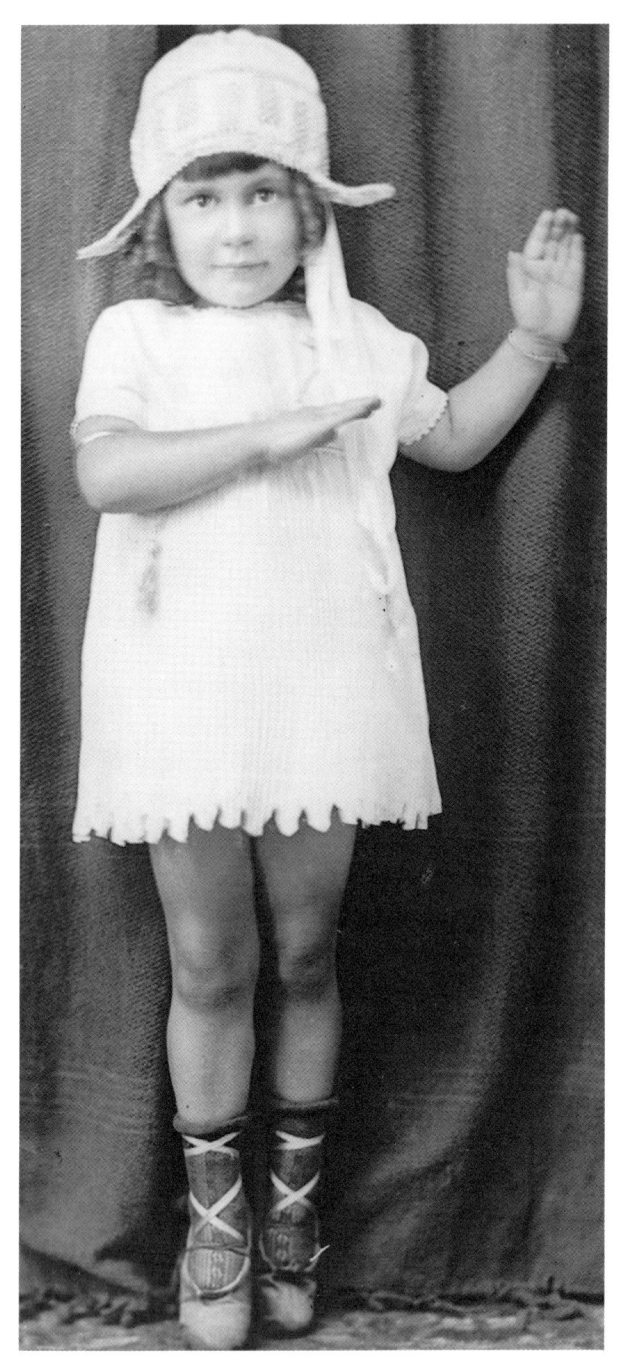

fox-trot through the evening in each other's arms. Most dance programs made varying compromises between old and new. The new dances seemed passing novelties, rather than serious challenges to the traditional repertoire, but there were growing numbers of jitterbugs, a new breed who rejected the tyranny of the dancing school and the ballroom steps it taught. Many favoured foxtrotting or jitterbugging in a city dance palace, while earlier the Charleston had outraged serious ballroom dancers.[55] Sporting clubs held dances for those with little to spend. Candle grease was used to lubricate rowing shed floors, and members did their own catering; supper at these affairs included rabbit sandwiches carefully disguised as chicken.[56]

Time-payment brought possession of the piano within the financial reach of the better-paid clerk or artisan, and at home in the evening friends and acquaintances gathered to engage in some hearty singing. The municipal bands were symbols of local identity and pride, and their achievements at the highest competitive level were evidence of a well-founded brass band culture. The frequent outdoor performances by municipal bands added to the gaiety and solemnity of civic life, whether they played in the park on weekends or, on more formal occasions, when they took part in processions and public ceremonies or helped raise funds for worthy causes.[57]

Two sporting activities in particular reflected the working-class character of inner-suburban life—boxing and dog-racing. In 1923 boxing promoter Pat McHugh converted the Coronation Theatre in Balmain Road to the Leichhardt Stadium. McHugh staged the first national title fight there in 1925, a bantamweight contest between Jimmy Semmens and Stan Thurston.[58] The stadium's capacity increased when its galvanised iron walls were replaced by a concrete structure in 1930. Working men from surrounding suburbs rolled up in strength to fill the stadium's 5,000 seats and cheer young raw talent struggling to get a shot at the big time.⁵⁹ Though Leichhardt Stadium remained the second main venue after Rushcutter's Bay, many of the country's best boxers fought there—Jack Carroll, Ron Richards, Fred Henneberry, Ambrose Palmer, Vic Patrick, Tommy Burns, Dave Sands and Jimmy Carruthers. One shilling would get you inside, two shillings would buy you a ringside seat, and for 35 years the Balmain Road stadium echoed to the roar of fight crowds. Boxing was the main drawcard but wrestling matches and vaudeville acts often featured on the same bill as a title fight. Italians turned up in strength in the 1950s to support boxing champion Carlo Marchini and Tony Magnifico.

For most boxers the monetary rewards were not high; payment was by the fight, not by the week, and very few were able to retain any wealth gained in this way. A welcome bonus was the shower of coins thrown into the ring by appreciative spectators. Boxers fought preliminaries under a string of different names, sometimes fighting in two different places on the one night. Ern Evans of Balmain was remembered dancing down the aisle at Leichhardt flanked by manager Jimmy Ryan and brother Fred as his Balmain supporters, decked out in their black and gold football guernseys, roared. Evans had many fights at Leichhardt, from four-rounders to an Australian bantamweight title in 1932, when he defeated Billy McAllister. He earned £25 for the title win, but had to pay his manager, seconds and sparring partner from the prize money.⁶⁰

Leichhardt Stadium closed in 1958; manager Herb McHugh blamed its demise on hotels remaining open to 10 p.m., betting on the dogs and trots, and the burden of heavy insurance premiums on boxers.⁶¹

The 'dogs' was a phenomenon of the 1920s. To own a greyhound was the ambition of many working-class men and kennels were to be found in the backyards of many inner-city terraces. Mechanical hare racing, as it was called, was first held under lights at Harold Park on 28 May 1927, but it was not until 1939 that a dog track was opened at Wentworth Park.⁶² The new sport barely had time to celebrate its successful beginnings when the Bavin government amended the *Gaming and Betting Act* to prevent betting after sunset. Without betting, greyhound racing collapsed but its fortunes changed with a new government. Jack Lang saw greyhounds

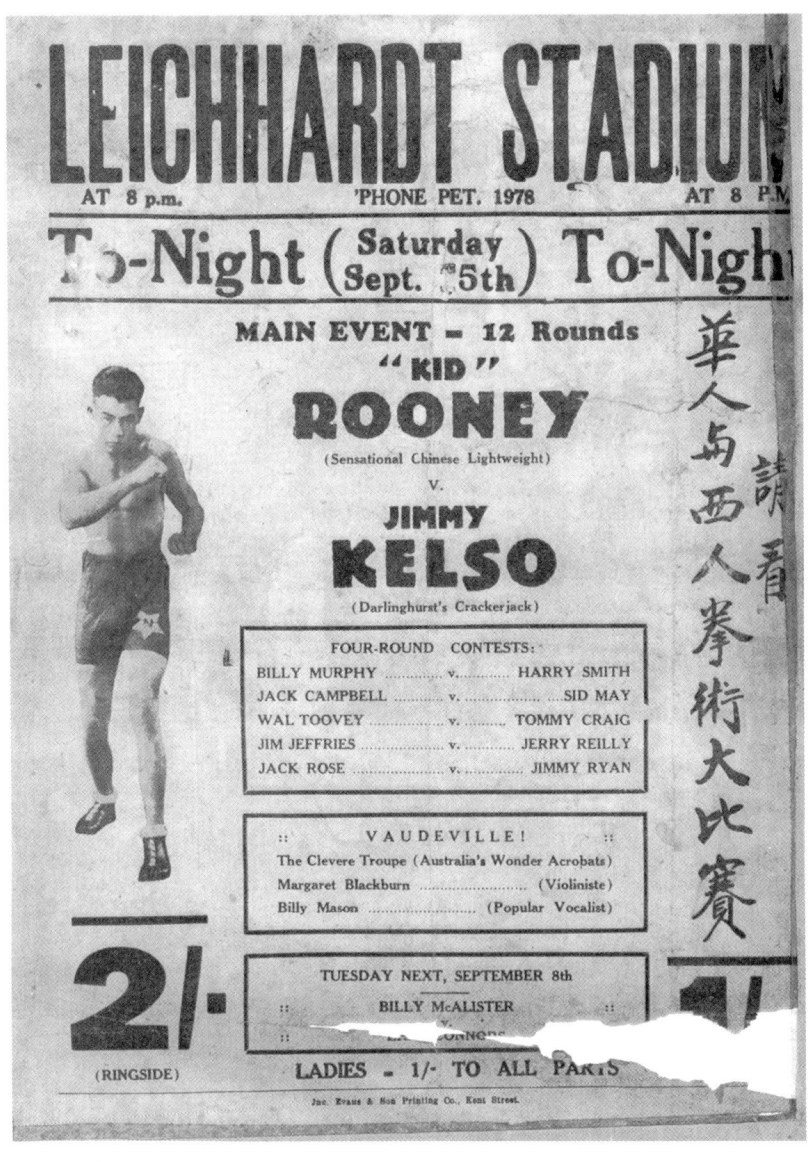

Boxing poster, 5 September 1932. Working men rolled up in strength to fill Leichhardt Stadium in Balmain Road. Between 1923 and 1958, the stadium was a major venue for boxing, second only to the Rushcutters Bay stadium. (Max Solling Collection)

The first dog race meeting held under lights at Harold Park on 28 May 1927. It was the ambition of many working men to own and race a greyhound. (Max Solling Collection)

as the working-man's racehorse, and announced that the previous government's policies were designed to rob the worker of his simple pleasure.[63] In the 1930s large crowds of men, most wearing hats, gathered at Harold Park to watch greyhounds pursue imitation hares. The Harold Park dog track closed in 1987 but greyhounds continue to race at Wentworth Park.[64]

Private promoters staged trotting races at Lillie Bridge from 1890 (much later renamed Harold Park), but in 1902 the non-proprietary New South Wales Trotting Club assumed control of the sport.[65] Trotting meetings frequently clashed with galloping events, and they struggled to compete, but trotting was unable to conduct night meetings. Without adequate prize money, the sport deteriorated and developed a reputation for corruption. This prompted the appointment of a Select Committee in 1938 to examine the conduct and administration of trotting in New South Wales.[66] Harness-racing at Harold Park flourished from 1949, when night trotting replaced day-time meetings. Crowd sizes swelled, with a record attendance of 50,341 at the 1961 Interdominion final.[67]

In the 1930s Rugby Union had become a more popular game in middle-class suburbs in winter but Rugby League remained solidly working class, flourishing in inner-city government and Catholic schools and nurtured by Police Boys Clubs. The fortunes of the Balmain Tigers was common knowledge, and the Leichhardt Wanderers and Codocks remained strong local clubs. In the depth of the depression hockey clubs were formed in Balmain and Glebe. The Glebe club emerged as a dominant force in the Sydney competition, winning the club championship on 26 occasions between 1948 and 1996. Since 1940 Glebe has been first-grade hockey premiers 24 times; its second-grade side has been premiers twenty times and the thirds have tasted premiership success on 16 occasions.[68]

People who achieved success in sport were often closely identified with particular localities, and locals bathed in their reflected glory. For some blue-collar workers, it was only in the sporting arena that they had any chance of achieving success.

Dawn Fraser epitomised the spirit of working people in Balmain, where she was born in 1937, the youngest of eight children in a poor family. She learned to swim in the local pool (which was later renamed the Dawn Fraser Pool) before establishing herself as one of Australia's greatest athletes. She was the first swimmer to win the 100 metres freestyle in three consecutive Olympics (1956, 1960, and 1964) and the first female to swim the 100 metres freestyle in under one minute. She won 30 Australian championships, eight Olympic and eight Commonwealth

Games medals, and was MLA for Balmain from 1988 to 1991. Her resistance to authority, affable roguishness and sometimes larrikin behaviour endeared her to the sporting public.[69]

Two personalities closely associated with the suburb of Leichhardt were Don Athaldo and Joe Marston. Don Lyons worked as a blacksmith in Leichhardt after the 1914–18 war and also operated a gymnasium there. Assuming the name of Don Athaldo, he offered correspondence courses that preached physical fitness. Although only 5 feet 5 inches tall and weighing twelve stone, the 'Pocket Atlas' made his reputation from spectacular demonstrations of strength and his flair for showmanship. Wearing a leopard skin and leather ankle-boots, he pulled a touring car with six passengers up the hill in William Street to Kings Cross.[70] Joe Marston, born in Leichhardt in 1926, attended Orange Grove Public School and in 1942, at the age of sixteen, he joined the Leichhardt–Annandale Football Club, making the first team in 1943. A paintbrush factory worker, at right-fullback Marston progressively represented Sydney, New South Wales and Australia between 1944 and 1949. He became a full-time professional with Preston North End in England from 1950 to 1955, and then rejoined Leichhardt–Annandale. Joe Marston made 35 appearances for Australia, captained it 24 times, and played for APIA from 1958 to 1964.[71]

Lew Hoad, the eldest of three sons of an electrician, was born in 1934. The Hoad family lived at 43 Wigram Road, Glebe, and a narrow lane separated their backyard from the four tennis courts of the Hereford Club. Lew was fascinated with the game being played behind his house and he practised in the morning and afternoon, hitting a tennis ball against a brick wall in the lane. He attended Glebe Public School and showed out as a fine footballer and cricketer with the local Police Boys Club, but tennis was his game.[72]

Hoad became a majestic player with a superb and flawless selection of strokes, and an intimidating presence on court. His serve and volleys were devastating and with his strong right wrist he hit both backhand and forehand at an unbelievable pace. Blond and powerfully built, Hoad won Wimbledon twice, was Australian, French and Italian singles champion, and a member of the Davis Cup team which took the trophy four times between 1952 and 1956. Hoad was widely liked for his cheerful disposition, his love of a drink and a joke, and an apparent refusal to take the game too seriously. A park in Glebe is named after him.[73]

Visions of a better post-war world   17

The decay of much housing in inner Sydney was condemned as an indictment of modern society and the Housing Improvement Board in New South Wales urged government in 1938 to adopt a bigger role in this area.[1] The Department of Post-War Reconstruction, established in 1942 by the federal Curtin government, spawned four major planning agencies, including the Commonwealth Housing Commission (CHC), whose report in 1944 emphasised that 'a dwelling of good standard and equipment is not only a need but the right of every citizen'.[2] The CHC promoted regional planning on a national scale because past development 'had been governed by the possibilities of profit-making rather than by the needs of the community'.[3] Those who could not afford to buy a house would be eligible for low-cost rental state government housing funded by the Commonwealth.

In allocating housing to low-income earners, the Housing Commission of New South Wales considered such things as insanitary, dangerous and condemned dwellings, eviction orders, overcrowding, divided families, excessive rentals and proximity to place of work. It promoted ideals of home ownership and the virtues of family life and domesticity.[4]

Planners were optimistic in 1945 that the newly created Cumberland County Council would develop a plan for Sydney's future. The Council estimated that 40,000 inner-suburban dwellings, one-third of the stock, were so bad they required immediate replacement:

> Obsolescence of these areas is due to outdated housing standards and dilapidation, while industrial penetration and lack of open space and the amenities have aggravated the condition. The existing street and subdivision patterns are so much below acceptable standards that rehabilitation of the area is not possible without a drastic clearance and the treatment of substantial areas at one time.[5]

The Cumberland County Plan, Sydney's metropolitan planning scheme produced in 1948, was strongly imbued with a sense of equity or social justice, reflecting the optimism and idealism of post-war years. Industry and retail activity would be moved to the outer suburbs where they would confer 'greater social benefits' on the working man and his family. The agenda of the Cumberland County Council was to replace housing, not improve it, and for acquisition of land by public authorities to ensure low income residents would benefit from new housing.[6] Poor housing, the Council believed, was the main source of the social ills that afflicted the inner city, and it urged immediate action:

> There can be no questioning the urgent need for ridding Sydney of its slums. If the cost to the nation, in the form of ill-health and premature death caused by the insanitary living conditions of these areas, of death or injury from accidents in their twisted streets, and of the vices and crimes which they have bred, could be assessed, there would be even greater cause for wonder that slum-clearance has been delayed so long that it should have been subordinated to less important works. About a quarter of a million people live in conditions which are almost intolerable.[7]

Inner-suburban communities, some observed, had been 'deeded by default to those who failed to fit acceptably into the expectations' of middle-class Sydney. Their 'miserable houses' horrified Judith Wright, who observed that landlords 'did as little as possible towards repairing them'.[8] The Housing Commission formulated plans for massive development of public housing and proposed radial expressway networks through neighbourhoods close to the city to complement its scheme of urban renewal. Growth of the city, the Department of Main Roads assumed, would result in the continued decay of inner-city housing. The radial expressway would improve the journey to work for the better-off car owners, but imposed a heavy social cost on the poor,

The post-war vision emphasised the right of every citizen to decent accommodation. Here, McGirr Court, a block of multi-unit brick Housing Commission flats in Nicholson Street, Balmain, is officially opened by the Minister for Housing, Clive Evatt, in 1949. (GPO Videodisc-1 Still 47582)

less articulate, working people concentrated close to the city. A car was beyond their financial reach.[9]

The Commission began its assault on Balmain by acquiring land in Glassop and Elliott streets, in the Lockhart and Laggan avenues precinct, in Curtis Road, College and Church streets, and in Nicholson Street. Between 1947 and 1951 a series of three- to five-storey brick buildings, altogether some 270 family units, were built on this land. Balmain Council expressed its concern in 1948 that residents displaced from resumed properties were not being given preference to flats at McGirr Court in Nicholson Street. 'The rentals for £2.7.0 and £2.7.6,' Mayor O'Connor protested at McGirr Court, 'can hardly be classed as worker's residences at worker's rentals.'[10] The member for Balmain, Mary Quirk, urged the Minister for Housing to build more working-men's flats for her constituents; however, planned pensioner housing in Waterview and Darling streets did not proceed because of high land prices.[11]

Leichhardt Council complained to the Commission in 1949 'that no housing for families with young children is being provided in this district and attention is drawn to the fact that young family units are the backbone of the community'. Some eighteen flats at 69 Marion Street, Leichhardt, Council argued, had inadequate provision for couples with young children.[12]

Old housing stock in Christie, Stirling and Bay streets, Glebe, was demolished by the Commission and 84 brick family units built there between 1952 and 1960 and nearby, in 1960, the City Council completed a major flat project—the twelve-storey John Byrne Court, containing 120 apartments. A further 58 units—at Clyne Place, Walsh Avenue, at 162–164 Glebe Road and 1 Palmerston Avenue—and a cul-de-sac of cottages in Crescent Street were all completed by 1953. In Lilyfield the Commission undertook major projects in Lilyfield and Balmain roads, and in Trevor, Helena and Edward streets. Altogether, 223 family units were completed in this precinct between 1950 and 1965.[13]

The Housing Commission considered multi-unit constructions the appropriate form for inner Sydney, while, further out, its energies were directed towards houses designed with large windows, modern fittings and lawns and gardens. The scale of Commission housing projects near the city was restricted by high land prices and the difficulty of justifying demolition of existing housing in the face of an acute shortage of accommodation. A revival of flat building in the mid-1950s was seen as a return to better times, but up to 1961 the Housing Commission had built less than 1500 brick walk-up flats in inner Sydney. Flats allowed single workers to live close to the city, free of the obligations of house and garden.[14] Rent control discouraged the building of private flats; a disincentive to private investment, it played a significant role in the continuing decay of inner-city housing. Building flats for rent resumed after the dismantling of rent control legislation began in 1954. Old inner-city houses were also being converted into flats, and up to 1968 the lingering effect of rent control meant that inner-city rents did not rise as much as elsewhere.[15]

The introduction of strata titles in 1961 made ownership of flats easier, and mortgagees found them a more attractive security than company title. These developments stimulated a flat-building boom between 1964 and 1973, a period when much housing erected between 1880 and 1914 faced the demolisher's hammer.[16]

In 1945 the New South Wales government appointed a Royal Commission of three to re-organise local government boundaries to secure 'proper economical and efficient Local

Government'.[17] The three Commissioners agreed to the need for change and to amalgamate some surrounding councils. The Bill encountered some opposition in the Legislative Council and a compromise was reached whereby the 67 local government areas in the country were consolidated into 39. Eight working-class areas, thought of as 'slum municipalities'—Alexandria, Darlington, Erskineville, Glebe, Newtown, Paddington, Redfern and Waterloo—were incorporated into the City of Sydney, raising its area to 11 square miles.[18] As these suburban municipalities were controlled by the state Labor machine, they were unable to resist amalgamation, and an election was set down for 4 December 1948. The municipalities of Annandale, Balmain and Leichhardt amalgamated to become the Municipality of Leichhardt, which now covered 3.8 square miles.

Expanding commerce or light industry in the city displaced many hard-core Labor voters. Aldermen sought to defend their wards from partial or total devastation, and the provision of low-income housing preoccupied their thoughts. Municipal Laborism in the City Council for about twenty years contributed significantly to the preservation of much of the inner-city, working-class residential areas.[19]

Municipal facilities in post-war Leichhardt were limited. Council maintained local ovals and swimming pools at Balmain and Leichhardt and contributed to baby health clinics. There were no municipal libraries in Leichhardt in 1947, and only eight within the metropolitan area.[20] The Sydney City Council opened a branch library at 191 Bridge Road, Glebe, on 15 September 1956 and, in 1968 when local government boundaries changed it became Leichhardt's first municipal library to be established after the war.[21] In the inter-war years, second-hand suburban bookshops, with their lending libraries, to some extent met the demand for popular literature, changing books for a penny each. The Leichhardt Library at 64 Renwick Street was opened in June 1972, and a home-bound service started in 1974. The branch library at Balmain Town Hall (370 Darling Street) opened on 1 May 1978. The Glebe Library closed in 1995 and a new library for Glebe was opened at 184–186 Glebe Road on 19 April 1997.[22]

In the 1930s another new institution directed at the reformation of city youth appeared. Police Commissioner W.J. Mackay urged the establishment of clubs to attract idle youth off the streets; there was, he said, a clear connection between youth unemployment and delinquency. Mackay hoped that the clubs would both reduce juvenile delinquency and enhance the public image of the police.[23] The first of these Police Boys Clubs opened at Woolloomooloo in 1937. A club at Leichhardt held its first meeting on 21 June 1937, was renamed Leichhardt Police Boys Club in 1938 and soon moved to the army drill hall in Hill Street. The wide range of sporting and recreational activities these clubs offered outside school hours, and in school holidays, attracted hundreds of working-class youth. Each club structured its program according to local needs, club facilities and resources and level of community support. Within six months of opening on 15 January 1938 Balmain Police Boys Club had 1,200 members and was unable to cope with the numbers wishing to join. Glebe, too, had trouble accommodating a massive influx of local youth. It took over premises abandoned by the Police Rowing Club in Federal Road, Glebe, in 1943, and by 1955 membership had swelled to 2,000.[24]

At the 1948 elections four Labor candidates each from Balmain, Leichhardt and Rozelle were elected but Annandale ward returned three non-Labor small businessmen, two of whom, John Cummings and Sydney Francis, had been stalwarts of the Progressive Party on Annandale

Above: Eddie Erwin (1907–1956). A councillor of Balmain (1941–48) and Leichhardt (1948–53), Erwin was Mayor of Leichhardt from 1950 to 1952. (Leichhardt Town Hall)
Centre: Daily Telegraph, 23 December 1952
Below: Daily Telegraph, 16 April 1953

WORK FOR MAYOR'S WIFE
21 men on job
Leichhardt Council has had to employ some of its staff at overtime rates because they had been working at ordinary rates for the Mayor's wife, a local government inspector alleges.
Council to meet

COUNCIL DISMISSED
Leichhardt sensation
The Governor (Sir John Northcott) has dismissed all members of Leichhardt Municipal Council and appointed an administrator to control the municipality.
Bribery reports probe

Council.[25] Most of the new Leichhardt councillors were solid Labor representatives. They included tram conductor George Harris, faction leader at Balmain; boilermaker Eddie Erwin, who controlled the Rozelle branch; and housewife Elizabeth Gallimore. Lilyfield resident Bill Colbourne was a leader of the extra-parliamentary ALP and general secretary of the Labor Council. There were two butchers, Jack Waite and Gilbert Lockhart; fireman Charles Laggan, mattress worker Les Moore; clerk Leo Newton; as well as an ironworker, a foreman and a shipwright.

Each ALP branch was a machine in the Tammany Hall mould where power tended to be more important than broad social programs. One powerful Labor faction had developed around Rozelle driver Michael Cashman, a Balmain and Leichhardt councillor and, after his death, his widow, Annie, continued the network established by this Irish Catholic family. Annie was elected to Leichhardt Council from 1956 to 1971 and was Mayor from 1963 to 1968.[26] The local machines operated on personal favours, debts and family ties, and rested ultimately on the resources of Leichhardt Council, which the machine could control.[27]

Leichhardt's first Mayor on the new council, Leo Newton, mirrored its traditional character. He was born in Day Street, Leichhardt, in 1904 and lived in the same street all his life. Educated at St Fiacre's, Leichhardt, and De la Salle, Ashfield, he joined the Leichhardt branch of the ALP in 1921 and worked as a clerk for the Balmain Electric Supply Co. A Leichhardt councillor from 1941 to 1953 and from 1956 to 1971, he had a passion for politics, for doing ordinary things for ordinary people. Like most of his colleagues on Council, he belonged to the conservative side of Labor politics; he was not a socialist.[28]

Another great Labor stalwart on the enlarged council was Jack Waite, who was first elected to Balmain Council in 1923 and was Mayor in 1936 and 1940. The Mullens Street butcher was an active member of the Colin Campbell Masonic Lodge and a Leichhardt councillor from 1948 to 1953. He had been a Balmain councillor for 20 years, having joined the local ALP branch in 1917.

In December 1952 a report of an investigation of Leichhardt Council's accounts and internal management by the Local Government Department was submitted to Council. Deputy Mayor Gallimore read a press statement rejecting claims that council work had been done for wives of aldermen, as well as allegations of bribery and other matters.[29] Former council employees who had resigned, it was alleged, had received gratuities. Eddie Erwin responded strongly to this allegation: 'I am a Labor Mayor and my job is to improve workers' conditions'.[30]

The Sydney press highlighted doubts about the legality of use of council materials and labour on the construction of a house owned by Erwin's wife at Eastwood.[31] On 15 April 1953 all the Leichhardt councillors were removed from office and H.W. Dane was appointed administrator.[32] The dismissal of Council revealed a range of malpractice and corruption, including the soliciting of bribes for the approval of building and development applications.[33] Erwin resigned from Council in December 1952, subsequently served a gaol term and died on 10 February 1956, aged 48 years. The administration of Leichhardt Council by H.W. Dane was completed on 28 November 1956.[34]

The composition of Leichhardt Council changed in December 1956, with only four members of the previous council—Elizabeth Gallimore, George Harris, Leo Newton and Charles Laggan—being returned. Marion Street garage proprietor Jack Deehan, first elected to Council in 1956, became Mayor, a position he retained until 1962.[35] With the election of Annie Cashman and Sabina Greenman, Leichhardt now had three female councillors but their numbers were reduced to two by Mrs Gallimore's death on 26 March 1958.[36] She was replaced in the Balmain ward by-election by Nick Origlass.

Port-oriented industries remained an integral part of Leichhardt Municipality's economy. Shipbuilding and port-servicing activities were major employers, and the workforce for these industries generally lived nearby. There were close links between aldermen of the 1950s and 1960s and local maritime and semi-maritime unions and service industries, but there had been a steady exodus of industrial firms from the municipality after the war, a movement accelerated by the closure of Mort's Dock in 1958.[37]

The introduction of containers into the overseas trade brought a radical change in the shape of the Sydney waterfront. The Maritime Services Board of New South Wales (MSB), with jurisdiction over Sydney's wharves and facilities, drew up its Ten Year Plan in 1966 for the development of new container berths.[38] The MSB's plan included terminals at Mort Bay, White Bay and Glebe Island, and under the legislative powers conferred upon the MSB, Leichhardt Council could not legally refuse container projects or even impose conditions of any real significance.[39] The Balmain berths lacked the necessary back-up area required for lorry space, and this ultimately forced the government to build a major terminal at Botany Bay.[40] In 1965 Leichhardt Council rejected an application by Associated Steamships Pty Ltd for a container facility at Mort's Dock, but on appeal in the court the facility was approved. Concerns about the White Bay terminal attracted 500 Balmain people to a public meeting on 27 September 1966.[41]

"Speak to me, Mort! I couldn't have squeezed you that hard!"

The closure of Mort's Dock, the municipality's largest single employer of labour, in 1958 was a sign of the changing industrial structure of inner Sydney. (*SMH*, 11 November 1958)

Blasting in the construction of White Bay terminal damaged houses and brought strong protests from the peninsula. Concerns were further heightened by the massive impact a chemical tank farm proposed by Swift & Co would have on the locality.[42] Industrial land users and some groups within Leichhardt Council welcomed container terminals and associated facilities as a source of employment and as a way of encouraging traditional marine servicing industries to remain in the district. But it was not a vision shared by the new middle class who were vociferous about a large-scale, impersonal, noisy and continuously operating terminal which required an endless flow of trucks to distribute its containers throughout the metropolitan area. In 1974 residents, supported by Nick Origlass, erected gates across streets leading to the Mort's Dock terminal so that at night and on weekends residents would have some respite from the noise.[43]

Membership of branches within Leichhardt municipality—Balmain, Glebe, Forest Lodge, Annandale, Rozelle, Glebe North, Lilyfield and Leichhardt—were filled by long-term residents of the area with a strong industrial, working-class background, anxious to see the retention of local industry. Their representatives on Council mirrored their views and during the 1960s they were anxious to arrest the decline in their working-class constituency and promote multi-unit development. The right-wing branches in Leichhardt possessed an influential trade-union membership, and had a strong public welfare commitment.[44] Operating largely on kinship and friendship networks, the rank and file accepted the decisions of party bosses mutely and regarded 'outsiders' with suspicion. There was also a fatalistic acceptance of external forces impinging on their community.[45] Influential Leichhardt councillors in the 1960s—Jack Deehan, Annie Cashman, Danny Casey and Les Rodwell—were socially conservative but adopted a pro-working-class welfarism stance. Between their world and Labor members with a left-wing perspective, who began to infiltrate local branches in the 1970s, there was a chasm of class, culture and age.

Meetings at Leichhardt Council were not occasions for debate and decision, but opportunities for Labor councillors to explain or justify decisions made within the confines of the caucus room. Meetings were held in strict secrecy and opposition aldermen were excluded. Once an issue was put to the vote Labor councillors were expected to adhere to caucus majority decisions at the subsequent council meeting; failure to do so could lead to suspension or expulsion from the party. Non-Labor aldermen or residents in the public gallery had no opportunity to make a contribution to the decision-making process.[46]

The first significant break with the tradition of caucus dominance came when Swift & Co. sought Council's permission to develop a tank farm for the storage of naphtha adjacent to the MSB's White Bay project.[47] At a Council meeting in December 1967 Balmain Labor aldermen Origlass and Wyner crossed the floor and voted against the caucus decision. Origlass and Wyner were expelled from the party, although Rozelle and Balmain branches supported them.[48] Until 1967 caucus had ensured that Council was not a decision-making body; 'crossing the floor' did not occur, and the ALP majority stifled even the most determined efforts at opposition by independent aldermen. Nick Origlass and Izzy Wyner formed Balmain Leichhardt Labor (BLL) to contest the forthcoming local government elections. Nineteen members of the Balmain branch were suspended over their refusal to accept the executive ruling on Origlass and Wyner, and they became core members of the BLL.[49] In December 1968 Origlass, Wyner and Alan Graham were elected to Council on the BLL ticket. Glebe came under the jurisdiction of Leichhardt Council on 1 August 1968 and H.J. Foley, J.L. McMahon and R.G. Walker were appointed Glebe's representatives on Council, and after December 1968 Foley, McMahon and Greg Johnston became Glebe's councillors.[50]

Nick Origlass and Izzy Wyner, both of them fearlessly and naturally egalitarian, were comrades in politics, unionism and local government for 60 years. Origlass, the second youngest of six children of an Italian father from Turin and an Irish mother from County Cork, was born

Above: Annie Cashman (1890–1976), Leichhardt councillor 1956 to 1971 and Mayor 1963 to 1968. (Leichhardt Town Hall)
Centre: Les Rodwell (1924–), Leichhardt councillor 1965 to 1984 and six times Mayor. (Leichhardt Town Hall)
Below: Daniel Casey (1923–), Leichhardt councillor 1965 to 1980. (Leichhardt Town Hall)

at Woodstock, Queensland, on 21 January 1908.[51] He left school early and was sacked from his first job with the Taxation Department in Brisbane for protesting against compulsory, unpaid classes after work. He joined the Communist Party in 1931 but was expelled soon afterwards. On the move for much of the 1930s, he resumed contact with the Trotskyites in Sydney in 1936.[52] Jim McClelland, one of Origlass's small group of Trotskyites, regarded him as a formidable figure but dogmatic and opinionated, with narrow views of the world and an absolute attachment to Trotskyist doctrine, patiently waiting for the inevitable demise of the capitalist State.[53] He settled in Balmain in 1942 and became a Federated Ironworkers delegate at Mort's Dock where he worked. Never one to shy away from confrontation, be it political or physical, he established a reputation as a determined speaker and was a central figure in the Balmain ironworkers' strike of 1945 which marked the end of communist control of the Federated Ironworkers.[54] Expelled from the union twice, first by the communists, then by the groupers, he joined the ALP in 1956.[55]

Confrontation is the Origlass way

Nick Origlass, (1908–1996), Leichhardt councillor from 1958 to 1980 and 1984 to 1996, Mayor 1971–72, 1972–73 and 1987–88. (By courtesy of John Shakespeare, *Sydney Morning Herald*, published *SMH*, 8 June 1989)

Elected to Leichhardt Council in 1958, Origlass represented Balmain Ward continuously to 1980, and then from 1984 to 1995, serving as Mayor in 1971–72, 1972–73 and 1987–88. The open-council system he introduced reflected his belief in grassroots participatory democracy. 'At Leichhardt,' he said, 'we get the biggest crowd of any Council in Sydney.'[56] They also had the longest meetings and if Origlass did not want to listen to someone, he turned off his hearing aid. Doug Spedding, when he was Mayor in 1988–89, had to control Origlass's pontifications. He claimed that 'the democracy Nick believes in is what he has got to say on an issue. Once he sets his mind on something, that's it.'[57] Nick Origlass died at Balmain on 17 May 1996.[58]

Izzy Wyner was born at Marrickville on 30 July 1916, the eldest of five children of Latvian and Estonian parents who moved to Rozelle in 1921. Before his cabinet-maker father vanished, leaving his mother to raise the children, he took Izzy to the 'dole dump' in Haymarket, where food was distributed to those hit by the depression, and introduced him to Jack Sylvester, local leader of the Unemployed Workers Movement.[59] Izzy, who with Origlass shared a common faith in Trotsky, became a delegate of the Painters and Dockers Union at Cockatoo Island; he subsequently wrote a history of the union.[60]

Wyner, who, with Origlass, was expelled from the ALP in 1968, was elected a Balmain Ward alderman on Leichhardt Council from 1959 to 1974, 1977 to 1980, and 1985 to 1991. An eloquent orator in the Council chamber, he was elected Mayor in 1989–90.[61]

18 A life apart: Italian Leichhardt

The social and physical landscape of Leichhardt in the nineteenth century was shaped by immigrants from Britain and Ireland. Their houses, hotels and churches reflected many of the characteristics of Britain, and much of Leichhardt's social life was derived from associations that immigrants brought with them.[1] By the 1914–18 war the number of residents born in the British Isles was small but their societies and clubs remained vibrant institutions. The character of Leichhardt was reshaped by immigrants after the 1939–45 war. As some of the working class abandoned their traditional strongholds, their place was increasingly being taken by people from continental Europe, mainly Italy, attracted by Leichhardt's cheap housing and proximity to unskilled work and factory jobs.[2]

Emigration had been an endemic phenomenon in Italy since the second half of the nineteenth century but Australia was an uncommon destination for Italians. Every year between 1876 and 1900 up to 300,000 itinerant Italian workers migrated to France, the United States and South America.[3] The first significant numbers of Italians arrived in the Australian colonies during the gold rush. Raffaello Carboni succumbed to gold fever and hoped to make his fortune at the Ballarat diggings. The articulate Italian patriot, with revolutionary experience, became caught up in events and played an important part in the Eureka revolt in 1854.[4]

Italians showed a distinct preference for small-scale entrepreneurial activity in Sydney, particularly in fruit and fish retailing, and were particularly visible as fruiterers in Kings Cross and in the Belmore Markets area.[5] Beyond the metropolitan area, Italians selected land near the Richmond River in northern New South Wales in 1882. They intensively cultivated their small farms and their community, which they called New Italy, had grown to 250 people by 1888.[6] The number of Italian-born immigrants seeking a new life in New South Wales grew steadily from 551 in 1881 to 1,577 in 1901, with a very high proportion from northern Italy, mostly from Lombardy and Piedmont. The Italian communities were very masculine ones; in 1901, for example, almost 90 per cent of these communities were men.[7]

The names of Italian immigrants, and their places of residence, can be found in the pages of *Sands's Sydney and Suburban Directory*. Ernesto Spagnoletti, who described himself as a 'Professor of Pianoforte', was a resident of Balmain and Glebe between 1858 and 1864. The well-to-do sent their offspring to Professor Spagnoletti, who composed a polka 'respectfully dedicated to the ladies of Balmain'. Another countryman, sawyer Pietro Sarina, settled in Balmain about 1868.[8] The first Italians to settle in Leichhardt, in about 1885, were fishmonger Angelo Pomabello and carpenter Luigi Viega, Rofe Street residents Angelo di Laurense and Andrea Fontana, Parramatta Road fruiterers the Bongiorno brothers, near whose shop could be found Oreste Vincenzini 'Teacher of piano and any description of Band instruments and Theory'.[9] Stationer John Bernasconi of Renwick Street appeared in the directory in 1889 and accountant Joseph Corti resided in Norton Street in 1894. Others with Leichhardt addresses were Antonio Rubino, Hugh Pedrotta and Albert Farmilio.

By 1914 Angelo Natoli, Giovanni Russo, Joseph Lamaro, Joseph and Giuseppe Serio, Arthur Sarina, Angelo and Giovanni Guiffre, Guy Lo Schiavo, Frank Merlino and Nicholas Catalano were conspicuous among Leichhardt's fruiterers and greengrocers. Emilio Reggitta operated as a dealer in White Street, while Peter Mairomati and Angelo Naaoli sold oysters at their Parramatta Road shops.[10]

Enterprising Italians with little capital were also proprietors of small businesses in adjoining municipalities. Fruit and vegetable shops operated by La Grega, Merlino and Palise, the billiard rooms of Edward Sala JP and the Palmisano brothers' oyster saloon were located along Darling Street, Balmain, about 1914. Ciro Voto was fishing locally from 1890, and six years earlier jeweller Farivanti Leoni was a Balmain resident. The sweet smells of Saporiti & Bardelini's confectionery wafted down Weston Street (Rozelle) in 1908 and Harry Licciardi traded as a Balmain greengrocer from 1912 and as a Glebe poulterer five years later.[11] In the mid-1890s Antony Timbaldi sold fish and oysters at his Glebe Road shop, Leon Tozzi was a Catherine Street hairdresser and Camillo Marina had done sufficiently well to be able to purchase Toxteth House in 1900.[12] In Glebe, as in Leichhardt, Italians were prominent as fruiterers. Numbered among Glebe's fruiterers were Filipo Cascio, Giacomo Costa, Giuseppe Nigro and Antoni Piconi. Giovanni Cincotta and the Arena brothers, Giuseppe and Sebastiano from Messina, were especially remembered as colourful identities along Glebe Road. A macaroni factory, owned by Nimzie Vivaldi, was listed in Parramatta Road in 1903, and medical practitioner G. Rioli hung up his brass plate at 242 Glebe Road in 1910.[13]

Italians also had a presence in Annandale in the years just before Federation—Torso's Fish & Oyster Saloon, costumiere Madam Mortelli, fruiterers Angelo Casamento and Robert Benedetto, Emma Rossi's Parramatta Road confectionery and Thomas Ricciardo, who taught singing at his Johnston Street residence from 1895 to 1897.[14]

Sculptors Achille Simonetti and Tomaso Sani and painter Giulio Anivitti enjoyed enviable reputations in Sydney. Colonial Architect James Barnet engaged Tomaso Sani to carve high-relief figures on the spandrels of the Pitt Street facade of the new General Post Office and to undertake other public statues. Born in Florence in 1839, he built a studio at 120 Trafalgar Street, Annandale, where he lived from 1894 to 1900. His sculpture was categorised as realistic in style with an underlying humour. The public figures in niches at the Lands Department building, Sydney, are examples of Sani's work.[15] A contemporary of Sani, Achille Simonetti, set up a studio at Balmain in 1874 and won prizes for sculpture. The talented and industrious Simonetti, born in Rome in 1838, became a fashionable Sydney sculptor and modelled busts of many of the city's notables. He died at Balmain in 1900.[16]

By 1914, when the Italian-Australian population had reached 10,000, the proportion of immigrants from southern and insular Italy had increased to 31 per cent, and the Italian-born were prominent in mining, fishing and foundries, keeping restaurants and wine shops, and selling fruit, fish and ice cream. The Italian intellectuals and professionals in Australia lived a life apart from their humbler countrymen.[17] About 1,000 Italians were living in the Sydney metropolitan area in 1914.

Many unmarried Italian labourers travelled long distances in search of work. An inquiry into lung diseases among Kalgoorlie miners in 1911 found that many northern Italian men returned to Italy late in life. Those who stayed and did marry often chose Irish-Australian women, often with children.[18]

The 1921 census registered only 8,135 Italian-born in Australia, with the percentage of women immigrants rising from 10 per cent in 1881 to 27 per cent in 1921. The restrictions on immigration imposed by the United States in 1921 and 1924, and propaganda promoting emigration to Australia, contributed to a net increase of 23,233 Italian immigrants between 1922 and 1930.[19] Before the 1914–18 war, waves of immigrants from the Lipari Islands, Sicily, Vicenza and Udine colonised the streets between Balmain Road and Hill Street in Leichhardt.[20] Chain migration accounted for much of Italian settlement in Leichhardt. The first migrant to arrive from a particular village, usually male, found somewhere to live and a livelihood. He was then joined by his wife, children, relatives and *paesani* (friends and neighbours from the native village). The Italian-born in the Leichhardt cluster, including Annandale and Petersham, numbered over 400 persons in 1933 and already constituted the major Italian concentration in Sydney. The main northern Italian group of Leichhardt consisted of interrelated families from Treviso province, but the largest number were from the Lipari Islands of Panarea, Sahna, Lipari and Stromboli, with others from Catania province in eastern Sicily, and from Friuli.[21] There was also a related group of fishermen in Balmain. These village colonies in Leichhardt retained links with their communities of origin and maintained specific dialects and cultural practices. The immigrant culture that emerged in Leichhardt was bonded by membership of political clubs, loyalty among *paesani* and occupational ties.

Italians experienced difficulty finding jobs in the cities in the inter-war years, and went into the countryside to work as farmers, agricultural labourers and itinerant construction workers; in 1933, 61 per cent of the Italian-born population lived in rural areas.[22] The narrow range of occupations followed by most Italians encouraged the growth of local concentrations and most, it seems, came out to join relatives and fellow villagers who had gone before.

A fascist regime seized power in Italy in 1922 and fascism marred relations between Italian migrants and Australians. The network of associations and clubs that sprang up were almost exclusively pro-fascist and the few anti-fascist clubs were also alienated from mainstream Australian life. The twenty Italian associations in Sydney in 1935 reflected the social and historical fragmentation of Italian migrants. They were all fascist-controlled, the most popular ones being the social clubs Roma, Venezia, Savoia, Piedmonte, La Rinascenza, Club Italia, and the oldest association, Circole Isole Eolie, founded in 1903, whose membership was restricted to people from the islands north of Sicily—mainly fruiterers and small businessmen. The Club Italia was a body for upper-class Italians—doctors, company executives and merchants.[23]

By the end of the 1939–45 war more than 10 per cent of Australia's Italian population (4,727 people) had experienced internment. The non-interned aliens and 14,000 prisoners of war were allowed to work freely in industry and on the land; they made an important contribution to the national war effort by taking the place of Australian labour.[24]

Pietro, Antonio and Galliano Melocco, born in the village of Toppo, near Friuli, came to Sydney—Pietro in 1908, and Antonio and the much younger Galliano in 1910. Pietro had studied at the Coopers' Union crafts school in New York and Antonio had been apprenticed as a mosaic worker in Paris. In 1912 they were mosaic workers at 37 Parramatta Road, Forest Lodge, and later opened a yard in Booth Street, Annandale.[25] The Melocco brothers established a reputation in the building trade for fine work in marble, mosaic and terrazzo, with Pietro the artist-designer, Antonio the master craftsman and Galliano the businessman. They are especially remembered for scagliola work on the columns in the Commonwealth Bank, Martin Place, the Tasman map at the entrance to the State Library and the mosaic and tile floor of the crypt of St Mary's Cathedral. After the 1939–45 war Galliano, a mechanical engineer, visited the United States where he first saw mobile concrete mixers, and on his return the brothers' company, Certified Concrete, introduced ready-mix concrete here. The Melocco brothers trained many workers who later became contractors, such as De Martin and Gasparini, and brought others out from Friuli to work for them.[26]

The Melocco brothers in 1912. Left to right, master craftsman Antonio (1887–1946), businessman Galliano (1897–1971) and artist/designer Pietro (1883–1961) built a reputation for outstanding fine work in marble, mosaic and terrazzo. (By courtesy of Bert Melocco)

After 1945 Australia embarked on a mass immigration program that changed the country's ethnic composition and national identity. Between 1947 and 1976 over 360,000 Italians arrived in Australia, though about 90,000 were to return home, making a net immigration of about 270,000.[27] Family issues, health, better economic conditions in Italy and a desire to establish a family there ranked high among the reasons that Italians returned home.[28] In the early post-war years waves of Italians and other southern Europeans, predominantly male, took board and lodgings in inner-city rooming houses, or found spare rooms of compatriots. The majority of Italians, aged between twenty and 40 years, were drawn from small villages in rural areas. Most came from an impoverished background and had not received any vocational training beyond the most basic level.[29] The 'typical' Italian migrant was a settler from the southern regions of Calabria, Sicily, Abruzzi and Campania, generally unskilled and unable to find a niche in post-war Italy.

On disembarking in Sydney, Italians sought areas of cheap housing, and proximity to employers of unskilled labour. In Leichhardt the cost of houses was lower than in surrounding suburbs, and the nucleus of an Italian community that had formed there also served as a magnet to the newly arrived. There was a demand in small near-city factories, employing four to six people, for workers in processing and general factory work and for builder's labourers. Larger concrete, terrazzo and excavation firms owned by De Martin & Gasparini, Cazac, Bayutti, Melocco and Fantuz employed up to 120 workers in the 1960s.[30] In 1966, for example, 86 per cent of all Italian-born workers were manual workers, with 65 per cent either unskilled or semi-skilled.[31] Italians brought with them a strong tradition of hard work, family cohesiveness and a will to succeed. Both husband and wife worked, preoccupied with attaining economic security they had never known. They endured hardship and drew their strength from a narrow social network of *paesani* and relatives who often lived nearby, creating a refuge against a generally unsympathetic and alien world outside. They kept to themselves, and spoke to each other since

Giuseppe and Annunziata Del Duca with their children (left to right) Francesco, Domenica, and Antonio, shortly after their arrival in Leichhardt in 1955. Photograph taken at Zuliani Studios, Leichhardt. (Max Solling Collection)

no one else could understand them; interaction between Italians and Australians was minimal.[32]

Giuseppe del Duca earned a living by the sweat of his brow, working on a farm in Calabria, Italy, and in September 1946 he married Annunziata Cammareri at Palma. The parents of the bride and groom were poor rural workers and their children received limited formal schooling. By 1951 Giuseppe and Annunziata, with three young children—Domenica, Antonio and Francesco—were finding it difficult to make ends meet. Giuseppe's brother, Domenico, had started a new life in Wollongong where he worked at the steel works. He wrote to Giuseppe that there were good job opportunities in Australia. Giuseppe came to Wollongong, where he lived with his brother and other compatriots from Palma, found a job and sent money back to support his family. After a year Giuseppe thought it would be a good place to live. He returned to his native land and the whole family boarded the *Napoletana* in Messina, Sicily, in August 1955 and arrived in Sydney a month later.

Giuseppe and another of his brothers, Carmelo, had earlier placed a deposit on a cottage in 25 Alfred Street, Leichhardt, and on their arrival the family was able to move into the house then occupied by Carmelo, a bachelor. Giuseppe found a job at the Cyclops toy factory in Leichhardt at £5 a week and Annunziata worked as a dressmaker at Pasadena in Broadway, and they set about paying off their house. All the children started school at St Fiacre's, and Antonio became an architect, Francesco, a solicitor and Domenica left school at Year 9 to sew dresses with her mother.

There was little spare room at 25 Alfred Street; Carmelo continued to live there for about five years and then he married Pasqualina, also from Palma; and Carmelo's mother, Domenica, arrived in 1958. In 1960 they sold their Alfred Street house and bought separate houses at 22 and 24 Wetherill Street, Leichhardt. The grandmother lived in each house for six months, and when Carmelo and Pasqualina had a baby she stayed with them to look after the child when they went to work.[33]

Between 1954 and 1961 Leichhardt was both a reception centre and transit camp for Italian migrants, as the number of Italian-born grew dramatically from 1,493 to 4,566. Dozens of interrelated families clustered together in a neighbourhood and an institutional structure slowly emerged to sustain this Italian residential concentration.

The Italian institutions that emerged in Leichhardt provided alienated migrants with an alternative society which had its own opportunities and contacts. The church, Father Adrian Pittarello wrote, was something with which Italian migrants could identify because they felt it to be 'part of themselves'.[34] But in the Irish-Catholic parishes in Australia they found the practice of religion, together with the social life surrounding it, culturally alien and unattractive. In Surry Hills the Scalabrian Fathers assumed responsibility for the pastoral care of a populous Italian parish, and in 1945 the Capuchin Fathers came to Leichhardt and were given the parish of St Fiacre.[35]

Feasts, balls, picnics and religious observance associated with particular saints were major activities of both regional and religious Italian groups. Linguistic or village groups preferred not just an Italian-speaking priest but one who came from their region. Italo-American Capuchins, Padre Enrico Kusnerick, Adalberto Salerno, Silvio Spighi and Anastasio Paoletti developed a distinctively Italian parish in Leichhardt. At St Fiacre's they celebrated the *feste* of San Bartolomeo, the Eolani saint; San Francesco, the Italian patron saint; San Giusto, patron saint of the Triestini, Giuliani and Dalmatians; and the Madonna del Rosario of the Lipari islanders.[36]

The Capuchins assisted migrants with their housing and employment, as well as with sponsorship, the finding of proxy brides and the establishment of a distinctively Christian Democratic ethnic press. Their social and religious committees engaged in fundraising and organised dances, and sporting teams, picnics and the screening of Italian films.[37] St Fiacre's became a unifying influence and a focus for Italian life in Leichhardt. Those who went to the missionary centre found friendship, guidance, moral and material support and a haven for a number of village saints unrecognised by local Australian parishes. Church attendance, however, increased for the celebration of Christmas, Easter, and on particular feast days and patron-saint days with their associated festivities.

The Capuchins established *La Fiamma* in 1947, attempting to counteract a communist newspaper, *Il Risveglio*. *La Fiamma* had a strongly religious flavour, and was so successful that within two years it had eliminated its communist rival. Dr Evasio Costanzo, who became editor in 1951, published B.A. Santamaria and displayed some sympathies with the Democratic Labor Party, but he described the newspaper's philosophy as Labor and socialist. By 1972 it had an average circulation of 25,000.

Italians did not challenge control of the Labor machine in Leichhardt. The New South Wales ALP was suspicious of migrant participation, and few Italians joined local branches. The transient nature of the Italian population (about one-third did not stay longer than five years in Leichhardt), together with the relatively small number of naturalisations, partially explains their low participation rate in local politics.[38] Jupp argues that the tightly controlled inner-city machine was a barrier to migrant participation.[39] In 1968 three Italians—Anthony Monticciola in Leichhardt, Len Bolzan in Lilyfield and George Lapaine in Annandale—were candidates at local government elections in Leichhardt. This was the first time Italians had stood; none was elected.[40]

It was the retailers rather than the residents who first mobilised themselves politically. Italian businessmen formed one-fifth of the membership of the Westgate Chamber of Commerce, and under the leadership of G.C. Gambotto in the late 1960s it became a vital local interest group.[41] However, retailers were reluctant to stand in local government elections against the ALP as most Italians were Labor supporters.

During the 1950s sporting and social clubs in Leichhardt—Giulia Sporting and Social

The Choro Italiano, founded by Fr Silvio Spighi (*centre front*) at St Fiacre's, Leichhardt, in 1954, provided music and sacred song in Italian for services held there for Italian migrants. Members were newly arrived, mainly from the Veneto region. Conductor Giovanni Pettenon is at left front and organist Patricia Nicoll (Fin), right front. (By Courtesy of Patricia Fin)

Club, the Club Miramare and Circolo Trieste—largely catered for a regionally based clientele. However, a more professional club was conceived to embrace a broader cross-section of the Italian community. The Associazone Polisportiva Italo Australiana (Apia) was founded in 1954 by Italians working at Kurnell Oil Refinery, with Giacomo (Jim) Bayutti as its driving force. Bayutti proudly announced that it was 'the first post-war Italian sporting association not financed or patronised by one person or authority . . . and which hopes to represent and guide Italian youth according to the greater ideals of the wider Italian community'.[42]

Based in a rented room in Norton Street, Leichhardt, in 1957, the club's declared aim was 'to establish, promote and encourage the sporting and social activities of Italian migrants in Australia and the assimilation of such migrants into the Australian community'. However, it was perceived as an elitist organisation, its executive comprised of established Italian businessmen and the post-war nouveaux riches.[43] The first floor of the avant-garde premises of the Apia Club at Fraser Street, Leichhardt, was opened on 19 March 1962, with 470 foundation members; the second floor was completed two years later. Italians produced many of the best soccer teams after the war, and in the 1962 and 1963 seasons, peak years for Australian soccer, the Apia Soccer Club—with Joe Marston, Giovanni Giacometti, Aduato Iglesias, Ricardo Campana, Cliff van Blerk, Johnny Wong, Stan Ackerly, Pat Hughes, George Nutall and Jim Sambrook—attracted crowds of 30,000 at semi-finals at the Sydney Sports Ground.

The role of the Apia Club went far beyond that of a social and sporting club; it became regarded by Sydney politicians as an authentic voice of Italian interests and, despite the narrowly recreational purpose implied in the title, it became a powerful vehicle for the expression of Italo-Australian opinions and attitudes.[44] Perceived as the Italian club by Italians and Australians, it was visited by representatives of both major political parties, including Whitlam, McMahon, Mulvihill, Wentworth and Hawke. Home soccer games at Lambert Park attracted crowds of about 7,000 and membership of the Apia Club reached a peak of 15,000. Although 60 per cent of its membership in 1980 was non-Italian, its governing body remained largely composed of Italian Australians. However as Italians moved further west, and the club's team was dropped from the National Soccer League, it began racking up a 9-million dollar debt, and closed in May 1996.[45]

A wide array of Italian businesses was operating in Leichhardt by 1962—seven Italian-born fruit vendors, six real estate and travel agents, six grocers, five restaurants, four cafes, four social/sports clubs, three barbers and three hairdresser, two cobblers (bootmakers), two butchers, two tailors, two pharmacies, and a cake shop, bakery, service station, jeweller, music shop and the San Remo night club. Expanding Italian enterprise led to the revival of the Leichhardt Chamber of Commerce in 1963 but few Italians joined.[46]

A high turnover rate in Leichhardt housing between 1959 and 1966 saw established real estate agents, Gallagher, Taylor and Hooker employ Italian-speaking staff, and new agents Montano, La Casa and Compagnon make their mark in the industry. The active local real estate market stimulated the emergence of offices at the southern end of Norton Street occupied by solicitors, tax consultants, business agents and accountants.[47]

The local Strand and Odeon theatres began screening Italian-language films during week nights, and in 1971 the *Westgate Weekly News* had a regular 'Pagina Italiana' dealing with social events. The *Glebe Weekly* translated its editorials into Italian, and G.C. Gambotto was responsible for the Italian contribution to the *Tiger*. Australian businesses adapted to meet Italian needs. Grace Bros imported Italian food specialties, and the Bank of New South Wales and Commonwealth Bank established savings bank agencies with local Italian businesses, all of which operated with extended hours. Though Leichhardt acquired a reputation as Sydney's 'Little Italy', in the period between 1961 and 1971 the number of Italian-born in the municipality never exceeded more than 25 per cent of the total population. The figures in Table 18 indicate the concentrations within the municipality.[48]

Table 18   Italian-born population in Leichhardt Municipality in 1971

Suburb	Number of Italians	Percentage
Leichhardt	2,580	15.2
Lilyfield	1,103	9.7
Annandale	586	6.00
Rozelle	247	2.2
Balmain	244	2.2
Glebe	243	1.7
Total	5,003	

Leichhardt had become the crucible of Italo-Australian identity in Sydney. Its range of institutions made it a place where all the needs of the Italian migrant could be met and where recent arrivals could find help in adjusting. Leichhardt Council became involved in the ethnic community, joining in a program to identify and cater for their needs. Small Italian enterprises continued to increase in the early 1970s and by 1976 there were 175 Italian businesses in Leichhardt; indeed, 52 per cent of the area's commercial establishments and social organisations were run by Italians. These businesses were located along a two-kilometre stretch of Parramatta Road, especially near the intersection of Norton Street.[49] In this precinct a plethora of businesses with an Italian heritage was to be found—just about all of the food outlets, butchers and delicatessens stocking imported Italian foods and condiments; optometrists; glass works; funeral directors; estate agents; and bridal, children's and babies' shops, all displaying the sign 'Si parla Italiano'. Leichhardt has an enduring symbolic power; its neon lights and signposting announce to all the world an Italian identity.[50] It was here that printers and publishers of the main Italian newspapers in Australia, *La Fiamma* and *Il Settegiorni* were located. The highest concentration of Italian residents in Leichhardt in 1976 was to be found in Catherine, Norton, Marion, Renwick, Excelsior and Elswick streets and in Balmain Road.

Frank Castiglione from Sicily, a Norton Street tax accountant, came to Leichhardt in

Presto Small Goods factory, Leichhardt, 1966. Italian food enriched the cuisine of the adopted country. (APA Collection, Still 22167, State Library of New South Wales)

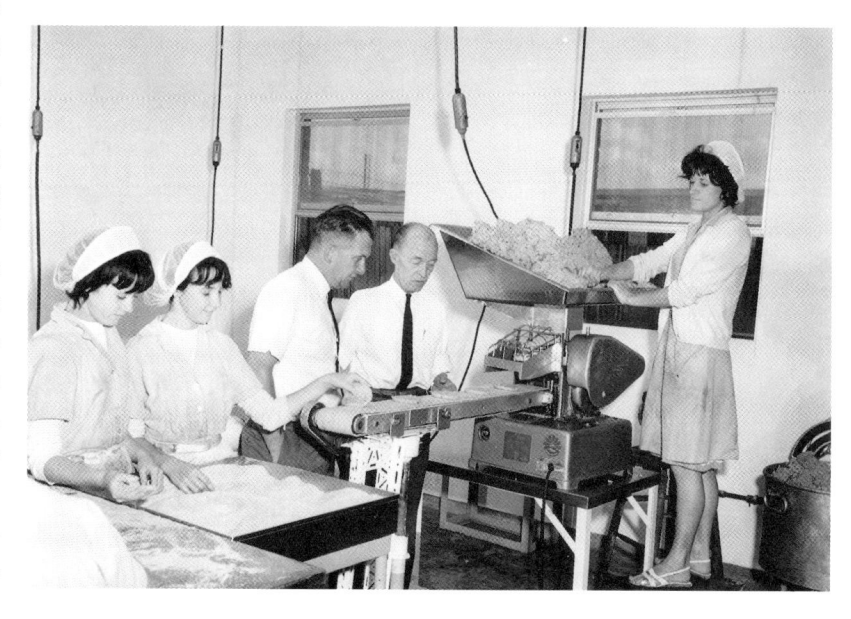

1952 and emerged as a father figure among the Italian community, someone to whom the newly arrived could go to sort out problems that confronted them.[51] Others took advantage of niches that became available with expansion of the Australian economy. Giacomo Bayutti rose in influence and was eventually appointed to the board of Qantas. Hopes of a better life induced most Italians to leave the place of their birth but the early years in their new land were generally difficult. 'It was a hard life,' said Nella Leone. 'We had no home, no money, no nothing. I worked at a factory and someone had to take care of my little son.'[52]

The Italian-born population in Leichhardt Municipality declined from 5,003 in 1971 to 3,922 five years later. As Italians established themselves, they tended to move away from the centre and the distinct clusters in Leichhardt. They gradually fanned out to Drummoyne (which in 1989 had the highest concentration—10.6 per cent of the total population), Ashfield, Haberfield, Concord and Burwood. Only 4 per cent of Leichhardt's population in 1989 were Italian-born. As Norton Street barber Vince Bontolillo observed in 1988, 'a lot of Italians are moving out. The old ones die and the young ones go to live somewhere cheaper or where they can build a good house. There are many young trendies moving into the area now'.[53] However, whatever the resident population, Leichhardt remains hallowed ground in Italian hearts, a link with their past and a place that opened up opportunities for industrious people.

According to the 1991 census, 1,872 people of Italian birth or background were living in the Leichhardt Local Government Area; this represented 3.2 per cent of its population. Other ethnic communities have left their own distinctive imprint on Leichhardt's landscape. In 1991 it had 673 Greek-born residents (1.2 per cent of the population), 505 people born in Vietnam, 453 from Yugoslavia and 442 Chinese. The number of Maltese-born residents, 600 in 1981, had declined to 263 in 1991.[54]

'Chardonnay Socialists' and 'yuppie Trotskyites': Leichhardt 1990

The combination of the depression, World War II and rent control contributed to the decay of neighbourhoods near the city. The status of Sydney's inner suburbs, like that of their inhabitants, was low for half a century. It was an environment described as 'smoky, dirty and crime-ridden', where no self-respecting person would live.[1] Inner-suburban streetscapes were seen as old and unfashionable at a time when Australian preferences were overwhelmingly for low-density suburban living.[2] Every suburb had its own social cachet: the names Balmain or Glebe represented the uttermost depth of social mediocrity. Those who wore a tie to work, and had ambitions of being accepted by the middle class, did not mention where they lived.

The suburban nuclear family, politicians claimed, was the bedrock on which the foundations of society were built in a world where the husband was the breadwinner and the energies of the wife were absorbed in home-making. Near the city the absence of hot running water and labour-saving devices made it tiring to prepare meals, bathe children and clean houses. Probably the most onerous of the wife's household tasks was the washing; clothes were boiled in a copper, then rinsed, wrung and pegged out on the clothesline and, when dry, they had to be ironed. Evenings were spent sewing, darning the heels of socks and knitting pullovers.[3]

The kind of neighbourliness that pervaded suburbs close to the city was the product of stable communities where big working-class families had stayed put for generations. It was a world where extended families were common, where three generations often lived in the same street, or in the same house and where aunts, uncles and cousins were part of the daily world. Neighbours did not need to get together, it was open house all year round as people dropped in for a cup of tea or a chat.[4] The vast majority walked rather than drove about their suburb. Money was never plentiful and, in times of need, a local could rely on the support of neighbours and relatives. Most children received an education at the local government schools, and large families meant that these were crowded places.[5] Streets and lanes, largely devoid of cars, were playgrounds, and a vigorous culture flourished here—handball, hopscotch and tennis were played and roughly made billycarts scooted down lanes. At local clubs, especially Police Boys Clubs, they could play football, cricket and other games.

A transitory population lived in a succession of rooms, or in often overcrowded flats. It was a lifestyle that disturbed the *Methodist*: 'Homes become just "rooms" in grim tenements, or cold, impersonal buildings. The one front door leads to "floors" where often enough the basement and attic become places of existence for whole families.'[6] Since there was nowhere to cook in some places, the occupants patronised dubiously clean cafes and hamburger joints. Owner-occupied houses in inner Sydney rose from 27 per cent in 1947 to 40 per cent in 1954 and 63 per cent in 1961.[7]

Leichhardt's population declined dramatically from 90,766 in 1947 to 71,388 in 1971. Rising real incomes enabled tenants to buy their own homes after the war, but few young couples whose circumstances permitted chose to raise their families in the inner city. Rising car ownership facilitated their exodus to intermediate or outer suburbs.[8] This out-migration left inner Sydney with a disproportionate number of older and poorer families. As sporting clubs lost members they complained that the inner city had become a transit camp 'where families pause long enough to save money to buy a home and then move on'.[9]

A working-class culture which lived and worked near the city for decades was undermined by a massive decline in manufacturing and service industries as the industrial structure of Sydney underwent profound changes. In Leichhardt Municipality the number of factories declined from 668 in 1945 to 462 in 1971 and to 210 in 1983, and at the same time as blue-collar jobs shifted to the western suburbs, office and professional jobs in Sydney grew. Structural changes in the workforce were closely associated with the transformation in the residential character of Leichhardt.[10]

Young professionals and other white-collar workers began moving into Paddington in the early 1960s seeking out Victorian and Federation housing with particular attributes—handmade bricks, ironwork, high and ornamental ceilings and a particular architectural style.[11] Paddington became a fashion symbol of urbane lifestyles, community diversity, architectural charm and historical significance. The proportion of blue-collar workers in the labour force in Sydney's inner suburbs fell by up to 15 per cent, compared with 5 per cent in the whole metropolis, between 1966 and 1971. At the same time the percentage of professional and upper-white collar workers in the Sydney population rose by 0.5 per cent, but in Paddington it rose by 7 per cent. Just behind were Balmain and Glebe with increases of 6 per cent and 5 per cent.[12] Balmain's spectacular harbour views and the short ferry trip to the city appealed to the new middle class and Glebe's proximity to the University of Sydney was an attraction. 'An army of young people is marching into Glebe,' wrote Sandra Jobson, 'buying up and renovating the houses, and hoping they have not made a mistake'.[13]

The term 'gentrification', borrowed from the inner-housing scene of London, has been used to describe this small-scale inner-city phenomenon. It involves two central notions—access to, and exclusive control over, real estate; and the displacement from property of less powerful residents. Some argue that this concept is inappropriate and inaccurate to explain the experience of inner-city areas of Australia.[14] A strong upward shift in occupational status and levels of owner occupancy is a useful barometer of this phenomenon, but census and other source materials are not sufficiently detailed to quantify, with any precision, the extent of inner-suburban change. A reliable barometer of an area's desirability, status and wealth—average house prices—reveals that these rose in Leichhardt municipality from $28,000 in 1977 to $70,000 in 1981. By 1988 average house prices had climbed to $190,000, and by 1994 to $255,000, placing home ownership beyond the financial reach of the average young family.[15]

In Glebe public renting and owner occupancy rose between 1966 and 1981 with a corresponding drop in private renting.[16] Far more dramatic tenure changes have taken place with boarding and lodging houses which have been converted and sold for single residency purposes.[17] The heightened demand of middle-class purchasers considerably raised sale prices of houses and rising house values have made renovation increasingly attractive. All inner-city local government areas had sizeable increases in house rents, with rises especially sharp in Leichhardt.[18]

Neighbourliness flowed from residential stability and the growing desirability of inner-city housing, and constant turnover of property, brought social upheaval for the traditional population as available low-priced rental accommodation was reduced.[19] The poor, disadvantaged and alienated were increasingly forced into the outreaches of the city as the number of cheap boarding and lodging houses declined. As private low-cost housing also declined traditional tenants had to pay higher rentals to remain in the area or find alternative accommodation elsewhere.[20] There was a bright side, however, for some respectable working-class citizens who were able to buy houses they had rented for years. Selling up at the right time, they reaped a handsome profit, making their final years the most comfortable time of their lives.[21]

Residents protest in Glebe against proposed high-rise development in Ferry Road, 1971. Professor Bernard Smith (with megaphone) was the president of the Glebe Society. (The *Glebe Weekly*, 10 March 1971)

Formation of local resident action groups between 1965 and 1971 signalled the arrival of the new middle class, though a few of the older residents did also join. These associations became cohesive bodies around which social networks were established and they were adept at using the media and mobilising their forces. Conservation policies were pursued to protect the urban heritage in which they had an economic stake and they assumed that their definition of the 'common good' was shared by the rest of the community.[22] While this was the case in anti-expressway battles, opposition to new blocks of flats operated against the interests of flat renters. Perhaps the demise of associations in Annandale and Leichhardt suggests that their influence and political clout may have been exaggerated, though residents' groups in Balmain and Glebe retain healthy memberships.

Middle-class residents and students were at the forefront of radical actions, the most visible being the alliance with the Builders Labourers Federation (BLF) with its socialist critique. BLF leader Jack Mundey was warm in his praise of resident activism, telling Balmain residents that labels like 'trendy' and 'silvertail' had little relevance in condemning activism. The most effective campaigns in protecting the environment, Mundey declared, were an alliance between the enlightened working class and the enlightened middle class.[23]

Something of the nature of political activism that pervaded the municipality in the 1970s is captured in this poem sent to the *Glebe Weekly*:

> The pioneers of conservation
> Catch the 433 past Central Station
> Dreaming of the ideal solution,
> For aircraft noise and lead pollution;
> Back at home their Balmain wives
> Are picking dill and chopping chives
> Julia takes a radical stand
> Between the Sèvres and the baby grand:
> 'I'll miss the seminar on child abuse,
> The microwave has blown a fuse'.
> It's Justin's birthday in three weeks
> Lucian's shopping for antiques —
> Some bijou pieces of Australiana,
> In which to grow their marijuana.
> There are forums, quorums, demonstrations,
> Vigils, fetes and remonstrations.
> Chuck the trucks, and plant some trees,
> Bring the Council to its knees.
> Laura's starting some radical action
> For lesbian truck drivers of Asian extraction.
> Save our skyline, save our beaches,
> Make life hell for sexist teachers,
> But renovate and speculate.
> Business is good in real estate.

The house price rise is meteoric
Since Toxteth Road became historic.[24]

The human dimensions of Leichhardt's changing character have attracted media attention, while social scientists and long-term residents are much more emphatic about the social and physical transformation taking place. The material fabric of the old terraces and houses has been lovingly restored but older residents lament that much of the warmth and energy that characterised inner-city living in the pre-TV era are largely gone as newer residents pursue a very different lifestyle.[25]

Politics, like property, were gentrified in the 1970s, prompting Paul Keating's derisive reference to the 'basket weavers of Balmain'.[26] Boilermakers and boatbuilders on the peninsula were now not as numerous as potters and poets. Journalist Peter Smark categorised Balmain's new residents in 1985 as 'a mix of Chardonnay Socialists whose anxieties over mortgages and divorces are blended with nostalgia for the Whitlam era (when they moved there) and a less bohemian group whose ambitions are more nakedly bound up with property prices, and whose Bible is *Vogue Living*'.[27]

Commercial redevelopment followed the gentrification phenomenon. Old inner-city shops and warehouses have been transformed into new establishments which sell goods and services desired by the gentrifiers, as well as by consumers living elsewhere. This newly built environment of refurbished housing, of specialty shops, eating places, bookshops, art galleries and so on, created a new and unique infrastructure of consumption, and one that symbolises the culture of consumerism.[28]

The pub, once a sort of colonised working-class institution, now seeks a wider clientele. In a municipality in a state of flux some pubs have remained blue-collar, places where the clientele believe a right uppercut to be repartee. Barry Green, a patron of the Forest Lodge, declared: 'We're all Tooheys boys here. It's the only pub in this area that hasn't gone bad.'[29] Drinkers can still wear shorts and thongs, and are not banned for life if they have a fight there. Within two blocks the Nag's Head and the British Lion, up-market boutique pubs, attract a more sophisticated clientele. The Nag's Head offers the serious drinker a choice of eleven beers on tap, and numerous Australian and imported beers.[30] Glebe Estate residents had always solidly supported the Australian Youth Hotel, but once they introduced new light fittings and furniture and polished floor boards, most of the traditional drinkers drifted elsewhere.[31] The old Riverview Hotel in Balmain hosted colourful personalities like Lennie McPherson and Stan 'the Man' Smith when Dawn Fraser was licensee. The new Riverview

Some pubs attracted a mix of old and new patrons. Here, Chardonnay Socialists inspect a traditional drinker. (Moir, *SMH*, 30 May 1985)

is different, renovated along the lines of a comfortable English pub, with new stained glass doors and black and white linoleum tiles on the floor in place of carpets.³² The London in Balmain, 'where old men in carpet slippers once fed their mangy dogs dark beer and chips under the table' underwent a million-dollar blackwood refit to become the New South Wales flagship for Coopers brewery.³³

Few of the new professionals and white-collar workers send their children to the local comprehensive co-educational high school. Their decision about where to send their offspring is dictated more by class and parental expectations than the child's aptitude or need. Some pursue the selective high school option with all possible coaching and cramming, or the special high school, but the fall-back is the private school.³⁴

The new residents display a clear preference for the more passive culture, be it drinking cappuccino in outside cafes and savouring the 'cosmopolitan atmosphere', or taking the dog for a walk. In the early 1970s, when English sheepdogs and Afghan hounds became thick on the pavement, locals acquired a motion known as the 'inner city dodge', a neat sidestep to avoid deposits left by dogs.³⁵ In the evenings small armies of dog walkers, complete with tennis racquet and ball, congregate in parks, and other available spaces, to exercise their dogs.

The largest number of people claiming no religion in 1986 were found in the inner-city communities. At Glebe Point, for example, 31 per cent of its population said they had no religion and growing secularisation near the city has left many churches under-utilised.³⁶

In 1985 the Department of Housing announced a proposal to provide public housing for long-time local residents on part of the former container facility and Australian National Line passenger terminal site (6.5 ha) at Mort Bay, with about one-half of the site being dedicated as park. It had been more than 30 years since any public housing had been constructed in Balmain.³⁷ The Mort Bay Action Group objected to the idea of Housing Commission development, arguing that the government was trying to squeeze too many people into Balmain. It wanted the entire site developed for parkland. Leichhardt Council zoned 3.82 hectares for open space and 3.5 hectares for residential development; 210 dwellings were built.³⁸

Leichhardt Council has become the scene of conflict over five industrial sites (covering 23 hectares or 7 per cent, of the Balmain peninsula), which once made Balmain a centre of

A number of traditional inner-city pubs acquired a new image to match a changing clientele. The Nag's Head in St John's Road, Forest Lodge, offers a choice of beers on tap and numerous Australian and imported beers. (Photograph by David Liddle)

manufacturing. Between 1976 and 1989 four of the sites—the Chemplex plant at Iron Cove, the nearby Balmain Power Station, the massive Unilever complex and Ampol's White Bay plant—had shut down. The only one of these sites still operating is the Caltex depot at Ballast Point. Balmain's population has been steadily declining, but when the site owners sought rezoning of their land in 1989, battle lines were drawn up.[39] The owners wanted to develop as much of their land as intensively as possible, spending about $500 million to provide housing for between 3,700 and 5,000 people. A group of local activists vigorously resisted rezoning, arguing that Balmain has less parkland than most areas, as well as major traffic problems and a high population density (1,038 residents per hectare).[40]

Leichhardt Council, under the control of Independents, closely considered submissions of local residents where redevelopment would be on a scale out of proportion to the existing environment.[41] Council, however, took a different view in September 1990 with the election of Bill Brady as Mayor. Brady believed rezoning was inevitable and that Council should not miss the opportunity of getting rid of the Caltex and Chemplex sites.[42]

In 1990 when David Hay, Minister for Planning, appointed Sean O'Toole as planning administrator for Balmain, Council did nothing, but residents, described by Hay as 'yuppie Trotskyites' were quick to invoke their property rights.[43] Balmain has demonstrated its capacity to defend itself against unwanted development. The Balmain Development Trust was formed, and to raise money for a court challenge, it held a $100-a-head dinner at the Sheraton Hotel with playwright David Williamson and broadcaster Robin Williams, both locals, the main speakers.[44] Mayor Brady asked the Local Government Association not to support the Balmain Development Trust, declaring he was 'on the side of the poor bugger in Leichhardt battling away at three jobs to try and pay off his mortgage, not the millionaires of Louisa Road'.[45] The Land and Environment Court dismissed the residents' action but the Court of Appeal overturned Justice Cripps' decision. The right of Council to hold a public hearing prevailed over Minister Hay's right to require Council to submit its environmental plans, and the appointment of O'Toole was found to be a denial of natural justice.[46] The *Glebe Weekly* greeted the decision as a 'Victory to the People', in which 'a group of residents had taken on Kerry Packer, Caltex, Ampol, the Electricity Commission and Unilever—and, to everyone's amazement, won'.[47]

The state government suffered its second defeat in the Court of Appeal in 1993 when the government again sought to ride roughshod over Leichhardt Council's planning powers. Proper consultation, the court held, meant Council should be given a reasonable opportunity to state its views.[48] In 1996 Council approved residential redevelopment of four of the five sites, with the Caltex site at Ballast Point awaiting rezoning.[49]

In 1990 Leichhardt's town planner told a public inquiry that Leichhardt was making a 'transition from an essentially mixed blue-collar industrial and residential suburb to an environmentally reformed and upgraded residential municipality'.[50] The municipality remains diverse and polarised socially, with blue-collar precincts surviving in Glebe, Leichhardt, Balmain, Rozelle and Lilyfield. Wealth and poverty live relatively close together, just as W.S. Jevons found in 1858.[51] The inner suburbs began as semi-rural resorts of the well-to-do, and with a renewed appreciation of city life, their transformation might be perceived as something like a return to their origins. The advantages of living ten minutes from the Opera House outweigh the lure of the housing of the northern suburbs. Some apartments in Balmain start at $1 million, and a projection of trends that have taken place in Glebe, a fairly characteristic inner suburb, suggest that growing concentrations of affluent people living near the city will continue.[52]

Traditional and new politics in Leichhardt

Overview

Blue-collar and clerical workers had been the backbone of Leichhardt's Labor branches for decades, but as the municipality's social structure experienced change from the early 1970s so too did the character of local politics. The new middle class moving into the area had a significant impact, participating in the Campaign for Better Council in 1971 that altered the composition of Leichhardt Council. The new councillors in 1971 encouraged public participation in Council's decision-making, 'opening up' council affairs to scrutiny. Improved town planning was a critical part of their agenda. The 1971 Open Council was a radical departure from the way Council had previously conducted its affairs. At the 1974 local government elections nine traditional Labor candidates were elected and they retained control of Council for the next six years, during which time many of the innovations introduced by their predecessors were dismantled. The traditional right-wing faction battled against those with a left-perspective for control of local Labor branches. By 1980 left-wing factions had the numbers to control four of the six wards, with traditional Labor retaining control of Glebe and Lilyfield. The 1980 Council embraced objectives not dissimilar from those of the new middle class and removed the barrier separating the public gallery from the council chamber, an important gesture that was symbolic of open local government. The 'open council' or participatory democracy adopted by Leichhardt was examined by a public inquiry in 1990.

The rise of the new middle class was an emerging phenomenon from the mid-1960s. Young, usually tertiary-educated, and socially aware, they generally had salaried jobs in large companies, universities or the public service, and had time to agitate on issues that most closely affected them.[1] John Roseth saw them as urbanites who rejected the environment in which they had been brought up. They came to the inner city looking for an alternative to the 'suburban' life.[2] The first sign of effective resident action came from the Paddington Society, formed in 1964. A middle-class and preservation-oriented group, it ran an elaborate campaign against a proposal to redesign the road system in Paddington which would effectively have destroyed Jersey Road.

Their protests brought about the appointment of architect Walter Bunning to adjudicate. In March 1968 he decided in favour of the residents and the Department of Main Roads' plans were shelved.[3]

The Balmain Association, which had its inaugural meeting on 4 November 1965, attracted 500 people to a public meeting on 27 September 1966 at which they voiced their concerns about the Maritime Services Board's proposals for a stopgap container terminal at White Bay. But despite their campaign, the Association was unable to persuade the Askin government to adopt Botany Bay as the major container facility.[4] In 1966 the Association's newsletter was expressing concern about the destruction of many 'historically and architecturally interesting buildings' at Mort's Dock, the use of the dock for steel discharge and the threatened demolition of the Stephens Street Wharf.[5] At the same time the Association produced a *Report on Alternative Container Shipping Schemes for Sydney*, and embarked on research which outlined the historical development of the Balmain peninsula.[6]

The first newsletter of the Glebe Society in July 1969 spelt out its aims:

> the Society will concern itself with the problems threatening Glebe as a pleasant place to live. Our approach will be two-pronged, to ensure that adequate thought and planning goes into new projects in the area and to preserve and conserve what is good in the already existing buildings and places of historic interest.[7]

The Glebe Society prepared *An Outline Plan for Glebe*, and Society member David Potter produced a monograph in 1972, *An Alternative to Inner Urban Expressways*.[8] According to Tony Strachan, its membership in 1971 comprised to a large extent the newly arrived professionals with relatively fewer of the old Glebe residents.[9] The interests of the new middle class were within an ideological framework of concern for the whole community and its future—opposition to expressways, unplanned and unrestricted unit development or 'unenlightened redevelopment without regard to architectural or historic merit'. Resident action groups sought to preserve the special character of their districts, and to ensure that any new development was in harmony with the existing physical fabric. They demanded a greater say in local matters that affected their lives and to achieve this they required access to the decision-making processes of Leichhardt Council.[10]

The destruction of 'Claremont', one of the 'Witches Houses' in Johnston Street, Annandale, and the threat of two eight-storey blocks of flats nearby, led to the formation of the Annandale Association in 1970. The Association claimed Council ignored residents' views. 'The monolithic opposition and personal vilification received from Council,' the Association observed, 'was unexpected and unwarranted.'[11] The relationship between Leichhardt Council and the other two local resident groups, too, was becoming strained. In 1968 the Balmain Association felt that, despite the efforts of their ward aldermen, 'the problems of our district continued to receive scant attention' at Council meetings.[12] In 1971 the Glebe Society took to the streets to protest against a proposed high-rise development in Ferry Road. It presented a petition to ward alderman H.J. Foley, who failed to pass it on to Council as promised. Society president Bernard Smith was quoted as saying that 'Ratepayers and citizens of Glebe would no longer tolerate Council's double dealing, their betrayal, or their arrogance. Foley let us down.'[13] It brought a swift response from Dr Foley, who castigated the Glebe Society as a gang of larrikins and dastardly plant tramplers.[14]

A little earlier the Balmain Association wrote that the performance of Council left a great deal to be desired: 'Many decisions have been imposed on Balmain by the Council . . . Little or no justification for decisions as they have been given by the ruling majority in Council – it is obvious that this state of affairs must not continue.'[15] Council made decisions in strict secrecy in the caucus room, never informing residents what issues were discussed there, or how they voted. Totally frustrated by their experiences with Council, the three resident action groups came to mistrust the Labor-dominated council. Concerned residents attended the inaugural meeting of the Leichhardt–Lilyfield Association on 5 November 1971. They pursued pressing local issues but within three years of election of a more sympathetic council in 1980, the Association had ceased to operate.[16]

Former Labor aldermen Origlass and Wyner were regarded as 'progressive' and 'responsive', and in gaining office in 1968 their Balmain Leichhardt Labor (BLL) group had adopted the slogan 'People come first', and depicted Labor councillors as 'tired old men' who did not adequately serve the residents.[17] The Glebe Society's constitution did not allow it to be associated with any political party, but its newsletter noted, 'this does not mean we are bound to support the existing aldermen and on their record we cannot'.[18]

Battle lines were being drawn up under the banner of the Campaign for Better Council (CBC), and most of the candidates were members of the resident action groups that actively supported them.[19] The

The team who stood under the banner of the Campaign for Better Council at Leichhardt Council elections on 18 September 1971. (The Glebe, 18 August 1971)

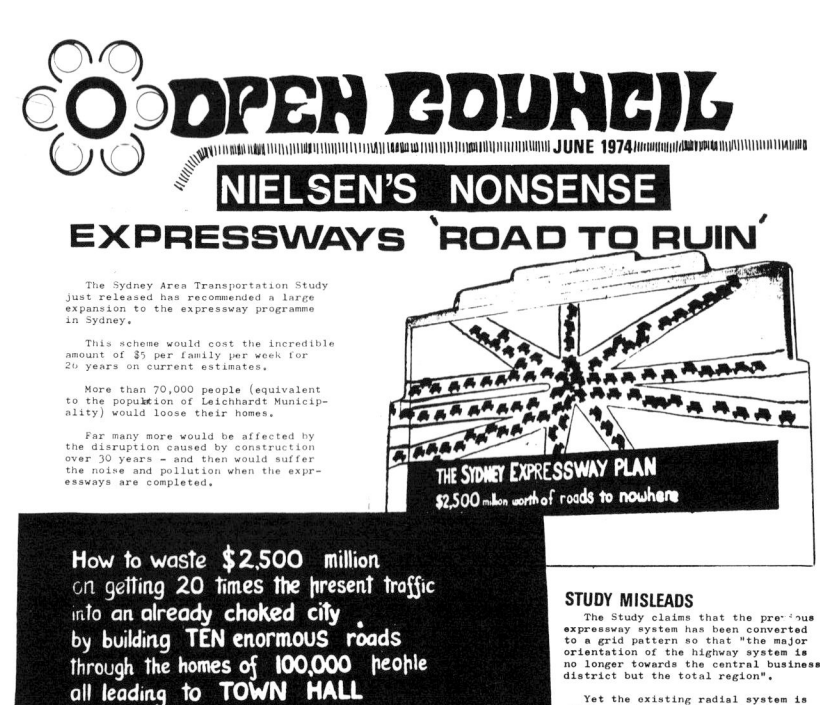

local press took an interest in readily definable issues—opposition to expressways, flat proposals, marinas and container terminals. The *Glebe Weekly* favoured election of CBC and BLL and ran a series of articles on their candidates who were presented as a credible alternative team.[20]

The *Sun* newspaper presented Leichhardt Council in an unflattering light:

> Mayor Rodwell described Leichhardt as a picture. Many ratepayers agree—they say a Council meeting is often better entertainment than the movies. Urgent calls for the police to restore order are not unusual . . . and Leichhardt Council by-laws inspectors carry guns to enforce the law.[21]

In the September 1971 election six CBC candidates—Eric Sandblom and David Young from Glebe, Philip Bray from Rozelle, Ern McIlveen from Lilyfield, and Bill Dougherty and Val Smart of Leichhardt—were elected to Council, and as a result of an informal coalition with the two BLL aldermen, they found themselves in control of the council chamber and Nick Origlass was elected Mayor.[22] Only four of the nine Labor aldermen remained on Council (Casey, Rodwell, Hume and Wilson). Introduction of preferential and non-compulsory voting meant only 26.5 per cent of the electorate cast their vote.[23]

Leichhardt Council's anti-expressway campaign through its newsletter *Open Council*, June 1974. (Max Solling Collection)

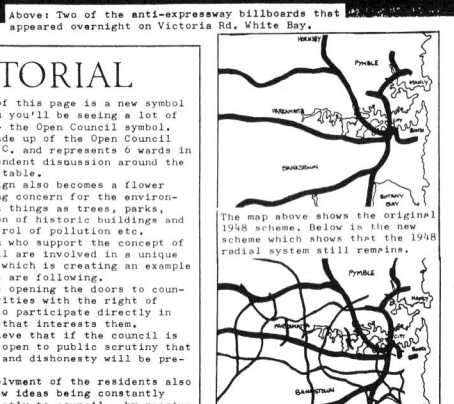

The CBC proposed extensive participation by residents in Council decision-making, in sharp contrast to the previous unco-operative and authoritarian Labor Council. At the first meeting of Council in October 1971, it was resolved to 'open up' Council and its meetings to public scrutiny, and give residents the right to speak freely at Council meetings and the opportunity to participate in their own government.[24] The first act of Council was a mayoral edict removing the barrier between the public gallery and council chamber. Community involvement was to be encouraged by giving both the public and the press access to council papers and agendas. The new council saw a need for improving local town planning, expressing opposition to expressways and controlling flat development, and interested persons were invited to participate in an array of newly established public committees.[25]

The CBC included opposition to the expressways in their platform under the slogan 'Save

Glebe'. Sydney's expressways were planned when the inner suburbs were designated as slums and, because of the low status accorded these suburbs, their residents were to bear the brunt of the 'greater good'.[26] The Department of Main Roads (DMR) began acquiring houses in the path of the north-western expressway in 1969, leaving them vacant and condemned, and later demolishing them. The new Leichhardt Council Urban Radial Expressway group was formed with a view to preventing demolition of houses and construction of expressways and Mayor Origlass, bedecked in full regalia, attracted considerable publicity by painting the proposed route of the expressway in Glebe.[27] The Glebe Society was delighted in 1970 when it succeeded in persuading the DMR to agree to have a portion of the north-western expressway driven underground beneath the Toxteth Estate.[28]

The official view of the inner-suburban communities came from Dr R.S. Neilsen, Director of the Sydney Area Transportation Study, who described areas such as Glebe, Annandale, Lilyfield and Leichhardt as 'old, stingy and should be torn down and the residents relocated'.[29] The route of the two proposed expressways carved Glebe into three distinct sections and would displace about 2,500 people.

Lyndhurst, an early Regency mansion in the expressway path, became a symbol of the anti-expressway movement, and as the DMR continued resuming properties in Glebe in 1972, Council formed a 'Save Lyndhurst Committee'. The main activists were students and middle-class residents who had the active support of Council and the resident action groups. Opposition to expressways took many forms. Confrontation was common at demolition sites, as was squatting in vacant DMR-affected houses, and Albert Mispel conducted what was virtually a one-man campaign disseminating information and lobbying the authorities.[30] After several confrontations between residents, police and demolishers in 1972, and the imposition of a 'green ban' by the Builders Labourers Federation (BLF) led by Jack Mundey, the DMR withdrew from Glebe.

Mundey, a charismatic radical, was able to 'spellbind an audience of any political persuasion with his eminently reasonable commonsense arguments'.[31] The green ban movement also espoused the ideas of the redistribution of wealth and power, and their bans 'demonstrate a refusal any longer to concede that the rich and powerful and entrenched interests have any unchallengeable right to make all the decisions . . . responsibility cannot be left to those whose obsession is with profits amassed by exploitation'.[32]

But the battle was far from over. The green bans were very much a response to insensitive official attitudes, especially towards predominantly working-class people close to the city. At Woolloomooloo, Jack Mundey wrote, proposed development would uproot 'hapless citizens' and distribute them around 'the far flung western and south-western outer suburbs'.[33]

In August 1973, Tom Uren, Federal Minister for Urban and Regional Development, announced that the government was 'moving towards a policy of opposition to inner city expressways' but the Askin government was anxious to push ahead with demolition and construction work.[34] The DMR was given orders to move into Fig Street, Ultimo, in October 1974 with bulldozers, chains and police, and here they were confronted by the BLF and anti-expressway groups.[35] The battles at Fig Street attracted national attention and the federal government, through the Commonwealth Roads Grants Act, withdrew finance from the project, forcing the New South Wales government to announce that no more work would take place until an inquiry was held.

The Church of England Glebe estate, which included 723 properties used as family dwellings and 27 commercial properties, was affected by a reservation for the western expressway, and in the late 1960s many of the long-term leases there were expiring.[36] The Archbishop of Sydney commented in 1968 that the diocese had a 'vast potential wealth in real estate which has not been developed to take advantage of the post-war rises in values'.[37] The Church of England was in an unenviable position: the low rentals it obtained meant little money was spent on maintenance of its properties, and it received adverse publicity in an ABC current affairs program which examined the plight of its tenants in Glebe.[38] Its response was to announce plans in October 1972 to sell part of the Glebe estate in order to help finance a city office development.[39] The Glebe Administration Board also submitted plans for redevelopment, including 'giant office blocks' in Glebe which were rejected by Leichhardt Council.

The Church submitted to the Royal Commission of Inquiry into Poverty in April 1973 that the Glebe estate would be an ideal place for government 'to experiment with the provisions of low-cost housing along planned lines' and Leichhardt Council urged intervention by the federal government.[40] Shortly after the federal Labor government was returned to office it purchased the Glebe estate with the passage of the *Glebe Lands (Appropriation) Act*, 1974.[41] It was a unique venture in Australia—for the scale of the rehabilitation scheme which involved the retention of a tract of Glebe composed largely of low-income families, and because it was the first time a government had acquired property to rehabilitate rather than to redevelop it. The Glebe Project demonstrated that the terraces could be refurbished for considerably less than the cost of a single high-rise unit.[42] Another inner-city working-class community was preserved in Woolloomooloo in 1975 when the Whitlam government again intervened on the side of the tenants. In 1985 the Glebe estate was transferred to the New South Wales Department of Housing.

The federal government acquisition in Glebe ended the threat posed by the expressways, something that was reinforced in 1976 when the National Trust and the Australian Heritage Commission declared Glebe a conservation area.

The council elected in 1971 set out to develop a new planning scheme. The Balmain Association, Glebe Society and Annandale Association believed a revised 'town plan' could effectively control development in the municipality, and each of the three resident action groups prepared its own plan.[43] The Town Planning Committee was established by the CBC, and a Draft Statutory Planning Scheme was developed from the 'Outline Plan' and exhibited before submission to the State Planning Authority (SPA). The plan was unique in that it neglected to include the DMR's north-western and western expressways.[44]

Divisions began to appear within the ranks of the CBC after the election of Origlass over Dougherty as Mayor, Council was criticised over time wasted by lengthy public debate at its meetings and Mayor Origlass was depicted as behaving in an authoritarian way at committee meetings. Within a year of their election, aldermen faced continuing ridicule in the pages of their former ally, the *Glebe Weekly*, which referred to Origlass and his team as 'Revolutionary Marxists'.[45]

At the 1974 elections the CBC candidates presented themselves under the Open Council banner. Their campaign lacked the energy they had generated three years earlier, perhaps affected by unrelenting criticism from the *Glebe Weekly*, and the ALP highlighted incidents of Council mismanagement and alleged squandering of ratepayers' money.[46] Though only 32.3 per cent of the electorate turned out to cast a vote, none of the six Open Council candidates was elected. The ALP won nine of the twelve seats, with the other three going to independents Dougherty and Spedding from Leichhardt Ward and Origlass from Balmain. Les Rodwell became Mayor, and machine boss Danny Casey his deputy.[47] The newly elected Labor council set about dismantling all the remnants of the Open Council experiment, and Council's only two qualified town planners, Pike and Falk, who were instrumental in completion of the Statutory Plan, were dismissed.[48] In November 1974 Council requested the SPA to suspend the Statutory Plan and return it, contending the plan was too restrictive and discouraged new flat development.[49]

The *National Times* gave an impressionistic overview of politics in Leichhardt in the early 1970s:

> Leichhardt . . . was rock-solid working-class Labor territory. The issues that mattered were the traditional industrial ones. You didn't complain about the noise from ship repairs yards and backyard factories because you were talking about the jobs held by the boys, who turned up at Labor Party branch meetings, or at least signed the attendance book when it was hawked around the pubs. Then the professionals, poets and junior executives moved in with their sandstock bricks and quarry tiles. In the municipal elections for 1971 Leichhardt Council was narrowly won by a coalition of greenies, civic reformers and radicals. This crowd scrapped the town plan of the earlier Labor council and began work on their own town plan. They were well-intentioned but sufficiently amateurish to lose the municipal elections of 1974. The old-style Labor machine might be rusting in the cogs but it could for the moment be cranked up enough to take on a few polite reformers.[50]

Dead people voting in municipal elections in Leichhardt was not an infrequent occurrence. (Gary Bennell's cartoon, Max Solling Collection)

Allegations of rigging postal votes in local elections did not disturb Mayor Rodwell, sales manager for a local timber yard, who was quoted as saying 'It's always on in local elections of course. People say "Elizabeth's going to be away. I'll vote for her". Every election it's on. It's common knowledge.'[51] The barrier between the public gallery and the aldermen in the chamber was re-erected, and residents were required to give notice in writing to the Town Clerk if they wished to speak. These speakers were given a few minutes at the end of a meeting. Disagreement from the gallery saw Deputy Mayor Casey climb over the barrier and invite an interjector to 'come outside'.[52]

The 1974 Labor council was pro-development, and in favour of more industry. Construction of cheap flats for working-class people would arrest the loss of good Labor voters who were being forced out. Rodwell declared: 'We must have progressive development. Pull down all the old dilapidated houses in Balmain and replace them with commercial and high rise. I don't want to live in a home unit, but plenty of others do . . . There's not much difference between 200 and 300 people per hectare, to be frank.'[53]

Recall of the Statutory Plan and its replacement by a new Outline Plan, and Council's refusal to permit public comment, angered resident action groups, who had formed the Leichhardt Planning Forum and participated on the Council Planning Committee. They began pamphleteering, alleging massive zoning changes and high-rise development. Council's response to strident public protests was to appoint Bill Sinclair, a businessman with travel agency interests, as a part-time public relations consultant on a salary of $15,000 a year. Rodwell told the press that Sinclair acted 'as a sort of ombudsman'.[54]

The SPA amended the planning scheme Council submitted, reducing population densities and effectively abandoning multi-storey development and reverting to walk-up flats. 'Now no one will want to do anything in Leichhardt,' said an exasperated Les Rodwell. 'The developers will stay well clear of us.'[55]

The bitter factionalism that characterised the Labor branches within Leichhardt Municipality is reflected in this 1982 poster. (Gary Bennell's cartoon, Max Solling Collection)

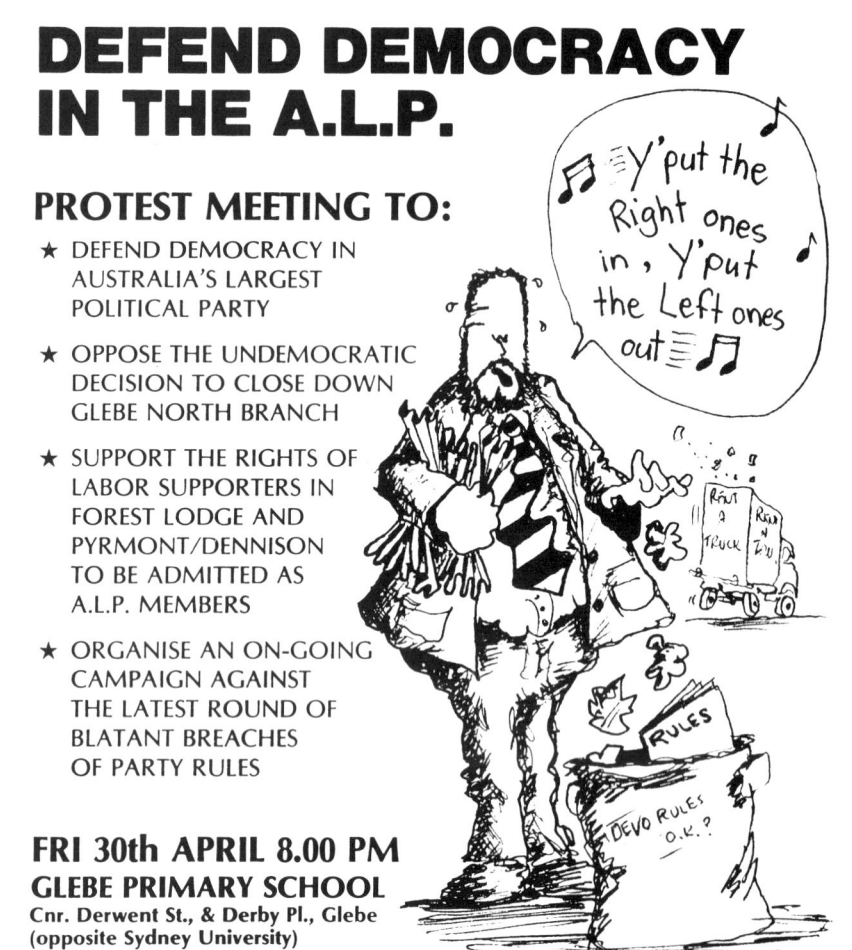

DEFEND DEMOCRACY IN THE A.L.P.

PROTEST MEETING TO:
★ DEFEND DEMOCRACY IN AUSTRALIA'S LARGEST POLITICAL PARTY
★ OPPOSE THE UNDEMOCRATIC DECISION TO CLOSE DOWN GLEBE NORTH BRANCH
★ SUPPORT THE RIGHTS OF LABOR SUPPORTERS IN FOREST LODGE AND PYRMONT/DENNISON TO BE ADMITTED AS A.L.P. MEMBERS
★ ORGANISE AN ON-GOING CAMPAIGN AGAINST THE LATEST ROUND OF BLATANT BREACHES OF PARTY RULES

FRI 30th APRIL 8.00 PM
GLEBE PRIMARY SCHOOL
Cnr. Derwent St., & Derby Pl., Glebe
(opposite Sydney University)

ALL PARTY MEMBERS AND THOSE REFUSED MEMBERSHIP ARE URGED TO ATTEND

Authorised by G. Bennell, 15 Carlisle St., Leichhardt

The new middle class, unable to exercise any influence through Council on the way the municipality developed, began to organise to make a concerted effort to infiltrate local ALP branches. The old guard rejected the applications of newcomers for a variety of reasons—'acted against the interest of the party', 'didn't live in the area' and so on—but such was the strength of the push that the left wing began to acquire a presence in the branches. The volatile nature of branch factionalism was reminiscent of the early years of the 1890s. The preselection for the federal seat of Sydney in 1975 saw Les McMahon, a former Leichhardt alderman, sponsored by Danny Casey, triumph over other contenders.[56]

The ALP municipal machine detailed alleged anti-Labor activities of resident action groups in a report. Attempts were first made in January 1972 for the party to adopt a ruling which would preclude members of 'Progress Associations' from ALP membership, and three years later the Glebe Society 'noted with amazement the attempt made by some ageing members of the local branch of the Labor Party to proscribe Labor Party members from being members of the Glebe Society' and were 'pleased to record that the attempt was unsuccessful'.[57]

The state executive of the ALP ignored the request to investigate local branches, especially Annandale, the most troublesome. A brawl broke out in Balmain in December 1976 as new recruits queued to take out membership tickets. Police were called and four left-wing supporters who had been hospitalised were threatened with expulsion because they had spoken to the press.[58] Efforts of the old guard to counteract the growing middle-class presence in the branches was not confined to Balmain. A Leichhardt long-time independent, Bill Dougherty, replaced the left-wing candidate when the state executive overturned the ballot.[59]

Loyalty and discipline were conditions of membership of local branches, and patronage and favours were the rewards. If you paid your dues you got promoted, and to succeed in the municipal arena it was an advantage to be Catholic. Most of the district's state and federal Labor parliamentarians since 1917 have been Catholic.[60]

The traditional branch member who played the game, after winning preselection for council elections, became an influential local figure and a street, lane or park might be dignified by his name. Under the machine, policy was formulated haphazardly, and it did not occur to its representatives on Council that the implications of high-rise development, expressway proposals or commercial industry needed to be examined in a more extensive and different way.[61]

The internal factionalism that emerged within the ALP overshadowed the municipal election in September 1977 where resident action groups failed to sponsor a municipality-wide team of independents. Balmain had become the focus for branch stacking and preselection credentialling between 1973 and 1980, when its membership swelled from about 70 to 700.[62] In August 1977 Danny Casey rolled up with 65 new recruits to join the Balmain branch; Peter Crawford and Peter Baldwin responded with 110 new applicants a month later.[63] Some 300 people attended the Balmain meeting in October 1977 to take out their tickets and so be eligible to vote at the AGM. Before the minutes were read, a fire extinguisher was thrown through the window and Balmain Town Hall was plunged into darkness. When the lights came on again, the Balmain branch books had disappeared.[64] New applicants were, however, issued with membership tickets, and by February 1978, forces marshalled by Baldwin and Crawford had control of Balmain.

The 1979 Planning Scheme largely duplicated the 1976 plan, promoting widespread development through the retention of high population densities. Developers rubbed their hands in glee. Public release of the 1979 plan not only created animosity between Council and the resident groups but also produced factionalism among Labor aldermen—Charlie Rocks, Anthony Kelly and Evan Jones came to form a progressive/left-wing breakaway group from the larger right-wing faction of Danny Casey, Les Rodwell, Ivor Cawley, George Millard, Bill Dougherty, Ernie Baldwin and Bob Heffernan. Rocks and Kelly came from the volatile Annandale branch, and Jones from Leichhardt.[65]

As preselection ballots loomed for the 1980 council elections, the machine feared it might lose control of caucus if Annandale, Balmain and Leichhardt returned left-wing candidates. As in-fighting intensified, the old guard accused Rocks, Kelly and Jones of breaking caucus (by objecting to a project in Annandale), and demanded their expulsion.[66] The left wing responded by filing counter-charges with the state executive against machine boss and Deputy Mayor, Danny Casey, claiming he had brought the party into disrepute through his association with

SMEAR TACTICS?
CASEY ATTACK FROM ALP LEFTISTS!

DAN CASEY ... "He's being crucified!"

Leichhardt's deputy mayor Dan Casey is in trouble "because he's too good-hearted."

"He's being crucified because of his good nature."

That's the view of Vic Sliteris, secretary of Casey's Rozelle East ALP branch

The *Glebe Weekly*, 26 September 1979

convicted criminals named in the Woodward Royal Commission into Drug Trafficking in New South Wales.[67]

The Royal Commission found that Casey's business, Balmain Welding Co., employed people with long criminal records but that there was no hard evidence linking Casey to drug trafficking. The state member for Balmain, Roger Degen, was also cleared.[68] During this time Casey was granted extended leave from Council, and with Casey absent, the old practice of block voting at caucus and council meetings gave way to debate. The sudden departure of Dougherty to Queensland further undermined caucus solidarity. Amid internal instability, ALP aldermen agreed to the appointment of an independent commissioner to investigate residents' complaints against the 1979 planning scheme.[69]

Peter Baldwin, an editor of *Challenge*, found gross irregularities in the membership records of Casey's Rozelle East branch and the Lilyfield branch of Mayor Rodwell. Before action was taken by the state executive on the findings, Baldwin was viciously beaten at his Marrickville home on 17 July 1980, and was hospitalised with a broken jaw and severe lacerations and bruises to the head.[70] The state executive, now unable to turn a blind eye to allegations of corruption and criminal activities, withdrew the charter of the Rozelle East and Lilyfield branches, and Casey resigned from the party.[71]

The September 1980 election became an emotionally charged affair, with newly endorsed left-wing Labor candidates running an anti-Casey campaign and focusing on the improper conduct of the old controllers of the machine. Candidates with a left-wing perspective won in Annandale (Hume, Greenland), Leichhardt (Jones, Roxborough), Rozelle (Floyd, Stevens) and Balmain (Crawford, O'Neill) and former rebel aldermen Evan Jones, a foreman estimator with the Public Works Department, was elected Mayor. The ruling clique had lost control, and only Glebe and Lilyfield remained loyal to surviving remnants of the old guard (Cawley, Millard, Rodwell and E. Baldwin).[72]

The apparatus of local government in Leichhardt, controlled by the ALP machine from 1974 to 1980, pursued policies in the allocation of resources and services that shaped public perception of how the municipality was run. Middle-class residents, excluded from the formal decision-making process, were forced to collectively organise and adopt non-conventional methods of protest to exert influence over an unsympathetic Labor-dominated council.[73]

The composition and policies of the 1980–84 council differed radically from those in control in 1974. The convictions of the 'new left' came to be translated into more open and public participation in municipal politics, upgrading of the local environment and responsible town planning. They again removed the barrier between the public gallery and council chamber. Eight of the twelve aldermen were white-collar and tertiary-educated.[74] Goals within Labor branches were being redefined, with priorities that were not dissimilar from those of the new middle class. An independent commissioner, Jim Coleman, who reported on a range of planning issues in 1981, condemned the 1979 plan, especially the residential densities, and recommended that the 1979 exhibited planning scheme be replaced with a more sensitive and socially responsive set of plans and policies.[75]

Following a 1980 report by local government inspectors that revealed gross mismanagement and machine corruption on Council, the internal management and personnel on Council were reorganised through the gradual introduction of a 'Corporate Planning Strategy'. Many changes were made and some machine stalwarts on Council either retired or resigned.[76]

A vigorous campaign was mounted in 1982 against a proposal by the DMR to construct a six-lane bridge and viaduct structure across the harbour, or a tunnel beneath it, linking the Gore Hill expressway to a proposed arterial route near Victoria Road, Rozelle. Leichhardt Council and the Combined Bridge Action Group, which were at the forefront of this campaign, rejoiced in December 1982 when the Minister for Roads announced the second crossing was not proceeding.[77]

The composition of Leichhardt Council changed at the April 1984 elections. The ALP lost Balmain to Open Councillors Origlass and Wyner, and Leichhardt to an independent and a Liberal. Glebe, Rozelle and Lilyfield, however, returned right-wing candidates, and Annandale elected Bill Brady, who was Mayor from 1984 to 1987. The retired vaudevillian, who had travelled the club circuit, had nothing but derision for the master creation of Origlass, Open Council. He complained of endless meetings, work inspections and reports but no decisions.[78] 'Meetings have just become a rabble,' said Brady. 'It's gotten to be a person who shouts the loudest that thinks he will win. We have kids crawling under our feet and people literally breathing down our necks asking how we are going to vote.'[79] Brady returned to the old secretive method of decision-making within the confines of the caucus room, rejecting the Open Council system.

Two rival ALP factions lined up against each other in September 1987, the 'Brady Bunch' gaining three representatives on Council (Brady, Page and Thompson) and the members' team two (Butler, Heffernan). A collection of two Open Councillors (Origlass, Wyner), two Community Independents (Hand, Leone), two from the Spedding group (Spedding, Smith) and a Liberal (Courtney) determined who wore the mayoral robes. Origlass, Spedding and Wyner were mayors between 1987 and 1990, and Bill Brady assumed the office in 1990 after a draw from a hat when the ballot with Larry Hand was tied at six each.[80] Resident activists did not warm to Mayor Brady's abrasive style: they labelled him a Stalinist because of his former presidency of the Australia–East Germany Friendship Society.[81]

Larry Hand, a former schoolteacher who was first elected to Council in 1984 as a Labor ward alderman for Annandale, was expelled from the ALP in 1987. Hand joined a leftish group that was dissatisfied with the performance of Council and formed the Community Independents. They took on Labor and survived, enjoying more electoral success than CBC candidates. The policy of the Community Independents embraced Open Council, social justice, support for the environment and better planning. During his years as Mayor from 1991 to 1995, Hand had a clear social agenda to improve the quality of life in the municipality. The acquisition of open

Rats in the Ranks. (Film Australia National Interest Program, Photography by Anthony Browell)

space for parkland, the reconstruction of the Dawn Fraser Baths and the Leichhardt Aquatic Centre were council initiatives during his mayoralty.[82] His critics argue that this period, when council reserves were drained, was not tempered by good financial management.[83] Hand also took a prominent role in Council's opposition to the third runway at Sydney Airport, sending council garbage trucks to block the airport to protest against aircraft noise.

No less than 62 candidates stood for the twelve seats at the 1991 elections. Groupings that called themselves True Blue, Liberal, Balmain Development Trust and Open Council each had a single representative elected to Council together with ungrouped boatbuilder Nick Masterman.[84] There were also four members of the 'Official Labor' team—librarian Kate Butler, president of the Labor Women's Committee from 1979 to 1986; Neil Macindoe, TAFE teacher and past-president of the Glebe Society; former mayor Evan Jones; and legal analyst/writer Trevor Snape. The Community Independents increased their number on Council to three—Hand, librarian Sue Stock and Rozelle activist Kath Hacking.[85]

An equally diverse group gained seats on Council at the September 1995 elections. For the first time Liberals won three seats—architect Harry Sidaway, first elected in 1991; administrator Christine Bourne; and Marcus Hewitt. Labor won three—Macindoe; electorate officer Kristine Cruden; and Evan Jones. There were three Community Independents—Hand, Stock and former Labor councillor Kate Butler; two No Aircraft Noise (NAN)—Maire Sheehan and Arthur Drew; and a True Blue, Bob Heffernan. An arrangement between the Liberals, NAN and True Blue, saw Irish-born TAFE teacher Maire Sheehan elected Mayor in 1995, the first female to occupy the mayoral chair since Annie Cashman in 1968.[86]

Leichhardt Council won recognition for its local government policies but decisions made beyond the municipality continued to impact adversely on the environment. The major issue challenging the community, wrote Mayor Sheehan:

> is damage to the environment and reduction in quality of life as a result of changed operations at Sydney Airport. Our residents have shown gritty spirit and determination and have been at the

forefront of the airport campaign to find an equitable solution. This campaign will continue on several fronts until a livable solution is reached.[87]

In 1996, for the first time, Leichhardt Council elected both a female Mayor, Kristine Cruden, and Deputy Mayor, Sue Stock.

Cameras were allowed into a variety of venues in 1994 to film shifting coalitions of Leichhardt councillors leading up to the mayoral election. The delightfully frank documentary *Rats in the Ranks* follows the manoeuvring and manipulation of contenders. Two ALP councillors do the unforgivable—they 'rat' on a colleague in the contest. The cast are the councillors themselves.[88]

Leichhardt councillors elected at the municipal election in September 1995. *Rear (left to right)*: Marcus Hewitt, Arthur Drew, Maire Sheehan, Kristine Cruden, Larry Hand, Sue Stock, Christine Bourne. *Front (left to right)*: Bob Heffernan, Neil Macindoe, Kate Butler, Evan Jones, Harry Sidaway. (Photograph by David Liddle)

Appendix A

Census figures

Population and habitation 1846–1901

	1846	1851	1861	1871	1881	1891	1901
Annandale (1894) (330 acres)							
Persons per acre (density)						13.82	23.19
Population						–	8,349
Residences						–	1,729
Balmain (1860) (938 acres)							
Persons per acre (density)	–	–	–	–	–	25.19	32.27
Population	1,337	1,397	3,482	6,272	15,063	23,475	30,077
Residences	296	–	737	1,391	3,430	5,138	6,028
Glebe (1859) (529 acres)							
Persons per acre (density)	–	–	–	–	–	32.77	36.87
Population	1,055	1,575	3,712	5,721	10,500	17,075	19,220
Residences	264	–	720	1,156	2,231	3,449	3,737
Leichhardt (1871) (1,300 acres 1872–1894) (1,120 acres 1894–1948)							
Persons per acre (density)	–	–	–	–	–	10.33	14.92
Population	–	–	–	–	1,866	17,067	17,454
Residences	–	–	–	–	–	3,605	3,393

Source: V&P NSWLC 1846, 1851.
V&P NSWLA 1862, 1872/3, 1883/4.
Report of eleventh census of NSW (1894).
Journal of NSWLC 1902.

APPENDIX A: CENSUS FIGURES

Population and habitation 1911–1947

	1911	1921	1933	1947
Annandale (1894) (330 acres) Persons per acre (density)				
Population	11,240	12,648	12,205	12,396
Residences	2,363	2,825	2,913	3,265
Balmain (1860) (938 acres)				
Population	32,038	32,104	28,272	28,398
Residences	6,464	6,866	6,524	7,335
Glebe (1859) (529 acres) Persons per acre (density)				
Population	21,943	22,754	19,874	20,510
Residences	4,202	4,337	4,456	5,848
Leichhardt (1871) (1,120 acres 1894–1948) Persons per acre (density)				
Population	24,254	29,356	30,209	29,462
Residences	4,909	6,047	6,647	6,928

Sydney at the Census 1911–1976, p 267.

Population and Habitation 1954–1976

Municipality of Leichhardt (as amalgamated in 1948)

	1954	1961	1966	1971	1976
Leichhardt (1948) (2,917? acres 1948)					
Population	64,919	61,951	59,325	71,338	62,540
Residences	17,593	17,672	17,773	24,334	24,085

Sydney at the Census 1911–1976, p 267.

Total population of Leichhardt Municipality 1947–1991

No	Year	Total population
1	1947	90,766
2	1954	64,919
3	1961	61,951
4	1966	59,325
5	1971	71,338
6	1976	62,550
7	1981	57,332
8	1986	56,303
9	1991	58,472

Leichhardt Profile, p 2.

(The years 1954, 1961 & 1966 do not include Glebe, then under the control of the City Council.)

Population changes by postcode area 1971–1986

Postcode area	1971	1976	1981	1986
Annandale	9,504	8,639	7,869	7,904
Balmain	14,982	12,791	12,051	11,966
Glebe	14,263	12,652	11,397	11,483
Leichhardt	24,784	22,115	20,368	18,473
Rozelle	7,544	6,257	5,554	6,384

Leichhardt Profile, p 3.

Comparison of densities in postcode areas in 1986

Postcode area	Population	Geographical area sq km	Population density per km^2
Annandale	7,904	1.00	7,904
Balmain	11,966	2.00	5,983
Glebe	11,483	2.00	5,741
Leichhardt	18,473	4.00	4,618
Rozelle	6,384	2.00	3,192

Leichhardt Profile, p 9.

Appendix B

Local elected representatives

Annandale 1894–1948

Mayors

John Young 1894–96.
Allen Taylor 1897–99, 1900–2.
William Wells 1900, 1902–3, 1907–9.
Owen Ridge 1904–6.
James Robertson 1910–12.
Thomas Colebrook 1913–14.
Edward Hogan 1915–17, 1923, 1931, 1932, 1938, 1942.
Frederick Smith 1918.
Arthur Packer 1919, 1920, 1921.
Charles Schofield 1922.
Walter Ridge 1924, 1925.
John Sharpe 1926, 1927, 1928, 1929, 1930.
Charles Winkworth 1933.
Matthew Smith 1933, 1934, 1935.
George Marshall 1936.
William Johnston 1937.
Sydney Francis 1939.
John Field 1940.
Percival McDonald 1941.
William Boyd 1941.
George Law 1943, 1944.
James Prendergast 1945, 1946, 1947, 1948.

Balmain 1860–1948

Chairmen 1860–1866

Ralph Mansfield 1860, 1865, 1866.
George Elliott 1861.
Nicol Stenhouse 1862.
Walter Church 1863, 1866.
Thomas Rowntree 1864.
Owen Evans 1864.

Mayors 1867–1948

John Booth 1867.
Henry Perdriau 1868, 1872, 1875.
Frederick Robinson 1869.
Josiah Mullens 1870.
Thomas Rowntree 1871.
George Elliott 1872.
Charles Mossman 1873.
Frederick Trouton 1873.
John Taylor 1874, 1877.
Solomon Hyam 1876.
James McDonald 1878, 1879.
Albert Elkington 1880.
William Hutchinson 1881, 1882.
James Cameron 1883, 1884.
Jacob Garrard 1885.
James Punch 1886.
William Burns 1887.
Edward Buchanan 1888, 1889.
George Clubb 1890, 1912, 1913.
James Brodie 1891.
James Wheeler 1892, 1893.
Henry Swan 1893, 1894, 1914, 1915.
Alexander Milne 1895, 1896, 1901.
George Murdoch 1897, 1898.
Henry Mills 1899, 1900.
Henry Cox 1902.
Alfred Crump 1903, 1904, 1910.
Matthew Cohen 1905, 1906, 1907, 1911.
William Laws 1908.
Thomas Minty 1909.
Henry Scott 1916, 1917.
Donald McKenzie 1918, 1919.
Reginald Thornton 1920, 1921, 1926, 1927, 1928.
William Wainwright 1922.
Bertie Wheeler 1923.
George Mullins 1924.
Thomas Harrington 1925.
Lyle Swan 1929, 1930, 1931.
Gilbert Storey 1933, 1934.
Cecil Stapleton 1935.
John Waite 1936, 1940.
Michael Cashman 1937, 1941.
Robert Brownlee 1938, 1942, 1943.
Herman Angelini 1939.
George Harris 1944.
Edward Erwin 1945.
Gilbert Lockhart 1946.
Charles Laggan 1947.
Richard O'Connor 1948.

Glebe 1859–1948

Chairman 1859–66

George Wigram Allen 1859–66.

Mayors 1867–1948

George Wigram Allen 1867–77.
John Seamer 1878.
William Cary 1879, 1896–97.
Thomas Dunn 1880, 1885–88.
Charles Field 1881.
Michael Chapman 1882–84.
Percy Lucas 1889, 1891, 1893, 1898–1900, 1906–8, 1925.
George Burcher 1890.
William Yeates 1892.
William Hutchinson 1894–95.
Henry MacNamara 1901.
Thomas Nosworthy 1902–3.
George Williamson 1904–5.
Stanley Cole 1909–10, 1915, 1920–22.
Ralph Stone 1916–17.
Henry Punter 1918, 1924.
Finlay Munro 1919.
William Tate 1923.
William Walsh 1926–29.
Francis Dick 1930.
Albert Ward 1931.
James Diver 1932.
Robert Gorman 1933.
Matthew Fitzpatrick 1934.
James Lahiff 1935.
Stephen McCormack 1936, 1939.
Horace Foley 1937, 1938.
Harold Splatt 1941–42.
Colin Colbourne 1943.
William Beasley 1944.
Colin Elphick 1945.
Albert Lawson 1946.
Cornelius O'Neill 1947.
Michael Ward 1948.

Leichhardt 1872–1948

(Including Annandale to 1894)

Mayors

Frank Beames 1872–74.
John Wetherill 1874–76.
Frederick Parsons 1876–78.
John Fraser 1878–79, 1880–81.
John Young 1879–80, 1884–86.
James Williams 1881–82.
William Pritchard 1882–84.
Thomas Madge 1883–84.
Samuel Davison 1886–87.
Benjamin Moore 1887–88, 1889–90, 1891–92, 1892–95.
Sydney Smith 1888–89.
Nathaniel Neal 1890–91, 1903–4, 1906–7.
William Wragge 1892–93, 1899–1900.
Robert Cropley 1893–94, 1895–98.
Alfred Hearn 1898–99.
James Treadgold 1900–3, 1909–10, 1913–14.
James Lonsdale 1904–5, 1908–9, 1910–11.
William Ainsworth 1905–6.
William Pearson 1907–9.
Thomas Hastings 1911–12, 1914–17.
Robert Connolly 1912–13.
Alfred Blackmore 1917–20.
William Lambert 1920–23, 1925.
Harry Breen 1924.
William Atkins 1926, 1931.
Andrew Campbell 1927–30, 1932, 1934, 1935, 1936.
William Stuart 1933, 1938, 1940–41, 1947.
William Bowmaker 1936–37.
William Dyer 1939.
Alexander O'Hare 1942–43.
Joseph Winchester 1944.
Thomas Reeves 1945, 1946.
Daniel Beck 1947, 1948.

Leichhardt 1949–

Mayors

Leo Newton 1949.
Edward Erwin 1950, 1951, 1952.
Charles Laggan 1953.
Administrator 1953–56.
John Deehan 1957, 1958, 1959, 1960, 1961, 1962.
Anne Cashman 1963, 1964, 1965, 1966, 1967, 1968.
Les Rodwell 1969, 1970, 1971, 1974, 1975, 1976, 1977, 1978, 1979.
Nicholas Origlass 1971–72, 1972–73, 1987–88.
William Dougherty 1973–74.
Evan Jones 1980–81, 1982, 1983, 1984.
John William Brady 1984, 1985, 1986, 1987, 1990–91.
Douglas Spedding 1988–89.
Isadore Wyner 1989–90.
Larry Hand 1991, 1992, 1993, 1994, 1995.
Maire Sheehan 1995–96.
Kristine Cruden 1996– .

Aldermen

(Alphabetically sorted)

Annandale 1894–1948

Abrams, Sydney 1903–05.
Blackhall, Horace 1945–48.
Boyd, William 1932–41.
Broad, Joseph 1895–1906.
Bull, William Junior 1897–1901.
Campbell, Alexander 1941–48.
Carbines, Robert 1926–28.
Carpenter, Albert 1926–28.
Chapman, Thomas 1908–22.
Clark, John 1912–19.
Cohen, Isaiah 1897–1904.
Colebrook, Thomas 1903–19, 1923–28.
Cox, William 1941–44.
Coyle, Thomas 1903–05, 1908–16.

Cummings, James 1908–22.
Cummings, John 1937–48.
Curtis, Richard 1898–1900.
Douglas, Thomas 1932–48.
Dwyer, Charles 1894–97.
Ferris, William 1894–1902.
Field, John 1934–41.
Francis, Sydney 1924–41.
Francis, William 1894–97.
Fraser, George 1908–12.
Fuller, Ernest 1926–31.
Guthrey, Albert 1894–97.
Hannan, John 1945–48.
Hartenstein, Theodore 1897.
Henley, William 1920–25.
Hogan, Edward 1906–44.
Horton, Alfred 1894–96.
Howe, Patrick 1926–37.
Howe, Stanislaus 1941–44.
Johnston, William 1924–41.
Landers, George 1907.
Law, George 1937–48.
Marshall, George 1926–48.
Martin, Thomas 1912–19.
Maxwell, John 1894–96, 1901.
McDonald, Percival 1932–40.
McDougall, Robert 1894.
McLaughlin, Henry 1932–40.
McLean, Archibald 1903–05.
McNamara, Michael 1933–1937.
Mitchell, Alfred 1906–07.

New, Ernest 1901–02.
Nicholson, Alfred 1942–44.
O'Brien, William 1902.
O'Donnell, John 1926–28.
Odgers, Reginald 1945–48.
Packer, Arthur 1908–24.
Prendergast, James 1941–48.
Pritchard, William 1894.
Ridge, Owen 1894–1912.
Ridge, Walter 1920–25.
Roberts, Wytham 1917–31.
Robertson, James 1901–25.
Rose, Herbert 1942.
Schofield, Charles 1906–25.
Service, James 1917–25, 1927–36.
Sharpe, John 1923–31.
Sinclair, Andrew 1920–24.
Smith, Frederick 1903–16.
Smith, George 1895–1907.
Smith, Matthew 1929–41.
Spies, Reginald 1941–48.
Starling, John 1902–07.
Taylor, Allan 1895–1906.
Tooker, Percy 1926–36.
Wells, William 1894–99, 1901–10.
Winkworth, Charles 1917–33.
Woods, William 1898–1901.
Yardley, Harry 1945–48.
Young, Francis 1894.
Young, John 1894–99.

Balmain 1860–1948

Abrahams, Barry 1932–34.
Adams, John 1893–94.
Angelini, Herman 1934–41.
Austin, William 1894–95.
Ballerum, Arthur 1920–22, 1926–28.
Barnes, John 1874.
Beattie, James 1860–66.
Beavis, Walter 1917–23.
Bogle, Alfred Henry 1922.
Booth, John 1862–63, 1865–69.
Bowen, Edward 1898–1910.
Briggs, Samuel 1885–87.
Broderick, Henry 1864–66.
Brodie, James 1889–94.
Broomfield, John 1874–75.
Brownlee, Robert 1923–25, 1929–48.
Buchanan, Edward 1885–89.
Burns, Samuel 1924–39.
Burns, William 1885–88.
Burt, James 1860.
Burt, William 1890–92, 1894–97.
Cameron, Ewen 1860–63.
Cameron, John 1881–86.
Campbell, Robert 1895–1916.

Carruthers, Charles 1887–89.
Cashman, Michael 1932–44.
Chidgey, George 1890–92.
Church, Walter 1862–65.
Clubb, George 1881–96, 1911–22.
Clubb, John 1889–1896.
Clymer, Charles 1887–89.
Cohen, John 1861–62.
Cohen, Matthew 1897–1919.
Copestake, Henry 1911.
Cox, Harry 1896–1910, 1917–19.
Crump, Alfred 1897–1910.
Davidson, William 1872–74.
Dingwall, George 1911–19.
Easton, David 1886–93.
Elkington, Albert 1876–82, 1888–90.
Elliott, George 1860–72.
Erwin, Edward 1941–48.
Etheridge, George 1872–1874.
Evans, Owen 1860–65.
Foy, William 1870–73.
Franki, James 1883–84.
Gallen, John 1919–28.
Gallimore, Elizabeth 1943–48.
Garrard, Jacob 1879–86.
Geddes John 1923–25.

Gould, Francis 1932–34.
Gow, Alexander 1876–79.
Gray, Robert 1864–66.
Hancock, Alfred 1872–79.
Harpur, Frederick 1876–78.
Harrington, Thomas 1923–28.
Harris, George 1941–48.
Harwood, Joseph 1908–9.
Hunter, Samuel 1932–37.
Hutchinson, William 1878–83.
Hyam, Solomon 1874–78.
Jesson, Thomas 1903–22.
Joseph, William 1944–48.
Jung, Leopold 1874–76.
Kenniff, Roger, 1882–86.
Laggan, Charles, 1941–48.
Laver, Grace 1944–48.
Laws, William 1902–1904.
Lockhart, Gilbert, 1941–48.
Looke, William 1872–86.
Maher, Albert Richard 1937–44.
Mansfield, Ralph 1860–67.
Marshall, William 1866–79.
McBeath, Peter 1867–68.
McClemens, John 1861–62.
McDonald, James 1872–95.
McGuire, Andrew 1887.
McIntosh, Francis 1926–34.
McKenzie, Donald 1914–19.
McMahon, John 1942–44.
McMahon, Michael 1937–42.
Middleton, William 1937–41.
Milham, George 1890–92.
Mills, Henry 1895–1913.
Milne, Alexander 1893–1911.
Milne, James 1885–87.
Minty, Thomas 1906–9.
Morgan, James 1920–22.
Mossman, Charles 1868–74.
Mullens, Josiah 1868–70.
Mullins, George 1923–25.
Murdoch, Gilbert 1895–1905.
O'Connor, Richard 1944–48.
O'Connor, William 1944–48.
Palmer, James 1860–63.
Perdriau, Henry 1865–76.
Peters, George 1909–19.
Punch, John 1878–93.

Ramsay, Edward 1864–65.
Reynolds, Andrew 1860–63.
Robinson, Frederick 1866–72.
Robinson, Robert 1924–38.
Rogers, David 1903–5.
Ronald, Rowan 1863–65.
Ross, William 1934–37.
Rowntree, Thomas 1860–64, 1870–72.
Schultz, William 1875–78.
Scott, Henry 1911–31.
Shiel, John 1923–31.
Smith, William 1879–81.
Springthorpe, John 1870–71.
Stapleton, Cecil 1932–37, 1941–43.
Stenhouse, Nicol 1861–63.
Stewart, George 1881–82.
Stock, Edward 1938–1941.
Stopford, Robert 1919.
Storey, Gilbert 1932–34.
Swan, Henry 1889–1908, 1911–22, 1926.
Swan, Lyle 1926–34.
Tancred, Patrick 1922–24.
Tatham, Herbert 1934–44.
Tayler, Christopher 1898–1901.
Taylor, Albert 1941–44.
Taylor, John 1872–80.
Thompson, William 1929–31.
Thornton, Reginald 1911–41.
Tidswell, Henry 1878.
Trainor, James 1934–41.
Trouton, Frederick 1872–75.
Vale, Frederick 1868–69.
Wainwright, William 1917–22.
Waite, John 1923–25, 1929–31, 1934–48.
Ward, Roger 1932–34.
Ward, William 1890–97.
Watson, John 1876–78.
Waugh, William 1920–22.
Wellfare, Edward 1944–48.
West, Harry 1937–41.
Wheeler, Bertie 1920–31.
Wheeler, James 1888–1902.
Williams, William 1897–1901.
Wise, John 1891–92.
Woolnough, Horace 1866–67.
Yeend, James 1870–72.
Young, George 1902, 1906–10.
Young, L.T. 1874–76.

Glebe 1859–1948

Abrams, Lewis 1893–98.
Alexander, John 1923–25.
Allen, George Wigram 1859–77.
Alleyn, William 1929–31.
Artlett, Frederick 1908–18.
Banks, Frederick 1897–1905.
Beasley, William 1941–48.

Blacket, Edmund 1859–70.
Brigg, Henry 1906–13, 1918–25.
Brown, George 1860–71.
Brown, Maurice 1902–13.
Bull, William 1876–84.
Burcher, George 1889–93.
Burton, Herbert 1942–44.
Burton, William 1889–93.
Caldwell, Alexander 1941–48.

Carlton, William 1929–35.
Cary, William 1878–82, 1892–1905.
Chapman, Henry 1886–90, 1905–10.
Chapman, Mervyn 1941–42.
Chapman, Michael 1866–74, 1878–92.
Chesterton, Percival 1942–44.
Clark, William 1872–75.
Colbourne, Colin 1941–48.
Cole, Stanley 1902–25.
Conlon, Michael 1884–94.
Davenport, Joseph 1871–74.
Davidson, Archibald 1917–23.
Dibbs, George 1871.
Dick, Francis 1925–35.
Diver, James 1925–28, 1930–39.
Doherty, Bernard 1934–37.
Duncan, Samuel 1886–94.
Dunn, Mary 1932–37.
Dunn, Thomas 1876–1907.
Dwyer, Cecil 1925–31.
Earl, Lancelot 1906–10.
Earnshaw, Ono 1859.
Ellis, James 1874–76.
Elphick, Colin 1944–48.
Elphinstone, David 1881–86.
Elphinstone, William 1861–64.
Emblem, Clarence 1925–39.
Field, Arthur 1911–27.
Field, Charles 1879–84.
Fitzpatrick, Matthew 1929–39.
Foley, Horace 1934–39.
Gill, Leo 1929–30.
Gillard, James 1865–67.
Gorman, Robert 1925–34.
Graham, James 1875–85.
Graham, Malcolm 1877.
Halliday, William 1929–31.
Harding, Charles 1920–27.
Harwood, Thomas 1861–65, 1867–69.
Hewitt, Robert 1941.
Hollingworth, Albert 1937–39.
Holt, James 1927–28, 1937–39.
Horne, Edward 1893–95.
Horne, John 1935–37.
Hosking, John 1914–23.
Howe, Joseph 1894–96.
Hutchinson, William 1893–97.
Jarrett, William 1860, 1872–75.
Jurd, Athol 1946–48.
Korff, John 1859–1865.
Lahiff, James 1927–39.
Law, Thomas 1889–1915.
Lawson, Albert 1942–48.
Lewis, Bert 1920–25.
Locke, John 1911–22.
Lucas, Percy 1880–1925.
MacNamara, Henry 1895–1901.
MacQueen, Norman 1923–25.
Mansfield, George 1866–77.
Martin, William 1923–25.

McCormack, Stephen 1932–39.
McDowell, Alick 1932–37.
McElhone, John 1925–28.
McEnnally, Robert 1915–17.
McNeill, Archibald 1894–98.
Meeks, John 1891–92.
Miller, Francis 1923–27.
Mitchell, David 1884–86.
Mitchell, William 1905–10.
Munro, Finlay 1917–20.
Munro, William 1865–72.
Murphy, John 1887–89.
Nosworthy, Thomas 1899–1907.
O'Leary, James 1941–44.
O'Leary, Patrick 1941–48.
O'Neill, Cornelius 1941–48.
Parton, William 1927–28.
Passau, Frederick 1874–76.
Pedersen, Ernest 1941–48.
Pinhey, William 1872–75.
Pitt, May 1941–45.
Punter, Henry 1914–25.
Redman, William 1875–77.
Reilly, John 1859–60, 1870–75.
Richardson, George 1914–20.
Robey, William 1897–1916.
Rock, Harry 1913, 1925–28.
Rohan, Hugh 1937–39.
Scott, Stephen 1905–07.
Seamer, John 1871–78, 1885–93.
Shannon, John 1932–39.
Simpson, James 1859–74.
Smith, Thomas Tipple 1859–60.
Splatt, Harold 1941–48.
Stanley, George 1944–48.
Stimson, Joseph 1895, 1907–19.
Stone, Benjamin 1920–23.
Stone, Ralph 1911–22.
Tate, George 1878.
Tate, William 1899–1904, 1908–13, 1920–25.
Thornley, Ambrose Junior 1887.
Thornley, Ambrose Senior 1859–64, 1868–83.
Tiley, John 1937–39.
Turner, Henry 1876–87.
Tye, Alfred 1876–78.
Vaughan, Henry 1883–85.
Walker, Joseph 1879–81.
Walsh, William 1925–31.
Walton, John 1859–60.
Ward, Albert 1925–39.
Ward, Michael 1942–48.
Wearne, Thomas 1879–88.
Wells, George 1879–83.
West, William 1896–1904.
Wilkinson, Frederick 1896–1901.
Williams, George 1871–77.
Williams, Phillip 1875.
Williamson, George 1898–1904.
Wood, John 1894–95.
Yeates, William 1877–79, 1887–94.

Leichhardt 1872–1948

(Including Annandale to 1894)

Ainsworth, William 1894–95, 1899–1907.
Anderson, David 1894–97.
Andrews, Leslie 1932–37.
Arguimbau, N. George 1879–85.
Atkins, William 1914–16, 1920–37.
Barrell, Albert 1872.
Bastard, William 1908–1910.
Beames, Frank 1872–74.
Beaumont, John 1914–17.
Beck, Daniel 1937–41, 1944–48.
Benton, George 1941–44.
Blackmore, Alfred 1912–1937.
Blackwell, William 1914–17, 1920–22.
Board, Arthur 1914–19.
Borley, William 1908–13.
Bowmaker, William 1917–41.
Breen, Harry 1917–28.
Brierley, Albert 1908.
Budd, William 1920–23.
Burrows, Henry 1874–75.
Campbell, Andrew 1919–41.
Campbell, John 1886–87.
Campbell, John 1920–37.
Carrington, Arthur 1904–7.
Chase, Henry 1879.
Colbourne, William 1941–44.
Colebrook, Thomas 1891–1901.
Collins, Ernest 1929–31.
Connolly, Robert 1906–7.
Conway, Patrick 1944–53.
Cook, Henry 1887–90.
Copley, Robert 1889–1903.
Cunningham, Robert 1896–97.
Davison, Samuel 1885–91.
De Boos, Vernon 1917–19.
Degen, Frank 1941–44.
Dyer, George 1897–1902.
Dyer, William 1925–41.
Evans, Frank 1929–31.
Evans, John 1883–85.
Falls, Francis 1895.
Ferris, William 1892–93.
Fisher, John 1929–31.
Fisher, William 1944–48.
Fletcher, Thomas 1898–1907.
Fraser, Angus 1903–7.
Fraser, John 1876–81.
Gibbs, Archibald 1904–7.
Gibson, Lincoln 1908–13, 1917–19.
Gow, Charles 1935–41, 1944–48.
Hannan, Thomas 1914–17.
Harler, John 1914–17.
Harris, Charles 1929–41.
Hastings, Thomas 1911–16.
Hearn, Alfred 1890–93, 1896–1907, 1911–13.
Hearn, Charles 1875–89.

Hogg, Thomas 1886.
Hollis, Percy 1944–48.
Horton, Arthur 1911–13.
Hudson, Roy 1932–41.
Hyde, Henry 1889–92.
Johnson, William 1920–28.
Keep, John 1874.
Kilpatrick, William 1914–17.
Knopp, Otto 1944.
Lambert, William 1912–35.
Langdale, John 1937–41.
Langshaw, William 1908–10.
Leece, Lionel 1941–44.
Linney, Charles 1872, 1879–81.
Little, Andrew 1889–92.
Lock, Richard 1917–19.
Lonsdale, James 1892–96, 1902–13, 1917–19.
Madge, Thomas 1881–83.
Marshall, Cornelius 1892–95.
McCredie, William 1886–89.
McDonald, Frank 1922–28.
McDonald, William 1873–78.
McLean, John 1917–19.
Meller, Monteith 1911–12.
Moore, Benjamin 1885–99.
Moore, Leslie 1944–48.
Mound, George 1896–1901.
Neale, Nathaniel 1885–98, 1902–06.
Newton, Leo 1941–48.
O'Hare, Alexander 1937–44.
O'Toole. Laurence 1894–1901.
Ogilvie, Charles 1937–41.
Osborn, John 1908–10.
Parker, Edwin 1944.
Parsons, Frederick 1872–78.
Pearson, William 1902–1910.
Powell, Mark 1897.
Precians, Eric 1941–44.
Pritchard, William 1879–83.
Reeves, Thomas 1944–48.
Retallack, Hylton 1911–13.
Ridge, Fred 1914–17, 1920–25.
Rodwell, George 1887–88.
Sadler, William 1888–90.
Scott, Edwin 1883–84.
Scott, Henry 1944–48.
Shelton, William 1894.
Shields, Charles 1920–28.
Simpson, John 1911–16.
Smith, Sydney 1886–91.
Steward, Herbert 1902–3.
Strang, Alexander 1941–44.
Stuart, William 1932–41.
Swadling, David 1923–41.
Tamsett, Edgar 1941–44.
Taylor, Henry 1878.
Thompson, John 1941–44.
Thoms, Peter 1922–28.
Treadgold, James 1892–1913.
Troup, William 1899–1900.

Walters, Henry 1903–10.
Wardrop, William 1917–19.
Westbrook, William 1899–1912.
Wetherill, John 1872–75.
Wheeler, Aaron 1872–74.
Whiting, John 1879–86.

Williams, James 1875–82.
Winchester, Joseph 1941–44.
Winkle, Thomas 1886–88.
Wragge, William 1888–1902.
Young, John 1879–87.

Leichhardt 1948–

Anderson, William 1956–62.
Armstrong, Robert 1956–59.
Baldwin, Ernest 1977–84.
Beaman, George 1950–53.
Bourne, Christine 1995– .
Brady, James 1956–71.
Brady, John William 1983–91.
Bray, Philip 1971–74.
Butler, Kate 1987–95, 1995– .
Callaghan, Michael 1956–59.
Campbell, John 1974–77.
Casey, Daniel 1965–80.
Cashman, Ann 1956–71.
Cashman, Michael 1950–53.
Cawley, Ivor 1974–87.
Colbourne, William 1948–50.
Conway, Patrick 1948–53.
Courtney, Geoffrey 1987–89.
Crawford, Peter 1980–84.
Crinion, Harold 1948–53.
Cruden, Kris 1995– .
Cummings, John 1948–50.
Deehan, John 1956–65.
Donaldson, William 1962–65.
Dougherty, William 1956–80.
Drew, Arthur 1995– .
Erwin, Edward 1948–53.
Floyd, Robyn 1980–84.
Foley, Horace 1968–71.
Francis, Sydney 1948–50.
Gallimore, Elizabeth 1948–53, 1956–58.
Gilmartin, William 1948–52.
Glover, Herbert 1956–59.
Graham, Alan 1968–71.
Greenland, Hall 1980–82.
Greenman, Sabina 1956–59.
Gunning, Denis 1959–68.
Hacking, Kath 1991–95.
Hammond, William 1948–52.
Hand, Larry 1984–95, 1995– .
Harris, George 1948–59.
Heffernan, Robert 1968–71, 1974–80, 1984– .
Hewitt, Marcus 1995– .
Higgins, Vincent 1950–53.
Hoy, Stanley 1974–77.
Hume, William 1971–74, 1980–84.
Innes, Richard 1959–1962.
Johnston, Gregory 1968–71.
Jones, Evan 1977–84, 1991– .

Keating, Frederick 1965–71.
Kelly, Anthony 1977–80.
Kirby, Geoffrey 1948–50.
Laggan, Charles 1948–53.
Leonard, George 1952–53.
Leone, Betty 1987–91.
Lewis, Elton 1956–62, 1965–68.
Lockhart, Gilbert 1948–53.
Lyons, Margaret 1984–87.
Macindoe, Neil 1991– .
Masterman, Nicholas 1991–94.
McIlveen, Ernest 1971–74.
McMahon, James 1968–71.
McVeigh, Carol 1984–97.
Millard, Stanley 1974–83.
Mitchell, Harry 1984–87.
Moore, Leslie 1948–53.
Newton, Leo 1948–53, 1956–71.
O'Brien, Christine 1994–95.
O'Malley, John 1950–53.
O'Neill, Nicholas 1980–84.
Origlass, Nicholas 1958–80, 1984–95.
Page, Sharon 1984–91.
Poole, Charles 1959–65, 1968–71.
Prendergast, James 1959–71.
Pursehouse, Ronald 1974–77.
Rocks, Charles 1977–80.
Rodwell, Leslie 1965–84.
Roxborough, Jock 1980–83.
Sandblom, Eric 1971–74.
Shaw, Charles 1968–71.
Sheehan, Maire 1995– .
Sidaway, Harry 1991– .
Skerritt, Frank 1962–65.
Smart, Val 1971–74.
Smith, Albert 1959–71.
Smith, Stephen 1987–91.
Snape, Trevor 1991–95.
Spedding, Douglas 1974–77, 1984–91.
Stevens, Geoffrey 1980–84.
Stock, Susan 1990–91, 1991– .
Straker, Robert 1965–68.
Styles, Helen 1991–95.
Taylor, Albert 1953, 1959–65.
Thompson, Brian 1984–91.
Turner, Herbert 1962–68.
Waite, John 1948–53.
Walker, Robert 1968.
Wilson, Peter 1971–77.
Wyner, Isadore 1959–74, 1977–80, 1984–91.
Young, David 1971–74.

Notes

Chapter 1

1 A Phillip, *The Voyage of Governor Phillip to Botany Bay* (ed J Stockdale, facsimile edn), Hutchinson Richmond, 1982, p 47.
2 A G L Shaw, *Convicts and the Colonies: A Study of Penal Transportation from Great Britain and Ireland to Australia and Other Parts of the Empire*, London, 1966.
3 Phillip to Sydney, 15 May 1788, *HRA*, 1, pp 16–32.
4 W Bradley, *A Voyage to NSW*, Sydney, 1969.
5 P G King, *Journal: 1787–1790*, Australian Documents Library, Sydney, 1980.
6 J Woolmington, *Aborigines in Colonial Society: 1788–1850*, Cassell Australia Ltd, Melbourne.
7 W E H Stanner, *White Man Got No Dreaming: Essays 1938–1973*, ANU Press, Canberra, 1979.
8 A Frost, 'NSW as Terra Nullius: The British Denial of Aboriginal Land Rights', *Historical Studies* 19, 1981, pp 513–523.
9 I and T Donaldson (eds), *Seeing the First Australians*, Allen & Unwin, Sydney, pp 16–17.
10 J P White and R Lampert, 'Creation & Discovery', D J Mulvaney and J P White (eds) *Australians to 1788*, Fairfax, Syme & Weldon, Sydney, 1987, pp 3–23.
11 Ibid, p 17.
12 P Turbet, *The Aborigines of the Sydney District Before 1788*, Kangaroo Press, Kenthurst, 1989.
13 A Ross, 'Tribal & Linguistic Boundaries: A Reassessment of the Evidence', G Asplin (ed) *A Difficult Infant: Sydney Before Macquarie*, NSWUP, 1988, p 43.
14 J Kohen and R J Lampert, 'Hunters & Fishers in the Sydney Region', D J Mulvaney and J P White (eds) *Australians to 1788*, pp 343–365.
15 J P White and R Lampert, 'How many people?', D J Mulvaney and J P White (eds) *Australians to 1788*, pp 115–117.
16 D Collins, *An Account of the English Colony in NSW*, vol. 1, Sydney 1975, London, 1798, p 488.
17 Kohen and Lampert, op cit (14), pp 352–355.
18 B Berzins, *The Coming of the Strangers, Life in Australia 1788–1822*, William Collins, State Library of NSW, 1988, p 15.
19 W E H Stanner, 'Religion, Totemism & Symbolism', R M and C H Berndt (eds) *Aboriginal Man in Australia*, Sydney, 1965.
20 Collins, op cit (16), p 454.
21 Kohen and Lampert, op cit (14), p 345.

22 Ibid, p 345.
23 Ross, op cit (13), pp 42–53.
24 D Plater, *Other Boundaries: Inner City Aboriginal Stories*, Leichhardt Council, 1993, p 25.
25 Collins op cit (16), pp 496–497.
26 J Hunter, *Historical Journal of the Transactions at Port Jackson and Norfolk Island*, Sydney, London, 1793, pp 340–341.
27 W E H Stanner (1977), 'The History of Indifference thus Begins', *Aboriginal History*, 1, p 17.
28 Berzins, op cit (18), p 39.
29 R Broome, *Aboriginal Australians Black Response to White Dominance 1788–1980*, Allen & Unwin, 1982, p 29.
30 *House of Commons Parliamentary Papers*, Report from the Select Committee on Aborigines (British Settlements): Together with the Minutes of Evidence, Appendix & Index, vol. 8, 1836.
31 R H W Reece, *Aborigines and Colonists, Aborigines and Colonial Society in NSW in the 1830s and 1840s*, SUP, 1974, p 17.
32 T van Bellingshausen, *The Voyage of Captain Bellingshausen to the Antarctic Seas 1819–1821*, ed F Debenham, London, 1945, 2 vols.
33 B Smith, *European Vision and the South Pacific*, Harper & Row, 1984, pp 169–176.
34 Reece, op cit (31), p 12.
35 A Bickford, 'Aboriginals in NSW after 1788', *History, Magazine of the RAHS*, 4 June 1989, p 9.
36 Broome, op cit (29), pp 58–62.
37 *V&P NSWLA* 1889, vol. 5.
38 L McMah, A Quantitative Analysis of the Aboriginal Rock Carvings in the District of Sydney, BA Hons thesis, University of Sydney, 1965.
39 C Lifu, The Leichhardt Aboriginal Heritage Report, Leichhardt Council.
40 Australian Archaeological Survey Consultants Pty Ltd, An Archaeological Investigation of Aboriginal Sites at Callan Point and Yurulbin Point: A Report to the Leichhardt Council, September 1995.

Chapter 2

1 B Berzins, *The Coming of the Strangers, Life in Australia 1788–1822*, Collins Australia/State Library of NSW, 1988, p 44.
2 J Hunter and J Bach, *An Historical Journal of Events at Sydney and at Sea 1787–1792 by Captain John Hunter*, A & R, Sydney, 1968, p 138. G Aplin, 'People in an Alien Landscape: Early Sydney's Environmental Context', G Aplin (ed) *Sydney Before Macquarie, A Difficult Infant*, NSWUP, 1988, pp 18–41.
3 T M Perry, *Australia's First Frontier: The Spread of Settlement in NSW 1788–1829*, MUP, 1963, pp 17–18.
4 W Tench, *A Complete Account of the Settlement at Port Jackson*, Angus & Robertson, 1961, p 81.
5 M Kartzoff, *Nature and a City: The Native Vegetation of the Sydney Area*, Edwards & Shaw, Sydney, 1969, pp 14–15. J R Dodson, 'Natural Vegetation', R J Harriman and E S Clifford (eds) *Atlas of NSW*, Central Mapping Authority, Bathurst, 1987, pp 94–95.
6 J F Campbell, 'The Valley of the Tank Stream', *JRAHS*, vol. 10 (1924), pp 64–103.
7 C Burton, 'Landscape Heritage', *Leichhardt Municipality Heritage Study*, vol. 1, McDonald McPhee Pty Ltd, 1990, pp 90–92.

Chapter 3

1. T M Perry, *Australia's First Frontier: The Spread of Settlement in NSW 1788–1829*, MUP, 1963, p 19.
2. Phillip to Grenville, 17 June 1790, *HRA*, 1, pp 179–180.
3. K W Robinson, 'Land', G J Abbott and N B Nairn (eds) *Economic Growth of Australia 1788–1821*, MUP, 1969.
4. L McLaughlan, 'Landed Peasantry or Landed Gentry: A Geography of Land Grants', G Aplin (ed) *Sydney Before Macquarie, A Difficult Infant*, NSWUP, 1988, p 130, p 142.
5. K S Inglis, *The Australian Colonists: An Exploration of Social History 1788–1870*, MUP, 1974. K Buckley and T Wheelwright, *No Paradise for Workers: Capitalism and the Common People in Australia 1788–1914*, OUP, 1988, pp 5–6.
6. E G Wakefield, *A Letter from Sydney, the Principal Town of Australasia*, London 1829.
7. C Lansbury, *Arcady in Australia, The Evocation of Australia in Nineteenth-Century English Literature*, MUP, 1970, pp 45–59.
8. J Philipp, *A Great View of Things: Edward Gibbon Wakefield*, Melbourne, 1971, p 91.
9. G J R Linge, *Industrial Awakening: A Geography of Australian Manufacturing 1788 to 1890*, ANU Press, 1979, p 90.
10. Lady Forbes, Reminiscences (nd), pp 46–47.
11. L A Meredith, *Notes & Sketches of NSW*, London, 1833, reprinted Melbourne, 1973, p 53.
12. J Broadbent, 'The Push East, Woolloomooloo Hill, the First Suburb', M Kelly (ed) *Sydney, City of Suburbs*, NSWUP, 1987.
13. B Dyster, 'Property, Prostration & Prudence: Business & Investment in Sydney 1838–1851', A Birch and D S Macmillan (eds) *Wealth & Progress*, p 51.
14. G C Mundy, *Our Antipodes*, London, 1852, pp 394–399.
15. J Raymond, *The NSW and General Post Office Directory 1833*.
16. *HRNSW*, vol 1, pt 1, Grenville to Phillip, 24 Aug 1789, encl Phillip's Additional Instructions, 20 Aug 1789, p 259.
17. J F Campbell, 'Notes on the Early History of the Glebe' *JRAHS*, vol. 15 (1929), p 298.
18. P L Reynolds and P V Flottmann, *Half a Thousand Acres: Balmain, A History of the Land Grant*, Balmain Association, 1976, pp 1–14.
19. *ADB*, vol 1, pp 51–52.
20. *Sydney Gazette*, 18 Feb 1828. *Aust* 7 May 1828. Church and Schools Corporation—Land Account, vol 1, NSWA 7/2708.
21. M Solling, 'Glebe 1790–1891 A Study of Patterns & Processes of Growth', MA thesis, Dept of Geography, University of Sydney, 1972, pp 19–21.
22. P Jeffrey, *LHJ* 15 (1986), pp 7–10.
23. Reynolds and Flottmann, op cit (18), pp 28–35.
24. F Low, *The City of Sydney Directory 1844–5*. SDC.
25. *Aust,* 21 May 1842, p 4.
26. SDC.
27. *Aust* 6 July 1841, p 3.
28. *SMH*, 14 March 1842.
29. Low, op cit (24).
30. Map, Land ownership in the Parishes of Petersham and Alexandria 1833, ML. W H Wells's map of the County of Cumberland 1840, ML.
31. C J Baker, *Sydney and Melbourne* (1845), p 135.
32. Low, op cit (24). SDC.
33. Solling, op cit (21), pp 40–45.

34   B Dyster, *Servant and Master: Building and Running the Grand Houses of Sydney 1788–1850*, NSWUP, 1989, pp 130–132.
35   McLaughlan, op cit (4), p 142.
36   A Roberts, *LHJ* 2 (1972), pp 20–34.
37   Dyster op cit (34), p 155.
38   *ADB*, vol 2, pp 20–22.
39   K J Cable, *LHJ* 8 (1979), p 3.
40   *ADB*, vol 1, pp 5–7.
41   G W D Allen, *Early Georgian Extracts from the Journal of George Allen (1800–77)*, Angus & Robertson, 1958, p 18.
42   Ibid, p 130.
43   Ibid, p 125.
44   J B Hirst, *Convict Society and its Enemies*, George Allen & Unwin, Sydney, 1983, p 59.
45   Dyster, op cit (34), *Servant and Master*, p 72.
46   Allen, op cit (41), p 126.
47   W Verge, *John Verge, Early Australian Architect: His Ledger and His Clients*, Sydney, 1962.
48   *ADB*, vol 1, pp 137–138.
49   J W Watson, 'Hereford House, Glebe', *JRAHS*, vol: 9, p 275. *SMH*, 19 April 1844, p 3.
50   *ADB*, vol 2, pp 51–52.
51   Verge, op cit (47).
52   C J Baker, *Sydney and Melbourne (1845)*, p 135.
53   T Shepherd, *Lectures on Landscape Gardening in Australia*, Sydney, 1836, p 86.
54   *Aust,* 21 May 1842, p 4.
55   P Reynolds, *LHJ* 13 (1984), pp 11–12.
56   *ADB*, vol 5, p 244.
57   P Reynolds, *LHJ* 14 (1985), pp 54–59.
58   Ibid, pp 37–41.
59   P Reynolds, *LHJ* 10 (1981), pp 4–8.
60   P Reynolds, *LHJ* 15 (1986), pp 44–47.
61   P Reynolds, *LHJ* 14 (1985), pp 36–37; SDC.
62   P Reynolds, *LHJ* 13 (1984), p 17.
63   P Reynolds, *LHJ* 12 (1983), p 7, pp 10–11.
64   'Return of Insolvents 1842–1849', *V&P NSWLC* 1849.
65   A Cusick, *LHJ* 16 (1989), pp 15–26.
66   SDC.
67   Vialoux and Reeves, *The Jubilee History of Leichhardt* (1921), pp 30–31.
68   *Sands's Sydney and Suburban Directory*, 1870.
69   Cusick, op cit (65), pp 19–23.
70   *ADB*, vol. 6, p 289.
71   Ibid, pp 324–5.
72   K Leong, *LHJ* 13 (1984), pp 4–6.
73   Ibid, pp 5–9.
74   *ADB*, vol 1, p 149. J H Watson, *Old Fellow*, 15 Aug 1924, pp 12–13.
75   M Roe, 'Colonial Society in Embryo', *Historical Studies* No 7 (1956), pp 149–159. B Dyster, 'The Fate of Colonial Conservatism on the Eve of the Gold Rush', *JRAHS*, vol. 54 (1968), p 347.
76   R D Altick, *Victorian People and Ideas*, J M Dent & Sons, London, 1974, pp 174–175.
77   W Westbrooke Burton, 'State of Society and of Crime in NSW During Six Years of Residence in that Colony', *Colonial Magazine and Commercial Maritime Journal,* vol. 1 (January–April 1840), p 433.

78 F Fowler, *Southern Lights and Shadows*, London, 1859, pp 7–8. SDC.
79 L A Meredith, *Notes and Sketches of NSW*, London, 1844, pp 52–53.
80 Low, op cit (24). Dyster, op cit (34), pp 47–58.
81 J Woolmington (ed), *Religion in Early Australia*, 1976.
82 K Inglis, op cit (5), pp 82–89.

Chapter 4

1 G P Walsh, 'The Geography of Manufacturing in Sydney, 1788–1851', *Business Archives and History*, vol. 3, pp 20–52. *SMH*, 16 November 1887, p 4.
2 C J Baker, *Sydney and Melbourne*, 1845, p 135.
3 S R Butlin, *Foundations of the Australian Monetary System*, MUP, 1968, p 225.
4 J Maclehose, *Maclehose's Picture of Sydney & Stranger's Guide in NSW*, 1838, p 70.
5 *Aust*, 13 September 1836, p 1. P L Reynolds and P V Flottmann, *Half a Thousand Acres*, Balmain Association, 1976, p 56.
6 *Aust*, 12 May 1840; 30 June 1840. *SMH*, 1 June 1840.
7 *Aust*, 4 May 1841, p 3; P Reynolds, *LHJ* 11 (1982), p 15.
8 *Aust*, 4 May 1841, p 3. (2/1)
9 J Hood, *Australia and the East*, London, 1844, p 85.
10 *Aust*, 1 June 1841, p 3.
11 B Dyster, *LHJ* 11 (1982), pp 6–7.
12 *Aust*, 9 March 1841, p 3. M Solling, *LHJ* 1 (1971), pp 14–17.
13 *Aust*, 27 January 1842, p 4.
14 R Mansfield, *Analytical View of the Census of NSW, for 1841*, Kent & Fairfax, Sydney, 1847, p 49.
15 SDC, ML D67.
16 Evidence of Thomas May and James Croft to the Select Committee on Slaughter Houses, *V and P NSWLC* 1848.
17 G J R Linge, *Industrial Awakening, A Geography of Australian Manufacturing, 1788 to 1890*, ANU, 1979, p 115.
18 Joan Kerr, *Our Great Victorian Architect, Edmund Thomas Blacket (1817–1883)*, National Trust, 1983, p 74–75. *V and P NSWLC 1850*, vol. 1, pp 447–450.
19 Mansfield, op cit (14), p 11.
20 F Low, *Directory of the City and District of Sydney, 1847*. W and F Ford, *Sydney Directory, 1851*.
21 *Aust*, 9 March 1841, p 3.
22 T T Smith, 'Evidence on the Building Act', *VandP NSWLC* 1838, Part 2, P 21.
23 *SMH*, 8 March 1851, p 2.
24 G Nicholls, 'Fowler Potteries', *Heritage*, 1, December 1984, pp 7–9.
25 *SM*, 4 April 1906, p 877.
26 *NSWPP* 1883, vol. 3, pp 202–204.
27 P Reynolds, *LHJ* 7 (1978), pp 3–9.
28 P Reynolds, *LHJ* 13 (1984), pp 30–31.
29 P Reynolds, *LHJ* 15 (1986), pp 44–45.
30 M Solling, 'Glebe, 1790–1891, A Study of Patterns and Processes of Growth' MA thesis, University of Sydney, 1972, p 50.
31 *SMH*, 6 November 1850.
32 *SMH*, 7 March 1851, p 2.
33 Reynolds and Flottmann, op cit (5), pp 71–84.
34 Solling, op cit (30), pp 90–93.

35 Solling, op cit (30), pp 50–51.
36 J A La Nauze, 'A Social Survey of Sydney in 1858', *Historical Studies* (1942–3), vol. 2, pp 264–268. W S Jevons, Remarks upon the Social Map of Sydney, Investigation into the City of Sydney 1858; and Pyrmont, Glebe, Camperdown, Sydney, 1858, B864 ML.
37 *V and P NSWLC* 1851, vol. 2. *V and P NSWLA* 1857, vol. 1. *V and P NSWLA* 1862, vol. 3.
38 Jevons, op cit (36).
39 *V and P NSWLA* 1859–60, vol. 4, p 8.
40 B Davidson, K Hamey and D Nicholls, *Called to the Bar, 150 years of Pubs in Balmain and Rozelle*, Balmain Association, 1991.
41 *V and P NSWLA* 1862, vol. 3.
42 G J Aplin, 'Models of Urban Change: Sydney 1820–1870', *Australian Geographical Studies*, vol. 20 (1982), pp 147–155.
43 L Lynch, 'T S Mort, His Dock and Balmain Labour', M Kelly (ed) *Nineteenth Century Sydney, Essays in Urban History*, SUP, 1978, pp 81–91.
44 F A Larcombe, *The Origins of Local Government in NSW, 1831–1858*, SUP, 1973, vol. 1, pp 199–239.
45 *SEM*, 9 April 1859.
46 *SMH*, 1 September 1859, p 5.
47 For gazettal of petitions and counter petitions see Larcombe, op cit (44), pp 270–271.
48 *SMH*, 5 April 1860, p 9.
49 A J C Mayne, 'A Most Pernicious Principle: the Local Government Franchise in Nineteenth Century Sydney', *Australian Journal of Politics and History*, vol. 27 (1987), pp 160–171.
50 *Govt Gazette*, 24 Dec 1864, p 2967.
51 R W Connell and T H Irving, *Class Structure in Australian History*, Longman, Melbourne, 1980, p 127.
52 D N Jeans, 'Town Planning in NSW, 1829–1842', *Australian Planning Institute Journal* (1965), vol. 3, pp 191–196.
53 W Aird, *The Water Supply, Sewerage and Drainage of Sydney* (1961), p 11.
54 'Report of the Commission to Enquire into the Supply of Water to Sydney and Suburbs', *V and P NSWLA* 1869, vol. 2.
55 D Clark, 'Worse than Physic: Sydney's Water Supply, 1788–1888', Kelly, op cit (43).
56 *Bradshaw's Almanac, 1864*, p 17.
57 W Maddock, *Visitor's Guide for Sydney* (1872).
58 G Mundy, *Our Antipodes: Or Residence and Rambles in the Australian Colonies, With a Glimpse of the Goldfields*, London, 1852.
59 *An Act to Consolidate and Amend the Laws Relating to the Licensing of Public Houses and to Regulate the Sale of Fermented and Spirituous Liquors in NSW, 2 October 1849*, Public Statutes of NSW, 1842–1851.
60 *SMH*, 14 February 1860, p 1; 15 February 1861, p 1.
61 S J Baker, *The Australian Language*, Currawong Press, 1978, Drinking, pp 225–233.
62 M Lake, 'The Politics of Respectability: Identifying the Masculinist Context', *Historical Studies*, vol. 22 No 86, pp 116–131.
63 Davidson, et al., op cit (40).
64 M Solling, *LHJ* 6 (1975), pp 10–15.
65 'Final Report of the Select Committee on Intemperance', *V and P NSWLC* 1855, vol. 1.
66 *V and P NSWLC* 1855, vol. 2, pp 976–1007.
67 'Select Committee on the Sale of Liquors Licensing Act Amendment Bill', *V and P NSWLA* 1870, vol. 2, p 867.
68 Evidence of Joseph Barnier before the Select Committee on the Sunday Sale of Liquors Prevention Bill, *V and P NSWLA* 1877–78, vol. 4.

69 Joan Kerr, op cit (18), pp 14–15.
70 K S Inglis, 'Religious Behaviour', S Encel and A F Davies (eds) *Australian Society* (1st edn 1965).
71 K S Inglis, *The Australian Colonists, An Exploration of Social History, 1788–1870*, MUP, 1974, p 80.
72 M Solling, *LHJ* 18 (1994), pp 3–12.
73 B T Dowd, 'Old St Benedict's of Abercrombie Place, Sydney', *JRAHS*, 34, pp 301–316.
74 St John's Bishopthorpe Pew Rent Account Book, 1893–1905.
75 T W Laquer, 'Sunday Schools and Social Control', R Bocock and K Thompson (eds) *Religion and Ideology*, Manchester University Press, 1985, pp 184–204.
76 *V and P NSWLA* 1862, vol. 3.
77 'Appendix' to the Report on National Education, 1862, *V and P NSWLA* 1863–64, vol. 4, p 1073.
78 GCM, 1 December 1859, *SM*, 23 February 1861, p 1.
79 *SM*, 17 January 1863, p 4.
80 W M Cowper, *The Autobiography and Reminiscences of William Macquarie Cowper*, Sydney, 1902, p 136.
81 Evidence of W Cowper and E Wise to the Select Committee on the Condition of the Working Classes of the Metropolis, *V and P NSWLA* 1859–60, vol. 4, p 203, pp 91–93.
82 *SM*, 26 August 1865, p 2.
83 A-M Jordens, *The Stenhouse Circle, Literary Life in Mid-Nineteenth Century Sydney*, MUP 1979, p 46.
84 *SM*, 31 January 1863, p 10; 14 March 1863, p 3; 5 May 1866, p 2; 9 May 1863, p 3; 6 June 1863, p 2; 27 May 1865, p 5.
85 *SM*, 23 February 1868, p 2.
86 *SMH*, 16 October 1860, p 6.
87 D Green and L Cromwell, *Mutual and or Welfare State: Australia's Friendly Societies*, Sydney, 1984, p xiv.
88 Inglis, op cit (71), pp 221–224.
89 *V and P NSWLA* 1870–71, vol. 4, p 833.

Chapter 5

1 '1851 and 1861 Census', *V and P NSWLC* 1851, vol. 2. *V and P NSWLA* 1862, vol. 3.
2 R J Johnston, *City and Society: An Outline for Urban Geography*, Penguin, 1980, p 224.
3 M Solling, *LHJ* 5 (1975), pp 3–8.
4 A J C Mayne, 'Commuter Travel and Class Mobility in Sydney 1858–1888', *AEHR*, vol. 21, 1, 1981, pp 53–65.
5 *V and P NSWLA* 1862, vol. 3. T A Coghlan, *General Report on the Eleventh Census of NSW*, Sydney, 1894.
6 *V and P NSWLA* 1883–84, vol. 8, p 65.
7 *J NSWLC*, 1902, part 2.
8 J Hood, *Australia and the East*, London, 1843, p 98.
9 G J Aplin, 'Models of Urban Change, Sydney 1820–1870', *Australian Geographical Studies*, vol. 20, (1982), pp 147–155.
10 S Fitzgerald, *Rising Damp, Sydney 1870–1890*, OUP, Melbourne, 1987, p 53.
11 W H Wells, *A Geographical Dictionary or Gazetteer of the Australian Colonies 1848* (facsimile), Council of Library of NSW, 1970, p 42.

12 'Select Committee on the Balmain Steam Ferry Company's Bill', *V and P NSWLC* 1853, vol. 2, p 281.
13 A M Prescott, *Sydney Ferry Fleets*, A M Prescott, 1984, p 8.
14 'Select Committee on Public Vehicles and Boats', *V and P NSWLA* 1870, vol. 2, p 971.
15 *The Echo*, 26 June 1890.
16 *SMH*, 6 Nov 1850.
17 S T Leigh, *S T Leigh and Co.'s Handbook in Sydney and Suburbs* (1867), p 59.
18 B Lennon and G Wotherspoon, 'Sydney's Trams 1861–1914: The Rise of an Urban Mass Transport System', G Wotherspoon (ed) *Sydney's Transport Studies in Urban History*, Hale & Iremonger, 1983, p 102.
19 I Badger, *Australian Horsedrawn Vehicles*, Sydney 1977, p 29.
20 'Select Committee on the Pyrmont Bridge Company Bill (amended)', *V and P NSWLA* 1858, vol. 2. Pyrmont Bridge Co—half-yearly meeting in *Govt Gazette*, 1863, p 1619.
21 *Sands,* 1858–59, 1867. *Bradshaw's Almanac* (1864), p 17.
22 Mayne, op cit (4), pp 53–65. W Maddock, *Visitors' Guide to Sydney* (1872).
23 Evidence of Thomas Hale, op cit (14), p 971.
24 G R Addison, *Balmain Almanac for 1878*, p 6. Petition for Bridge between Balmain and The Glebe, *V and P NSWLA* 1875, vol. 3, p 819.
25 *SM,* 23 June 1888, p 1323.
26 W C Taylor, *Jottings on Australia* (1872), p 55.
27 *SMH,* 6 July 1881, p 5.
28 'Report of the Select Committee on the Sydney Tramway and Omnibus Co.'s Bill', *V and P NSWLA* 1879–80, vol. 5, pp 277–288.
29 P Clarke, *The New Chum in Australia: Or the Scenery, Life and Manners of Australians*.
30 'Select Committee on the Balmain Tramway Bill', *V and P NSWLA* 1885–86, vol. 8, pp 737–742.
31 R Willson et al., *The Red Lines*, Sydney, 1970, pp 8–10.
32 'Evidence of J A Brodie to Royal Commission on City and Suburban Railways', *V and P NSWLA* 1891–92, vol. 5, pp 18–21.
33 D Audley, 'Sydney's Horse Bus Industry in 1889', Wotherspoon, op cit (18), p 88.
34 *SMH*, 2 February 1887, p 13.
35 'Evidence of Walter Macdougall to Royal Commission on the Extension of the Railway to the Suburbs of Sydney', *V and P NSWLA* 1891–92, vol. 5, pp 27–29.
36 Evidence of Benjamin Moore, op cit (35), pp 14–15.
37 L G Lynch, 'A Community Study—Balmain *c.*1860–1894', PhD thesis University of Sydney, 1982, p 307.
38 Evidence of Walter Macdougall, op cit (35), p 27.
39 Prescott, op cit (13),p 12.
40 *SMH,* 25 July 1896, p 9.
41 The *Glebe Gazette*, 8 August 1903, p 2.
42 *NSWSR* 1887, p 307.
43 M Bray and M Rimmer, *Delivering the Goods: A History of the Transport Workers' Union in NSW 1888–1986*, Allen & Unwin, 1987, p 8.
44 *Newsletter of RAHS,* May 1974, p 5.
45 G Davison, 'The Australian Energy System in 1888, Australia 1888', *Bulletin* No 10 (September 1982), p 19.
46 Lennon and Wotherspoon, op cit (18), pp 101–114.
47 A Atkinson and A Aveling (eds), 'Work', *Australians 1838*, Fairfax, Syme & Weldon, 1988, pp 132–134.
48 J Birmingham, 'Brick-making and Other Clay-using Industries', chapter 2 , pp 53–94, and

D Jeans, The Building Industry: Materials and Styles, chapter 3, J Birmingham, I Jack, and D Jeans, *Industrial Archaeology in Australian Rural Industry*, Heinemann, 1983, pp 95–118.

49 A Coolican, 'Solidarity and Sectionalism in the Sydney Building Trades: The Role of the Building Trades Council 1886–1895', *Labour History*, 54 (May 1988), p 17.
50 N G Butlin, *Investment in Australia, Economic Development 1861–1900*, OUP, 1964, pp 283–286.
51 J Inglis, *Our Australian Cousins*, London 1886, pp 147–148.
52 Butlin, op cit (50), pp 211–214.
53 'Select Committee of Sydney Water Reserves', *V and P NSWLA* 1863–64, vol. 4, p 663.
54 *SMH*, 8 February 1851, p 2.
55 GCM, 19 November 1860. BCM, 13 January 1862, 4 May 1864, 31 August 1880.
56 'Commission Appointed to Inquire into the Supply of Water to Sydney and Suburbs', *V and P NSWLA* 1869, vol. 2.
57 'Sydney City and Suburban Sewage and Health Board—Second Progress Report', *V and P NSWLA* 1875, vol. 394–395.
58 D Clark, '"Worse than Physic": Sydney's Water Supply 1788–1888', M Kelly (ed) *Nineteenth Century Sydney: Essays in Urban History*, SUP, 1978, p 64.
59 *The Empire,* 21 June 1869, p 3.
60 'Sydney City and Suburban Sewage and Health Board—Eleventh Progress Report', *V and P NSWLA* 1875–76, vol. 5, p 618.
61 *V and P NSWLA* 1889, vol. 4, p 905.
62 'Evidence of Percy Charles Lucas to the Select Committee on the Claim of Glebe Borough Council in Respect of Sewerage Works', *V and P NSWLA* 1901, vol. 3, p 1140.
63 Select Committee, op cit (62), pp 1129–1156.
64 'Evidence of E H Buchanan, B Moore and P Lucas to the Parliamentary Standing Committee on Public Works—Proposed Drainage Works for the Western Suburbs', *V and P NSWLA* 1889, vol. 4, p 905.
65 N Thorpe, 'Water Supply and Sewerage', D Fraser (ed) *Sydney: From Settlement to City*, Engineers Australia Pty Ltd, 1989, p 34.
66 'Appendix 2, Deaths and Death-rate in NSW 1872–1887, to Report on Proposed Drainage Works for the Western Suburbs', *V and P NSWLA* 1889, vol. 4, p 905.
67 Thorpe, op cit (65), p 35.
68 *The Roadmakers: A History of Main Roads in NSW*, Department of Main Roads, 1976, pp 44–48.
69 J Ginswick, 'Foundations of the Australian Gas Light Company', *JRAHS*, 45 (1959), p 232. GCM, 7 September 1860, 19 November 1860. Leigh, op cit (17), p 59.
70 BCM, 29 December 1874.
71 A Garran (ed), *Picturesque Atlas of Australia*, Sydney, 1888, p 85.
72 *NSWSR 1890*.
73 F A Larcombe, *The Stabilisation of Local Government in NSW 1858–1906*, SUP, 1976, vol. 2, pp 203–204.

Chapter 6

1 Petitions. For details of petitions and dates of incorporations see F A Larcombe, *The Origins of Local Government in NSW 1831–1858* (Sydney 1973), vol. 1, p 270.
2 *SEM*, 9 April 1859.
3 *NSWGG,* 10 October 1870, pp 2169–70; 3 April 1871, pp 765–66.

4 *NSWGG* 14 December 1871, p 2829. A Vialoux and C M Reeves, The *Jubilee History of Leichhardt* (1923), p 23.
5 *NSWGG,* 24 December 1864, p 2967. *JNSWLC* 1867–68, vol. 15, p 309; 1868–69, vol. 16 pp 175–181, 1872; vol. 21 pp 473–487.
6 Vialoux and Reeves, op cit (4), p 33. *Balmain Municipal Council Souvenir to Commemorate the 50th Anniversary of the Incorporation of the Municipality of Balmain 1860–1910*, pp 29–30.
7 *NSWSR* 1875, p 223; *1878*, p 255.
8 *NSWSR* 1861, 1862, 1865, 1867, 1870.
9 *V and P NSWLA* 1875–76, vol. 4, p 911.
10 F A Larcombe, *The Stabilization of Local Government in NSW 1858–1906, A History of Local Government in NSW*, vol. 2, pp 188–9.
11 *V and P NSWLA* 1873–74, vol. 5, pp 135–40.
12 *NSWGG* 1862, p 2293; p 1865, p 1459.
13 GCM, 1859–1870. BCM, 1860–1870.
14 GCM, 6 May 1861.
15 GCM, 6 July 1868, p 399. LCM, 4 March 1872.
16 *NSWSR* 1878, p 255.
17 *SMH, 17* September 1888.
18 'Select Committee on the Working of Municipalities', *V and P NSWLA* 1873–74, vol. 5.
19 *NSWSR* 1885, 1888, p 320.
20 *NSWSR* 1885, 1888.
21 *NSWSR 1884*, 1885.
22 *V and P NSWLA* 1888–89 vol. 3, p 1085. *SMH*, 1 December 1887, p 11.
23 *SMH*, 9 December 1887, p 4.
24 *SMH,* 30 December 1887, p 3.
25 *DT,* 12,13, 15, 17, 19 October 1898. Larcombe, op cit (10), p 185.
26 T A Coghlan, *Wealth and Progress of NSW*, 1892, pp 455–6.
27 Larcombe, op cit (10), p 185.
28 *DT,* 15 October 1898.
29 *ATCJ*, 24 July 1880, pp 168–9. 'Select Committee on Glebe Borough Bill', *V and P NSWLA* 1878–89, vol. 7, pp 797–802.
30 *BO,* 1 September 1888, p 3. *SM,* 13 October 1888, p 774. 'Select Committee on Leichhardt Council Chambers (Mortgage) Bill', *V and P NSWLA* 1887–88, vol. 2, pp 957–963.
31 *WSWB,* 23 September 1899, p 6. *ATCJ*, 18 November 1899.
32 M Solling, *LHJ* 15 (1986), pp 35–42.
33 'Evidence of T Colebrook, G Clubb, F Artlett and J Treadgold to the Royal Commission on Greater Sydney', *NSWPP* 1913, vol. 81 (2), pp 398–400, pp 242–3, pp 156–163, pp 401–2.
34 *NSWSR 1888*.
35 A Roberts, 'The Development of the Suburb of Annandale 1876–1899', University of Sydney BA (Hons) 1970, pp 45–49.
36 *SMH,* 3 December 1926. *SMH,* 22 May 1933.
37 Vialoux and Reeves, op cit (4), pp 46–8.
38 Ibid, p 48.
39 GCM, 21 October 1867, p 354; 19 Oct, p 414.
40 'Sydney City and Suburban Sewerage and Health Board—Second Progress Report', *V and P NSWLA* 1875, vol. 4, pp 394–5.
41 'Parliamentary Standing Committee on Public Works—Proposed Drainage and Works for the Western Suburbs', *V and P NSWLA* 1889, vol. 4, p 905.
42 Second Progress Report, op cit (40), pp 372–3.

43 L Lynch, 'A Community Study—Balmain c.1860–1894', PhD Thesis, University of Sydney 1981, pp 266–268.
44 Ibid, p 267.
45 *V and P NSWLA* 1889, vol. 4, pp 905–1128.
46 'Select Committee on the Claim of Glebe Borough Council in Respect of Sewerage Works', *V and P NSWLA* 1901, vol. 3, pp 1129–1156.
47 'Eleventh Report of City of Sydney Suburban Sewage and Health Board' *V and P NSWLA* 1875–6 vol. 5 p 618.
48 *SM*, 26 October 1865, p 961.
49 *V and P NSWLA* 1876–77, vol. 3, p 695–787.
50 *V and P NSWLA* 1872–73, vol. 3, p 249.
51 *V and P NSWLA* 1875–76, vol. 5, p 318.
52 *V and P NSWLA* 1859–60, vol. 4, p 4.
53 *V and P NSWLA* 1875–76, vol. 5.
54 Ibid.
55 J H L Cumpston, *The History of Diphtheria, Scarlet Fever, Measles and Whooping Cough in Australia 1788–1925*, Commonwealth Department of Health 1927. Scarlet Fever *V and P NSWLA* 1875–76, vol. 6.
56 *NSWLA* 1892–93, vol. 3. *V and P NSWLA* 1883, vol. 2, p 964. *V and P NSWLA* 1900, vol. 2.
57 P H Curson, *Times of Crisis*, SUP 1985, pp 16–20.
58 GCM, 14 April 1870, p 528.
59 Lynch, op cit (43), p 246.
60 *NSWGG*, 12 December 1892, pp 9747–9756.
61 *NSWGG*, 2 January 1894, pp 3–4. Roberts, op cit (35), pp 36–43.
62 Larcombe, op cit (10), p 291.
63 *The Empire*, 22 June 1869. *SMH*, 27 October 1880, p 3.
64 GCM, 7 March 1881.
65 *V and P NSWLA* 1900, vol. 1, p 20.
66 GCM, Library, 21 March 1901, p 104. GCM, 4 February 1907, 6 May 1907.
67 *NSWSR* 1912, p 414.
68 A Hamill, 1884–1984, *Celebrating a Centenary—Balmain Swimming Club* (1984).
69 Vialoux and Reeves, op cit (4), p 78.
70 GCM, 31 March 1879, p 257; 21 March 1912, p 322; 2 January 1900, p 123.
71 C Cunneen, 'Hands off the parks!' The Provision of Parks and Playgrounds, J Roe (ed) *Twentieth Century Sydney Studies in Urban and Social History*, Hale & Iremonger 1980, pp 105–119.
72 *ATCJ*, 29 July 1882 p 227.
73 P Jeffrey, *LHJ* 15 (1986), pp 30–1.
74 G Jetis, 'Leichhardt North (Lilyfield), A Historical Study', BArch thesis, University of NSW, 1984, p 80.
75 *Souvenir* . . . op cit (6), pp 63–64.
76 *Old Balmain (Leichhardt) Cemetery Act*, 1941.
77 J Ginswick, Foundations of the Australian Gas Light Company, *JRAHS*, vol. 45, pp 226–265.
78 Lynch, op cit (43), pp 296–8. GCM 19 October 1860.
79 Larcombe, op cit (10), p 204.
80 Lynch, op cit (43), p 299.
81 *SMH*, 13 February 1905, p 5. *SMH*, 29 December 1911, p 6.
82 Vialoux and Reeves, p 47.
83 *Souvenir*, op cit (6), p 63.

84 *SMH*, 9 April 1900, p 5.
85 S Fitzgerald, *Sydney 1842–1992*, Hale & Iremonger, 1992, p 265.
86 *SMH*, 20 November 1933, p 5. *The Australasian Engineer*, 8 August 1932. *Construction Review*, July 1935, p 20.
87 Larcombe, op cit (10), pp 68–70.
88 H E Maiden, *The History of Local Government in NSW*, A & R, 1966, p 220.
89 F Larcombe, *The Advancement of Local Government in NSW 1906 to the Present, A History of Local Government in NSW*, vol. 3, pp 159–210.
90 Royal Commission on Greater Sydney, *NSWPP*, 1913, vol. 81 (2).
91 Larcombe, op cit (89), p 110.

Chapter 7

1 *Sands* for 1880, 1882, 1884, 1886, 1888, 1889.
2 *V and P NSWLA* 1862, vol. 3; 1872–73, vol. 3; 1883–84, vol. 8. T A Coghlan, *General Report on the Eleventh Census of NSW* (1894).
3 M Solling, *LHJ* 5 (1975), pp 3–8.
4 N G Butlin, *Investment in Australian Economic Development 1861–1900*, CUP, 1964, p 279.
5 *Sands* 1865, 1866, 1867, 1868.
6 *Aust*, 27 January 1842, p 4. Registered Lease Book 38 No 20; LTO Plan 1478 (L).
7 M Solling, 'Glebe 1790–1891, A Study of Patterns and Processes of Growth', MA Thesis, University of Sydney, 1972, p 37. *SM*, 27 February 1869, p 4.
8 *SMH*, 23 January 1856, p 7. LTO Plan 321 (W).
9 'Report on Housing on Bishopthorpe Estate' by E T Blacket, 29 December 1863, Church of England Property Trust, Norton Smith Papers, ML A5372. Bishopthorpe Estate 1839–1877, NSWA 4/806.1.
10 LTO Registered Leases, Bishopthorpe 1857–1874.
11 B and K Smith, *The Architectural Character of Victorian Glebe, Sydney*, University Co-op Bookshop, Sydney, 1973, pp 29–30.
12 Proceedings of Sixth Synod of Diocese of Sydney, NSW, 26–31 August 1883, p 46.
13 *SMH*, 9 February 1857, p 2; 7 July 1857.
14 Reuss and Browne, Town of Waterview, the Site of T S Mort's Dry Dock (appended to evidence of F H Reuss, Select Committee on the Waterview Patent Slip Bill), *V and P NSWLA* 1867–68, vol. 4.
15 'Minutes of Evidence, Select Committee on the Waterview Dry Dock Bill', *V and P NSWLC* 1855, vol. 3.
16 L Lynch, 'T S Mort, His Dock and Balmain Labour', M Kelly (ed) *Nineteenth Century Sydney, Essays in Urban History*, SUP, 1978, pp 83–84.
17 LTO Bk 27 No 96.
18 *The Empire*, 30 August 1859, p 7.
19 LTO Plan 313 (W). Bishopthorpe Rate Book 1868–69, NSWA.
20 LTO Bk 80 Nos 832–834. LTO Roll Plan 733.
21 Forest Lodge Ward Rate Book 1889, NSWA.
22 S Fitzgerald, *Rising Damp, Sydney 1870–90* OUP 1987, p 33.
23 'Sydney Public Abattoir', *V and P NSWLC* 1850, pp 447–450. *SMH*, 7 January 1859, p 4.
24 'Evidence of W A Hutchinson, Royal Commission into Noxious and Offensive Trades', *JNSWLC* 1883, vol. 3, pp 177–299.
25 P Mazza, 'Historical Development of Rozelle East', BArch thesis, University of NSW, 1986, pp 301–303.

26 LTO TT Purchasers Index, 1867–1880.
27 The *Bulletin*, 26 June 1880, p 3.
28 L G Lynch, 'A Community Study—Balmain *c.*1860–1894', PhD thesis, University of Sydney, 1981, p 197.
29 Mazza, op cit (25), pp 302–303.
30 Ibid, pp 155–130, pp 199–203, pp 221–223.
31 J Bates, *Gathering the Strands for Rozelle Public School*, published by author, 1980, p 19.
32 Butlin, op cit (4), pp 267–273.
33 G P Jones, *The Road I Came 1915*, p 53, ML.
34 C Burton,' Housing the Glebe: Architects, Builders and Styles 1828–1915', MA thesis University of Sydney, 1979, pp 41–42, pp 49–52.
35 Butlin, op cit (4), pp 285–286. LTO TT Purchasers Index 1860–1890.
36 W S Jevons, 'Remarks upon the Social Map of Sydney, Investigations into the City of Sydney 1858; and Pyrmont, Glebe, Camperdown (Sydney 1858)', B864, ML.
37 Smith, op cit (11), p 31, pp 39–45.
38 Ibid, pp 70–75. M Lewis, 'The Terrace Form', in *Fitzroy: Melbourne's First Suburb*, Hyland Home, 1989, pp 94–101.
39 R V Jackson, 'Owner Occupation of Houses in Sydney 1871 to 1891', in *Australian Economic History Review*, vol. 10 No 2, p 148.
40 Butlin, op cit (4), pp 249–253.
41 LTO TT Purchasers Index 1873–1890.
42 Lynch, op cit (28), pp 202–203.
43 'Evidence of W Jarrett to Select Committee on Assisted Immigration', *V and P NSWLA* 1879–80, vol. 5, p 751.
44 P Reynolds, *LHJ* 17 (1993), pp 53–55.
45 *ADB*, 6, pp 454–455.
46 L Muir, 'Shady Acres, Politicians, Developers and the Design of Sydney's Public Transport System 1873–1891', PhD thesis, Department of Geography, University of Sydney, 1994, p 119.
47 'A Roberts, The Development of the Suburb of Annandale', BA Hons, University of Sydney, 1970, pp 11–13.
48 Muir, op cit (46), p 119.
49 A Roberts, *LHJ* 9 (1980), pp 9–12.
50 *ATCJ,* 12 January 1878, p 64.
51 *SMH*, 17 November 1877.
52 Roberts, op cit (47), p 11.
53 Ibid, p 57.
54 LTO OST Vendors Index and TT Purchasers Index 1877–1885.
55 Burton, op cit (34), pp 41–42.
56 Ibid, pp 66–68.
57 *V and P NSWLA* 1872–73, vol. 3. *Sands* for 1873.
58 *ISN*, 16 June 1864.
59 A Cusick, *LHJ* 16 (1989), pp 37–38.
60 *V and P NSWLA* 1883–84, vol. 8.
61 Cusick, op cit (59), pp 23–24.
62 Vialoux and Reeves, *The Jubilee History of Leichhardt* (1921), p 32.
63 *V and P NSWLA* 1883–84, vol. 8. Coghlan, op cit (2). *JNSWLC,* 1902, Part 2.
64 P Reynolds, *LHJ* 17, p 53, p 56.
65 Ibid, p 57.
66 For potted biographies see Reynolds, op cit (64), pp 53–56.

67 Reynolds, op cit (64), p 56.
68 Ibid, p 51.
69 Jackson, op cit (39), p 141.
70 *Sands* for 1882, 1886, 1890.
71 *Sands* for 1886.
72 L Muir, op cit (46), p 239.
73 Reynolds, op cit (64), p 60.
74 Cusick, op cit (59), pp 56–59.
75 Ibid, pp 28–29.
76 Ibid, p 38.
77 G Jetis, 'Leichhardt North (Lilyfield), A Historical Study', BArch thesis, University of NSW, 1984, pp 64–69.
78 Cusick, op cit (59), pp 68–71. Muir, op cit (46), pp 322–323.
79 Cusick, op cit (59), pp 37–38, p 43.
80 S G Carrick, 'Leichhardt South, A History, The Road to Parramatta, 1788–1988', BArch thesis, University of NSW, 1988, pp 76–80.
81 Ibid, pp 73–75.
82 D J Truman, 'Leichhardt East: A History, The Biggers and Piperston Estates, 1794–1986', BArch thesis, University of NSW, 1986, pp 133–138.
83 Jetis, op cit (77), p 28, pp 70–74.
84 Truman, op cit (82), pp 85–93.
85 Ibid, pp 156–162, pp 133–138.
86 Ibid, pp 183–184.
87 G Best, *Mid-Victorian Britain 1851–1875*, Panther, p 34.
88 P Reynolds, *The Initial Landholders* (unpub).
89 Ibid.
90 Ibid. P Reynolds, *Balmain: 1800–1882, The Gilchrist Settlement, A Basic Search Plan* [Map], Balmain Association, 1976.
91 Mazza, op cit (25), pp 20–22.
92 Ibid, p 303. E Russell, *Drummoyne, A Western Suburb's History from 1794*, Drummoyne Council, 1971, p 122.
93 J Kerr, *Our Great Victorian Architect, Edmund Thomas Blacket (1817–1883)*, p 42. J Bates, *Gathering the Strands . . . for Rozelle Public School*, pub by the author, Balmain, 1980, p 7, p 16, p 37.
94 Mazza, op cit (25), pp 20–27.
95 Ibid, pp 115–130.
96 *Sands* for 1882, 1886, 1890.
97 Reynolds, op cit (90).
98 J-C Bertoni, 'Historical Development of Rozelle West', BArch, University of NSW, 1985, pp 16–79.
99 *The Times* (London), 30 March 1899.
100 Bertoni, op cit (98), pp 72–73, pp 76–80. *Sands* for 1882, 1886, 1890.
101 Bertoni, op cit (98), pp 16–29.
102 Ibid, pp 30–43.
103 Ibid, pp 60–64, 55–59.
104 P Jeffrey, *LHJ* 15 (1986), pp 7–10.
105 K Leong, *LHJ* 14 (1986), pp 5–9. D I McDonald, *LHJ* 3 (1972), pp 5–6.
106 LTO Roll Plan 607. Bishopthorpe Ward Rate Book, 1889, NSWA.
107 D Allen, *Early Georgian: Extracts from the Journal of George Allen (1800–1877)*, Halstead Press, Sydney, 1958, pp 134–136.

108 *SMH*, 24 March 1884, p 11. Mills and Pile Papers 1879–1898, A2737, ML.
109 S McGlynn, *Urbanisation in Australian History*, Nelson 1970, pp 25–30.
110 Solling, op cit (7), p 103.
111 LTO TT Purchasers Index.
112 J Niland, 'The Birth of the Movement for an Eight Hour Working Day in NSW', *Australian Journal of Politics and History*, vol. 14 (1968), p 77.
113 'Evidence before Select Committee on Assisted Immigration', *V and P NSWLA* 1879–80, vol. 5, p 751.
114 LTO TT Purchasers Index.
115 R V Jackson, 'House Building and the Age Structure of the Population in NSW 1861–1900', *Australian Economic History Review*, vol. 14, pp 143–159.
116 *JNSWLC* 1902, Part 2.
117 J Flower, *LHJ* 8 (1979), pp 4–9.
118 C McNamara, *LHJ* 15 (1986), p 4.
119 *V and P NSWLA* 1872–73, vol. 3 and 1883–84, vol. 8. Coghlan, op cit (2). *JNSWLC* 1902, Part 2.
120 Coghlan, op cit (2).
121 *JNSWLC* 1902, Part 2.
122 Burton, op cit (34), pp 41–42.
123 L Hoefschmit, 'Ambrose Thornley Junior', BArch thesis, University of NSW, 1976.
124 Burton, op cit (34), pp 55–59.
125 R Wilson and N Patrick, *LHJ* 3 (1972), pp 15–16.
126 R Irving et al., 'The Abbey, Annandale', *Fine Houses of Sydney*, Methuen Australia, Sydney, 1982, pp 57–65.
127 Ibid, p 61.
128 LTO TT Purchasers Index 1882–1900.
129 *JNSWLC* 1902, Part 2. *Census of Commonwealth of Australia* 1921, vols 1, 3.
130 Reynolds, op cit (64), pp 67–71.
131 LTO TT Purchasers Index.
132 A Coolican, 'Solidarity and Sectionalism in the Sydney Building Trades: The Role of the Building Trades Council 1886–1895', *Labour History*, 54 (May 1988), p 17.
133 G Nicholls, 'Fowler Potteries', *Heritage* 1 (December 1984), pp 7–9.
134 *Sands and Kenny's Commercial and General Sydney Directory* for 1858–59.
135 Cusick, op cit (59), p 38. *Sands* for 1882.
136 G Davison, *The Rise and Fall of Marvellous Melbourne*, MUP, 1979, p 51. W Gemmell, *And So We Graft from Six to Six: The Brickmakers of NSW*, A & R, 1986, pp 17–23.
137 Gemmell, op cit (136), pp 17–23.
138 Ibid, pp 65–69.
139 *ADB*, vol. 3, pp 193–194. R and N Selfe, *John Booth of Balmain, Reminiscences by His Family*, published by the authors, n d.
140 *Sands* for 1891, p 900.
141 *Sands* for 1882, 1886, 1891.
142 *Sands* for 1896.
143 *JNSWLC* 1902, Part 2.
144 Muir, op cit (46), p 37.
145 Ibid, p 239.
146 G Curr, 'Liberalism, Localism and Suburban Development in Melbourne 1870–1900', *Historical Studies* No 74 (1980), pp 41–58. Muir, op cit (46), pp 119–121.
147 M Solling, *LHJ* 15 (1986), pp 35–36.
148 Roberts, op cit (47), p 44.

149 *Glebe Lodge No 96 1881–1981: A Review of the First 100 years of Glebe Lodge* (1981).
150 *Sands* for 1886, 1890.
151 Coghlan, op cit (2). *JNSWLC* 1902, Part 2.
152 *Sands* for 1894.
153 NSW Supreme Court, Probate Office.
154 *ADB*, vol. 4, pp 414–415. H E Holt, *An Energetic Colonist, A Biographical Account of the Activities of the Late Thomas Holt MLC*, Hawthorne Press, Melbourne, 1972.
155 *ADB*, vol. 6, pp 138–139.
156 *ADB*, vol. 3, pp 24–25. JA Froude, *Oceana or England and her Colonies* (1886), pp 194–195.
157 Reynolds, op cit (90).
158 *ADB*, vol. 5, pp 389–390.
159 *ADB*, vol. 5, pp 299–301. A Barnard, *Visions and Profits, Studies in the Business Career of T S Mort*, Melbourne, 1961.
160 Reynolds, op cit (88).
161 LTO TT Purchasers Index 1868–1900.
162 Muir, op cit (46), p 270. *Sands* for 1880. *SM*, 28 February 1906, p 570.
163 Muir, op cit (46), pp 118–120, pp 47–49.
164 *JNSWLC* 1902, Part 2.
165 *SMH*, 26 September 1885. M T Daly, *Sydney Boom, Sydney Bust*, Sydney 1982, p 156.
166 Davison, op cit (136) p 151. T A Coghlan, *Labour and Industry in Australia*, vol. 2, pp 793–794.
167 'Evidence of Joseph Stimson to Select Committee on Increase in House Rents', *V and P NSWLA* 1911–12, vol. 3, pp 783–784.
168 C Fox, *Working Australia*, Allen & Unwin, 1991, pp 79–80. P G McCarthy, 'Wages in Australia 1891 to 1914', *Australian Economic History Review* (March 1970), pp 56–76.
169 Jackson, op cit (39), p 141.
170 Lynch, op cit (28), p 186.
171 Solling, op cit (7), p 114. Carrick, op cit (80), p 175.
172 J A La Nauze, 'A Social Survey of Sydney in 1858', *Historical Studies* (1942–43), vol. 2, pp 264–268. G Aplin, 'The Rise of Suburban Sydney', M Kelly (ed) *Sydney, City of Suburbs*, NSWUP, 1987.
173 M Solling, *LHJ* 1 (1971), pp 14–25.

Chapter 8

1 J R McGuanne, 'Humours and Pastimes of Early Sydney', *JRAHS* 1, pp 34–42.
2 F Engels, *The Condition of the Working Class in England 1845*, Granada, 1969, p 133.
3 *V and P NSWLA* 1870–71, vol. 4, p 70.
4 *Sands* for 1870, 1880.
5 P Bailey, 'Parasexuality and Glamour: The Victorian Barmaid as Cultural Prototype', *Gender and History*, 2 (Summer 1990), pp 150–1.
6 F B Boyce, *The Drink Problem in Australia: The Plagues of Alcohol and the Remedies*, London, 1893, p 139.
7 Bailey, op cit (5), p 150.
8 J M Freeland, *The Australian Pub*, Melbourne, 1966, p 141.
9 R Broome, *Treasure in Earthen Vessels: Protestant Christianity in NSW Society 1900–1914*, UQP 1980, pp 141–149.
10 Ibid, p 141, p 147.
11 A E Dingle, '"The Truly Magnificent Thirst"; An Historical Survey of Australian Drinking Habits', *Historical Studies,* vol. 19 No 75 (October 1980), pp 227–249.

12 *Sands* for 1884, 1886, 1888 and 1890.
13 *Sands* for 1884.
14 'Report of the Intoxicating Drink Inquiry Commission', *V and P NSWLA* 1887–88, vol. 7.
15 *Church Standard,* 17 June 1899. 'NSW Police Department Report 1900', *V and P NSWLA* 1901, vol. 2.
16 *Sands* 1880–90.
17 Broome, op cit (9), p 126, p 128.
18 'Evidence of Rev J Barmier to Select Committee on Sunday Sale of Liquors Prevention Bill', *V and P NSWLA* 1877–78, vol. 4, p 893.
19 *V and P NSWLA* 1877–78, vol. 7, p 153.
20 *V and P NSWLA* 1877–78, vol. 4, p 893.
21 *SMH*, 22 March 1879, p 14.
22 'NSW Police Department Report 1904', *V and P NSWLA* 1905, vol. 3.
23 J F Flitcroft, Interview with M Solling, 30 April 1983.
24 'Royal Commission to Inquire into a Charge Against Sergeant James Hogg of the Police Force', *JNSWLC* Session 1902, part 2, pp 9–36.
25 'Evidence to Select Committee on Tied Houses', *V and P NSWLA* 1901, vol. 6, p 801.
26 Ibid, pp 801.
27 'Evidence of S Davoren', op cit (25), pp 814–818.
28 'Evidence of J M Toohey', op cit (25), p 884.
29 *NSWPD*, 30 October 1905, vol. 20, p 2591.
30 Broome, op cit (9), pp 156–7.
31 Tooth Town Barrel Beer Books 1900–1914.
32 List of acquisition of freehold titles by Tooth's.
33 G T Caldwell, 'From Pub to Club: The History of Drinking Attitudes in NSW (1900–1945) and the Growth of Registered Clubs', *ANUHJ*, vol. 9 (Dec, 1972), p 25.
34 *SMH*, 12 June 1916, p 10.
35 Caldwell, op cit (33), p 25.
36 P Spearritt, *Sydney Since the Twenties*, Hale & Iremonger, 1978, pp 231–5.
37 B Gammage and P Spearritt (eds), *Australians 1938,* pp 356–7.
38 J M Freeland, *The Australian Pub*, Melbourne, 1966, p 179.
39 Caldwell, op cit (33), pp 25–26.
40 *SMH*, 23 May 1928, 31 May 1928.
41 Caldwell, op cit (33), pp 28–29.
42 Royal Commission on Liquor Laws in NSW, 'Report', *NSWPP* 1954, vol. 1, pp 51–155.
43 *SMH*, 5 February 1862, p 1. *SMH*, 7 February 1863, p 12.
44 Broome, op cit (9), pp 144–5.
45 B Davidson, K Hamey and D Nicholls, *Called to the Bar*, Balmain Association, 1991.
46 M Solling, *LHJ* 6 (1975), pp 10–15.
47 *SMH*, 20 July 1985, pp 6–10; 30 May 1985, p 5.
48 *SMH*, 29 September 1990, p19.
49 I Matheson, 'A Question of Conscience: Denominational Education in South-East NSW 1863–1885', 60 *JRAHS*, p 170.
50 B K Hyams and B Bessant, *Schools for the People? An Introduction to The History of State Education in Australia*, Longman, 1972.
51 Annual Report 1862 *V and P NSWLA* 1863–64 vol. 4, p 1073.
52 R J W Selleck, 'State Education and Culture', F B Smith (ed) *Australian Cultural History*, ANU 1988, p 79.
53 'Evidence to Select Committee on Education', *V and P NSWLC* 1844.
54 Selleck, op cit (52), p 80.

55 *ATCJ,* 20 April 1878, p 744.
56 P O'Farrell, *The Catholic Church and Community in Australia. A History*, Nelson 1977, pp 92–3.
57 'Annual Report 1869', *V and P NSWLA* 1870 vol. 2, p 629.
58 J Burnswoods and J Fletcher, *Sydney and the Bush, A Pictorial History of Education in NSW*, Department of Education, 1980, p 45.
59 'Annual Report 1878', *V and P NSWLA* 1875–76 vol. 5, p 115.
60 Graeme Davison, 'The Dimensions of Mobility in Nineteenth Century Australia', *Australia 1888 Bulletin No 2* (1979), p 8, p 12.
61 *SM,* 15 April 1876. R I Francis, 'Schools from the Pupils' Point of View: NSW in the late Colonial Period', *ANZHES Journal,* vol. 8 No 2 (1979), p 28.
62 K Buckley and T Wheelwright, *No Paradise for Workers: Capitalism and the Common People in Australia 1788–1914*, OUP 1988, p 162.
63 'Annual Report 1880', *V and P NSWLA* 1880–81 vol. 2, p 221: 'Annual Report 1885', *V and P NSWLA* 1885–86 vol. 4, p 1, 'Annual Report 1900', *V and P NSWLA* 1901 vol. 3, p 771.
64 B V Hill, 'Training State School Teachers in NSW 1880–1904' A D Spaull (ed) *Australian Teachers: From Colonial Schoolmasters to Militant Professionals*, Melbourne 1977, pp 62–80.
65 'Annual Report 1880', *V and P NSWLA* 1880–81 vol. 2, 1892–93 vol. 3, 'Annual Report 1900', *V and P NSWLA* 1901 vol. 3.
66 P Reynolds, *LHJ* 19 (1995), pp 16–18.
67 Burnswoods and Fletcher, op cit (58), p 103.
68 *Kegworth Public School—Centenary Booklet 1887–1987*, p 6.
69 *The Birchgrove Public School—Centenary Booklet 1885–1985,* p 11.
70 'Annual Report 1886', *V and P NSWLA* 1887, vol. 3, p 555.
71 Op cit (69), p 11.
72 Op cit (68), p 8.
73 Ibid, p 6.
74 *Our History, Annandale Public School 1886–1986*, p 65, p 73.
75 *The Wheeling Years, The Sisters of the Good Samaritan 1857–1957.*
76 *Freeman's Journal,* 29 September 1877.
77 O'Farrell, op cit (56). p 182. J Flower, *LHJ* 8 (1979), pp 8–9.
78 *St Augustine's Church, Balmain, Centenary Booklet 1848–1948,* p 34. H N Birt, *Benedictine Pioneers in Australia*, 2 vols (London 1911).
79 R Fogarty, *Catholic Education in Australia, 1806–1950*, MUP 1959, vol. 2, p 258.
80 O'Farrell, op cit (56), p 211.
81 Fogarty, op cit (79), p 258.
82 Sisters of the Good Samaritan Archives, Glebe.
83 Ibid.
84 A Cusick, *LHJ* 16 (1989), p 40.
85 *St Fiacre's Primary School Leichhardt Centenary Booklet 1894–1994*, p 6.
86 Fogarty, op cit (79), p 357.
87 M Warner, *Visions, Dreams and Memories, The Christian Brothers and Balmain* (1990), p 19.
88 Ibid, p 67.
89 S G Firth, 'Social Values in the NSW Primary Schools 1880–1914: An Analysis of School Texts', R J W Selleck, *Melbourne Studies in Education* (1970), p 137.
90 D Cole '"The Crimson Thread of Kinship": Ethnic Ideas in Australia 1870–1914', *Historical Studies*, vol. 14 No 56 (1971), pp 511–525.
91 S Firth and J Hoorn, 'From Empire Day to Cracker Night', P Spearritt and D Walker (eds) *Australian Popular Culture*, Allen & Unwin, Sydney 1979, pp 17–38.
92 S Macintyre, *The Oxford History of Australia*, OUP 1986, vol. 4 1901–1942, p 133.
93 'Annual Report 1891', *V and P NSWLA* 1892–93 vol. 3, p 779.

94 B Gammage, *The Broken Years, Australian Soldiers in the Great War*, Penguin Books 1974, pp 1–3.
95 Firth, op cit 89, pp 123–159.
96 M Solling, *LHJ* 9 (1980), pp 18–20.
97 J Ramsland, *Children of the Back Lanes: Destitute and Neglected Children in Colonial NSW*, NSWUP, 1986, p 98.
98 J Fletcher and J Burnswoods, *Government Schools in NSW 1848–1983*.
99 Burnswoods and Fletcher, op cit (58), p 164.
100 Reminiscences of John McGlynn, pupil at Glebe Public School 1915 to 1923, 9 November 1992.
101 Fletcher and Burnswoods, op cit (98).
102 Burnswoods and Fletcher, op cit (58), p 140, pp 162–5.
103 Ibid, p 173.
104 'Annual Report 1880', *V and P NSWLA* 1880–81 vol. 2; 'Annual Report 1891' *V and P NSWLA* 1892–93 vol. 3, 'Annual Report 1900', *V and P NSWLA*; 1901 vol. 3.
105 Burnswoods and Fletcher, op cit (58), p 176.
106 Ibid, p 140. Op cit (74), p 63. Op cit (69) p 27. Op cit (68), pp 17–18.
107 Op cit (68), p 18.
108 Op cit (69), p 31.
109 Abstracts of Returns of School Attendance 1900, 1937 NSWSA X1002, X1947.
110 Abstracts of Returns of School Attendance 1900, 1910, 1921, 1931, 1937 NSWSA X1002, X1012, X1934, X1942, X1947.
111 *Balmain Primary School,* (1994). P Reynolds, *On the Pigeon Ground, Balmain Public School, 1859–1961, Balmain Historical Monograph No 1* (LHJ, 1995).
112 Abstracts of Returns of School Attendance 1900, 1910, 1921, 1931, 1937 NSWSA X1002, X1012, X1934, X1942, X1947.
113 Burnswoods and Fletcher, op cit (58), p 224.
114 Abstracts of Returns of School Attendance 1900, 1937 NSWSA X1002, X1947.
115 Op cit (74), p 70. Op cit (69), p 35. Op cit (68), p 18.
116 *Married Women (Lecturers and Teachers) Act 1932*.
117 S Macintyre, *Winners and Losers, The Pursuit of Social Justice in Australian History*, Allen & Unwin, Sydney, 1985, pp 98–9.
118 P H Karmel, 'Some Arithmetic of Education', E L French (ed) *Melbourne Studies in Education in 1966*, MUP, 1967, p 6. B Bessant and A D Spaull, *Politics of Schooling*, Melbourne Pitman, 1976, Chapter 2.
119 *Commonwealth of Australia Census 1947*.
120 The *National Times*, 14–19 January 1974, p 13. H Kendig, *New Life for Old Suburbs*, Allen & Unwin, Sydney, 1979. *Commonwealth of Australia Census 1976*.
121 Burnswoods and Fletcher, op cit (58), p 213.
122 A Barcan, *A History of Australian Education*, OUP, Melbourne, p 369.
123 Macintyre, op cit (117), p 101.
124 Burnswoods and Fletcher, op cit (58), p 212.
125 Ibid, p 215.
126 Fletcher and Burnswoods, op cit (98). *Glebe High School, The First Ten Years* (1989), p 72.
127 P Spearritt, *Sydney Since the Twenties*, pp 207–208.
128 G Bolton, *The Oxford History of Australia*, OUP, Melbourne, 1990, p 114.
129 R W Connell et al., *Making the Difference: Schools, Families and Social Division* (Allen & Unwin, 1982).
130 Anglican churches generally occupied prominent sites while Primitive Methodist chapels and Salvation Army barracks were found in poor, less desirable localities.

131 P Reynolds, *LHJ* 19 (1995), pp 16–22. R Withycombe, 'Church of England Attitudes to Social Questions in the Diocese of Sydney *c*.1856–1866', *JRAHS* 47, p 104. M Askew, 'Praying, Paying and Obeying', V Burgmann and J Lee (eds), *Constructing a Culture*, Penguin, 1988.

132 '1871 Census', *V and P NSWLA* 1873–74, vol. 3.

133 Op cit (78), p 16, p 21.

134 W W Phillips, 'Religious Profession and Practice in New South Wales 1850–1901: The Statistical Evidence', *Historical Studies* (1972), vol. 15, pp 378–400.

135 G Davison, L W McCarty and A McLeary (eds), *Australians 1888*, Fairfax Syme and Weldon, 1988, pp 350–354.

136 Annual Reports of the Glebe Presbyterian Church 1875–1909 (Ferguson Memorial Library).

137 D Hilliard, 'Anglicanism', S L Goldberg and F B Smith (eds), *Australian Cultural History*, CUP, Sydney, 1988, p 16.

138 Joan Kerr, *Our Great Victorian Architect, Edmund Thomas Blacket (1817–1883)*, National Trust of Australia (NSW), 1983.

139 J Barrett, *That Better Country, The Religious Aspect of Life in Eastern Australia 1835–1850*, MUP, 1966, pp 153–154.

140 K S Inglis, *The Australian Colonists, An Exploration of Social History 1788–1870*, MUP, 1974, p 80.

141 Withycombe, op cit (131), p 104.

142 *ADB*, vol. 7, pp 85–86.

143 J Cashman, *St Mary's Balmain, For Which to Give Thanks*, GSBE, UNSW, 1986, pp 10–11.

144 J K Wright, *St John's Church, Balmain* (St John's Balmain Centenary Committee, 1981), p 20.

145 St John's Bishopthorpe, Glebe, Service Book, Register 1866–1902. All Saints' Anglican Church, Leichhardt Jubilee Booklet 1882–1932, pp 2–6.

146 M Solling, *LHJ* 4 (1973), p 11. D S Macmillan, *Scotland and Australia 1788–1850*, Clarendon Press, Oxford, 1967.

147 Presbyterian Church of Australia, NSW Blue Book—Minutes of Proceedings of the General Assembly 1901.

148 *The Presbyterian*, 11 February 1898. J Cameron, *Centenary History of the Presbyterian Church in NSW*, Sydney, 1905.

149 *ADB*, vol. 3, pp 466–467. *ADB*, vol. 4, p 302. Solling, op cit (146), p 10.

150 A Roberts and E Malcolm, *Hunter Baillie: A History of the Presbyterian Church in Annandale* (1973), pp 12–16. J Williams, *LHJ* 17 (1993), pp 3–14.

151 R B Walker 'Presbyterian Church and People in the Colony of NSW in the Late Nineteenth Century', *Journal of Religious History* (1962), vol. 2, p 49.

152 R B Walker, 'The Growth and Typology of the Wesleyan Methodist Church in NSW 1812–1901', *Journal of Religious History* (1971), vol. 6, pp 331–345. J Colwell, *The Illustrated History of Methodism*, W Brooks, Sydney, 1904.

153 *SMH*, 12 May 1928, p 18. *Weekly Advocate*, 13 December 1890, p 315. *SMH*, 19 June 1936, p 10. *ADB*, vol. 4, p 234.

154 R Broome, op cit (9), p 134.

155 The *Methodist*, 4 March 1905.

156 W G Taylor, *Life Story of an Australian Evangelist*, Epworth Press, London, 1920, pp 118–122. Circuit Books Glebe 1882–84, Annual Report of Glebe Road Wesleyan Church 1883.

157 *ADB*, vol. 12, pp 188–189.

158 W A Stewart, *Early History of the Loyal Orange Institution NSW*, Grand Lodge NSW, Sydney, 1926. *SMH*, 5 March 1879, p 1. L G Lynch, 'A Community Study—Balmain *c*.1860–1894', PhD thesis, University of Sydney, 1981, p 458.

159 E Rule Taylor, *A Brief History of the Balmain Masonic Lodge*, S T Leigh & Co, Sydney, 1909.

Glebe Lodge No 96 1881–1981: A Review of the First Hundred Years of Glebe Lodge (1981). *Lodge Wentworth No 89 1881–1891: Centenary History* (1981).

160 O'Farrell, op cit (56), pp 180–184. *Australian Catholic Directory*.

161 P O'Farrell, *The Irish in Australia*, UNSW Press, 1986, pp 22–53. C McConville, 'Catholics and Mobility in Melbourne and Sydney 1861–1891', *Australia 1888 Bulletin No 2* (1979), pp 55–65.

162 W W Phillips, 'The Social Composition of Religious Denominations in Late Nineteenth Century Australia', *Church Heritage* (1985), pp 77–94.

163 J Hagan and K Turner, *A History of the Labor Party in NSW 1891–1991*, Longman Cheshire, 1991, pp 25–26.

164 J Fletcher, *St James Church, Forest Lodge: A Chronicle 1877–1977*, p 7.

165 Sydney Diocesan Archives, St Mary's Cathedral, Leichhardt, St Fiacre's Church 1896, 1916, Box C 2418.

166 Sydney Diocesan Archives, Balmain, St Augustine's 1915, 1918, Folder C1629–2 (1857–1918).

167 Broome, op cit (9), p xiii.

168 Hagan and Turner, op cit (163), p 114, p 122.

169 B Ussher, 'The Salvation War', G Davison, D Dunstan and C McConville, *The Outcasts of Melbourne*, Allen & Unwin, Sydney, 1985.

170 B Bolton, *Booth's Drum, The Salvation Army in Australia 1880–1980*, Hodder & Stoughton, Sydney, 1980, pp 12–16.

171 W Phillips, *Defending 'A Christian Country', Churchmen and Society in NSW in the 1880s and After*, UQP, 1981, p 41, p 75.

172 F G Clancy, 'The Primitive Methodist Church in NSW 1845–1902', MA thesis, Macquarie Univ, 1985. H Carruthers, *Rehoboth Methodist Church, Forest Lodge Primitive Methodist Circuit* (1921).

173 *SMH*, 25 January 1894.

174 G L Lockley, 'The Foundation, Development and Influence of Congregationalism in Australia, with Emphasis on the Nineteenth Century', PhD thesis, University of Queensland, 1966.

175 A C Prior, *Some Fell on Good Ground: A History of the Beginning and Development of the Baptist Church in NSW 1831–1965*, Baptist Union of NSW, 1966.

176 C Booth, *Life and Labour of the People in London, Final Volume: Notes on Social Influences and Conclusion*, Macmillan, London, 1903, p 205.

177 Broome, op cit (9), p xi. J Jackson, 'Moving House and Changing Churches: the Case of the Melbourne Congregationalists', *Historical Studies* 74 (1980), pp 74–85.

178 The *Methodist*, 23 September 1899, p 8.

179 *Churchman*, 7 August 1896. P Kaldor, *A Gulf Too Deep? The Protestant Churches and the Urban Working Class in Australia* (1983), pp 22–33.

180 J E Carruthers, *Suburban Methodism* (Sydney, 1901).

181 F B Boyce, *Fourscore Years and Seven, The Memoirs of Archdeacon Boyce*, A and R, Sydney, 1934, pp 97–102.

182 *ADB*, vol. 12, pp 64–65. D Wright and E G Clancy, *The Methodists: A History of Methodism in NSW*, Allen & Unwin, 1993, p 114.

183 Wright and Clancy, op cit (182), pp 114–115. The *Methodist*, 7 November 1903, pp 3–4; 5 March 1904, p 10.

184 T W Lacquer, *Religion and Respectability: Sunday Schools and Working Class Culture 1788–1850*, New Haven, 1976. J D Bollen, *Protestantism and Social Reform in NSW, 1890–1910*, MUP, 1972, Appendix, Table 4, p 186.

185 Davison, et al., op cit (135), p 225.

186 M Gilmore, *Old Days, Old Ways*, Sydney, 1934, pp 66–70.

187 S Humphries, *Hooligans or Rebels: An Oral History of Working Class Children and Youth 1889–1939*, Blackwell, Oxford, 1981, p 131.
188 General Returns—Minutes of NSW Methodist Conference. Proceedings of the General Assembly of the Presbyterian Church of Australia.
189 Minutes of NSW Methodists Conference 1890, 1900, 1910, 1920. Bollen, op cit (184), p 186.
190 Minutes of Proceedings of Presbyterian Church of Australia, NSW Blue Book 1901. J Williams, *LHJ* 16 (1989), pp 7–14.
191 St John's Bishopthorpe, Glebe, Sunday School Journal 1899–1906. R Best, *Annals from Aidan's in Annandale* (1992), p 32.
192 St Mary's, Balmain, Annual Report 1897–98. *All Souls', Leichhardt, Parish Paper*, 1 October 1907–1 June 1909.
193 The honour rolls and memorials reflect the extent of involvement by their respective communities.
194 *All Souls' Church of England Leichhardt, Jubilee 1822–1932*, p 7.
195 Roberts and Malcolm, op cit (150), p 25.
196 Best, op cit (191), pp 36–37. Roberts and Malcolm, op cit (150), pp 25–26.
197 T A Coghlan, *Report on the Eleventh Census of NSW*, Sydney, 1894. *1933 Census, Commonwealth of Australia*.
198 Phillips, op cit (171), pp 378–400.
199 C McConville, *Croppies, Celts and Catholics: The Irish in Australia*, Edward Arnold, 1987, p 68.
200 Minutes of Proceedings of Presbyterian Church of Australia – NSW General Assembly 1881.
201 Ibid, 1911.
202 Ibid, 1931.
203 All Souls', Leichhardt, Service Book Register 1922, 1930, 1940.
204 St John's, Balmain North, Service Book Register, 1905, 1910, 1920, 1930, 1940.
205 St John's Bishopthorpe, Glebe, Service Book Register 1915, 1920, 1930, 1940. K Percival, *A History of St John's Glebe* (1987), pp 89–143.
206 General Returns—Minutes of NSW Methodist Conference 1883, 1890, 1900, 1910, 1930.
207 Ibid, 1900, 1910, 1940.
208 Ibid, 1910, 1940. *The Leichhardt Story, Leichhardt Methodist Mission*, Leichhardt, 1963.
209 J Owen, *The Heart of the City, The First 125 Years of the Sydney City Mission*, Kangaroo Press, 1987, pp 11–46.
210 P Kaldor, '"Benevolent Picknicking"?—A Case Study of Community Work under Church Auspices', M Urban Studies, Macquarie Univ, 1981, pp 57–66.
211 Fletcher, op cit (164), p 15.
212 The *Methodist*, 25 May 1929, p 16.
213 B G Judd, *He That Doeth: The Life Story of Archdeacon R B S Hammond*, Marshall Morgan & Scott, London, 1951, p 57.
214 The *Methodist*, 12 July 1941, p 1.
215 M Solling, *LHJ* 18 (1994), p 10.
216 Solling, *LHJ* 4 (1973), p 13.
217 *Report of Inner City Commission of Inquiry 1969*, Church of England in Australia, Diocese of Sydney p 10, p 14.
218 R J Horvath, G Harrison and R M Dowling, *Sydney, A Social Atlas* (1989), p 82.
219 H Mol, *The Faith of Australians,* Allen & Unwin, 1985.
220 *SMH,* 17 April 1995, p 3.

Chapter 9

1. SDC.
2. *SMH*, 29 June 1881, p 6. W Maddock, *Visitor's Guide to Sydney* (1872), p 89. 'PSCPW with Minutes of Evidence and Plans Relating to the Removal of the Public Abattoir from Glebe Island', *V and P NSWLA* 1902, vol. 3, p 7.
3. *SMH*, 24 August 1853.
4. *ISN*, 7 October 1854.
5. L G Lynch, 'A Community Study, Balmain 1860–1894', PhD thesis, University of Sydney, 1981, pp 115–123.
6. L Lynch, 'T S Mort, His Dock and Balmain Labour', M Kelly (ed) *Nineteenth Century Sydney*, SUP, 1978.
7. *NSWSR* 1889. S Fitzgerald, *Rising Damp, Sydney 1870–1890*, OUP 1987, pp 157–158.
8. R Morris, 'The NSW Ship Painters And Dockers 1900–1914: A Small Union and the Institutionalisation of Industrial Relations', *Labour History* No 43 (1982), pp 14–15.
9. I Wyner, *With Banner Unfurled, The Early Years of the Ship Painters' and Dockers' Union*, Hale & Iremonger, Sydney, 1983, pp 28–29.
10. L Brignell, *Mort's Dock and Engineering Company Site—Balmain, Report to the Heritage Council of NSW 1984*, pp 9–13.
11. *ADB*, vol. 3, pp 193–194. P Reynolds, *LHJ* 20 (1996), pp 24–30.
12. *SMH*, 23 June 1866. G J R Linge, *Industrial Awakening, A Geography of Australian Manufacturing 1788–1890*, ANU Press, 1979, p 475. *ADB* vol. 8, p 431.
13. R Markey, *The Making of the Labor Party in NSW 1880–1900*, UNSW Press, 1988, pp 28–31.
14. *NSWSR* 1889.
15. *NSWSR* 1881, 1883, 1887, 1888.
16. *Sands* for 1889.
17. P Proudfoot, 'The Extension of Maritime Activity in Sydney: Pyrmont, Glebe Island and Balmain 1890–1950', *The Great Circle*, vol. 10 (1988), pp 110–135. 'PSCPW relating to the Proposed Goods Railway from Flemington to Belmore and Wardell Road to Glebe Island and Darling Island', *NSWPP* 1910, vol. 3, p viii. 'PSCPW on Authorised Goods Line Darling Harbour to Rozelle', *NSWPP* 1914–15, vol. 5, pp 691–721.
18. Sydney Harbour Trust Commissioners, Annual Report 1914.
19. Proudfoot, op cit (17), p 112.
20. *NSWSR 1880, 1888.*
21. *SM,* 23 June 1888, p 1323.
22. *Sands* for 1889. The *Echo*, 26 June 1890. *DT*, 9 January 1889.
23. *Sands* for 1882.
24. 'Leichhardt: A History of Its Progress', The *Echo*, 17 July 1890.
25. *Sands* for 1889.
26. 'Final report on the Sydney City and Suburban Sewerage Health Board', *V and P NSWLA* 1875–76, vol. 8, pp 551–659.
27. 'Returns under the *Census and Industrial Returns Act 1891*, *V and P NSWLA* 1891–92, vol. 7, pp 1079–1118.
28. 'Select Committee on the Employment of Children', *V and P NSWLA* 1875–76, vol. 6, pp 889–890.
29. Ibid, pp 916–918.
30. G P Walsh, 'Factories and Factory Workers in NSW 1788–1900', *Labour History* No 21 (1971), pp 1–16.
31. 'Report on the Working of the *Factories and Shops Act 1900*', *V and P NSWLA* 1901, vol. 6, pp 716–746.

32 G J R Linge, 'The Forging of an Industrial Nation: Manufacturing in Australia 1788–1913', J M Powell and M Williams (eds) *Australian Space, Australian Time*, OUP, 1975, pp 163–165.
33 D N Jeans, 'The Incorporation of Australia', D N Jeans (ed) *Space and Society*, SUP, 1987, pp 16–18.
34 P Spearritt, *Sydney Since the Twenties*, Hale & Iremonger, 1978, pp 117–121.
35 K Bak, *A Lever and Kitchen Album*, Lever & Kitchen Pty Ltd, 1988, pp 18–24.
36 P Reynolds, *The Coal Mine under the Harbour, Balmain Places 2* (1986). Royal Commission of Inquiry on Coal and Shale Mines in the State of NSW, 'Report and Minutes', *NSWPP* 1926, vol. 3, pp 163–176.
37 K Hamey, 'Heritage Aspects of the Peninsula Power Stations', *Balmain Association News Sheet*, December 1993, p 3. D Godden & Associates and Heritage Consultants, *The Significance of White Bay and Balmain Power Stations to Sydney's Industrial Heritage, A Report to the Electricity Commission of NSW 1989*, p 21.
38 S Fitzgerald, *Sydney 1842–1992*, Hale & Iremonger, 1992, p 235. Godden et al., p 34.
39 R Thornton and A W Sommerville, *Retrospect, Municipality of Balmain 1860–1935*, pp 39–51.
40 *Sands* for 1912, 1918.
41 *Sands* for 1918
42 *ADB*, vol. 11, pp 187–188.
43 *Sands* for 1932–33. A Vialoux and C M Reeves, *The Jubilee History of Leichhardt 1921*, pp 49–50, 79–80, 86–87.
44 *Sands* for 1918.
45 *ADB*, vol. 7, pp 225–226.
46 *Sands* for 1932–33.
47 Calculated from *Sands* for 1932–33. Factory numbers in *NSW Year Book 1944–45*, p 617.
48 *NSW Year Book 1944–45*, p 615.
49 Spearritt, op cit (34), pp 115–118. M Logan, 'Manufacturing Decentralisation in the Sydney Metropolitan Area', *Economic Geography* 40 (1964), pp 151–161.
50 R Horvath, *Sydney: A Social Atlas* (1989), p 44.
51 *Inner Voice*, March 1986, p 8. *Leichhardt Municipality Population Profile* (Leichhardt Council), 1990
52 F Low, *The City of Sydney Directory 1844–45*; F Low, *The City of Sydney Directory 1847*; W and F Ford, *Sydney Directory 1851*; *Waugh & Cox's Directory of Sydney and Its Suburbs 1855*.
53 *Sands* for 1880, 1886, 1888.
54 *Sands* for 1893, 1904.
55 *Sands* for 1900.
56 *Balmain Municipal Council Souvenir to Commemorate the 50th Anniversary of the Incorporation of the Municipality of Balmain 1860–1910*, pp 73–80. *Sands* for 1884.
57 'Leichhardt: A History of Its Progress', op cit (24).
58 Ford, op cit (52). Waugh and Cox, op cit (52)
59 Surveyor John Heady, Field Book—Glebe 1861–62, Department of Lands.
60 *Sands* for 1890.
61 Balmain Municipal Council, op cit (56). M Salmon, 'Balmain: One of the Most Important Suburbs of Sydney', *ATCJ*, 10 December 1902, pp 26–27.
62 *Sands* for 1890. The *Echo* 26 June 1890.
63 *Sands* for 1928.
64 *Sands* for 1890.
65 'Leichhardt, Annandale and Camperdown', *ATCJ*, 18 November 1899, pp 32–39. *Sands* for 1910.
66 *Sands* for 1910. Mills and Pile Papers 1879–1898, A2737, ML.
67 B Kingston, *Basket, Bag and Trolley, A History of Shopping in Australia*, OUP 1994, pp 44–45.

68 D Kernohan, Interview with M Solling, 27 January 1984.
69 P Reynolds, 'Corner Shops—a Record of their Genesis and Location', unpublished, 1995.
70 *Sands* for 1895, 1932–33.
71 Reynolds, op cit (69).
72 Kernohan, interview.
73 The number of retailers is based on *Sands* for 1918 and 1932–33.
74 *Sands* for 1932–33.
75 B Little, '"Up the Street" and "Down the Street"—Shopping Locally', *Heritage 1* (December 1984), pp 5–7.
76 *Sands* for 1903, 1932–33.
77 *Sands* for 1915, 1920, 1925.
78 Compiled from *Sands* for 1932–33.
79 Kingston, op cit (67), p 58.
80 F Pollon, *Shopkeepers and Shoppers*, Retail Traders Association of NSW, 1989.
81 N Brash, *The Model Store 1885–1985, Grace Bros*, Weldon—N Brash, 1985, p 13. *ADB*, vol. 9, p 65.
82 S Oulds, Interview with P Reynolds, 16 November 1995.
83 *Sands* for 1918.

Chapter 10

1 L J Hume, 'Working Class Movements in Sydney and Melbourne Before the Gold Rushes', *Historical Studies*, vol. 9 no 35 (1960), pp 263–278.
2 R A Gollan, *Radical Working Class Politics: A Study of Eastern Australia 1850–1910*, MUP, 1960, pp 69–84. 'Labor' is used throughout this chapter.
3 J Niland, 'The Birth of the Movement for an Eight Hour Working Day in NSW', *AJPH*, vol. 14 no 1 (1968), pp 75–87.
4 K D Buckley, *The Amalgamated Engineers in Australia 1852–1900*, Canberra, 1970, Chapter 1.
5 J Niland, 'In Search of Shorter Hours, The 1861 and 1874 Iron Trades Disputes', *Labour History* 12 (1967) pp 3–15.
6 R Markey, *The Making of the Labor Party in NSW 1880–1900*, NSWUP, 1988, pp 136–170.
7 B Nairn, *Civilising Capitalism. The Labor Movement in NSW 1870–1900*, ANU Press, 1973, pp 8–19.
8 Markey, op cit (6), pp 28–55.
9 G N Hawker, *The Parliament of NSW 1856–1965*, Government Printer, Sydney, 1971, pp 1–10.
10 P Loveday, 'The Legislative Council of New South Wales 1856–1870', *Historical Studies* 44 (April 1965).
11 Hawker, op cit (9), p 15.
12 Ibid.
13 P Loveday and A W Martin, *Parliament, Factions and Parties: The First Thirty Years of Responsible Government in NSW 1856–1889*, MUP, 1966, p 1.
14 Ibid, p 52.
15 A W Martin, 'The Legislative Assembly of NSW 1856–1900', *AJPH* 2 (1956). Hawker, op cit (9), p 16.
16 *ADB*, vol. 1, p 199; *SMH*, 7, 10, 14, 15 June 1859.
17 *ADB*, vol. 6, pp 138–9; *SMH*, 30 May 1881.
18 *SMH*, 13 December 1869, p 5; *SMH*, 20 February 1872, p 5.
19 *SMH*, 10, 12 December 1874.

20 *SMH*, 24, 27 March 1875.
21 *ADB*, vol. 4, p 234.
22 *SMH*, 24 October 1877, p 7.
23 *Bulletin*, 30 October 1880, p 3.
24 L Lynch, 'A Community Study—Balmain *c*.1860–1894', PhD thesis, University of Sydney, 1982, pp 511–513.
25 Loveday and Martin, op cit (13). A W Martin and P Wardle, *Members of the Legislative Assembly of NSW 1856–1901*, Canberra, 1959.
26 TLC minutes, 15, 22 October 1873.
27 Martin, op cit (15).
28 Lynch, op cit (24), pp 375–378. J Niland, op cit (5), pp 3–15.
29 J Hagan and K Turner, *A History of the Labor Party in NSW 1891–1991*, Longman Cheshire, 1991, p 15. Markey, op cit (6), pp 28–30.
30 S Fitzgerald, *Rising Damp, Sydney 1870–1890*, OUP, 1987, p 154.
31 'Evidence of J A Brodie and P C Lucas, Mayors of Balmain and Glebe, to the Royal Commission on City and Suburban Railways', *V and P NSWLA* 1891–2 vol. 5, pp 18–22, pp 22–23. G P Walsh, 'Factories and Factory Workers in NSW 1788–1900', *Labour History* 21 (1971) pp 1–16.
32 G Davison, 'The Australian Energy System in 1888', *Australia 1888, Bulletin* 10 (1982) pp 7, 9.
33 'Report of NSW Agent-General on Immigration from the United Kingdom', *V and P NSWLA* 1883–4, vol. 6, pp 4–12.
34 P G Macarthy, 'Labor and the Living Wage 1890–1910', *AJPH* vol. 13 (1967), pp 67–89.
35 S Fisher, 'The Family and the Sydney Economy in the Late Nineteenth Century', P Grimshaw, C McConville and E McEwen (eds) *Families in Colonial Australia*, Allen & Unwin, 1985, pp 153–162.
36 G Davison, 'Capital Cities', G Davison, J W McCarty and A McLeary (eds), *Australians 1888*, p 102.
37 Loveday, op cit (10), pp 16–19.
38 Nairn, op cit (7), pp 28–31.
39 Ibid, pp 20–32.
40 R Gollan, *Radical and Working Class Politics: A Study of Eastern Australia 1850–1910*, MUP, 1960, pp 128–135.
41 Nairn, op cit (7), pp 42–47.
42 R Markey, op cit (6), pp 175–6. L Lynch, op cit (24), pp 506–507. I. Wyner, *With Banner Unfurled*, Hale & Iremonger, 1983, pp 16–17, 102–108, 201–203.
43 *Australian Workman*, 4, 11, 18 April 1891.
44 Lynch, op cit (24), p 510.
45 Nairn, op cit (7), pp 59.
46 Ibid, pp 61–3.
47 *Bulletin*, 18 March 1893, pp 6–7.
48 R Markey, 'The Aristocracy of Labour and Productive Reorganisation in NSW *c*.1880–1900', *Australian Economic History Review* vol. 28 (1988), pp 43–59. R Gray, *The Aristocracy of Labour in Nineteenth-Century Britain c.1850–1914*, Macmillan, London, 1981, Chapter 4.
49 K Buckley and E Wheelwright, *No Paradise for Workers: Capitalism and the Common People in Australia 1788–1914*, OUP, 1988, pp 141–143.
50 Ibid. V Burgmann, *'In our Time', Socialism and the Rise of Labor 1885–1905*, Allen & Unwin, 1985, pp 7–18.
51 Buckley and Wheelwright, op cit (49), pp 160–161
52 L G Churchward, 'The American Influence on the Australian Labour Movement', *Historical Studies* vol. 5 (1952), pp 258–266.

53 *ADB*, vol. 4, pp 241–242.
54 P J O'Farrell, 'The Australian Socialist League and the Labour Movement 1887–1891', *Historical Studies* vol. 8 (1958), pp 152–65. Buckley and Wheelwright, op cit (49), pp 125–126.
55 V Burgmann, op cit (50), pp 363–7.
56 *ADB,* vol. 9 pp 393–400.
57 Burgmann, op cit (50), p 49.
58 *ADB,* vol. 9 pp 340–347.
59 V Burgmann, op cit (50), p 36, p 56.
60 The *Workman,* 21 February 1891.
61 F Cotton, 'Millennium or Pandemonium?' in *The Prophet of San Francisco: Inaugural Address to the Land Nationalisation Associates of NSW*, Bathurst 1888.
62 B Scates, '"Millennium or Pandemonium?": Radicalism in the Labour Movement in Sydney 1889–1899', *Labour History* 50 (1986), pp 77–83.
63 Burgmann, op cit (50), p 49.
64 F Picard, 'Henry George and the Labour Split of 1891', *Historical Studies* 21 (1953), pp 45–63.
65 Scates, op cit (62), pp 89–94.
66 'Royal Commission on Strikes, Sydney 1891', *NSWPP* 1891 Second Session, p 1002. Precis of evidence, pp 244–246.
67 Scates, op cit (62), p 78.
68 Lynch, op cit (24), pp 506–509.
69 *Australian Workman,* 3, 5 December 1891.
70 Scates, op cit (62), pp 85–6.
71 *Australian Workman,* 12 March 1892.
72 Buckley and Wheelwright, op cit (49), pp 185–198.
73 C A Hughes and B D Graham, *Voting for the NSW Legislative Assembly 1890–1964*, ANU, 1975 pp 19–44.
74 Ibid, pp 63–85
75 Hagan and Turner, op cit (29), p 26.
76 Nairn, op cit (7), pp 80–3, 101–103.
77 P Ford, *Cardinal Moran and the ALP*, MUP, 1965, pp 265–267, 270–271.
78 R Gollan, 'The Ideology of the Labour Movement', pp 206–226, K Buckley and E Wheelwright (eds) *Essays in the Political Economy of Australian Capitalism*, ANZ Book Co. 1975, vol. 1 .
79 R W Connell and T H Irving, *Class Structure in Australian History*, Longman Cheshire, 1980, p 197. Markey, op cit (6), pp 230–256.
80 Hagan and Turner, op cit (29), pp 25–26.
81 Ibid, pp 26–31.
82 R N Ebbels, *The Australian Labor Movement 1850–1907*, Australasian Book Society, 1960, p 232.
83 Ibid, pp 28–31.
84 The occupations of these early councillors were quarryman, carpenter, plasterer, blacksmith and brickmaker.
85 R Markey, 'The Emergence of the Labor Party at the Municipal Level in NSW 1891–1900', *AJPH* 31 (1985), pp 408–417. Markey, op cit (6), pp 233–235.
86 *SMH,* 24 January 1908, p 6. *SMH,* 30 January 1911, p 3.
87 *ADB,* vol. 12, p 494.
88 *ADB,* vol. 10, pp 11–12.
89 *SMH,* 6 November 1925, p 12.
90 *SMH,* 14 December 1938, p 19.
91 *DT,* 19 July 1894, p 5.

92 *ADB*, vol. 7, pp 562–564.
93 *SMH,* 16 March 1918, 13 April 1918.
94 *DT,* 22 June 1894. *SMH,* 30 July 1918.
95 *ADB*, vol. 9, pp 110–112. J D Bollen, *Protestantism and Social Reform in NSW 1890–1910*, MUP, 1972, p 160, pp 164–165.
96 *ADB,* vol. 9, p 374. Nairn, op cit (7), pp 27–28.
97 *ADB,* vol. 9, pp 325–6.
98 R Broome, *Treasure in Earthen Vessels. Protestant Christianity in NSW Society 1900–1914*, UQP, 1980, p 117.
99 Ibid, p 109.
100 Ibid, pp 118–119.
101 Bollen, op cit (95), p 149.
102 *DT,* 20, 22 July 1904.
103 *DT,* 11 August 1904, p 4.
104 Bollen, op cit (95), p 167.
105 Hagan and Turner, op cit (29), pp 53, 55.
106 Hughes and Graham, op cit (73), pp 146–160. Hagan and Turner, op cit (29), p 262.
107 Ibid, p 101.
108 *ADB,* vol. 9, pp 544–545.
109 *ADB,* vol. 12, pp 106–108.
110 Loveday, op cit (10), p 98.
111 Hagan and Turner, op cit (29), p 108.
112 Loveday, op cit (10), p 98
113 Hagan and Turner, op cit (29), p 112.

Chapter 11

1 C J Baker, *Sydney and Melbourne* (1845), p 135.
2 *SMH*, 6 November 1850.
3 M Solling, *LHJ* 1 (1971), pp 14–17.
4 *SMH*, 8 March 1851, p 2.
5 'Report from the Select Committee on Slaughter Houses 1848', *V and P NSWLC* 1848.
6 'Evidence of Dr F Campbell to Select Committee on Slaughter Houses', *V and P NSWLC* 1848. *SMH*, 7 June 1848, pp 2–3.
7 A J C Mayne, *Fever, Squalor and Vice: Sanitation and Social Policy in Victorian Sydney*, UQP, St Lucia, 1982, pp 23–36.
8 P H Curson, *Times of Crisis*, SUP, 1985, pp 58–61.
9 Mayne, op cit (7), p 27.
10 T A Coghlan, T*he Wealth and Progress of NSW 1886–87*, Sydney, 1887, p 177.
11 Mayne, op cit (7), p 24.
12 S Fisher, 'The Pastoral Interest and Sydney's Public Health', *Historical Studies* 78 (1982), p 74.
13 D G Hamilton, *Hand in Hand: The Story of the Royal Alexandra Hospital for Children, Sydney*, Ferguson, 1979, pp 10–35.
14 *BO*, 3 May 1916.
15 *V and P NSWLA* 1876–77, vol. 8, p 540.
16 '11th Progress Report, Sydney City and Suburban Sewage and Health Board', *V and P NSWLA* 1875–76, vol. 5, p 586.
17 F B Boyce, *Fourscore Years and Seven, The Memoirs of Archdeacon Boyce*, Angus & Roberston, Sydney 1934, p 97.

18 M Solling, *LHJ* 15 (1986), p 37.
19 'PSCPW, Report together with Minutes of Evidence Relating to the Proposed Drainage Works for the Western Suburbs', *V and P NSWLA* 1889, vol. 4, pp 83–85.
20 Ibid, pp 73–82.
21 M Lewis, 'Milk, Mothers and Infant Welfare', J Roe (ed) *Twentieth Century Sydney: Studies in Urban and Social History*, Hale & Iremonger, 1980, pp 193–194.
22 'Royal Commission into Noxious and Offensive Trades', *JNSWLC* 1883, vol. 3, pp 177–299.
23 L G Lynch, 'A Community Study, Balmain 1860–1894', PhD thesis, University of Sydney, 1981, pp 257–260.
24 'Board Appointed to Inquire into and Report upon the Condition and Management of the Public Abattoir, Glebe Island', *V and P NSWLA* 1878–79, vol. 7, pp 497–618, and 1879–80, vol. 5, pp 871–980.
25 Lynch, op cit (23), pp 261–262.
26 'Evidence of G F Williamson to Select Committee on the Abattoir, Glebe Island', *NSWPP* 1902, vol. 3, pp 665–833.
27 Lynch, op cit (23), pp 254–256.
28 'Select Committee on Balmain General Cemetery', *V and P NSWLA* 1881, vol. 5, p 140.
29 'Progress Report of the Royal Commission on City and Suburban Railways', *V and P NSWLA* 1891–92, vol. 5, p 2141.
30 'Report Relating to the Proposed Railway to Connect the North Shore with Port Jackson', *V and P NSWLA* 1889, vol. 2, p 324.
31 F M Jones, 'The Aesthetic of the Nineteenth-Century Industrial Town', H J Dyos (ed) *The Study of Urban History*, Edward Arnold, London, 1968, pp 171–182.
32 M Cannon, *Life in the Cities*, Thomas Nelson, 1975, pp 128–177. D Dunstan, 'Dirt and Disease', G Davison, D Dunstan and C McConville, *The Outcasts of Melbourne*, Allen & Unwin, 1985, pp 140–171.
33 *ATCJ*, 18 November 1899, pp 32–39; 10 December 1902, pp 26–37. 'Royal Commission into Noxious and Offensive Trades', *JNSWLC* 1883, vol. 3, pp 177–299.
34 *Sands* for 1885.
35 'Report on the Outbreak of Typhoid Fever in Municipal District of Leichhardt Due to Polluted Milk', *V and P NSWLA* 1885–86, vol. 4, pp 585–608.
36 Lewis, op cit (21), p 197.
37 Board of Health Minute Book 1890–1891, NSWA 4937, p 498.
38 Lewis, op cit (21), p 197.
39 *Sands* for 1918, 1932–33.
40 F Adams, *The Australians* (1893).
41 'Report on the Outbreak of Plague at Sydney', *V and P NSWLA* 1900, vol. 2. Fourteen cases of plague were notified in Balmain in 1900, see Register, Notification and Prevention Of Infectious Disease (Leichhardt Central Library).
42 M Kelly, 'Picturesque and Pestilential: The Sydney Slum Observed 1860–1900', M Kelly (ed) *Nineteenth-Century Sydney: Essays in Urban History*, SUP, 1978, pp 61–80.
43 Curson, op cit (8), pp 140–147.
44 M Kelly, *A Certain Sydney 1900*, Doak Press, pp 1–9.
45 A O'Brien, *Poverty's Prison, The Poor in NSW 1880–1918*, MUP, 1988, p 20.
46 'Royal Commission for the Improvement of the City of Sydney and Its Suburbs', *V and P NSWLA* 1909, vol. 5, pp 379–703.
47 *ADB*, vol. 8, pp 513–515.
48 M T Daly, *Sydney Boom, Sydney Bust*, Allen & Unwin, 1982, pp 186–187.
49 'Select Committee on Increase in Home Rents', *V and P NSWLA* 1911–12, vol. 3, pp 783–784.

50 R F Irvine, 'Commission of Inquiry into the Question of the Housing of Workmen in Europe and America', *NSWPP* 1913, vol. 2, pp 7–141.
51 B Kingston, *My Wife, My Mother and Poor Mary Ann: Women and Work in Australia*, Thomas Nelson, 1977, pp 56–73.
52 'Royal Commission on the Decline of the Birth-Rate and on the Mortality of Infants in NSW', *NSWPP* 1904, vol. 4.
53 Josephine Law, Interview with M Solling, 19 July 1991.
54 P Spearritt, 'The Kindergarten Movement: Tradition and Change', D E Edgar (ed) *Social Change in Australia, Readings in Sociology*, Cheshire, Melbourne, 1974, pp 583–596.
55 R Harrison, *The Sydney Kindergarten Teachers College 1897–1981*, Sydney Teachers College Graduates Association), p 43, p 361.
56 Lewis, op cit (21), p 200.
57 Ibid.

Chapter 12

1 W W Phillips, 'The Social Composition of Religious Denominations in Late-Nineteenth-Century Australia', *Church Heritage* (1985), pp 77–94. The *Methodist*, 23 September 1899, p 8.
2 '1901 Census', *JNSWLC* 1902, part 2, p 1179. *ATCJ*, 28 January 1909.
3 *The Australian Handbook 1900*, p 169. *EN*, 20 October 1917.
4 W Harris, *Where to Live ABC Guide to Sydney* (1918), p 38, p 45. Vialoux and Reeves, *The Jubilee History of Leichhardt* (1921).
5 R Markey, *The Making of the Labor Party in NSW*, NSWUP, 1988, pp 19–27.
6 F Adams, *The Australians, A Social Sketch*, London, 1892.
7 E W Burgess, 'The Growth of the City: An Introduction to a Research Project', R E Park, E W Burgess and R McKenzie (eds) *The City*, Chicago, 1925, reprinted 1967, pp 55–56.
8 H M Franklyn, *A Glance at Australia in 1880*, Melbourne, 1881, p 66.
9 W F Morrison (ed), *Aldine Centennial History of NSW*. E Digby, *Australian Men of Mark*, C Maxwell, Melbourne, 1888.
10 W D Rubenstein, 'The Top Wealth Holders in NSW 1817–1939', *Australian Economic History Review* (vol. 20) 1980. E H Knibbs, *The Private Wealth of Australia and Its Growth*, Commonwealth Bureau of Statistics, Melbourne, 1918.
11 'Evidence to the Royal Commission on City and Suburban Railways 1891', *V and P NSWLA* 1891–92, vol. 5.
12 C Fox, *Working Australia*, Allen & Unwin, 1991, pp 79–82.
13 J F Flitcroft, Interview with M Solling, 30 April 1983.
14 H Furniss, *Australian Sketches*, London, 1888, p 51.
15 *V and P NSWLA* 1900, vol. 2, p 3.
16 H M Moran, *Viewless Winds*, London, 1939, pp 17–18.
17 J McCalman, 'Class and Respectability in a Working Class Suburb: Richmond, Victoria, Before the Great War', *Historical Studies*, vol. 20 (No 78), pp 90–103.
18 S Fisher, 'The Family and the Sydney Economy', *1888* (Bulletin No 9), pp 83–87.
19 R Samuel 'Comers and Goers', H J Dyos and M Wolff (eds) *The Victorian City*, vol. 1, pp 123–166. G Davison, 'Sydney and the Bush: An Urban Context for the Australian Legend', *Historical Studies*, vol. 18 (1978).
20 R B Walker, 'Aspects of Working-Class Life in Industrial Sydney in 1913', *Labour History* No 58 (May 1990), p 42.

21 D Kernohan, Interview with M Solling, 27 January 1984.
22 Ibid.
23 W Mitchell, 'Home Life at the Hungry Mile: Sydney Wharf Labourers and Their Families 1900–1914', *Labour History* No 33 (1977), p 92.
24 'Report of Inquiry into Grain Sacks Regulation Bill', *V and P NSWLA* 1906, vol. 2, pp 51–197.
25 Mitchell, op cit (23), p 94.
26 'Evidence of John Gildea and John McMahon to the Inquiry into Grain Sacks Regulation Bill', *V and P NSWLA* 1906, vol. 2, pp 58–61.
27 B Kingston, *My Wife, My Daughter and Poor Mary Ann*, Nelson, 1975, p 46.
28 Fox, op cit (12), pp 66–69.
29 J Rickard, *Class and Politics, NSW, Victoria and the Early Commonwealth 1890–1910*, ANU Press, Canberra, 1976, pp 291–292.
30 'Evidence of Mary Edwards Before the Royal Commission on Female and Juvenile Labour in Factories and Shops', *NSWPP* 1911–12, vol. 2, pp 38–41.
31 J Carroll, 'Mateship and Egalitarianism; The Failure of Upper Middle Class Nerve', J Carroll (ed) *Intruders in the Bush, The Australian Quest for Identity*, OUP, 1982, pp 143–153.
32 R Broome, *Treasure in Earthen Vessels. Protestant Christianity in NSW 1900–1914*, UQP, 1980, pp 1–19.
33 D G Green and L G Cromwell, *Mutual Aid or Welfare State: Australia's Friendly Societies*, Allen & Unwin, 1984, p 13.
34 A O'Brien, *Poverty's Prison, The Poor in NSW 1880–1918*, MUP, 1988, p 18.
35 Green and Cromwell, op cit (33), p 14.
36 'Report of the Registrar of Friendly Societies 1897', *V and P NSWLA* 1900, vol. 6, p 947.
37 Vialoux and Reeves, op cit (4), pp 81–85.
38 Green and Cromwell, op cit (33), p 145.
39 Vialoux and Reeves, op cit (4), p 83.
40 R Markey, 'NSW Trade Unions and the "Co-operative Principle" in the 1890s', *Labour History* No 49 (1985), pp 54–55.
41 Balmain Co-operative Society 1877–1894, NSWA 10/4264 (K).
42 R W Connell and T H Irving, *Class Structure in Australian History*, Longman Cheshire, 1980, p 189.
43 *SM*, 23 November 1910, p 28.
44 P Spearritt, *Sydney Since the Twenties*, Hale & Iremonger, 1978, pp 231–235.
45 *The Sydney Sportsman*, 25 December 1907, p 6; 29 April 1908, p 6; 8 July 1908, p 6.
46 *SM,* 28 October 1865, p 4.
47 *SMH*, 3 December 1880, p 5; 9 February 1894. J Lack, 'Working Class Leisure', *VHJ* 49 (1978), pp 49–65.
48 D Bythell, 'Class Community and Culture: The Case of the Brass Band in Newcastle', *Labour History* No 67 (1994), pp 144–155.
49 *SM*, 17 May 1911, p 54.
50 *State Electoral Rolls* for Annandale, Balmain and Glebe 1910, 1917.
51 L Burge, Interview with M Solling, 1 May 1980.
52 For examples of crowd disorder see the *Bulletin*, 27 July 1911, p 27; 5 June 1913, p 28; 2 August 1917, p 32.
53 M Solling, *The Boatshed on Blackwattle Bay: Glebe Rowing Club 1879–1993* (1993), pp 22–25.
54 *SM,* 6 March 1886, p 501.
55 *SM,* 10 October 1887, p 729.
56 *SM,* 15 July 1903, p 186; 22 July 1903, p 251.

Chapter 13

1. *Argus*, 1 August 1914.
2. *The Official History of Australia in the War 1914–1918*, Sydney, 1921–42, vol. 11, p 13.
3. The *Australian Worker*, 6 August 1914.
4. BCM, 4 August 1914, p 164; GCM, 3 August 1914, p 443.
5. B Gammage, *The Broken Years, Australian Soldiers in the Great War*, Penguin Books, 1975, p 7.
6. L L Robson, *The First AIF, A Study of its Recruitment 1914–1918*, MUP, 1982, pp 20–45.
7. S Garton, *Out of Luck, Poor Australians and Social Welfare*, Allen & Unwin, 1990, p 113.
8. Gammage, op cit (5), p 9.
9. H Matthews, *Saints and Soldiers*, Sydney, 1918, p 81.
10. S Macintyre, *The Oxford History of Australia*, OUP, 1986, vol. 4, 1901–1942, pp 147–149.
11. Gammage, op cit (5), p 97.
12. *Argus*, 8 May 1915.
13. Gammage, op cit (5), p 110.
14. Robson, op cit (6), p 42.
15. D Kent, 'The Anzac Book, C E W Bean as Editor and Image Maker', *Historical Studies* No 84 (1985), pp 376–390. A Thomson, 'Steadfast until Death? C E W Bean and the Representation of Australian Military Manhood', *Historical Studies* No 93 (1989), pp 462–478.
16. DT, 22 June 1915, p 6.
17. DT, 25 May 1915, p 8.
18. DT, 4 June 1915, p 9.
19. DT, 26 May 1915, p 10; 1 June 1915, p 9; 18 June 1915, p 6.
20. SMH, 24 May 1915, p 5.
21. SMH, 24 May 1915, p 5.
22. DT, 25 May 1915, p 10; SMH, 24 May 1915, p 5.
23. I Turner, '1914–1919', F Crowley (ed) *A New History of Australia*, Heinemann, Melbourne, 1974, p 318.
24. Robson, op cit (6), p 54.
25. LCM, 5 July 1915, p 339.
26. M McKernan, *The Australian People and the Great War*, Melbourne, 1980, pp 98–105.
27. Robson, op cit (6), p 69. SMH, 15 February 1916. W H Gough, Interview with M Solling, 23 May 1978.
28. MOA, 3 June 1916, p 4.
29. SMH, 24 May 1916, p 10.
30. SMH, 12 June 1916, p 10.
31. BCM, 17 August 1915, p 299. LCM, 5 July 1915, p 335.
32. MOA, 29 April 1916, p 3; 8 January 1916, p 3; 6 May 1916, p 3.
33. MOA, 22 April 1916, p 3.
34. SM, 3 December 1913, p 30.
35. McKernan, op cit (26), p 157.
36. SMH, 15 January 1916, p 16.
37. G Fischer, '"Negative Integration" and an Australian Road to Modernity: Interpreting the Australian Homefront Experience in World War I', *Historical Studies* No 104 (1995), pp 469–470.
38. Robson, op cit (6), pp 62–81.
39. *Argus*, 11 January 1916.
40. DT, 10 November 1916.
41. SMH, 18 October 1916, p 12.
42. SMH, 19 October 1916, p 10.

43 J Damousi, 'Socialist Women and Gendered Space, The Anti-Conscription and Anti-War Campaigns of 1914–1918', *Labour History* No 60, p 9.
44 *SMH*, 24 October 1916, p 8.
45 *SMH*, 10 October 1916, p 10.
46 *SMH*, 18 October 1916, p 12.
47 *SMH*, 24 October 1916, p 8.
48 *SMH*, 17 October 1916, p 7.
49 A Spaull, 'The Response of Australian Schools to the Two World Wars', *An Anzac Muster, Monash Publications in History No 14*, p 136.
50 D Coward, 'Crime and Punishment: The Great Strike in NSW', J Iremonger, J Merrit and G Osborne, *Strikes: Studies in Twentieth Century Australian Social History*, Angus & Robertson and Australian Society for Study of Labour History, Cremorne, 1973, pp 52–54.
51 *SMH*, 3 August 1917.
52 Damousi, op cit (43), p 9.
53 *DT*, 17 December 1917, p 5.
54 Damousi, op cit (43), p 9.
55 Letter from H D Murray dated 29 August 1917 in possession of M Solling.
56 Gammage, op cit (5), p 268.
57 Ibid, p 117.
58 Ibid, p 182.
59 *SMH*, 20 July 1918, p 11.
60 R Best, *Annals from St Aidan's in Annandale* (1992), p 37.
61 *ADB*, vol. 8, p 180.
62 A Vialoux and C M Reeves, *The Jubilee History of Leichhardt 1871–1921*, p 91.
63 *SMH*, 12 November 1918.
64 Robson, op cit (6), pp 202–203.
65 J McKay, 'Putting the Digger on a Pedestal', *Historic Environment,* vol. 3 (1986), pp 5–9. K S Inglis and J Phillips, 'War Memorials in Australia and New Zealand, A Comparative Survey', *Australian Historical Studies* No 96 (1991), pp 179–191.
66 *SMH*, 24 April 1916, p 3, p 8.
67 Balmain Honour Book 1914–1918, Draft (Leichhardt Council).
68 *SM*, 4 July 1917, p 8.
69 *All Souls' Church of England, Leichhardt, Jubilee 1882–1932*, p 7.
70 A Carolan, 'Winged Victory, Two Sculptors', *Marrickville Heritage Society Journal* No 5, pp 43–44.
71 *SMH*, 5 December 1921, p 10.

Chapter 14

1 *NSWSR* 1861, 1862, 1865, 1870, 1878. *V and P NSWLA* 1873–74, vol. 5, pp 135–140.
2 *Balmain Municipal Council Souvenir to Commemorate the 50th Anniversary of the Incorporation of the Municipality of Balmain 1860–1910*, p 11.
3 *GCM*, 3 August 1885.
4 G Curr, 'Liberalism, Localism and Suburban Development in Melbourne 1870–1890', *Historical Studies* No 74 (1980), p 43.
5 *GCM*, 30 December 1867, p 364. For details of counter petitions see F A Larcombe, *The Origins of Local Government in NSW 1831–1858*, Sydney, 1973, pp 270–271.

6 A Vialoux and C M Reeves, *The Jubilee History of Leichhardt December 1871–December 1921*, pp 9–13.
7 A Roberts, 'The Development of the Suburb of Annandale 1876–1899', University of Sydney, BA (Hons), 1970, pp 40–45.
8 *SMH*, 10 February 1879, p 8, p 9; 11 February 1879, p 3.
9 A J C Mayne, '"A Most Pernicious Principle": The Local Government Franchise in Nineteenth Century Sydney', *AJPH* 27 (1981), pp 160–171.
10 R A Wild, *Australian Community Studies and Beyond*, Allen & Unwin, 1981, p 197.
11 *V and P NSWLA* 1911–12, vol. 3, p 121.
12 *V and P NSWLA* 1893, vol. 2, pp 109–111.
13 GCM, 13 July 1881. LCM, 27 February 1893, p 142.
14 BCM, 5 December 1893, p 153.
15 LCM, 8 February 1894, pp 204–207.
16 R Markey, 'The Emergence of the Labor Party at the Municipal Level in NSW 1891–1900', *AJPH* 31 (1985), pp 408–417.
17 L G Lynch, 'A Community Study—Balmain 1860–1894', University of Sydney, PhD thesis, 1982, pp 250–253.
18 *SMH*, 19 October 1926, p 10.
19 R Thornton and A W Sommerville, *Retrospect, Municipality of Balmain 1860–1935*, pp 23–25.
20 M Solling, 'Biographical Register of Local Elected Representatives', unpublished.
21 *Sunday News*, 12 July 1925. *SMH*, 19 June 1930, p 6.
22 G Dawson, J W McCarty and A McLeary (eds), *Australians 1888* Fairfax Syme Weldon Associates, 1988, p 359.
23 Solling, op cit (20).
24 *SMH*, 22 April 1937, p 8.
25 Solling, op cit (20).
26 *SMH*, 12 May 1928, p 18.
27 *SMH*, 6 August 1945, p 12.
28 Solling, op cit (20).
29 A Jakubowics, 'The City Game: Urban Ideology and Social Conflict', J Edgar (ed) *Social Change in Australia: Readings in Sociology*, Melbourne, 1974. J Hagan and K Turner, *A History of the Labor Party in NSW 1891–1991*, Longman, Cheshire, 1991, pp 27–32.
30 F A Larcombe, *The Advancement of Local Government in NSW 1906 to the Present*, SUP, 1978, vol. 3, p 392.
31 *SMH*, 24 January 1908, p 6; 3 February 1908, p 8.
32 *SMH*, 30 January 1911, p 10.
33 *SMH*, 30 January 1911, p 10; 4 December 1922, p 10.
34 'Select Committee on System of Local Government for Greater Sydney', *V and P NSWLA* 1911–12, vol. 3, p 124.
35 'Royal Commission on Greater Sydney', *NSWPP* 1913 (2), pp 242–3.
36 Ibid, p 309, pp 401–402; pp 163–163.
37 Larcombe, op cit (30), p 393.
38 *NSWPP* 1915–16 vol. 4, p 509.
39 *SMH*, 9 December 1915.
40 *NSWPP* 1915–16, vol. 4, p 499.
41 *SMH*, 2 February 1920, p 3, p 8.
42 *SMH*, 30 January 1911, p 10; 4 December 1922, p 10.
43 *SMH*, 7 December 1925, p 3, pp 11–12
44 *Sane Democracy League,* pamphlet (1926), pp 20–21.
45 *Australian National Review*, 18 February 1925, p 18; 28 November 1927, pp 18–19.

46 M Hogan, 'The Sydney Style, NSW Labor and the Catholic Church', *Labour History* 36 (1979), p 40.
47 Larcombe, op cit (30), p 396.
48 *Labour Daily*, 3 Dec, 4 December 1928. *Sunday Sun*, 2 December 1928.
49 *SMH*, 7 August 1928, p 7.
50 *SMH*, 19 March 1929, p 17; 28 November 1928, p 14; 19 June 1929, p 15.
51 J M McCalman, *Struggletown, Public and Private Life in Richmond 1900–1965*, MUP, 1984, p 36.
52 *SMH*, 13 May 1931, p 13; 11 February 1931, p 6. Larcombe, op cit (30), pp 366–367.
53 Larcombe, op cit (30), p 369.
54 Hogan, p 46.
55 A Parkin, 'Party Organisation and Machine Politics: The ALP in Perspective', A Parkin and J Warhurst (eds) *Machine Politics in the Australian Labor Party*, Allen & Unwin, 1983, p 25.
56 R F I Smith, 'Collingwood, Wren Left-Overs and Political Change: Aspects of Local Level in the 1970s', *Labour History* 30 (1976), pp 42–57.
57 Solling, op cit (20).
58 *DT*, 3 December 1934, p 9.
59 *SMH*, 22, 25, 26, 28 June 1935.
60 *SMH*, 14 December 1938; 25 March 1939, p 3; 1 June 1939, p 11.
61 *SMH*, 7 December 1925, p 3.
62 *DT*, 3 December 1934, p 9.
63 *SMH*, 3 December 1928, p 14; 6 December 1937, p 8.
64 *SMH*, 8 December 1941, p 8.
65 *SMH*, 4 December 1944, p 6.
66 *SMH*, 2 February 1920, p 3.
67 N Massey, 'A Century of Laborism and the State 1891–1993: An Historical Interpretation', *Labour History* 66 (1994), p 49.
68 *ADB*, vol. 8, pp 562–563.
69 *SMH*, 18 August 1944, p 10.
70 *SMH*, 4 December 1944, p 6; 6 December 1948.

Chapter 15

1 H McQueen, 'The Spanish Influenza Pandemic in Australia 1918–19', J Roe (ed) *Social Policy in Australia: Some Perspectives 1901–75*, Cassell, 1976, pp 131–147.
2 A G Butler, *Official History of the Australian Army Medical Services in the 1914–18 War*, vol. 3, (1943), pp 50–187, pp 769–963.
3 H McQueen, 'Shoot the Bolshevik! Hang the Profiteer', E L Wheelwright and K Buckley (eds) *Essays in the Political Economy of Australian Capitalism*, Sydney, 1978, vol. 2, p 199.
4 Royal Commission on the Basic Wage, 'Report', Commonwealth of Australia, *CPP* 1920–21, vols 4–5. K M Reiger, '"Clean and Comfortable and Respectable": Working-class Aspirations and the Australian 1920 Royal Commission on the Basic Wage', *History Workshop* (1989), vol. 27, pp 86–105.
5 *Commonwealth Arbitration Reports*, 15, p 838.
6 *Census of the Commonwealth of Australia* 1911, vols 1–3.
7 Ibid, 1933, vols 1–3.
8 P Spearritt, *Sydney Since the Twenties*, Hale & Iremonger, 1978, p 50.
9 R Freestone, 'The Great Lever of Social Reform: The Garden Suburb 1900–1930', M Kelly (ed) *Sydney, City of Suburbs*, NSWUP, 1987, pp 53–76. Spearritt, op cit (8), pp 46–51.

10 Spearritt op cit (8), pp 141–174.
11 T Kass, 'Cheaper than Rent: Aspects of the Growth of Owner-Occupation in Sydney 1911–1966', op cit 9, p 80, p 86.
12 GCM, 5 May 1919, p 132; 2 August 1920, p 180.
13 S Macintyre, *The Oxford History of Australia 1901–1942*, OUP, 1986, vol. 4, pp 213–214.
14 Spearritt, op cit (8), p 75. N H Dick, 'Housing and Slum Clearance in NSW', *Australian Quarterly*, December 1935, p 81.
15 M Kelly, 'Introduction', Kelly, op cit (9), p 3.
16 *SMH*, 13 September 1924.
17 P Spearitt, 'Sydney's Slums: Middle-Class Reformers and the Labor Response', *Labour History* (1974) No 26, pp 65–81.
18 *SMH*, 25 July 1935.
19 *Australian Worker*, 20 October 1935; 25 September 1935.
20 V Kelly, *A Man of the People: From Boilermaker to Governor-General, The Career of the Rt Hon Sir William McKell*, Sydney, 1971.
21 E Spratt, *Eddie Ward, Firebrand of East Sydney*, Adelaide, 1965. E C Fry, 'Growth of an Australian Metropolis', R S Parker and P N Troy (eds) *The Politics of Urban Growth*, Canberra, 1972, p 18.
22 R Park, *The Harp in the South*, Angus & Robertson, Sydney, 1948, p 188, p 48.
23 *SMH*, 20 February 1932, p 9.
24 G R Gerlach, 'Housing Improvement in NSW', *Building* 361 (1937), p 29.
25 M Hogan, *The Sectarian Strand, Religion in Australian History*, Penguin Books, 1987, p 191.
26 M Solling, *The Boatshed on Blackwattle Bay 1879–1993*, Southwood Press, 1993, pp 63–64.
27 M Hogan, 'The Sydney Style, NSW Labor and the Catholic Church', *Labour History* 36 (1979), p 40.
28 G T Caldwell, 'From Pub to Club: The History of Drinking Attitudes in NSW (1900–1945) and the Growth of Registered Clubs', *ANU Historical Journal*, vol. 9 (December 1972), pp 24–31.
29 S Garton, 'Patterns of Policing in NSW', *JRAHS* (1991), vol. 77, pp 16–29.
30 R Broome, *Treasure in Earthen Vessels: Protestant Christianity in NSW Society 1900–1914*, UQP, 1980, pp 141–157. Garton, op cit (29), p 23.
31 R Hogg and H Golder, 'Policing Sydney in the Late Nineteenth Century', M Finnane (ed) *Policing Australia: Historical Perspectives*, NSWUP, 1987, pp 60–73.
32 Garton, op cit (29), p 23.
33 A McCoy, *Drug Traffic, Narcotics and Organised Crime in Australia*, Sydney, 1980, pp 114–116.
34 A McCoy, 'Two Cities and Their Syndicates: A Comparative Urban History of Organised Crime', J Davidson (ed) *The Sydney–Melbourne Book,* Allen & Unwin, 1986, p 107.
35 R G Blissett, Interview with M Solling, 8 March 1996.
36 D Hickie, *Chow Hayes, Gunman*, Angus & Robertson, Sydney, pp 113–121.
37 McCoy, op cit (33), pp 167–69.
38 R G Blissett, Interview with M Solling, 6 April 1995.
39 McCoy, op cit (33), p 149.
40 'Report of the NSW Royal Commission into Allegations against Police in Connection with the Suppression of Illicit Betting', *NSWPP* 1936–37, vol. 1, pp 417–557; vol. 3, pp 1–1499.
41 McCoy, op cit (33), p 114.
42 H Radi, '1920–1929', F K Crowley (ed) *A New History of Australia*, Melbourne, 1974, pp 357–358.
43 M Dixon, 'The Timber Strike of 1929', *Historical Studies No 40* (1963), p 480.
44 *SMH*, 28 March 1929, p 15.
45 D van den Broek, *LHJ* 19 (1995), pp 3–8.

46 Ibid, p 6.
47 Ibid, p 5.
48 Ibid, p 7.
49 Ibid.
50 GCM, 1 August 1929, p 64. *SMH*, 21 August 1929, p 15.
51 *SMH*, 2 August 1929, p 11.
52 Van den Broek, op cit (45), p 8.
53 GCM, 19 December 1929.
54 GCM, 9 July 1929. LCM, 10 February 1932.
55 *NSWPD*, vol. 27, 3668, 26 June 1931.
56 R Walker, 'Mr Lang's Dole: The Administration of Food Relief in NSW 1930–1932', *Labour History* No 51 (1986), pp 70–82.
57 'Report of the Royal Commission on Child Endowment and Family Allowances 1929', *Australian PP* 1929, vol. 2, p 105.
58 S Macintyre, 'Australian Responses to Unemployment in the Last Depression in Australia', J Roe (ed), *Unemployment: Are These Lessons from History?*, Hale & Iremonger, 1985.
59 *SMH*, 26 February 1934, p 10. J Worthy, 'A Good Working Man's Home: Annandale in the Depression 1929–36', BA Hons thesis, University of NSW, 1986, p 80–84.
60 *Sands's Sydney and Suburban Directory* for 1915.
61 Worthy, op cit (59), p 89.
62 N Wheatley, 'The Unemployed Who Kicked: A Study of the Political Struggles and Organisations in the Great Depression', MA Hons thesis, Macquarie Univ, 1975.
63 A Johnson, *Bread and Roses, A Personal History of the Three Militant Women and Their Friends 1902–1988*, Left Book Club, 1990, p 37.
64 N Wheatley, 'Meeting Them at the Door: Radicalism, Militancy and the Anti-eviction Campaign of 1931', J Roe (ed) *Twentieth-Century Sydney*, Hale & Iremonger, 1980.
65 N Wheatley, 'All in the Same Boat? Sydney's Rich and Poor in the Great Depression', V Burgmann and J Lee (eds) *Making a Life*, Penguin Books, 1988, p 214. BCM, 30 March 1932; 19 August 1930. LCM, 28 January 1931.
66 BCM, 13 October 1931, p 47.
67 LCM, 13 August 1930; 12 August 1931.
68 ACM, 2 March 1931; 12 October 1931; 20 July 1931; 14 March 1931.
69 N Wheatley, op cit (62).
70 GCM, 20 November 1930, p 9.
71 Ibid, 18 April 1929, p 25; 20 June 1929, p 47.
72 *SMH*, 8 August 1930, p 12.
73 Johnson, op cit (63), p 38.
74 *SMH*, 30 June 1931, p 13; 15 July 1931.
75 S Moran, *Reminiscences of a Rebel*, Chippendale Alternative Publishing, 1979, pp 8–10.
76 W Lowenstein, *Weevils in the Flour*, Hyland, 1978, pp 214–215.
77 Blissett, op cit (38).
78 *SMH*, 7 May 1993, p 12. See also S Moran's 'Recollection' in *SMH*, 1 May 1993, p 1.
79 P Spearritt, 'Depression Statistics', J Mackinolty (ed) *The Wasted Years, Australia's Great Depression*, Allen & Unwin, 1981, pp 194–211.
80 J Wright, 'Forty Years and Australian Cities', *Community* No 7 (February 1975), pp 2–3.
81 *SMH*, 22 August 1930, p 10.
82 Balmain Infectious Diseases Register 1899–1938 (Leichhardt Council Library).
83 P Spearritt, op cit (79), pp 194–211.

Chapter 16

1. R Cashman and S Gibbs (eds), *Early Cricket in Sydney 1803 to 1856*, NSW Cricket Association, 1991, p 198. T V Hickie, *They Ran with the Ball: How Rugby Football Began in Australia*, Longman, 1993, p 38.
2. 'Public House Sports', *The Oxford Companion to Australian Sport*, OUP 2nd edn, 1994, p 339.
3. B C Peck, Recollections of Sydney (1850), p 95 (bathing house). Plan of Avona (Glebe) and Grounds, ML M3/811.1823 (1879).
4. A Garran, *Picturesque Atlas of Australasia* (1888), p 96.
5. H Lawson, 'A Song of Southern Writers', C Roderick (ed) *Henry Lawson Collected Verse*, Angus and Robertson, Sydney, 1967.
6. W Vamplew and B Stoddart (eds), *Sport in Australia: A Social History*, CUP, 1994, pp 1–18.
7. A K McKenzie, 'Local Cricket in Australia', J C Davis (ed) *Australian Cricket Annual 1896*.
8. A G Moyes, *Australian Cricket: A History* Angus & Robertson, 1959, pp 118–128.
9. M Bonnell, R Cashman and J Rodgers, *Making the Grade: 100 Years of Grade Cricket in Sydney 1893–94 to 1993–94*, NSW Cricket Association, 1994, p 20, p 26.
10. Hickie, op cit (1), p 159.
11. M Solling, *LHJ* 8 (1979), pp 26–27.
12. P Moseley, 'The Game: Early Soccer Scenery in NSW', *Sporting Traditions* (May 1992), vol. 8, p 143.
13. S Grant, *Jack Pollard's Soccer Records*, Sydney, 1974.
14. 'Is Football Brutalising', *Sunday Times*, 10 May 1896, p 7; 17 May 1896, p 2; 24 May 1896, p 2.
15. M P Sharp, 'Australian Football in Sydney Before 1914', *Sporting Traditions* (November 1987), vol. 4, p 40.
16. 'The Sports of Australia—Cycling', *ISN*, 26 July 1888, pp 8–13. *NSW Motorists and Cyclists Annual 1905*, pp 170–172.
17. M Solling, *The Boatshed on Blackwattle Bay, Glebe Rowing Club 1879–1993*, Glebe Rowing Club, 1993, pp 84–85.
18. G Inglis, *Sport and Pastime in Australia*, Methuen, 1912, p 213.
19. *SM*, 11 November 1876, p 629.
20. B Stannard, *The Blue-Water Bushmen*, Angus & Robertson, 1981, pp 12–14.
21. A Hamill, *1884–1984 Celebrating a Centenary—Balmain Swimming Club*, Balmain Swimming Club, 1984.
22. W F Morrison, *Aldine Centennial History of NSW* (1888).
23. A Roberts, 'An Ancient Game in a New Land: Bowling and Society in NSW to 1912', *JRAHS*, Vol. 65, pp 109–127.
24. G T Caldwell, 'From Pub to Club, The History of Drinking Attitudes in NSW (1900–1945) and the Growth of Registered Clubs', *ANU Historical Journal*, vol. 9 (December 1972), p 25.
25. Tooth's Town Barrel Beer Books 1900–1914.
26. C Cunneen, 'The Rugby War; The Early History of Rugby League in NSW 1907–1915', R Cashman and M McKernan (eds) *Sport in History: The Making of Sporting Traditions*, Brisbane, 1979, p 295.
27. *SM*, 25 March 1908, p 89.
28. *SMH*, 10 January 1908, p 7.
29. Ibid.
30. *SM*, 26 April 1911, p 60.
31. *SMH*, 18 September 1911, p 4; 26 August 1912, p 5.
32. P Reynolds, *LHJ J* 7 (1978), pp 18–20.
33. *The Oxford Companion to Australian Sport*, OUP 2nd edn, 1994, p 173, pp 83–84.

34 Ibid.
35 Cunneen, op cit (26), p 295.
36 *The Referee*, 25 July 1917, p12. Glebe District Rugby League Club Annual Report 1917.
37 *Oxford,* op cit (33), p 173, pp 83–84.
38 Ibid.
39 R Cashman, A Weaver and S Glass, *Wicket Women, Cricket and Women in Australia*, UNSWP, 1991, p 91.
40 ACM, 13 October 1930.
41 P Spearritt, *Sydney Since the Twenties*, Hale & Iremonger, 1978, pp 231–235.
42 D Collins, 'The Movie Octopus', P Spearrit and D Walker (eds) *Australian Popular Culture*, Allen & Unwin, 1979, pp 102–105.
43 *Sydney Sportsman,* 29 April 1908, p 6; 18 June 1908, p 6.
44 Collins, op cit (42), p 103.
45 T B Brown, Interview with M Solling, 20 April 1981.
46 *SMH*, 17 July 1920.
47 Collins, op cit (42), p 103.
48 'Eighth Report of the Commissioner of Taxation 1920–23', *CPP* 1923–24, pp 2–3.
49 P Spearritt, op cit (41), 231–235.
50 R Thorne and K Cork, *For All the Kings Men, The Kings Theatres of Sydney*, Australian Theatre Historical Society, Campbelltown, 1991, pp 40–41. M Quinn, *LHJ* 5 (1975), pp 15–18.
51 *Sands's Sydney and Suburban Directory* for 1930.
52 Scrap Book of Dancing School Advertisements held by M Solling.
53 B Gammage and P Spearritt (eds), *Australians 1838*, Fairfax, Syme, Weldon, 1987, p 1902.
54 Scrap Book, op cit (52).
55 Gammage and Spearritt, op cit (53), p 356.
56 Solling, op cit (17), p 132.
57 D Bythell, 'Class Community and Culture: The Case of the Brass Band in Newcastle', *Labour History* 67 (November 1994), pp 144–155.
58 *Australian Ring,* March 1963, p 1.
59 *SMH*, 6 February 1995, p 2. P Corris, *Lords of the Ring*, Cassell, Sydney, 1980, pp 119–121.
60 W Lowenstein, *Weevils in the Flour: An Oral Record of the 1930s Depression in Australia*, Hyland, Melbourne, 1978, p 239.
61 *SMH*, 6 February 1995, p 2.
62 Oxford, op cit (33), p 193.
63 J O'Hara, *A Mug's Game: A History of Gaming and Betting in Australia*, UNSW Press, 1988, pp 186–187. 'NSW Royal Commission into Greyhound Racing and Fruit Machines' *NSWPP* 1932, vol. 1, pp 993–1082
64 *SMH*, 21 September 1987, p 52.
65 O'Hara, op cit (63), pp 185–186.
66 'Select Committee into the Conduct and Administration of Trotting in NSW', *NSWPP*, 1938–40.
67 G Brown, *100 years of Trotting 1877–1977*, Whitcombe & Tombs, Sydney, 1981) pp 244–246.
68 M Solling and H Wark, *Under the Arches: A History of the Glebe District Hockey Club to 1993*, Glebe District Hockey Club, 1994, pp 172–173, p 178.
69 *Oxford*, op cit (33), p 173.
70 *ADB*, vol. 13, p 82.
71 *Oxford*, op cit (33), p 274.
72 L Hoad and J Pollard, *My Game*, Hodder & Stoughton, 1958, pp 26–36.
73 *SMH*, 8 November 1990, p 52; 5 July 1994, p 1; 6 July 1994, pp 55–56.

Chapter 17

1. 'Report of the Housing Improvement Board of NSW', *NSWPP* 1938–39–40, pp 49–78.
2. Commonwealth Housing Commission, Ministry of Post-War Reconstruction, Final Report, Canberra, 25 August 1944, p 8.
3. Commonwealth Housing Commission, Final Report, 1945, p 26.
4. 'Report of the Housing Commission of NSW', *NSWPP* 1943–44, vol. 1.
5. Cumberland County Council, *Report on the Planning Scheme for the County of Cumberland*, NSW (Sydney, 1948), p 33.
6. P N Troy (ed), *Equity in the City*, Allen & Unwin, 1981, pp 148–149.
7. Cumberland County Council, op cit (5), p 68.
8. A Jakubowicz, 'The City Game: Urban Ideology and Social Conflict, Or Who gets the Goodies and Who Pays the Cost?', D E Edgar (ed) *Social Change in Australia: Readings in Sociology*, Cheshire Publishing, 1974, p 332. J Wright, 'Forty Years and Australian Cities', *Community No 7* (February 1975), p 2.
9. R J Cain, 'Transportation, Planning and Conflict in Sydney: A Case Study of Inner-City Expressways in Glebe', BSc thesis, University of NSW, 1975, pp 21–30.
10. BCM, 6 January 1948, p 374.
11. Ibid, 16 March 1948, p 392.
12. LCM, 11 October 1949, p 142.
13. P Ashton, *The Accidental City: Planning Sydney Since 1788*, Sydney City Council, 1993, p 86. 'Report of the Housing Commission of NSW', *NSWPP* 1950–51–52, vol. 3, p 31; *NSWPP* 1953–54, vol. 2, p 1829.
14. R Cardew, 'Flats in Sydney: The Thirty Per Cent Solution?', J Roe (ed), *Twentieth-Century Sydney Studies in Urban and Social History*, Hale & Iremonger, 1980, pp 72–83.
15. H Kendig, *New Life for Old Suburbs*, Allen & Unwin, 1979, pp 112–113. Royal 'Commission of Enquiry on the Landlord & Tenant (Amendment) Act 1948', *NSWPP* 1961.
16. Cardew, op cit (14), pp 79–80.
17. 'Royal Commission of Enquiry into the Question of the Boundaries of the Local Government Areas in the County of Cumberland', *NSWPP* 1945–46, vol. 1, pp 481–508.
18. F A Larcombe, *The Advancement of Local Government in NSW 1906 to the Present*, vol. 3 (SUP, 1978), pp 114–120.
19. Ashton, op cit (13), p 66.
20. C Allport, 'The Unrealised Promise: Plans for Sydney Housing in the Forties', Roe, op cit (14), p 55.
21. Records of Sydney City Library.
22. Records of Leichhardt Library.
23. *ADB*, vol. 10, p 296.
24. Records of the Federation of NSW Police Citizens Youth Clubs, Surry Hills.
25. *SMH*, 6 December 1948, p 4.
26. A Jakubowicz, 'A New Politics of Suburbia', *Current Affairs Bulletin*, April 1972, p 346. S Ball, 'Balmain 1945–1975: A Case Study of the Town Planning Processes at the Local Level', BA Hons, Department of Government, University of Sydney, 1975.
27. T Wheelwright, 'NSW: The Dominant Right', A Parkin and J Warhurst (eds) *Machine Politics in the ALP*, Allen & Unwin, 1983, pp 48–51.
28. *SMH*, 4 August 1989, p 27.
29. LCM, 23 December 1952, p 738.
30. *DM*, 18 December 1952. *DT*, 16, 18 December 1952. *SMH*, 17 December 1952.
31. *DT*, 16 December 1952.
32. *NSWGG*, Proclamation of 15 April 1953. LCM, 15 April 1953, p 821.

33 The *Sun,* 16 and 17 April 1953. *DT,* 16 April 1953.
34 LCM, 28 November 1956, p 1421. *SMH*, 11 February 1956, p 48.
35 *SMH*, 3 December 1956, p 6. LCM, 11 December 1956, p 1422.
36 *SMH*, 27 March 1958.
37 R Johnston, 'Participation in Local Government: Leichhardt 1971–74', R Lucy (ed) *The Pieces of Politics*, Macmillan, 1979, pp 233–234.
38 Maritime Services Board, *A Ten Year Port Redevelopment Plan* (September 1966), p 32.
39 Cumberland County Council: Planning Scheme Ordinance (1963), Section 31(b).
40 J Bach, *A Maritime History of Australia*, Nelson, 1976, p 407.
41 *Newsletter* (Balmain Association), October 1966.
42 Ibid, August 1967.
43 Ibid, June 1975.
44 Wheelwright, op cit (27), pp 58–59.
45 M McAllister, 'Community Organisations and Local Politics in Glebe', Research Project 1974, Government III, University of Sydney, p 11.
46 B Engels, 'The Gentrification of Glebe: The Residential Restructuring of An Inner Sydney Suburb, 1960 to 1980', PhD thesis, Department of Geography, University of Sydney, 1989, p 463.
47 *Newsletter* (Balmain Assoc), June 1967; February 1968.
48 A Jakubowicz, 'The Split in the Balmain Branch of the ALP: A Study in the Politics of a Small Community', Research Essay, 1968, Government II, Department of Government, University of Sydney.
49 Johnston, op cit (37), p 236.
50 *SMH*, 6 December 1968.
51 *SMH*, 14 December 1985, p 40.
52 S Short, *Laurie Short: A Political Life*, Allen & Unwin, 1992, pp 32–33, pp 54–65. P Beilhars, 'Trotskyism in Australia—Notes from a Talk with Ted Tripp (1976)', *Labour History* 62 (May 1992), pp 133–137.
53 J McClelland, *Stirring the Possum—A Political Autobiography*, Penguin Books, 1988, pp 75–76. R Gollan, *Revolutionaries and Reformists*, ANU, 1975, pp 136–139
54 D Gollan, 'The Balmain Ironworkers Strike of 1945, Part 1', *Labour History* 22 (May 1972), pp 23–41. D Gollan, 'The Balmain Ironworkers Strike of 1945, Part 2', *Labour History* 23 (November 1972), pp 62–73.
55 *SMH*, 25 August 1956, p 4.
56 *SMH*, 8 June 1989, p 2.
57 *SMH*, 8 June 1989, p 15.
58 *SMH*, 20 May 1966, p 6. I Wyner, 'N Origlass (1908–1996)', *The Hummer, Bulletin of the Sydney Branch, Australian Society for the Study of Labour History,* vol. 2 No 6 (Winter 1966), pp 29–36
59 *SMH*, 14 December 1985, p 40.
60 I Wyner, *With Banner Unfurled: The Early Years of the Ship Painters' and Dockers' Union*, Hale & Iremonger, 1983.
61 *SMH*, 14 December 1985, p 40.

Chapter 18

1 F L Crowley, 'The British Contribution to the Australian Population 1860–1919', *Universities' Studies in Political History*, vol. 2 (1954), pp 55–88.

2   S Castles, C Alcorso, G Rando and E Vasta (eds), *Australia's Italians: Culture and Community in a Changing Society*, Allen & Unwin, Sydney, 1992, pp 35–55.

3   R Pascoe, 'Italian Settlement until 1914', J Jupp (ed) *The Australian People: An Encyclopedia of the Nation, Its People and Their Origins*, Angus & Robertson, Sydney, 1988, pp 596–598.

4   *ADB*, vol. 3, p 352.

5   J Walforth, 'Residential Concentration of Non-British Minorities in Nineteenth-Century Sydney', *Australian Geographical Studies* (1974) 12, pp 207–218.

6   F C Clifford, *Richmond River District of NSW: New Italy, A Brief Sketch of a New and Thriving Colony*, Government Printer, Sydney, 1889.

7   H Ware, *A Profile of the Italian Community in Australia*, Australian Institute of Multicultural Affairs, 1981, p 12.

8   *SMH*, 12 February 1858, p 1; 7 February 1857. St Mary's Balmain, Parish Register.

9   G Giovenco, Index to Italians in Leichhardt (Leichhardt Library).

10 Ibid.

11 Ibid.

12 W G Verge, *John Verge*, Sydney, 1963.

13 Giovenco, op cit (9).

14 Ibid.

15 *Sands's Sydney and Suburban Directory for 1894, 1900. ADB*, vol. 6, pp 86–87.

16 *ADB*, vol. 6, pp 125–126.

17 Ware, op cit (7), p 12.

18 R Pascoe, *Buongiorno Australia: Our Italian Heritage*, Greenhouse Publications, Melbourne, 1987, Chapter 5.

19 G Cresciani, 'Italian Immigrants 1920–1945', Jupp, op cit (3), p 608.

20 R Valente, 'The Post-War Leichhardt Italian Community', MA Thesis, University of Sydney, 1977, p 3.

21 C Cronin, *The Sting of Change: The Sicilian Family in Sicily and Australia*, Chicago, 1970.
    I H Burnley, 'Italian Settlement in Sydney 1920–1978', *Australian Geographical Studies* (1981), vol. 19, p 180.

22 Ware, op cit (7), p 13.

23 Cresciani, op cit (19), p 610.

24 Ibid, p 611.

25 *Sands's Sydney and Suburban Directory for 1912, 1916.*

26 Melocco Bros 1908–1958 (50th anniversary booklet).

27 Castles et al., op cit (2), pp 41–43.

28 S L Thompson, *Australia Through Italian Eyes: A Study of Settlers Returning from Australia to Italy*, OUP, Melbourne, 1980.

29 I H Burnley, 'Italian Community Life in Sydney', Jupp, op cit (3), pp 628–630.

30 Valente, op cit (20), p 23.

31 M di Nicola, 'The Political Impact of Italian Migrants in Leichhardt 1961–1973', BA Hons Thesis, University of Sydney, 1973, p 6.

32 Valente, op cit (20), p 46.

33 F Del Duca, Interview with M Solling, 5 July 1996.

34 A Pittarello, *Soup without Salt: The Australian Catholic Church and the Italian Migrant*, Centre for Migration Studies, Sydney, 1980, p 83.

35 Valente, op cit (20), p 25.

36 Ibid, p 27.

37 Ibid, p 28.

38 M di Nicola, 'The Political Impact of Italian Migrants in Leichhardt 1961–1973', J Jupp (ed) *Ethnic Politics in Australia*, Allen & Unwin, Sydney, 1984.

39 J Jupp, B York, and A McRabbie, *The Political Participation of Ethnic Minorities in Australia*, AGPS, Canberra, 1989, p 37.
40 Di Nicola, op cit (31), pp 31–33.
41 M di Nicola, 'The Political Impact of Italian Migrants in Leichhardt 1961–1973', BA Hons Thesis, University of Sydney, 1973, pp 14–15.
42 Valente, op cit (20), p 29.
43 Di Nicola, op cit (31), p 18. Valente, op cit (20), p 30.
44 Valente, op cit (20), p 30.
45 *SMH*, 2 March 1996, p 27, p 32.
46 Burnley, op cit (21), p 183.
47 Valente, op cit (20), pp 22–23.
48 Di Nicola, op cit (31), pp 2–3, p 9.
49 Burnley, op cit (21), p 184.
50 Castles et al., op cit (2), p 91.
51 Del Duca, op cit (33).
52 *Western Suburbs Courier*, 17 July 1989, p 9.
53 *Eastern Herald*, 19 May 1988, p 4.
54 *1991 Census of Population and Housing NSW*, Statistical Local Area, Leichhardt.

Chapter 19

1 P Spearritt, 'Sydney's Slums: Middle Class Reformers and the Labor Response', *Labour History* (1974) No 26, pp 65–81.
2 W S Logan, 'Gentrification in Inner Melbourne: Problems of Analysis', *Australian Geographical Studies*, vol. 20 (April 1982), p 66.
3 B Gammage, P Spearritt (eds), *Australian 1938*, Fairfax Syme & Weldon, 1988, pp 200–201.
4 *SMH Good Weekend*, 6 July 1985, p 13.
5 See government school enrolments in Chapter 8.
6 The *Methodist*, 16 October 1954, p 1.
7 H Kendig, *New Life for Old Suburbs*, Allen & Unwin, 1979, p 112.
8 I H Burnley, 'Immigration', D N Jeans (ed) *Space and Society*, SUP, vol. 2, p 123.
9 M Solling and H Wark, *Under the Arches: A History of the Glebe District Hockey Club to 1993*, Glebe District Hockey Club, 1994, p 53.
10 R Horvath, *Sydney, A Social Atlas*, Division of National Mapping, Canberra, 1989, p 44.
11 P Fisher, 'How the Trendy Twees Expelled the Blue Collars and Ethnics', *National Times*, 14–19 January 1974, p 13.
12 P Spearritt, *Sydney Since the Twenties*, Hale & Iremonger, 1978, p 215. Kendig, op cit (7), p 125.
13 *SMH*, 7 December 1968, p 18.
14 Logan, op cit (2), p 71.
15 *SMH*, 4 February 1995, p 65.
16 R Horvath and B Engels, 'The Residential Restructuring of Inner Sydney', I Burnley and J Forrest (eds) *Living in Cities*, Allen & Unwin, 1985, p 157.
17 Ibid.
18 Kendig, op cit (7), p 129.
19 K Legge, 'All Our Changing Days on The Avenue', the *Australian Magazine*, 12–13 March 1994, p 10.
20 M Berry, 'Urbanisation and Social Change: Australia in the Twentieth Century', S Encel and L Bryson (eds) *Australian Society*, 4th edn, 1984, pp 52–53.

21. J McCalman, 'Fitzroy 1989', *Fitzroy: Melbourne's First Suburb*, Hyland, 1989, pp 316–319.
22. M McAllister, 'Community Organisation and Local Politics in Glebe', Government III, Research Essay, University of Sydney, 1975, p 14.
23. *Balmain Association Newsletter* No 121 (June 1982).
24. *Glebe Weekly*, 28 November 1979.
25. *SMH Good Weekend,* 6 July 1985, p 13.
26. Legge, op cit (19), p 11.
27. *SMH*, 30 May 1985, p 5.
28. P Mullins, 'Household Consumerism and Metropolitan Development', P Troy (ed) *Australian Cities, Issues, Strategies and Policies for Urban Australia in the 1990s*, CUP, 1995, p 105.
29. *SMH*, 29 September 1990, p 19.
30. Ibid.
31. *SMH*, 20 July 1985, p 8.
32. Ibid, p 7.
33. *SMH*, 23 February 1991, p 47.
34. *SMH*, 2 June 1996, p 20.
35. *SMH*, 13 July 1992, p 13.
36. Horvath, op cit (10), p 82.
37. Mort Bay Housing 1985, NSW Department of Housing.
38. *SMH*, 20 July 1985; 4 September 1985.
39. For a comprehensive analysis of the battles over the five sites, see T Bonyhady, 'The Battle for Balmain', Troy, op cit (28), pp 112–141.
40. *SMH*, 23 February 1991, p 41, p 47.
41. Bonyhady, op cit (39), p 115.
42. *Glebe Weekly,* 23 May 1990, p 3; 6 June 1990, p 1.
43. *SMH*, 1 September 1990, p 9. *Glebe Weekly,* 5 September 1990, p 2.
44. *SMH*, 6 September 1990, p 9.
45. *Eastern Herald*, 21 February 1991, p 2. *SMH*, 14 January 1991, p 4.
46. Bonyhady, op cit (39), pp 131–132.
47. *Glebe Weekly,* 20 February 1991, p 1.
48. Bonyhady, op cit (39), pp 138–139.
49. *Glebe Weekly,* 18 September 1996, p 5.
50. Leichhardt Public Enquiry 1990–91, *Report to the Hon G P Peacocke, Minister for Local Government*, p 26.
51. W S Jevons, 'Remarks upon the Social Map of Sydney 1858', MS B864, ML. J A La Nauze, 'A Social Survey of Sydney in 1858', *Historical Studies* (1942–43), vol. 2, pp 264–268.
52. *SMH Spectrum*, 5 October 1996, p 6.

Chapter 20

1. T Dare, 'The Rise of the Middle Class', *Australian*, 9 October 1973, p 11; 10 October 1973, p 13; 11 October 1973, p 13; 12 October 1973, p 15.
2. J Roseth, 'The Inner Suburbs', Paper Presented to 44th ANZAAS Conference, Sydney 1972, p 4.
3. Z Nittim, 'The Coalition of Resident Action Groups, J Roe (ed) *Twentieth Century Sydney, Studies in Urban & Social History*, Hale & Iremonger, Sydney, 1980, p 232.
4. *Balmain Association Newsletter*, vol. 1 No 10 (October 1967).
5. Ibid, vol. 1 No 2 (June 1966).
6. P Reynolds and R Irving, *Balmain in Time*, Balmain Association, 1971. P L Reynolds and

P V Flottmann, *Half a Thousand Acres: Balmain, a History of the Land Grant*, Balmain Association, 1976.

7   *Glebe Society Bulletin*, vol. 1 No 1 (July 1969); 20 June 1969, p 13.
8   The Glebe Society, *An Outline Plan for Glebe*.
9   A Strachan, H Johnston and E Duek-Cohen, *Local Civic Groups and Planning*, UNSW, Civic Design Society, 1971. A Jakubowicz, 'A New Politics of Suburbia', *Current Affairs Bulletin* (April 1972), pp 338–351.
10 B and K Smith, *The Architectural Character of Glebe, Sydney*, University Co-op Book Shop, 1973. R A Wild, *Australian Community Studies and Beyond*, A & R, Sydney, 1981, pp 198–199.
11 *Annandale Association Newsletter*, vol. 1 No 2 (March 1970); vol. 1 No 6 (July 1970).
12 R Johnston, 'Participation in Local Government: Leichhardt 1971–74', R Lucy (ed) *The Pieces of Politics*, p 244.
13 *Glebe Weekly*, 10 March 1971.
14 *Glebe Society Bulletin*, vol. 3 No 3, 1971.
15 *Balmain Association Newsletter*, vol. 1 No 16, December 1968.
16 M di Nicola, 'The Political Impact of Italian Migrants in Leichhardt 1961–1973', BA Hons, University of Sydney, 1973, p 14.
17 R Johnston, op cit (12), p 241.
18 M McAllister, 'Community Organisations and Local Politics in Glebe', Government III, University of Sydney, 1975, p 14.
19 J Power, 'The New Politics in the Old Suburbs', *Quadrant*, vol. 13, pp 60–65.
20 *Glebe Weekly*, 21 July 1971; 11 August 1971.
21 *Sun*, 7 September 1971.
22 R Johnston, op cit (12), pp 246–147. B Engels, 'The Gentrification of Glebe: The Residential Restructuring of an Inner Sydney Suburb 1960 to 1986', PhD thesis, University of Sydney, 1989, pp 468–473.
23 Engels, op cit (22), p 473.
24 R Johnston, op cit (12), p 247.
25 Engels, op cit (22), p 478.
26 McAllister, op cit (18), pp 16–17.
27 R Cain, 'Transportation, Planning and Conflict in Sydney: A Case Study of Inner-City Expressways in Glebe', BSc Thesis, University of NSW, 1975, pp 65–72.
28 L Sandercock, *Cities for Sale*, MUP, 1977, p 206.
29 *Glebe Society Bulletin*, No 4, 1974.
30 McAllister, op cit (18), pp 16–17.
31 R Roddewig, *Green Bans*, Hale & Iremonger, Sydney 1978, p 12.
32 P Thomas, *Taming the Concrete Jungle*, BLF, Sydney, 1973, p 131.
33 J Mundey, 'From Red to Green: Citizen Worker Alliance', D Hutton (ed) *Green Politics in Australia*, Angus & Robertson, Sydney, 1987, p 113.
34 Cain, op cit (27), p 76.
35 Ibid, pp 85–86.
36 Jackson Teece Chesterman Willis, *The Church of England Lands, Glebe, A Report to the Department of Urban and Regional Development* (July 1973).
37 Archdeacon C Goodwin, 'How the Church Will Change the Face of Sydney', *Sun-Herald*, 13 October 1968, p 56.
38 L Mortimer and C Burke, *The Glebe Health and Welfare Survey*, RPA Hospital, 1974, p 33.
39 Ibid, p 34.
40 'Church of England Submission to the Royal Commission of Enquiry into Poverty' as quoted in the *Royal Australian Planning Institute Journal*, vol. 15 No 1 (1977), p 5.
41 McAllister, op cit (18), p 10.

42 C Wagner, 'Sydney's Glebe Project: An Essay in Urban Rehabilitation', *Royal Australian Planning Institute Journal*, vol. 15 No 1 (February 1977), pp 1–24.
43 P Pike, 'Local Government Goes Local: The Leichhardt Experiment 1971–1974', *Community* (June 1976), pp 6–7.
44 R Johnston, op cit (12), p 252.
45 *Glebe Weekly*, 30 August 1973.
46 *Glebe Weekly*, 5 September 1974; 12 September 1974.
47 Engels, op cit (22), p 488.
48 Leichhardt Council, Staff Committee Report, 5 November 1974, p 4.
49 Leichhardt Council Business Papers 19 November 1974, p 395. *Glebe Weekly*, 30 June 1976.
50 *NT*, 9–14 August 1976, p 7.
51 Ibid.
52 Ibid.
53 Ibid.
54 Ibid.
55 Ibid.
56 T Wheelwright, 'NSW: The Dominant Right', A Parkin and J Warhurst (eds) *Machine Politics in the Australian Labor Party*, Allen & Unwin, Sydney, 1983, p 50.
57 *Glebe Weekly*, 27 January 1972. *Glebe Society Bulletin*, No 6, 1975.
58 Engels, op cit (22), p 498. *NT*, 27 December 1976, p 1.
59 *Challenge*, July 1977, p 8.
60 J Ryder, *A Biographical Register of the Commonwealth Parliament 1901–1972*, Canberra, 1975. H Radi, P Spearritt and E Hinton, *Biographical Register of the NSW Parliament 1901–1970*, Canberra, 1979.
61 R F I Smith, 'Collingwood, Wren Leftovers and Political Change: Aspects of Local Level Politics in the 1970s', *Labour History* 30 (May 1976), pp 42–47.
62 Wheelwright, op cit (56), p 49.
63 Ibid, p 50.
64 *NT*, 17 October 1977, p 12.
65 *Glebe Weekly*, 6 February 1980. Engels, op cit (22), p 506.
66 Engels, op cit (22), p 507.
67 *NT*, 15 September 1979, p 15; 10 February 1980, p 32. *NSW Parliament, The Hon Mr Justice Woodward, Further Report of the Royal Commission into Drug Trafficking*, Government Printer, Sydney, 1980.
68 Engels, op cit (22), pp 507–509.
69 Ibid p 509.
70 *Challenge*, October 1979; June 1980. The *Bulletin*, 6 August 1980. Wheelwright, op cit (56), pp 50–51.
71 *Challenge*, August 1980. The *Bulletin*, 6 August 1980.
72 Engels, op cit (22), p 510.
73 Ibid, p 513.
74 Ibid.
75 J Coleman, *Report to Council on the Objections to the 1979 Planning Scheme*, Leichhardt Council, 1981, p 39.
76 Leichhardt Council, 'Corporate Structural Reorganisation', Internal Policy Document 1983, pp 2–3.
77 *Balmain Association Newsletter*, June 1982.
78 *SMH*, 8 June 1989, p 2, p 15.
79 *SMH*, 8 June 1989, p 15.
80 *SMH*, 6 September 1990, p 9. *Glebe Weekly*, 26 September 1990, p 7.

81 *Eastern Herald,* 21 February 1991, p 2.
82 *SMH Spectrum,* 29 June 1996, p 5.
83 Ibid.
84 *Glebe Weekly,* 11 September 1991, pp 38–39.
85 Ibid.
86 'Leichhardt, Camera, Action', *SMH Spectrum,* 29 June 1996, pp 4, 5.
87 Leichhardt Municipal Council, *Annual Report 1994–1995,* pp 4–5.
88 *SMH Spectrum,* 29 June 1996, pp 4–5.

Index

abattoirs 29, 62, 70, 121, 151–2
Abbey, The 86
Aborigines 1–7
adult franchise 184–5
alcohol *see* liquor
Allen, George Wigram 19–20, 90, 136, 178
animal life 2, 3
Annandale Association 240, 244
Annandale House 18
anti-German sentiment 171–2
Anzacs 169–70, 176
Archdall, Canon Mervyn 110
architects 71
Athaldo, Don 213
Australian Protestant Defence Association (APDA) 145, 146
Australian Socialist League (ASL) 141

Balmain: appears on the map 14; early attraction of 16
Balmain, William 14–15
Balmain Association 240, 241, 244
Balmain Co-operative Grocery Society Ltd 132–3
Balmain Development Trust 237
banks 73, 130 *see also* lending institutions
Baptists 114
Beale, Octavius 127–8
bicycles 204
Birch Grove House 15–16, 21
Bishopgate 27, 31
Bishopthorpe 31, 69
Blake, Robert 30
blood sports 202
boatbuilding 21, 121, 122–3
Booth, John 90
bowling 205
Bowman, James 20
boxing 165, 210–11
Brady, Bill 249
brass bands 165
Brenan, John Ryan 23

brickmaking 75, 87–8, 124
bridges 45, 46, 71
bubonic plague 61, 62, 66, 154
Buchanan, Edward Harman 85
Builders Labourers Federation (BLF) 234
building and construction 29, 31, 51–2, 68–9, 71, 72, 74, 76, 78–9, 88
building industry 84–7, 89–90
building materials 18
building regulations 35
building societies 72–3
buses *see* omnibuses

cadet corps 104, 173
Callan Park Hospital 71, 83
Campaign for Better Council (CBC) 241–3, 244–5
capital 72
Capuchins 227
Carmichael, Ambrose Campbell 145
carters 49–50
Casey, Danny 248
cash-and-carry 132
Cashman, Annie 218
casualties 174
Catholics 112–13, 117, 119, 143, 193
cemeteries 152
charities 118
childbirth 155
cholera 150
Christianity *see* religion
Church of England 244
churches 25, 38–9, 81, 98, 100, 109–20, 205
cinemas 209, 229
class culture 167
clerical workers 158–9
coal 126
Cole, S.L. 184
Colebrook, Thomas 182
commerce 128–33, 217
commercial redevelopment 235
Congregationalists 114

311

conscription 148, 172–3, 174, 176
containerisation 128–9, 219–20
contractors 51–2
convicts 11–12, 13, 20
co-operative societies 164
corner stores 131–2, 161–2
corruption 218–19
councillors 178–80, 186, 218
councils 34, 55–7, 60–1, 183–4 *see also* government, local
cricket 202–3, 207
crime 194–5
Cumberland County Plan 214–15
Currey, William 176

dairies 153–4
dancing 209–10
death rates 151
Del Duca family 226
delinquents 160
demographics 43
Department of Main Roads (DMR) 243
depressions 22, 27, 200
development 30–1, 237
diphtheria 150, 200
dockyards 69, 121, 123
dog-racing 211–12
domestic service 162–3
drainage *see* essential services
drunkenness 40, 97
Dunn, Mary Ann 187
Durham House 21

economic prosperity 17
education 99–108
electricity 65, 126–7
Elphinstone, David 75, 86
Elswick 22–3
employment 125, 128
enlistment 116
enrolments in schools 106–7, 108
essential services 34, 43, 52–4, 61–2, 64–5, 66, 151
estate system 27
evening schools 105
eviction 199–200
expressways, 242–3, 244

factionalism 135, 247
factories 121–33, 138
family life 36
fascism 224
fauna 2
ferries 17, 21, 36, 44, 48–9, 51
fire 2
flats 216, 232, 246
flora 2, 9, 10
Foley, Dr H.J. 186
food relief 197–8
football 165–7, 202–3, 204, 205–7, 212
Fowler, Lilian 187

Fraser, Dawn 212–13
Freemasons 112–13
friendly societies 41, 163–4

gangs 194–5
gardens 75
Garrard, Jacob 136–7
gas supply 64–5
gentrification 232–3, 235
George, Henry 140, 141, 142
Gilchrist, John 14–15, 16
Glebe: appears on the map 14; early attraction of 16–17
Glebe Island Bridge 44
Glebe Society 240, 241, 243, 244
gold rush 30, 31
government 135; local 34, 35, 55–67, 89, 179, 185, 217, 248, 250 *see also* councils; self- 34
Grant, John 142
grants 11, 14, 22
Greater Sydney 66–7, 184
green bans 243
Griffith, Arthur Hill 145–6

Hammond, R.B.S. 118
Hancock, Alfred 71
Hand, Larry 249
Harold Park 212
Hart, Charles 142
Hawthorne, John 145
Hereford House 20
Hoad, Lew 213
Hogan, Edward 182
Hogue, J.A. 146
Holman, W.A. 141
Holt, Thomas 90
home ownership 77, 91
horses 17, 35, 43, 44, 45, 46, 47–8, 49–50
hospitals 150
Houghton, Thomas 146
housing 28, 33, 51, 87, 155, 200, 214–16, 228, 233, 236–7, 244
Housing Commission 214–16
Hughes, William Morris 141
human impact 2

ill-health 150, 151
immigrants 12, 32–3, 140, 141, 158, 222–30
incinerators 66
indebtedness 185
industrial enterprise 34
industrialisation 123, 124, 128
industries 75, 108, 121–33, 138, 219
infant welfare 156
infectious diseases 61, 62–3, 66, 106, 149, 150, 153–4, 190, 200
influenza 62, 106, 190
Iron Cove Bridge 71
Italians 222–30

Johnston, George 18
Johnston, Robert 18–19

Keegan, Tom 147
kerbing and guttering 56
kindergartens 156

Labor Leagues 139, 143, 144, 180
labourers 138–9, 162
landholding 26
land values 57
languages 4–5
larrikins 159–60
law and order 39–40
lay preachers 112
Leichhardt, Municipality of, grants in 14
leisure activities 202–13
lending institutions 72–4, 88 see also banks
libraries 63–4, 217
lighting 35, 54, 65
Lillie Bridge 212
liquor 94, 96, 97, 98, 112, 193, 195
living standards 26, 171, 174
loyalty 185
Lucas, P.C. 181
Lyndhurst 20, 243

Manning, William Montagu 90
manufacturing 128
manure 50
Maritime Services Board (MSB) 219
maritime unions 122
Marston, Joe 213
mass entertainment 208
McDonald, James 85
measles 62, 150
Melocco brothers 225
Methodists 112, 117
middle classes 29, 239, 240, 246
migration to the suburbs 28
milk 62, 154
missionary activity 115
Mitchell, James Sutherland 30
morality 39–41
Mort, Thomas Sutcliffe 30, 121–2
Mort's Dock 121–2, 137–8, 181, 219
motherhood 156
moving 161
Mundey, Jack 243
municipal facilities 217
municipalities 35, 178–9, 184
music 209, 210

neighbourhood 231–2
newspapers 41
Newton, Leo 218
Norton, James 22–3

omnibuses 17, 35, 44, 45–6, 47–8
Orangemen 112, 146

organised labour 135
Origlass, Nick 220–1
overcrowding 30, 42, 150, 155

Paling, William Henry 90
parks 64, 202, 237, 250
parliament 135
patriotism 171
pawnshops 198
Pemulwuy 5
Perry, Samuel 23
Phillip, Captain Arthur 1–2, 5
piano manufacture 128
picture shows 96, 164–5, 208–9
piggeries 152
playing fields 202
police 39, 194, 195
Police Boys Clubs 217
politics 134, 135, 141, 178–87, 235, 239–51
pollution 62, 126, 153
population 14, 28, 33, 43, 63, 68, 155, 190–1, 232
poverty 28, 36, 39, 150, 154, 198, 237
Presbyterians 111–12, 117
Primitives 114
prohibition 193
protectionism 142
Protestantism, militant 145, 146, 205
Protestants 117, 118
public buildings 129–30
public health 60–7, 150
public houses 22, 32, 36, 37–8, 93–9, 165, 171, 194, 205, 235–6
public reserves 64, 202
public schools see education; schools
public transport see transportation
public works 57
pubs see public houses
pushes 160

Ragged Schools 104–5
railway line 43–4
rates 56, 57, 58
rats 154
recreation grounds 64
recruitment 168, 171, 172
registered clubs 97
religion 38, 109–20, 236
rents 91, 161, 191–2, 200, 216, 233
resident action groups 246, 249
residential development 21, 68, 69, 70
respectability 23–4, 25, 157, 158–9
retailers 129–33, 179, 227–8
roads 34, 35, 44, 53–4, 56, 74, 215
road transport 17, 35, 44
rowing 167, 204–5
Rowntree, Captain Thomas Stephenson 30, 121
rubbish removal see essential services
Rugby League see football
Rugby Union see football

sailing 205
salaries *see* wages
Salvation Army 113–14
sanitation *see* essential services
sawmills 123–4
scarlatina 150
scarlet fever 200
schools 39, 99–108, 156, 173–4, 236
servants 20, 33–4, 162–3
sewerage *see* essential services
shipbuilding 125, 219
shops 77
slaughterhouses 28–9, 149
slums 192–3
smallpox 5, 62, 150
Smart, Thomas 90
smells 153
soap manufacture 126, 127
soccer 203–4, 228
social geography 92
socialism 142, 143
social status 24–5
society 12–14, 31–2
soils 8, 11
SP bookmaking 195
sport 171, 202–4, 212, 228
St Phillip's 27–8, 86
status 159
Stonemason's Society 142
Storey, John 147–8
streets *see* roads
strikes 138, 139, 174, 196–7
subdivisions 26–7, 69–71, 76–7, 78, 79, 82 ,191
    see also suburban development
suburban development 30, 36, 42–54, 63, 68–91
Sunday school 115–16
supermarkets 132
Swan, Henry Brisbane 181
swimming pools 64, 205, 217
Sydney City Mission 118

taxes 140
teachers 101, 107, 115
temperance 40, 97, 137, 171
tennis 213
terraces 72, 80, 91, 192, 235
Thornley, Ambrose Junior 86
Thornton, Reginald 181
timber industry 85, 121, 127
topography 9–10, 149
town halls 58–9, 180
Toxteth Park 19, 83–4
Trades and Labor Council (TLC) 134, 139
tradesmen 12, 17–18, 29–30
trade unions *see* unions
trams 44–5, 46–7, 48, 51
transportation 17, 21, 35–6, 42–51, 77, 81, 215
trotting races 212
trucking 128–9
typhoid 149, 150, 153

Unemployed Workers Movement (UWM) 198–200
unemployment 28, 57, 161, 169, 171, 180, 192, 197, 200–1
unionism 136, 139, 143–4, 162
unions 122, 134–48, 162, 198
urban change 160
urban economy 192

vegetation 2, 9–10
vigilante committee 181
villas 20, 26, 75, 80
voluntary movement 41

wages 29, 60, 161, 174, 190, 198
Waite, Jack 218
Wakefield, Edward Gibbon 12
walking 35, 43
war 168–77
War Precautions Regulations 172
Ward, Eddie 193
wards 63
water supply 34, 35, 52, 61, 151
Waterview House 21
wealth 17, 22, 24–5, 34, 237
welfare 197–8, 199
Whaleyborough 78
wharfage 124
wharves 21
White Bay Power Station 126–7, 129
white settlement 3
women 155–6, 161, 163, 184, 187, 197, 202, 207
wool industry 26
working classes 40, 163, 168–9, 232
working conditions 174
Wyner, Izzy 221

Young, John 73–4, 86, 91
youth 217